*Hermeneutics and
Modern Philosophy*

BRICE R. WACHTERHAUSER, *Editor*

Hermeneutics and Modern Philosophy

State University of New York Press

Published by State University of New York Press, Albany
©1986 State University of New York

For information, address State University of New York Press,
State University Plaza, Albany, N.Y., 12246

Library of Congress Cataloging-in-Publication Data
Hermeneutics and modern philosophy.
   Bibliography: p.
   Includes index.
   1. Hermeneutics.   2. Gadamer, Hans George, 1900-
3. Heidegger, Martin, 1889-1976.   I. Wachterhauser.
Brice R., 1953-
BD241.H365   1986   149   86-14572
ISBN 0-88076-295-4
ISBN 0-88076-296-2 (pbk.)

10 9 8 7 6 5 4 3 2 1

Contents

HERMENEUTICS AND 'POST–MODERNISM'

Preface

I originally began work on this volume in the summer of 1981. Along the way, many changes have taken place and I have incurred many debts - more than I can recount. Thanks are certainly due to the NEH for giving me a stipend to attend a seminar for college teachers on the history of hermeneutics at the University of Iowa in 1981. Jerry Bruns, the director of the seminar, was very supportive of my plans and helped me to see a clearer outline of its final form. Merold Westphal and David Hoy also deserve a special word, for in addition to making their work available to me they provided advice and much-needed support at some of the darker moments of the volume's development. I must also thank Augustana Research Foundation for a summer grant in 1982, which enabled me to write my article for this volume. Reiner Wiehl and Hans-Georg Gadamer are to be thanked for their support and for their willingness to take time from their busy schedules to discuss my work for this volume. Kathleen Wright deserves special mention not only for her insightful and tactful advice, but also for her willingness to read a draft of my translation of Reiner Wiehl's article. She saved it from many errors and gave me a better idea of what translation is about. Robert Dostal also deserves thanks for his friendly and judicious advice. The Board on Faculty Research at Saint Joseph's University supplied me with a summer grant in 1984 and a grant-in-aid in 1986 which enabled me to finish much of the work for this volume. My thanks to the board and to the university. Joy Ansky and Carolyn McNasby did the tedious work of typing the bibliography, and Joanne Devlin and Ethel Ritter have typed and retyped many parts of the manuscript. They deserve a great deal more than thanks. Without their tireless efforts this volume

1

could have been delayed indefinitely. Finally, to all those who have helped along the way and especially to the authors who entrusted their work to me, I thank you for your confidence, patience and commitment to this project.

Acknowledgements

This volume would not have been possible without the permission to reprint several key articles from various sources. Richard Bernstein's "From Hermeneutics to Praxis" appears with permission from the author and *The Review of Metaphysics*, where it appeared in volume 35: (1982): 823–45. Wolfhart Pannenberg's "Hermeneutics and Universal History" originally appeared in the *Journal for Theology and Church* 4 (1967): 122–52. It is reprinted with permission from the author, who now holds the rights. Marjorie Grene's "The Paradoxes of Historicity" was published originally in the *Review of Metaphysics* 32 (1978): 15–36. It is reprinted with the kind permission of the review and the author. Jürgen Habermas's "A Review of Gadamer's *Truth and Method*" is reprinted with permission from *Understanding and Social Inquiry*, edited by Fred R. Dallmayr and Thomas McCarthy, Notre Dame: University of Notre Dame Press, 1977, pp. 335–64. Copyright 1977 by Notre Dame Press. Hans-Georg Gadamer's "On the Scope and Function of Hermeneutical Reflection" is reprinted with permission from *Philosophical Hermeneutics*, edited by David Linge, Berkeley: University of California Press, 1976, pp. 18–43. Copyright by the University of California Press, 1976. Paul Ricoeur's "Hermeneutics and the Critique of Ideology" is reprinted with permission from *Hermeneutics and the Human Sciences*, edited by John B. Thompson. Cambridge: Cambridge University Press, 1981, pp. 63–100. Richard Bernstein's "What is the Difference that Makes a Difference? Gadamer, Habermas, and Rorty" was originally published by the Philosophy of Science Association, vol. 2 (1982). It is reprinted with permission from the author and PSA. Hans-Georg Gadamer's "Text and Interpretation", translated by Dennis J. Schmidt, is reprinted with the kind permission of the author. My thanks also are extended to Dennis J. Schmidt, who agreed to have his translation used in this volume. David C. Hoy's "Must We Say What We Mean? the Grammatological Critique of Hermeneutics" is reprinted with permission from the author and *The University of Ottawa Quarterly*, where it appeared originally in volume 50 (1980): 411–26. Finally, John Caputo's essay "Hermeneutics as the Recovery of Man" is reprinted with permission from the author and *Man and World*, where it originally appeared in volume 15 (1982): 343–67.

INTRODUCTION

HISTORY AND LANGUAGE IN UNDERSTANDING

B RICE R. WA CHTERHAUSER

1

'Hermeneutics' is a term bandied about a great deal today. Like all such catchwords that enjoy a period of popularity it has taken on a life of its own. So much so that it is now used in so many different contexts with so many different meanings that it no longer has a univocal meaning. This is probably no accident, for hermeneutics represents not so much a highly honed, well-established theory of understanding or a long-standing, well-defined tradition of philosophy as it does a family of concerns and critical perspectives that is just beginning to emerge as a program of thought and research. This does not mean that hermeneutics lacks critical force on the current cultural scene. On the contrary, both a casual acquaintance with the widespread use of the term and a deeper grasp of the philosophical issues behind it indicate that hermeneutics wields considerable critical power indeed. Despite the facts that there are many debates within the movement and that hermeneutics is not firmly united behind a single theory or personality, advocates of hermeneutics share a family of critical concerns and perspectives that make their philosophical program a strongly unified one. Hermenetucial thinkers can be characterized quite generally by their common concern to resist the idea of the human intellect as a wordless and timeless source of insight. The human intellect, *pace* Plato, Aristotle, Augustine, Aquinas, Descartes, Spinoza, et alia, does not have the capacity for a "pure" seeing of reality "in itself," a wordless intuition of reality *sub specie aeternitatis*. Instead, hermeneutical theories of understanding argue that all human understanding is never 'without words' and never 'outside of time'. On the contrary, what is distinctive about human understand-

5

ing is that it is always in terms of some evolving linguistic framework that has been worked out over time in terms of some historically conditioned set of concerns and practices. In short, hermeneutical thinkers argue that language and history are always both conditions and limits of understanding.

These two themes, history and language, run like dual leitmotifs throughout hermeneutical literature. Hermeneutical thinkers see history and language functioning as special types of transcendental conditions of all understanding. To borrow a phrase from Habermas, history and language are seen as "transitory a prioris"[1] of thought. But because these a prioris are transitory in nature, that is, always different in different contexts, they necessarily evade a final theoretical account of how they function in this transcendental capacity. Unlike Kant's three critiques, which sought apodictic certainty regarding the necessary conditions of three clearly delineated types of understanding, hermeneutics pursues no such transcendental project. To begin with, the emphasis on the changing "grids" of language and history precludes a definitive, apodictic account. Hermeneutical thinkers argue against the assumption that understanding takes places in terms of conditions that are always and everywhere the same. Secondly, hermeneutics' "quasitranscendental" account of history and language shows itself in the rejection of the Kantian thesis that the human intellect operates according to strictly differentiated rules for clearly distinguishable realms of understanding. Human understanding cannot be so easily parsed into compartments, and neither is its essence to be a follower of rules. Thirdly, hermeneutical accounts differ from strict transcendental accounts in that they do not ground intelligibility in the private sphere of a pregiven, essentially changeless subject but in the public sphere of evolving, linguistically mediated practice. In short, hermeneutics does not seek the conditions of intelligibility as such, as if understanding were always and everywhere the same. Rather its account of the transcendental conditions of history and language remain necessarily general and in principle open precisely because the desire to take change seriously demands it. Thus hermeneutical thinkers find themselves in the difficult position of trying to be general enough in their "transcendental" investigations to leave room for unforeseen changes, yet specific enough to give a convincing account of our actual experience of thinking and incisive enough to demonstrate the critical power of hermeneutical reflection.

2

Such "quasitranscendental" accounts usually take as their point of departure the concept of 'historicity' (*Geschichtlichkeit*).[2] 'Historicity' is the term most often used to denote our participation in and intractable belonging to history. It is no exaggeration to say that the notion of 'historicity' is perhaps hermeneutics' most central and most compelling claim. 'Historicity' does not refer to the incontestable but obvious fact that we live out our lives in time. It refers instead to the thesis that who we *are* is through and through historical. This concept refers to the claim that the relation between being human and finding ourselves in particular historical circumstances is not accidental but rather essential or 'ontological'. This means that what we *are* cannot be reduced to a noumenal, ahistorical core such as a transcendental ego or, more broadly, to a human nature that is the same in all historical circumstances. Rather, who we are is a function of the historical circumstances and community we find ourselves in, the historical language we speak, the historically evolving habits and practices we appropriate, the temporally conditioned problems we take seriously, and the historically conditioned choices we make. According to the hermeneutical perspective, human beings are neither given an immutable essence by God or nature, nor do we make ourselves (at least not as isolated individuals), but we are rather the particular mode of historical existence we in part find ourselves in and in part shape in cooperation with others. In short, hermeneutics defends the ontological claim that human beings *are* their history.

The thesis of historicity is central to a hermeneutical theory of understanding because advocates of philosophical hermeneutics insist that our historicity colors all our rational activities, that is, our ability to order and make sense of our world. What this implies is that all human knowledge-claims bear within them an essential relation to the historical process out of which they emerge. This implies much more than the trivial claim that any knowledge-claim will show certain 'accidental' traces of the historical context in which it was formulated, such as the language, grammar, and style of its author; it involves the more radical claim that the very meaning and validity of any knowledge-claim is inextricably intertwined with the historical situation of both its formulators and evaluators. Thus hermeneutical thinkers would argue that there are no knowledge-claims that can claim to be true *sub specie aeternitatis*, but they claim only to be "true" in a "pragmatic"[3] sense of being the best solution at the present time to a problem that has been generated out of a set of historically mediated understandings, interests, and practices. For example, the initial formulation and critical acceptance of Newton's physics were carried out in terms of a historically mediated set of understandings and concerns. It implies equally, however, that *our* assessment of Newton's physics, which is, of course, very different than that of his contemporaries and immediate successors, is different precisely because of the changed historical circumstances, brought about in large part by quantum mechanics and Einstein's general theory of relativity. This difference is not simply a difference in the scientific sophistication with which we understand Newton; it is a difference in our grasp of the meaning and scope of Newton's truth claims. Hence we understand Newton differently although we certainly understand Newton. If this situation is paradigmatic for all knowledge-claims, as hermeneutical thinkers are inclined to argue, then knowledge is not so much an ahistorical reconstruction of reality *sub specie aeternitatis* but a way of seeing things from the standpoint of a historically mediated set of concerns and preunderstandings, which is subject to inevitable change whenever our historically mediated standpoint shifts its focus. Hence it can be said that although new knowledge-claims may evolve internally and dialectically from previous knowledge claims, they do not necessarily move toward better and better ahistorical representations of reality but according to the ever-changing theoretical and practical demands of the present and relative to the understandings of the past. For example, just as there seems to be no one Plato but only a history of interpretation of Plato (Aristotle, Porphyry, Plotinus, Augustine, Shaftesbury, Kant, Rousseau, Schleiermacher, Friedländer, Cornford, Ryle, Vlastos, et alia) so many contemporary philosophers of science have argued plausibly that there is no theory-free perspective on natural realities that science attempts of discover and reconstruct, but only the process of science itself, which attempts to understand natural entities from the perspective of this or that evolving theoretical framework.[4] Consequently, there is no theory-free standpoint or set of rules by which we could evaluate new theoretical proposals. Instead, we must rely on something like an emerging consensus of scientists working in the field regarding the 'validity', 'fruitfulness', and 'cogency' of new developments within the field. That this is an inherently fallible and historically mediated process has been shown repeatedly by postempiricist philosophers of science like Kuhn,

Feyerabend, Polanyi, Lakatos, and company. Quite generally hermeneutical philosophers concur that we never see anything in historical vacuum but rather from the standpoint of a present that has been irrevocably shaped by the past and that carries within it implicit interests in the future. Hence a hermeneutical thinker like Gadamer claims that "understanding itself is not to be thought of so much as an action of subjectivity, but as the entering into an event of transmission in which past and present are constantly mediated."[5] In short, it is history that determines our possibilities for understanding ourselves and our world.

It is important if one wants to understand the thesis that "history determines our possibilities of understanding" to place the emphasis on the word "possibilities" rather than on the word "determines." To place it on the latter is to give the false impression that hermeneutics advocates a kind of historical determinism in the sense that what we understand is simply a function of what our past has preprogrammed us to understand. If, however, the past determines *possibilities* of understanding, then we can see how the past may *limit* the number of possible ways we can come to understand something but it does not lock us into a predetermined grasp of some issue. Our relation to history makes our understanding "finite"[6] in the sense that it limits the perspectives from which a phenomenon can show itself, but it still allows for the possibility that it is up to us to work out these understandings and to explore their hidden riches and limitations. Of course we will do this in ways that are inevitably influenced by a host of factors, but we are still responsible to a large extent for the way we appropriate our past as we project ourselves toward our future.

3

A principle vehicle by which the past is transported into the present and carried over into the future is language. Our involvement in language is responsible for the fact that all understanding occurs in a historical context where our historically formed present informs our interpretation of any topic or subject. It is the "institution" of language that ensures that all understanding is historically mediated. For example, by learning our native tongue or by learning a specialized language of some field of study we inherit with it a past we have not shaped. Moreover this same language, which we participate in unconsciously and implicitly long before we begin to see any of its limitations, shapes our own attempts to understand in a variety of ways. Language, so to speak, goes out ahead of the reflective understanding and shapes our grasp of the subject matter.[7]

This is not to say that language imprisons the understanding, in the sense that the reflective understanding can never break through a specific linguistic tradition and criticize it incisively. Language does not turn us into windowless monads, which must depend on some mysterious "preestablished harmony" to account for our ability to interact effectively with that which is different and other. But it is to say that in transcending the limitations of any one mode of speaking and seeing, we never transcend the fundamental linguisticality (*Sprachlichkeit*)[8] of our own understanding. Even our most incisive and radical critiques of certain linguistic traditions remain engaged in a language that itself has limitations and blind spots and hence awaits its own critique. Exchanging one language for another more critical and refined language never implies that we have somehow transcended our inextricable belonging to language in general. No matter how often we rise to self-criticism and self-transcendence our fundamental "belongingness" (*Zugehörigkeit*)[9] to language does not change. As we have already intimated, this does not imply that language involves us in a linguistic solipcism or relativism such that every language or way of speaking about something cuts us off from reality and makes it impossible to communicate and understand other ways of speaking about things, but it does imply that our grasp of anything can never be final, exhaustive, or otherwise unlimited; our understanding never reaches a point where it so thoroughly grasps the subject matter and so commands the many different ways of speaking about it that it can claim that its current, hard-won understanding is free from all the limitations of the language in which it is expressed. On the contrary, all language makes our grasp of things inherently *finite*. We never understand without words, and there are no linguistic accounts that cannot, in principle, be criticized, sharpened, developed, and even eventually transcended.

Moreover, if "linguisticality" is part and parcel of who we are, then it is not the case that we can first understand apart from some historically formed language, for example, by means of a wordless intuition, and then subsequently formulate that understanding in words as if language were simply a tool that we master and control with varying degrees of proficiency. On the contrary, we always understand in terms of some historically shaped language, and long before we control any sphere of discourse it has already shaped our understanding. "For language is not only an object in our hands, it is the reservoir of tradition and the medium in and through which we exist and perceive our world."[10] If this is so, then understanding no more occurs in a pure, logical space of the mind that is free of words than anyone learns a language by hooking up certain perfectly clear 'intuitions' or 'experiences' with a set of arbitrary signs that somehow stand in for them and represent them. On the contrary, we first understand by learning how to get around in certain speech communities.

The test of this understanding is not whether we have learned how to associate certain words with certain 'inner' experiences but rather whether we can successfully "do things with words" in the communities with which we share a language. In other words, understanding is not measured in a "private space" before the "eye of the mind," but it is measured in the public space of discourse. This implies that the criteria of understanding are pragmatic and linguistic; understanding a phenomenon means being able to talk about it in terms common to some community and, more important, being able to relate that talk to other sorts of language usage in the community. For example, understanding what natural science is about does not depend on having an insight into the essence or nature of science, as if science were a timeless universal. Rather, I understand what natural science is about when I am able, for example, not only to demonstrate that I can talk about science in terms of its own vocabulary and distinguish it from the ideological clichés that often surround it, but, more importantly, it can be said that I understand what science is about when I can talk about how the scientist's language of gathering data, theory-construction, experimentation, theory refinement, and so on, relates to and is different from other modes of speaking and acting, such as literature, morality, or business. In short, it is by being at home in these languages (and the practices surrounding them) and moving between them with relative ease and not in terms of having some alinguistic vision into the essence of science, that distinguishes those who understand science from those who do not. In other words, what science "means" depends on the changing linguistic and practical contexts from which it is understood. On this view, science "means" many things; one thing in relation to philosophy, another in relation to business, yet another when we relate it to politics or literature, and so on, but there is no "essence" of science "underneath" the varing perspectives on it. Moreover, there is no one linguistic perspective that is primary, say the working scientist's own perspective, that all other perspectives must measure themselves against. To insist on such a privileged understanding would be arbitrary in that it would ignore the way in which science is simply one human activity among many, and it would ignore the fact that we have never had an understanding that has been developed exclusively from any one perspective. Rather, all understanding of science at any time in history has always been in terms of the cultural and linguistic context in which it functions.

4

The emphasis on language and history that leads to an insistence on the finite, conditioned, and situated nature of all understanding has a considerable critical payoff. If we go back to our first general claim about hermeneutical thinkers, namely that they resist the notion that one can grasp reality 'in itself' or *sub specie aeternitatis*, I think we can begin to see this more clearly. The ideal of grasping a reality "in itself" presupposes that we can make sense of what reality would be like independent of its relation to time, to ourselves, or to anything else for that matter. But do we even have an idea of any such reality "in itself"? It seems clear that we do not. Take any instance of understanding and examine whether or not it has been grasped *an sich*. It becomes clear very quickly that all thematic understanding depends on other temporally mediated understandings that we take for granted whenever understanding takes place at all.

This leads hermeneutical thinkers to a 'holistic', or, more accurately, a 'contextualist' theory of meaning. The meaning of any phenomenon or proposition depends on the 'whole' of which it is a 'part' or, in other words, it depends on the 'context' in which it has a 'function.' It is slightly less confusing to call hermeneutics a contextualist theory rather than a holistic theory of meaning because hermeneutical theorists do not believe that we ever really grasp the entire whole of which anything is a part. This Hegelian emphasis, if taken seriously, would mean that the meaning of any one thing could not be grasped apart from a grasp of everything else. Now it seems clear that we certainly do grasp the meaning of things, not relative to the whole of everything else but relative to the limited whole of the context in which the subject matter plays its part. For example, we understand a social reality like education by studying how it functions in our society, economically, psychologically, ideologically, and so on. In short, we understand it by placing it in a context in which it has a function in terms of other realities that we already understand in some way.

This implies that all understanding will necessarily be an understanding relative to the standpoint of the inquirer. It is we who decide what the relevant context for understanding will be. More significantly, however, contextualism implies that the meaning of what we understand will change as the context and its constituents change. It is in this sense that we can think of history and language, to borrow Habermas's phrase again, as "transitory *a priois*" of all understanding. Our historicity and linguisticality are the transcendental conditions of any understanding, but because they are continually shifting, all understanding is an interpretive act, that is, a finite grasp of something from a relative perspective and never a complete or otherwise final vision of things.

This contextualist theory of meaning is also directed against 'foundationalist' epistemologies. Many philosophers have thought, following Plato, Aristotle, Descartes, et alia, that true knowledge demands some kind of certainty. Certainty can be had, it is claimed, only if we can discover certain self-evident first truths that can act as a 'foundation' for all other knowledge-claims in the sense that all other knowledge-claims can be deduced from these foundational truths. Hermeneutical theorists argue, however, that the rationalistic ideal of discovering a set of self-evident 'foundational' truths from which all legitimate knowledge-claims would follow by strict logical inference is impossible to achieve.[11] Foundationalism founders on the historical fact that the knowledge-claims of any science or philosophy to date cannot be adequately analyzed in terms of a deductive relationship between certain self-evident 'first truths' and the body of actual knowledge-claims that constitutes the findings of the discipline. This is so because certain sciences simply do not have 'first truths'—biology, for example—but more fundamentally because the relations between the various knowledge-claims of a science cannot be understood solely in terms of their deductive connections. How the knowledge-claims of any one discipline are related to each other seems, in many instances, to be a much more pragmatic affair involving the conceptual and practical needs of the discipline at the time. For example, a theory may be accepted almost solely because it suggests a concrete research program, whereas its competitors do not. The overwhelming popularity of behaviorism as a research program in psychology is a good case in point. In such cases questions about whether this theory can be deduced from certain "first truths" of the discipline, or even from other theoretical postulates operative at other points within the discipline are mute. What counted (and still counts) in the case of behaviorism was the theoretical elegance of eliminating the stubborn imponderability of consciousness and the enormously fruitful research program that behaviorism suggested.

Moreover, foundationalism fails because it cannot make good its claim to have discovered a set of truly *self-evident* first truths. Such claims to self-evidence and priority seem to rest on the possibility of grasping such truths *an sich*, that is, simply by themselves without having to situate them in an historically mediated context of understanding. But in point of fact such truths are never grasped *an sich* in a context-free, presuppositionless manner. Instead they seem to be inseparable from a circular logic of parts and wholes; they are always understood with regard to the function they play in the broader conceptual framework of which they are a part. In short, such truths are not self-evident in themselves but they are understood within a certain way of looking at a set of problems. Thus such truths may be seen as first truths only in the sense of being *contingent* starting points for some inquiry. For example, Descartes's *cogito* is the first truth of his system, but it is not a self-evident, absolute starting point from which all his other claims follow with strict logical necessity. Descartes cannot, for example, validly deduce the existence of God or the existence of the external world from the starting point of his own indubitable thinking. Moreover, the *cogito* is not a first truth in the sense that its 'truth' can be grasped *an sich* either without presuppositions or in isolation from the rest of Descartes' philosophy. This can be seen from the fact that no one has ever understood Descartes' *cogito* in any depth without understanding how it functions in the rest of his philosophy. It is only by seeing how it works in Descartes' search for an indubitable foundation for the new science of Galileo, which simultaneously would allow for the special metaphysical status of the soul and incorporate the rational indispensability of God, that we begin to plumb the depths of Descartes' "I think." Moreover this cannot be done without presuppositions that are largely taken for granted. The fact that Descartes saw the *cogito* as a thing or a substance, albeit a thinking thing (*res cogitans*), shows that he himself was operating with metaphysical presuppositions about the unified and selfsame nature of the self, which someone like Hume was able to point out and criticize incisively.

These examples suggest, I think, that there can be no radical beginnings from truths that are somehow self-grounding or self-justifying. The meaning of any truth claim seems to depend on an implicit con-

text of meaning that it takes for granted. The very attempt to formulate a presuppositionless philosophy or science founders on the
fact that all meaningful statements have a deep linguistic history,
which makes the analysis of their meaning (their interpretation) an
"endless task."[12] There is no bedrock of first truths to discover, just
more interpretation or more 'talk', which may indeed be useful, illuminating, and necessary depending on the context, but such interpretation never begins with or culminates in a set of self-justifying
propositions.

It might be said, however, that even more than a rejection of a foundationalism based on indubitable, self-justifying, or self-interpreting
first truths, hermeneutical thinkers like Heidegger and Gadamer are
concerned to rule out a kind of "foundationalism of the subject," or
what has been called "methodological solipcism." Descartes and
Kant may be seen as representatives of this tradition. Methodological
solipsism seeks a basis for knowledge in the thinking subject in that it
assumes that rational consciousness has priviledged access to its own
contents and 'autonomy' with respect to its own rational activitiy.
This implies that consciousness can be inherently certain about its
own content and that it has the power, moreover, to be self-
legislating and self-regulating regarding its own rational activity.
What this amounts to in practice is the assumption that rational beings can so know and control the conditions of their own reason that
we can develop a set of criteria, rules, or categories that are sufficient
to determine unequivocally and for all times and places the difference
between such things as meaningful and meaningless statements,
valid and invalid intepretations, true and false knowledge-claims,
and so on. In short, methodological solipcism assumes that consciousness is a completely free and autonomous master of its own
cognitive activity and is not, at least in principle, dependent on the
contingent events in nature and history. Hermeneutical thinkers like
Heidegger and Gadamer challenge this Cartesian/Kantian assumption.

Descartes and Kant assumed that although our bodies might be
part of a contingent world of nature and history (and hence dependent on changes that occurred within these realms), the intellect is,
nevertheless, free or autonomous in principle from such 'accidents'
or contingencies, at least as far as its own proper activities are concerned.[13] This is to say that although we may not have been born with
"innate ideas"[14] that would provide us with a self-justifying foundation for all thought, we can nevertheless discover wholly within
ourselves the proper 'criteria' or 'rules' for all essential cognitive ac-

tivities. These 'rules', moreover, would lead, if we believe Descartes, to an indubitable knowledge of reality or, if we follow Kant, to an apodictic science of appearances, a sure and final knowledge of our moral responsibilities and a definitive grasp of the canons of taste.

In our century this Cartesian/Kantian tradition of looking for the 'eternal', 'noncontingent' rules of all thought has remained strong, particularly in the heirs to Husserl's transcendental phenomenology and in the descendents of the logical positivists. Hermeneutics, however, understands itself as a critique of this notion of a noncontingent, 'autonomous' intellect. Instead of seeing our various cognitive activities as being in principle able to liberate themselves from the contingencies of nature and history,[15] hermeneutical thinkers have insisted on the 'finite', 'dependent', and 'contingent' nature of all understanding.

If this is so, then the view that sufficient criteria of meaning, knowledge, and truth can be found within or generated from consciousness alone (for example, Descartes's clear and distinct ideas) is an inherently deceptive epistemological standpoint. It hides from us the actual contingent conditions that make our thinking possible. According to Heidegger and Gadamer the actual historical circumstances provide a set of tacit preunderstandings and concerns in terms of which any act of understanding is ultimately made possible. This implies that understanding is never simply a function of what goes on in consciousness. When we understand there is always an unconscious element we take for granted and over against which we understand. This entails, moreover, that understanding never can be exhaustively analyzed in terms of a set of *a priori* rules which the intellect formulates autonomously and then simply follows. Understanding always depends, in part, on social standards which evolve historically and which the individual neither produces nor controls. If this is so we are never in the position to give a presuppositionless reconstruction of some reality. Because we can never make explicit to ourselves everything on which our own understanding depends we can never claim with confidence that our understanding is without presuppositions.

5

If we turn to the history of this notion of a historically situated, linguistically mediated, contextualist and antifoundationalist theory of understanding, the name of Hegel immediately comes to mind.

Not only was Hegel the first to insist that "the truth is the whole" and, thereby, to suggest that the meaning of anything is inescapably contextual, but more important Hegel was also the first to gain prominence (*pace* Vico and Herder) for insisting that reason cannot be understood apart from its past or in isolation from the historically mediated languages it speaks. Moreover, Hegel argued that reason has no true starting points (other than its desire and drive to comprehend the world) that can act as self-justifying foundations and from which the truth can be deduced in an ahistorical fashion.[16] In general Hegel seems to be the first prominent thinker in the Western tradition to suggest that our ability to understand our world does not rest on some timeless ability of reason that conceives reality according to strict rules or fixed archetypes of intelligibility like Kant's categories or Plato's Forms. Hegel contends that human consciousness is a historically emerging reality that has different capacities and limitations at various times. His *Phenomenology of Spirit* is a bold attempt to outline that history.

But the *Phenomenology* is also an attempt to show that history has its own logic. Human reason has not evolved willy-nilly as the outcome of a series of accidents that the human race has suffered. Hegel insists that consciousness, despite its historical course of development, has been driven all along by a deep and immanent logic that has worked itself out in the history of Western civilization. It is this same historically developing logic that, according to Hegel, is finally culminating and coming to full self-awareness in his own philosophy. Thus Hegel's *Phenomenology* is also the attempt to show how each preceding stage of this 'logical' history prepared the ground for and was taken up into each succeeding stage.

But Hegel also argued that human reason can reach a point where it is no longer essentially affected by history. Hegel's notion of "absolute knowing" implies that reason can perform the Munchhausian feat of extracting itself from the swamp of history. This means that reason can attain the capacity to so thoroughly grasp itself and its conditions that it no longer passively suffers its development in any sense but actually attains a complete freedom to control and direct it. Hegel's position on "absolute knowing" implies that history ceases to be a real conditioning and limiting factor of human life.

Many thinkers have argued that Hegel failed to appreciate adequately our contingent relation to history. Philosophers like Marx and Nietzsche argued that the mind was rooted in nature and history and not nature and history in the mind.[17] Kierkegaard, too, claimed that

Hegel forgot the existing individual and his or her contingent relation to time. But as important as Hegel, Marx, Nietzsche, and Kierkegaard are for the development of hermeneutics, it was Wilhelm Dilthey (1833–1911) who explicitly tried to turn historicity into a transcendental condition of human thought.

Dilthey sought to understand the theoretical basis of the *Geisteswissenschaften*. He wanted to show that the humanities and the social sciences offered us a valid form of knowledge. Indeed, he insisted that these disciplines offered a form of knowledge that was categorically different from the knowledge of the natural sciences and one that, moreover, demonstrated that human beings were something more than 'mere' mechanical entities. Unlike natural entities human beings have the capacity for self-interpretation (*Selbstbesinnung*). This implies that we have the capacity to define and shape our own lives in response to the historical situations we find ourselves in. Hence history and our response to history becomes the key, for Dilthey, to unlock the secrets of human life. "Not through introspection but only through history do we come to know ourselves."[18] In this spirit, Dilthey sought to complete the Kantian project by developing "a critique of historical instead of 'pure' reason."[19] In attempting this critique, Dilthey made historicity into a transcendental condition of historical understanding. Only insofar as we are beings who make history do we have the capacity to understand it.

Yet despite the fact that Dilthey made 'historicity' the explicit focus of a theory of understanding, many hermeneutical thinkers have argued that Dilthey too failed to think out the notion of historicity consistently.[20] For example, Dilthey claimed, on the one hand, that "the totality of man is only history,"[21] and he also claimed that "It is in no way possible to go back behind the relativity of historical consciousness. . . . The type 'man' dissolves and changes in the process of history."[22] This implies that history knows no single logic of development and man has no ahistorical core. On the other hand, however, Dilthey seemed to ignore the role of historicity in his accounts of the historian's own ability to comprehend the past. Dilthey argued that the historian could achieve 'objective validity' in her results through an act of 'empathy' (*sich hineinfühlen*) whereby the historian pulled herself out of her own immersion in history and transposed herself into the lives of others. This seems to be a very questionable methodological principle because, if one really takes

seriously the thesis that we are through and through historical beings, then we cannot guarantee in principle that the historian will be
in a historical position which will allow for sufficient common ground
between the historian and her subject matter to make such imaginative
empathy possible. It would seem that if Dilthey was going to assert the
radical thesis that "the totality of man is only history," then he should
have also applied it to the historian herself. This would have forced him
to admit that the historian is also a historical being whose own historical
standpoint influences and shapes the results of her historical
research. Dilthey, however, equivocated in coming to such a conclusion. He maintained, despite admissions from time to time of the
historicity of the historian and the relativity of her perspective, that
the historian can transcend her own history in order to reconstruct
the past veridically, *"wie es eigentlich gewesen war"* (Ranke). Instead of
seeing the historian's goal as a kind of 'dialogue' with the past, that
is, to illuminate the past according to our present needs, Dilthey conceived the historian along Cartesian lines as someone who can free
herself from the influence of her own historical context in order to
reconstruct and represent the past as it actually was.

For these reasons thinkers like Heidegger and Gadamer have accused
Dilthey of failing to think through the implications of historicity consistently. This supposed failure on Dilthey's part may be seen,
however, as philosophically significant. I mean by this that Dilthey's
alleged inconsistency shows us something more than a problem with
regard to the internal coherence of Dilthey's thought. The problem
inherent in Dilthey's work seems to suggest that the problem of the
historicity of human understanding cannot be adequately comprehended in terms of the relativism and objectivism within which he
worked. This is so because there seems to be a genuine paradox inherent to the problem of historicity; namely, it seems possible to
know the past as genuinely different than our own time and to
distinguish better and worse, 'truer' or 'falser' accounts of it, while at
the same time never achieving an account that is free from the influences of the inquirer's own historical situation, that is, one that
succeeds in veridically reconstructing the past as a presuppositionless
object of scientific investigation. Even in the best accounts, elements
of the inquirer's historically contingent interests and conceptual
frame of reference are always present. It seems that Dilthey's thought
ran aground on this evident paradox because he failed to develop a
conceptual framework that would have allowed him to develop a

theory of understanding that went beyond the rubrics of relativism and objectivism in which he worked.[23] Dilthey remained trapped in the dichotomy of either relativism or objectivism, (as does much contemporary work on hermeneutics). As a result he could not see any way to give historicity its due without opening what he conceived as the Pandora's box of relativism.

6

The first thinker to address this paradox more adequately was Martin Heidegger. Heidegger's *Being and Time*[24] is not only an attempt to revive the question of Being, particularly in its relation to time, but it is also an attempt to develop an ontology of understanding that would ground our understanding in our "being-in-the-world."[25] Heidegger argued that our own type of historical existence, or what he called "being-in-the-world," affected, both positively and negatively, our understanding of everything. According to Heidegger, it is not a set of ahistorical rules or categories of the understanding that makes understanding possible, but it is the different "interested" ways and practices, the different concerns[26] and commitments through which we experience reality, that make it intelligible. As these concerns and commitments change over the course of history, so will our apprehension of reality.

Heidegger argues that previous accounts of knowledge, meaning, and understanding were fundamentally distorted because they either ignored or blithely explained away the influences of historicity on the very constitution of knowledge, meaning, and understanding. Because of this oversight the nature of the thinker was so misrepresented that the epistemologies that stemmed from these accounts were fundamentally mistaken. For example, Heidegger argues that a certain language about the self such as we find throughout the Western tradition of philosophy in figures such as Plato, Augustine, Descartes, Kant, and Husserl tends to obscure something fundamental about us. Talk of a purely spiritual soul, an ahistorical *cogito* or a transcendental ego obscures the way in which human beings are always deeply rooted in their historical circumstances. In order to rectify this oversight and the concomitant distortions it engendered, Heidegger attempts to develop a new vocabulary for speaking about human beings. His term for human being(s) is *Dasein.*[27] This term, which translates literally as "there-being," graphically insists on the contingent situatedness of our condition in space and time. We always happen to find ourselves in a set of spatio-temporal circumstances that are never entirely of our own making and that we cannot leave behind at will. Finding oneself in some set of circumstances is an ontological characteristic of human beings. This is to say that although it may be 'incidental' or 'accidental' that we are born in the particular place and time we happened to have been born in, it is not accidental that every human being has such a contingent point of entry into the world. Moreover living out our lives in the particular circumstances we find ourselves in is 'accidental' in the sense that all of us can change these circumstances at least to some extent, but what is not 'accidental' but rather essential and constitutive of our being is that we always find ourselves in some particular set of circumstances. In short, we cannot evade the fundamental finitude and contingency of our lives. In Heidegger's terms, we find ourselves "thrown"[28] into a world that disposes over us in innumerable ways and with which we always have to come to terms.

This implies, I think, that we experience ourselves most fundamentally not as autonomous rational agents but as a part of a natural world that is not of our own making but on which we are dependent in all our acting and suffering. Try as we may to escape or ignore this fundamental relation to reality, we can never leave it behind even when we adopt a "disinterested," theoretical attitude towards it. All our interaction with nature takes place over against this primordial relationship in terms of the concern or care it generates.[29]

More important, however, for hermeneutics, is the fact that our 'thrownness' involves an inextricable relation to history. In fact, our relation to history is more 'primordial' than our relation to nature. Although there is a sense in which we are natural beings before we are historical beings. After all, at birth, history is a mere possibility for us, whereas we are never not natural beings. Nevertheless, we are thrown into a historically mediated culture in terms of which we come to understand not only ourselves but nature itself. Because we come to undersatnd nature only through a historical matrix, history is, in a sense, more primordial than nature. The languages we speak, the practices we unconsciously appropriate, the institutions we live out our lives in, the theoretical debates we inherit, and so forth, all form a loosely packed amalgam of meaningful relations that we can never entirely objectify and that we always presuppose in our thematic understanding of anything whatsoever.

This highly complex conglomeration of historically mediated relations, which Heidegger calls having a "world,"[30] can never be traced back to a foundation of first principles from which all other knowledge-claims can be deduced, and neither does it rest on a set of a priori rules or intuited structures of consciousness in terms of which all our understanding can be organized. Instead it is a continually changing reality, something like Theseus' ship, that has a kind of loose temporal continuity with itself but no underlying identity. Similarly, like a ship in which we have set sail and which we gradually redesign in the course of our voyage, we can never simply leave our 'world', that is, this system of meaningful relations behind. Rather, participation in this system of relations is the precondition of all understanding and the gradual modification of it is its inevitable outcome. In this sense, Heidegger argues that being creatures who are "thrown" means that we have always already inherited a way of understanding that is so inextricably part of us that it constitutes our very being itself.[31] This is to say that the role of preunderstanding in human life is never incidental or in any way optional for us. Human beings always have inherited a way of looking at things around them long before they begin to modify that way of looking and understanding. Our lives become defined by these preunderstandings; in this sense, we *are* our preunderstandings and we do not simply have them in the way we have a coat or a pair of shoes. For example, we might say that Kant's involvement in the 'world' of eighteenth-century Europe enabled him to develop the particular epistemology, metaphysics, and morality he did. All understanding presupposes participation in varying conglomerations of preunderstandings in terms of which we grasp things as meaning such and such, portending this or that, suggesting certain consequences, and so forth, but it never presupposes an ahistorical grasp of a reality *sub specie aeternitatis*.

Given this 'situatedness', Heidegger argues that our very ability to understand at all comes from our participation in the contexts that make reality meaningful in the first place.[32] In short, all "new" understanding depends on our ability to relate new phenomena to our already existing set of understandings and concerns that, for purposes of understanding, we take for granted. It may be said that preunderstandings function like landmarks in otherwise unfamiliar territory. It is by them that we find our way, even when we have not thoroughly examined their nature. The point here is that preunderstandings are not usually, if ever, clear, well-justified beliefs or knowledge-claims that we have already established and from which we build up a cumulative body of knowledge; they are simply understandings we take for granted and treat *in practice* as being beyond the need for justification, even though they may harbor errors, distortions, simplications, and so forth. Heidegger was one of the first in this century to remind us that understanding something or explaining something successfully does not involve tracing back certain propositions to other propositions that are self-evident and self-justifying and from which we can deduce the *explanadum*. Rather all understanding and explanation termintates in the taken-for-granted preunderstandings of the context in which both the *interpretandum* and the *interpretans* share.

But if understanding anything over against an inherited set of preunderstandings is a condition of all understanding, it is also the case that these preunderstandings change in the course of our inquiries as we gradually remake our historical circumstances. This points us to the well-known "hermeneutical circle." The hermeneutical circle involves the "contextualist" claim that the 'parts' of some larger reality can be understood only in terms of the 'whole' of that reality, and the 'whole' of that reality can be understood only in terms of its parts. This is to say that understanding any phenomenon means, first of all, situating it in a larger context in which it has its function and, in turn, it also means letting our grasp of this particular phenomenon influence our grasp of the whole context. In a book, for example, we understand a chapter by understanding how it functions in the overall plan of the book, but our understanding of the chapter is equally indispensable for our grasp of the whole work.

This circular relation serves a purpose outside a limited descriptive concern with the logic of textual interpretation. It is meant to depict a structural feature of the way in which human knowledge evolves within a given historical-linguistic framework without ever jumping out of that framework in a great leap of reflection. Thus, for example, a new argument or position against a traditional position will always be understood, at least initially, over against that traditional position, but it may also succeed in transforming our understanding of that position. Heidegger's own work in *Being and Time* attempts just that: Neo-Kantianism and particularly Husserls's ideal of a presuppositionless philosophy is the anvil on which Heidegger attempts to hammer out a position that will transform and supersede our sense of transcendental philosophy. One could also cite Aristotle's attempt to work out his position on knowledge vis-a-vis Plato. His terms and his problems are clearly indebted to Plato, but he also pointed to problems that Plato did not consider and hence in a sense he pointed us beyond Plato. The same could be said for Kant's relation to empiricism and rationalism. He used empiricism and rationalism to change our sense of the meaning of these two philosophical traditions. This is not to say that everyone accepted Kant's critique of his predecessors (anymore than everyone has accepted Aristotle's departure from Plato), but it is the case that these traditions after Kant (and after Aristotle) were irrevocably changed in that no one could ignore their critique of their predecessors and still be considered responsible philosophers. The broader lesson to be learned from these examples is that human understanding seems to go forth and transform itself only over against a past or a tradition in terms of which it always understands itself, even when it attempts to leave that past behind. In short, the hermeneutical circle reminds us that although the past is no straightjacket or cage, there are no truly "new" beginnings.

If this is so then the task that the hermeneutical philosopher must face is the task of describing how something like valid knowledge-claims can emerge from such an apparently circular process. Heidegger is fully aware of this problem and the challenge it presents:

> In a scientific proof, we may not presuppose what it is our task to provide grounds for. But if interpretation must in any case already operate in that which is understood, and if it must draw its nurture from this, how is it to bring any scientific results to maturity without moving in a circle, especially if, moreover, the understanding which is presupposed still operates within our common information about man and the world? Yet according to the most elementary rules of logic, this circle is a *circulus vitiosus*.[35]

Some have thought that Heidegger's rhetorical question in this passage are indeed unanswerable. If we are immersed in our pre-understandings, then a vicious kind of relativism must follow. These same preunderstandings must block us off from the possibility of grasping anything as it really is.

One can argue, however, that Heidegger is not really a 'relativist' at all but a 'perspectivist.' Relativism has many forms that I won't discuss here,[34] but one classic form of relativism, which Heidegger clearly avoids, rests on the distinction between appearances and reality. On this view human understanding either grasps the mere appearances of things that are "for us" and hence relative to our species-specific and historically mediated perspective or it grasps reality "in itself," that is, as it is apart from the "foreign" influences of our contingent ways of grasping it. On this view of understanding, any theory of understanding must be called "relativist" if it denies the possibility of somehow climbing out of our own historical and human point of view and grasping things as they really are in themselves.

This view of relativism rests on two fundamental assumptions that Heidegger challenges. It assumes, to begin with, that our most common everyday relation to things is a relation to the mere appearances and not to things themselves. Hence all understanding based on these appearances of reality is mere opinion (*doxa*, as Plato called it) and as such inherently untrustworthy. Secondly, on this view our pre-understandings are seen as nothing other than barriers or roadblocks in the path toward a true grasp of the things themselves. Heidegger argues, however, that such an account of relativism and the basic assumptions about understanding that it presupposes is wrong on a number of accounts. It is wrong, to begin with, in that it conceives our fundamental relation to reality as one of being fundamentally estranged from reality, shut off by the barrier of our own thoughts. This ignores the fact that our most basic, fundamental, and primitive relation to reality is one of being-in-the-world where we have an intimate contact with and access to things. This intimate, ineluctable relation to things does not preclude the possibility of error, deception, and estrangement from reality, but Heidegger suggests that the very possibility of being shut off from reality, of being fundamentally mistaken about this or that reality, presupposes a prior access and openness to reality in terms of which this being mistaken can be recognized and (perhaps) corrected.

This kind of classic relativism is also mistaken in that it insists, very precipitously, that our preunderstandings cannot be as anything but roadblocks or barriers in the path of understanding. Heidegger argues that our preunderstandings are not so much roadblocks around which we must detour but more like a medium or fabric of semantic relations in which things qua intelligible realities already exist and which makes it possible for us to understand them by virtue of their 'situation' in this medium.

> In interpreting, we do not, so to speak, throw a 'signification' over some naked thing which is present-at-hand, we do not

stick a value on it; but when something within-the-world is encountered as such, the thing in question already has an involvement which is disclosed in our understanding of the
world, and this involvement is one which gets laid out by the
interpretation.[35]

In other words, reality is not lurking behind our historically mediated
understanding, but instead reality shows itself *through* our preunderstanding.

Heidegger's main contribution to hermeneutical thought can be described as an attempt to give us a way to think about our own thinking
that avoids the suggestion that our situatedness in history leads to a
skeptical relativism. If our preunderstandings are not like the barriers
that block our access to things and over which we must jump in order to
understand things as they truly are, then there is no problem of
relativism as we have described it. Instead, by being historical, by inheriting a set of linguistically mediated preunderstandings, we gain the
possibility of having a meaningful world. It is only because we take so
much for granted, only because there is so much implicitly understood
in the very ways we inherit a historical world that we can understand
anything new or challenging.

From this perspective Heidegger's position amounts to a perspec-
tivism and not a skeptical relativism. Things show themselves from a
certain perspective; things themselves are made manifest in this implicitly meaningful context, not "in themselves" or as pregiven
atomic particulars, but as they really exist in time, that is, in relation
to us in a context of meaningful relations with other things. Of
course, our historically mediated perspective on things will have
limitations, but the fact that any perspective has limitations does not
imply that our perspectives cut us off from reality. Just because we
always understand reality from some perspective does *not* imply that
what we understand is, really, our own perspective and not reality.
On the contrary, we understand *from* a perspective but *what* we
understand is still reality.

We can better understand this point about our fundamentally
unalienable contact with reality through a brief consideration of
Heidegger's appropriation of Husserl's theory of the intentional
nature of consciouness. Consciousness, according to Husserl, always
"intends" a determinate something as its object.[36] Consciousness is always, for example, a thinking about . . . , a feeling that . . . , a wishing
for . . . , a remembering how . . . , and so forth. In this sense "consciousness is" in Husserl's famous formula "always a consciousness

of something.'' Heidegger translated Husserl's thesis that ''consciousness is always a consciousness of . . . '' into the claim that we are *always already (''immer schon'')* in the world with others and with things. This is a very Husserlian move in spirit even though Heidegger attempts to make its language less Cartesian, more concrete and more arresting. When Husserl claimed that consciousness is always consciousness of something he meant to combat the view that consciousness is, first of all, closed in on itself, dwelling totally within the inner space of its own ''ideas'' and ''experiences'' and only subsequently (if at all) in contact with ''external'' reality. This view of consciousness as a ''closed box''[37] is false, for it ignores the subtle but unavoidable fact that we are *always already* with things and others in a world we have not chosen and from which we cannot in any kind of radical way short of complete madness cut ourselves off. If consciousness were a ''closed box,'' we would indeed be faced with the old (unanswerable) skeptical problem of the external world, that is, it would indeed be a fundamental mystery how consciousness could know anything other than its own contents. But if consciousness is not essentially monadic, but rather intentional and inalienably 'worldly', then we have a way to explain how despite the fact that our consciousness of the world is never without preunderstandings, it is nevertheless a consciousness *of reality.* Of course it is a consciousness of reality relative to this or that perspective, but if perspectives are not barriers but vantage points on reality, then it is precisely by relating some reality to many different contexts or viewpoints that we gain a sense of the complexity, richness, or inexhaustibility of the real.

Heidegger wishes to be clear that just because we grasp reality from this or that historically mediated perspective—just because all understanding operates in a hermeneutical circle—it does not allow us to be arbitrary; reality does not mean whatever I take it to mean. The awareness of the hermeneutical circles demands, on the contrary, that we come into the circle ''in the right way;''[38] it does not allow us to avoid the hard empirical work of learning how things really are with the world, but it is a finite discovery of how things are from a particular perspective at a particular time. Meaning is neither arbitrarily imposed from without nor discovered as a brute fact. Rather it is worked out in a finite historical context in a dialectical fashion. Heidegger writes:

> To be sure, we genuinely take hold of this possibility only
> when in our interpretation, we have understood that our first,

last, and constant task is never to allow our fore-having, fore-sight, and fore-conception to be presented to us by fancies and popular conceptions, but rather to make the scientific theme secure by working out these fore-structures in terms of the things themselves.[39]

Considering what we have already said this appeal to the "things themselves" should not be understood as an appeal to things "in themselves" but as an appeal to 'deep' interpretations as opposed to 'superficial' interpretatons of things worked out in terms of "fancies and popular conceptions." A deep understanding of things worked out "scientifically" in terms of the "things themselves" does not assume an ahistorical notion of science and neither is it a metaphysical distinction conceived along lines of idealistic or realistic ontologies. Rather, it is a working, practical distinction between accounts that see things superficially, namely, accounts that fail to plumb the depths of preunderstanding and that settle for an understanding in terms of "fancies and popular conceptions," and deep accounts that work out an understanding of the subject matter that addresses everything that shows itself in light of a specific preunderstanding. In this sense, Heidegger is not asking us to do the impossible, that is, to step outside our preunderstandings and view things as such or, as Gadamer sometimes phrases it, "from a perspective that is no perspective at all," but he is asking us to look deeply at things as they present themselves from the horizon of our preunderstandings.

A very important source of these preunderstandings, according to Heidegger, is language. In *Being and Time* Heidegger associates language with reason. This can be seen in such claims as "language already conceals within itself a developed mode of conceiving."[40] Hence for Heidegger language is a principle source of our pre-understandings. More fundamental, however, is Heidegger's attempt to connect the hermeneutical function of language with the traditional notions of *logos*.[41] The *logos*, for the Greeks, was intimately connected with the reason or the essence of things. But it was also related etymologically to language and speech. Heidegger sees this as no mere accident but insists rather that it is language (*logos*) in both its function as speech ("*legein*") and its designative function ("*legmenon*") that allows us to see the reaon (ratio) of things in terms of their relatedness to each other and to us.[42]

Heidegger understands the thesis that it is language that makes possible rational activity in that it is language that first makes it possible for us to understand things as more than mere objects to which we react blindly and mechanically and instead makes possible the designation of something as a specific such and such.[43] In short, it is language that gives us the ability to understand things as a certain *sort* or *type* of thing. As such, it is langauge that enables us to identify things as belonging to certain historically varied classes, which then enables us to think of them in general and shared terms. Heidegger calls this function of language the 'apophantic' function of language. Language is apophantic in the sense that it "lets an entity be seen from itself."[44] In other words, language allows us to grasp things in both their complex similarity to an distinctiveness from other things. Language allows the world to be seen as something more than a mere conglomeration of brutely given and fundamentally unintelligible particulars and transforms it into a semantic world where both the differences and similarities can be seen, preserved, explored, and deepened.

We should be warned, however, that Heidegger's emphasis on the semantic function of language does not commit him to a *Sprachidealismus*, which sees language as imposing a meaning on an indifferent and forever foreign reality. As Heidegger pointed out, interpretation does not involve "throw[ing] a signification over some naked things."[45] On the contrary, language and reality are mutually illuminating according to Heidegger; changes in the world necessitate changes in language, and changes in language affect what we are able to grasp about the world. Language lives and grows through our attempts to respond to reality as it shows itself in a variety of ways. By searching for new ways to speak about new situations and experiences language develops. Of course, in each situation where understanding is sought there is a linguistically mediated preunderstanding that casts the subject matter of speech in a certain light; but this 'light' or perspective is not, as it were, "the last word," for speech goes forward in the attempt to adjust itself simultaneously to reality and to other linguistic accounts of the same phenomenon. In the process, new meanings can emerge that can, in turn, be tested in terms of previous linguistic accounts and in terms of the reality they make visible. In short, the dialectic of language operates according to the pattern of the hermeneutical circle.

Reason, on this model, is something like the ability both to allow language to organize and illuminate reality *and* to develop the possibilities inherent in certain ways of speaking toward new and deeper insights. This linguistically mediated process of reason is the activity of interpretation itself.[45] By seeking ever new ways to interpret our linguistically mediated world, the life of reason itself goes forth. It is in this sense that Gadamer insists that the "work of understanding and interpreting always remains meaningful. In this is demonstrated the superior universality with which reason is elevated above the limits of every given system of language. The hermeneutical experience is the corrective through which thinking reason escapes the power of the linguistic even while it is itself linguistically constituted."[46] The cutting edge of rational activity itself seems to exist in our ability, on the one hand, to become thoroughly familiar with a way of speaking about some reality and, on the other hand, to see new ways of speaking and understanding that are implicit in those familiar patterns of speech. Something like linguistic imagination is necessary to rational activity because "whoever has language 'has' the world."[47]

7

Gadamer's contribution to hermeneutics may be described as an enormously suggestive attempt to extend Heidegger's insight into the linguistically mediated nature of human understanding. Gadamer's jumping-off point for this project is a critique of the thesis that language is essentially an instrument or tool we use to express thoughts that are fully developed prior to their articulation in speech.[48] According to the 'instrumental' view we use language incidentally to express essentially private thoughts in a public realm, but language is not the very medium of thought itself. Gadamer points out that language really is not like a tool or instrument we can pick up and put down at will. We may choose a word or phrase, but we do not choose either to use or not use language. All thought is linguistic. Thinking may not be reducible to language or linguistic behavior, but it is, nevertheless, inseparable from it. We never have a "pure" thought that is wordless and that is then incidentally expressed in language. Thought may begin with vague hunches and intuitions, but one wordless hunch is like another. Rather, in finding 'the right words" we have the thought (and hence an understanding of the object) for the first time.[49] Thought comes to fruition in language and not just to outward expression. It is first by articulating a thought in some language that the thought itself becomes distinct and understandable. In short, our consciousness of the world is a linguistic consciousness that we can never leave behind to achieve a wordless condition of so-called pure thought.

Language, according to Gadamer, is a medium within which we move and understand ourselves and the world from various perspectives.[50] As a medium, language should not be understood as a straightjacket, but it is an intersubjective fabric of semantic relations that both makes possible and limits understanding. It is in this sense that Gadamer claims that "being that can be understood is language."[51] "In language the reality beyond every individual consciousness becomes visible."[52] This understanding is always limited or finite in that every linguistic account is bound to be selective both in what it emphasizes about a phenomenon and in terms of the clarity and suggestiveness by which it allows the phenomenon to be seen. But the same conditions that make language a limiting factor in understanding also make it a necessary condition of any possible understanding. Having a complex and nuanced language is a necessary condition for understanding what something is and how it is related to other realities. Our understanding of some phenomenon will vary in sophistication and depth in direct proportion to both the number of different ways we have of speaking about it and in our intralinguistic ability to relate these ways of speaking to one another.

But if language is not adequately understood as an instrument or tool we use incidentally when the need arises, neither is language a mere "sign." Gadamer criticizes the notion of language as a mere sign because it suggests—wrongly, he thinks—that the way we think is in terms of arbitrarily chosen signs that stand in for concepts, which in turn point to fully determinate, pregiven realities. The notion that thought moves from reality, to a concept, to a sign, and back again ignores the fact that we never have a concept apart from some linguistic account of it, nor do we ever have an alinguistic insight into reality. The notion of language as sign ignores the fact that it is first through language that we acquire a meaningful system of relations in terms of which anything can show itself as meaningful in any way at all. Gadamer would say that it is only through language that we have a world. The world does not stand over against language as a pregiven intelligible entity in its own right. The world in its brute givenness is not intelligible at all. Rather it is only by coming into language that any reality itself becomes meaningful as this or that.[53] Only through language does a set of common, repeatable meanings emerge that enables me to share with others a common sense of what the world is about. It is this shared sense of things that enables me to assume points of implicit agreement between myself and those I speak with, listen to, or read, which in turn makes our conversation and mutual understanding possible.

Given this inexhaustible and ever-shifting linguistic backdrop of understanding, Gadamer argues that all understanding presupposes a set of linguistically mediated prejudices and prejudgments (*"Vorurteile"*) that provide a vantage point from which we understand reality. According to Gadamer, "Prejudices in the literal sense of the word, constitute the intitial directedness of our whole ability to experience. Prejudices are the biases of our openness to the world."[54] This is perhaps Gadamer's most controversial thesis. In emphasizing the role that linguistically mediated prejudices play in all thought, Gadamer is *not* advocating parochial, uncritical, or undisciplined thought. He is, however, attempting to challenge certain Enlightenment assumptions about the ahistorical autonomy of rational activity and to suggest instead that all knowledge-claims necessarily presuppose a dialectical history. Gadamer points out that any knowledge-claim can be adequately understood only from within a tradition. No knowledge-claim stands alone, *an sich*, but presupposes a way of speaking about its subject matter that stretches back into the past and toward the future. If this is so, the question that arises is How are we to understand the development of understanding from this dialectical and linguistically mediated process? What conditions make possible the emergence of a new insight from a process that appears self-referential and locked into the past?

Gadamer's answer to this question, depends on his notion of language as dialogue or conversation (*"Gespräch"*). Gadamer conceives language primarily a living dialogue or conversation and only secondarily as a deposit of grammatical rules and lexigraphically secure meanings. "Language has its true being only in conversation, in the exercise of understanding between people."[55] This implies that deep, adequate views of things cannot in a strict sense be guaranteed at all, even by 'method', but can be worked out only in conversation. Talk, 'mere talk' is the source of our growing awareness of how things really are in the world. This is to say that only by coming to terms internally with the language of a sphere of inquiry, that is, only from the point of view of actual dialogue in the field, does the subject matter of the field begin to emerge and take on recognizable meaning and adequate intelligibility. Even practitioners of the same 'method' have need of a genuine exchange of viewpoints if they are to secure a firm grasp on the subject matter. Thus Gadamer would say that such academic practices as giving papers, entering into debates and dialogues, asking questions, and so forth, are all part of working out our preunderstandings in light of the things themselves. 'Talk' or dialogue is not an incidental condition of inquiry; it is the very life of inquiry, discovery, and truth itself.[56]

Gadamer stresses dialogue as the real life of inquiry and not certain formal rules of dialogue like logic and grammar, or 'method' because he thinks that over and above these rules and methods (but not necessarily contrary to them) the twists and turns of dialogue itself help bring the subject matter to light. This means that in the course of a real, open conversation, that is, a conversation where the participants actually devote themselves to understanding the issue and not simply to 'scoring points' or 'defending' a position, that, for example, insights, metaphors, and frameworks can emerge that may suggest new ways of seeing the subject matter, or new conceptual vocabularies can be hammered out that will help move a discussion onto new ground. Further, it is only through 'talk' that different ways of 'grouping' the data may emerge that may enable new insights to be gained or new questions to be asked that will reveal some inadequacy or theoretical breakthrough. In all these ways, conversation is necessary to gaining a deeper, more adequate understanding of things.

The very generality and seeming "emptiness" of Gadamer's claim that all inquiry develops only through dialogue or conversation is intentional and significant. By saying little he intends to imply much. By keeping his claim general and necessarily vague Gadamer emphasizes that there is no one method on which all our research should be modeled. Neither does he think that there ever will be any such method. Our very "linguisticality" and "finitude" make it impossible for us to escape the linguistically mediated nature of our contact with reality and the necessarily "perspectival" and limited understanding this engenders. This means that we can never shake ourselves free of language through the development of something like the 'perfect' research method or the most rigorous set of a-historical criteria for judging disputes in all our disciplines.

We can make better sense of this role that conversation or dialogue can play in working out new insights by pointing to a number of features about language and history and their relationship to the subject matter of any inquiry. To begin with Gadamer often cites a line from Hans Lipps that any linguistic account or 'word' always carries with it a "circle of the unexpressed";[57] or, as Gadamer phrases it, an "infinity of the unsaid."[58] This implies that any linguistic account is never entirely clear and univocal but carries within it unspoken meanings and possibilities of understanding and critique to be explored and articulated. It is important to stress that these 'ambiguities' are not necessarily deficiencies but sources of possible meaning that can cast a new light on the very subject matter of discourse. This implies that one way that knowledge advances is by looking for that which is implicit and unsaid in an account, whether as a source of criticism or as positive continuation of what was said.

This notion of every linguistic account containing possibilities for questioning and development also points to its relation to history itself. I mean by this that often historical circumstances themselves have a way of opening up critical insight into a linguistic account or penetrating into the circle of the unexpressed and advancing understanding. For example, the events of the French Revolution showed the young Hegel some of the problems inherent in Kant's deontological account of morality. The Reign of Terror convinced the young Hegel that a 'universal' account of an 'autonomous' practical reason could never do justice to the 'contingent' demands of a 'heteronomous' moral life. In general, historical circumstances often cast a subject matter in a certain light, which in turn makes obvious the shortcomings of some linguistic account of it. In this way history and language are dialectically related in a process that gives rise again and again to new insights. This leads Gadamer to say, on the one hand, that all understanding presupposes both historically and linguistically mediated preunderstanding and, on the other hand, to insist that understanding takes place only when the inquirer doggedly pursues the logic of the subject matter itself. Thus, for example, if we are interested in a phenomenon like friendship or duty, it will be possible to understand it only if we first of all examine the linguistic accounts associated with these phenomena in our culture. But it is equally important that we actually look to the experience of friendship or duty itself in order to test the accuracy, coherence and depth of that language.

In all of our concerns with these phenomena it is not language on which we explicitly focus our attention, but rather the linguistically mediated *content* of language. It is the content of linguistic accounts, the subject matter of a discourse, that actually prompts and sustains our dialogue with one another. Language becomes a theme of inquiry only when understanding breaks down or become otherwise problematic. This is so because in speaking a certain language and in appropriating, say, a certain traditional way of speaking about a phenomenon, I am not cut off from reality but I am, instead, always already with things. Language is a medium in which we have contact with things and each other. We live and think *in* language and never just *with* language. Because language does not estrange us from reality but gives us meaningful contact with it, we tend to overlook the role of language as such and focus our attention instead on the realities it makes manifest. These realities, themes, or subject matters are furthermore historically mediated concerns, issues, and perspectives, in which the discussants share a common interest that sustain and direct their discourse. Gadamer calls these realities, concerns, issues, perspectives, *Sachen*.[59]

The German "*die Sache*" can be translated in many different ways as object, phenomenon, concern, issue, case, or things, just to mention a few. What Gadamer seems to have in mind is that the '*Sachen*' of discourse are always some shared topic of concern, in which the conversants have some kind of vested interest, that they wish to understand for some purpose. Language always directs us to these concerns or issues that make up our world in such a direct and forceful way that language itself seems to disappear behind the concerns and topics that animate and give focus to our conversations. Moreover, it is by openly trying to understand concerns like justice, duty, love, freedom, friendship, understanding, explanation, and so forth, that the life of language goes forth and develops itself in dialectical fashion.

Gadamer's model for this process of understanding is drawn largely from the Platonic dialogue.[60] Socrates' inquiries almost always involved an investigation of the language of some phenomenon—particularly that of the poets and 'common-sense' politicians of his day—and a determined effort to question both the implications of that language and the logic of the subject matter itself. The results, of course, are rarely definitive, but the point that Gadamer wants to stress is that the insights into a certain phenomenon which emerge in the course of the dialogue are inseparable from the dialogical situation and the conditions that make it possible. What is generated in the course of the dialogue are not ahistorical truths, *pace* Plato, but an insight into the subject matter that is relative to both a certain way of speaking and a way of being concerned about the phenomenon in question. Moreover, what emerges is something previously unseen about the phenomenon in question, something that transcends the expectation of the interlocutors. This is so in the sense that the truth that emerges was not necessarily expected by either interlocutor, but it emerged from a set of linguistic and philosophical presuppositions in which they participated without complete understanding. In Gadamer's words, "what emerged in its truth is the *logos*, and this is neither yours or mine, but rather exceeds the subjective opinion of the partners in discussion to such an extent that even the leader of the discussion always remains the ignorant one."[61] In this sense, the participants are carried along in a historical or linguistic "event" that gives rise to an advance in understanding, which itself can be further analyzed, built upon and, perhaps, someday superceded.

Gadamer calls this an "event" (*Geschehen*)[62] of understanding because he wishes to emphasize the fact that what emerges from a genuine conversation is not the *subjective accomplishment* of one of the interlocutors. Neither is it, strictly speaking, their joint accomplishment. Rather it is something that *happens* to them in a way they had not anticipated and that they could not control. Of course, each participant in a discussion may make a contribution to its outcome, but the point is that the outcome can never be analyzed solely in terms of either an individual or joint subjective accomplishment. Rather, language itself has a way of carrying the participants along in a dialogue, in a process, that exceeds their subjective awareness. For example, in the *Euthyphro* something emerges both about Euthyphro's relation to Greek religion and Socrates' relation to authority of which neither Euthyphro nor Socrates seemed transparently aware. Moreover, after the dialogue—if it or some semblance of it actually took place—it is not clear exactly how much of this insight into their respective relations to Greek religion and authority actually sank into either Euthyphro or Socrates. What is clear, however, is that through the dialogue itself something about both Euthyphro and Socrates, as well as Greek religion and Greek morality, emerged, something that, moreover, was not accessible before. In short, some truth was made manifest through their dialogue whether they were able to acknowledge it or not.

Now this 'event' could take place only because Socrates and Euthyphro shared a certain familiarity with the language(s) of religion and morality in their society. This is to say they shared a tradition (or traditions) all of which they did not necessarily accept or believe but which they took for granted in their conversation.

Gadamer would describe this involvement of both discussants in a tradition as a *"Wirkungsgeschichte"*[63] or 'history of effects.' This is to say that both Socrates and Euthyphro participated in a fabric of linguistic and social practices that served as the backdrop of their discussion of piety or holiness. Both of them were affected by this tradition, albeit in different ways, as much as they were trying to affect its interpretation and ultimate direction. In this sense they were part of an ongoing cultural phenomenon, and this participation was a precondition of their understanding each other in any way. Gadamer would argue that such participation in a *Wirkungsgeschichte* was not unique to Euthyphro and Socrates or to discussants in a "precritical," "unenlightened" society, but a condition of any human attempt to understand any phenomenon.

Socrates and Euthyphro were not, however, simply passive sufferers of these traditions; they were also trying to extend them in various ways and criticize them in others. They had an active interest in these traditions that was motivated by their *present* perception of their needs and the needs of their culture. They interpreted these traditions and understood them, at least in part, through these concerns and interests. Gadamer would say that they *applied* these traditions to their own situation and he would point out that all interpretation involves application of a historically mediated tradition to the present needs and perspectives of the interpreter.[64] This is to say that in addition to always having been possibly shaped by a *Wirkungsgeschichte* of a tradition we also contribute actively to that tradition by applying it to our current situation. The need for application testifies to our ineluctable historicity in the sense that in addition to always having a past that affects us in innumerably complex ways we also have a present that is always in some ways different from the past and that is animated by concerns and interests that drive it toward the future. Thus the past shapes us, but we contribute to its outcome by responding to it in light of our current needs and interests.

In this sense Gadamer argues that all interpretation involves a fusion of horizons (*"Horizontsverschmelzung"*) between the past and present.[65] All interpretation takes place not only in terms of an implicit involvement in a tradition but also with an eye to how that past can be applied to our current theoretical and practical concerns. If we are temporal then we can no sooner divorce ourselves completely from the past than we can ignore our present concerns and perspectives. It can be said that it is precisely this need for application that prevents the past from turning into a sterile deposit of irrelevant facts or an ossified orthodoxy. The need for application, brought about by the ever-changing needs of the present, is what drives traditions forward, sometimes, of course, even to their breaking points.[66]

This emphasis on application suggests that we never understand in a 'disinterested' fashion but only in terms of some theoretical/pragmatic framework in terms of which certain understandings, theories, solutions recommend themselves, almost as a matter of course. To emphasize this 'interested' character of 'rational' activity Gadamer attempts to revive the Aristotelian notion of *phronesis* or practical wisdom.[67] In so doing he emphasizes the claim that reason and judgment cannot function without making a type of value-assessment about the 'significance' or 'importance' of a knowledge-claim for the present circumstances. Reason makes these kinds of judgments in light of the explicit and implicit needs and priorities of the particular historical community in which it functions. The *phronimos*, or person with practical wisdom, supposedly sees with intuitive clarity what is called for, what is needed, what is possible in a specific moral or political situation in a way akin to our ability to grasp essential differences between geometrical figures.[68] According to Gadamer, it is the self-understanding of the historical community of the *phronimos* that gives rise to its members' ability to make putatively self-evident judgments about what is real, likely, plausible, needed, important, problematical, and so forth.[69] According to Gadamer, this is an inherent aspect of all rational understanding. Gadamer points out, however, that, unlike the rules of deductive argumentation, the rational criteria of such judgments changes as the self-understanding of the historically situated community changes. What this means for Gadamer is that our rational ability to make such judgments does not rest on some deep, permanent structure, transcendental reason or human nature, but rather it depends on our changing self-understanding. As this self-understanding changes it gives rise to a new sense of our needs, priorities, and possibilities. Insofar as such historically shifting 'prejudgments' are essential to any understanding, the human community is not, according to Gadamer, asymptotically approaching the same body of universal truths. Instead, we are moving "in fits and starts" toward epistemic goals that shift as our needs and priorities change.[70] In this manner, Gadamer wishes to point out that the human sciences have never been really guided by the ideal of universal reason or objectivity but instead have always been guided by the 'practical' needs of the historical community, which have been their final arbiter in matters of dispute.

Gadamer takes this insight so seriously that he proposes that the epistemic ideal of universal reason and objectivity in the human sciences should be replaced with the moral ideal of "practical wisdom."[71] Gadamer argues for this substitution not only because the ideal of objectivity or universal reason cannot be approached in light of our 'situatedness' in language and history but because he thinks that the human sciences themselves have always had a broadly construed 'moral' goal. All of our disputes about reason, knowledge, sex, art, religion, and so forth, are disputes, which, at bottom are disputes about the kind of life human beings ought to form for themselves. Gadamer wants to be clear about what it is we are really arguing about and what is at stake in these disputes. Despite the daunting complexity of these debates, we should not lose sight of their overarching moral significance. Only this insight will save us from pedantry and pseudo-science. For this reason Gadamer has written that "hermeneutical philosophy is the heir of the older tradition of practical philosophy."[72] Moreover, its primary task is to "justify this way of reason against the domination of technology based on sciences."[73]

Gadamer wishes to remind us that technology, say in the form of computer science, will never solve the debates in the human sciences that have practical impact on our lives. Conflicts arise repeatedly because we are always confronted with a variety of contradictory linguistic accounts of our situation which contain a myriad of practical possibilities. Technology will not free us from our many ways of speaking about ourselves. It will not decide for us which of these ways of speaking will be authoritative for us and it will not decide how we are to actualize our practical possibilities. Conflicting possibilities of understanding in the human sciences must be and should be settled ultimately on nonscientific, moral grounds.[74] We cope with this situation as best we can through *phronesis*, that is, a fallible, historically-informed judgement about what is 'best' now. Roughly speaking, if understanding occurs only by relating the concerns of a text or disputes about an issue to our human concerns and these concerns can be traced back only to historically informed judgments about what is important, needful, plausible, problematic, and so on, for a specific historic community, then ultimately disputes within or between communities will have to be decided by going back to these concerns and deciding which of the competing claims, if any, really is more important, needful plausible, problematic, and so on *at the present time*. This is important because Gadamer suggests that the way disputes are settled is never by simply applying a set of ahistorical criteria but by sustained dialogue about which perspectives in a dispute really reflect both the best theoretical and practical responses to the questions inherited from a tradition and the best response to our needs of self-understanding and self-development at the present time. For example, it can be argued that Kant's philosophy took Europe by storm not because it was without internal problems or blindspots, but because it best addressed many theoretical problems inherited from the traditions of rationalism and empiricism *and* because it suggested profound practical implications for human freedom that resonated deeply with the perceived political and cultural needs of the time. This is, of course, a simplification, but the point is that there are never ahistorical criteria available that will settle our debates. We must instead rely on pragmatic criteria of the moment. In the final analysis, this is what has always been behind all cultural change.

Of course, solutions arrived at by such means are always tentative and rarely satisfactory to everyone. An act of *phronesis* which enjoys consensus depends on the right historical 'circumstances' as much as anything else does, and, certainly, the successful adjudication of our disputes is evasive and rare indeed.[75] What is more, such practical decisions can, more often than not, only be implemented by wielding power of some sort or another. Consequently, the exercise of *phronesis* often creates divisions and disputes. Be that as it may, Gadamer insists that we cannot escape making practical judgements about our past and the direction in which it is taking us. Because we are finite historical beings who always stand within a tradition, because we cannot walk away from our present, and because we must make choices toward some future, we can no sooner escape *phronesis* than we can escape our own humanity. It is one of Gadamer's deepest concerns to remind Western humanity that despite the fact that we have achieved a great deal technical mastery over our environment and are daily tempted to embrace the illusion that all questions of human existence will eventually be resolved through the same scientific means that have given us our technologically based comforts, we should not forget our historical finitude and our own responsibility for the future of our species on this planet. "The ancient Greek 'know thyself' still holds good for us as well. For it means 'know that you are no god, but a human being'."[76] It is to promote this kind of awareness so rare in our technological society, to which Gadamer has devoted so many of his writings. Gadamer wishes to promote a dialogue or conversation that would help us reach greater consensus on who we were, who we are, and who we will be, in order to help us realize our need for current application of those traditions to our future. Only by recognizing this as our task and by freely taking it up do we have a chance, in Gadamer's opinion, to prevent the demise of the humanistic tradition.

8

Many critical questions could (and should) be asked at this point. But introductions are sometimes better confined to presenting a sketch of the concerns that a work addresses. This is what I have attempted to do. The debates and dialogues that hermeneutics has raised are widely represented in this volume. The intent of this collection is to provide an insight into the contemporary status of hermeneutics, as it stems from thinkers like Heidegger and Gadamer. I have chosen Heidegger and Gadamer for they are clearly the seminal thinkers in this field. But the title I have chosen also intentionally juxtaposes hermeneutics and modern philosophy. By 'modern philosophy' I do not simply mean the period in the history of philosophy from Descartes up to and (depending on your philosophical tradition) possibly including Kant, but I mean to include contemporary philosophy as well. I have chosen this broad perspective because hermeneutics addresses a number of concerns (some of which I have attempted to outline above) that have been seminal to modernity. It was, in part, to bring this *Wirkungsgeschichte* to mind that the title was chosen. But also the title is significant because hermeneutics has been seen by some to mark a departure from the tradition of modern philosophy.[77] Of course, if it is such a departure hermeneutics cannot pretend that it is really starting anew. On the contrary, if it really does mark a departure it will be a departure only in the sense that one tradition is dialectically evolving into another and not in the sense of a 'clean' break with the past. From our perspective, however, we cannot tell what hermeneutics may portend. We can only attempt to continue the discussion with as much clarity and vigor as we can muster.

It is for these purposes of dialogue and conversation on the meaning and direction of philosophical hermeneutics that this volume has been assembled. If it generates debates that move this tradition of philosophy forward, it will repay, I think, the efforts of its many contributors.

The collection begins with a section that concentrates on the concept of historicity in understanding. Merold Westphal's "Hegel and Gadamer" provides a very clear and useful introduction to this theme both in terms of Gadamer's theory of understanding and in terms of the historical indebtedness of Gadamer to the critique of rationalist, empiricist, and Kantian epistemology, which was formulated by Hegel, Husserl, and the existentialists. Westphal argues that Gadamer understands our relation to the past as a "tension-filled proximity," that is neither slavish imitation nor complete freedom from history. History forms a horizon of possibilities which gives us a finite but open perspective from which to view reality. Westphal illustrates this thesis by pointing out, on the one hand, Gadamer's acceptance of both Hegel's understanding of the transcendental subject as "a speaker of a language" and his repudiation of the Cartesian thesis that 'method' can 'desituate' the inquirer. But, on the other hand, Westphal points to Gadamer's rejection of the Hegelian claim to absolute knowledge, which is no longer viable for our historical situation. By showing this "polar tension" in Gadamer's thought, Westphal hopes to show how "openness to tradition and respect for its authority need not involve an uncritical conservativism that worships the past."[78]

Richard J. Bernstein's "From Hermeneutics to Praxis" is next. Like Westphal, Bernstein accepts Gadamer's thesis regarding the 'historicity' of understanding but his point of departure is an analysis of *phronesis* and the problems associated with the 'appropriation' of a tradition for our present purposes. Bernstein suggests quite plausibly that Gadamer's understanding of Aristotle's notion of *phronesis* itself provides a model for understanding what Gadamer means by 'appropriation' or 'application'. By a careful study of Aristotle we learn how our own understanding of application has been deformed by the model of "the application of science to technical tasks." In a critical vein, however, Bernstein feels that Gadamer's own claims regarding *phronesis*, when pressed "lead us beyond philosophical hermeneutics."[79] Bernstein complains that however sympathetic we may be to Gadamer's critique of objectivism and foundationalism, we cannot skirt the question of the proper basis or standards for our critical endeavors. He notes, through a careful exposition of the concept of *phronesis* in its original Aristotelian context, that the conditions that made "practical wisdom" possible in Aristotle's day no longer hold today. Bernstein rightly points out that Aristotle assumed a widespread consensus regarding ethical matters that we cannot pretend exists in the contemporary world. This relative degree of uniformity of opinion gave Aristotle good grounds for placing confidence in *phronesis*. But in our pluralistic, relativistic and individualistic society such confidence would be misplaced. This leads Bernstein to conclude that Gadamer is unjustified in thinking that *phronesis* is always possible in any situation. According to Bernstein, hermeneutics leaves us with the unfinished and daunting task of actually creating a new set of political conditions in our society that will enable an open and rational dialogue. In short, hermeneutics points us beyond itself to the need for political praxis.

Wolfhart Pannenberg's "Hermeneutic and Universal History" follows Bernstein. In addition to pointing out the relevance of hermeneutics for theological concerns, Pannenberg asks a crucial philosophical question for hermeneutics: What must the interpreter assume about the relation between his own finite standpoint in history and history as a completed temporal process in order to criticize or apply the past to the present in a nonarbitrary way? Pannenberg criticizes Gadamer for not realizing the Hegelian implications of his own position. Pannenberg argues that every critique or application of a historical tradition presupposes that the thinker has an insight into the ultimate direction or goal of 'universal history.' Without at least an intimation of this direction we would have no way to link the present with the past; we would have no way to grasp the overall direction of our temporality, of which the past and present are merely 'moments'. But we can in fact grasp some such connection between past and present, so Pannenberg concludes that every finite point of departure contains within it at least an intimation of the truth of the whole. Pannenberg suggests that our critiques and applications of the past are always critiques that point out that a certain development strays from that goal (however provisional our grasp of it may be) or applications that attempt to show that this application is called for in light of a certain immanent goal. Without some such knowledge how could we justify our criticism or application of the past as anything other than arbitrary? Insofar as we are willing to defend our criticism as nonarbitrary we necessarily assume, Pannenberg thinks, that we are not totally immersed in our own present standpoint, but have instead some perspective, however tentative, on the ultimate direction of universal history. If this is so, then Gadamer and Heidegger are wrong to insist that human historicity entails the denial of any transhistorical standards of inquiry. If Pannenberg is right, the possibility of objectively valid criticisms or appropriations of the past seems defensible because as participants in history we also share in the ultimate goal of history, of which our present standpoint is a part. If this is so then we must find a way, Pannenberg argues, to formulate a philosophy of universal history that does justice to human finitude, while not denying us the possibility of universally valid insights.

Charles Larmore's paper, "Tradition, Objectivity, and Hermeneutics" also is concerned with the claims of hermeneutical thinkers to have disposed of the notion of "objective knowledge." In addition to a helpful discussion of some of the epistemological implications of Gadamer's position, Larmore focuses attention on how all inquiry presupposes a body of well-established and rationally justifiable beliefs that, despite our historicity, gives us a touchstone for determining the objective validity of any new knowledge-claim. Larmore's standard for judging any new knowledge-claim is coherence with "our more significant and steadfast beliefs." Larmore argues that Gadamer as well considers "coherence a constant standard of rationality." Hence he concludes "that a recognition of the historicity of knowledge-claims in no way forces us to give up the pursuit of objectivity."[80]

Marjorie Grene's essay "The Paradoxes of Historicity" closes off this section on the concept of historicity. She raises, as her title suggests, certain problems and paradoxes that any theory of understanding that emphasizes historicity as its point of departure must confront. Although she is sympathetic to the claim that human existence is historical, she complains that such a view ignores natural conditioning factors that, at the very least, play a complementary role in making us what we are. So much so, she insists that any view of human existence which ignores these natural factors distorts our situation by leaving us with "the image of a human world shorn of any roots in nature and a natural world devoid of places for humanity to show itself."[81] This distortion would be serious enough in itself but it also stands in the way of finding a solution to a problem Grene thinks is more pressing still. She asks whether the thesis of the historicity of understanding is not self-defeating in the sense that it seems to claim that all understanding is *caused* by its socio-temporal milieu, including the understanding that grasps this fact. Such a view seems to leave no room for the idea that insight into persons must not reduce them to causal conditioning factors but preserve their irreducible, historical uniqueness. Appeals to 'historicity', contrary to what many of its proponents think, will not solve the problem of cultural determinism. Grene suggests that our inability to solve this problem comes from the cavalier way in which philosophers on both sides of *Erklären/Verstehen* controversy have refused to explore the relation between nature and history. Grene proposes that we begin to think about human beings *in* nature and *in* history but not reducible to either. This entails, she thinks, the need to develop

> a concept, not of two different types of explanation, nor of two ways of being, but a number of levels of explanation, complementary to, but not contradictory of, one another and, accordingly of ways of being that exhibit among themselves analogously complementary relations. We need to show from within the hermeneutical circle, how both its own level of interpretation, which relies on culture-based meanings and their interpretation and reinterpretation by human beings in their worlds, and poorer but indispensable levels of explanation causal or otherwise scientific, can, and do, coexist and cooperate.[82]

Only then, she contends, will we have a notion of what it means to be human which is neither reductivistic nor another "opiate of the intellectuals."

Kathleen Wright's article "Gadamer: The Speculative Structures of Language" opens the next section, which focuses on the role of language in understanding for philosophical hermeneutics. Wright begins by exploring the complex dynamic betwen Hegel and Heidegger in Gadamer's understanding of language. She points out that despite Gadamer's more immediate proximity to Heidegger Gadamer turns to Hegel to understand the notion of the I-Thou structure of language. Gadamer makes this move, which is a move in favor of Hegel's concept of *Geist*, because Heidegger's philosophy lacks a notion of the authentic reciprocity so characteristic of our involvement with language. Language involves reciprocity in that, according to Gadamer, "[L]anguage has its true being only in conversation . . . " This is to say that our deepest relations to language is not that of a mere 'sign' or 'tool' to express our thoughts. Instead we stand in the midst of a language, rich in meaning, which always confronts us with something to say, that is, some way of perceiving reality to which we must respond, like another person's moral demands on us. For example, we can experience the language of, say, the philosophical traditions of the West as languages which make a claim on us that demands that we allow them to question our lives. When we do this, we experience something fundamental about language which we often ignore, when we objectify and distance ourselves from this language by turning it into an object of research or criticism. This does not imply that Gadamer deprecates research and criticism. Quite the contrary. But he wishes to remind us that before we criticize and objectify our language it has always appropriated us to some extent. Only as conversation, with a reciprocal I-Thou structure, do we understand how we stand with respect to language. This emphasis on conversation is also linked to Gadamer's notion of language as a 'center' or a medium shared by participants in a tradition, which binds them together in a common understanding, and indeed, which binds the world together as a "web of meaning". To understand further the way in which language is a 'center' which binds us together with each other and reality, Wright takes up Gadamer's claim that language is "speculative." In using the term "speculative" Gadamer is looking to the etymological sense of the term "speculative," which derives from *speculum* or mirror. Language is speculative in that reality gets "reflected" in it and through it. It is through language that the world is shown to us in all its many-sided dimensions. Language is like a mirror which holds up to us an image of the real, which, qua image, is logically distinct, but which nevertheless belongs inseparably to that which it reflects. In this way, Gadamer wants to suggest that any linguistic account of a phenomenon offers us a finite perspective on some reality which nevertheless is not a mere appearance of the real but a viable reflection of the real. So it is that by understanding the language of some phenomenon we understand the phenomenon itself but without ever exhausting it or precluding the possibility of developing new ways of speaking about it. Wright explores these ideas with a conceptual subtlety and attention to historical detail that defies summary. Suffice it to say that she offers us an in-depth look not only at part of the history of Gadamer's thoughts on language, but at some of its more profound nuances as well.

Brice Wachterhauser's essay "Must We Be What We Say? Gadamer on Truth in the Human Sciences" stays with the theme of Gadamer's reflections on language but it attempts to explore the implications of his theory of language for the problem of truth and self-knowledge. The paper argues that although Gadamer seems to lack any fully developed theory of truth, his thoughts on this subject point to some interesting criticisms of the traditional theories of truth, that is, correspondence and coherence theories of truth, particularly as they pertain to truths about the self. It raises critical questions, however, about whether Gadamer's historicistic and pragmatic understanding of knowledge-claims about ourselves does not lead to formidable problems regarding the possibility of antinomial or contradictory truths about the nature of the self.

The next section features the relation between hermeneutics and critical theory. Perhaps no other debate, that hermeneutics has generated, has received more attention than the debate between Gadamer and Habermas. In a number of exchanges Habermas and Gadamer have squared off against each other in ways that have been very interesting and fruitful for both parties.

It is interesting to note that since their first *Auseinandersetzung* Gadamer and Habermas have moved closer to each other's position. In very general terms, Habermas has become less transcendental and Gadamer has become more concerned to defend the 'univocal understanding' and 'truth-claims' of hermeneutical inquiry.[83] However, Habermas originally raised the criticism that Gadamer's understanding of language as an "event of tradition," which we essentially 'suffer,' commits him, in effect, to a kind of "idealism of linguisticality" that effectively undercut the possibility of gaining a critical distance from the oppressive and inhuman aspects of our socio-cultural traditions. Habermas argues that Gadamer "denies the power of reflection. The latter proves itself, however, in being able to reject the claim of tradition. Reflection dissolves substantiality because it not only confirms, but also breaks up, dogmatic forces. Authority and knowledge do not converge."[84] Moreover, Habermas criticizes Gadamer for obscuring our relation to the powerful, quasilinguistic forces of society that influence our thought, such as the institutions that regulate labor and perpetrate various forms of domination. We need to distance ourselves from these forces and criticize them rationally because they often operate nearly unnoticed and often lead to conclusions that tend to legitimate these institutions without rational justification. Habermas worries about a conservative tendency he claims to find in Gadamer's works to accept at least some authority as rational qua authority. According to Habermas, authority as such can never be rational but authority must justify itself before the demands of practical rationality or else be rejected.[85] Furthermore, Habermas claims that Gadamer is wrong to suggest that a mere linguistic reappraisal of the forces which shapes our social life is sufficient to transform them. Habermas claims that this ignores the need for political praxis, as well as the need to work out transcendental conditions of knowledge that would enable us to justify our criticisms before a universal court of reason.

Gadamer has responded to these criticisms by pointing out that he has never been an advocate of any version *Sprachidealismus* either in the sense of claiming that the only reality is language or in the sense that a mere linguistic reappraisal of any social reality can suffice, by itself, to transform that reality. Gadamer, however, argued (and continues to argue to this day) that our 'linguisticality' precludes a notion of rationality that claims that it grasps reality in itself apart from any linguistically mediated perspective. Instead, all understanding takes place in terms of some historically mediated language (or languages). This implies the rejection of Habermas's "opposition and separation between the ongoing natural 'tradition' and the reflective appropriation of it."[86] This means that we can never step out of a linguistic tradition and criticize it from a transcendental perspective that would give us alinguistic insights into the final truth of that tradition. But this poses no threat in principle to the possibility of rational criticism. The power of tradition can never be entirely broken through reflection but we can certainly criticize a tradition from within. When we do so we extend and/or transform a linguistic tradition without suspending or neutralizing completly its power over us. This is plain to Gadamer because human finitude makes it impossible for us simply to make a clean break with the past. Instead, we always criticize particular aspects of it for particular practical purposes. In this sense we are a 'dialogue' with our past (and sometimes against it as well). This means, despite our undisputed ability of rational criticism, human beings will always stand in an inescapable relation to authority. But Gadamer is quick to point out that this relation is "basically ambivalent"[87], that is, we need neither accept it wholesale nor reject it root and branch. Instead we criticize and develop the authoritative linguistic traditions of our society through the exercise of practical reason which always seeks to operate on a consensus of what is really important for us at the present moment and in the foreseeable future.

Paul Ricoeur's "Hermeneutics and the Critique of Ideology" ends this section with a careful summary and critical assessment of the Habermas-Gadamer debate. Ricoeur argues that ultimately there is no fundamental conflict between these two thinkers, although each has something to learn from the other in order to round out their respective philosophical programs. He describes Gadamer's concern as 'metacritical.' This means that Gadamer's understands hermeneutics to point to that "deep common accord" (tragendes Einverständnis) that we have with tradition and which "precedes and envelops" all criticism.[88] Habermas, on the other hand, is suspicious of this "deep common accord" particularly as a paradigm for understanding the social sciences, which have always taken as their point of departure the confrontation with the ideologies that distort human communication in the interests of the institutions of domination and power. In order to break the power of ideology, our grasp of the past must pass through an explanatory phase where the distorting and oppressive features of the past are unmasked and explained for what they really are. Only when this is done are we in a position to understand our past with the openness and trust which Gadamer's "deep common accord" presupposes. But precisely because ideology has been so dominant in our lives a trust in a "deep common accord" is more a goal of inquiry for Habermas than a metacritical presupposition. Ricoeur argues, however, that Habermas and Gadamer are not fundamentally incompatable; each position speaks from a different 'place' and "raises in its on way a legitimate claim."[89] Ricoeur complains that Gadamer fails to appreciate the "alienating distantiation" from the past that we experience in addition to the deep common accord with tradition. It is the *tension* between this alienation from tradition and the *deep common accord* with tradition that opens up the possibility of a dialectic of acceptance and criticism vis-a-vis the past that Gadamer fails to explore. As a result, Gadamer has not incorporated into his account of hermeneutics a detailed and compelling account of the possibility and need for critique as an integral part of hermeneutics. In order to find ourselves in the past, we must disassemble our immediate relation to the past. We do this by explaining what actually took place and thereby distinguishing a 'true' from a 'false' consciousness of it. On the other hand, however, Ricoeur points out that Habermas's own claims regarding the 'interests' implicit in human knowledge have a hermeneutical basis; they disclose themselves as ontological moments of human understanding rather than as empirical facts or theoretical postulates. He also asks whether Habermas's interest in emancipation is really incompatible with Gadamer's ethical interests in finitude. Apparently they are not because Habermas's own work shows a connection between our need for a proper grasp of our understanding of the past in order to realize the past's communicative possibilities for a society where consensus is arrived at without coercion. What is more, hermeneutics and critical theory also converge in their concern to criticize the ideological function of technology and social planning. Moreover, they converge in their concern to revitalize the traditions of practical wisdom and political responsibility. Quite generally, hermeneutics' cultural concern with the past is not and should not be seen as incompatible with critical theory's political concern for the future. Human beings have never found it necessary to "choose between reminiscence and hope"[90] but, Ricoeur points out to do justice to both reminiscence and hope, a thinker must occupy different positions in the horizon of history. Hence, Ricoeur claims, hermeneutics and critical theory are and must remain distinct but they are by no means separated by an unbridgeable chasm.

The last section is entitled "Hermeneutics and Postmodernism." Postmodernism is a many-faceted cultural phenomenon, but philosophically it is usually associated with the rejection of the idea that there are 'foundations' or self-justifying starting points for human understanding.[91] In some cases, 'postmodernists' have rejected the ideas of foundations, truth, reality, consensus, and objectivity altogether. It should be pointed out, however, that hermeneutics stands in an ambivalent relation to postmodernist tendencies of thought. On the one hand, hermeneutical thinkers have categorically rejected the idea that there are self-evident 'foundations' for human understanding. But they have often not gone so far as to reject the meaningfulness of such notions of 'understanding reality', 'grasping the truth', or 'reaching consensus' about some important matter. What they have often done is argued that a 'postfoundationalist' theory of understanding demands the revision but not the rejection of our ideas of reality, truth, and consensus.

Richard Bernstein's "What is the Difference that Makes a Difference? Gadamer, Habermas, and Rorty" opens this section. He gives, as Bernstein so often does, a careful and very perceptive interpretation of each of these thinkers. It is worth noting that although Rorty can be given credit for developing hermeneutical insights in certain postmodernist directions,[92] other representatives of a hermeneutical bent of mind, like Gadamer and Habermas, have not necessarily traveled down this road. Bernstein suggests, however, that for all their differences, which can never be "*aufgehoben* into a grand synthesis",[93] what these three thinkers have in common may ultimately be more significant than their differences. According to Bernstein, it is their "nonfoundational pragmatic humanism,"[94] that is, their commitment to pragmatic theories of understanding and conflict dispute and their ultimate commitment to communities of open dialogue that makes their philosophical contributions strongly unified and humanistic. In this regard, Bernstein suggests, Gadamer, Habermas, and Rorty are all different than many postmodernistic theorists who seem indifferent to ideals like 'dialogue' and 'community' and instead seem contemptuous of humanistic ideals, even to the extent of prophesying the end of humanism and the death of 'man'.

Hans-Georg Gadamer's "Text and Interpretation" is a fitting follow up piece to Bernstein's. In this essay Gadamer gives us a very lucid, updated version of his position, in which he is at pains to distinguish philosophical hermeneutics from recent developments in French thought, particularly those of Derrida. Gadamer begins with an analysis of the phenomenon that in any interpretation of the meaning of an artwork, a historical period or a philosophical problem there is always a surplus of meaning never entirely captured and exhausted in the interpretation. This makes interpretation a never ending task that each generation must take up anew. Gadamer connects this insight with Heidegger's quest for Being: "Being does not unfold totally in its self-manifestation, but rather withholds itself and withdraws with the same originality with which it manifests itself."[95] Hence Gadamer claims that his own hermeneutical "efforts were directed toward not forgetting the limit that is implied in every hermeneutical experience of meaning."[96] This surplus of meaning is, however, by no means a barrier to mutual understanding. Instead real conversation, and the real understanding between people which emerges from it, is made possible and sustained by the 'play' between the said and unsaid in all our experiences of meaning. This experience does not entail a Derridean scepticism regarding an univocal meaning of an utterance or a text but the realization that all communication is never complete. Communication is an interpretive process that can always, in principle, be continued. This realization, however, does not imply, *pace* Nietzsche and Derrida, "that interpretation is an insertion [einlegen] of meaning and not a discovery [finden] of meaning."[97] The meaning of the text itself is not lost in the warp and woof of 'intertextuality', despite the fact that we never know the text *an sich* but always only have a linguistically mediated perspective on the text. "The text itself", Gadamer claims, "still remains the firm point of relation over and against . . . the possibilities of interpretation that are directed toward the text."[98] Gadamer suggests that texts have a way of regulating their own interpretation; they speak for themselves, as it were, and oppose arbitrary insertions of meaning. According to Gadamer this happens, in part, because texts are arranged internally for their readers; they are arranged with interpretation in mind. Hence they give us hints and directions for reading and they censure our misreadings by leading us into incoherence. Moreover, Gadamer argues that texts always point beyond themselves to a reality, an ineluctable access to which they presuppose and share with their prospective readers. It is by moving between the text and the reality it discusses that we come to understand what a text is saying, that is, its meaning. When we do so, the text qua text disappears behind the meaning which emerges from it. Moreover, the distinction between interpretation and text disappears in the sense that the former merges with the latter to form what Gadamer calls an "univocal understanding"[99] of meaning. In this sense, the text normally guides understanding only as its *penultimate* point of reference. In the final analysis the text disappears as a mere means to a "communicative event",[100] in which we experience reality as both revealed and concealed. Despite this dynamic between revelation and concealment, Gadamer suggests that what is revealed can be univocally understood although never finally exhausted.

David Hoy's "Must We Mean What We Say? The Grammatological Critique of Hermeneutics" follows Gadamer's far ranging discussion. Hoy addresses the critique of hermeneutics which eminates from Derrida and his followers. He focuses attention on five issues: the continuity of history, the commensurability of discourse, the principle of charity in translation, the issue of communality between author and reader and the possibility of progress and consensus in interpretation. And he tries to point out the sometimes subtle but important differences between hermeneutics and grammatology. Hoy wants to focus on the general direction of this grammatological critique as well as some of its shortcomings. Hoy does not settle these controversies but he does point to issues, the deeper examination of which should lead to fruitful results. What Hoy succeeds in showing, I think, is that the jury is still very much out on this debate. Hoy also raises questions about the difference between a methodology relying on intentionality and one relying on intertextuality. Here too he shows effectively, I think, that there are important issues to be discussed which have by no means been settled. One key advantage

of Hoy's work is that he not only compares hermeneutics and grammatology but he also compares them to important issues raised in the
writings of Stanley Cavell and John Searle. Hoy thus suggests important points of contact between what are often seen as divergent
philosophical programs.

John Caputo's "Hermeneutics as the Recovery of Man" continues
to try to differentiate hermeneutics from postmodernist strains of
thought. Caputo's particular target is Derrida's claim that Heidegger
(and his understanding of hermeneutics) fails, contrary to his own
claims, to break out of the circle of metaphysics, with its quest for
secure foundations for thought and action. Derrida has claimed,
despite Heidegger's emphasis on the open, temporal and non-
essential nature of *Dasein*, that his quest for a "fundamental ontology" which distinguishes between primordial or more fundamental structures of our being and derivative or secondary structures of
our being, is within the pale of metaphysical thinking. This is supposedly so because it is still looking for something permanent and
foundational to give human life a secure orientation.[101] But Caputo
argues that Heidegger's quest for understanding is not a quest to fix
the "essence" of man, no matter how attenuated that essence may be
conceived to be. Rather, Heidegger is seeking to discover a truth
which calls us back to our own inner freedom for possibilities of self-
development, a freedom which we often suppress but cannot escape.
Caputo makes his case through an analysis of the concept of "repetition". In general, this concept points to the act of going back into the
past to retrieve one's true self, which has somehow been lost. Caputo
distinguishes Platonic recollection from Husserlian reduction and
Kierkegaardian repetition. He shows through a detailed, technical
analysis of Plato and Husserl that they do indeed fall victim to the
charges which Derrida has brought against the "metaphysics of
presence". In Plato and Husserl the goal is to somehow transfix the
self in universal truths which make its freedom a secondary feature.
Kierkegaard, on the other hand, develops an understanding of the
existing individual's relation to the past and to eternity that escapes
this charge. In Kierkegaard, we retrieve the self out of the past in
order to repeat the call to freedom, i.e., to exist by choosing without
assurance that the life we choose is sanctioned by some type of
ultimate authority. In short we are called back to the *Angst* of human
finitude. It is this existential notion of "repetition", Caputo argues,
that Heidegger uses to criticize the philosophical tradition and to
transform Husserl's program for his own purposes. The result,

Caputo thinks, is not a metaphysics but a higher form of humanism which calls us back again and again to the "existential imperative to become oneself."[102]

Gianni Vattimo's "Hermeneutics and Nihilism: An Apology for Aesthetic Consciousness" may be said to function as a postmodernist response to the previous four papers' attempt to keep hermeneutics from moving in a postmodernistic direction. Vattimo complains that thinkers like Apel, Jauss and Ricoeur, who have developed Gadamer's hermeneutical insights, "seem ever so distant from its Heideggerian origins".[103] Vattimo claims that even Gadamer himself has not thought through the meaning of Heidegger's reflection on Being for hermeneutics. Vattimo argues that there is a consistent nihilistic theme running throughout Heidegger's writings. In a word, this theme is the rejection of any metaphysical foundation for thought and practice. The history of metaphysics shows us that, despite our attempts to find such a foundation, Being continually withdraws behind the many fleeting interpretations of its meaning. Instead of disclosing itself in terms of "causes and principles . . . having established which we could finally explain to ourselves what is happening . . .",[104] (thereby offering us some sort of support and guidance for our lives) we are only confronted with the ephemerality of everything including ourselves and every interpretation we offer of our own situation. Contrary to Gadamer, Vattimo argues that history does not offer itself to us as a continuous event, in which we participate and which we can understand univocally, even if never finally. Instead what we have been attempting to "re-collect" from our past "tends to identify itself with nothingness, with the fleeting traits of an existence enclosed by the boundaries of birth and death."[105] The consequence of this is that our efforts at self interpretation must be understood "aesthetically." Vattimo means by this that every interpretation of our condition must forgo any appeal to continuity with tradition in order to justify its "vision." Like every work of art, which despite its undisputed indebtedness to the past, provides its own vision and standard of uniqueness which it alone creates and sustains, so every interpretation of our condition (or any aspect of it) cannot appeal to transhistorical standards to justify itself. At best such interpretations work, like a work of art, by appealing to contingent and fleeting standards of the historical context in which it speaks. Vattimo argues that if we look for more than this we will miss the meaning of art and the meaning of interpretation. Art confronts us with the "mortality" of all things. Although works of art often capture a "world" or system

of meaningful relations whose life it is able to extend through the artistic medium beyond its historical origin, art shows us by this very act of historical transmission, the fleeting nature of all human worlds. Although art gives a specific interpretation of human life (say that of David's Enlightenment Classicism) a transhistorical ideality, it bears deep testimony to the ephermeral nature of all human understanding. It is precisely because art *decontextualizes* a world of meanings that it bears poignant witness to the ephemerality of all human institutions, aspirations, and understandings. Even the physical medium of the artwork itself is subject to decay. Like art and the "world" it depicts, every interpretation is groundless, that is, without ultimate justification. Accordingly, all such interpretations will inevitably be transcended and forgotten. There are no transhistorical standards or truths to undergird it and to give succeeding interpretations any claim to either superiority over the past or continuity with it. This, Vattimo claims, is the nihilistic lesson of hermeneutics. If he is right, then much recent work will need "critical revision ''[106] in light of its failure to think through all the nihilistic implications of its Heideggarian starting point.

The last article in the anthology is by Reiner Wiehl, Gadamer's successor at Heidelberg. Wiehl, too, is concerned with the nihilistic implications of hermeneutics, but not in order to bring about a "critical revision" of work already done in the field but in order to criticize hermeneutics for failing to make good its claims to provide an adequate model for philosophical knowledge. "Heidegger, Hermeneutics, and Ontology" argues that although hermeneutics has claimed to provide something like a universal ontology of understanding, it has not presented a full fledged ontology, which he understands as "an interrelated whole, a system of ontological principles formulated with respect to a definite manifold of beings, which is, in turn, determined by these principles."[107] He adds to this criterion the requirement that this ontology be presented systematically in terms of a well-defined set of logical principles. According to Wiehl, hermeneutics fails to pass this test. Instead, hermeneutics has left the door open to numerous incompatible understandings of its own claims to be an ontology. Wiehl explores in detail what he calls the "many-sided ambiguity"[108] of Gadamer's hermeneutics. Similarly, Wiehl criticizes Heidegger's quest to "think the unthought in the history of metaphysics."[109] Wiehl argues that Heidegger has shackled philosophy with an impossible task, that is, to think the unthought in metaphysics without bringing it into the pale of metaphysical thinking. At best, Wiehl thinks Heidegger presents us with a contingent point of departure for contemporary ontological thinking, whose task, as Wiehl sees it, we have outlined above. In sum, Wiehl wonders whether hermeneutics in either its Heideggarian or Gadamerian variations has really transcended traditional philosophy's quest for a self-grounded, well-defined, logically rigorous, and systematically articulated conception of reality.

All of these issues show us, I think, not only something of the range of topics which philosophical hermeneutics addresses but also something of its controversial and critical claims. These issues are, I think, on the cutting edge of hermeneutics as a philosophical movement. How these issues are resolved, if they can be resolved at all, will determine the future of the movement. One thing we can be sure of is that history and language will not stand still. The issues and controversies implicit in hermeneutics are in many ways the issues of modern philosophy. They contain within themselves our past and they carry us toward our future.

NOTES

1. Jürgen Habermas, *Towards a Rational Society*, trans. Jeremy J. Shapiro (Boston, 1970), p. 84. Quoted in Merold Westphal, "Hegel and Gadamer," p. 67.

2. 'Geschichtlichkeit' is first found in German with Hegel. Thereafter it is found almost exclusively in theological writers like C. J. Nitzsch and F. P. Schleiermacher and in Hegelian circles in such writers as K. Rosenkranz and R. Haym. It surfaces again as a central philosophical concept in the correspondence between Grafen P. Yorck von Wartenburg and W. Dilthey, which took place from 1877 to 1897. Heidegger seems to have inherited the concept from Dilthey, and it is Heidegger who seems to have made it the widely used concept it has become today. For more information see Joachim Ritter, ed., *Historisches Wörterbuch der Philosophie* (Basel: Schwabe & Co., 1974), 3: 403–8.

3. Although the classic hermeneutical thinkers like Dilthey, Heidegger, and Gadamer did not study American pragmatists like James, Pierce, Dewey, and Royce, their affinities have been pointed out by writers like Apel, Bernstein, Habermas, and Rorty. See K.O. Apel, *Towards a Transformation of Philosophy* (London: Routledge & Kegan Paul, 1980), pp. 77–136; J. Habermas, *Knowledge and Human Interests* (Boston: Beacon, 1971, pp. 65–161; R. Rorty, *Philosophy*

and the Mirror of Nature (Princeton: Princeton University Press, 1980),m pp. 3–13; and R. Bernstein, "What is the Difference that Makes a Difference? Gadamer, Habermas, Rorty," pp. 343–376.

4. Thomas Kuhn, *The Structure of Scientific Revolutions* (Chicago: University of Chicago Press, 1970).

5. Hans-Georg Gadamer, *Wahrheit und Methode* (Tübingen: J.C.B. Mohr [Paul Siebeck], 1960), pp. 274, 275. English translation, *Truth and Method* (New York: Seabury Press, 1975), p. 258. Hereafter cited as *WM* and *TM* respectively.

6. *WM*, pp. 94, 114, 126, 218ff., 260, 339 f., 401ff.; and *TM*, pp. 88, 109, 205ff, 244, 320f., 414f.

7. "We are always already biased in our thinking and knowing by our linguistic interpretation of the world. To grow into this linguistic interpretation means to grow up in the world. To this extent language is the real mark of our finitude. It is always out beyond us." Hans-Georg Gadamer, *Philosophical Hermeneutics*, edited by David E. Linge. Berkeley: University of California Press (1976), p. 64. Hereafter cited as *PH*. Compare also *WM*, pp. 252, 359, 380ff., 404ff. and *TM*, pp. 237, 340, 363ff., 387ff.

8. *WM*, p. 367ff.; and *TM*, p. 351ff.

9. *WM*, pp. 123ff, 153, 247; and *TM*, pp. 115ff, 142, 232.

10. Hans-Georg Gadamer, "On the Scope and Function of Hermeneutical Reflection" in this volume, p. 286. Similarly, "we never find ourselves as consciousness over against the world and, as it were, grasp after a goal of understanding in a wordless condition. Rather in all our knowledge of ourselves and in all knowledge of the world we are always already encompassed by the language that is our own." *PH*, p. 62. Compare also, *WM*, p. 391 and *TM*, p. 375.

11. For a very good discussion and summary of the case against 'foundationalism' see Richard Bernstein's *Beyond Objectivism and Relativism: Science, Hermeneutics, and Praxis* (Philadelphia: University of Pennsylvania Press, 1983), pp. 16–25.

12. The affinities between this aspect of hermeneutics and Neo-Kantianism has been pointed out but not sufficiently explored, in my opinion.

13. "For as regards reason . . . I should like to hold that it is to be found complete in each of us and to follow the common opinion of philosophers who say that 'more' or 'less' apply only in the field of 'accidents' and not as between the 'forms' or natures of 'individuals' of the same species." Descartes, *Discourse on Method*, trans E. Anscombe and P. Geach, in *Descartes' Philosophical Writings* (New York: Bobbs-Mererill, 1971), p. 7.

14. Descartes, it seems, denied that "innate ideas" were necessarily with us from birth. Instead, what is with us "by nature" is "a certain disposition or propensity for contracting them" that is synonomous with "the faculty of thinking." This faculty is so constituted that it can grasp certain "eternal truths" and build up a sure knowledge upon them. See Descartes's *Notes against a Program*, in *Oeuvres*, edited by Charles Adam and Paul Tannery, VIII B, pp. 357–59.

15. Hermeneutical thinkers have often overlooked certain 'natural' conditioning factors like biology in favor of more 'cultural' conditioning factors like history. This 'imbalance' needs further exploration and/or justification. See Marjorie Grene, "The Paradoxes of Historicity," pp. 168–189.

16. Compare the preface to *Phenomenology of Spirit*, trans. A.V. Miller (Oxford: Oxford University Press, 1977).

17. Martin Heidegger, *What Is a Thing?* (Chicago: Regnery, 1967), p. 48.

18. Wilhelm Dilthey, *Gesammelte Schriften*, Volume 7 (Leipzig and Berlin: Teubner, 1924), p. 279. Hereafter cited as *GS*. Cited in Richard Palmer, *Hermeneutics* (Evanston, 1969).

19. *GS*, 5: XXI.

20. Cf. *WM*, pp. 205ff, and *TM*, pp. 192ff. Gadamer accuses Dilthey of being essentially Hegelian in that he overlooks the connection between the historical roots of *Geist* and its inevitable finitude. In short, both Hegel and Dilthey agree that the mind is not limited in principle by history either in its potential scope or in its transparency. See *WM*, pp. 215, 216; and *TM*, p. 202.

21. *GS*, 8: 166.

22. Ibid., p. 6.

23. For a developed theory of understanding that takes this transcendence of relativism and objectivism as its point of departure, see Richard Bernstein's *Beyond Objectivism and Relativism: Science, Hermeneutics and Praxis*. Philadelphia: University of Pennsylvania Press: 1983.

24. Martin Heidegger, *Sein und Zeit* (Tübingen: Max Wiemeyer Verlag, 1977). English translation *Being and Time*, by J. Macquarrie and C. Robinson (New York: Harper & Row), 1962. Hereafter cited as *SZ* and *BT* respectively.

25. *SZ*, pp. 52 ff; and *BT*, pp. 78 ff.

26. Heidegger's emphasis on 'care' (*Sorge*) as the fundamental way in which human beings exist in the world precludes accounts of understanding that insist on the 'objective' and 'disinterested' nature of understanding. Cf. *SZ* pp. 180 ff; and *BT* pp. 225 ff.

27. Cf. *SZ* pp. 42ff; and *BT*, pp. 67 ff.

28. Cf. *SZ* pp. 135, 179, 221; and BT, pp. 174, 223, 224, and 264.

29. Heidegger's preoccupation with time and history inclines him, perhaps, not to emphasize our relation to nature in *Being and Time*. There can be no doubt, however, that our relation to nature constitutes an important aspect of our contingent "there-being". Cf. *SZ*, pp. 71, 381, 413; and *BT*, pp. 100, 101, 433, 466.

30. *SZ*, pp. 52 ff; and *BT*, 78 ff.

31. Cf. *SZ*, pp. 142–48; and *BT*, pp. 182–88.

32. *SZ*, pp. 150 ff; and *BT*, pp. 191 ff.

33. *SZ*, p. 152; and *BT*, p. 194.

34. Cf. Joseph Margolis, "The Nature and Strategies of Relativism" *Mind* 92 (October 1983): 548–67.

35. *SZ*, p. 150; and *BT*, p. 190, p. 191.

36. Cf. Edmund Husserl, *Ideas Pertaining to a Pure Phenomenology and to a Phenomenological Philosophy*, translated by F. Kersten (The Hague: Martinus Nijhoff, 1983), pp. 199ff.

37. Cf. *SZ*, p. 62; and *BT*, p. 89.

38. *SZ*, p. 153; and *BT*, p. 195.

39. *SZ*, p. 150, 154; and *BT*, p. 191. For a detailed discussion of the distinctions Heidegger draws between fore-having, fore-sight and fore-conception, see Herbert Dreyfus' "Hermeneutics and Holism," *Review of Metaphysics* 34 (September 1980).

40. *SZ*, p. 157; and *BT*, p. 199.

41. Cf. *SZ*, p. 34 ff, p. 159 ff; and *BT*, p. 58 ff, p. 201 ff.

42. *SZ*, p. 34 and *BT*, p. 58.

43. Cf. *SZ*, pp. 160 ff; and *BT*, pp. 203 ff.

44. *SZ*, pp. 154–61; and *BT*, p. 196–203. Heidegger draws a distinction between the "apophantic 'as'" and "existential-hermeneutical 'as'." The latter is more primordial in the sense that we always already understand something through "circumspection" and "care" before articulation makes it visible.

45. *SZ*, p. 62 and *BT*, p. 89.

46. *WM*, p. 380; and *TM*, p. 363.

47. *WM*, p. 426; and *TM*, p. 411. See also *PH*, pp. 15, 16.

48. *WM*, pp. 318 ff, 394, 409 ff, 422 f; and *TM*, pp. 364 ff, 377, 392 ff, 404 f.

49. *WM*, p. 394; and *TM*, p. 377.

50. Cf. *WM*, pp. 361 ff, and 432ff; and *TM*, pp. 345 ff and 414 ff.

51. "Sein, dass verstanden werden kann, ist Sprache." *WM* , p. 450; *TM*, p. 432.

52. *WM*, p. 425; *TM*, p. 407

53. *WM*, p. 394; *TM*, p. 377

54. *PH*, p. 9.

55. *WM*, p. 422 *TM*, p. 404.

56. *WM*, p. 465; *TM*, p. 447.

57. Hans Lipps, *Untersuchungen zu einer hermeneutischen Logik* (Frankfurt: Klostermann, 1938), p. 71. Quoted in *PH*, p. 17.

58. CF. *WM*, pp. 443–44; *TM*, pp. 424–25.

59. '*Die Sache*' can mean simply the subject matter of some discourse, but it also can be variously translated as 'things' as in Husserl's motto "zu den Sachen selbst" or as 'objects' which is the meaning implicit in the imperative "Reden wir sachlich!" or "Speak objectively!" Alternatively, it can be translated as 'concerns' in the sense that it is often said in German "das ist nicht meine Sache"—"that's none of my business," "that's not my concern"—or as "interest' in the sense of "was uns angeht"—"that which pertains to us." Gadamer also has the Latin term *causa* or 'case' in mind as in a legal 'case' or as in "this is the 'case'." Here a complex state of affairs seems to be denoted. Gadamer appeals to various meanings in various contexts but in all cases he wants to emphasize, it seems, our involvement and interest in that which we seek to understand.

60. Cf. Hans-George Gadamer, *Dialogue and Dialectic*, trans. P. Christopher Smith (New Haven: Yale University Press), 1980.

61. *WM*, p. 350; *TM*, p. 332.

62. *WM*, pp. 94, 293, 355 f, 396, 403f, 447, 496; *TM*, pp. 8, 276, 336 f, 379, 386 f, 429, 476.

63. *WM*, pp. 287 ff, 323f, 328, 348 f, 366f, 432, 448 f; *TM*, pp. 267ff, 305 f, 310, 324 f, 351 f, 414, 429 f.

64. *WM*, pp. 27 f, 173, 290 ff, 298 ff, 312 ff, 315 f, 322 f, f381, 491; *TM*, pp. 29 ff, 163, 274 f, 281 f, 294 ff, 297 f, 303 f, 364 f, 472.

65. *WM*, pp. 289 f, 356 f, 375; *TM*, pp. 273 f, 337 f, 358.

66. The issues of what gives a tradition 'unity' and 'identity' and of how traditions arise and die are issues that hermeneutical philosophers need to explore in greater depth.

67. *WM*, pp. 17 ff, 297 ff, 392 f, 511; *TM*, pp. 20 ff, 278 ff, 376 f, 490.

68. Aristotle, *Nichomachean Ethics*, 1142a, 25–30.

69. *WM*, pp. 295 ff; *TM*, pp. 278 ff.

70. *WM*, p. 92; *TM*, p. 179.

71. *WM*, pp. 295 ff, 311, 321; *TM*, pp. 278 ff, 293, 303.

72. Hans-Georg Gadamer, "Hermeneutics and Social Science," *Cultural Hermeneutics* 2 (1975): 316.

73. Ibid.

74. *WM*, pp. XXV, 246; *TM*, pp. XXV, 231.

75. See Richard Bernstein's "From Hermeneutics to Praxis," pp. 000–000.

76. Hans-Georg Gadamer, *Reason in the Age of Science*. Trans. by Frederick G. Lawrence. Cambridge: MIT Press, 1981, p. 52.

77. Richard Rorty, *Philosophy and the Mirror of Nature*. Princeton: Princeton University Press, 1980, pp. 315ff. Hereafter cited as *PMN*.

78. See p. 82.

79. See p. 102.

80. See p. 96.

81. See p. 82.

82. Ibid.

83. For a short bibliographical history of this debate, see Footnote 1 to Paul Ricoeur's "Hermeneutics and the Critique of Ideology," p. 338. See also for a concise summary of the direction in which this debate has moved Robert Dostal's, "The World Never Lost" forthcoming in *Philosophy and Phenomenological Research*.

84. See p. 264.

85. See p. 265ff.

86. See p. 286.

87. See p. 290.

88. See p. 314.

89. See p. 325.

90. See p. 337.

91. Cf. Richard Rorty, "Habermas and Lyotard on PostModernity," *Praxis International*, 4 no. 1 (April, 1984).

92. Cf. *PMN*, pp. 315ff.

93. See p. 369.

94. See p. 370.

95. See p. 382.

96. Ibid.

97. See p. 388.

98. Ibid.

99. See p. 394.

100. See p. 396. Gadamer admits that there are some texts that function differently than this account suggests. He calls them "eminent texts." He has in mind certain literary texts, like lyric poetry, where the text creates rather than mediates meaning. See, for example, Gadamer's "The Eminent Text and Its Truth," *Bulletin of the Midwest Modern Language Association*, 13 (1980), pp. 3–23 and "Philosophie und Literature." *Was ist Literatur?* (*Phänomenologische Forschungen*, 11) ed. Ernst Orth (Frieburg: Albert, 1981), pp. 18–34. English translation by A.J. Steinbock in *Man and World*, 18, No. 3, (1985), pp. 241–259.

101. See p. 439.

102. See p. 437.

103. See p. 447.

104. See pp. 450–51.

105. See p. 453.

106. See p. 447.

107. See p. 471.

108. See p. 468.

109. See pp. 460–61.

Hermeneutics and History

I

HEGEL AND GADAMER

MEROLD WESTPHAL

At the heart of Hans-Georg Gadamer's philosophical hermeneutics is the claim that the "fundamental prejudice of the Enlightenment is the prejudice against prejudice itself, which deprives tradition of its authority."[1] He counters with the claim that "the prejudices of the individual, far more than his judgments, constitute the historical reality of his being," and he seeks to bring about a "rehabilitation of authority and tradition."[2]

No one has understood this as a call for resurgent bigotry. The etymological sense of prejudice as pre-judgment (*Vor-urteil*) and thus as the fore-sight that guides all sight, has been noticed.[3] But the charge has been made that philosophical hermeneutics represents an uncritical conservatism vis-a-vis the past. To this Gadamer responds that being open to tradition, allowing it to address us and make its claim upon us *before* we make it into an object over which we preside as subjects, is not the same as blindly accepting everything it says. Perhaps there is no better example of what Gadamer means than his own relation to Hegel.

Gadamer describes the relation as a "tension-filled proximity."[4] We are not likely to improve on that formula. Gadamer is powerfully drawn to Hegel's thought as a source of insight he cannot do without. At the same time he sees it as a seductive force that he must use every energy at his disposal to resist, lest it lead him to forsake his own deepest insights. Still it would not be helpful to call him ambivalent, as if he isn't able to make up his mind and vascillates, finding Hegelian dialectic attractive on Monday, Wednesday, and Friday, but dangerous on Tuesday, Thursday, and Saturday. It is just because he knows who he is and where he stands that he finds it necessary to say both yes and no to Hegel.

One way to express this is to see contemporary debates as reenactments of debates in which Hegel took part. In the debate over whether the full self-transparency of self-consciousness can provide a foundation for philosophy as a rigorous science, Gadamer (with Heidegger) plays Kant to Husserl's Hegel and comes down consistently on the side of the unsurpassable finitude of human cognition. But in the debate over whether an energetics of nature creates a boundary beyond which hermeneutical understanding cannot pass, needing to give way to a more nearly natural scientific way of thinking, Gadamer plays Hegel to Habermas's Marx.[5] His proximity to Hegel is indeed tension filled.

THE POST-TRANSCENDENTAL
UNDERSTANDING OF KNOWLEDGE

An important part of this proximity arises from an agreement that the nature of the finitude of human knowledge is to be understood in existentialist rather than empiricist terms. The question is whether it is ultimately the sense-bound character or the situation-bound character of knowledge that renders it finite.

Empiricism sees cognitive limitations in quantitative and spatial terms. There are some areas (metaphysics) into which our capacities will not reach, and some portions of those areas that they will reach will remain at any given time unexplored. But this latter limitation is in principle remediable, and the sense-based knowledge we gain through exploration of the sensible world is territory genuinely brought under our control. We have objective knowledge. This remains the case even if no definitive answers can be given to problems about induction and confirmation.

By contrast, existentialism sees the limitations of human knowledge in qualitative and nonspatial terms. While asserting that no territory can be ruled out of bounds to human investigation a priori, it even more vigorously insists that there is no territory where the situatedness of human cognition does not place a qualification on the knowledge achieved.

This second view is common ground shared by representatives of philosophical traditions that often disagree among themselves sharply on other issues. Among these can be mentioned Marxism; the sociology of knowledge; the Frankfurt school; pragmatism;

phenomenology; hermeneutics (including Gadamer); and, I shall argue, Hegel. To label this view 'existentialist' is not to suggest a monopoly on the part of those who claim or merit that title. It is rather to note the combination in the existentialist tradition of the theme of human finitude on the one hand, and its explication in terms of being in a situation on the other. This applies to Heidegger's analysis of being-in-the-world as much as to the analyses of Jaspers, Marcel, Merleau-Ponty, and Sartre, who explicitly use the term 'situation'.[6]

Most often reference is to the so-called *Geisteswissenschaften*, where the claims of situation epistemology are most easily supported. But epistemological existentialism is not limited to what we call the humanities and social sciences; it extends to the natural sciences as well. When Marcuse and Habermas can debate not whether but how the natural sciences function as ideology, when Heidegger can suggest that the exact sciences give us correct answers but in so doing direct us away from the truth, when Whitehead similarly suggests that Cartesian-Galilean science leads us metaphysically astray because of the fallacy of misplaced concreteness, when Husserl suggests that all of the sciences have their foundation in the life-world, when Gadamer claims that the methodical character of the natural sciences requires both a historical derivation and an epistemological restriction, and when even within the philosophy of science it is increasingly doubted that there are any theory-free data, it is clear that the philosophical issue is broader than the conflict of political ideologies in the human sciences.[7]

It is clear that for any philosophy that gives what I've been calling an existentialist interpretation to the finitude of human knowledge, transcendental philosophy can be only preliminary and in no sense final. This is not because there is no a priori element in our knowledge, but because the situatedness of knowing implies that beneath the necessity and universality of the a priori elements there lies a contingency that renders them particular.

Thus, for example, Habermas speaks of a "transitory a priori structure" underlying our knowledge, because "apparently the empirical conditions under which transcendental rules take shape and determine the constitutive order of a life-world are themselves the result of a socialization process." He concludes that "a radial critique of knowledge is possible only as social theory."[8]

Gadamer agrees, for this is the point of his "defense" of prejudice. With reference to the hermeneutical circle as described by Heidegger, he writes, "It is not so much our judgments as it is our prejudices that constitute our being . . . the historicity of our existence entails that prejudices in the literal sense of the word, constitute the initial directedness of our whole ability to experience. Prejudices are biases of our openness to the world. They are simply conditions whereby we experience something—whereby what we encounter says something to us."[9] For Gadamer the concept of prejudice and that of tradition are closely linked, as is clear in this summary of his views by Ricoeur.

> A human being discovers his finitude in the fact that, first of all, he finds himself within a tradition or traditions. Because history precedes me and my reflection, because I belong to history before I belong to myself, prejudgment also precedes judgment, and submission to traditions precedes their examination. The regime of historical consciousness is that of a consciousness exposed to the effect of history [wirkungsgeschichtliches Bewusstsein]. If therefore we cannot extract ourselves from historical becoming, or place ourselves at a distance from it in such a way that the past becomes an object for us, then we must confess that we are always situated within history in such a fashion that our consciousness never has the freedom to bring itself face to face with the past by an act of sovereign independence.[10]

This kind of conclusion, along with the implication it has for the possibility of our being free to bring ourselves directly face to face with any object of knowledge at all, is what has pulled contemporary hermeneutics away from Husserlian phenomenology. David Linge has written, "The life-world was overlooked by constitutional analysis as Husserl had practiced it [though it] functioned precisely as the horizon of intentional objects without even becoming thematic itself. How could the phenomenologist's own enterprise avoid presupposing the self-evident validity of a life-world in which his praxis had its meaning? Indeed, this life-world, present as a nonobjectified horizon of meaning, seems to encompass transcendental subjectivity itself and in this sense threatens to displace it as the absolute foundation of experience. The ego at this point appears to be 'in' the life-world."[11]

This is exactly the conclusion that Gadamer wishes us to draw. One way he puts it is to give to philosophical hermeneutics the task of moving "back along the path of Hegel's phenomenology of mind until we discover in all that is subjective the substantiality that determines it."[12] The main point Gadamer wants to make about the life-world that grounds the transcendental ego, thereby giving substantiality to the subjective, is its linguistic nature. "for language is not only an object in our hands, it is the reservoir of tradition and the medium in and through which we exist and perceive our world." This means we can speak of the "linguistic constitution of the world".[13] It also means we must speak of the historically conditioned constitution of the world; for as the "reservoir of tradition," each particular language is both a specific and a changing "medium in and through which we exist and perceive our world."

This central theme of post-transcendental philosophy, that all human knowledge is inextricably situated in some historically specific life-world or other, makes the question of history and truth the central philosophical problem. It is not merely an issue for the methodology of the *Geisteswissenschaften* or even for a general epistemology. It concerns our very being. For historicity seems to be as essential to our nature as truth is to our destiny or calling (*Bestimmung*). But if being historically situated means that our knowing is always perspectivally partial (disclosure entailing concealment) and not merely quantitatively partial, is there not a discrepancy between our nature and our destiny? Are not epistemological existentialism and the "vertigo of relativity" it brings with it just the Sartrean conclusion that we are a useless passion coming at us from another direction?[14]

Rather than try to answer these questions at this point, we need to note that Hegel stands with Gadamer in this post-transcendental tradition. In fact, it is to him that we owe its first clear formulation. As early as his essay on natural law he expects "to see the empirical condition of the world reflected in the ideal mirror of science," because "the condition of all sciences will express also the condition of the world."[15]

Though it is especially the political-ethical sciences he has in mind here, he means it when he says *all* the sciences are historically conditioned, and he applies this idea to systematic philosophy as a whole. Throughout his career as a philosopher Hegel remarks with wonder at the new era that has dawned for European civilization in his own lifetime.[16] And he regularly states that this birth of a new historical epoch has epistemological significance. Thus, for example, in the preface to the first edition of the *Science of Logic* he complains that "logic shows no traces so far of the new spirit which has arisen in the sciences no less than in the world of actuality." This cannot last, however, for "once the substantial form of the spirit has inwardly reconstituted itself, all attempts to preserve the forms of an earlier culture are utterly in vain." What is now called for is "the labour required for a scientific elaboration of the new principle."[17] Much too little attention has been given to this clear indication that when Hegel calls philosophy "its own time comprehended in thoughts,"[18] he means not only his political philosophy but also his Logic itself!

We get an equally clear statement (and more) in the *Phenomenology*. It's goal is "to show that now is the time for philosophy to be raised to the status of a Science." The reason this hasn't already happened is not that Hegel's predecessors were not as clever as he, but because they lived too soon. It will therefore be necessary for this treatise on knowledge to take account of "the stage which self-conscious Spirit has presently reached." Once the question is put "it is not difficult to see that ours is a birth-time and a period of transition to a new era." Again the task is to articulate the significance of the new era by bringing the whole, rich content of spirit's life into a systematic knowledge structured by the principles of spirit's latest advance.[19]

But the *Phenomenology* contains more than this programmatic commitment to incorporating history into epistemology. It inaugurates the post-transcendental era by teaching us to ask a new question: Who is the transcendental subject? Both the answer implied in chapter 1 Sense-Certainty, and the explicit answer of chapter 4 The Truth of Self-Certainty, make the same point: the transcendental subject, or the totality of conditions of possible experience, is a particular perspective on the world by virtue of being historically situated.

The phenomenological critique of sense-certainty's claim to immediacy in knowing brings to light not only the mediated character of sense perception, which thereby has the status of interpretation, but also the central role of language in this mediation. Especially when read against the background of the Jena lectures on the philosophy of spirit, this analysis both teaches us to ask Who is the transcendental subject? and to answer by saying that, the transcendental subject is the speaker of a language, or perhaps, the transcendental subject is language itself. And because language is always some specific language and never language in general, we find reflection on consciousness turning into reflection on language, which in turn become reflection on tradition. The I is not fundamental here. Individual consciousness is rather the vehicle of the tradition embedded in language. As Hegel puts it, "Through consciousness Spirit intervenes in the way the world is ruled," and language is "the true being of Spirit as Spirit in general."[20]

This is but one of two Hegelian routes to the Gadamerian conclusions that "understanding is not to be thought of so much as an action of one's subjectivity, but as the placing of oneself within a process of tradition. . . .The anticipation of meaning that governs our understanding of a text is not an act of subjectivity, but proceeds from the communality that binds us to the tradition."[21] When Hegel turns from the interpretations of sense perception to the more sophisticated interpretations of the understanding, which we would call natural science, a second "transcendental deduction" of the post-transcendental perspective occurs.

Here the often neglected continuity of chapters 3 and 4 of the *Phenomenology* is crucial. The latter contains the famous section on lordship and bondage as these emerge from the fundamental human desire for recognition. The ineradicable need for reciprocal recognition is what leads to the revolutionary definition of Spirit as " 'I' that is 'We' and 'We' that is 'I'."[22] But the *Phenomenology* has not abandoned the task, clearly announced in preface and introduction alike, of solving the problem of knowledge. We have already noted that in the Jena lectures Spirit replaces the transcendental ego of Kantian-Fictean idealism. Here, too, the emergence of Spirit has epistemic meaning. For in chapter 3 Hegel gives an essentially Kantian interpretation of understanding, leading to the conclusion that every consciousness is a self-consciousness, that the world is *given* only to the self, which *takes* it in a certain way. But that self is no individual, theoretical self, as the Cartesian assumptions of the transcendental tradition take for granted. The concrete human self is a desiring as well as a judging self, and because the desire for recognition is what distinguished human from animal desire, the social, interactive self that is We as much as I and thus Spirit is the subject of any concrete and thus fully adequate knowing. But Spirit is no static structure and the struggle for recognition has many historical moments. The theory of knowledge inescapably becomes the history of Sprit. The transcendental framework is *aufgehoben* through asking the question Who is the transcendental subject?[23]

THE CRITIQUE OF METHOD

The proximity of Hegel and Gadamer finds expression in a second important agreement. If the situational interpretation of cognitional human finitude gives rise to a post-transcendental self-understanding threatened by "the vertigo of relativity," some will seek to desituate themselves by recourse to method.[24] This can be called the Cartesian strategy, for Descartes makes it clear in the *Discourse* that the goal of his method is not just the power of predictability but the transcendence of tradition, with its interminable disputes. Hegel and Gadamer are united in uncompromising opposition to the Cartesian strategy and to the paradigmatic privilege of mathematics and the matematico-experimental sciences that belongs with it.

In Hegel's case, it is immediately after noting the historically situated character of the Logic that he repudiates any borrowing of method from "a subordinate science like mathematics."[25] His reference is to the critique of mathematical (geometrical) knowledge in the preface to the *Phenomenology*. The key word is 'external'. In geometry I set out to prove a theorem. Because this goal guides the construction of the proof, "an external purpose governs this activity." Correspondingly, in this mathematical cognition "insight is an activity external to the thing; it follows that the true thing is altered by it." The result may be "true propositions," but "the content is false ." For, to put it one way, the subject matter that can be treated in this way is lifeless in itself, incapable of being adequate to the philosophical concept. Or, to put in the other way, this external knowing "proceeds on the surface, does not touch the thing itself. . . . and therefore fails to comprehend it."[26]

By explicitly repudiating the idea that philosophy can borrow its method from mathematics, Hegel makes it clear that his critique is not merely directed toward mathematics but toward any method modeled after it and sharing its character. That character has two closely related features, a purpose that comes from the knowing subject rather than the subject matter, and, consequently concepts and procedures that are external to the subject matter and imposed upon it rather than arising from within it. This subjectivity of thinking and this independence of the object thought can be called the creation of subject and object, for the relation between knower and known it entails is by no means universal or necessary. Calculative thinking, rooted in the desire to control, is a specific, historical project. Like Heidegger's analysis, Hegel's shows it to be a road taken, but not necessarily.[27]

In the *Science of Logic* Hegel reemphasizes the connection between externality and subjectivity in seeking to look beyond them. What is needed is "the point of view which no longer takes the determinations of thought to be only an instrument and a means" of the knower's purposes; "more important is the further point connected with it, namely that it is usual to regard them as an external form."[28] This also must go. It must be replaced by the method that is no method, which no longer allows an external relation between method and content because the method of knowing is at once "the manner peculiar to cognition" and "the *objective* manner, or rather the *substantiality*, of *things*" being known.[29] By contrast to external reflection "it can only be the nature of the content itself which spontaneously develops itself in a scientific method of knowing. . . . This spiritual movement . . . is the absolute method of knowing and at the same time is the immanent soul of the content itself."[30] Perhaps it is a bit misleading to speak of the method arising by spontaneous generation. But the point Hegel wants to make is the same as when he says that true philosophical knowledge "demands surrender to the life of the object, or, what amounts to the same thing, confronting and expressing *its* inner necessity."[31] And it is the same point once again when he says of true philosophic knowledge, "It is not *we* who frame the concepts."[32]

Hegel's analysis of the Concept as the union of Universality, Particularity, and Individuality is in terms of the freedom whose most immediate forms are friendship and love. Because this includes a theory of the theoretical as well as the practical self, we can say that Hegel attempts to spell out a relation of loving intersubjectivity between knower and known.[33] We can even speak here of epistemological nonviolence. For "the universal is therefore *free* power; it is itself and takes its other within its embrace, but without *doing violence* to it . . . for it bears itself towards its other as towards *its own self*."[34] This golden rule of the theoretical self is in striking contrast to the triumph of Cartesian method, whose inner secret Kant betrays when he admits that the scientific revolution assumed "that reason has insight only into that which it produces after a plan of its own, and that it must not allow itself to be kept, as it were, in nature's leading strings, but must itself show the way . . . *constraining nature to give answer to questions of reason's own determining*."[35]

This methodical violence Hegel abjures, so that knowledge will let the known be itself and show itself as itself. But such an encounter of loving and nonviolent intersubjectivity, in which the knower's openness means "surrender to the life of the object," can only occur in the world. Both knower and known belong to the closeness of a situation. The former has not become a subject outside the world for whom the world in its totality has become object, over which it presides like a judge and from whom it demands answers like a prosecuting attorney. The methodical attempt to desituate the knowing self turns out to be not so much a form of escape as of aggression. It arises from the will to dominate.

The same themes recur in Gadamer's critique of the Cartesian strategy. He tells us that "the title of *Truth and Method* never intended that the antithesis it implies should be mutually exclusive."[36] But the title does not imply an antithesis, so that even if the 'and' in it isn't the 'and' of 'black and white', it is surely closer to that 'and' than to the one in 'love and marriage.' He repeatedly insists that the hermeneutical problem is not one of method but rather of truth (and of being);[37] but his regular introduction of hermeneutics, with reference to the way a work of art seizes us and makes a truth-claim upon us, makes it clear that he is concerned with kinds of truth not available to method.[38]

No more than Hegel does Gadamer propose that the sciences whose glory is their method forsake their Cartesian heritage. He wants them rather to acknowledge its meaning. Only by becoming aware of their estrangement from natural consciousness, of the price they have paid for the achievements made possible thereby, of the presuppositions guiding the entire enterprise, and of the necessary return to the larger language context in which they are but one of the language games played, can they regain their integrity.[39]

When all this is fully brought to light the cognitive primacy of methodically secured science will be undermined.[40] The concept of experience will be freed from the concept of science. With the concepts of life and the life-world, respectively, Dilthey and Husserl were in a position to achieve this freedom. But their Cartesian roots were too deep, and the ideal of science governs both the concept of history grounded in romantic hermeneutics and the concept of philosophy grounded in intentional analysis.[41] What Gadamer says about experimental and historico-critical methods applies with at least equal force to the methods Dilthey and Husserl derive from Schleiermacher and Brentano, namely that they "are concerned to guarantee, through the objectivity of their approach, that these basic experiences can be repeated by anyone."[42]

But this denial of the historical nature of experience, which Hegel had already spelled out so emphatically in the *Phenomenology*, this attempt to desituate the knower, remains plausible only as long as self-deception about the logic of question and answer is allowed to prevail. As an example Gadamer points to the objective answers statistical research can give to precisely formulated questions. Everything is under the strict governance of method except the choice of questions to be asked. This shows that "science always stands under definite conditions of methodological abstraction and that the successes of modern sciences rest on the fact that other possibilities for questioning are concealed by abstraction. This fact comes out clearly in the case of statistics, for the anticipatory character of the questions statistics answer make it particularly suitable for propaganda purposes. . . . Thus what is established by statistics seems to be a language of facts, but which questions these facts answer and which facts would begin to speak if other questions were asked are heremeneutical questions."[43] The Kantian claim that the questions asked are of "reason's own determining" only serves the self-deception that remains oblivious to the historically specific purposes that guide such questioning. By calling itself reason this particular project seeks to hide from itself its own finitude.

Because "there is no such thing as a method of learning to ask questions,"[44] science is delivered over to history and tradition at its very foundation, the selection of questions to be asked. Moreover, the particular historical project at work in the sciences, which have come to be paradigmatic, is not hard to identify. Bacon already formulated it at the birth of modern science with the slogan Knowledge Is Power. For this reason the concepts of method and of control are intimately connected as Gadamer restates Hegel's objection to the "external purpose" that governs any methodical inquiry that is not a "surrender to the life of the object."[45]

This "surrender" Gadamer expresses in terms of the distinction between openness to the truth claims placed upon us by text or tradition and knowledge as domination (Scheler), in which appropriation means taking possession of the subject matter and placing it at our disposal. For every true question, he holds, involves the openness that puts ourselves in question.[46] Such true questioning is unknown by the knowledge that rests upon objectifying procedures in the investigation of its subject matter. "Abstracted out of the fundamental relation to the world that is given in the linguistic nature of our experience of it, it seeks to become certain about entities by methodically organizing its knowledge of the world. Consequently it condemns as heresy all knowledge that does not allow of this kind of certainty and hence is not able to serve the growing domination of being. As against this, we have endeavored to liberate the mode of being of art and history, and the experience which corresponds to them, from the ontological prejudice that is contained in the ideal of scientific objectivity."[47]

Because hermeneutics "does not intend an absolute mastery over being by the one who understands,"[48] it finds in the Greek understanding of theoria a further account of the openness that surrenders to the object. As the Greeks understood it, theory meant being so present to the object as to be "outside oneself." "This kind of being present is a self-forgetfulness." It "arises from the attention to the object," which, in turn makes it "possible to forget one's own purpose." Instead of being a "self-determination of the subjective consciousness," theory is rather "a true sharing, not something active, but something passive (pathos), namely being totally involved in and carried away by what one sees."[49] But it would be a mistake to interpret this passivity as inertia or listlessness. For this passivity is the activity of "uninterrupted listening."[50]

THE DISPUTE OVER ABSOLUTE KNOWLEDGE

It can be said that the concept of life is central to Hegel's attempt "to distance himself critically from the subjectivity of modern philosophy."[51] But the crucial form of life in and through which this occurs is human social life. For this reason much of what Gadamer appreciates in Hegel is implicit in his regular praise of the concept of objective spirit, the I that is We and vice versa. This concept enables Hegel to break with the individualized self-consciousness fundamental to idealist transcendentalism, including Kantian moral philosophy, which rests on the moral certitudes of the Cartesian ego.[53] It is the same concept with its critique of subject and object that assists Gadamer in the attempt to free himself from post-Kantian Cartesianism, whether in Schleiermacher, neo-Kantianism, or Husserlian phenomenology.[54] By recognizing that there is a reason in history greater than that of the individual, this concept not only opens up our understanding of understanding to history, but also permits the reappropriation of the Greek *logos* tradition of a rationality above that of individual self-consciousness. Ancient substantiality and modern subjectivity are united in a relationship that deepens and enriches both.[55]

But proximity gives way to tension when Hegel seeks to go beyond objective spirit to absolute spirit, to that knowledge of spirit by itself, which can be called absolute knowledge. Here, in Gadamer's view, Hegel's struggle with the Cartesian spirit proves itself to be halfhearted, and he succumbs to it in a threefold manner. First, he remains within the transcendental framework in that knowledge of the world and knowledge of knowing the world are inseparable. Or, to put it another way, knowledge remains self-knowledge, even if the self is not the static, individualized self of the earlier tradition, but the expanded self expressed in the notions of *nous* and spirit.[56] Next, there is the idea of "the transparency of the idea to itself or spirit's self-consciousness," which represents the "self-apotheosis of thought implied in Hegel's idea of truth."[57] Finally, there is the notion that when knowledge is this kind of self-knowledge, the certainty of the self's full transparency to itself, philosophy can be science as the "perfection of experience." The philosophy that in its anti-Cartesian moments is a "self-defense against the sciences" turns out to claim the status of science for itself, a claim "which ultimately is founded upon Descartes' idea of method and which, within the framework of transcendental philosophy, is developed from the principle of self-consciousness."[58]

There are, to be sure, important differences between Hegel's philosophical science and the sciences against which it is meant to stand as a self-defense. Its method seeks to be immanent rather than external. It seeks to deal with the whole rather than some part of the real.[59] Most important, it does not seek to ground itself in a timeless, desituated ego, but holds fast to the notion that the true subject of human knowledge is the historically situated social self. It is at this point that Hegel is perhaps most ingenious. Biblical eschatology becomes the key as he regularly relates the notion of science to that of the kingdom, meaning the Kingdom of God. Then, instead of seeking to make thought absolute by freeing it from all conditioning by life, he puts the question of the cognitive implications of the fulfillment of historical life in the Kingdom of God. As we have already seen, he makes thought in both his *Phenomenology* and his *Science of Logic* relative to the new age that has dawned in his own lifetime, but instead of producing vertigo, this relativity is affirmed simultaneously with the claim of scientific status for both works. This is possible because the route to absolute knowledge is not that of fleeing every historical situation, but that of being born in the absolute historical situation, the Kingdom in which history achieves its goal. And it is precisely the birth of that Kingdom that Hegel believes the tumult of his own times to represent.[60]

But whatever awe we may experience before the grandeur of Hegel's project, Gadamer finds it irrelevant to our situation. It shatters, and we need to understand why. "The ancient Greek, 'Know thyself!' still holds good for us as well, for it means, "know that you are no god, but a human being.' What self-knowledge really is is not the perfect self-transparency of knowledge but the insight that we have to accept the limits posed for finite natures."[61] In other words, scientific philosophy as absolute knowledge is *hubris*.

As it stands this charge is mere assertion. To support it Gadamer finds it necessary to turn his phenomenology of the hermeneutical situation against Hegel. Whereas for much of the journey Hegel has been, in Gadamer's view, a major partner in the development of this understanding of understanding, he now becomes its target. Not surprisingly it is the historical and linguistic character of understanding to which Gadamer appeals.

With reference to history Gadamer emphasizes both the openness and the opaqueness of the historical situation. There are two aspects, in turn, to the openness of historical experience, general and specific. Against Hegel's insistence that knowledge be self-knowledge and experience become science in order that absolute knowledge be possible, the openness of historical experience in general is affirmed. "We can now understand why Hegel's application to history, insofar as he saw it as part of the absolute self-consciousness of philosophy, does not do justice to the hermeneutical consciousness. The nature of experience is conceived in terms of that which goes beyond it; for experience itself can never be science. . . . The truth of experience always contains an orientation towards new experience."[62] This means that historical experience has the marks of what Hegel calls the "bad infinite," and that historical understanding is given over to the "tireless self-correction" of the Socratic dialogues, which join "the metaphysical question concerning the infinite and absolute with the ineradicable finitude of the questioner."[63]

More specifically, the openness of history is evidenced in that at best partial realization of the fulfillment Hegel claimed for his historical moment. Gadamer willingly grants that the final principle of history has emerged. Since Hegel's time "history is not to be based upon a new principle. The principle of freedom is unimpugnable and irrevocable. It is not longer possible for anyone still to affirm the unfreedom of humanity. The principle that all are free never again can be shaken. But does this mean that on account of this, history has come to an end? Are all human beings actually free? Has not history since then been a matter of just this, that the historical conduct of man has to translate the principle of freedom into reality? Obviously this points to the unending march of world history into the openness of its future tasks and gives no becalming assurance that everything is already in order."[64]

Hegel might reply that the last sentence is dogmatic and without foundation. Biblical eschatology in both its Jewish and Christian forms envisages a decisive fulfillment of history's goal, which, while not violating the general character of historical experience, would put us in a situation so different from all previous situations that their finitude would be overcome. Does not Paul promise that in that day we shall know as we are known by God?[65] Gadamer might well grant the theoretical possibility of such a historical transcendence of the normal limits of historical understanding. (How else avoid the charge of blatant dogmatism?) But his response to Hegel's actual claim would not be changed. It would take an eschatological transition far more dramatic than anything that took place in Hegel's life or since to merit being called the Kingdom of God. The promise of "liberty and justice" for all would have to become a reality and not merely a promise and a dream.

In addition to this openness of the historical situation, there is also its opaqueness. "It is precisely our experience of history that we are located so completely within it that we can in a certain sense always say, We don't know what is happening to us."[66] The point can be put in Hegelian terms. "That the consciousness of the individual . . . . is no match for reason in history Hegel had illuminatingly demonstrated in his famous doctrine about the cunning of reason (*List der Vernunft*). But must not this knowledge of the finitude and limitedness of the individual who stands as an agent in history affect any individual who thinks? What must this mean for the claim of philosophic thought to truth?"[67] This is not to say that reflection is utterly impotent, only that it is finite. "Reflection on a given preunderstanding brings before me something that otherwise happens *behind my back*. Something—but not everything, for what I have called *wirkungsgeschichtliches Bewusstsein* is inescapably more *being* than consciousness, and being is never fully manifest."[68]

Beyond its historical character, Gadamer sees the linguistic character of experience as a barrier to the possibility of its being perfected as science. The same linguisticality of all understanding, including philosophical reflection, which drives beyond the Cartesian-transcendental perspective in the first place keeps us from returning to it at the level of spirit, as Hegel wishes to do. This is the meaning of Gadamer's claim that "dialectic must retrieve itself in hermeneutics."[69] The claim of the dialectic of Hegel's Logic to be scientific may well be consistent. "It is another question, however, whether that purpose, which he proposes for his Logic as transcendental logic, is justified convincingly when even he himself relies on the natural logic which he finds in the 'logical instinct' of language."[70]

It seems that Gadamer never tires of finding new ways to make this point, including the following:

1. The multiplicity of languages implies the multiplicity of logics and places the scientific status of any particular logic in question.[71]

2. The categories of thought presuppose language as the home of thought, and we can never reflect ourselves out of that home. Since language is not an instrument in the service of our purposes but the medium in which we live, it can never be objectified so that it ceases to surround us and define a limited horizon for our thinking.[72]

3. This becomes even clearer if we notice that even the speculative proposition, which Hegel so carefully distinguishes from ordinary predication, needs to be interpreted. Philosophical reflection is language that points to what it cannot fully say.[73]

4. This point in turn is deepened by the realization that philosophical discourse not only implies ongoing philosophical discourse (interpretation), and thus its own finitude, but it also implies an ongoing dialogue with nonphilosophical discourse. The language of philosophy is always in dialogue with the language of the world.[74]

5. Finally there is the face that language places us within tradition and thereby within history. The linguistic character of experience implies its historical character and all the implications of finitude already noted with reference to the latter.[75]

6. All five of these points are implied by and summed up in the conversational nature of language, which Gadamer indicates by speaking of the logic of question and answer. This logic limits the dogmatic claims of Hegelian Logic by calling attention to the historical situatedness of language and the unending conversation it represents, both within and among ourselves. Because objective spirit is this conversation it can never become absolute spirit. The truth of absolute spirit is precisely the finitude of the questioner. We are "exposed" to the questions that "befall" us in art, religion, and philosophy. In fact, "these questions hold us in suspense." As long

as we allow ourselves to be addressed by these questions the conversation continues, and as long as this happens, dialectic will need to retrieve itself in hermeneutics, because speculation will remain open to new interpretation.[76]

Though mostly spelled out in essays subsequent to *Truth and Method*, this critique of the Hegelian doctrines of absolute spirit and absolute knowledge from the perspective of the historical and linguistic character of objective spirit relies entirely on themes developed carefully in Gadamer's magnum opus. The more recent of these essays, however, include a third line of argument against Hegel, one derived from what Ricoeur calls the hermeneutics of suspicion. This was not a part of Gadamer's project originally, and much of the Gadamer-Habermas debate, with the larger discussion of hermeneutics in relation to ideology critique, is best understood as the challenging of a "hermeneutics of recovery" with a "hermeneutics of suspicion." Like Ricoeur, Gadamer does not see in the arguments of Marx, Nietzsche, and Freud (along with Schopenhauer and Bergson) a limit to the hermeneutical claim to universality. Suspicion is to be incorporated into hermeneutics.

The possibility of including suspicion in the hermeneutical task is grounded in a refusal to make the Cartesian assumption that the mind is more easily known than the body. In the transcendental tradition up through Husserl this becomes the assumption that consciousness is fully transparent to itself, once it makes the decision to become reflective. By accepting the critique of this position, which stems from Habermas and the "school of suspicion," Gadamer broadens the hermeneutical perspective by indicating yet another way (beyond history and language) in which revealing and concealing are the convex and concave sides of the same curve even for reflective self-consciousness. If there is always more going on "behind the back" of consciousness than it can get out in front of itself, so to speak, this refers not only to the impossibility of thematizing the horizon of one's thinking without remainder, or making the background of perception the foreground without creating a new background. In addition to the implicit, the unconscious also makes its home "behind my back." The attempt to understand must include the search for meanings unnoticed (because unwelcome) by those in whom they function.

So far as Hegel is concerned, this means that in addition to the ordinary opacity of historical life and the "tacit dimension" involved in every conversation, there is also the unconscious as a barrier to the full transparency of self-consciousness. Whether one speaks of repression or bad faith, the shared rationalizations of ideology are as intractable as the personal ones of neurosis, leaving the self-consciousness of spirit always in need of therapy.[77]

This third argument against Hegel plays a relatively minor role, and perhaps this is fitting. For to the degree that he can base his quarrel with Hegel on perspectives developed in the first place with help from Hegel, the quarrel becomes an example of the immanent critique that Hegel's own theory of dialectical "method" requires. This, in turn, is perhaps the best way of indicating how openness to tradition and respect for its authority need not involve an uncritical conservatism that worships the past. As long as distance and involvement, tension and proximity are kept in polar tension, the conversation continues.

NOTES

The following abbreviations are used in the footnotes below for referring to English translations of the works of Hegel and Gadamer:

PS   = *Hegel, Phenomenology of Spirit*, trans. A. V. Miller (Oxford, 1977).
SL   = *Hegel, Science of Logic*, trans. A. V. Miller (New York, 1969).
TM   = *Truth and Method*, trans. Barden and Cumming (New York, 1975).
PH   = *Philosophical Hermeneutics*, trans. David E. Linge (Berkeley, 1976).
HD   = *Hegel's Dialectic*, trans. P. Christopher Smith (New Haven, 1976).
RAS = *Reason in the Age of Science*, trans. Frederick G. Lawrence (Cambridge, 1981).

1. *TM*, pp. 239–40. Cf. p. 244, "The overcoming of all prejudices, this global demand of the enlightenment, will prove to be itself a prejudice."
2. Ibid. p. 245.
3. The notion of fore-sight along with the related notions of fore-having and fore-conception are part of Heidegger's analysis of understanding in *Being and Time*, par. 32. Habermas is getting at a closely related theme when he speaks of the "transitory a priori structure" of modern science and technology. *Towards a Rational Society*, trans. Jeremy J. Shapiro (Boston, 1970, p. 84. It is the historically conditioned a priori of experience that Gadamer indicates with the notion of prejudice, not the putatively universal and necessary a priori of Kant. Thus for him language becomes a "contingent absolute." See n. 20, below.
4. *RAS*, p. 53. Thus Gadamer has the intent of "learning something from Hegel" but by no means that of "renewing his perspective." p. 27. There is

"no question of Hegel discipleship, but of interiorizing the challenge that he represents." p. 50.

5. On Gadamer's Kantianism, see *TM*, pp. xxiv, 88–89, 245, 460–91; and *PH*, pp. 130–77. The language of hermeneutics and energetics comes from Ricoeur's *Freud and Philosophy*. The debate with Habermas begins with the latter's "A Review of Gadamer's *Truth and Method*" in *Understanding and Social Inquiry*, ed. Dallmayr and McCarthy (Notre Dame, 1977). Then come Gadamer's essays in *PH*, "The Universality of the Hermeneutical Problem," and "On the Scope and Function of Hermeneutical Reflection." Habermas's reply is "The Hermeneutic Claim to Universality" in Josef Bleicher, *Contemporary Hermeneutics: Hermeneutics as Method, Philosophy and Critique* (London, 1980). Most of this debate is found in *Hermeneutics and Ideologiekritik* (Frankfurt, 1971), which also contains Gadamer's "Replik" to the whole debate, including the last-mentioned essay of Habermas. For helpful analysis of the debate see Thomas McCarthy, *The Critical Theory of Jürgen Habermas* (Cambridge, 1981), chap. 3; Paul Ricoeur, "Ethics and Culture: Habermas and Gadamer in Dialogue," *Philosphy Today* v. 17 (1973): 153–65; and the relevant chapters of Bleicher.

6. Protests that Heidegger is no existentialist have their point. They are also one of the best illustrations of the Heideggerian point that revealing necessarily involves concealing.

7. Husserl, incidentally, is willing to take quite literally his own claim that "all" sciences are involved. He explicitly includes geometry, and Merleau-Ponty, agreeing, writes, "When I think the Pythagorean theorem and recognize it as true, it is clear that this truth is not for this moment only. Nevertheless later progress in knowledge will show that it is not yet a final, unconditioned evidence and that, if the Pythagorean theorem and the Euclidian system once appeared as final, unconditioned evidences, that is itself the mark of a certain cultural epoch. Later developments would not annul the Pythagorean theorem but would put it back in its place as a partial, and also an abstract, truth. Thus here also we do not have a timeless truth but rather the recovery of one time by another time." *The Primacy of Perception*, ed. James M. Edie (Evanston, 1964), p. 20.

8. See n. 3 above; McCarthy, p. 161; and *Knowledge and Human Interests*, trans. Jeremy J. Shapiro (Boston, 1971), p. vii.

9. *PH*, p. 9.

10. Ricoeur, "Ethics and Culture," p. 157.

11. See editor's introduction to *PH*, p. xliv.

12. *TM*, p. 269.

13. *PH*, pp. 29 and 13. Cf. pp. 13–16, 19, 25, 29–32, 35; *TM*, pp. 345–447, and *RAS*, p. 4.

14. It is Berger and Luckman who speak of the "vertigo of relativity" in *The Social Construction of Reality* (Gerden City, 1966), p. 5.

15. *Natural Law*, trans. T.M. Knox (n.p., 1975), p. 58.

16. See Shlomo Avineri, *Hegel's Theory of the Modern State* (Cambridge, 1972), ch. 4, "The New Era."

17. *SL*, pp. 26–27.

18. Hegel, *Philosophy of Right*. Translated by T.M. Knox, New York: Oxford University Press, 1967. See "Preface."

19. *PS*, pp. 3-8.

20. For these quotations, for the emergence of the question Who is the transcendental subject? and for a detailed analysis of the linguistic character of perception, see Merold Westphal, *History and Truth in Hegel's Phenomenology* (Atlantic Highlands, 1979), chapters 2-3. Cf. Habermas's summary of Gadamer's position, "At the level of objective spirit, language becomes a contingent absolute." Dallmayr and McCarthy, "Review of Gadamer's *Truth and Method*," p. 359.

21. *TM*, pp. 258 and 261. Cf. *TM*, xvi, "My real concern was and is philosophic: not what we do or what we ought to do, but what happens to us over and above our wanting and doing."

22. *PS*, p. 110.

23. Cf. Westphal, *History and Truth in Hegel's Phenomenology*, chapters 4-8. For Gadamer's appreciation of the anti-Cartesian character of Hegel's concept of spirit, see *HD*, pp. 35-36, 54-59, and 77-78.

24. According to McCarthy, Habermas is the latest to attempt this in the form of scientific social theory. "Habermas' counterposition [to Gadamer] is an attempt to mitigate the radically situational character of understanding through the introduction of theoretical elements; the theories of communication and social evolution are meant to reduce the context dependency of the basic categories and assumptions of critical theory." *Critical Theory*, p. 193.

25. *SL*, p. 27.

26. *PS*, pp. 25-28. Cf. p. 32; and for Gadamer's appreciation, see *HD*, pp. 16-17; and *RAS* p. 6, where he describes philosophy down through Hegel as "a self-defense against the sciences." N.B. Whereas for Kant there is an insuperable barrier between the human subject and the thing in itself (*"das Ding an sich"*), for Hegel it is method that erects the barrier between the knowing subject and the thing itself (*"die Sache selbst"*). This is why the transition from *Verstand* to *Vernunft* can have such a different meaning for the two.

27. Cf. *RAS*, p. 41. On the view Hegel seeks to overcome, "the truth of the object is not an intelligibility or meaning it can reveal to us but rather a brute otherness which we must forge weapons to overcome. Abstract universals are those weapons, by means of which we hope to deprive the object of its original independence and render it subject to our purposes and interests. Knowing is the desire to master and dominate. Without any specific reference to technological purposes and interests, Hegel has described the essence of calculative thinking." Merold Westphal, "Hegel's Theory of the Concept," in *Art and Logic in Hegel's Philosophy*, ed. Steinkraus and Schmitz (New Jersey: Humanities Press, 1980), esp. pp. 116-17.

28. *SL*, p. 36.

29. Ibid, p. 826. Hegel's italics.

30. Ibid, pp. 27-28. Cf. *HD*, pp. 5-7, 19, and 27.

31. *PS*, p. 32. My italics. He goes on to speak of being "absorbed in its object" and "immersed in the material."

32. *The Logic of Hegel*, trans. William Wallace, 2d ed. (1892, rpt. London, 1959), par. 163, Second *Zusatz*. Cf. the *Zusatze* to paragraphs 166, 175, and 181.

I have used 'concepts' where Wallace uses 'notions'. Hegel is most emphatic here. What is to be noted is "dass *wir* die Begriffe gar nicht bilden." Cf. *RAS*, p. 17.

33. For the argument in support of this conclusion, see "Hegel's Theory of the Concept."

34. *SL*, p. 603. Hegel's italics.

35. *Critique of Pure Reason*, B xiii. Kant's verb *nötigen* may also be translated as "coerce" or "compel."

36. *PH*, p. 26. Cf. preface to the second edition.

37. For example, *TM*, p. xi.

38. Compare *PH*, pp. 4–5 and 18–19 with *TM*, first part.

39. *PH*, p. 39; *TM*, p. 407; and *TAS*, pp. 70–71.

40. This includes the human sciences that seek legitimacy by going Cartesian. Whether they turn to the *Port Royal Logic*, or to Hume and Mill, or to Schleiermacher and Dilthey, Gadamer wants to expose the inadequacy of their self-understanding. See *TM*, pp. 19, 5, and 147–234. When Gadamer favorably quotes Heidegger's claim that the natural sciences have "strayed into the legitimate task of grasping the present-at-hand in its essential unintelligibility," he comes close to Hegel's formulations in terms of true propositions about an inferior subject matter. See *TM*, p. 230; and n. 26 above.

41. On the "unresolved Cartesianism" of both Dilthey and Husserl, see *TM*, pp. 210–29. In Gadamer's view Husserl's *Crisis* is not a joining of Heidegger, who has no wish to ground either history or philosophy as science, but rather a deflection of the anti-Cartesian thrust of Heidegger's thought by making the life-world into an object for phenomenological descrition rather than the subject of even philosophical reflection. See *TM*, pp. 225–27; and *PH*, pp. xliii–xlv.

42. *TM*, p. 311.

43. *PH*, p. 11. Statistics level themselves to propaganda because 'they let facts speak and hence simulate an objectivity that in reality depends on the legitimacy of the questions asked." *TM*, p. 268. On the logic of question and answer in general see *TM*, p. 325 ff.

44. *TM*, p. 329. Cf. *RAS*, p. 47.

45. The domination motif is especially strong in *RAS*. See pp. 3, 14–17, 23, and 70–71.

46. *TM*, pp. 277–78, 321–27, and 340–41. Some of these texts, especially the first, would be appealed to by those who see hermeneutics as uncritical acceptance of tradition. Apart from reading them in the light of other comments Gadamer makes and his own critical conversation with the philosophical tradition, what needs to be noted is the specific role these statements have in polemic against the will to power in the Cartesian tradition.

47. *TM*, p. 433.

48. Ibid., p. xxiii.

49. Ibid, p. 111. Cf. *RAS*, p. 77 and 17–18, where *theoria* is "complete self-donation."

50. *TM*, p. 422.

51. *HD*, p. 29.

52. *RAS*, pp. 61–63.

53. Ibid, pp. 14–15, 30–33.
54. Ibid, pp. 39–41.
55. Ibid, pp. 14–15, 46.
56. *TM*, pp. 318–20; and *HD*, pp. 11–13.
57. *HD*, pp. 110.
58. *TM*, p. 318; *RAS*, pp. 6 and 13; *HD*, p. 79. Cf. *RAS*, p. 46, where Gadamer even speaks of Hegel's "methodological compulsion."
59. See *RAS*, p. 1.
60. On this eschatological strategy for overcoming historical relativism within history, see Westphal, *History and Truth in Hegel's Phenomenology*, chapters 2 and 8, especially sections 2C and 8B.
61. *RAS*, p. 52.
62. *TM*, pp. 318–19.
63. *RAS*, pp. 40 and 59–60.
64. Ibid., p. 37. Cf. p. 10.
65. 1 Cor. 13:12 (NEB): "Now we see only puzzling reflections in a mirror, but then we shall see face to face. My knowledge now is partial; then it will be whole, like God's knowledge of me."
66. *RAS*, p. 36.
67. Ibid., p. 46.
68. *PH*, p. 38. Gadamer's italics. The reference to what happens "behind my back" is meant to evoke *PS*, p. 56, where Hegel describes the scientific status of the *Phenomenology* in terms of overcoming this hiddenness, that is, of making consciousness fully transparent to itself.
69. *HD*, p. 99.
70. Ibid., p. 91. Cf. pp. 31–33, 112; and *RAS*, p. 12.
71. *HD*, p. 93.
72. Ibid., pp. 94–97; and *RAS*, p. 50. Cf. *RAS*, p. 11.
73. *HD*, p. 96. Cf. p. 113, where Gadamer says that if we listen to language we will hear what Hegel didn't and couldn't say.
74. *HD*, p. 116.
75. *RAS*, p. 50.
76. Ibid., p. 53. Cf. pp. 20, 46–47, 57–60, and 106–8.
77. Reference to the "tacit dimension" suggests that more attention needs to be given to the relation of Gadamer and Polanyi than has been given to date. For Gadamer's incorporation of the suspicion critique of Hegel, see *RAS*, pp. 13, 49, 54, 58, 100–4, and 108.

FROM HERMENEUTICS TO PRAXIS

RICHARD J. BERNSTEIN

One of the most important and central claims in Hans-Georg Gadamer's philosophical hermeneutics is that all understanding involves not only interpretation, but also application. Against an older tradition that divided up hermeneutics into *subtilitas intelligendi* ("understanding"), *subtilitas explicandi* ("interpretation"), and *subtilitas applicandi* ("application"), a primary thesis of *Truth and Method* is that these are not three independent activities to be relegated to different subdisciplines, but rather they are internally related. They are all moments of the single process of understanding. I want to explore this integration of the moment of application into hermeneutic understanding, which Gadamer calls "the rediscovery of the fundamental hermeneutic problem."[1] For it not only takes us to the heart of what is distinctive about philosophical hermeneutics, but it reveals some of the deep problems and tensions implicit in hermeneutics. First, I want to note some of the central features of what Gadamer means by philosophical hermeneutics. Then I can specify the problem that he is confronting when dealing with application. This will enable us to see what Gadamer seeks to appropriate from Aristotle, and especially from Aristotle's analysis of *phronesis* in book 6 of the *Nichomachean Ethics*, in elucidating the sense in which all understanding involves application. Gadamer certainly realizes that "Aristotle is not concerned with the hermeneutical problem and certainly not with its historical dimension, but with the right estimation of the role that reason has to play in moral action,"[2] and yet Gadamer claims that "if we relate Aristotle's description of the ethical phenomenon and especially the virtue of moral knowledge to our own investigation, we find Aristotle's analysis is in fact a kind of model   the problems of hermeneutics."[3] But Gadamer's own understanding, interpretation, and appropriation of Aristotle has much richer consequences. It is itself a model of what he means by hermeneutical understanding. It is an exemplar of effective-historical consciousness (*Wirkungs-geschichtliches Bewusstsein*), the fusion of horizons (*Horizontversch-melzung*), the positive role of temporal distance, how understanding is part of the process of the coming into being of meaning, the way in which tradition "speaks to us" and makes a "claim to truth" upon us, and what it means to say that "the interpreter dealing with a traditional text seeks to apply it to himself." Furthermore, when we see how Gadamer appropriates Aristotle's text, we gain a deeper understanding of why the *Geisteswissenschaften* are moral-practical disciplines in the sense in which the *Ethics* and the *Politics* are practical disciplines, and why Gadamer thinks that "hermeneutic philosophy is the heir of the older tradition of practical philosophy," whose chief task is to "justify this way of reason and defend practical and political reason against the domination of technology based on science."[4] Gadamer's   own   understanding   of   philosophical hermeneutics can itself be interpreted as a series of footnotes and reflections on his decisive intellectual encounter with Aristotle, an encounter to which he frequently refers and that was initiated by his participation in Heidegger's seminar on the *Nichomachean Ethics*.[5]

In order to orient our discussion, it is important to recall some of the primary characteristics of philosophical hermeneutics. As Gadamer frequently reiterates, "the hermeneutic phenomenon is basically not a problem of method at all. It is not concerned with a method of understanding, by means of which texts are subjected to scientific investigation like all other objects of experience. It is not concerned primarily with amassing ratified knowledge that satisfies the methodological ideal of science—yet it is concerned, here too, with knowledge and with truth."[6] The task is to elucidate the distinctive type of *knowledge and truth* that is realized whenever we authentically understand.[7] From Gadamer's perspective, it has been the obsession with *Method*, and with thinking that the primary task of hermeneutics is to specify a distinctive method of the *Geisteswissenschaften* that can rival the scientific method of the *Naturwissenschaften*, which plagued and distorted nineteenth-century hermeneutics. This led to a view of understanding as primarily a psychological subjective activity, as involving some sort of empathy where we can overcome and leap out of our own historical situation and identify ourselves with the intentions of the authors of texts or the intentions of the historical actors whom we are studying. There was a "latent Cartesianism" in this tradition and an acceptance of the basic dichotomy between what is objective and subjective.[8] But it is just this dichotomy that Gadamer seeks to question and undermine. According to Gadamer, it is only with Heidegger that the full dimensions of understanding were fully realized. Implicit in Heidegger and explicit in Gadamer are two central claims: the ontological primacy of hermeneutics and its universality. We are "thrown" into the world as beings who understand; and understanding itself is not one type of activity of a subject but may properly be said to underlie all activities.

When Gadamer introduces the concept of play and tells us that play is "the clue to ontological explanation,"[9] he is seeking to show us that there is a more primordial mode of being for understanding our being in the world—an alternative to the Cartesian persuasion that rivets our attention on the subjective attitudes toward what is presumably objective. "Play has its own essence which is independent of the consciousness of those who play." "The players are not subjects of play; instead play merely reaches presentation through the players."[10] Play has its own rhythm, its own buoyancy, its distinctive to-and-fro movement. This mode of being of play is what Gadamer takes to be characteristic of our relation with works of art, texts, and indeed anything that is handed down to us. Gadamer introduces the concept of play in order to highlight the subtle dialectical and dialogical relation that exists between the interpreter and what he seeks to interpret. We misconceive this relation if we think that we are merely subjects or spectators standing over and against what is objective and what exists *an sich*. We participate in the works of art, texts, and tradition that we encounter, and it is only through understanding that their meaning and truth is realized. The aim of hermeneutical understanding is to open ourselves to what texts and tradition "say to us," to open ourselves to their meaning and the claim to truth that they make upon us.[11] But what Gadamer stresses, building on Heidegger, is that we do *not* do this by forgetting or seeking to bracket our own historicity, our own forestructures, prejudgments, and prejudices. Here we touch upon one of the most controversial features of Gadamer's philosophic hermeneutics, viz., his *apologia* for prejudice against the Enlightenment's "prejudice against prejudice."[12] As Gadamer tells us:

> It is not so much our judgments as it is our prejudices that constitute our being. This is a provocative formulation, for I am using it to restore to its rightful place as a positive concept of pre-

judice that was driven out of our linguistic usage by the French and English Enlightenment. . . . Prejudices are not necessarily unjustified and erroneous, so that they inevitably distort the truth. In fact, the historicity of our existence entails that prejudices, in the literal sense of the word, constitute the initial directedness of our whole ability to experience. Prejudices are biases of our openness to the world. They are simply the conditions whereby we experience something—whereby what we encounter says something to us.[13]

Gadamer does want to make the all-important distinction between "blind prejudices," which are unjustified, and those "justified prejudices that are productive of knowledge"—what we might call "enabling prejudices." This does not diminish the thrust of his claim that *both* sorts of prejudice are constitutive of what we are. But then how do we distinguish between these types of prejudice or prejudgment? One answer is clearly ruled out. We cannot do this by a solitary or monological act of pure self-reflection where we bracket or suspend judgment about *all* of our prejudices. This is what is ontologically impossible—for what we *are*, and what is revelatory of our human finitude—is that prejudices are constitutive of our being. Indeed the answer that Gadamer gives to the question of how we make this distinction between blind and enabling prejudices is the very one that Descartes rejected from serious consideration. It is only through the dialogical encounter with what is handed down to us that we can test and *risk* our prejudices. Unlike Descartes (and Hegel), Gadamer sees this as a constant open task, not one that can ever achieve finality or closure. For Gadamer then, there is a threefold temporal character to prejudices. They are themselves inherited from tradition and shape what we are, whether we are aware of this or not. It is because our prejudices themselves have their source in the very tradition that we seek to understand that we can account for the *affinity* (*Zugehörigkeit*) that we have with tradition. Although inherited from tradition, they are constitutive of what we are *now*. But there is also a projective or anticipatory aspect of our prejudices and prejudgments, a dimension highlighted by Heidegger's own emphasis on fore-structures, that is, on fore-having, fore-sight, and fore-conceptions.[14] It is through the hermeneutical circle of understanding that we call upon these fore-structures, which enable us to understand and at the same time discriminate critically between blind and enabling prejudices.

We can begin to see where Gadamer is leading us and why the problem of application is so important for him. On the one hand,

Gadamer tells us that hermeneutic understanding is always tempered to the "thing itself" that we are trying to understand. We seek nothing less than to understand the *same* text of the same piece of tradition. But the *meaning* of what we seek to understand is not self-contained, it does not exist *an sich*. The meaning of a text or of tradition is only realized through the happening (*pathos*) of understanding. But such understanding is only possible because of the prejudices and prejudgments that are constitutive of what we are—our own historicity. This is why Gadamer tells us that to understand is always to understand *differently*. There is a play, a to-and-fro movement that occurs in all understanding in which both what we seek to understand and our prejudices are dynamically involved with each other. Unlike those who think that such appropriation or application to our hermeneutical situation reveals a distortion or a deficiency that is to be overcome, it is the positive enabling roles of prejudgments and prejudices that become thematic for philosophical hermeneutics.

It is in this context that the problem of application becomes so central for Gadamer. It is here that we can see why Aristotle's analysis of *phronesis* is so important for him. For *phronesis* is a form of reasoning and knowledge that involves a distinctive mediation between the universal and the particular. This mediation is not accomplished by any appeal to technical rules or Method (in the Cartesian sense), or by the subsumption of a pregiven determinate universal to a particular case. What Gadamer emphasizes about *phronesis* is that it is a form of reasoning, yielding a type of "ethical know-how" in which both what is universal and what is particular are *codetermined*. Furthermore, *phronesis* involves a "peculiar interlacing of being and knowledge, determination through one's own becoming."[15] It is not to be identified with or confused with the type of "objective knowledge" that is detached from one's own being and becoming. Just as *phronesis* determines what the *phronimos* becomes, Gadamer wants to make a similar claim for all authentic understanding, that is, that it is not detached from the interpreter but constitutive of his or her *praxis*. Understanding for Gadamer is a form of *phronesis*.

We gain a subtler comprehension of what this means by noting the contrasts that Gadamer highlights when he explores the ways in which Aristotle distinguishes *phronesis* from the other "intellectual virtues," especially from *episteme* and *techne*. *Episteme*, scientific knowledge, is knowledge of what is universal, of what exists "of necessity" and takes the form of the scientific demonstration. The subject matter, the form, the telos, the way in which *episteme* is learned and taught differ from *phronesis*, the form of reasoning appropriate to *praxis*, where there is always a mediation between the universal and the particular that involves deliberation and choice. But it is not primarily the contrast between *episteme* and *phronesis* that Gadamer takes to be instructive for hermeneutics, but rather the careful ways in which Aristotle distinguishes *techne* (technical know-how) from *phronesis* (ethical know-how). And here Gadamer stresses three contrasts. (1) *Techne*, or "a technique is learned and can be forgotten; we can lose a skill. But ethical 'reason' can neither be learned nor forgotten. . . . By contrast, the subject of ethical reason, of *phronesis*, man always finds himself in an 'acting situation' and he is always obliged to use ethical knowledge and apply it according to the exigencies of his concrete situation.[16] (2) There is a different conceptual relation between means and ends in *techne* and *phronesis*. The end of ethical know-how, unlike a technique, is not a "particular thing or product" but rather the "*complete* ethical rectitude of a life time."[17] Even more important, while technical activity does not require that the means that allow it to arrive at an end be weighed anew on each occasion, this is what is required in ethical know-how. In ethical know-how there can be no prior knowledge of the right means by which we realize the end. For the end itself is only concretely specified in deliberating about the means appropriate to *this* particular situation.[18] (3) *Phronesis*, unlike *techne*, is a distinctive type of "knowledge-for-the-sake-of-oneself." This is indicated when Aristotle considers the variants of *phronesis*, especially *synesis* ("understanding"). "It appears in the fact of concern, not about myself, but about the other person. Thus it is a moral judgment. . . . The question here, then, is not of a general kind of knowledge, but of its specification at a particular moment. This knowledge also is not in any sense technical knowledge or the application of such. . . . . The person with understanding does not know and judge as one who stands apart and unaffected; but rather, as one united by a specific bond with the other, he thinks with the other and undergoes the situation with him."[19]

What does this analysis of *phronesis* and the ways in which it differs from both *episteme* and *techne* have to do with the problems of hermeneutics? The analogy that Gadamer draws, the reason why he thinks it is a "model of the problems of hermeneutics," is that just as application is not a subsequent or occasional part of *phronesis* where we relate some pregiven determinate universal to a particular situation, this is true for *all* understanding. And just as with *phronesis* there is always a mediation between the universal and the particular in which both are codetermined and become integral to the very being of the *phronimos*, this is what Gadamer claims is characteristic of all authentic understanding.

> The interpreter dealing with a traditional text seeks to apply it to himself. But this does not mean that the text is given for him as something universal, that he understands it as such and only afterwards uses it for particular application. Rather, the interpreter seeks no more than to understand this universal thing, the text; i.e., to understand what this piece of tradition says, what constitutes the meaning and the importance of the text. In order to understand that, he must not seek to disregard himself and his particular hermeneutical situation. He must relate the text to this situation, if he wants to understand at all.[20]

What is striking about this passage is that it applies perfectly to the way in which Gadamer himself understands, interprets, and appropriates Aristotle's text. This is what I meant earlier when I said that Aristotle's analysis of *phronesis* is not only a model of the problems of hermeneutics, but that Gadamer's interpretation of Aristotle is itself a model or exemplar of what is meant by hermeneutical understanding. In the passage quoted above, Gadamer tells us that if we are to understand what a text or a piece of tradition says, then we must not seek to disregard ourselves and our hermeneutical situation. This is characteristic of the way in which Gadamer approaches Aristotle. For what Gadamer takes to be basic for *our* hermeneutical situation is that we are confronted with a world in which there has been a "domination of technology based on science," that there is a "false idolatry of the expert," a "scientific mystification of the modern society of specialization," and a dangerous "inner longing in our society to find in science a substitute for lost orientations."[21] It is this problematic that orients Gadamer's questioning of Aristotle's text, for Gadamer's central claim is that there has been a forgetfulness and deformation of what *praxis* really is.

Indeed it is through the dialogical encounter with Aristotle's text that we risk and test our own deeply entrenched prejudices that hinder us from grasping the autonomy and integrity of *phronesis*. This doesn't mean that we approach Aristotle without any prejudices and prejudgments. What enables us to understand Aristotle and appropriate the "truth" of what he says is that we ourselves have been shaped by this effective history. It is not a nostalgic return to Aristotle that Gadamer is advocating, but rather an appropriation of Aristotle's own insights to our concrete situation. Gadamer's interpretation of Aristotle illustrates what he means by the fusion of horizons. We are, of course, questioning Aristotle's text from our own historical horizon. But we distort the very idea of a horizon if we think it is self-contained, that we are prisoners enclosed within it. "The historical movement of human life consists in the fact that it is never utterly bound to any one standpoint, and hence can never have a truly closed horizon."[22] We come to understand what Aristotle is saying and at the same time come to a deeper understanding of our own situation when we are sensitive to Aristotle's own confrontation with the "professional lawmakers whose function at that time corresponded to the role of the expert in modern scientific society."[23] By appropriating the "truth" of what Aristotle says, especially the way in which he distinguishes practical reason from theoretical and technical reason, we thereby enlarge our own horizon. It is this fusion of horizons that enables us to risk and test our own prejudices. For the dialogical encounter with Aristotle allows us to see how the contemporary understanding of *praxis* has become deformed. We can learn from Aristotle what "practice" really is, why it is not to be identified with the "application of science to technical tasks." Gadamer realizes that in modern society *techne* itself has been transformed, but this only highlights the importance of what we can learn from Aristotle about *praxis* and *phronesis*. He tells us:

> In a scientific culture such as ours the fields of *techne* and art are much more expanded. Thus the fields of mastering means to pre-given ends have been rendered even more monological and controllable. The crucial change is that practical wisdom can no longer be promoted by personal contact and the mutual exchange of views among the citizens. Not only has craftmanship been replaced by industrial work; many forms of our daily life are technologically organized so that they no longer require personal decision. In modern technological society public opinion itself has in a new and really decisive way become the object of very complicated techniques—and this, I think, is the main problem facing our civilization.[24]

The temporal distance between ourselves and Aristotle is not a negative barrier to understanding, but rather positive and productive for understanding. By opening ourselves to what this "piece of tradition" says and to the claim to truth that it makes upon us, we bring to life new meanings of the text. "Understanding must be conceived as part of the process of the coming into being of meaning."[25] And this understanding, like *phronesis*, is a form of moral-practical knowledge that becomes constitutive of what we are in the process of becoming. What Gadamer seeks to show is that authentic hermeneutical understanding truly humanizes us, it becomes integrated in our very being just as *phronesis* itself shapes the being of the *phronimos*.

This emphasis on the moment of appropriation in hermeneutical understanding enables us to see why Gadamer thinks that the *Geisteswissenschaften*—when authentically practiced—are moral-practical disciplines. As hermeneutical disciplines, they are not concerned with amassing "theoretical" knowledge of what is strange and alien. Rather they involve the type of appropriation characteristic of *phronesis*. The type of knowledge and truth that they yield is practical knowledge and truth that shapes our *praxis*. This also helps to clarify why the "chief task" of philosophical hermeneutics is to "correct the peculiar falsehood of modern consciousness" and "to defend practical and political reason against the domination of technology based on science." It is in this sense that "hermeneutic philosophy is the heir of the older tradition of practical philosophy."[26]

This fusion of hermeneutics and *praxis* through the appropriation of *phronesis* has much broader ramifications. For in a number of different contexts we can discern how a variety of thinkers have been led to a reinterpretation or appreciation of the tradition of practical philosophy in order to come to a critical understanding of modern society. It is an underlying theme in the work of Hannah Arendt and Jürgen Habermas, both of whom share Gadamer's concern sharply to distinguish the technical from the practical. The attempt to clarify and restore the integrity of practical reasoning surfaces in such recent critical appraisals as Richard Rorty's *Philosophy and the Mirror of Nature*, Alasdair MacIntyre's *After Virtue*, and Hilary Putnam's *Meaning and the Moral Sciences*. Differences among these thinkers are as important as the common themes that run through their work. But I do think we are witnessing a new turn in the conversation of philosophy and in the understanding of human rationality where there is a recovery and appropriation of the types of practical reasoning, knowledge, and wisdom that are characteristic of *phronesis*.

I have indicated that Gadamer's appropriation of this tradition of practical philosophy is not without problems and tensions. If we take

Gadamer seriously and press his own claims, then they lead us beyond philosophical hermeneutics. Before I begin my immanent critique, it is important to remember that in *Truth and Method* Gadamer's primary concern is with the understanding and interpretation of works of art, texts, and tradition, with "what is handed down to us." Ethics and politics are not in the foreground of his investigations. Even his discussion of Aristotle is introduced only insofar as it helps to illuminate the hermeneutical phenomenon. But it is also clear that if we pay close attention to Gadamer's writings before and after the publication of *Truth and Method*, there has been an underlying and pervasive concern with ethics and politics—especially with what we can learn from Greek philosophy. In his writings since the publication of *Truth and Method*, Gadamer has returned again and again to the dialectical interplay of hermeneutics and *praxis*. I emphasize this because when we enlarge our horizon and consider the implications of what he is saying for a contemporary understanding of ethics and politics, then a number of difficulties come into sharp relief.

Let me begin with a consideration of the meaning of *truth* for Gadamer, then move to his conception of *criticism*. This will allow us to take a closer look at some of the difficulties with his understanding of *phronesis*. Finally we can turn to Gadamer's reflections on dialogue and its implications for politics. Truth is not only basic for the entire project of philosophical hermeneutics, but it turns out to be one of the most elusive concepts in Gadamer. After all, the primary intention of *Truth and Method* is to defend and elucidate the legitimacy of speaking of the truth of works of art, texts, and tradition. Gadamer tells us that it was not his intention to play off Method against Truth, but rather to show that there is a "different type of knowledge and truth" that is not exhausted by achievements of scientific method and that is only available to us through hermeneutical understanding.[27] This appeal to truth—a truth that transcends our own historical horizon—is absolutely essential in order to distinguish philosophical hermeneutics from a historicist form of relativism. Gadamer concludes *Truth and Method* with strong claims about this distinctive type of truth.

> Thus there is undoubtedly no understanding that is free of all prejudices, however much the will of our knowledge must be directed towards escaping their thrall. It has emerged throughout our investigation that the certainty that is imparted by the use of scientific methods does not suffice to guarantee truth. This is so especially of the human sciences, but this does not mean a

diminution of their scientific quality, but on the contrary, a justification of the claim to special humane significance that they have always made. The fact that in the knowing involved in them the knower's own being is involved marks, certainly, the limitation of 'method,' but not that of science. Rather, what the tool of method does not achieve must—and effectively can—be achieved by a discipline of questioning and research, a discipline that guarantees truth [*die Wahrheit verbürgt*].[28]

But what precisely does "truth" mean here? And what does it mean to say that there is a discipline of questioning and research that "guarantees truth "? It is much easier to say what "truth" does not mean than to give a positive account. It may seem curious (although I do not think it is accidental) that in a work *Truth and Method*, the topic of truth never becomes fully thematic and is discussed only briefly toward the very end of the book.[29] It is clear, however, that like Hegel and Heidegger, Gadamer criticizes the notion of truth as correspondence, as *adequatio intellectus et rei*, at least in regard to the distinctive type of truth that is achieved through hermeneutical understanding. What Gadamer means by "truth" is a blending of motifs that have resonances in Hegel and Heidegger. For like Hegel, Gadamer seeks to show that there is a truth that is revealed in the process of experience (*Erfahrung*) and that emerges in the dialogical encounter with the very tradition that has shaped us. Even the passage quoted above echoes the typical Hegelian movement from *Gewissheit* (certainty) to *Wahrheit* (truth). And like Heidegger, Gadamer also seeks to recover the notion of *alethia* as disclosedness (*Erschlossenheit*) and unconcealment (*Unverborgenheit*). There is even a parallel between Heidegger's claim that *Dasein* is "equally in truth and in untruth" and Gadamer's claim that prejudices (both true and untrue prejudices) are constitutive of our being. But Gadamer also distances himself from both Hegel and Heidegger. He categorically rejects what Hegel himself took to be the ground for his conception of truth, viz., that "truth is the whole" that is finally revealed in *Wissenschaft*, the absolute knowledge that completes and overcomes experience.[30] Gadamer also stands in an uneasy relation with Heidegger, for he knows all too well where Heidegger's meditations on *alethia* can lead us. He writes, "When science expands into a total technocracy and this brings on the 'cosmic night' of the 'forgetfulness of being,'" the nihilism that Nietzsche prophesied, then may one look at the last fading light of the sun that is set in the evening sky, instead of turning around to look for the first shimmer of its return?'' And with explicit reference to Heidegger, he tells us "what man needs is not only a persistent asking of ultimate questions, but the sense of what is feasible, what is possible, what is correct, here and now,"[31] But even if we play out the similarities and differences with Hegel and Heidegger, the precise meaning of truth for Gadamer still eludes us. What is even more problematic and revealing is that if we closely examine the way in which Gadamer appeals to "truth," he is employing a concept of truth that he never fully makes explicit. His typical phrasing is to speak of the "claim to truth" (Anspruch auf Wahrheit) that works of art, texts, and tradition make upon us. Gadamer never says (and it would certainly distort his meaning) that something is true simply because it is handed down to us. What he is always doing is seeking to appropriate critically what is handed down ,to us. This is just as evident in his claims about the tradition of practical philosophy as it is in his criticism of the "Enlightenment's prejudice against prejudice." When Gadamer, for example, says, "When Aristotle, in the sixth book of the Nichomachean Ethics, distinguishes the manner of 'practical' knowledge . . . from theoretical and technical knowledge, he expresses, in my opinion, one of the greatest truths by which the Greeks throw light upon the 'scientific' mystification of modern society of specialization,'[32] he is not telling us that this is one of the greatest truths simply because it is what Aristotle's text says. Rather it is true because Gadamer thinks we can now give convincing arguments to show why it is true. The force is not simply on what tradition says to us, or even of the "claim to truth" that it makes upon us, but on the validation of such claims by critical arguments. Gadamer has warned us against deifying tradition and thinking that it is something simply given.[33] Furthermore, tradition is not a seamless whole. There are conflicting traditions making conflicting claims of truth upon us. If we take our own historicity seriously, then the challenge that always confronts us is to give the best possible reasons and arguments that are appropriate to our hermeneutical situation in order to validate claims to truth. Gadamer himself makes this point forcefully in his friendly quarrel with Leo Strauss. Commenting on a theme that Gadamer shares with Strauss—the importance of the concept of friendship in Aristotle's ethics for recognizing the limitations of modern ethics—he asks, "Does this insight emerge because we 'read' the classics with an eye that is trained by historical science, reconstructing their meaning, as it were, and then considering it possible, trusting that they are right?

Or do we see truth in them, because we are thinking ourselves as we try to understand them, i.e. because what they say seems true to us when we consider the corresponding modern theories that are invoked?''[34] There is no ambiguity in how Gadamer answers his own question. But then this casts the entire question of truth in a very different light. For when it comes to the validation of claims to truth and the correct interpretations of texts, then the essential issue concerns reasons and arguments that are, of course, fallible and are anticipatory in the sense that they can be challenged and criticized by future argumentation. In effect, I am suggesting that what Gadamer himself is appealing to is a concept of truth that comes down to what can be argumentatively validated by the community of interpreters who open themselves to what is "handed down" *says* to us. This does not mean that there is some transcendental or ahistorical perspective from which we can evaluate competing claims to truth. We judge and evaluate such claims by the standards and practices that have been hammered out in the course of history. If I am right in pursuing this line of thought, that is implicit in Gadamer, then it is extraordinarily misleading—and betrays his own best insights—to say that there is any discipline that "guarantees truth." Rather we can only seek to justify claims to truth by giving the strongest arguments that we can show why something is true—and this is in fact what Gadamer himself does.

The point that I am making about the concept of truth that is implicit in Gadamer is closely related to the allied concept of criticism. Gadamer tells us, "It is a grave misunderstanding to assume that emphasis on the essential factor of tradition which enters into all understanding implies an uncritical acceptance of tradition and sociopolitical conservatism. . . . In truth the confrontation of our historic tradition is always a critical challenge of this tradition. . . . Every experience is such a confrontation."[35] But even if we acknowledge what he is saying here and appreciate that this is characteristic of the way in which Gadamer always approaches tradition, there is a problem that Gadamer does not squarely confront. Implicitly or explicitly all criticism appeals to some principles, standards, or criteria. Gadamer is extremely incisive in exposing the fallacy of thinking that such principles, standards, or criteria can be removed from our own historicity and in showing that there is an essential openness and indeterminacy about them. But even if we grant him everything he wants to say about human finitude rooted in historicity, this does not lessen the burden of the question of what is and what ought to be the basis for the critical evaluation of the problems of modernity. One can be extraordinarily sympathetic with Gadamer's critique of objectivism, foundationalism, the search for some Archimedian point that somehow stands outside of our historical situation. But if we take the theme of application or appropriation seriously and speak about *our* hermeneutical situation, then we must still address the question of what is the basis for our critical judgments. When Gadamer tells us that ''the concept of *'praxis'* which was developed in the last two centuries is an awful deformation of what practice really is,'' or when he speaks of ''the peculiar falsehood of modern consciousness: the idolatry of scientific method and the anonymous authority of the sciences,''[36] he is himself appealing to critical standards and norms of what practice really is, and what is truly a human life—standards and norms that demand rational justification and argumentation. It is not *sufficient* to give a justification that directs us to tradition. What is required is a form of argumentation. It is not *sufficient* to give a justification that directs us to tradition. What is required is a form of argumentation that seeks to *warrant* what is valid in this tradition.

Characteristically, when questions are raised about the validity of standards and norms that are to serve as the basis for criticism, Gadamer tells us that they too are handed down to us and need to be recovered from tradition. But this response is not adequate. Consider again what Gadamer highlights in his appropriation of *phronesis*—the distinctive type of mediaton of the universal and the particular. Let us focus our attention on the universal element that is mediated in *phronesis*. Gadamer's meaning is illustrated by his interpretation of the role of natural law in Aristotle. In the realm of *praxis*, natural law is not to be thought of as a law that is eternal, immutable, and fully determinate. He tells us, ''For according to Aristotle, the idea of an immutable natural law applies only to the divine world, and he declares that with us humans natural law is in the last analysis just as inconstant as positive law.[37] While natural law is not to be reduced to or confused with positive law, it requies interpretation and specification in concrete particular situations of *praxis*. Finding justice in a concrete situation demands perfecting law with equity (*epieikeia*): ''It follows, then, according to Aristotle that the idea of natural law serves only a critical function. Nothing in the idea authorizes us to use it dogmatically by attributing the inviolability of natural law to particular and concrete juridical contents.''[38] The claim that Gadamer makes about Aristotle's understanding of natural law (the universal element), which is essentially open to interpretation and is only concretely specified when related and mediated in a concrete ethical situation, is paradigmatic for the application of all ethical principles and norms. But what Aristotle stresses and Gadamer realizes is that what is required for the exercise of *phronesis*, and what keeps it from degenerating into the mere cleverness of the *deinos*, is the existence of such a *nomos* in the polis or community. Given a community in which there is a living shared acceptance of ethical principles and norms, then *phronesis*, and what keeps it from degenerating into the mere cleverness of the *deinos*, is the existence of such a *nomos* in the polis or community. Given a community in which there is a living shared acceptance of ethical principles and norms, then *phronesis* as the mediation of such universals in concrete particular situations makes sense. But what has become so problematic for us today, what is characteristic of our hermeneutical situation, is that there is so much confusion and uncertainty (some may even say chaos) about what are the norms or the "universals" that ought to govern our practical lives. What Gadamer himself realizes (but I don't think he squarely faces the issues that it raises) is that we are living in a time when the very conditions required for exercise of *phronesis*—the shared acceptance and stability of universal principles and laws—are themselves breaking down. Furthermore, Gadamer does not adequately clarify the type of discourse that is appropriate when questions about the validity of basic norms (or universals) are raised. When pressed on these questions, Gadamer deals with a different issue. He typically stresses that such universals are inherited from tradition, that they are essentially open, that they require the type of mediation in which their meaning is specified in the application to concrete practical situations. But this doesn't clarify the issue of what are the norms that are to serve as the universals that are to be mediated and codetermined in particular situations. Nor does it clarify how we are to evaluate a situation in which we are forced to question the validity of such norms. If we follow out the logic of Gadamer's own line of thought, if we are really concerned with "the sense of what is feasible, what is possible, what is correct, here and now," then this demands that we turn our attention to the question of how we can nurture and foster the types of community required for the exercise of *phronesis*. Indeed, there is a paradox that stands at the center of Gadamer's thinking about *praxis*. For on the one hand, he acutely analyzes the deformation of *praxis* in the contemporary world and shows how the main problem facing our civilization is one in which the very possibility for the exercise of *phronesis* is undermined; and yet on the other hand he seems to suggest that, regardless of the type of community in which we live, *phronesis* is always a real possibility. Just as Aristotle saw the continuity and movement from ethics to politics, one would think that this is a movement necessitated by Gadamer's own appropriation of *phronesis*. But Gadamer stops short of facing the issue of what is to be done when the *polis* or community itself is "corrupt"—when there is a breakdown of its *nomos* and of a rational discourse about the norms that ought to govern our practical lives.[39]

In defense of Gadamer, one can see why he stops short of confronting the practical issues of our hermeneutical situation. We can read his philosophical hermeneutics as a profound mediation on the meaning of human finitude, as a constant warning against the excesses of what he calls "planning reason," a caution that philosophy must give up the ideal of an "infinite intellect." Like Heidegger, there is a deep skepticism about the human will and the belief that we can *make* or engineer such communities in which there are living shared universal principles. The claims of his philosophical hermeneutics are at once bold and extremely modest. They are bold insofar as hermeneutics has the task of defending practical and political reason against the various attacks and deformations of it in the contemporary world. But hermeneutic philosophy—or any form of philosophy—cannot *solve* the problems of society or politics. It is dangerous to submit to the temptation of playing the prophet. This is the way to dogmatism. But even if one accepts Gadamer's cautions about prophesy and dogmatism, still there is a practical task that confronts us and to which Gadamer's own investigations lead, seeking to nurture the type of dialogical communities in which *phronesis* becomes a living reality.

The major point of this immanent critique of philosophical hermeneutics—that it leads us to practical tasks that take us beyond hermeneutics—can be approached from a different perspective. Thus far I have been concentrating on Gadamer's appropriation of the "truth" in Aristotle's understanding of *praxis* and *phronesis*, but a full-scale analysis of Gadamer's philosophical hermeneutics would require seeing how it represents a blending and appropriation of both Aristotelian and Platonic themes. Here I want to discuss briefly the most important theme that Gadamer appropriates from Plato—the centrality of dialogue and conversation.

A conversation or a dialogue, Gadamer tells us, "is a process of two people understanding each other. Thus it is characteristic of every true conversation that each opens himself to the other person, truly accepts his point of view as worthy of consideration and gets inside the other to such an extent that he understands not a particular individual, but what he says. The thing that has to be grasped is the objective rightness or otherwise of his opinion, so that they can agree with each other on the subject."[40] When Gadamer introduces the concept of play as the clue to ontological explanation, this has its full realization in his understanding of dialogue and conversation.

> Now I contend that the basic constitution of the game, to be filled with its spirit—the spirit of buoyancy, freedom and the joy of success—and to fulfill him who is playing, is structurally related to the constitution of the dialogue in which language is a reality. When one enters into a dialogue with another person and then is carried further by the dialogue, it is no longer the will of the individual person, holding itself back or exposing itself, that is determinative. Rather, the law of the subject matter is at issue in the dialogue and elicits statement and counterstatement and in the end plays them into each other.[41]

Dialogue itself is fundamental for grasping what is distinctive about hermeneutical understanding. Gadamer is, of course, aware of the disanalogies between the dialogue that we have with texts and tradition and that which occurs with other persons. "Texts are 'permanently fixed expressions of life' which have to be understood, and that means that one partner in the hermeneutical conversation, the text is expressed only through the other partner, the interpreter."[42] Nevertheless the conversation, questioning, and dialogue with texts and tradition is like a living conversation or dialogue "in that it is the common object that unites the partners, the text and the interpreter."[43] The conversation or dialogue that he takes to be the quintessence of hermeneutical understanding always evokes the memory of a living conversation or dialogue between persons. But consider what he stresses in his analysis of dialogue and conversation—it is the mutuality, the respect required, the genuine seeking to understand what the other is saying, the openness to test and evaluate our own opinions through such an encounter. And in

Gadamer's distinctive understanding of practical philosophy he blends this concept of dialogue that he finds illustrated in the Platonic Dialogues with his understanding of *phronesis*. But here too there are strong practical and political implications that Gadamer fails to pursue. For Gadamer can be read as showing us that what we truly are, what is most characteristic of our humanity, is that we are dialogical or conversational beings. According to Gadamer's reading of the history of philosophy, this is the idea that he finds at the very beginning of Western philosophy and that in our time again is the most central lesson of the philosophic tradition.

But if we are really to appropriate this central idea to our historical situation, then it points us toward important practical and political tasks. It would be a gross distortion to imagine that we might conceive of the entire political realm organized on the principle of dialogue or conversation, considering the fragile conditions that are required for genuine dialogue and conversation. Nevertheless, if we think out what is required for such dialogue based on mutual understanding, respect, a willingness to listen and test one's opinions and prejudices, a mutual seeking of the objective rightness of what is said, then this provides us a powerful regulative ideal that can orient our practical and political lives. If the quintessence of what we are is to be dialogical—and this is not just the privilege of the few—then whatever the limitations of the practical realization of this ideal, it nevertheless can and should give practical orientation to our lives. We must ask what is it that blocks and distorts such dialogue, and what is to be done, "what is feasible, what is possible, what is correct, here and now" to make much genuine dialogue a living reality.[44]

Let me conclude by underscoring the main point of my critique of Gadamer's philosophical hermeneutics. I do think that one of his profoundest insights has been the linkage (or fusion) of hermeneutics and *praxis*, and his claim that all understanding involves appropriation to our own concrete historical situation. But if we pursue the logic of his own argument, if we probe what he means by truth and criticism, or the common ethical and political principles required for the virtue of *phronesis*, or the type of polis or community that it demands, or the implications of what he has to say about dialogue or conversation, then the thrust of his reflections is to lead us beyond philosophical hermeneutics. They lead us—with a deepened understanding of human finitude—to the genuinely practical task of concretely realizing in our historical situation what he has so nobly defended as being central to our humanity.

NOTES

1. See Gadamer's discussion of application in the section entitled, "The Rediscovery of the Fundamental Hermeneutic Problem," pp. 274ff. *Truth and Method* (New York, The Seabury Press, 1975). The expression "application" (*Anwendung*) is used to translate the corresponding Latin term. This translation can be misleading. For example, when we speak of "applied physics" or "applied mathematics" we normally want to distinguish between the pure or theoretical disciplines and their applications. We do not think of the applications as integral or internally related to the corresponding pure disciplines. We can call this the "technical" sense of application. But, as we shall see, for Gadamer this is *not* what is distinctive about application as it pertains to understanding. Such application is integral to all understanding. The English expression "appropriation" better conveys what Gadamer means—especially when we think of appropriation as transforming and becoming constitutive of the individual who understands.

Unless otherwise noted, all page references in the text are to *Truth and Method*. I have also given references to the German text *Wahrheit and Methode*, 4. *Auflage* (Tübingen: J.C.B. Mohr [Paul Siebeck], 1975).

2. *TM*, p. 278; *WM*, p. 295.

3. *TM*, p. 299; *WM*, p. 307. Gadamer also discusses the Hermeneutical Problem and Aristotle's *Ethics* in "The Problem of Historical Consciousness," which is reprinted in *Interpretive Social Science: A Reader*, ed. P. Rabinow and W. M. Sullivan (Berkeley: University of California Press, 1979), pp. 135ff.

4. "Hermeneutics and Social Science," *Cultural Hermeneutics*, 2 (1975): 316.

5. See the essay "Hermeneutics and Historicism," included in *Truth and Method*, p. 498. See also "Heidegger and Marburg Theology," *Philosophical Hermeneutics*, ed. by D.E. Linge (Berkeley: University of California Press, 1976), p. 201.

6. *TM*, xi; *WM*, xxvii.

7. Cf. "The Problem of Historical Consciousness" where Gadamer says, "It is useless to restrict the elucidation of the nature of the human sciences to a purely methodological question: it is a question not simply of defining a specific method, but rather, of recognizing an entirely different notion of knowledge and truth." P. 113.

8. There is a parallel between Wittgenstein's critique of the attempt to reduce understanding to "psychological processes" in *The Philosophical Investigations*, and Gadamer's critique of this type of psychological reductionism in the context of hermeneutics. Both stress the essential linguistic character of understanding. See Gadamer's discussion of Wittgenstein in his essay, "The Phenomenological Tradition," *Philosophical Hermeneutics*, pp. 173 ff.

9. *TM*, p. 91; *WM*, p. 87.

10. *TM*, p. 92; *WM*, p. 98.

11. Gadamer tells us, "The best definition for hermeneutics is: to let what is alienated by the character of the written word or by the character of being distantiated by cultural or historical distances speak again. This is

hermeneutics: to let what seems to be far and alienated speak again." Practical Philosophy as a Model of the Human Sciences," *Research in Phenomenology* IX: p. 83.

12. *TM*, p. 240; *WM*, p. 255.

13. "The Universality of the Hermeneutical Problem," *Philosophical Hermeneutics*, p. 9. See also the analysis of prejudices in *TM*, pp. 235ff; *WM*, pp. 250ff. The German word that is translated as "prejudice" is *Vorurteil*. This can be translated as "prejudgment" in order to avoid the exclusively prejorative meaning that "prejudice" conveys in English. Gadamer's main point is to emphasize that *pre*-judices or *pre*-judgements are *pre*-conditions for all understanding. But for Gadamer, *both* negative or unfounded prejudices and positive or justified prejudices are constitutive of our being. He tells us, "This recognition that all understanding inevitably involves some prejudice gives the hermeneutical problem its real thrust,"*TM* p. 239; *WM*, p. 254.

14. Gadamer cites Heidegger's description of the hermeneutical circle from *Being and Time*, which stresses the anticipatory dimension of all fore structures. See *TM*, pp. 235 ff.; *WM*, pp. 250 ff. See also "The Problem of Historical Consciousness," pp.148 ff.

15. "The Problem of Historical Consciousness," p. 107.

16. Ibid., p. 140.

17. Ibid., p. 140.

18. According to Gadamer, *phronesis* involves a knowledge of both ends and means. See his discussion of this point in "The Problem of Historical Consciousness," p. 143; and *Truth and Method*, pp. 286ff.; *WM*, pp. 304 ff.

19. *TM*, p. 288; *WM*, p. 306.

20. *TM*, p. 289; *WM*, p. 307.

21. See "Hermeneutics and Social Science."

22. *TM*, p. 271; *WM*, p. 288.

23. "Hermeneutics and Social Science," p. 312.

24. Ibid., p. 313.

25. *TM*, p. 247; *WM*, p. 157.

26. "Hermeneutics and Social Science", p. 316.

27. There is a problem that arises in Gadamer's frequent appeals to a "different kind of knowledge and truth." Gadamer never provides a detailed analysis of the type of knowledge and truth that is appropriate to the natural sciences. Consequently, it is never quite clear what is *common* to these *different* kinds of knowledge and truth. Furthermore, there are conflicting tendencies in what he does say. At times Gadamer suggests that these two types of truth are compatible as long as we are aware of the limits and proper domain of scientific method. But there is also a strain in Gadamer's thinking that suggests that Method is never sufficient to achieve and guarantee truth. Although Gadamer, in some of the papers that he has published since *Truth and Method*, acknowledges the recovery of the hermeneutical dimension of the natural sciences, he does not fully appreciate the extent to which the very idea of Method (as an adequate way of characterizing the natural sciences) has been called into question by developments in the postempiricist philosophy of science. The issue here is not denying that there are important differences be-

tween the *Naturwissenschaften* and the *Geisteswissenschaften*, but rather questioning whether the contrast between Method and Truth is helpful in illuminating these differences. For a discussion of the hermeneutical dimensions of the natural sciences, see Mary Hesse, "In Defence of Objectivity" *Revolutions & Reconstructions in the Philosophy of Science* (Brighton, Sussex: Harvester Press, 1980).

28. *TM*, p. 447; *WM*, p. 465.

29. For a discussion of the concept of truth, see also "*Wahrheit in den Geisteswissenschaften,*" and "*Was ist Wahrheit?*", *Kleine Schriften*, I (Tübingen: J.C.B. Mohr [Paul Siebeck], 1967).

30. Concerning Hegel, Gadamer writes:

> For Hegel, it is necessary, of course, that the movement of consciousness, experience should lead to a self-knowledge that no longer has anything different or alien to itself. For him the perfection of experience is 'science', the certainty of itself in knowledge. Hence his criterion of experience is that of self-knowledge. That is why the dialectic of experience must end with the overcoming of all experience, which is attained in absolute knowledge, i.e., in the complete identity of consciousness and object. We can now understand why Hegel's application to history, insofar as he saw it as part of the absolute self-consciousness of philosophy, does not do justice to the hermeneutical consciousness. The nature of experience is conceived in terms of that which goes beyond it; for experience itself can never be science. It is the absolute antithesis to knowledge and to that kind of instruction that follows from general theoretical or technical knowledge. The truth of experience always contains an orientation towards new experience. . . . The dialectic of experience has its own fulfillment not in definitive knowledge, but in that openness to experience that is encouraged by experience itself. (*TM*, p. 318; *WM*, p. 337).

31. *TM*, XXV; *WM*, XXV.

32. "The Problem of Historical Consciousness," p. 107. Gadamer typically links truth (*Wahrheit*) with the thing (*Sache*) itself. He tells us, "I repeat again what I have often insisted upon: every hermeneutical understanding begins and ends with the 'thing itself'." ("The Problem of Historical Consciousness," p. 159.) In appealing to the thing itself, Gadamer does *not* mean Kant's *Ding-an-sich*. Rather he *plays* on the associations of what is suggested by Aristotle in the *Ethics* when he tells us that the appropriate form of knowledge and reasoning is conditioned by the subject matter what it treats; the way in which Hegel in the *Phenomenology of Spirit* is always directing us to *Sache* in order to reveal the dialectical movement of consciousness (*Bewusstsein*): the significance of the call for the "return to things themselves" in Husserl; and the way in which this demand is radically transformed in Heidegger's "hermeneutics of facticity." But this appeal to the *Sache* is not sufficient to clarify the concept (*Begriff*) of truth. For the question can always be asked, When do we have a *true* understanding of the thing (*Sache*) itself? Gadamer implicitly recognizes that this is always a proper question when he emphasizes that our anticipatory interpretations "may not conform to what

the thing is" ("The Problem of Historical Consciousness," p. 149). The crucial point as it pertains to truth is that however prominent the thing itself may be in testing our prejudices, a *true* (although not a final) understanding of the thing itself must be *warranted by the appropriate forms of argumentation* that are intended to show that we have properly grasped what the thing itself says.

33. See Gadamer's discussion of the concept of tradition in *TM*, pp. 245ff.; *WM*, pp. 261ff. It is instructive to compare Gadamer's understanding of tradition with that of Alasdair MacIntyre when he says, "A tradition then not only embodies the narrative of an argument, but is only to be recovered by an argumentative retelling of that narrative which will itself be in conflict with other argumentative retellings. Every tradition therefore is always in danger of lapsing into incoherence and when a tradition does so lapse it sometimes can only be recovered by a revolutionary reconstitution." "Epistemological Crises, Dramatic Narrative and the Philosophy of Science," *The Monist* 60 (1977): 461.

34. *TM*, p. 485; *WM*, p. 507.

35. "The Problem of Historical Consciousness," p. 108.

36. "Hermeneutics and Social Science," p. 312; p. 316.

37. "The Problem of Historical Consciousness," p. 141.

38. Ibid., p. 142.

39. Gadamer does approach this problem of corruption indirectly. This can be seen in his perceptive interpretations of Plato's *Dialogues*, especially the *Republic*, for the central "political" problem that Plato confronts is the *corruption* of the polis. Gadamer says the following about the *Republic*.

> Thus the exposition of this ideal state in the *Republic serves in educating the political human being, but the Republic* is not meant as a manual on educational methods and materials, and it does not point out the goal of the educational process to the educator. In the background of this work, on the state is a real educational state, the community of Plato's academy. The *Republic* exemplifies the purpose of the academy. This community of students applying themselves rigorously to mathematics and dialectic is no apolitical society of scholars. Instead, the work done here is intended to lead to the result which remained unattainable for the current sophistic paideia, with its encyclopedic instruction and arbitrary moralistic reformulations of the educational content of ancient poetry. It is intended to lead to a new discovery of justice in one's own soul and thus to *the shaping of the political human being. This* education, however, the actual education to participation in the state, is anything but a total manipulation of the soul, a rigorous leading of it to a predetermined goal. Instead, precisely in extending its questioning behind the supposedly valid traditional moral ideas, it is in itself the new experience of justice. Thus this education is not authoritative instruction based on an ideal organization at all: rather it lives from questioning alone. "Plato and the Poets." *Dialogue and Dialectic* (New Haven: Yale University Press, 1980), p. 52. See also "Plato's Educational State" in *Dialogue and Dialectic*.

The "moral" that can be drawn from this for *our* hermeneutical situation is that the *political* task of the philosopher is to help revive that deep sense of questioning that can lead to a discovery "of justice in one's own soul and thus to *the shaping of the political human being.*" My quarrel with Gadamer is not to suggest that he is wrong about this; on the contrary, I think he is essentially right. But rather, I want to emphasize the Hegelian point that the "discovery of justice in one's own soul" is only the *beginning* of "the shaping of the political human being." This discovery is in danger of becoming merely "abstract" unless one confronts the concrete practical tasks of shaping or reshaping the actual polis or community.

40. *TM*, p. 347; *WM*, p. 363.

41. "Man and Language," *Philosophical Hermeneutics*, p. 66.

42. *TM*, p. 349; *WM*, p. 365.

43. *TM*, p. 349; *WM*, p. 365. Gadamer's acknowledgement of the difference between a living dialogue, where the other person can literally answer questions, and the hermeneutical dialogue, where "the text is expressed only through the other partner, the interpreter" opens a pandora's box of problems for philosophical hermeneutics. It is fundamental for Gadamer's understanding of philosophical hermeneutics that although we always understand and interpret *differently, nevertheless we are interpreting the same* text, the same "universal thing." "To understand a text always means to apply it to ourselves and to know that, even if it must always be understood in different ways, it is still the same text presenting itself to us in these different ways (*TM*, p. 359; *WM*, p. 375). But if the interpreter must not only open himself or herself to what the text "says to us" and the "claim to truth" that it makes upon us but is also the linguistic medium for answering for the text, then this raises questions concerning what sense if any we can speak of the *same* text, the same "universal thing." For it is not the text *an sich* that answers the interpreter, but only the text as understood, and all understanding is conditioned by our prejudices and prejudgments. This is a point that was already pressed by Nietzsche and that has become so central for poststructuralist thinking. And as Nietzsche showed, this can lead to a questioning of the very idea of truth, and the "claim to truth" that texts and tradition make upon us. This also raises problems in an ethical and political context concerning what sense, if any, we can speak of the *same* universal principles, laws, or norms that are mediated by *phronesis*.

44. Many critics (and defenders) of Gadamer stress the conservative implications of his philosophical hermeneutics. Certainly, Gadamer seeks to *conserve* the "truth" that speaks to us through tradition, although he strongly denies that the emphasis on the essential factor of tradition in all understanding, implies an uncritical acceptance of tradition or a "socio-political conservatism." But what has been neglected in the *latent* radical strain implicit in Gadamer's understanding of hermeneutics as a practical philosophy. This is reflected in his emphasis in recent yeras on freedom and solidarity that embraces *all of humanity.* He tells us, "For there is no higher principle of reason than that of freedom. Thus the opinion of Hegel and thus our own opinion as well. No higher principle is thinkable than that of the freedom of all, and we understand actual history from the perspective of this principle; as the ever-to-be renewed and the never-ending struggle for this freedom." *Reason in the*

Age of Science (Cambridge, MA: MIT Press, 1982), p. 9. And in a passage that echoes The Frankfurt School's radical interpretation of Hegel, Gadamer writes: "The principle that all are free never again can be shaken. But does this mean that on account of this, history has come to an end? Are all human beings actually free? Has not history since then been a matter of just this, that the historical conduct of many has to translate the principle of freedom into reality? Obviously this points to the unending march of world history into the openness of its future tasks and gives no becalming assurance that everything is already in order" (Ibid., p. 37).

Concerning the principle of solidarity, Gadamer tells us "genuine solidarity, authentic community, should be realized" (Ibid., p. 80). In summarizing his answer to the question, What is practice? he writes: "practice is conducting oneself and acting in solidarity. Solidarity, however, is the decisive condition and basis of all social reason. There is a saying of Heraclitus, the 'weeping' philosopher: The *logos* is common to all, but people behave as if each had a private reason. Does this have to remain this way?" (Ibid., p. 87).

HERMENEUTICS AND UNIVERSAL HISTORY

1

The early Protestant doctrine of the clarity of Scripture, by means of which Luther made the authority of Scripture independent of interpretation by an ecclesiastical teaching office, has become problematical in modern times in two respects. For Luther and early Protestantism, the literal sense (*sensus literalis*) of the biblical writings passed at the same time for the historical sense (*sensus historicus*); and, on the other hand, his own conception of the doctrine of the Gospel (*doctrina evangelii*) coincided with the content of Scripture understood literally (*ad litteram*). Since that time, however, a gulf has opened up between the literal meaning of the biblical writings and the historical course of events to which they refer, on the one hand; and, on the other hand, the distance separating our period and any possible theology today from the time of primitive Christianity and the various theological conceptions of the New Testament witnesses can no longer be overlooked.

With respect to the difference between the biblical texts and the events to which they point, we have to do with the central problem of historical study. With respect to the distance between primitive Christianity and our age, we have to do with the central problem of hermeneutics. The two are closely related and probably form a single theme. Whether or not that is actually the case should be clarified in the course of our reflections. In any event, both gaps—the one between the biblical texts and the events of the history of Jesus and his community, which henceforth have to be sought out by going behind the texts; as well as the other one between the biblical writings, as witnesses of an age long past, and our own present age—have arisen from one and the same methodological requirement, namely, the principle that the biblical texts are to be interpreted in accordance with the intention of their authors, and thus with reference to the situation in which they were written. This requirement was occasionally expressed as early as the sixteenth century by Matthias Flacius and Joachim Camerarius. It was J. S. Semler (1725–91) however, who, after the attempts of Grotius and Lightfoot, succeeded in winning general recognition for the principle within theological exegesis. This development in turn opened up the possibility of noting the various *tendencies* within the biblical writings in their portrayal and interpretation of the Christ-event and its consequences. This "tendence criticism" (*Tendenzkritik*), which was methodically elaborated for the first time by F. C. Baur, forced one to go behind the text to form a picture of the actual course of events. In that way, the proper content of Scripture (its *res*), the actual history of Jesus, was separated from the biblical texts as something to be sought out behind them. The same methodological requirement that led to this result, namely, the requirement that the texts be interpreted relative to the time of their origin, also produced an awareness of the distance between the intellectual milieu of the New Testament writings and the spirit of the age contemporaneous with any given interpreter. This consciousness gave rise in the eighteenth century to the special hermeneutical problem of the modern era, the task of achieving an understanding that spans the historical distance between primitive Christianity and the present time.

The distinction between going behind the texts by means of historical investigation and building hermeneutical bridges from them to some present time can claim no more than limited validity. Upon deeper consideration, these two prove to be aspects of a single theme. Nor is it easy to tell whether the totality that embraces both should be called hermeneutics or history. Modern historical investigation, which inquires after what lies behind the texts, has itself arisen in connection with the tasks of interpreting texts. To this extent it seems as if the hermeneutical theme includes historical inquiry as a subordinate element. On the other hand, historical inquiry goes beyond the text, nevertheless, because it asks about what lies behind it, and it even includes the specifically hermeneutical theme in itself insofar as the event sought in inquiring behind the texts does not manifest itself for what it really is when taken as an isolated fact, but does so only within universal continuities of events and of meanings, i.e., only within the horizon of universal history, which, incidentally, also embraces the present era of the investigator. This latter point is often overlooked and can also be neglected, to a certain extent, in dealing with history. Of course, every event has its peculiar character and meaning only within the nexus of events to which it belongs from the very beginning. But this is at first a matter of the proximate environment of the event and not immediately of universal history. This observation is correct insofar as it may suffice for the understanding of average events and figures, to see them within the horizon of their epoch and life-setting. This life-setting and this epoch, however, have their meaning only within more comprehensive continuities. Even significant individual occurrences and historical figures require for their evaluation a view of the broader continuities that extended beyond their narrower life-setting and epoch. The more significant an occurrence or a figure is, the more comprehensive must be the nexus of events to which one has to relate it in order to do justice to its true significance, at least in an appropriate way. It is to such notable occurrences and figures, in turn, that the remaining events of an epoch are referred. To that extent, we can justify in a general way our assertion that the event sought for in inquiring behind the texts reveals its true visage only within universal continuities of events and of meaning. To that extent, however, the historical quest, as a quest for universal history, includes on its part the specifically hermeneutical theme, namely, the relationship of a text (or event) of the past to the present age of the interpreter.

Thus, there proves to be a certain competition between the hermeneutical and universal-historical ways of looking at things. Both have to do with texts. Both arrive at the interpreter's present on the basis of the text and draw the interpreter into the interpretation of the text. However, the hermeneutical outlook apparently moves solely between the past text and the present interpreter, whereas the universal-historical outlook first goes back behind the text and considers the essential content (*Sache*), that is, the event being inquired into behind the text,[1] in its universal-historical context of meaning, including also the interpreter's own present era. The universal-historical approach thus makes a detour, the detour of going behind the text to the underlying event that the text attests, in order to build a bridge to the era contemporaneous with the interpreter (or historian).

The competition between hermeneutic and universal-historical methods can nevertheless also signify a convergence; for the correct resolution of both tasks must actually lead to the same results. In the course of its struggles with the text it is dealing with, the hermeneutic endeavor would have to take the step behind the text back to the essential content it expresses, because that is demanded by the intention of the texts themselves in that, for example, they say something about an event distinct from themselves and so point away from themselves to this event. To that extent, understanding of the text itself, namely, of its assertion, necessarily leads to the movement back behind the text, and thus, in our case, to the properly historical formulation of the question of the relationship of its theme to the time of the investigator, because when one investigates a historical object, that object is always already viewed from the perspective of the present time. The historian may forget this in his drive for "objectivity" and in his passionate quest to know "how it really happened." As a result of this passion, historical discussions easily fall under the suspicion (viewed from the standpoint of the hermeneutical task) that the things being spoken about have been placed at a distance from the speakers themselves as something that is simply over and done with. If it were actually the case that the historical outlook, because it objectified the past, destroyed the living relationship of the present with what has been handed down by tradition, then the problem of the historical distance that is always created anew by historical thinking could be overcome only on an entirely different intellectual basis. But as a universal-historical conception of events, historical investigation cannot represent the events it seeks to reconstruct in going behind their texts as something merely past, but, on the contrary, must grasp them in the continuity of meaning in which they stand, which connects them with the present age of the historian. Insofar as historical work always implies the problem of universal history, it by no means deals with the dead remains of the past, as is sometimes asserted, as though the past of the historian were comparable to that of the caretaker of a cemetery.[2]

2

The insight concerning the relationship between historical and hermeneutical problems has recently been advanced by the hermeneutical work of Hans-Georg Gadamer.[3] In order to to evaluate the step Gadamer's work has taken, and which also prompts certain counterquestions to him, we must first of all have before us the history of our theme within the discipline of hermeneutics.

It has already been mentioned that the modern historical method has developed out of the hermeneutical task of interpreting texts. The relationship between the two was subsequently reversed. Philology became an auxiliary science to that of history.[4] This development is to a certain extent the result of consistency of procedure, because textual interpretation had taught itself to view the texts as merely historical documents. Therefore, it is very questionable whether one can share Bultmann's judgment: "But the result was simply that philology lost its real subject matter, the interpretation of texts for the sake of understanding them."[5] This judgment is questionable because it is just this interpretation of the text for the sake of understanding it that led to the historical step of going behind the texts because of the methodological requirement of understanding every author on the basis of the situation of his time. This requirement led, as we saw, to the discernment of the fundamental "tendency" inherent in every text in relation to its essential content, so that henceforth the essential content dealt with by a text had to be distinguished from the way in which this found expression in language. This was to be accomplished precisely through reflection upon the "tendency" of the text. Because in the "process" of the development of "tendency criticism" textual interpretation itself succeeded in inquiring behind the text, it could very well be the case that hermeneutics here has sublimated itself (*sich aufhebt*) into history and continues to exist only as an auxiliary science to history.

Such a sublimation [*Aufhebung*], however else it might be regarded, is nevertheless incomplete so long as the historical outlook has not been broadened into universal history. If history uses the texts at its disposal only as documents of the period of their origination, then the text retains a dimension that has not entered into historical understanding. This is particularly clear in the case of works of art, but also with respect to religious texts. If one describes the Greek tragedies of the fifth century only as expressions of the classical period of Greek history, then he has obviously not touched the artistic truth of the works of Aeschylus or Sophocles, which speak to man regardless of his place in time. These works are more than simply expressions of the Greek spirit of the fifth century, for they created an image of human behavior that has proved its formative power in our cultural tradition. Just as little are the Pauline letters exhausted in being taken as merely expressions of the situation of primitive Christianity. As long as there is a Christian church, someone will find in these texts, despite all changes of time, something that still brings to consciousness the true situation of man before God. The same thing could be exemplified with legal, mathematical, or philosophical works. To all appearances such texts have a dimension that is not accessible to historical inquiry, at least so long as those "generally human" contents are not themselves recognized as historical structures (law, religion, art, philosophy), and as long as, on the other hand, the historical interrogation of such texts limits itself to the period of their origin. As opposed to such a restricted formulation of the historical question, however, the transmitted texts contain a surplus because their truth continues to be effective beyond the situation of their origin. Just for this reason they are able to make a "direct appeal." To evaluate them as mere documents of a long bygone age constitutes an abridgment. This is true even of historiographical works. Herodotus's historical treatise, as he states in the introduction, intended to set up a monument to the deeds of the heroes of his time, and he obviously believed that these deeds contained in an exemplary way something of what it means to be human universally. Historiography itself never wants to portray a completed epoch of the past merely as past. That would not be worth the effort. Quite the contrary, historiography is guided by an interest in the present.

The fact that transmitted texts of the widest variety are not exhausted when they are used as nothing more than sources for the period of their origination is the basis of a relative independence of hermeneutics over against historical research. So long as historical science treats universal history as a marginal problem and remains content with more narrowly defined tasks, it has no right to view hermeneutics as a mere auxiliary discipline but will rather itself remain only a branch of hermeneutics. To be sure, this final conclusion had not yet been drawn by even the most significant theoreticians of hermeneutics in the nineteenth century, Schleiermacher and Dilthey. History and hermeneutics remained juxtaposed.

Schleiermacher's hermeneutics arose out of a theological interest in connection with the task of interpreting Scripture, and not with reference to the historical task.[6] This does not mean that Schleiermacher laid claim to special principles of interpretation for the biblical writings. On the contrary, the biblical texts were to be interpreted in accordance with such rules as had general validity. Here, as elsewhere, Schleiermacher explained, the general takes precedence over the particular.[7] His point of departure is to be found, however, in the understanding, not in the first instance of texts, but of oral speech and the thought expressed in it.[8] In this way, Schleiermacher became the first to view hermeneutics as a science of understanding as such, something reaching beyond the task of interpreting given texts. Reciprocal understanding is grounded in man's "consciousness of kind" (*Gattungsbewusstsein*, lit. "species consciousness"), which links single individuals to each other insofar as it involves each of them in the generally human and in what is meaningful for man as such.[9] As Niebuhr has shown, Schleiermacher's conception of hermeneutics is grounded in his idea of the common consciousness of kind. Only by means of the common consciousness of kind is it possible to understand not only the words but also the gestures, inflections, mimicry, and total behavior of another person. It enables us to grasp in our own self-consciousness, in the mode of feeling, the meaning of the words and gestures of the other person. Thus, intuition, empathy with the other on the basis of common participation in humanity, is the foundation of all understanding.

Nevertheless, Schleiermacher did not develop a universal hermeneutic of interrelatedness, corresponding to such general considerations as have just been mentioned. Rather, he immediately turned back to the traditional task of the interpretation of texts. This task obviously did not appear to him to be essentially different from the task of understanding oral conversation. The fact that Schleiermacher did not find any additional problem in this transition from the dialogical understanding of oral exchange to the interpretation of transmitted texts shows that he was not aware of the true depth of the problem of historical understanding.[10] Comprehending the particularity of an author—beyond the general character of the grammatical structure of his language—was simply a psychological, not a historical, task for Schleiermacher. This has had its effects, through Dilthey, down to the present time, even if today we no longer speak of a psychological but of existentialist interpretation. Schleiermacher's theory of psychological interpretation was at first intended simply to lead to the determination of the individual style of an author's linguistic usage, but later it was also to lead to the reconstruction of the origin of a text from the mental processes of the author.[11] The object of understanding is now no longer a specific, essential content (*Sache*) expressed in the text, but rather "the process of emergence from the inwardness of thought into language."[12] In order to accomplish that kind of psychological reconstruction of a text as formed by the thought of its author, one must put himself into the place of the author, entering into the particular conditions of his peculiar characteristics and situations. For only by means of such empathetic understanding is it possible, as Schleiermacher stressed in 1829, "*correctly to reproduce that creative act*, [to show] how the necessities of the moment could have influenced the living fund of language, hovering before the author, in precisely the way it did and not otherwise."[13]

The psychological intention of Schleiermacher's hermeneutics was retained by Dilthey. Understanding appeared to him, too, as a "psychological imitation," which had as its task the reconstruction of the "creative process" by which some work originated. In order to characterize the relationship of a text to its author, Dilthey used the concept of "expression" (*Ausdruck*), which at the same time constituted the point of departure for overcoming the psychological conception of the hermeneutical task. The concept of "expression" had already been employed in Droysen's historiographical works and may go back to Hegel.[14] Dilthey not only saw texts as "expressions" of the intentions and thoughts of their authors, but understood all events in general as expressions of the acting persons. The sphere of hermeneutics was in this way widened to an amazing degree. It now included not only oral discourse, as in Schleiermacher, but even the wordless event or the remaining traces of it. Dilthey could comprehend all the events of history as expressions of human behavior because he held—calling upon Vico for support—that all historical events are to be understood as workings of the human spirit in which the historian also shares, so that he can always imagine the possibility that he himself could produce similar effects. Dilthey writes: "The first condition for the possibility of historical science lies in the fact that I myself am a historical being: that he who investigates history is the same [!] as he who makes history."[15] Doubts cannot be suppressed at this point. It is really extremely questionable that any average historian, *by virtue of his having the same psychic nature*, can "empathize" with any activity of men of earlier time he pleases whether they be criminals, founders of religion, or rulers. Besides this, history does not have to deal with unique occurrence only with respect to how men acted, but also with respect of what happened to them.[16] It is simply not the case that the historian may concern himself only with man's mental activity and leave the rest to physics.

The reference of the past to the interpreter's present can no more be called into question for Dilthey than for Schleiermacher. Both of them seem rather to have presupposed this reference: the identity of life and the possibilities of experience on the part of the interpreter and on the part of the men of the past is the common element that from the outset connects the interpreted past and the present. The interpreter can therefore find in the past only what is also accessible to present experience, at least as a possibility. The preunderstanding of life and the possibilities of experience thus determines and limits the interpretation from the *start*.

However, Dilthey's idea that the possibilities of life are really first revealed to us by history stands in tension with what has just been stated. This idea, for its part, is closely related to the psychology of expression. Just as the individual, according to Dilthey, is unable to know himself through introspection, but know himself only from the forms he produces, so the possibilities of the human soul generally are to be understood only from the forms in which it has expressed itself at some time or another. To that extent, contemporary life is directed for its own possibilites to that which earlier generations have given form as human possibilities and thus made accessible to the comprehending recollection (*der verstehenden Besinnung*).

Bultmann fastened on to this side of Dilthey's thought. To be sure, he also sought a structure of man's being—now no longer a psychological kind, but an existential one—on the basis of which the possibilities of human activities and experience were to be understood. But the existential structure of man's being, according to Bultmann, is at once marked by the fact that the one who understands deals with his text as a questioner because questionableness [*Fraglichkeit*) determines the very structure of human existence. In this sense, Bultmann says that interpretation always requires "the interpreter's relationship in his life to the essential content which is directly or indirectly expressed in the text."[17] Which content this is depends upon the interest of the interpretation.[18] This interest can be directed toward the historical reconstruction of a course of events; it can be psychologically or aesthetically oriented . Lastly, it "can be established by an interest in history, as the sphere of life in which human existence moves, in which it attains its possibilities and develops them."[19] It is with such considerations in mind that Bultmann turns to the interpretation of New Testament texts. Because he thinks of God, of whose actions the New Testament witnesses speak, only in connection with man, only as the one who is asked about in the questionableness of human existence, the pre-understanding of an exegesis of the New Testament must consist in "the inquiry into the understanding of human existence which finds expression in the Scriptures."[20] Thus, for Bultmann, the necessity of an existentialist interpretation follows as a consequence of the fact that we know God as the one about whom man asks in the questionableness of his own existence. This is the conclusion of the essay he wrote in 1925, "What Does it Mean to Speak of God?"[21] and it forms the basis of the program of an existentialist interpretation of the New Testament writings.

Although Bultmann's emphasis on the questionability of human existence as the presupposition of interrogating a transmitted text about the possibilities of human existence and self understanding does tie in with Dilthey's recognition that man attains knowledge of his own possibilities only by means of a comprehending perception (*verstehende Wahrnehmung*) of the forms produced by men in history,[22] it nevertheless surpasses Dilthey's psychological interpretation in a fundamental way. This is particularly evident in the fact that Bultmann replaces the questionable requirement of an empathetic interpretation with "the simple fact that the presupposition for understanding is the interpreters' relationship in his life to the essential content which is directly or indirectly expressed in the text."[23] Thus, the questioning without which the text could not be understood as an answer is the only presupposition of understanding. Accordingly, the "preunderstanding" of Bultmann's existentialist interpretation is also to be conceived in terms of the questioning character (*Fraglichkeit*) of human existence. With respect to the New Testament, it consists in "the *inquiry* into the understanding of human existence that finds expression in the Scriptures."[24] Thus, the preunderstanding involved does not, as has been repeatedly misunderstood, prescribe answers of an already determinate content in the sense of a prejudgment. At least, that is not the hermeneutical intention of Bultmann's concept of preunderstanding. Rather, the questioning character of the preunderstanding makes room for a revision of any given preconception about the essential content of a text by means of the confrontation with the text itself. In spite of this, the considerations against Dilthey's attempt to undergird all historical forms with a general psychological typology must be raised, in part at least, against Bultmann, too.

Existentialist interpretation, like the psychological interpretation of Schleiermacher and Dilthey, also restricts the question about the contemporary significance of the past to that which a transmitted text expresses concerning the question of human existence. Although the intention is not to tone down the particular thing the text has to say, but, on the contrary, to bring it into view for the sake of contemporary understanding, nevertheless that content is constricted from the outset: anything other than possibilities of human existence cannot become relevant for existentialist interpretation. Or better: absolutely everything becomes relevant, but only *as* the possibility of an understanding of human existence. Now, it is very much a question whether such a treatment allows the texts being interpreted still to say what they themselves have to say: for example, the New Testament texts deal (at least at the explicit level) with many other matters than possibilities of understanding human existence, although everything that they do deal with will *also* be an element of a New Testament author's understanding of existence. Yet this latter element is not always intended. The New Testament writings deal also, indeed primarily, with God and his works in the events of the world and its history. Whatever they say about man is conditioned by this perspective. Bultmann's way of formulating his question forces him to proceed the other way round. He must regard the statements about God, the world, and history as merely the *expression* of an underlying understanding of human existence. In a certain sense this procedure is doubtless appropriate, because the statements involved unquestionably always *also* have such an expressive value. But this value comes into view only when one takes the statements about God, world, and history, not in their direct intention (*intentio recta*) but rather according to an indirect intention (*intentio obliqua*), that is, by understanding them through reflection upon their character as expressions of this or that author. Such a hermeneutical obscuring of the *intentio recta* of the statements about God, the world, and history in favor of the meaning of the text as an expression of an understanding of human existence evidences an anthropological constriction in the formulation of the question, in the preunderstanding. Is it not true that the question concerning the possibilities of human existence is after all always referred for its clarification to the questions about the world, about society, and beyond both of these, about God? Is it not the case that man cannot expect an answer to the question about himself without knowledge of the world, of society, of history, and of God? If this is the case, however, then self-understanding cannot become thematic irrespective of previous understanding of the world and also, in a certain sense, of God.[25] The understanding of the world and of God are not merely the *expression* of man's question concerning himself, but, on the contrary, the relationship to the world, to society, and to God is what first *mediates* man to himself. Only by means of the mediation of these relationships does he gain his self-understanding.

The existentialist constriction of the hermeneutical theme raises the further question of whether the historical distance between the texts to be understood and the interpreter's own time is retained in all its profundity if one subjects the texts to an anthropocentric understanding of existence, as do Dilthey and Bultmann.[26] How could that be possible if the texts, quite the other way around, express precisely the priority of the understanding of God and of the world over the self-understanding of man? It is just at this point that the historical distance between the New Testament texts and Bultmann's intellectual situation stands out quite clearly, and perhaps it is here that a question is put to our contemporary modes of thought. If this distance is obscured beforehand by an existentialist mode of inquiry, then the attempt to build a hermeneutical bridge, which is supposed to set the text in all its antiquity in relationship to the present, cannot succeed.

Texts coming from a past epoch demand, nevertheless, an interpretation that links the historically past *as such* with the time of the interpreter. What happened then (*das Damalige*) cannot be stripped of its "then-ness" (*Damaligkeit*) and in such a way construed as a contemporary possibility; for in that case its "then-ness" would be missing. On the contrary, it must be related to the present precisely in its character as having happened then. This undertaking is meaningful, to be sure, only so long as the present age does not regard itself as self-sufficient but asks about its historical heritage for the sake of giving shape to human existence in the present. That contemporary man can become aware of and comprehend his own possibilities of existence only by means of such questioning, is the pioneering idea that Bultmann's hermeneutics shares with Dilthey and Heidegger.[27] In the fact that the interrogation of transmitted texts is indispensable for the understanding of contemporary possibilities of human existence, Bultmann sees, conversely, that man is questioned by the tradition—and that is his own further step. "True understanding would therefore be to listen to the *question* which is imposed in the writing to be interpreted, to the claim which is met in the writing."[28] Bultmann himself found the difference between his way and that of Dilthey in the fact that the interpreter not only observes the variations of human life aesthetically[29]—a method of observaton that leads to relativism[30]—but rather experiences from history a "claim," a question concerning his own self-understanding, and in that way is summoned to responsible "decision."

This basic idea of Bultmann's points beyond the existentialist limitations of his formulation of the question. If a transmitted text, precisely in its character of having happened then, can make a claim upon the interpreter, then one obviously cannot set boundaries around this claim (for instance, by means of reflection upon the intellectual situation of the present), but the interpreter must instead expose himself utterly to the particularity of what happened then. He must apprehend the past situation to which the text refers in its disparity from his own present and may relate that situation to the present only in its disparateness. The preunderstanding or the interpreter's formulation of the question would thereby be set in motion by the text in a way that is no longer reflected in Bultmann's thought. If the historical distance of what happened in the past is retained, then the link connecting the events and forms of the past to the present can scarcely be found anywhere else than in the continuity of history itself, which joins today with yesterday. The hermeneutical formulation of the question would thus expand into the question of universal history.

Bultmann, of course, did not take this step. He did not even relativize the preunderstanding of the existentialist analytic in relation to the historical context within which it arose. Accordingly, the "claim" of the historical heritage is not discussed in its substantive diversity but is referred to the formal "either-or" of the authenticity or inauthenticity of human existence, to the true or false understanding of existence, to being at one's own disposal or the renunciation of this in faith.[31] The fruitful start toward apprehension of the conditioning of man by history, precisely in recognition of the fact that the past confronts the understanding of existence on the part of those who come after with a claim, a question, was not carried through in its full consequences. It is true that this fundamental idea of Bultmann's is tied up with his view of the "Word" or the "proclamation." The proclamation allows the claim that appeared in Jesus, through which the possibility of a believing understanding of existence is disclosed, to be heard by contemporary men. But it is just this idea that is neutralized by the reference to the formal either-or of the understanding of existence. Gadamer could remark about this that in Bultmann the summons of the Christian proclamation released "almost a privative experience of human self-disposal."[32] It is a fact that the substantive bearing of the claim of Jesus and of the proclamation of him is misplaced by referring it to the formal structure of human existence. It is characteristic that what is decisive for Bultmann is simply the "that" of the claim, and not any specific content. This seems to confirm the contention that the claim of the Christian proclamation does not disclose any new content but only releases that "privative experience of human self-disposal."[33]

Ernst Fuchs and Gerhard Ebeling have taken up Bultmann's suggestive but incompletely developed idea of the "claim" with which a transmitted text confronts the interpreter.[34] For Fuchs, the "claim" or "Word" of the New Testament texts to us includes the "support" that faith needs and on which it can ground itself. "Jesus anticipates us in that he meets us in the *Word*."[35] The character of the text as address becomes for Fuchs the center of the hermeneutical theme. In this connection, Fuchs can appeal to the later writings of Heidegger where the "dimension of language" is opened up,[36] but he clearly finds the decisive idea already indicated in the analysis of the call of conscience in *Being and Time*.[37] According to Fuchs, man exists as man "linguistically between call and answer."[38] Man is already constituted as such in understanding the call: [T]he I that speaks within the realm of mankind is always an I that has already been called."[39] Fuchs's discussion of language and address is often related, in a dubiously direct way, to ethics. In that way one leaps on occasion from the breadth of the problem of language into the area of the traditional theme of Law and Gospel.[40] This is reminiscent of the abrupt relationship in which the "question" and "claim" a text directs at the interpreter stands to the either-or of authentic versus inauthentic existence in Bultmann's writings. Yet Fuchs sees that man hears the "call" upon which his existence is oriented from out of the historical context in which he stands. Thus he can say: "History is . . . essentially 'saga,' and thus the history of language. The language which is carried to us from history is fundamentally that *essential* language in which we from time to time answer 'with ourselves.'"[41] In this way, however, history places "our given self-understanding linguistically in question."[42]

3

The comprehensive critique of the hermeneutical tradition and the analysis of the process of understanding in Hans-Georg Gadamer's work *Wahrheit und Methode* (1960) largely corresponds to the hermeneutic of the language event that was opened up by Fuchs and likewise by Ebeling. Here, too, it is a matter of keeping in view, without prior restrictions, the claim laid upon the bearer, reader, observer, or interpreter, as the actual center of the hermeneutical theme. For precisely this reason, Gadamer struggles to maintain without effacement the difference between the historical situation of the text to be interpreted and the interpreter's present era. For it is just this difference that articulates the claim the text makes upon contemporary understanding. Thus, hermeneutical and historical motifs, in the narrower sense, interpenetrate in Gadamer's thought. In this case, historical difference acquires decisive significance for the structure of the process of understanding itself. With Schleiermacher, this difference remained outside the hermeneutical considerations as a merely external presupposition of understanding. In Dilthey and even more clearly in Bultmann we found starting points for taking up the historical difference between text and interpreter into hermeneutical thought. In Dilthey, there was the idea that man can gain knowledge of what is human only from history. And in Bultmann this idea was sharpened to the extent that the historically formed factor, for instance, something transmitted by a text, confronts those who live in the present with a specific claim upon their self-understanding. Nevertheless, such starting points for appropriating the historical difference between text and interpreter into hermeneutical thought are consistently developed for the first time in Gadamer's work.

Gadamer, too, developed a theory of the linguisticality (*Sprachlichkeit*) of understanding. He achieved this by way of a critical discussion of Dilthey's hermeneutic. He spotted the difficulty of that position in the fact that Dilthey did not conceive deeply enough as a hermeneutical structure the historical character of understanding something handed down from the past.[43] But it is precisely the temporal distance of the interpreter from the situation in which the text originated that immediately opens up for the first time the possibility of conceiving the process of understanding as one of interpretation.[44] In any case, this temporal distance is fundamentally taken into account by Gadamer with respect to the hermeneutical relation, so that he can say: "the hermeneutically schooled consciousness will . . . include historical consciousness."[45] Of course, it will also have to "think of its *own* historicness at the same time," so that "the reality of history is exhibited in the process of understanding itself."[46]

Gadamer excellently describes the way in which the past and present are brought into relation to each other in the process of understanding as a "fusion of horizons" (*Horizontverschmelzung*)[47] The horizons of the interpreter and of the text to be interpreted are different at first, but that is only their initial position, so to speak, in the process of interpretation. The interpreter's own horizon is not fixed, but capable of movement and expansion. In the process of understanding, the interpreter's horizon is widened in such a way that the initially strange matter along with its own horizon can be appropriated into the expanded horizon he attains as he understands. In the interpreter's encounter with his text, a new horizon is formed, "a single horizon which includes everything which the historical consciousness contains within itself."[48] To place oneself into the strange situation that is to be understood always means, therefore, "the elevation to a higher universality, which overcomes not only one's own particularity, but also that of the other."[49] That corresponds to a successful conversation insofar as the agreement reached in conversation represents "a transformation into mutual possession, in which one does not remain what he was."[50] What occurs in conversation is precisely the fusion of horizons by means of an elevation of the partners to a new, comprehensive horizon that comprises the two originally separate horizons. Despite the analogy to a conversation, however, interpretation in the proper sense can hardly be designated a "conversation with the text," as it is by Gadamer.[51] Although in a conversation the partner takes care to avoid premature absorption into the other's horizon, in the case of the interpretation of a text the interpreter himself must see that the peculiar form, the alien horizon of the text, is allowed to assert itself in contrast to the horizon he brings with him. Gadamer himself calls attention to the fact that

> every encounter with the tradition that is effected by the historical consciousness experiences in itself the tension between the text and the present. The hermeneutical task consists not in concealing this tension by a naive assimilation, but rather in deliberately developing it.
>
> For this reason, the projection of a historical horizon that is distinct from the horizon of the present era necessarily belongs to the hermeneutical procedure. The historical consciousness is aware of its own otherness and therefore contrasts the horizon of the tradition with its own. On the other hand, however, it reunites itself with the contrasting horizon in order to mediate itself to itself in the unity of the historical horizon produced in this way. The projection of the historical horizon is therefore only one *phase* in the achievement of understanding, and . . . is overtaken by the present's own horizon of understanding.[52]

In this masterly description of understanding as a fusion of horizons, historical thinking is in fact incorporated into the hermeneutical achievement. Whether the hermeneutical formulation of the question, in the narrower sense, is not thereby burst through and displayed by universal-historical thinking is something we must take up shortly. Before we do this, however, the advances that this conception of hermeneutics makes over the hermeneutics of Dilthey and Bultmann should be highlighted.

1. Gadamer does not begin by relating the text to be understood to a presupposed understanding of the structure of human existence by way of the formulation of the question (preunderstanding) but rather is concerned first to grasp the strange object that is to be understood precisely in its *distance* from the total horizon the interpreter brings with him. "The hermeneutical task consists not in concealing this tension by a naive assimilation, but rather in deliberately developing it."[53] In this way, there is some prospect of overcoming any constriction of viewpoint that may be lodged in the very formulation of the question a person brings with him.

2. The agreement that is striven for in the accomplishment of understanding takes shape through the formation of a comprehensive horizon that comprises the two, at first alien, contrasting horizons of the interpreter and his text. This comprehensive horizon is formed in every case only in the course of the process of understanding itself. It is precisely what understanding consists in. The comprehensive horizon is not already presupposed (as a preunderstanding) in the formulation of the question.

3. The distinction between (questioning) preunderstanding and (projecting) preconception is superseded in Gadamer by the idea of the horizon that the interpreter brings with him. By this means, not only the given preconception but also the formulation of the question are set in motion, because the horizon that the interpreter brings with him is not a rigid presupposition. "The horizon is rather something into which we move, and which moves with us. Horizons change for the one who moves."[54] Thus, after the interpreter becomes aware of the temporal distance between the text and the horizon he has brought with him (1), he builds up a new, comprehensive horizon (2), and thereby succeeds in moving beyond the limits of his original preconception and formulation of the question (3).

In applying these insights to the interpretation of New Testament texts, the interpreter must first of all attain clarity about the difference between his own intellectual situation, the situation of "modern man" in which he shares, and the horizon of the New Testament authors with whom he has become occupied. He will then attempt—but that is always a creative act!—to achieve a synthesis, to formulate a comprehensive horizon of understanding within which both the intellectual world of modern man will each have its place and can thus be related to each other. Everything depends here on the newly projected horizon being wide enough to comprehend not only "something" of the texts, but all of their complex riches.

Such an application already presupposes that the comprehensive horizon formed in the process of understanding will also be explicitly formulated as such. This would be a way of distinguishing between an interpretation that is to be carried out methodically and an unreflective mode of understanding such as that which occurs in a conversation. In a successful conversation, the partners understand one another without being obliged to articulate explicitly the comprehensive horizon within which their understanding takes place. Rather, one is assured of complete mutual agreement by reaching agreement on this or that particular subordinate theme. Such agreement on a particular point constitutes the test, so to speak, of an anticipatory certainty of mutual understanding of the whole. Only rarely will that totality, within which one reaches agreement, become itself the subject of conversation. This will happen especially when the presupposed agreement is endangered.

An unreflective interpretation of a tradition may proceed in a similar way. In a methodical execution of an interpretation, however, the process of understanding must be reflected upon because only in that way can the correctness of the interpretation be tested. The comprehensive horizon of understanding must be formulated so that one can test whether or not it is capable of including both the horizon of the text and the contemporary horizon of the interpreter. To be sure, the effort to formulate that most comprehensive horizon within which a person lives his own life has still other roots than the technical requirements of a methodical interpretation of a transmitted text. Man can become sure of the wholeness of his own life only through being linked with the whole of reality generally. And he can become conscious of it. Even the agreement reached in a conversation is propelled by a quest for the one all-embracing truth, although this is not always articulated as a theme. This same quest for the unity of truth provides the impulse for projecting comprehensive horizons. That the particular requirements of methodical interpretation provoke such projections only makes plain the fact that the methodical interpretation of what has been transmitted shares in the basic human task of understanding reality as a whole.

The projection of a total understanding of reality that, in view of the distance between the interpreter and the tradition he is interpreting, can be only a historically differentiated one, and, thus, a mediation of the present by the totality of history, is not the consequence Gadamer draws from his description of understanding as a fusion of horizons. With the form of Hegel's philosophy of spirit in mind,[55] he regards such an undertaking as claiming "to perform a total mediation of history and the present"[56] Against this, Gadmer insists on the "openness . . . in which experience is acquired."[56] He points to the negative character of the process of experience, in the course of which, "false generalizations are continually refuted by experience."[58] and thus arrives at the thesis that experience stands in irreducible contrast to knowledge.[59] One can object to this thesis that experience nevertheless tends toward knowledge insofar as it opens itself to new knowledge. Still, it remains true for the one who is experienced and who knows about being overtaken by continually new experiences, that they can never regard as complete the knowledge they possess or that they may somehow attain. To that extent, Gadamer is right when he observes that genuine experience is "that experience in which man becomes aware of his finitude."[60] With this, Gadamer has formulated the state of affairs that does in fact separate all possible contemporary thought from Hegel, and that makes any simple repetition of Hegel's system impossible; finitude as the vantage point of thought, and the openness of the future. But how can the mediation, in thought, of history to contemporary life still succeed? Gadamer attempts to do justice to this hermeneutical task by reflecting on the linguisticality of the hermeneutical experience instead of attempting a total mediation of the present by means of history.

Gadamer finds the model of the hermeneutical process in conversation.[61] His demand that the interpreter ascertain the question to which the text was an answer is not to be disputed. But Gadamer combines with this the statement that text (that is, the answer to that question which is to be reconstructed) "itself" poses a "question, and thereby brings our supposition into the open."[62] "The reconstruction of the question to which the text is supposed to be the answer stands itself within a question through which we seek the answer to the question posed to us by the tradition." The reconstructed question, to which the text is supposed to be the answer, passes over into the question "which the tradition is for us."[63] Manifestly, the latter has to do with the question whether the text can still be an answer for us. The stylistic device of speaking about a "question" that the text poses to the reader and interpreter has, to be sure, no more value than that of an image that expresses the peculiar inescapability of the context of tradition within which one stands, whether he relates himself to it positively or negatively.[64] Gadamer himself concedes that the text does *not* speak to us "as a thou," because "we, the ones who comprehend, must on our part first enable it to speak."[65] What this last insight means, however, is precisely that talk about the "question" the text poses to us can only be metaphorical: the text becomes a question only for the one who asks questions; it does not have this character in and of itself.

Before we follow up these considerations, which press in the direction of the distinction between interpretation and conversation, it must be expressly emphasized that Gadamer is right in understanding the hermeneutical process as a linguistic process. The fusion of horizons that occurs in understanding is inconceivable without linguistic expression, even if this fusion is perhaps not to be flatly designated, with Gadamer, as "the proper effect" of language.[66] The process of understanding indeed has to do with "the coming-into-language [*zur-Sprache-kommen*] of the essential content itself," insofar as the "understanding of the essential content . . . necessarily [attains] linguistic form."[67] Language is truly "the universal medium in which understanding itself is accomplished," insofar as in understanding the essential content that is to be understood enters language.[68] Thus, it is also the essence of tradition "to exist in the medium of language."[69]

Yet, even if one gladly agrees with these vigorous remarks about the linguisticality of understanding, the concealment of the difference between the interpretation of a text and a conversation renders Gadamer's argument suspect. The interpretation of a transmitted content does not become a lanaguage event (*Sprachgeschehen*) by the fact that someone speaks to me, as is the case in conversation. Rather, it becomes such only when *the interpreter* finds the language that unites him with the text. To that extent, the fusion of horizons, too, is not in the first instance something produced by language, but, on the contrary, the formation of a new manner of speaking is the expression of the fusion of horizons accomplished by understanding. The hermeneutical process is certainly articulated in language. But this is much more a matter of the creative formation of language by the interpreter than of being called by a "thou." The text does not "speak," but rather the interpreter finds a linguistic expression that combines the essential content of the text with his own contemporary horizon. It is always a matter of formulating the essential content of a text, in other words, of formulating as assertion (*Aussage*). And here we reach the point at which we can no longer follow Gadamer.

Gadamer would like to separate the language event of understanding from the predicative function (*Aussagefunktion*) of language.[70] The concept of "assertion" stands, in his opinion, "in an extreme contrast to the essence of hermeneutical experience and the linguisticality of human experience of the world generally." Plato, as well as Hegel, is reproached for having rested his dialectic "in essence on the subordination of language to the 'assertion.'"[71]

How does Gadamer establish such a negative assessment of the assertion? He maintains that the furnishing of assertions is not an appropriate way of "saying [*Sagen*] what one means," because the language event of an understanding holds together "what is said [*das Gesagte*] with an infinity of what is unsaid [*das Ungesagte*] in the unity of one meaning," and in this way gives it to be understood.[72] Precisely in this way "what is unsaid and what is to be said" are brought into language.[73] The words will thereby "express a relationship to the totality of being, and allow it to enter into language." In contrast to that, anyone who only "repeats what has been said" (*Gesagtes weitersagt*) will unavoidably and without exception "change the sense of what has been said," because precisely in the repetition the unspoken context of the meaning of the original utterance disappears.[74] For Gadamer, this point is demonstrated with particular clarity in the process of a judicial hearing. The "statements" that are recorded are already reduced, severed from their unsaid but accompanying horizon of meaning, with the result that their meaning is from the outset a "distorted meaning" in comparison with the original speech.[75] Thus, Gadamer concludes: "In the assertion, the horizon of meaning of what actually wants to be said is concealed with methodical exactitude,"[76] precisely by its abstraction from the background of what is unsaid.

For a closer understanding of the devaluation of the predicative character of language as this is established by Gadamer, attention may be called to the different basis Gerhard Ebeling gives for countering an understanding of language from the standpoint of the assertion. Ebeling distinguishes between the predicative function of language and its communicative function in relations between persons.[77] Although one fully acknowledges the concern to free the essence of language from the narrowness of an abstract view of the world as a mere instance of assertion, one must nevertheless ask, in view of Ebelings, "not this . . . but rather that," whether the rubric "communication" is meant to include within itself the element of assertion, too, or whether—as appears to be the case in his discussion—it is to be set in opposition to the assertion. In the latter case, one would have to object that reference to content and relation to persons always belong together: that personal association arises within the horizon of common substantive interests, just as, conversely, all relationships to substantive matters are already socially conditioned. Accordingly, the personal dimension of language (as communication) is accessible only in its concrete substantiveness (with which, at any rate, its predicative character is connected). Gadamer seems to have seen this connection quite clearly. He does not place the character of language as personal communication in opposition to the understanding of language based on assertion but rather opposes the latter to the "infinity of what is unsaid,"[78] which forms the horizon of meaning and of situational understanding of the spoken word, where as the assertion allows this horizon to disappear.

Gadamer's reference to the unspoken horizon of meaning of every spoken word is, at first glance, convincing. The primary hermeneutical task consists precisely in restoring the word of a transmitted text to its original, if also unspoken, context of meaning, in order to understand it from within its original situation, the situation of its author in which he composed the text we now have. Nevertheless, *in the first place*, such a procedure can begin only from an exact grasp of what is stated. The implicit, unspoken horizon of meaning is accessible to the understanding only on the basis of the assertion and not without it. And, *in the second place*, the interpreter can become clearly conscious of the unity of that background of meaning made accessible by assertions, only if this unity, for its part, also becomes the content of assertions. Gadamer's correct insight, that every spoken word has an infinite, unspoken background of meaning, does not therefore demolish the significance of the assertion for the spoken word and for an understanding of it, because that background of meaning can be grasped only on the basis of the assertion, and it will then—in the course of the interpretation—be itself turned into something that is asserted. Gadamer's arguments affect only an abstract handling of assertions that does not pay attention to their unspoken horizon of meaning (including the personal relationships within which the word in question was originally spoken or written). If one follows Gadamer's argument, as indeed one must, then one will not somehow go beyond or behind the assertion form of language, but will instead, as an interpreter, also convert into the form of assertion the unspoken horizon that accompanied the original assertion. Precisely by means of interpretation, to the extent that interpretation really intends to understand the author, *everything* must be turned into assertion; everything that was involved in the formulation of a text— nuances, or frames of reference, of which the author himself was partly unaware—must be made explicit. The interpreted text is precisely the text that has been *objectified* with respect to the previously unanticipated proportions of its horizon of meaning.[79]

Gadamer himself cannot really get away from the predicative sense of language. Following the anthropological suggestions of Scheler, Plessner, and Gehlen, he understands language as an expression of the freedom in relation to its environment (*Umweltfreiheit*) that characterizes all human behavior.[80]

> The peculiar objectivity [*Sachlichkeit*] of language is a consequence of its relationship to the world. What enters into language are states of affairs [*Sachverhalte*], i.e., an objective content [*Sache*] that is related in such and such ways [*sich so und so verhalt*]. Therein is acknowledged the independent existence of the other, which presupposes that it has its own measure of the distance between the objective content and what is being said about it. That something can be lifted out as a state of affairs in itself and be made into the content of an *assertion* which others also understand, depends upon this distance.[81]

These sentences provide an excellent description of the significance of the predicative structure of language. For one thing, they express the very objectivity that is the specific characteristic of the human, open-to-the-world (*weltoffen*) mode of relationship. In addition to that, however, Gadamer also says that the possibility of men reaching an understanding among each other depends upon the predicative structure, upon the separability of the intended objective content from the one making the assertion. "That something can be lifted out as a state of affairs in itself and made into the content of an assertion which others also understand, depends upon this distance." Thus, without assertion, without the objectification that always occurs in the assertion, men cannot come to an understanding among themselves about something. Without assertions, there is no language. To be sure, the assertion itself is not understood as long as its unspoken horizon of meaning is disregarded. For that reason, the *interpretation* of the assertion must take into account the situation in which it arose, and to that extent the interpretation goes *behind the assertion* to its original conditions in order to be able to understand the assertion.

The priority of the assertion for hermeneutics is further confirmed by Gadamer's finding that understanding always means "coming to an understanding with reference to an objective content [*Sache*]."[82] "Carrying on a conversation means to place oneself under the guidance of the objective content toward which the conversants are directed."[83] The objectivity of language that is expressed in the form of the assertion thus constitutes the meaning of the conversation, too. A conversation has to do with bringing the objective content into language, that is, putting it into the form of an assertion. When people come to an understanding on the objective content, they also understand each other. This matter of having reference to the objective content applies to the interpreter's craft, too. Although, as we saw, interpretation has a different structure from a conversation, it also has to do with bringing out of the assertions of the text themselves the essential content (including the unspoken horizon of meaning that accompanies it) that they intended and putting this into the form of assertion.

4

It is a peculiar spectacle to see how an incisive and penetrating author has his hands full trying to keep his thoughts from going in the direction they inherently want to go. Gadamer's book offers this kind of spectacle when he strives to avoid the Hegelian total mediation of the truth of the present by means of history. As was noted, the point about the finitude of human experience that can never be sublimated into absolute knowledge provides a very good reason for this concern. But strangely enough, the phenomena that Gadamer describes move time and again in the direction of a universal conception of history, something that he would like to avoid in view of the Hegelian system. This applies first of all to Gadamer's new formulation of the hermeneutical event as a "fusion of horizons." If interpretation has to do with the relationship between the then and the now in such a way that the difference between them is preserved when the hermeneutical bridge is built; and if, further, one must inquire behind the text into its unspoken horizon of meaning, into its historical situation, so that the first task of the interpreter is to project the historical horizon to which the text is native; then the only way that the historical situation of the text can be adequately linked to the interpreter's present is by investigating the historical continuity between the present and the past situation from which the text stems. This means that the text can only be understood in connection with the totality of history that links the past to the present, and indeed not only to what currently exists today, but also to the horizon of the future based on what is presently possible, because the meaning of the present becomes clear only in the light of the future. Only a conception of the actual course of history linking the past with the present situation and its horizon of the future can form the comprehensive horizon within which the interpreter's limited horizon of the present and the historical horizon of the text fuse together. For only in that way are the past and the present preserved in their historical uniqueness and difference in contrast to one another within the comprehensive horizon. Nevertheless, they are preserved in such a way that they are as moments that enter into the unity of a comprehensive continuity of history that embraces them both.

Gadamer himself has seen that the description of understanding as a fusion of horizons moves in the direction just indicated.[84] He is of the opinion, however, that he can escape this tendency by being able to avoid the "speculative claim of a philosophy of world history,"[85] through reflection upon the experience of the linguisticality of transmitted tradition. We have reviewed this attempt and have seen that this route does not bring us to the desired goal without doing violence to the phenomenon of language itself. The objectivity of the human experience of the world, which constitutes such a thing as language as a specifically human mode of behavior in the first place, and which is expressed in a particular way within language itself in its predicative character, excludes an unmediated relationship of the present to the "claim" of a transmitted text. Understanding is always mediated by the essential content expressed by the text. But always this content is brought into language in the text only within the totality of a horizon that remains unspoken, which is not the interpreter's horizon of the present but is rather connected with the particular historical situation within which the text originated. So reflection upon the relationship between the interpreter and the text leads back to the historical difference between their horizons, which is to be bridged over by means of a fusion of horizons. *Consideration of the linguisticality of this relationship by itself is, thus, unable to accomplish this bridging.* The bridging must occur within the realm of the stated content itself as this becomes visible in its historicalness, so that the art, religion, law, and even such an apparently nonhistorical matter as mathematics, are to be understood as contents that have undergone historical development and have been historically structured both in essence and in concept: art as creative projection; law as positive deposition; religion as having become historic and mediated by its forms; mathematics as the instrument of mastering the world by means of abstraction. The concept of truth itself is essentially to be conceived as history.[86] This by no means signifies its relativistic dissolution but certainly does mean that it is impossible to conceive of the unity of truth as a timeless identity of a given essential content. It can be conceived only as the whole of a historical career. Always it is the merely abstract concepts of man, nature, architecture, law, etc., that are thought of as timelessly identical. Their timeless generality consists precisely in their abstractness, however, and therewith also their merely *provisional* truth. They all attain their authentic truth only by their sublimation in the history of the essential content intended by them. This does not call into question the fact that all knowledge begins with abstract, general representations of its object, but such preliminary, unavoidable, and abstract representations must allow themselves to be sublimated into a differentiated understanding of this object in its historical movement.

Only by devaluing the predicative structure of language[87]—which he is himself nevertheless elsewhere compelled to acknowledge as a primary phenomenon[88]—can Gadamer get around the fact that the understanding of the essential content of a text requires a projection of the history of this content (at least an intellectual history of man's understanding of it), because only within the horizon of such a projection can the historically conditioned perspective of the text on this content and the interpreter's contemporary perspective on it be properly brought into relation to each other. Because, also, the various subject matters (*Sachbereiche*) are in turn connected to each other, the hermeneutical task requires not only projections of the history of this or that particular subject matter, but also universal-historical projections that encompass the changing associations of all the various subject matters. Only within the context of universal history can the "then" of the text be bound to the "today" of the interpreter in such a way that the temporal, historical difference between them is not eliminated but rather preserved and bridged over in the nexus of events linking them both. For even the delimitation of the subject matter about which a transmitted text is to be interrogated can mean that the formulation of the question would be constricted by the presupposition of a modern division of subject matters that would do violence to the perspective of the text itself.

It is true that the motivation of an actual interest in associating with transmitted texts is the fact that the contemporary perspective on a given matter (*Sache*) has become questionable. This perspective is not a fixed datum that the interpreter has to take over en bloc simply in order to distance himself from the alien perspective of his text as a still inadequate standpoint. On the contrary, the transmitted texts—in highly varying degrees, to be sure—cause the interpreter himself to be concerned about his current understanding of the matter he is interested in. Because the truth about such a matter is not given with final and absolutely universal validity even in a contemporary perspective on it, but rather remains in question and open to further experience, even transmitted texts can therefore become the occasion for noting new aspects of this matter that have not been given adequate recognition in the current perspective. Even if the transmitted text in its historical sense can never simplistically provide the model solution to the substantive issue in its contemporary form, it may nevertheless provide the impetus for a better, creative mastery of it. That is the significance of the hermeneutical requirement that the transmitted text be related not merely to a currently *available* horizon on some matter, but to the present age's horizon of the future, in order that it might be related to the questionableness of the current understanding of this matter and thus, perhaps, discover new possibilities for a contemporary understanding of this matter itself. Herein lies the justification of the idea of turning toward the present on the basis of the "claim" made by a transmitted text, which, since Bultmann, had played so great a role in theological hermeneutics— and surely it was not by accident that this development happened precisely here.[89] It is true that such a claim is itself always questionable. It must prove itself anew in every period by the power the transmitted material exhibit in relation to the contemporary state of the problem. But the face that such a power of disclosure can proceed from a transmitted text at all is linked to the fact that the current understanding of the matter in question is not yet absolute but is itself

bound to a finite perspective and is thus submitted to questionableness. In its questionability, and in view of the openness of the
future, the current understanding of a matter is referred to tradition.
This means that the matter about which one is presently concerned
cannot be understood without looking back to what was written and
spoken about it in the past.

Here we hit upon the significance of the *application* of what has been
transmitted, on which Gadamer has laid special emphasis. It forms a
phase of the hermeneutical task, which is forced upon legal and
theological hermeneutics especially, but which is nevertheless essential
for hermeneutics of all the cultural sciences.[90] Insofar as it is precisely
the application that has the "task of mediating the then to the
now,"[91] because it goes beyond the historically ascertained self-
understanding of the text to the contemporary possibilities, it flows
once again into the problem of universal history. For the "fabric composed of custom and tradition," on which the philologist as well as
the lawyers and theologians weave,[92] is for its part the hermeneutical
object of the historian.[93] His act of application consists in projecting
the "unity of the totality of tradition" by going beyond the text of his
widely varying "sources,"[94] but he thereby projects the horizon
within which the jurist and the philologist already move. Only the unity of the totality of tradition provides the horizon—this is what is to be
concluded, beyond the points Gadamer has made—for an assessment
of the results of applications made in working with the transmitted
texts, even though philological or legal interpretation of texts, on the
other hand, can burst through a specific, overly narrow projection of
the totality of tradition and thus, likewise, have a critical function to
observe over against it. The latter point does not cancel the fact that
the appropriateness of the application of a transmitted text to a current substantive problem cannot be scrutinized without reflecting
upon the historical difference between the present and the past situations, and on that which nevertheless links the two together. Indeed,
just such historical reflection on the totality of tradition may, under certain conditions, free one for the first time for the present's particular
possibilities of action and thus, also, for the particularity of a present
application of what has been transmitted.[95] It cannot be disputed that
a projection of universal history, by means of its speculative claim,
can also obscure such possibilities instead of opening them up. But
that simply demonstrates the finitude that, just as it qualifies all
human thought, naturally also inheres in projections of universal

history. What it means in concrete cases is that we are summoned to produce ever better projections of universal history.

Here, in closing, we just return once more to Hegel. Gadamer correctly points out that Hegel's system of the absolute idea had overleaped the irreducible finitude of experience. Closely related to that is the further fact that the future could no longer be thought of as an open one, from Hegel's standpoint, insofar as its openness would consist in its continuously bringing forth surprising experiences. Also related to the failure to recognize the irreducible finitude of experience is the further failure to recognize the impossibility of taking account of the contingent and the individual by means of the universal. All these points indicate the limits of Hegel's philosophy and, thus, of his philosophy of history, too. But the task of a philosophy or a theology of world history dare not be sacrificed on account of the failure of the Hegelian solution, as it is by Gadamer for the sake of a hermeneutical ontology within the horizon of language.[96] This conception remains exposed to the criticism that it understands the nexuses of events abstractly, namely in abstraction from the predicative function of language by means of which the word points beyond itself as a "mere" word. It was shown that by virtue of its predicative character, language leads back to the problem of universal history. Instead of avoiding this problem, we must instead ask how it is possible today to develop a conception of universal history that, in contrast to Hegel's, would preserve the finitude of human experience and thereby the openness of the future as well as the intrinsic claim of the individual. The task thus formulated may seem like that of squaring the circle, because the totality of history could come into view only from the perspective of its end, so that there would then be just as little need to speak of a further future as there would be to speak of the finitude of human experience. But the Hegelian conception of history is not in fact the only possible one, because the end of history can also be understood as something that is itself only *provisionally* known, and in reflecting upon this provisional character of our knowledge of the end of history, the horizon of the future could be held open and the finitude of human experience preserved. It is precisely this understanding of history as something whose totality is given by the fact that its end has become accessible in a provisional and anticipatory way that is to be gathered today from the history of Jesus in its relationship to the Israelite-Jewish tradition. Hegel was unable to see this because the eschatological character of the message of Jesus remained hidden to him, as was the case with the New Testament exegesis of his time. To this extent, we have here a paradigm of the way philology, on the basis of transmitted texts (though not on the basis of just any text one pleases!) can not only call into question a given conception of universal history but can also point the way for its replacement by means of a better projection. That is certainly related in this instance to the fact that the biblical tradition constitutes the origin of universal historical thought as such. For this reason, a deeper understanding of this tradition can provide the impetus for projections of universal history that do more justice to reality.

The possibility of taking a new look at the problem of universal history, on the basis of the original eschatological meaning of the history of Jesus as an anticipation of the end, is relevant in the context of our considerations, because the hermeneutical theme itself leads back to the problem of universal history. This is so because it appears that an understanding of transmitted texts in their historical differentiation from the present cannot be adequately and methodically carried out apart from universal historical thought, which, to be sure, must include the horizon of an open future and with this the possibilities of action in the present. The significance of Gadamer's book lies in its having forcefully demonstrated that this whole problem is inescapable for hermeneutical thought, partly by his explicit reference to the task of mediating to the present the past to which the text belongs; and partly, also, by his own futile attempt to avoid the universal-historical consequences of his own description of understanding. It is precisely the impasse that a hermeneutical ontology runs into when it tries to establish its independence from the philosophy (or theology) of history that points all the more emphatically to the task of elevating the hermeneutical theme, whose own logic moves it toward the universal-historical perspective, into a projection of a universal history, which goes beyond the inadequacies of the Hegelian conception.

NOTES

Originally published as "Hermeneutik und Universalgeschichte," *ZThK* 60 (1963): 90–121. A translation by Paul J. Achtemeier appeared in Wolfhart Pannenberg et al., *History and Hermeneutic*, Journal for Theology and Church 4 (New York: Harper Torchbooks, 1967), pp. 122–52.

1. The essential content stated by a text is not, of course, always a specific event. That is only the case with texts that speak of occurrences and persons, as well as of their significance. The essential content of a text can also be a mathematical truth, a natural entity, a technical construction, or a philosophical idea. The fact that all these contents are for their part also historically conditioned is another question and can occupy us only marginally. With regard to the biblical texts, however, we have to do in every case with testimonies to specific events and their inherent meaning. The inquiry that presses behind them to their essential content will to that extent be a quest for the actual course of events and will thus be historical.

2. So, for instance, Otto Weber, *Grundlagen der Dogmatik* (Neukirchen Kreis Moers, 1955–62), 2 (1962), pp. 106f, who appeals for support to Reinhard Wittram, *Das Interesse an der Geschichte* (Göttingen, 1958), p. 16, passim. In any case, even Weber has to admit in view of the contemporaneous character of the historical quest itself "that history is not 'dead' in every sense" (p. 108).

3. Hans-Georg Gadamer, *Wahrheit und Methode; Grundzüge einer philosophischen Hermeneutik* (Tübingen, 1960; [2]1965). Supplementing this book is Gadamer's article "Hermeneutik und Historismus," *Philosophische Rundschau* 9 (1962): pp. 241–76 (reissued as an appendix to the second edition of *Wahrheit und Methode*, pp. 477–512).

4. Gadamer, *Wahrheit und Methode*, p. 320.

5. Bultmann, "The Problem of Hermeneutics," in *Essays on Old Testament Hermeneutics*, ed. Claus Westermann (London: SCM Press and Richmond: John Knox Press, 1963), p. 237.

6. Gadamer, *Wahrheit und Methode*, p. 185

7. Friedrich D. E. Schleiermacher, *Hermeneutik*, newly edited from the manuscripts and introduced by Heinz Kimmerle, Abhandlungen der Heidelberger Akademie der Wissenschaften, Philosophisch-historische Klasse 2 (Heidelberg, 1959), p. 55 (= first draft of 1810). Kompendium of 1819, secs. 3–5 (Schleiermacher, *Hermeneutik*, pp. 8of.).

9. Richard R. Niebuhr, "Schleiermacher on Language and Feeling," *Theology Today* 17 (1960), 150–67, esp. 153ff. [The translation of *Gattungsbewusstsein* as "consciousness of kind" is taken from Richard R. Niebuhr, ibid, p. 153. He also gives "fellow feeling" in his *Schleiermacher on Christ and Religion* (New York: Charles Scribner's Sons, 1964), p. 127.—Trans.]

10. Kimmerle writes in his introduction to Schleiermacher's *Hermeneutik* (p. 16) that Schleiermacher did not see "that knowledge of historical relationships (*Zusammenhänge*) belongs to the process of understanding itself" and does not constitute merely its presupposition. Cf. also Gadamer, *Wahrheit und Methode*, p. 179.

11. Since the Academy courses, "Über den Begriff der Hermeneutik," etc., 1829.

12. Schleiermacher, *Hermeneutik*, Introduction, p. 23. Kimmerle sees a loss of substance in this development (ibid). This development was already posed as a problem, however, in the earlier distinction between the general meaning of words and the individual nuance (cf. *Aphorismen* from 1805 and 1809, p. 34). The question of how the one passes over to the other was to be solved later by means of psychological construction. Nevertheless, it was Schleier-

macher's opinion already at an early stage that the concrete assertion is to be taken as "an empirical modification of an ideal quantity" (Schleiermacher, *Hermeneutik*, 23), as is clear from the passage indicated.

13. Schleiermacher, *Hermeneutik*, p. 138.

14. Georg W. F. Hegel, *The Phenomenology of Mind*, trans. George Lichtheim (New York: Harper Torchbooks, 1960), pp. 179ff. ("Force and Understanding, etc."). Cf. also Gadamer, *Wahrheit und Methode*, p. 193. On J. G. Droysen's *Outline of the Principles of History*, trans. E. Benjamin Andrews (Boston: Ginn and Co., 1893), sec. 9, pp. 12f. and the corresponding section in Droysen's *Historik; Vorlesungen über Enzyklopädie und Methodologie der Geschichte*, ed. R. Hübner (Munich, ³1958), pp. 21ff., cf. Gadamer, *Wahrheit und Methode*, p. 204. But see already Schleiermacher, *Grundriss der philosophischen Ethik*, ed. D. A. Twesten (Berlin, 1841), sec. 61, p. 64.

15. Wilhelm Dilthey, *Gesammelte Schriften* (Leipzig and Stuttgart, 1927; ²1948), 7, p. 278; on which see Gadamer, *Wahrheit und Methode*, p. 209.

16. Cf. Bultmann's argument against Collingwood in *The Presence of Eternity: History and Eschatology* (New York: Harper and Brothers, 1957), pp. 136ff.

17. Rudolf Bultmann, "The Problem of Hermeneutics," in Westermann, *Essays*, p. 241 [trans. slightly altered].

18. Ibid., pp. 243f.

19. Ibid., p. 253.

20. Ibid., p. 258.

21. Rudolf Bultmann, *Faith and Understanding* I, trans. by Louise Pettibone Smith (London: SCM Press and New York: Harper and Row, 1969), pp. 53–65.

22. Bultmann, in Westermann, *Essays*, pp. 250f.

23. Ibid., p. 241 (trans. slightly altered).

24. Ibid., p. 258 (italics mine).

25. I certainly agree with Bultmann that God can be thought of today only as the one who is asked about in the questionableness of human existence. But even if, since the beginning of the modern era, God can only be thought of by beginning with man, he must nevertheless be conceived of as the indispensable *presupposition* of human self-understanding, and not merely as the *expression* of man's questionableness. To that extent, however, the understanding of God logically (not psychologically) precedes the understanding of the self. Incidentally, the inappropriateness of a proof for the existence of God that proceeds from an understanding of the self also stems from this point. The objective priority of the understanding of God over the understanding of the self manifests itself in the fact that God is experienced in the world as the ground of a total view of the world and of man in it, in relation to the whole current experience of reality. The questionableness of human existence is essentially involved in the relationship to the world insofar as the wholeness of human existence is to be attained only in relation to the wholeness of the world. Therefore man cannot acquiesce in any answer to the questionableness of his existence that does not include his relationship to the world, and that does not render his experience of the world (even that of physics!) intelligible as a whole.

26. See Bultmann's statements about man as the "subject of history" in *Presence* pp. 138ff.

27. On Bultmann, in Westermann, *Essays*, pp. 251ff., cf. Heidegger, *Being and Time*, trans. John Macquarrie and Edward Robinson (London: SCM Press and New York: Harper and Row, 1962), pp. 434f.

28. Bultmann, in Westermann, *Essays*, p. 226.

29. Bultmann specifically abjures the "aesthetic standpoint" of Dilthey's historical understanding in *Presence*, pp. 125ff. He can nevertheless also emphasize (in Westermann, *Essays*, pp. 250f., in the context of the passage mentioned in n. 27, above) that Dilthey, through his idea that only history shows man what he is, because only the abundance of historical forms reveals the possibilities of human existence, actually points beyond the aesthetic standpoint.

30. Bultmann, *Presence*, p. 148.

31. Ibid., 140ff., 148; on the second alternative, cf. pp. 150ff., and especially the discussion in the essay, "New Testament and Mythology," in H. W. Bartsch, ed., *Kerygma and Myth* I (London: S.P.C.K., 1963), pp. 1–44.

32. Gadamer, "Hermeneutik und Historismus," p. 261 (= *Wahrheit und Methode* [²1965], p. 497).

33. Compare, on this point, the discussion concerning the knowledge that the self that has taken over responsibility for itself = being at one's own disposal?) has of the "other possibility" of faith that it has thus rejected, in "The Problem of Natural Theology," *Faith and Understanding* I (London: SCM Press and New York: Harper and Row, 1969), pp. 313ff. On the whole problem of the bare "that" in Bultmann's thought with respect to the event of salvation itself as well as to the proclamation, cf. Gerhard Ebeling, *Theology and Proclamation* (London: Collins and Philadelphia: Fortress Press 1966), pp. 36ff., 48, 67ff., 118f.

34. Fuchs emphasized this relationship himself in the supplement to his *Hermeneutik* (Bad Cannstatt, ²1958), p. 6: "Bultmann's term 'address' [*Anrede*] provides sufficient reason for regarding faith as a 'speech-event'"

35. Ibid., p. 75.

36. Ibid., pp. 70f.

37. Ibid., p. 64. To that extent, Fuchs rightly defends himself against the conjecture, most recently repeated by Gadamer (*Wahrheit und Methode* [²1965], p. 498), that he has been particularly influenced by the "later" Heidegger (ibid., *Ergänzungsheft*, p. 5).

38. Fuchs, *Hermeneutik* [²1958], p. 133.

39. Ibid.

40. Cf. Efnst Fuchs, *Zum Hermeneutischen Problem in der Theologie* (Tübingen, 1959), pp. 282f., 190f., 193; as well as *Hermeneutik*, pp. 133, 147.

41. Fuchs, *Hermeneutik*, p. 137.

42. Ibid., p. 138.

43. Gadamer, *Wahrheit und Methode*, p. 228.

44. Ibid., pp. 280f.

45. Ibid., p. 282.

46. Ibid., p. 283.

47. Ibid., pp. 286–90.
48. Ibid., p. 288.
49. Ibid.
50. Ibid., p. 360.
51. Ibid., p. 350.
52. Ibid., p. 290.
53. Ibid.
54. Ibid, p. 288.
55. The whole work of Gadamer's is engaged in a partly open, partly tacit debate with Hegel. As early as the transition to the second section, which deals with the hermeneutics of the cultural sciences, Gadamer remarks that Hegel points beyond "the whole dimension" within which Schleiermacher posed the problem of understanding. Hegel recognized, according to Gadamer, that "the essence of the historical spirit is not in the restoration of the past, but in a mediation of it by thought to contemporary life" (ibid., p. 161). He sees it as his "task . . . to follow Hegel more than Schleiermacher" (ibid., p. 162), and in fact the theory of understanding as a fusion of horizons has its home on the ground of the Hegelian dialectic (cf. ibid., p. 290). Nevertheless, Gadamer shuns the "speculative claims of a philosophy of world history" (ibid., p. 343), because he sees—with good reason—in Hegel's attempt to sublimate history into "the absolute self-consciousness of philosophy" (ibid., p. 338) a contradiction to the finitude of human experience (ibid., pp. 339f.). For that reason, he is at pains to prove that it is linguisticality, instead of universal history, that provides "mediation of past and present" (ibid., p. 451), with the explicit allusion that in this way a misguided ideal of objectivity in the cultural sciences as well as "the idealistic spiritualism of a metaphysics of the infinite in the style of Hegel" should be avoided (ibid.).
56. Ibid., p. 328.
57. Ibid., p. 335.
58. Ibid.
59. Ibid., p. 338.
60. Ibid., p. 340.
61. Ibid., pp. 344ff.
62. Ibid., p. 356.
63. Ibid.
64. To be more exact, this should say: "to specific traditional contents." For one cannot take a position with reference to the whole context of tradition within which he stands, because he can find no standpoint that would be situated completely outside this totality.
65. Gadamer, Wahrheit und Methode, p. 359.
66. Ibid., p. 359.
67. Ibid., p. 360.
68. Ibid., p. 366.
69. Ibid., p. 367.
70. Ibid., p. 444.
71. Ibid.

72. Ibid.

73. Ibid., p. 445.

74. Ibid.

75. Ibid., p. 444.

76. Ibid.

77. Gerhard Ebeling, "Word of God and Hermeneutic," in *Word and Faith* (London: SCM Press and Philadelphia: Fortress Press, 1963), pp. 305–32, esp. pp. 326f. Ebeling emphasises the mutual relatedness of the content and power of a word in an event "to which at least two belong" and continues: "The basic structure of word is therefore *not assertion*—that is an abstract variety of the word-event—*but appraisal*, certainly not in the colorless sense of information, but in the pregnant sense of participation and communion" (ibid., p. 326, italic mine). Furthermore, communication is defined as promise. As such, it occurs in its purest form when "in word the speaker pledges and imparts himself to the other and opens a future to him by awakening faith within him" (ibid., p. 327). Friedrich Gogarten (*Der Mensch zwischen Gott und Welt* [Stuttgart, 1956], pp. 234ff.), in discussing the concept "Word of God," had already emphasized, in a way analogous to Ebeling's distinction, the personal character of the word as gift and demand (ibid., p. 241), with stress on the power (ibid.) of this word and its character as a divine "promise of himself to us" (ibid., p. 246), as opposed to an understanding of the word as "a means of communication and understanding" (ibid., p. 244).

78. Gadamer, *Wahrheit und Methode*, p. 444.

79. This sentence deliberately links the by now infamous word "objectify" with a quantitative viewpoint. The question of the given "proportions" of the objectification and objectifiability could perhaps (as I suggested already in *Theologische Literaturzeitung* 83 [1958], cols. 327ff.) avoid the false alternative between, on the one hand, the scientific ideal of absolute objectivity (as a complete disregard of everything subjective), which has not once proven attainable in the natural sciences or in mathematics, and, on the other hand, the illusion of a totally nonobjectifying discourse, which is probably equally unattainable. In opposition to the faddish, sloganeering demand for "overcoming" objectifying thinking, Martin Landmann has rightly pointed out that the ability to *objectify*, to grasp the encountered reality in its (of course, only relative, greater or lesser) independence over against the experiencing subjectivity, characterizes the distinctively human relationship to the world, namely, man's specific objectivity, which is based on his extensive freedom from instinctual drives (*Philosophische Anthropologie* [Berlin, 1955], pp. 215f., 219f.). Cf. also Jürgen Moltmann, *Ev Th* 22 (1962), pp. 45ff, as well as the way Gadamer links up with the relational anthropology [*Verhaltensanthropologie*] referred to in the text above.

80. Gadamer, *Wahrheit und Methode*, pp. 420ff.

81. Ibid., p. 421.

82. Ibid., p. 361.

83. Ibid., p. 349.

84. Ibid., p. 324.

85. Ibid., p. 343.

86. On this, see my article "What is Truth?" in *Basic Questions of Theology* Vol. 2. New York: Harper Torchbooks.

87. Gadamer calls the assertion a "de-naturing" of the occurrence of understanding (*Wahrheit und Methode*, p. 445), with the exception of the poetic assertion, which, however, is assertion (*Aussage*) in another sense, viz., as expression (*Ausdruck*).

88. Ibid., p. 421.

89. The tradition with which theology has to do claims for itself in a special way that it reveals the true situation of man and the truth of reality generally.

90. Gadamer, *Wahrheit und Methode*, pp. 290–323.

91. Ibid., p. 316.

92. Ibid., p. 321.

93. Ibid., pp. 322f.

94. Ibid., p. 322.

95. Of course that does not mean leaping clear of the context of tradition as such, as though historical research freed one in principle from the power of tradition!

96. *Wahrheit und Methode*, pp. 415ff.

TRADITION, OBJECTIVITY, AND HERMENEUTICS*

CHARLES LARMORE

Originally hermeneutics was the theory of how we are to interpret texts. But already among the German romantics, who contributed so much to hermeneutic theory, and especially with Schleiermacher, who was the greatest hermeneutic theorist, this definition underwent a significant extension. We implicitly rely upon hermeneutic principles, Schleiermacher observed, even in our conversations with others. Toward the end of the nineteenth century Dilthey further broadened the scope of hermeneutic theory to cover all meaningful human action: in his view hermeneutic principles lay at the basis of all the historical sciences. Finally, in the beginning of this century, Heidegger gave to the idea of hermeneutics its maximal extension by characterizing hermeneutic understanding as a necessary feature, not just of our experience of others, but of all human experience whatsoever. It is just this all-encompassing sense of "hermeneutics" that we find elaborated in Gadamer's *Wahrheit und Methode*.

One reaction to this conceptual inflation would be to suspect that the term "hermeneutics" has lost any concrete sense it once had and has come to function as a mere slogan. In many cases this reaction would indeed be valid. But I suggest that within this confusing terminological development there lies an important idea. The expansion of the hermeneutical perspective to include all forms of knowledge and experience stems from the realization that *epistemologically* the interpretation of texts does not differ from other forms of knowledge and, in particular, from the knowledge that the natural sciences give us. This proposal may appear wrongheaded in light of the rather

*I am gratefully indebted to discussions with Isaac Levi for many of the ideas in this essay.

147

disparaging view that Heidegger and Gadamer have displayed toward epistemology. Nonetheless, I shall show that their hermeneutical perspective, their insistence on the "historicity" of all knowledge-claims, consists in both a justified epistemological critique of certain earlier views about the nature of knowledge and an unjustified epistemological position of historical relativism. It may also be objected that in *Wahrheit und Methode* Gadamer restricted the scope of his hermeneutical perspective to the *Geisteswissenschaften*, in contrast to the *Naturwissenschaften*. While this is so, his more recent writings have often come to discard this restriction, and thus he has come to espouse the more general position that in effect Heidegger held all along.[1]

The greater part of this essay will be devoted to analyzing the general epistemological position underlying Gadamer's hermeneutics. My reconstruction of his position will show in passing that at this level of generality there are indeed no epistemological differences between textual interpretation and other forms of knowledge. But my chief aim will be to establish the following critical point: although the "historicity" of all knowledge-claims (a concept that I shall explicate) does undermine certain important epistemological views, it does not imply, either in textual interpretation or elsewhere, the historical relativism that Gadamer in fact embraces. Morever, I shall sketch how the historicity of knowledge-claims can be reconciled with the epistemological position that I shall contrast with relativism and shall call "objectivism": namely, the view that there are universally correct conditions for "knowledge" and "acceptable theory" that it makes sense for us to pursue. After this general discussion I shall turn to examine the more specific and characteristic claims that Gadamer has made about textual interpretation. Although in some of them there is an element of truth, they are motivated primarily, I shall show, by his relativism.

Like most relativistic philosophers, Gadamer has based his conclusions on certain contextual and historical features of our knowledge-claims. In arguing that a recognition of these features need not force us to give up the ideal of objectivity, I shall in effect be outlining a theory of the relation between tradition and objective knowledge. This theory will indicate that history and objectivity are far less antagonistic than either Gadamer or the ahistorical epistemologists he opposes have assumed.

THE HISTORICITY OF KNOWLEDGE-CLAIMS

The method of interpreting Scripture does not widely differ from the method of interpreting nature—in fact, it is almost the same. For as the interpretation of nature consists in the examination of the history of nature, and therefrom deducing definitions of natural phenomena on certain fixed axioms, so Scriptural interpretation proceeds by the examination of Scripture, and inferring the intention of its authors as a legitimate conclusion from its fundamental principles.[2]

As this passage from Spinoza's *Tractatus Theologico-Politicus* indicates, the idea that no significant epistemological difference divides the interpretation of texts from other forms of knowledge is by no means a novel one. Nonetheless, the universalistic claims that Gadamer has made for the hermeneutical perspective, his insistence that this perspective illuminates all forms of human knowledge, differ from Spinoza's position, for better and for worse, in significant respects. The two important differences that I shall emphasize are Gadamer's just recognition of the historicity of all knowledge claims, and the unjustified historical relativism to which this insight leads him. I shall reserve to the end of this paper a discussion of a third difference—his claim that the author's intention does not form the object of textual interpretation.

What is meant by the "historicity" or historical character (*Geschichtlichkeit*) of all knowledge-claims? There are two quite different things for which Gadamer (following Heidegger) uses this term. First of all, the "historicity" of knowledge-claims has to do with an important feature of the relation between tradition and the justification of beliefs. To see what this relation is, we must begin by noting that Gadamer has a "contextualist" view of the justification of belief. We are never able to expose all of our beliefs to critical scrutiny at any one time. On the contrary, the critical examination of some beliefs must always take place against the background of other beliefs that, at least for the purpose of this task, are held constant and immune to revision.[3] But, in addition to this promising account of justification, Gadamer also insists that these background-beliefs are, to a significant extent, socially shared beliefs that belong to a historical tradition in advance of their ever becoming our own beliefs. This is the idea that he exploits to argue that all inquiry proceeds with some dependence upon tradition. But there are two distinct claims here that his argument does not fully distinguish: (1) our dependence upon tradition is a *psychological* one, consisting in the fact that many of these traditional beliefs are ones that we did not *develop* or indeed could not have developed on our own; (2) our dependence upon tradition is also an *epistemological* one, consisting in the fact that there will always be some of these traditional beliefs that we have never had occasion to *appraise* on our own.[4] The first claim is incontravertible, but it is also one that no philosopher has ever really denied. If we elaborate our own beliefs in order to solve problems, and if the formulation of a problem cannot be separated from beliefs about the subject matter involved, then to some extent our individual elaboration of beliefs must always proceed against the background of beliefs we have acquired from others in our social environment and tradition. But equally clearly this first claim, even in conjunction with the contextualist account of justification, does not imply the second claim, which does challenge what many philosophers have said that they have accomplished. Even if we were not responsible for elaborating all of our beliefs, we might still succeed in critically examining them all. Given a contextualist account of justification, this total critical examination could not, of course, occur at one time: the examination of some beliefs would require that others, in that context, be withheld from examination. But why could not critical reflection, proceeding in a piecemeal, context-by-context fashion, thus take in the totality of our beliefs? I see no reason why such an ideal is inconsistent. There is no valid philosophical argument to demonstrate that it is necessarily unrealizable. But nor do I think that Gadamer believes he has such an argument. His proclaimed aim is only to describe what actually does happen in inquiry,[5] and any real acquaintance with inquiry indicates that no one has ever realized this ideal of full critical reflection upon the totality of his beliefs. Although, among others, numerous philosophers from Plato to Spinoza and certainly beyond have claimed to have attained this ideal in their own thought, it has not been difficult to discover elements in their thought that they never critically examined. This fact that no one ever becomes fully transparent to himself and is always somewhat bound up in tradition in unsuspected or unscrutinized ways may require no more profound explanation than that we have limited capacities, a limited time to develop them in, and other interests besides just the pursuit of truth. But an awareness of just these limitations should make us reasonably skeptical of any claims to have completely attained that ideal of self-transparency. To express this point Gadamer often resorts to the terminology of Husserl's *Krisis der europaischen Wissenschaften*, saying that our deployment of "method" never completely redeems our involvement in historical "life-world."[6]

Thus, Gadamer is right, I believe, to insist that we exercise some control over our beliefs only by participating at the same time in a tradition—in both of the senses of such participation that I have distinguished. For those of our background-beliefs that belong to tradition he chooses the very misleading label of "prejudices" (*Vorurteile*). But, in virtue of other things he says, it is clear that he means this term to be understood primarily in its etymological sense of "pre-judgment" (*Vor-urteil*). "Prejudices" are simply those traditional beliefs that logically precede or underlie the judgments at which, in some particular context, we arrive. Gadamer does not deny that inquiry should proceed as much as possible on the basis of "legitimate" prejudices, those whose validity we come to recognize;[7] nor does he claim that *any particular* traditional background-belief of ours *must* remain withdrawn from critical attention; he claims only that there will always be some that we have not critically examined.

Now the precise force of Gadamer's argument must be kept in mind. Although we must recognize that the ideal that at least epistemologically we can completely neutralize the force of tradition by subjecting all of our beliefs to critical examination will not be realized, we do not thereby have reason to discard that ideal as one worth pursuing as far as possible. As I shall have occasion to emphasize later, an ideal ought to be rejected, not if it is unrealizable, but only if we can never have good reason to believe that we are getting closer to realizing it. Nonetheless, we should not let the ideal of self-transparency skew our perception of what, with every likelihood, inquiry will always be. We should acknowledge, unlike Kant, that under the basic conditions in which human beings find themselves, heteronomy need not always stand *opposed* to autonomy. The justification of some beliefs requires that other beliefs be taken as true; and because our capacities are finite, these background beliefs will always include some beliefs that we have not explicitly justified. The "autonomy" that we may exercise in critically evaluating our beliefs will always be "heteronomously" dependent on other beliefs, some of which are withheld from scrutiny in this particular context, but, even more important, others that have not met critical reflection at all but are ours simply because certain historical traditions are ours as well. We, as knowing subjects, can never assume the position of fully constitutive subjects with total epistemological control over our beliefs. This is the idea that justly motivated Heidegger's and Gadamer's critique of Kantian and neo-Kantian epistemology.[8]

The second thing that Gadamer means by the "historicity" of knowledge-claims is that not only beliefs about the world, but also beliefs about the standards for accepting beliefs have changed through history, and, moreover, that the acceptance of different standards in different historical contexts was in some sense "justified."[9] In order to lend greater precision to this discussion, I believe that we must first distinguish, unlike Gadamer, the different kinds of cognitive standards that may have changed historically. I shall suggest a somewhat rough classification of three kinds, which I shall call epistemological, theoretical, and rationality standards. Epistemological standards form the conditions that all beliefs must satisfy in order to count as *knowledge*. Theories, or articulated systems of beliefs, if they are to count as knowledge, will have to satisfy these epistemological standards. But not all beliefs process the systematicity that makes them (in the proper sense of the term) theories or parts of theories. Thus there must be further theoretical standards that beliefs must satisfy if they are to count as constituting *acceptable* theories. Among such theoretical standards there will be standards of empirical adequacy that go beyond those which beliefs must fulfill simply to count as knowledge: to be acceptable as a correct theory, a system of beliefs must successfully explain some hitherto unexplained fact, but this is not something we demand of an atheoretical belief such as "I have two hands" for it to be knowledge. Another theoretical standard may be explanatory adequacy. It would stipulate how "deep" a theory must be, what level of entities and processes it must appeal to, if it is to be recognized as an acceptable theory. By distinguishing these two kinds of cognitive standards, I do not mean, however, to suggest that they are unrelated. On the contrary, the chief justification for any theoretical standard would seem to be that its satisfaction will make the theory a more likely basis for acquiring more knowledge in the future. Finally, there are what I have called rationality standards. By "rationality" I shall mean a set of criteria that lie at a higher level of generality than those criteria to which we appeal for justifying first-order beliefs. If it is true that not only first-order beliefs, but also what have been accepted as epistemological and theoretical standards have undergone historical change, then whatever attempts were made to justify these second-order beliefs must have involved some conception of which ones it was in those contexts *rational* to choose.

Gadamer is obviously right that history has witnessed different conceptions of what ought to be our epistemological and theoretical standards. (He tends to attribute these different conceptions chiefly to distinct historical periods, but this is just a residue of Hegelian *Zeitgeist* theories; diversity of accepted standards is to be found within "historical periods" as well.) Before exploring the full ramifications of this historical fact in the light of the distinctions that I have just drawn, however, I shall first turn to Gadamer's claim that a recognition of the historicity of knowledge-claims must lead us to reject the ideal of "objectivity." Once we have seen the relativism to which Gadamer retreats, we shall be better able to clarify in what sense cognitive standards have proven historically variable.

HISTORY AND OBJECTIVITY

In *Wahrheit und Methode* Gadamer invokes the historicity of knowledge-claims in order to criticize the ideal of "objectivity," which attempts to interpret human action and belief have generally sought to attain. In this book he restricts the scope of this historicity to the interpretative sciences alone, and so here he is inclined to contrast their character with the "objectivity" of the natural sciences. But because, as I indicated before, his later writings seem to sanction the extension of the same epistemological ideas to the natural sciences, he would presumably deny at least full objectivity to them as well. In any case, it will be plain that the aspects of the *Geisteswissenschaften* that arouse his scepticism about their objectivity figure equally among the natural sciences.

What we are to make of Gadamer's claims depends, of course, upon what he means by "objectivity." If the "objectivity" of inquiry requires the complete epistemological neutralization of historical tradition, in the way that we have seen to be highly improbable; or if it means the permanence of what are accepted as epistemological and theoretical standards, then his scepticism about "objectivity" will be justified. But what he apparently considers the only alternative to objectivity indicates that he has something else in mind with this term. In effect, Gadamer's position is that we would have reason to call inquiry "objective" only if the following two conditions were satisfied: (1) there is a correct set of conditions for justifying beliefs and accepting theories, which inquiry aims to ascertain and satisfy; and (2) the attempt to accomplish this aim forms a task worth pursuing: that is, it will be possible for us to have a good reason to believe that we are making progress in achieving this goal. These conditions form indeed, I suggest, a viable definition of objectivity. But Gadamer believes that the historicity of knowledge-claims prevents these conditions from being fulfillable. In textual interpretation as well as elsewhere, he says, this historicity implies that there is no sense to our saying we understand a certain subject-matter *better* than others do: we simply understand it *differently*.[10] In other words, for Gadamer the only alternative to objectivism, or the pursuit of objectivity, is relativism. Because he follows Hegel (wrongly, I have urged) in assuming that the important differences among beliefs (about the world and about cognitive standards) lie always *between* different historical epochs rather than *within* them, the kind of relativism he embraces is a historical relativism.[11] Both of the aspects of historicity that I distinguished above fuel this relativism. Because different historical periods have different standards for accepting beliefs and because, he urges, there is no rational basis to prefer our standards to those of other times, and because in any case the totality of our beliefs never lies under our complete epistemological control, we should simply recognize our historical finitude and, in all good conscience, continue to apply our own merely historically specific standards.[12] What he reproaches nineteenth-century German historicism with is not its relativism, but rather its confidence that its own claims had somehow transcended this relativism.[13] Thus, in the case of textual interpretation, he insists that we should give up the idea that our aim is to discover what the text itself means and that different interpretations may be rated better or worse to the extent that they approximate that goal.[14] Interpretations cannot have that as their goal, he says, *because* they cannot escape their historicity.

As I have indicated, Gadamer derives his denial of the possibility of objective inquiry from both the aspects of historicity that I have distinguished: our inability ever to gain complete epistemological control over all of our beliefs and the fact (which I shall shortly clarify further) that accepted cognitive standards have changed through history. I shall examine in this order what are, therefore, his two arguments for relativism.

Now the mere fact that unexamined assumptions will always play some role in shaping inquiry does not, of course, entail that they, or the beliefs depending on them, will be false. Unexamined beliefs, and the other beliefs that depend on them, need not fail to meet the correct conditions or justification just because those beliefs are unexamined: similarly, accepted standards for accepting beliefs or theories need not fail to coincide with the correct standards just because they are unexamined. But, as I noted above, the objectivity of inquiry requires that we have *good reason* to believe we are *getting closer* to meeting and ascertaining such correct standards. Gadamer's argument is that the presence of unexamined background beliefs must undermine any right to claim that there is good reason to believe that other beliefs that may depend on them satisfy or coincide with the correct conditions of justification. In other words, if objectivity consists in the pursuit of a goal toward which we will never have good reason to believe we are advancing, then relativism will be the more sensible view of the nature of inquiry.

The proper response to this argument, I believe, is that a modest but reasonable epistemology will require that beliefs should be subjected to critical examination only if there is some problem that casts doubt upon them.[16] The beliefs that we have uncritically taken over from our environment and tradition do not, for that reason alone, demand critical reflection. Until there arises some problem that puts them into question, we have every right to consider those beliefs of ours that may depend on them as satisfying or belonging among the correct standards of justification. It is not, I must stress, that absence of serious doubt justifies or entitles us to *accept* beliefs, but rather that it entitles us not to *reject* or *suspend* beliefs that, for whatever reasons, we already have. In other words, unexamined beliefs that we have had no reason to question are not ones we therefore have good reason to accept; rather, they are beliefs we already have for which precisely the question of justification has not yet arisen. They are, for the time being, simply beliefs that we have. Consequently, other beliefs that we otherwise have good reason to accept and that also depend on such unexamined background-beliefs do not thereby cease to be acceptable. In short, the objectivity of inquiry, or the possibility of having good reasons to believe that our present beliefs constitute knowledge or acceptable theory or the standards for determining these does not require, as Gadamer suggests,[17] that we transcend our place in history and ensure that these beliefs escape all logical possibility of error. It requires only that we do not now have any evidence indicating that they are false. This account of objectivity thus appeals to the very "*Lebensgewissheit*," or certainty that is shaken only by actual problems, which Gadamer (mistakenly) contrasts with scientific objectivity.[18]

Now there is one way in which the existence of unexamined background-beliefs could play a role in leading us to conclude that some form of inquiry fails to be objective. If these beliefs resisted critical reflection even when they were confronted with problems that warranted their examination, there would be no good reason to suppose that to this extent such inquiry was getting closer to satisfying the correct conditions of justification. But while this sort of thing may happen because (for instance) our interests stand in the way, there is no basis to suppose, as (we have seen) Gadamer himself acknowledges, that it *must* happen. Some forms of inquiry may at times thus lose some of their objectivity, but nothing in principle prevents them from moving beyond this stage.

Gadamer's second reason for yielding to relativism lies to his concern for how not only beliefs about the world but also beliefs about what constitute the standards for accepting beliefs have undergone historical change.[19] It is indisputable that different historical periods (and, I would add, the same historical periods) have witnessed different conceptions of what ought to be our epistemological and theoretical standards. But, equally obviously, this mere variability of belief does not entail relativism or impugn our right to claim that our beliefs, if better justified than those of others, are more likely to be the correct ones. (We may think that beliefs are more likely to be correct ones without being the ones we accept as correct if they fail to resolve further problems whose solution we consider mandatory for acceptance). Just as historical disagreements about the nature of mass or about the nature of Shakespeare's political views do not preclude there being correct answers to these questions, so historical disagreements about the proper epistemological or theoretical standards for justifying beliefs (for example, Should the fundamental laws of mechanics be derivable *a priori*, posited as conventions, or empirically corroborated? Should the author's intention play a critical role in the interpretation of the meaning of a text?) do not preclude there being correct answers to these questions as well. Nor do they undermine our claim that our answers are the correct ones, if (among other things) we have reason to prefer our answers to theirs. Despite his lack of precision in this area, I do not believe that Gadamer's relativism turns on any ignorance of this rather elementary point. He seems far more concerned with how the acceptance of different and even contrary epistemological or theoretical standards has, in different historical contexts, been thought to be and, more important, was in fact *justified*. Thus, for example, he has argued that a certain theory of aesthetic genius (however questionable in its own right) did indeed justify Schleiermacher in adopting the author's intention as what a successful interpretation of a text's meaning should reconstruct;[20] and he has similarly argued that the distinctive cognitive standards governing modern physics are justified by our interest in the technical control of nature.[21] Without necessarily sharing Gadamer's understanding of these two examples, I believe we can agree with his general claim that in different historical contexts the acceptance of different epistemological or theoretical standards has been thought to be and often has been justified. (This kind of historicity has generally been overlooked by classical epistemology, which has been more concerned to secure acontextual justifications for the standards for accepting beliefs.[22]) The contextual factors to which such justification may appeal would include the general world-view of those accepting these standards, the actual state of their knowledge, their actual prospects (given their other beliefs and resources) of acquiring more knowledge on the basis of these standards, and so forth. Thus, the contextualist theory of justification, mentioned above, applies not only to first-order beliefs, but to epistemological and theoretical standards as well.

Now the contextual justifiability of different standards should lead us to relativism only if it prevents the two conditions for the pursuit of objectivity, described above, from being fulfillable: that is, only if it implies either that no such thing as "the correct" standards can exist, or that, even if they do exist, we will never have good reason to believe we are making progress in ascertaining them. I shall begin with the first condition. Just as first-order beliefs may be justified (relative to their context) without being true (because some of the pertinent contextual beliefs may be false or the evidence incomplete), so different second-order beliefs about what epistemological or theoretical standards should be accepted may be justified in different historical contexts while there could still remain one set of such standards that is the correct one. There may be some doubt, however, about just how exact this parallel between first-order and second-order beliefs can be. First-order beliefs can be justifiable (in a context) while false, because their truth or falsity consists in their correspondence to reality, and not in their justifiability (in any given context). But, it may be asked, can a similar distinction be drawn between the contextual justifiability of standards for accepting first-order beliefs and something to be called their "correctness"? To what in reality can such standards be said to "correspond"? If the role of theoretical standards, for example, is that their satisfaction should enable us to acquire further knowledge, will not this utilitarian character of theirs make them essentially dependent on context? The best way to see that these doubts are unfounded is to recognize that second-order methodological beliefs do carry substantive commitments about the way the world is. The demand that theories explain hitherto unexplained facts entails, if the satisfaction of that demand is thought to give us theories that will prove more successful at getting us further knowledge, that the world itself must be structured so as to support the connection between this standard's fulfillment and the future performance of theories. Clearly, then, to the extent that standards for accepting beliefs imply beliefs about the world, they can be justified (in a context) and yet still fail to correspond to the world; they can fail to be correct.

What then of the second condition? Can we ever have reason to believe that, although the epistemological and theoretical standards accepted by others were justified in their historical context, the different standards that we accept are more likely to be true? Only if we can, will objectivity be an ideal worth pursuing. We can make such a claim about the superiority of our standards, I believe, only if the following is true. The rationality standards that justified, in their context, the acceptance of these lower-level standards must belong to the rationality standards to which we appeal when justifying our choice of such standards. Only then will our assertion that, despite their epistemological and theoretical standards having been justified (in their context), our standards are "rationality preferable" have an unambiguous and unparochial sense. Here I can do no more than suggest that there has always been a shared rationality standard with the generality suitable for choosing other cognitive standards: overall *coherence*, or the mutual adjustment between our choice of epistemological or theoretical standards and everything else that we believe (including other such standards that we already hold). More exactly, a standard coheres with our given beliefs to the extent that they give reason to suppose that its adoption will move us closer to achieving our cognitive goals, the pursuit of truth and the avoidance of error. Coherence, then, underlies what I described as the *contextualist* justification of epistemological and theoretical standards. This idea of rationality does not require, however, that an epistemological or theoretical standard cohere with indiscriminately everything that we believe. The choice of such standards will frequently lead us to revise or reject some of our previous beliefs. Instead, rationality enjoins that we strive for overall and mutual coherence, and thus that any new standard cohere with our more significant and steadfast beliefs. Moreover, even if such a standard should fail to be compatible with some of our more important beliefs, we need not automatically reject it. There is also the possibility that we could accept the standard (while casting aside those important beliefs) if its acceptance, in the light of other beliefs held constant, would appear more fruitful in pursuing our cognitive goals than its rejection. This norm of coherence constitutes a sense of rationality that, I again wish to insist, has been universally shared. No doubt rationality has often meant more than just this, but not only have these surplus meanings not been universally accepted, they have also been advanced on the basis of how they *cohere* with other beliefs that were accepted.[23]

Dependence on this shared standard of rationality will not suffice by itself, however, if we are to have the right to claim that our epistemological and theoretical standards are superior to those of others, even if they were justified in their context. In addition, the contetxtual beliefs of ours by which we justify (successfully) either the acceptance of a standard not shared by them or the rejection of a standard of theirs not shared by us (or both) must be ones that they could have come to share without first (as the case may be) either accepting our standard or rejecting their standard. The point, put more simply, is that here as elsewhere one belief is rationally prefereable to another only if the acceptance of the evidence for preferring it does not depend on our having first accepted that belief itself. So long as no such "neutral" evidence is available, the two beliefs are "incommensurable," and the proper response is then to suspend judgment between them. Of course, the fact that two beliefs are incommensurable with respect to a given set of evidence does not imply that they must remain so, if we succeed in finding further evidence that will permit a decision between them. That is why suspension of judgement can serve as a prelude to further inquiry. So it could well turn out that in come cases our preferred standards are, given the available evidence, incommensurable with the different ones held by others. To learn that that is so would be indeed to learn something from history.

Now if there were no universal conception of rationality or if cognitive standards were *inalterably* incommensurable with one another although justified in different contexts, any hope of legitimately claiming that some standards are more likely to be the correct ones than others would have to vanish. Objectivity would become an ideal that we would never have any reason to believe we had come closer to attaining, and thus an ideal it would make no sense to pursue. Then relativism would appear the far more plausible view of inquiry than objectivism. However, not only is there no indication that either of these suppositions is true, but Gadamer himself does not seem really to believe that either of them is true. Although he frequently characterizes reason (*Vernunft*) as historically situated,[24] actually he is referring to the fact that the beliefs to which we apply our reason have an inescapably historical character. Indeed, both his reconstructions of how the beliefs of others led them to choose different epistemological and theoretical standards (for example, his account of how romantic hermeneutics depended on theories of aesthetic genius) and his own epistemological reflections suggest that he, too, considers coherence a constant standard of rationality.[25] As for inalterable incommensurability, Gadamer like so many others has only asserted but has not shown that cases of it have occurred. Moreover, his efforts to argue the superiority of his own hermeneutical principles to those of Schleiermacher indicate that he does not really believe, at least in this case, that it has occurred. Thus, recognizing how the acceptance of different epistemological and theoretical standards has indeed been justified in different historical contexts does not make relativism any more plausible.[26] And so we may conclude in general that a recognition of the historicity of knowledge-claims, in both the senses that Gadamer has been right to emphasize, in no way forces us to give up the pursuit of objectivity.

TEXTUAL INTERPRETATION

Nothing in these epistemological reflections upon objectivity and historical tradition makes them any less applicable to the natural sciences than to the interpretative sciences. Both Spinoza and Gadamer had some glimpse of their epistemological unity, although they wrongly emphasized either objectivity or history at the expense of the other. I shall now turn to consider the specific account that Gadamer has given of textual interpretation both in its own right and in view of the general epistemological results we have achieved.

Gadamer has insisted a number of times that he is not proposing any *principles* of interpretation but only describing what actually happens in the interpretation. This is very far from the truth. The three most striking theses that Gadamer has advanced about textual interpretation consist in criticisms that he has directed against Schleiermacher's theory of hermeneutics. Although he regards Schleiermacher's mistakes as characteristic of nineteenth-century romantic hermeneutics in general, the views in question may be found as well in Spinoza and many others. This is not surprising, because the positions that come under Gadamer's attack are ones that most of us are naturally inclined to hold. They are that textual interpretation is concerned with determining the meaning, and not the truth, of what has been said or written; that it has as its object what the author intended or meant to say; and that it attempts to reconstruct the author's meaning as it actually was, without confusing it with our own views about its subject matter. In part his criticisms of the first two views can be regarded as shifts of emphasis that, while untenable as they stand, nonetheless point to something important, though something that Schleiermacher and others did not fail to perceive. But they are also motivated by the historical relativism that comes to full expression in his criticism of the third view.

According to Gadamer, we do not really begin to understand a text until we enter a conversation with it about its subject matter; in other words, interpretation is concerned not simply with the meaning of a text, but also with the truth of what it says.[27] Now, indeed, we will not usually succeed in reconstructing the meaning of a text unless we make use of our own knowledge about its subject matter. This is because in general what a person wants to say about a certain subject, whatever its degree of truth, rarely lacks some systematic connection to what that subject matter is actually like. And thus our own best beliefs about that subject matter can often provide us with some clues to the author's intention, even if our aim is to determine what he meant and not whether what he meant is true. But this does not seem to be the idea that Gadamer has in mind (and not merely because he does not share the view that the object of textual interpretation is the author's meaning). Instead, he maintains that involvement with the subject matter that a text addresses is the *goal* of interpretation. In one way this claim makes a justified point. It raises the pertinent but too often neglected question why we should be *interested* in determining what a text means. Far too many interpretations of texts give no indication why they were worth undertaking. Certainly one reason for interpreting a text lies in the assumption that it offers us the opportunity to learn something about the subject matter with which it is concerned. And much of literary criticism appears pointless precisely because of an unfortunately widespread belief that literature does not form a mode of knowledge. For having challenged the prejudice, solidified by modern literary criticism more than anyone else, that literature cannot and does not aim to give us knowledge of the world and ourselves, Gadamer deserves our thanks. But he is wrong to suggest that to become involved with the subject matter of a text must always be why we are interested in interpreting it; instead, for example, we may want to use the text to reconstruct larger historical developments of which it is only a symptom. But, more fundamentally, the determination of a text's meaning must always remain the *proximate* goal of interpretation, a distinct project logically (if not temporally) prior to its use in the pursuit of different *ulterior* goals, such as evaluating the truth of what it says. We must, to use Hirsch's terms, distinguish the text's *meaning* from its *significance*, the different ways this meaning may be utilized in our further projects.[28] We cannot enter a conversation with a text about its subject matter except to the extent that we believe we have reconstructed its perspective on that subject matter; otherwise, there is simply no sense to talking about agreeing or disagreeing with the text; carrying it further; or applying it, as Gadamer says, to our own situation. This point became firmly established in the Schleiermacher tradition through August Boeckh's distinction between the separate tasks of "interpretation" and "criticism."[29] And Gadamer himself may well have perceived it, without acknowledging it, when he claims that interpretation, by which again he means a conversation with the text about its subject matter, consists in a fusion of the text's horizon (its meaning, presumed to be already reconstructed) with the interpreter's horizon.[30] What had led Gadamer, despite himself, to deny this point is at bottom his historical relativism: because every interpretation of a text's meaning is merely our own construal of it, without any objective claim to being preferable, there is really no difference between what it means and how it is significant to us. I shall have more to say about this when I come to Gadamer's third hermeneutic principle.

The second criticism that Gadamer has lodged against Schleiermacher's hermeneutics is that it fell into "psychologism" by presenting the *author's* meaning (*mens auctoris*) as the object of interpretation. In his view, it is instead the *text's* meaning that we must try to grasp.[31] Once again, an important point underlies Gadamer's position, but his dichotomy between authorial meaning and textual meaning is untenable. What a text means need not, it is true, coincide with everything that the author had in mind, either before or even during its composition. But it is difficult to conceive what textual meaning could be apart from the author's meaning as it came to expression *in* what he wrote down as the text. If what the author meant in the act of composing the text is irrelevant to what the text itself means, we would have no good reason to invoke the known beliefs of the author as well as the meaning of other texts he wrote, in order to ascertain the meaning of this text. The relevance of these facts consists in what they share in common with the text's meaning: their link to the mind of the author. What other reason would we have to believe that the interpretation of Wordsworth's Lucy poems would turn more readily to other things that he wrote, instead of to the love lyrics of Burns or Shelley? In fact, if textual meaning did not coincide with what the author meant to say, what right would we have to presume that one part of a text illuminates the meaning of another part of the *same* text or even that there is a *single* text involved? Our belief that texts are likely to possess some sort of interconnectedness (whether or not it amounts to systematicity or even consistency) depends on our parallel but more fundamental belief that minds have this property. To be sure, nothing guarantees that an author will prove the best interpreter of his work; it may contain meanings of which he is unaware. But this fact implies only that in the writings of texts as in our other actions we do not necessarily have an immediate and apodictic access to the full range of our intentions. It is also true that our intentions are shaped in large part by our other beliefs, some of which will no doubt lie outside of our critical control, and this form of "heteronomy" will often find expression in the texts themselves. But the fact that our intentions are never fully autonomous does not prevent them from constituting the meaning of the actions they inspire (as opposed, of course, to their "significance").[32]

Thus, Gadamer's rejection of equating textual meaning with authorial meaning points to some important considerations. The meaning of a text need not simply reflect whatever was in the author's mind, nor need it be something of which the author was fully aware or in full control. But not only did Schleiermacher himself understand these points perfectly well,[33] he also saw more clearly than Gadamer that, for all that, the meaning of a text still consists in what its author meant. Once again, the commitment pushing Gadamer beyond his valid insights and into an untenable position is his historical relativism. Positing the *mens auctoris* as the object of interpretation would insinuate, he insists, that there is an independent fact of the matter about which our interpretations should be trying to be as objective as possible, instead of recognizing, as he says, that texts are never interpreted "better," only "differently."[34]

Let us turn then to Gadamer's third criticism of Schleiermacher, one that forms his outright espousal of just this relativism. He directs it against Schleiermacher's idea that interpretation aims to reconstruct the meaning of a text as it was actually conceived and thus to avoid substituting any of our own conceptions about its subject matter for those that find expression in the text itself. We should give up, he insists, the goal of ascertaining what a text originally meant, because every interpretation we propose will depend necessarily upon our own historically determined beliefs. A frank awareness of our historicity requires, in his mind, that we discard Schleiermacher's ideal of reconstruction and recognize that all interpretation is integration, assigning a meaning to the text that reconciles or "mediates" it with our own conception about its subject matter.[35] Now Gadamer's view of interpretation as integration is unsatisfactory first because it slights the way we may read a text in order to challenge some of our most deeply held convictions. The more fundamental mistake in this view is that it turns on the historicistic relativism that we have seen to be unjustified. It is undeniable that the interpretations we give will reflect our historical and cultural situation. They will be marked not only by their reliance upon beliefs, which we and not others are in a position to consider justified, but also by their subordination to standards of acceptability whose justification may also prove historically or culturally specific. But, as the general argument of the previous section goes to show, none of this entails that historical relativism forms the most plausible view of textual interpretation.

If Gadamer believes that it does, that is because he assumes that one interpretation could be objectively preferable to another only if it could rise above its historical circumstances. This attitude reveals that despite his appeals that we take history more seriously, Gadamer himself does not take it seriously enough. In common with those epistemologists who have ignored history, he takes for granted that history and objectivity form antithetical dimensions of human experience. Like they, he fails to recognize that the human pursuit of objectivity can and must take place through the vicissitudes of history. Despite the burden of relativism that he carries, there are in fact a few passages of *Wahrheit und Methode* where Gadamer works his way through to just this insight. Far from necessarily withholding us from the truth, he can say, belonging to history often makes possible our very access to truth.[36] This is the path that an historical epistemology must follow.

NOTES

1. See, for example, Gadamer's "Philosophie oder Wissenschaft-Theorie?" in *Vernunft im Zeitalter der Wissenschaft* (Frankfurt, 1976), exp. pp. 140–45; "Rhetorik, Hermeneutik und Ideologiekritik" and "Replik," both in Apel et al., eds., *Hermeneutik und Ideologiekritik* (Frankfurt, 1971), pp. 79, 289; and *Wahrheit und Methode*, 3d edition (Tubingen, 1972), pp. 521–23. (Subsequent references to this work, henceforth abbreviated *WM*, will be given in the text.) Gadamer continues to believe that the "historicity" of belief is more pronounced in the human sciences than in the natural sciences.

2. Spinoza, *A Theological-Political Treatise* (New York, 1951), Chap. 7, p. 99 (Elwes transl.).

3. *WM*, pp. 423ff.

4. Ibid., pp. 284f.

5. Ibid., p. 483.

6. Ibid., p. xxvii.

7. Ibid., p. 263.

8. Unfortunately, Gadamer often succombs to the opposite extreme by asserting that understanding consists not so much in individual initiative as in the acceptance of tradition (ibid., pp. 274–75). Instead of emphasizing either the active and innovational or the passive and traditional aspects of inquiry at the expense of the other, we must learn to see how both aspects work together. For more detailed criticisms of Gadamer on this score, see M. Frank, *Das Individuelle Allgemeine* (Frankfurt, 1977), p. 20ff, and my essay "Moral Judgment," *Review of Metaphysics* 35, no. 2 (December 1981): 275–96, as well as my parallel critique of Heidegger (whose *Sein* becomes Gadamer's '*Überlieferung*) in "The Concept of the Constitutive Subject", in C. Maccabe, ed., *The Talking Cure: Essays in Psychoanalysis and Language* (London 1981), pp. 108–31.

9. *WM*, pp. 260, 448, and 515.

10. Ibid., pp. 280 and 355.

11. Cf.: "Eine jede Zeit wird einen Überlieferten Text auf ihre Weise verstehen müssen. . . . Nicht nur gelegentlich, sondern immer Übertrifft der Sinn eines Textes seinen Autor. Daher ist Verstehen kein nur reproduktives, sondern stets auch ein produktives Verhalten. Es ist vielleicht nicht richtig, für dieses produktive Moment, das im Verstehen liegt, von Besserwissen zu

reden. . . . Es genügt zu sagen, dass man *anders* versteht, *wenn man überhaupt versteht''* (Ibid., p. 280).

12. Ibid., p. 343f.

13. Ibid., pp. 283, 500, and 505.

14. Ibid., p. 269.

15. Ibid., p. 250.

16. Cf. C.S. Pierce, *Philosophical Writings* ed. J. Buchler (New York, 1955), pp. 10ff., 256ff. Although a commonplace of pragmatist philosophy, this idea represents a valuable step in appreciating the compatibility of tradition and objective knowledge.

17. WM, p. 250.

18. Ibid., p. 225. Observe that (contrary to Peirce) this pragmatist epistemology will not automatically eliminate the doubts raised by universal scepticism, because these doubts may refer to genuine problems confronting our beliefs about what constitutes reliable sources of knowledge.

19. The subsequent four paragraphs are based on comments that I gave on a paper by Marx Wartofsky at a meeting of the Conference on Methods in New York City (December 1981). I am grateful to Wartofsky for helping me to think about the relations between history and knowledge.

20. WM, pp. 180 and 280.

21. Ibid., pp. 427ff.

22. The *realist* idea of truth so often advocated by classical epistemology—the view that truth is a nonepistemic notion, having to do with the way the world is in itself apart from how we conceive of it, and so not relative to any particular conception of the world we may come to have—explains why all methods for attaining the truth, which we may adopt, can be subject to justifiable revision. Truth, so understood, is not defined relative to what any method, now or in the long run, will tell us. To this extent, classical epistemology had the means at its disposal for recognizing the historicity of knowledge-claims. Moreover, something like this realist conception of truth is needed, I believe, to bring together our legitimate desire for objectivity and the thoroughgoing revisability and historicity of belief. Recent philosophers such as Putnam have rejected this view as ''metaphysical'', as invoking a distinction (between the truth and what our conception of the world would be at ''the ideal limit'' or under ''ideal epistemic conditions'' that makes no difference for inquiry. (Cf. H. Putnam, *Reason, Truth and History* [Cambridge University Press 1981]. p. 49ff.) But the force of this objection depends on the sense we attach to this ''ideal limit''. If, on the one hand, we at the present describe the ideal limit of inquiry in any determinate way at all, as including some particular beliefs or methods, we shall be saying that these are unrevisable. A realist, nonepistemic conception of truth, by contrast, tells us that every belief and every method or standard for appraising beliefs is in principle subject to revision. Here the distinction between truth and what our conception of the world is at the ideal limit will clearly make a difference for how we conduct inquiry. If, on the other hand, nothing is assumed about the content of this ''ideal limit'', then this ideal limit bears the same absolutely transcendent relation to inquiry as we now conceive of it, which is the essential and distinctive feature of the nonepistemic conception of truth. So either

we admit that some beliefs or methods are immune to revision or we must accept the nonepistemic conception of truth, by whatever name.

23. Thus, for foundationalists in epistemology "rationality" has generally demanded that some beliefs must be incorrigible because, in virtue of other beliefs that they hold about knowledge, this fact seems required if knowledge is to be possible. (They generally believed that the justification of belief must ultimately fall back upon particular self-warranting beliefs; I have already suggested in the preceding text why this need not be so: justification must instead lead back to already accepted beliefs that no problem at the time leads us to question). Incidentally, the view of rationality I have suggested indicates that coherence as a rationality standard should not be confused with coherence as an epistemological standard (on the difference of levels here, cf. A. Goldman, "The Internalist Conception of Justification," *Midwest Studies in Philosophy* 4 [Minneapolis, 1980], esp. pp. 48–49). The general coherentist contextualism that I have laid out conforms, I believe, to Hegel's method in the *Phenomenology of Mind*. More recent examples of it can be found in L. Laudan, *Progress and its Problems* (Berkeley, 1977), p. 157f.; K. Lehrer, *Knowledge* (Oxford, 1974), chapter 8, and especially I. Levi, *The Enterprise of Knowledge* (Cambridge, 1980).

24. *WM*, p. 260.

25. Ibid., p. 423.

26. The same argument applies to the case where the different cognitive standards of others, instead of being contextually justified, formed unexamined assumptions that they had no reason to scrutinize but that we have come to have reason to revise or reject.

27. *WM*, p. 276.

28. E. D. Hirsh, Jr., *Validity in Interpretation* (New Haven, 1967), pp. 8ff.

29. August Boeckh, *On Interpretation and Criticism*, trans. J. P. Pritchard (Norman, 1968).

30. *WM*, p. 289.

31. Ibid., pp. 354f.

32. Although aware that intentions may be unconscious, Hirsch still exaggerates the autonomy of authorial intentions by asserting that they are simply what the author "wills" (cf. *Validity in Interpretation*, Hirsch, p. 31).

33. Thus, the recognition that the author's intentions may be to some extent unconscious underlies Schleiermacher's maxim that we may have to understand the author better than he understood himself. And the extent to which the author's intentions are shaped by tradition, over which he generally will not have full critical control, is covered by "grammatical" interpretation, as opposed to "psychological" interpretation, which focuses on how the author elaborates this tradition in an individual way, by means of a "style." Cf. F. Schleiermacher, *Hermeneutik und Kritik*, ed. Frank (Frankfurt: Suhrkomp 1974), pp. 94 104ff, 168ff.

34. Cf. "Normbegriffe wie die Meinung des Verfassers oder das Verständnis des ursprünglichen Lesers repräsentieren in Wahrheit nur eine leere Stelle, die sich von Gelegenheit zu Gelegenheit des Verstehens ausfüllt" (*WM*, p. 373).

35. Ibid., pp. 158ff.

36. Ibid., p. 515.

THE PARADOXES OF HISTORICITY*

MARJORIE GRENE

The remarks that follow are concerned, not with historiography, nor yet with history as the broad sweep of human events, but with the historicity of the person. Despite Heidegger's disclaimer of the bearing of his ontological analysis on "anthropological" questions, I would say that I am concerned with *Geschichtlichkeit* in a sense related to that in which Heidegger used that term in *Sein und Zeit:* that is, with the concept of human being as temporal, with the articulation of a concept of personal history. Admittedly, the existence of a human society, itself a historical entity, is a necessary condition for the existence of a human individual. But it is the temporality of *the person* that interests me, as distinct from the wider range of social, regional, or human history.

1

To what extent and in what sense is the being of a person a historical way of being? To what extent? Comprehensively and fundamentally. To be a person is to be a history. In what respect? In two respects, opposed but related. On the one hand, being a person is an achievement of a living individual belonging to a natural kind whose genetic endowment and possible behaviors provide the necessary conditions for that achievement. On the other hand, a human being becomes the person he is within, and as one expression of, a complex network of artifacts—language, ritual, social institutions, styles of art and architecture, cosmologies and myths—that

*This paper was prepared for a conference entitled "History and Anthropology," held at the Werner-Reimersstiftung, 31 August-September, 1977.

constitute a culture. A culture, of course, is itself a sedimentation of the actions of past persons; but it is, nevertheless, preexistent with respect to the development of any particular person. Great innovators may change their societies, but they have to be born into, and grow up in, *some* society, however radically they may come to alter, perhaps even to destroy it. Admittedly, the distinction between nature and culture is a commonplace; I am trying to introduce it here, however, not as a simple dichotomy, but as an internal relation essential in its integrity to the being of human beings. Helmuth Plessner has spoken of the natural artificiality of man:[1] a human being is an individual member of the species *homo sapiens*, to whose development, even as a living thing, inherence in an artifactual medium is necessary. It is our nature to need the artificial; we come to ourselves not only as users of, but as dwellers within, a tightly woven net of artifacts. Even for his physiological development, for the achievement of reproduction, sustenance, rest, and so on, a human being needs, in general, a roof over his head, a language (a local habitation and a name?), theories of some kind about the way things are, at least minimal apprenticeship in a trade or calling, etc. Thus human nature, being dependent on culture, is itself historical. For a culture is a historical artifact interiorized in the life history of each of its participants, and to be one of those participants consists precisely in that process of interiorization. That is the chief lesson, for example, of Adolf Portmann's study of the first year of life, or, as he calls it, the year of the social uterus. Our young, like those of other higher mammals, are born with their senses wide awake, yet, like the lower mammals, and unlike other higher forms, they have to hug the nest, lying recumbent, in order (again unlike kittens or puppies) to assimilate, in their dependency, the structure of their immediate human community. Only in the second year of life, when they have learned to walk and to speak, will they enter on a course of what will eventually be responsible actions. In its natural as well as cultural aspect, humanity is something to be achieved, and the person is the history of that achievement. It is in this dual, yet single, sense that the being of the person is historical.

Other organisims, too, it may be objected, have, or are, their life histories. This baboon *is* his life history from birth to death, so is this goldfinch, so is every sexually reproducing organism. Yet although "natural history" is still an intelligible term, historicity (*Geschichtlichkeit*) seems to be a concept uniquely applicable to the human case. I don't know enough of nineteenth-century intellectual history to be able to say, exactly, how this change of meaning came about, nor do I want do so. But let me try to state very crudely what I mean, or what I take anyone to mean who may in our day want to formulate this far from novel thesis. Take as a starting point, for the moment, A. J. P. Kenny's definition of mind, but permit me to adapt it for a definition of "person."[3] To be potentially a person, let me say, "is to have the capacity to acquire the ability to operate with symbols, in such a way that it is one's own activity that makes them symbols and confers meaning upon them." To be actually a person is to be engaged in the process of acquiring and exercising this ability. And that is what it is to exist historically in a uniquely human sense. But then, one may object, why not define "person" in relation to the understanding and the making of symbols, as Cassirer did, for example, in his *Essay on Man*?[4] The answer is that this would be too easy a reversion to a slightly different formulation of the past phrase *animal rationale*. We don't just *have* rationality or language or symbol systems as our portable property. We come to ourselves within symbol systems. They have us as much as we have them. The human individual comes to be himself not only within the limits of his particular genetic endowment (an endowment shared, with wide individual variation, by all human beings, though in its chance collocation peculiar to each), but also within the limits prescribed by this particular cultural world or worlds. It is within the limits prescribed by both these constraints that he is what he becomes, and as he becomes it. Mute, inglorious Miltons are not Miltons, nor are verse-spewing computers poets, except by relation to the misguided human beings who spend *their* life histories programming them. Neither a biological existence nor a formal symbol system in itself constitutes a human being, but only the way in which, in a given case, the former comes to express the latter. And that is what I mean by historical existence; it is in the sense that I want to assert, as premise for the problems I shall discuss, the primacy of historicity.

Let me try now to explicate this thesis by setting it into a relation to the argument of the Transcendental Analytic. For it seems to me that it is our assimilation and reinterpretation of Kant's argument that best shows where both our philosophical principles and our philosophical problems lie. Before I do this, however, I should perhaps say why, because I want to stress the historicity of the human, I revert to Kant, rather than starting from Hegel, who himself asserted the distinction between the natural, which merely survives, and the human, which exists historically. There are two substantive reasons (apart from an insuperable antipathy contracted many years ago).

On the one hand, Hegel's cut between the merely living and human is made in terms of a static nature as against a historical conception of humanity. Kant's critical philosophy, too, admittedly, is preevolutionary, but he was sympathetic to a possible evolutionary theory: see his review of Moscati's essay.[5] Hegelian nature, however, is dogmatically alleged to go round and round, not to develop. And once one has rejected on principle the very possibility of organic evolution, it seems to me, one has set up the kind of cosmology that we, in our post-Darwinian time, simply cannot use. Not that philosophical anthropology is, or should be, evolutionary; indeed, it is important (as we shall see later) to set strict limits to evolutionary explanation. But we cannot properly see these limits unless we first accept evolutionary theory in the domain for which it *is* explanatory and look for what Plessner has called the monopolies of man within the constraints of an evolving, not a static, nature.[6] On the other hand, secondly, Hegel's conception of history radically bypasses what is, in my view, the central concern of philosophical anthropology: that is, precisely, the historicity of the *person*. Hegel happily sends the passions, that is, the individual, or all individuals except world-historical ones, into the field to do battle for the *Weltgeist*. My colleagues tell me Hegel is full of concrete empirical insights despite the system; I can only say, with Kierkegaard, that the system is intolerable, and all it contains is polluted by its arrogant dogmatism. So excuse me, please, from taking that dismal detour, and let me go back to Kant.

Kant, too, you may say, is excessively systematic. Of course. But, in particular, in the *Critique of Pure Reason*, and there, in particular, in the Transcendental Analytic, one finds the groping of a great philosophical explorer, beside which the insistence on system is trivial. There is something in the thesis of Heidegger's early Kant book: Kant has been seeking, and finding, an insight from which he himself, at least in part, turned back.[7] And we can see our own philosophical position, both its strength and its weakness, better, if we look back in the late twentieth century at Kant's major moves in the Analytic. It is the outcome of the eighteenth century we still have to wrestle with. So, begging the pardon of my colleagues more at-

tuned than I to the Dialectical Dream, let me try sketchily what I have
tried a couple of times before: to put the central problem(s) of the
philosophy of the person in relation to the Transcendental Deduction.

Kant's reply to Hume, although it did not, as he proclaimed,
establish once for all a stable body of apodictic knowledge, did
demonstrate irrefutably that the very objectivity of our experience
depends upon, is made possible by, the concepts and principles that
we have always already legislated for it. In Kant's terms, these concepts and principles are valid, of course, only within the limits of experience: for appearances, not for things-in-themselves. But experience *is* experience, intelligent orientation in a world of objects,
only by virtue of *our* ordering of what would otherwise be an inchoate
sensory mass. The synthesis of the manifold is a human synthesis,
the product of the legislative activity of mind. This Kantian discovery
is incontrovertible. The role of agency in knowledge, or, more
generally, of the way in which we make sense of our surroundings—
this thesis, however we interpret it, and whatever we do with it, is
not to be denied.

Experience, then, is possible only through categorization. Kant's
categories, however, the pure concepts through which the mind has
always already organized experience, depend, in their turn, on the
Transcendental Unity of Apperception, the pinnacle of the regressive
argument of the Deduction. That is to say, the orderliness of nature,
as experienced, is possible only through the possibility that I could attach to any experience an "I think." Thus, what the structure of objective experience rests on, in the last analysis, is a bare possibility, an
"I might," where the "I" in the case is, in turn, a bare fact that, an
"I" that is no "I." Yet to go further, to read into this bare possibility
any actual self-like character would be, in Kant's view, to commit
paralogism, to fall once more into the illusions of an irresponsible
metaphysical speculation. Thus the objectivity of experience, subtly
and elaborately vindicated in the Deduction, hangs, nevertheless,
from a very slender thread.

Kant could maintain his position with respect to the TUA and,
therefore, the whole foundation of objectivity, I believe, only because
he was confident, at the same time, of the primacy of practical reason.
We know ourselves morally, though never theoretically, as real
centers of responsible action. And he could maintain, in turn, the
delicate separation, yet harmony, of theoretical and practical reason
only because he believed, and believed we would all always believe,

in an all-good, all-powerful God, who made us so that, fallen, we must live in two worlds, yet within an ordered creation, where the divisions of sensibility from intellection, of theoretical from practical reason, of constitutive theory from regulative, judgment, would be reconciled at last. Lacking that theistic solace, we can achieve no such equilibrium. Yet we cannot afford, either, to turn our backs on Kant's fundamental insight.

What, then, should we do? I think we may take as valid the general bent of the Deduction but challenge the adequacy of the Transcendental Unity to accomplish its work. What can a bare possibility that . . . do? Who is the TUA, and what is its power? "*The* human mind" no longer carries the force it had in the Enlightenment. There *are* human minds, or, better, human persons, cast contingently into one human situation or another. The unity of the human mind is a poor abstraction compared with its rich diversity.

Suppose, then, we take the unifying principle behind our categorization of experience to be, not a bare fact, that I could . . . , but a real, live, bodily sentient, historical human being. What happens? A number of things. First, the synthetic a priori that make objective experience possible are historicized. Each society, each group of language users, in a limited way each human being, has *its* categories and principles. There is no fixed and eternal system of human reason, no guarantee that any principle in its exact formulation has always legislated and will always legislate for all human experience of nature. Second, the "I think" of the Transcendental Unity, fleshed in as the activity of a live, thinking, hoping, desiring being, loses its aseptic isolation from *praxis*. It is an "I feel," "I ought," "I respect," "I hope," as much as an "I think." Cognition is *one* kind of *praxis*—the kind Kant knew and analyzed best—and one kind that needs to be carefully hedged in from the intrusion of the more immediately practical. But it is one kind of *praxis* all the same, in the sense that it is one of the ways in which, relying on our own self imposed rules for working in symbol-systems, we try to make sense of our surroundings. Morality, art, religion, theoretical knowledge are all *praxeis* of this general kind. In this sense, we may perhaps say that the primacy of practical reason is vindicated—not, however, in the subjectivist fashion initiated by Fichte, nor yet in Kant's dichotomous way. Far from limiting reason to make room for faith, as Kant alleged he had done, we need to articulate carefully the field of the practical so as to preserve within it a place for rationality, or at least reasonableness.

We could do worse than to rely here on Peirce's ordering of his three phenomenological sciences.[8] Logic (including epistemology) is a branch of ethics, because learning how to know is a part of learning how to act (knowledge being a certain kind of action). But then, if we follow this reasoning through, ethics, in turn, becomes a branch of aesthetics, because our belief about how we ought to act depends finally on the kind of life we admire. In this second Peircean move, however, we go beyond the primacy of the practical, in any overarching eternal sense, and assert the primacy of historicity. For what a person ultimately admires expresses the kind of person he, historically and contingently, is, as one unique expression of the culture in which, as this child of this time, he happens to participate.

Our transposition of the TUA into twentieth-century thought, therefore, issues in the recognition of the historicity of the person as primary. But there are also further consequences of this transposition that we must note here and to which our argument will have to return in its concluding section. In order to protect his synthetic a prioris from metaphysical *Schwärmerei*, Kant erected a sharp barrier between the appearances for which they legislate and the things-*in*-themselves that lie beyond our ken. A living, situated, historical person, however, finds himself bodily, within a real world of things themselves. He is not just appeared to, as a pure consciousness might be, threatened, attracted, lured, frustrated. . . . Thus it is not appearances, this side of a barrier separating them from the really real, but other bodily entities and real events that are the targets of his cognitive inquiry, as well as his moral, aesthetic, or even religious undertakings. Not, indeed, things-*in*-themselves, divided from appearances, nor appearances cut off from things-*in*-themselves, but things themselves appearing one way and another in the light of our ways of understanding them: these are the targets of real, diversified inquiry by puzzled people trying to make sense in given historical ways of given historically emergent problems. As against Kant's situation, however, where, granted the restriction of knowledge to appearances, we could achieve universal and necessary knowledge of the formal structure of those appearances, in so far as the mind has imposed it on them, we are in a less stable state. For if it is real things we find ourselves among and try to cope with, we cannot claim apodicticity in our conceptions with respect to them. We can, indeed, *hope* to understand things themselves, but we approach that understanding, at best, asymptotically and can never assert with logical certainty that we have achieved it. The barrier has fallen that divided appearance from reality, but what Kant called the high road of science has turned into a steep, winding, rocky, and interminable path. And yet, thanks to Kant, we are not back with Humaean blind custom: we do give order to nature, and it is the very heart of our rationality (nor just our habit) that we do so. But, like Hume and unlike Kant, we never know for sure that we have done the job right. That's not tragic: it only means that being human is a precarious and never-ending task. Who that thought well ever thought otherwise?

There are two main lessons, then, to be learned from a latter-day rereading of the Deduction: the primacy of historicity and, along with it, the restoration of reality. Each of these principles, however (the second insofar as it follows from and depends on the first) issues in serious difficulties. In what follows I shall try, sketchily, to state these difficulties and to suggest a direction for their resolution.

2

First, the stress on historicity seems to be self-undermining. *Geschichtlichkeit* in *Sein und Zeit*, it's true, makes its appearance only when the formidable apparatus of *Daseinsanalyse* has already ensnared the reader, and long after the hermeneutical circle has safely been established.[9] But let's look at the matter outside that protective context, as it occurs by now in relatively everyday thinking.

I am reflecting here on the philosophical problem of the person, not on social science, or on history as a discipline. But the familiar debate about the methodology of the social sciences may serve as a starting point for the problem I want to state, or better, to remind you of. In these discussions, it was claimed (with variations that for present purposes I may ignore) that while the subject matter of natural science is to be dealt with in terms of general covering laws, usually understood as causal explanations, the subject matter of social science—persons, their actions and institutions—must be treated by a different method, which includes, in particular, *Verstehen*.[10] And this is supposed to be so because the subject matter of the social sciences is a class of unique events, in contrast to the more readily generalizable data of natural science. Except in number, every electron is identical with any electron, but not every revolution is the French Revolution, nor is the present inflation identical except in number with the German inflation of 1922. So it seems one can mark off a place for the understanding of human events—and a fortiori human persons—exempt from the reductivist moves attempted by many philosophers and methodologists. All that is causal is subject to science and nonhistorical; all that is historical is noncausal and safe from the reductive attacks of science and metascience.

What the stress on historicity seems to accomplish, however, is the very opposite of this comforting bisection. To explain human actions or human beliefs historically is precisely to explain them causally. Take two humdrum examples. All of us who have taught philosophy, in the United States at least, know the response of students in introductory courses: "I just believe this because I was conditioned to." Here historical explanation consists in reducing significance to insignificance, in reducing knowledge claims to effects of propaganda, indoctrination, and the like. Or take a popular rendering of the dogmas of social science: "Crime is a disease produced by a sick society." Here historical explanation wipes out responsible action by excusing it, by making it the predictable effect of specific causes, and removing its responsible core. In either kind of case, what we have is precisely the equation of the historical with the causal, and so, in terms of the contrast of natural science and *Verstehende Wissenschaft*, with the nonhistorical. Thus the stress on historicity seems to generate its own contradiction. If human beliefs, attitudes, actions are primarily historical, then they are wholly amenable to covering law type causal explanations, and nothing is left to be understood. All diachronic explanation is causal-deterministic; historical explanation is causal-deterministic. If this is a defensible or, worse, an inescapable, inference, then the thesis of the primacy of historicity destroys itself. The reliance on historicity, rather than providing an adequate ground for a philosophy of the person, proves to be yet another form of intellectual suicide.

Can we avoid this self-destruction? I shall mention here five ways in which the attempt may be made to avoid it, with objections to all of them.

(1) To begin with, if, while recognizing Heidegger's objection to "philosophical anthropology," I am, nevertheless, borrowing the concept of *Geschichtlichkeit* from *Sein und Zeit*, I must, of course, admit that the temporality of diachronic explanation is *Innerzeitigkeit*, not primordial *Zeitlichkeit*.[11] The temporality of human being lies at a more fundamental level, ontologically, than the one-darned-thing-after-another of cause-and-effect explanation. That sounds nice—or nasty, depending on one's philosophical predilections—but it doesn't really help. For if the concept of the temporality of *Dasein* has anything to offer us—and, as a matter of fact, I believe it has—we have to be able to defend it against such common attacks as those just

mentioned, not only with a Heideggerian sneer, but with something resembling an argument. Behaviorism, popular psychological and sociological jargon: all these belong to *das Man*. Yet it is not enough to say so and assume a superior stand from the ground (or the abyss) of authenticity. For one thing, everybody, however authentic, remains in the everyday, and so it seems to be incumbent even on the most faithful Heideggerian to understand, *existentiell, his* everyday. And the self-denial of historicity, whether by denying meaning or absolving agents of responsibility, is a striking feature of our everyday world, too ubiquitous to be ignored. Besides, who is to say he is authentic, any more than, without succumbing to spiritual pride, a Christian could affirm that he was saved? No, to defend the primacy of historicity we have to come out in the marketplace and discuss openly the grounds of its inability to defend itself. As dwellers in our world we, too, are subject to the same self-destructive lines of thought. We are cast into a world where persons appear to be neither copies of the divine spirit nor, to most of us, mere molecules in motion. They appear to be first and foremost histories. Yet this conception, which comes naturally to many of us, threatens itself in our minds with its self-destroying reduction to pure cause-and-effect sequences. It is characteristic of our time and place and therefore of ourselves to think this way. Let's face it, not wave it away.

(2) Given, then, that this is a problem to be taken seriously, how can we deal with it less condescendingly and indirectly than Heideggerian hermeneutics would do? There are several ways in which people have tried to insulate causality and so keep it from taking place. One, analogous to the suggestion of Manfred Eigen with respect to the origin of life, is to say: it's all right, there's always some room for chance, and so for noncausality, and so for the humanly historical, for the uniqueness of this action by this agency and of this life history as a sum total of unique actions. This resort to chance can mean one of two things, neither of which is adequate to solve our problem. Either (A), we may say, this happened by "chance" when the causes are hidden. If I knew in detail every determining factor in my past and back into the past of my parents, etc., I could explain causally every move I make. But that's too much to expect of a less than Laplacean intelligence. So, being happily ignorant, I remain, within these limits, happily free to accept a limited historicity. Such a "refuge in ignorance" accomplishes nothing. Historicity becomes an illusion supported by the want of knowledge, one more opiate of the intellectuals. Or (B), we may say that causation is not complete, there are

areas really left for chance within a not quite totally determined universe. It used to be fashionable to fall back on the "principle of indeterminacy" to back up this position. Within an account of scientific explanation more adequate than the crude "causal law" view I am concerned with here, such arguments can be shown to be invalid. But to argue this in the present context would take me too far afield. Let us continue here to suppose, with Whitehead in *Science and the Modern World*, for example,[13] and with many others, that scientific explanation is causal, and that quantum mechanics has put a limit on explanation in this sense. There is not thoroughgoing causality but real chance in nature. Does that help? Of course not. To be a human history is not to be—exclusively—a set of curious chances. Koko's story is precisely a parody of existence. There *is* an element of such chance occurrences in every life; that's why the *Mikado* is funny. But we don't really believe our lives are, except in periods of natural or historical horror, composed so mechanically and absurdly of nothing but such tos-and-fros. That's why Koko's tale is funny and neither tragic nor just unthinkable. But if we are to retain the concept of historicity as primary to the being of persons, curious chances have to be seen to operate within a context that makes sense *as* a history, not a kaleidoscope of odd and amusing shapes.

(3) How else, then, can we safely keep history from collapse? G. E. M. Anscombe, in her inaugural lecture *Causality and Determination*, has presented a possible avenue of escape that looks, at first sight, more viable than those so far presented.[14] The thesis that we can ask for a cause of anything, she argues, does not entail a universal determination of the sort characteristic of Kantian nature. Applying this suggestion to the situation we are considering, we could perhaps argue that, even though any given segment of any given personal history may be causally explained, that does not mean that we have to interpret the whole of any human life, let alone human existence as such, in these rigorous causal terms. That is a crude summary of an elegant and plausible argument, which may be convincing, even in the long run, if one has the solace of inhabiting a traditionally theistic universe and a stably Aristotelian society. Outside that doubly protected conceptual framework, however, it seems to me Professor Anscombe's argument won't take us much further than did the resort to chance. If we can ask for a causal explanation in *any* historical situation, then we can ask for a causal explanation in *every* historical situa-

tion, and we are back with the reduction of the historical to the causal.

(4) Yet another possibility has been suggested to me by Professor A. J. M. Milne of the University of Durham.[15] Although between nature and culture all my actions may be read as caused, the cultural component in these cases is itself the product of past personal histories, of responsible choices on the part of other human beings: in my case, for instance, of my midwestern, reformed Jewish, English (or American)-speaking, democratic egalitarian (or, if one prefers, bourgeois-capitalistic and self-deceptively oppressive) ancestors. That's a comfort for the moment—but not for long. For the sins of the fathers can, in turn, be read as the effects of earlier "actions" in turn reducible to effects of earlier causes, and so on ad infinitum. If Professor Anscombe's seeming way out is subject to universalization, Professor Milne's is subject to extension, backwards in time, to an infinite regress.

(5) Where are we, then? At an impasse? In a way. I said I would list possible ways of evading the self-destruction of the thesis that historicity is primary to the being of persons. The fifth is a return to the first, though, I hope, with a difference. If we are to accept the primacy of historicity—and I believe we must—then each of us, insofar as he is a person, is one history, born into his world and destined to die at, and as, its close. Again, please, this is of course no solipcism. Each of us is one expression of a more than individual history, of the symbol systems that constitute his society and, therewith, himself. Being-in-the-world always entails, in Plessner's terms, an *Innenwelt*, an *Aussenwelt*, and a *Mitwelt*.[16] Nor is the relation between these three components additive, as I have just expressed it. Speech, alas, is irredeemably linear; existence, though also in a sense linear, is nevertheless structured in many dimensions, at least the three just mentioned: inner-, outer-, with-. Never mind these complications; my point here is simply that each of us, however pervasively an expression of his society, does exist within his own hermeneutical circle, which must somehow be saved from predation by causal thinking. We cannot get outside that circle, whatever argument we may use to make it more habitable. We have to ask, then, from within the hermeneutical circle, if there is any way to answer the critic who chooses to interpret historicity in purely causal terms. Only, I think, by reinstating the *natural* foundation of the historical in a way that modern philosophy has largely failed to do.

3

This brings me to part three of these reflections, and to the second aspect of my proposed transposition of the Transcendental Deduction into a new coordinate system. To historicize the TUA, I suggested, means at the same time to restore the reality of things, not as a network of phenomena only, but as things themselves, which we try to know. But these are also the real things *among* which we have to count *ourselves*. It is the difficulty of that transposition that constitutes the difficulty of the path suggested under point five. Can we, in fact, without losing our hold on nature, bring the reading of nature into culture? Can we affirm the primacy of historicity, while seeing historical existence as one form of natural existence? Remaining within the hermeneutical circle, can we found it on nature? Or does the stress on historicity destroy nature, and so make this recourse, too, impossible?

To put my problem once more: what is crucial here in the rereading of the Deduction that I have suggested is not only (1) that we interpret the categories and principles as the constitution of its world by a live, historically situated human being and (2) by that means restore, at the same time, the reality of the things themselves that are the targets of the person's efforts to make sense of his surroundings, but that (3) these real targets are acknowledged at the same time to be the milieu of the person's own constituting activities, the *Umwelt*, if you like, within which *Welt*, and a fortiori *In-der-welt-Sein*, is possible—and more than that: in such a way that the person is seen to be a unit in the very nature he seeks to know. *We* are real things, too, not only constituting, but constituted. True, a personal history is not just another life history, like a baboon's or a goldfinch's, nor indeed is it a life history plus some other superadded something, but it *is* a *life* history, though of a peculiar kind. That is what we have to be able to say; to elaborate this thesis, in fact, is the chief task of philosophical anthropology. Only if we can place ourselves, not, indeed, securely (for what is human is qua human not secure), but yet without blatant contradiction, *within* nature, only then can we save the concept of historicity from the self-destruction to which it seems so readily susceptible.

Yet, if we look around us, philosophically, at the chief styles of thinking that have come about—historically—under the aegis of historicity, we find an insulation of the human from the natural that makes this indispensable step a very difficult one to take. Let me take Heidegger and Wittgenstein here as representative: Heidegger, obviously, as in *Sein und Zeit*, the philosopher of historicity, and Wittgenstein for two reasons. First, he is trying to show the individual how he copes, especially as language user, in his everyday world; language games are forms of life, not in a biological, but in a practical sense, in a sense related to the *Sich-vorweg-sein*, as well as the *Schonsein-in*, of *Sein und Zeit*. And, second, in the context of the history of philosophy, Wittgenstein, like Heidegger, is trying to find an egress from the dead end of a tradition, to let the fly out of the fly bottle.

Now, both of these thinkers share, for their followers, a strength, from my point of view, a radical weakness. They share an inability to place man within an organized nature, to show how the human power of constituting order can be itself one unique kind of natural order. For both Heidegger (of *Sein und Zeit*) and Wittgenstein (of the *Investigations* period), all order is human order. So it was, too, of course, for Kant, except in the as-if concessions of the *Critique of Judgment*. But that is just what, from within a historical situation, despite the stress on historicity, and, indeed, somehow by means of the stress on historicity, we need to change. That is what, in the last analysis, the historicization of the Transcendental Deduction ought to have accomplished. Yet it has not done so. On the contrary, the stress on historicity seems to entail ignoring nature, if not denying it, to a human artifact. How? And what can be done about it?

Although Heidegger, even in *Sein und Zeit*, was not interested in *Dasein* except as an avenue to *Sein*, he did seem to many to be offering the foundation of a philosophical theory (although he would have denied it was a theory) of the person (although he would have rejected such a corrupt, traditional term). Under the protection of a heavy ontological carapace, he seemed to be constructing a well-articulated organism that represented with radical adequacy the being of human being in its true form—true in Heidegger's sense, in that Being here both uncovers and hides itself. And different though his style of thinking was, Wittgenstein in the *Investigations* period was, it seems, working at a similar task. He was showing, rather than proving, how, as language users and perceivers and agents, we do what we do—and never mind threats from philosophers who distort or misunderstand the jobs that speakers uncorrupted by philosophy and perceivers and agents, in fact, get on with in their ordinary lives. There is, in both cases, a self-contained presentation of what it *is* to be a person, which bypasses the strained arguments of professional philosophers, past and present. The scandal of philosophy, says Heidegger, is not that no one has proved the reality of the external world, but that anyone still thinks he needs to try. Philosophy, says Wittgenstein, is always after symbol systems or secret, inner thoughts; we should be able to stop that kind of silliness whenever we like. Unless one is a philosopher with a sceptical bent—and there will always be some—these seem sound prescriptions. At the same time, both these prescriptions depend for their efficacy, it seems to me, on a naive acceptance of the cut between *Naturwissenschaft* and *Geisteswissenschaft*. Granted once more, of course, Heidegger would deny any connection of his thinking with "Geist" or "Geisteswissen- schaften," and I don't know if Wittgenstein was influenced by the Rickert-Windelband school, as Heidegger certainly was by Dilthey. It does seem clear, however, that both what has called itself hermeneutical philosophy and the method of the late Wittgenstein (which is close to it) rest on the acceptance of some such horizontal cut between the scientific and the human or historical. And it is precisely that dichotomy that proves unstable. We still have the im- age of a human world shorn of any roots in nature and a natural world devoid of places for humanity to show itself.

What we need, however, in place of this dichotomy, is a concept, not of two different kinds of explanation, nor of two says of being, but of a number of levels of explanation, complementary to, but not contradictory of, one another and, accordingly, of ways of being that exhibit among themselves analogously complementary relations. We need to show, from within the hermeneutical circle, how both its own level of interpretation, which relies on culture-based meanings and their interpretation and reinterpretation by human beings in their worlds, and poorer but indispensable levels of explanation, causal or otherwise scientific, can, and do, coexist and cooperate. In other words, we need to show how historicity, as necessary condition for, and defining principle of, human being, can be within, not over against, nature, in a way superior to, while at the same time depen- dent on, the possibilities left open by the organization of the natural world within which man as an artifact-needing, culture-dwelling *animal* has become a possibility and, for the moment, an actuality. The problem is, how, without abandoning a base in historicity, we can move from Wittgenstein or Heidegger to such an altered style of thinking.

About Wittgensteinian thinking, two very brief remarks may suffice here. First, Wittgenstein's philosophical therapy was directed against the cramp of latter-day empiricism. But empiricism, with its secret in- ner sensations and empty formal systems, is already so well insulated against the outside world that to overcome it may mean to restore an activity, or family of activities, still very narrowly anthropocentric or even academic. Wittgenstein himself asked some profound questions about the differences between men and other animals, yet the concept of "forms of life" remains a marginal one, simply equated, in at least one passage, with "activity."[17] The question of a wider, living nature in its relation to human life can remain unasked. It is as if a catatonic patient were persuaded to move about his room: that's already an achievement; one doesn't push him then and there into cross-country skiing. Secondly, however, the "form of life" concept could be expanded, one would suppose, to provide a more articulate philosophical framework for the human activities set free by Wittgenstein's therapeutic techniques. We *could* reflect more explicitly, for example, on speaking or seeing as forms of life without returning to the arid empiricist routines from which Wittgenstein had set us free. (At least one writer once tried this, if not very successfully.)[18] There is a realistic rendering of Wittgenstein that might lead us in this direction. I don't see, in principle, why not.

Sein und Zeit is a more difficult case. On the one hand, Heidegger gives us what sounds like a "realistic" account of perception: we hear the roaring motorcyles, . . . the crackling fire.[19] So it is as if, as real perceivers, we are situated among real things, and it must then be as animals, one would suppose, that we have ears to hear them. On the other hand, Heidegger emphatically rejects biology as well as psychology and social science as sources for insight into the being of human being.[20] He tells us, too, that events or entities cut off from a relation to Dasein are conceivable: "Nur solang Dasein ist, 'gibt es' Sein."[21] Granted, he has systematically and radically sidestepped the cul-de-sac of Cartesian consciousness, yet he still keeps existence prisoner within itself, and that was precisely Descartes's deepest and most fundamental error. In *The End of Philosophy* Heidegger (rightly) attacks Hegel and Husserl for the subjectivistic medium within which their thought remains confined.[22] But is he really exempt from the same object? In an essay entitled "Psychiatry and Philosophy," Erwin Strauss reproached Heidegger for failing to give us, between *existentialia* and the concepts subsumed under *Vorhandenheit*, what he calls *animalia*.[23] This criticism is justified. Not everything that is not flatly Cartesian *res extensa* is related intrinsically to Dasein's concerns *as* Dasein. We, like other animals, have our ecological niche, not all of which is artifactual and human. Heidegger was a countryman who should have known that. But it seems that the Todnauberg was there for him to ski on as much as the Aula was there for him to lecture in. Surely personal existence, however, is intelligible only as one style of bodily lived existence, as much as lived existence is one style (or a family of styles) of existence as such. Unless nature is prior (*ontologically* prior) to personal history, our account of the latter seems self-defeating and ephemeral. The hermeneutical circle can remain only a dizzying Being-to-Death, not, as it must minimally be, Being-to-Death-within-life.

Why does Heidegger refuse to articulate Dasein into the living world? He might have said that such a tactic would be merely ontic, not ontological—or empirical, not philosophical. And, indeed, he does remark that he could have dealt with *Leiblichkeit*, at least, if not with nature, but didn't want to.[24] Further, where he calls *Leben* a privation of *Dasein*,[25] it is plain that he is ignoring, rather than deprecating, a biological perspective, because what he calls *Leben* here is clearly the *Leben* of *Lebensphilosophie*, which, like Wittgenstein's "forms of life," is, in fact, just human activity. It is *Dasein* less rigorously thought through and, in that sense, a privation. This is to overlook the possibility of *animalia* rather than to reject them. But to do this constitutes an *ontological* omission, not a reasoned dismissal of ontic claims from an ontological analysis. And I think that may well have been the case. To support this claim, let me look for a moment at Heidegger's account of the basic structure of *Dasein* and consider its possible historical origin.

Consider the three prepositions that characterize *Sorge: in, (sich) vorweg,* and *bei.* Because *Sorge* is to be read as temporality, one is inclined to identify these with the three temporal *ecstases,* past, future, present. But let's think of them for a moment from a different point of view. We have here a threefold unity: a *Dreieinigkeit,* but a *Dreieinigkeit* that is human-all-too-human rather than divine. Traditionally, of course, the being of man was ground in the being of God. God was *causa essendi, ratio intelligendi,* and *ordo vivendi,* and these three aspects of divine being were reflected in human nature insofar as man was a creature, made by God the Father, insofar as the truth of God's being, and of Being as such, was revealed to him through Christ, and insofar as the order of human life was guided by the Holy Ghost. What is man with God's causality, revelation, and grace removed? Instead of being made, he has been thrown into the world where he simply finds himself: *"wo er als geworfen sich befindet."* His understanding, secondly, is not, as it was for Augustine, Christ the teacher teaching within, but the projection of his own existence, essentially in relation to his own nonexistence (as *Sein zum Tode*). And, finally, the order he lives by is first and foremost keeping up with the Joneses: he is, not this very soul chosen by grace, but the They. (Unless, of course, swaying over the abyss of nothingness, he pulls himself up to authenticity and even, heroically, finds a Destiny). Thus man, unprotected by the Trinity, is his own trinity. Orphaned by the Divine father, he is not yet able to grasp his own being as one way among many others of living, an embodied, animate life history.

One of the strangest sections of *Sein und Zeit*, it seems to me, is the *cura* story, which is fetched in, rather arbitrarily, in order to justify the term *Sorge* as shorthand for *sich-Vorweg-sein-im-Schon-Sein-in-einer-Welt-als-Sein-bei-Innerweltlichem Seienden*. But in that very story, it was clay, *humus*, from which man was fashioned, and that is why Earth demanded that he be called after *humus*, *homo*. Heidegger took up the cause of Care, who made the creature, but forgot the material it was fashioned from, which is, after all, just as necessary to shaping its existence as is the "spirit," the breath of life, that Jove infused in it. Without clay, without embodiment, there is no humanity.

Human being, as Being-in-a-world, in other words, is possible only as the achievement of a certain kind of living being, with certain organic endowments and a certain kind of biological as well as social environment. *Animalia* are a necessary presupposition of *existentialia*. Note, however, I am not now preposing to replace the principle of the primacy of historicity by a principle of the primacy of life. What we have to recognize is the place cleared *within* nature for the possibility of the human, that is, historical, or historicizing-historicized, nature. There have been recurrent attempts to understand human beings purely biologically, and, in particular, in terms of a theory of evolution. Whether in evolutionary ethics, evolutionary epistemology, or a functionalist theory of social organization, however, these are mistaken extrapolations from a theory of change in the genetic composition of populations to fields where some reference to human symbol systems is fundamental to the questions asked, let alone the answers given. R. C. Lewontin, in a recent paper, "Adaptation," has traced very clearly the line that needs to be drawn. First, he points out, even in organic evolution, although in the long run it is the environment that is controlling, organisms do not simply change passively with changing environments:

> The simple view that the external environment changes by some dynamic of its own and is tracked by the organisms takes no account of the effect that organisms have on the environ-

ment. The activity of all living forms transforms the external world in ways that both promote and inhibit the organisms's life. Nest building, trail and boundary marking, the creation of entire habitats as in the dam-building activity of beavers, all increase the possibilities of life for their creators. On the other hand, the universal character of organisms is that they are self-limited in their increase because they quickly use up food and space resources. In this way, the environment is a product of the organism, just as the organism is a product of the environment. The organism adapts the environment in the short term to its own needs, as, for example, by nest building, but in the long term the organism must adapt to an environment that is changing, partly by the organism's own activity, in ways that are distinctive to the species.[26]

This kind of interaction, however, has become so massive in the human case, that the usual biological relation has been fundamentally transformed:

The relation between organism and environment has become virtually reversed in adaptation. Cultural invention replaces genetic change as the effective source of variation. Consciousness makes analysis and deliberate alternations in practice possible. As a result, the adaptation of environment to organism has become the dominant adaptation to an almost independently changing environment was dominant, the line leading to Homo sapiens passed to a stage where conscious activity made adaptation of the environment to the organism's needs an integral part of the biological evolution of the species. As Engels observed . . . , the human hand is as much a product of human labor as it is an instrument of that labor. Finally the human species has passed to the stage where adaptation of the environment to the organism has come to be completely dominant, marking off Homo sapiens from all other life. It is this phenomenon, rather than any lucky change in the external world, that is responsible for the rapid expansion of the human species in historical time.[27]

It is within these boundary conditions that personal existence, as in each case a personal history, takes place. It is in each case still a life history, but a biologically anomalous one, dependent on a certain degree of sheltering from the immediate pressures of organism-environment interaction, or on a skewing of these relations that allows a space within which the symbol-making and symbol-accepting activities of the person can develop. Such activities can be adequately described only as activities of living things, but of living things so situated as to be able to achieve the cultural conditions that are equally necessary to their existence as the kinds of living things they are. Thus, there are constraints in the organization of nature that are presupposed in the organization of human nature. And an account of the way(s) in which we constitute the order of our world demands that we take account, at the same time, of the kinds of order that enter into our constitution as animals capable of such idiosyncratic activities. The biological does not constitute the cultural, but it establishes the area within which the cultural becomes, and remains, possible. Human beings have not, of course, always known very much or very accurately about the complex underlying order of living on which their own lives depend. But their being within nature, not simply against or above it, has certainly been a constituent part of most people's view of their own nature. And given what we now know about the biological mechanisms on which any life, including human life, depends, we need, in our philosophical reflection on the question what it is to be a person, to take reasoned account of the existence and character of these foundations. Not historicity cut off from life, nor life devouring and denying historicity, is what we need to think about, but historicity as one life-style, one peculiar to our kind, as the kind of animals we happen to be.

There are contemporary thinkers, unfortunately less influential than those I have alluded to, who can assist us in this task.[28] What I have been trying to do here is simply to clear a path for these more hopeful styles of thinking by considering two difficulties that have prevented our listening more attentively to what their proponents have tried to tell us, and so from building on the foundations that they might provide: the difficulties, first, of the way in which an emphasis on the historicity of the person seems, at least in popular thinking, to destroy itself, and, second, of the way in which an emphasis on historicity has either cut us off from nature or humanized the natural and so dissolved it. In the first case, the human is reduced to the nonhuman; in the second, the nonhuman is either ignored or assimilated to the human. It is between this latter-day dogmatism on the one hand and latter-day scepticism on the other that philosophical anthropology needs to steer its course.

NOTES

1. Helmuth Plessner, *Die Stufen des Organischen und der Mensh*, 2d ed. (Berlin: Walter de Gruyter and Co., 1965), pp. 309ff.

2. See, e.g., Adolf Portmann, *Zoologie und das neue Bild des Menschen* (Munich: Rowohlts Deutsche Enzyklopadie, 1956), pp. 29–80, esp. 68ff., "Das Extra-Uterine Frühjahr."

3. A. J. P. Kenny et al., *The Development of Mind* (Edinburgh: Edinburgh University Press, 1973), p. 47.

4. Ernst Cassirer, *An Essay on Man* (Garden City, New York: Doubleday and Co., 1953), p. 44.

5. Immanuel Kant, "Recension von Moscatis Schrift: Von dem korperlichen wesentlichen Unterschiede zwischen der Struktur der Thiere and Menschen," in *Gesammelte Schriften*, ed., Königlich Preussischen Akademie der Wissenschaften, 8 vols. (Berlin: G. Reimer, 1902–12), 2: 421–25.

6. See, e.g., Helmuth Plessner, *Philosophische Anthropologie* (Frankfurt: S. Fischer Verlag, 1970), p. 49.

7. Martin Heidegger, *Kant und das Problem der Metaphysik* (Bonn: Cohen, 1929).

8. Charles S. Peirce, *Collected Papers*, eds. Charles Hartshorne and Paul Weiss, 6 vols. (Cambridge: Harvard University Press, 1931–1958), 5: pars. 35 and 36.

9. Martin Heidegger, *Sein und Zeit*, 3d ed. (Halle: Max Niemeyer, 1931), pp. 372 ff.

10. One may take as a convenient starting point H. Rickert, *Grenzen der naturwissenschaftlichen Begriffsbildung*, 2ed. (Tübingen: Mohr, 1902; 1st ed., 1896).

11. See Heidegger, *Sein und Zeit*, pp. 411ff.

12. Manfred Eign, "The Self-Organization of Matter and the Evolution of Biological Macromolecules," *Die Naturwissenschaften* 58 (1971):465–523.

13. Alfred North Whitehead, *Science and the Modern World* (New York: Macmillan, 1925), see, e.g., p. 343, p. 131.

14. G. E. M Anscombe, *Causality and Determination* (Cambridge: Cambridge University Press, 1971).

15. Personal communication, September 1976.

16. Plessner, *Stufen*, pp. 293 ff.

17. Ludwig Wittgenstein, *Philosophical Investigations*, trans. G. E. M. Anscombe (Oxford: Basil Blackwell, 1958), 1 par. 23, p. 11.

18. John Holloway, *Language and Intelligence* (London: Macmillan, 1951).

19. Heidegger, *Sein und Zeit*, p. 163.

20. Ibid., pp. 49–50. Cf. "Brief uber den Humanismus," in *Wegmarken* (Frankfurt: Klostermann, 1967), pp. 145–94, pp. 155–56.

21. Ibid., p. 212.

22. Idem. "Das Ende der Philosophie und die Aufgabe des Denkens," in *Zur Sache des Denkens* (Tübingen: Max Niemeyer Verlag, 1969), pp.61–80.

23. Erwin W. Straus, "Psychiatry and Philosophy," in *Psychiatry and Philosophy*, ed. Maurice Natanson (New York: Springer-Verlag, 1969), pp. 1–84, esp. pp. 3–18.

24. Heidegger, *Sein und Zeit*, p. 108.

25. Ibid., pp. 46–50.

26. Richard C. Lewontin, "Adaptation," MS, p. 6.

27. Ibid., pp. 6–7.

28. I have in mind especially Plessner, to whose work I have already alluded, and Merleau-Ponty (Maurice Merleau-Ponty, La Structure du Comportement [Paris: Presses Universitaires de France, 1942? and *La Phenomenologie de la Perception* [Paris: Gallimard, 1945]).

Hermeneutics and Language

II

GADAMER: THE SPECULATIVE
STRUCTURE OF LANGUAGE*

Heidegger, who first described the idea of understanding as the universal determinateness of There-being (Dasein) means the very projective character of understanding, ie, the futural character of There-being (Dasein). I shall not deny, however, that within the universal context of the elements of understanding I have emphasized the element of the assimilation of what is past and handed down. What does the end of metaphysics as a science mean? What does its ending in science mean?[1]

—Hans-Georg Gadamer, Truth and Method

It is rare to find in Gadamer's writings an explicit statement of how he understands himself to differ from Heidegger. He is clearly in agreement with Heidegger about the importance of understanding the tradition of Western metaphysics, which begins with Plato and comes to completion in Hegel's *Encyclopedia of Philosophical Sciences*. That for Heidegger understanding is oriented primarily to the future, where for Gadamer it is directed to the past, is therefore for Gadamer simply a difference of emphasis. Yet Gadamer's reason for recalling and responding to the tradition seems to differ radically from that of Heidegger. Although Heidegger does indeed respond to the tradition, his reason for doing so is in order to overcome the tradition of Western metaphysics and in particular the language of metaphysics. For Heidegger, what thinking (*Denken*) is to commemorate and bring to remembrance (*Andenken*), namely, being in its difference from beings, has been consistently overlooked and hence forgotten within

---

*I would like to express my gratitude to the NEH for the grant that enabled me to write this paper as part of a larger study of the problem of language in Gadamer and Heidegger.

the tradition of Western metaphysics is to understand (*Verstehen*) it through appropriating it in a hermeneutical conversation.

As Heidegger has said, and Gadamer has reiterated, Heidegger's relation to the tradition is misunderstood if the overcoming (*Überwindung*) of metaphysics is taken simply to mean its destruction (*Destruktion*). Instead one can get over (*Verwinden*) the tradition only by coming to terms with it. Throughout Gadamer's lifelong conversation with Heidegger, Gadamer has maintained that Heidegger has failed to come to terms with both Plato and Hegel. For Heidegger, the metaphysics that begins to reach its completion in Hegel begins with Plato and his doctrine of truth. Gadamer has questioned whether Heidegger has understood the relation between the said and the unsaid in Plato, that is, the nature of Platonic dialogue. So too he has questioned whether Heidegger has understood the speculative in Hegel, that is, the speculative structure of language. The emphasis Gadamer places within *Truth and Method* on the assimilation of what is past and handed down must be understood within the context of the questions he has raised about Heidegger's understanding of the tradition of Western metaphysics. Yet at issue in Gadamer's conversation with Heidegger is more than how to understand Plato and Hegel, and therefore the tradition of Western metaphysics. Rather the very nature of a *hermeneutical conversation* with the written tradition is at issue.

In the following paper I shall presuppose, as background, this lifelong conversation between Gadamer and Heidegger as the unsaid in *Truth and Method*, which enables a better understanding of what Gadamer says there about hermeneutical conversation. I shall focus here only on what Gadamer, in contrast to Heidegger, perceives to be the truth of Hegel insofar as it sheds light on two issues discussed in *Truth and Method*: first, the I-Thou structure of language taken as the event of language, and second, language as a center. Although I shall show that on both these issues Gadamer begins in agreement with Heidegger and ends in agreement with Hegel, I shall not argue that Gadamer's turn from Heidegger to Hegel signifies a fundamental disagreement and break with Heidegger's understanding of language. Instead in following Hegel to the extent that he does, Gadamer understands himself to be developing further a possibility opened up by Heidegger's understanding of language. Instead in following Hegel to the extent that he does, Gadamer understands himself to be developing further a possibility opened up by Heidegger's understanding of language yet that remains unrealized by Heidegger in his attempt to overcome the language of metaphysics. As early as 1916, at the end of his *Habilitationsschrift* on Duns Scotus, Heidegger acknowledges the need to come to terms with Hegel's philosophical system.[1] In 1971, in his essay "Hegel and Heidegger," Gadamer notes: "It is striking how persistently Heidegger's thought circles around Hegel and how he continues to this day to seek new ways of demarcating his own thought from Hegel's."[2] In *Truth and Method*, Gadamer presents a concept of language that he claims supplements the concept of language worked out by Heidegger by conjoining it with Hegel's concept of the speculative structure of language freed from Hegel's systematic metaphysics.

Given the complexities of the lifelong conversation between Gadamer and Heidegger, and the limits of this paper, it is not possible here to consider Heidegger's objections to Gadamer's concept of a hermeneutical conversation, its I-Thou structure, and the speculative structure of language. Nor is it possible to do justice to Heidegger's reasons for dissociating his own path of thinking from that hermeneutical phenomenology that was his starting point in *Being and Time* and that remains Gadamer's starting point in *Truth in Method*. Further whether or not Heidegger has understood the speculative in Hegel will not be decided here. Nor will it be possible to account for Gadamer's reasons for limiting the extent to which he is in agreement with Hegel. Rather this paper can only take up Gadamer's appropriation of Hegel with respect to the speculative structure of language and conclude with Gadamer's understanding of the relation between the language of thinking and the language of poetry.

THE EVENT OF LANGUAGE AND ITS I-THOU STRUCTURE

Gadamer introduces the theme of language at the start of part 2 of *Truth and Method*: "In the field of semantics, in particular, we are confronted with the problem of the unconscious nature of our own use of language. How do we discover that there is a difference between our own customary usage and that of the text?"[3] In speaking of the "unconscious nature" of our own use of language, Gadamer does not mean to imply that we cannot question this use because language is forever destined by its very nature to elude us and to cause us to mistake the meaning of the text.[4] Rather he is calling attention to the forgetfulness of language in our use of it and thus is raising the question of the mode of being of language. This question was first raised by Heidegger in *Being and Time*: "In the last resort, philosophical research must resolve to ask what kind of Being goes with language in general. Is it a kind of equipment ready-to-hand within-the-world, or has it Dasein's kind of Being, or is it neither of these?"[5] His differentiation of modes of being (*Seinsmodi*) can be helpful in clarifying Gadamer's answer to this question.

By the *unconscious* nature of of our own use of language, Gadamer is referring to the fact that language in use is not an object present or present-at-hand (*Vorhandensein*) for a subject or consciousness. In this respect language in use appears to be similar to a tool in use. Let us recall Heidegger's example of the use of a hammer in *Being and Time*.[6] When we are hammering, we are not conscious of the hammer as such but attend rather to what we are doing with the hammer. Similarly, when we are doing things with words, for example, promising, we are not conscious of the meaning of the words as such but are engaged rather in what we are doing with the words. Further, like a tool, language may become an object for a subject but only if an interruption occurs that inhibits its further use. Such is, for exmaple, the case in the linguistic science of Saussure when language (*langue*), itself only a part of human speech (*language*), is studied in abstraction from human speech and speaking (*parole*).[7] But is language a tool, something ready-to-hand (*Zuhandensein*)? If we take language either as a complex of interrelated signs (*langue*) or as a complex of locutionary, illocutionary, and perlocutionary acts (*parole*),[8] we mistake the *means* of communication for the *event* of communication. Language is human speech. Based on the distinctions worked out in *Being and Time*, language must be understood in terms of the mode of Being of *Dasein*, or more explicitly *Mitdasein*. In the words of Hölderlin: "We are a conversation." In *Truth and Method*, we find Gadamer in agreement with Heidegger: "[L]anguage has its true being only in conversation, in the exercise of understanding between people."[9]

There is, however, within Gadamer's agreement with Heidegger, especially in the emphasis he gives to the event of understanding, an indication of where he begins to turn away from Heidegger's way to language. Let us recall Hölderlin's poem "Celebration of Peace" and the context of the statement that "we are a conversation" (*Gespräch* is translated here as "discourse"):

> Much, from the morning onwards,
> Since we have been a discourse and have heard from one another,
> Has human kind learnt; but soon we shall be song.[10]

Where Heidegger's way to language turns to Hölderlin and to poetry as song, Gadamer's way to language turns to Hegel to elaborate further the structure of conversation taken as the event of language. While Heidegger looks forward with the help of Hölderlin to an experience of language that is to come, Gadamer looks back with the help of Hegel to the conversation that we have been and continue to be: "The hermeneutical experience is concerned with what has been transmitted in tradition. This is what is to be experienced. But tradition is not simply a process that we learn to know and to be in command of through experience; it is language, i.e., it expresses itself like a 'Thou'."[11] Although in agreement with Heidegger that language is essentially conversation, Gadamer turns to Hegel to work out the I-Thou structure of conversation taken as the event of language.

In order explain why Gadamer turns from Heidegger to Hegel to understand the I-Thou structure of conversation, we must examine Heidegger's description of *everyday* being with another (*Mitdasein*), which is presented in section 26 of *Being and Time*. There he distinguishes two extremes of solicitude (*Fürsorge*), an inauthentic and an authentic way of everyday being with another. The first way is that which "leaps in and dominates."[12] It takes the other into one's care such that care is taken away from the other and instead provided for the other. This way of being with another dominates inappropriately and is an authentic I-Thou relation. The second way of being with another is said to be that which "leaps forth and liberates."[13] It takes the other into one's care in order for the other to develop the ability to take care of himself. The other is taken into one's care "not in order to take away his 'care' but rather to give it back to him authentically as such for the first time."[14] Teaching would be an example of an everyday relation between an I and a Thou that is authentic.

What is striking about Heidegger's characterization of authentic everyday being with another is that liberation into authenticity is not truly reciprocal. At best the end of the other's liberation into authenticity is the means whereby I maintain my already attained authenticity. Further, my authenticity comes about only in the experience of primordial and radical individualization in the face of my ownmost, nonrelational possibility, in being towards my death.[15] It is difficult to see and indeed Heidegger never says in *Being and Time* how authentic *Dasein* overcomes the lack of reciprocity characteristic of authentic everyday being with another. It is therefore not surprising to find that authentic discourse (*Rede*) is said to be about things rather than to be about matters (*die Sache*) of mutual concern within a conversation where the exchange is reciprocal and the aim is to reach agreement. In *Being and Time*, human speech with others is described only in its inauthentic form, as idle chatter (*Gerede*). While Heidegger maintains in his writings after *Being and Time* that we are a conversation, one looks in vain for an alternative conception of the I-Thou relation that would overcome the one-sidedness characteristic of being with another as it is presented in *Being and Time* and would therefore satisfy the conditions for a reciprocal conversation.[16]

In *Truth and Method*, Gadamer looks instead to Hegel's master-slave dialectic and to his concept of *Geist* for the structure of an I-Thou relation appropriate for the give-and-take of a reciprocal conversation. We should be reminded that for Gadamer the works and deeds handed down to us as tradition speak to us as a Thou. His discussion of the three forms of actual I-Thou relations in *Truth and Method* serves to clarify the conditions necessary for the interpretation of these works and deeds, that is, for a hermeneutical conversation with the written tradition. Further, what is at issue is not the otherness of the author. The task at hand is not for the interpreter to come to understand the author as a Thou in his difference from the interpreter. Rather the ''meaningful content [of the text] detached from all bonds of the meaning individual [the author and his intentions],''[17] is the subject and the subject matter (*die Sache*) of the hermeneutical conversation. This is what speaks to us as a person, as a Thou. Finally we should note that when Gadamer argues that the first two forms of I-Thou relations lack morality, he bases this claim on two distinct although related criteria. First of all, there is the question whether there is evidence of explicit or implicit domination of the Thou by the I. Secondly, there is the question of how the meaningful content of the tradition is taken: as a general truth, as a particular truth, or as a truth claim made to and on the interpreter whose task is to question it in its application to himself.

Gadamer first discusses that concept of interpretation modeled after an actual I-Thou relation where the I "seeks to discover things that are typical in the behaviour of one's fellow men and is able to make predictions concerning another person on the basis of experience."[18] In this relation the other is taken as something typical in the sense of generalizable and predictable. Further, the I, which objectifies another, a Thou, claims only to be interested in understanding *human nature in general* (Menschenkenntnis).[19] When this form of I-Thou relation is made the basis of a hermeneutical conversation with the written tradition, we find that "someone who understands the tradition in this way makes it an object, i.e., he confronts it in a free and uninvolved way, and, by methodically excluding all subjective elements in regard to it, he discovers what it contains."[20]

Throughout *Truth and Method* Gadamer criticizes this concept of interpretation that he finds particularly prevalent in the social sciences in their imitation of the method of the natural sciences. He argues that this reification of the Thou of tradition reduces the meaningful content of the tradition to a means in service of ends independent of the meaningful content. Further, he argues that the claim on the part of the interpreter to be value-free and uninvolved conceals the intent to dominate the Thou of tradition. A reciprocal conversation with what the tradition says to us is impossible for one who "detaches himself from the continuing action of tradition, in which he himself has his historical reality."[21] In his generalizations about the content of the written tradition, the interpreter fails to let the written tradition speak for itself. A monologue takes the place of a conversation with the Thou of tradition.

Gadamer next discusses another concept of interpretation modeled after a second form of actual I-Thou relation, namely, one where the I acknowledges the Thou to be a person yet remains within this relation self-related and without reciprocation. This relation is the same as that described by Heidegger as everyday authentic being with another, and it is Hegel's master-slave dialectic that provides insight into the self-relatedness and lack of reciprocity basic to this relation. Here we find that "one claims to express the other's claim and even to understand the other better than the other understands himself. In this way the 'Thou' loses the immediacy with which it makes its claim. It is understood, but this means that it is anticipated and intercepted and intercepted reflectively from the standpoint of the other person [namely, of the I]."[23] Gadamer suggests two examples of everyday relations between an I and a Thou that exhibit this kind of self-relatedness: first, the servant who tyrannizes the master through serving him; and second, charitable or welfare work, which includes "the educative relationship, an authoritative form of welfare work."[23] In these examples, the one who claims to serve is at the same time "reflecting himself out of his relation to the other and so becoming unreachable by him. By understanding the other, by claiming to know him, one takes from him all justification of his own claim."[24] When this form of I-Thou relation is made the basis of a hermeneutical conversation with the written tradition, the following results: "Just as in a conversation, when we have discovered the standpoint and horizon of the other person, his ideas become intelligible, without our necessarily having to agree with him, the person who thinks historically comes to understand the meaning of what has been handed down, without necessarily agreeing with it, or seeing himself in it."[25]

Here Gadamer, with his customary reticence, does not refer directly to Heidegger and his concept of authentic everyday solicitude as presented in *Being and Time*, but rather to Dilthey and his concept of historical consciousness. Historical consciousness "seeks in the otherness of the past not the instantiation of a general law, but something historically unique."[26] In what sense can an interpretation of the written tradition that claims to understand it so to speak within its own historical horizon be basically self-related? First of all, by understanding the meaningful content of the tradition as other and unique to its historical time, the interpreter distances and dissociates himself from the actual claim made by the text, namely, that what it claims is and remains true. The meaning of the text is determined for its time rather than for the time of the interpreter. As such the interpreter does not see himself in the text and is freed from the responsibility of answering to it. Secondly, while the interpreter dissociates himself from the truth claim actually made by the meaningful content of the tradition, he also claims to be able to say what it says, what the past means. Without allowing it to speak *to* the interpreter, the interpreter speaks *for* it and claims to do so in a free and unprejudiced way. Although this concept of a hermeneutical conversation with the written tradition is more than a monologue, it remains one-sided and fails to realize that reciprocity which we call the give-and-take of conversation.

According to Gadamer, each of these two forms of I-Thou relation have acted as models for the relation between an interpreter and the meaningful content of the written tradition. Yet both fail to do justice to interpretation taken as the event of understanding and thus to the conversation that we are. In the name of freedom from prejudice, the interpreter denies that he is historically affected—both *in* what he understands the text to mean and *by* what he understands the text to question.[27] If the meaningful content of the written tradition is taken as an instantiation of a general law or as a historically unique instance, then the *moment of application* in the event of understanding is deferred. The text is questioned, but not the questioner. Thus to deny the necessity with which one's own prejudices come into play in the event of understanding is to deny the possibility that the truth of one's own prejudices come into question.

At issue for Gadamer is the truth of the Enlightenment prejudice against prejudice. He argues that the claim to be free from prejudice is in reality a denial of tradition, both that the *I* or individual interpreter stands within a tradition and that *we* stand together within a tradition. To do justice to the way we stand together within a tradition, Gadamer proposes as a third form of the I-Thou relation Hegel's concept of *Geist*, that is, "the I which is a we and the we which is an I"[28] In this relation, the I not only recognizes the Thou to be a person but also listens to what the Thou has to say. The I is open to the Thou and to the truth of what the Thou claims. Ready to experience the limitations of its own original understanding of that which is called into question by the Thou, the I is a questioner open to questions; it is open-minded and prepared to change its mind. The truth is that which emerges in the course of this conversation. It is no longer that originally claimed by the I or that originally claimed by the Thou, but rather that which emerges out of the give-and-take of conversation.

To illustrate how this form of I-Thou relation provides a basis for the interpretation of the meaningful content of the written tradition, Gadamer once more follows Hegel further who points us back to the Platonic dialogues as exemplifying the art of conducting a true conversation: "[Here] language, in the process of question and answer, giving and taking, talking at cross purposes and seeing each other's point, performs that communication of meaning which, with respect to the written tradition, is the task of hermeneutics."[29] Gadamer does not mean to suggest that the task of hermeneutics is to presume the role of Socrates and to cross-examine the written tradition as Socrates does the opinions of his interlocutors. Rather the task of hermeneutics is to enter into a conversation with what is written by assuming the role of an interlocutor in a Platonic dialogue. As a listening reader we allow ourselves to be cross-examined by what is written and handed down to be understood. While it was Schleiermacher who first spoke of hermeneutics as a conversation, for Gadamer "it is more than a metaphor, it is a memory of what originally was the case, to describe the work of hermeneutics as a conversation with the text."[30]

For Gadamer, the event of understanding is ultimately the event of language: "Being which can be understood, is language."[31] Understanding takes place and is realized only in and as a reciprocal conversation. In a hermeneutical conversation with the text, the meaning that is communicated, that comes to be understood, is the meaning that emerges in common. In the give-and-take of a reciprocal conversation language is the center (*Mitte*) that brings about the meaning that is common. It makes possible a fusion of the "horizons" of the interpreter and the text into a common horizon wherein not only the issues questioned by the text are open to issues of common concern but also the response to these issues is responsible and open for what is common and can be agreed upon. Language, as conversation, is the medium (*Mitte*) that joins the I to the Thou and the Thou to the I as a we.

Beginning with the question of the mode of being appropriate to language, we found that Gadamer is in agreement with Heidegger that language is essentially, that is, has its true being only in conversation. We found further that it is Hegel rather than Heidegger who aids Gadamer in working out the I-Thou structure required for a hermeneutical conversation with the written tradition that is truly reciprocal. To what extent can Gadamer claim in turning from Heidegger to Hegel to be nonetheless supplementing what Heidegger has said about language?

Let us consider Heidegger's talk "Hölderlin and the Essence of Poetry" (1936).[32] In this talk Heidegger reflects on the following lines from an unfinished poem by Hölderlin, entitled "Conciliator, You That No Longer Believed In. . ." as providing an answer to the question how language occurs:

Much has man learnt.
Many of the heavenly ones has he named.
Since we have been a conversation
And have been able to hear from one another.[33]

According to Heidegger, Hölderlin's poem tells us that language occurs essentially (*wesentlich*) as conversation, whereby speaking mediates a coming together and coming to terms with one another. Moreover Hölderlin's poem tells us that being able to hear from one another is not a consequence of being a conversation, but rather that being able to listen to one another is the presupposition for being a conversation. Further Heidegger understands Hölderlin's poem to say that in being a (*ein*) conversation, we are a single (*ein*) conversation, that in reaching agreement about one and the same (*das Eine und Selbe*) we are united (*einig*) and thus authentically a we. Finally Heidegger understands Hölderlin's poem to say that both being a single conversation and being historical "are alike ancient, they belong together and are the same."[34] Clearly Gadamer agrees thus far with Heidegger and develops further in *Truth and Method* the answer suggested by Hölderlin's poem to the question of how language occurs.

In this same talk, however, Heidegger goes on to determine more specifically the conversation that we are. This conversation takes place between man and the gods, the "heavenly ones." For Heidegger it is only insofar as the gods have addressed us and we have responded to this address that we are a conversation: "And this to the extent that it is precisely in the naming of the gods, and in the transmutation of the world into word, that the real conversation, which we ourselves are, consists."[35] For Gadamer, the conversation that we are is not limited to our response to the address of the gods. Rather it concerns all that which is written by humankind and handed down to be understood. Further the transmutation of the world into word takes place with or without the naming of the gods, that is, independently in the exercise of understanding between people.

In "Hölderlin and the Essence of Poetry," Heidegger asks how the conversation that we are is to begin and who is to accomplish this beginning. Behind this question lies his conviction that the gods (or god) have fled and that poetry alone, the originary language (*Ursprache*), makes language (*Sprache*) and therefore conversation (*Gespräch*) possible. According to Heidegger, it is Hölderlin, who commemorates and brings to remembrance (*Andenken*) in his poetry the need for a new beginning both to institute the conversation that we are and to found our being historical. A new beginning is called for insofar as metaphysics, beginning with Plato and coming to completion with Hegel, is the history of the forgetfulness of being in its difference from beings. The essence of poetry, therefore, is "*worthafte*

Stiftung des Seins,''[36] the bestowing of being in and through the word.

Gadamer argues in *Truth and Method* first that: "the poetic statement as such is speculative, in that the linguistic event of the poetic
word expresses its own relationship to being,"[37] and second, that it is
not only the essence of poetry, in particular the essence of Hölderlin's
poetry, that bestows being in and through the word. Instead what
Heidegger discloses as the essence of language in poetry *belongs
together* with the essence of language in philosophy. For it is the
speculative structure of language as such, including that of Plato and
Hegel when properly understood, that bestows being in and through
the word.

THE CENTER OF LANGUAGE AND ITS SPECULATIVE STRUCTURE

In *Truth and Method*, Gadamer announces the task of the section on
the speculative structure of language to be the following: "The
linguistic nature of the human experience of the world was the guideline along which Greek metaphysics since Plato's 'flight into the
logoi' developed its thinking about being. We must enquire *how far*
the answer given there—an answer that lasted until Hegel—does
justice to the problem we are concerned with."[38] Gadamer's problem
is how language as a center mediates that meaning which becomes
common. The answer which Gadamer refers to is *metaphysical* and
takes the complete and actual identity of thought and being—thought
thinking itself—to be the infinite "which human thought regards as
its fulfilled potential, its divinity."[39] To be sure, this metaphysical
answer includes the recognition that for finite human beings this
identity takes place discursively through the mediation of language.
Yet in the end language as such is transcended in the ultimate identity
of thought and being that serves throughout as the measure and standard of truth. Gadamer's own answer is different: "It is the center of
language *alone* that, related to the totality of beings, mediates the
finite, historical nature of man to himself and to the world."[40] It
would be mistaken to assume that Gadamer's response remains
traditionally metaphysical and simply substitutes language in place of
the various absolutes that have served to govern our thinking about
ourselves and the world we find ourselves in. For Gadamer, language
is a center (*Mitte*), not an end (*telos*). It is a medium (*Mitte*), not a
ground (*arche*).

The traditional metaphysical answer that takes language as
ultimately to be transcended has many forms, two of which are the

subject of Gadamer's particular attention, both here and elsewhere. These are the views of Plato and Hegel on language. These must be examined together, according to Gadamer, for not only does Hegel's "dialectic of the determinations of thought [his *Logic*] as well as his dialectic of the forms of knowledge [his *Phenomenology*] explicitly repeat the total mediation between thought and being that was formerly the natural element of Greek thought,"[41] but also "whoever wants to learn from the Greeks has always first to learn from Hegel."[42] However what accounts for Gadamer's lifelong interest in Plato and in Hegel is not the mediated immediacy of the one as a whole, be it the complete articulation of the *logos* or the absolute identity of the subject (thinking) and the object (thinking's thinking), but rather their understanding of dialectic as mediation and how language discloses. For according to Gadamer: "[T]here is in the hermeneutical experience something that resembles a dialectic, an activity of the thing itself, an activity that, unlike the methodology of modern science, is a passivity (*ein Erleiden*), an understanding [that is] an event."[43] Following Hegel, Gadamer calls that which resembles a dialectic within hermeneutics the speculative.

In order to understand what Gadamer means when he calls language speculative in a hermeneutical conversation, we need to consider what he has said about "the emergence of the concept of language in the history of Western thought." In that section of *Truth and Method* which bears this title, Gadamer has prepared the hermeneutical situation of the question of language "in regard to fore-having, fore-sight and fore-conception."[44] by presenting "important turning-points in European thought concerning language."[45] There he has argued that the epoch-making decision to think of language as a mere tool of communication follows from a suppression of a legitimate question as early as Plato's discussion of language in the *Cratylus*. This question is "whether the word is nothing but a 'pure sign' ("*reines Zeichen*') or has something about it of the 'image' ('Bild', [eikon])."[46] Because in the course of the *Cratylus* "the argument that the word is a copy (*Abbild*) is worked out there ad absurdum, the only alternative seems to be that it is a sign (*semeiion* or *semainon*)."[47] In questioning this dominate preconception about the being of language, Gadamer points to its origin in a *metaphysical* position, that of Plato, where "the true being of things is to be investigated 'without names',[48] because "it is not the word, but number that is the true paradigm of the poetic."[49] Alongside this dominate preconception about the nature of language, Gadamer brings forth evidence for an alternative conception of language within the tradition of Western metaphysics. Both the Christian idea of *verbum* and the Aristotelian idea of *epagoge* present another possibility for understanding language that enables Gadamer to recover "the phenomenon of language out of its immersion in the ideality of meaning."[50]

In the section on the speculative structure of language, Gadamer takes up the alternative suppressed in the *Cratylus*, namely, that language has something about it of the image, where image (*Bild*) is more than a copy (*Abbild*): "The word is not just a sign. In a sense that is hard to grasp it is almost something like an image (*Abbild*)."[51] Gadamer deliberately chooses the term "speculative" as it was used in Germany around 1800 and, most important, by Hegel to characterize that structure of language that bestows being in and through the word. In this choice, Gadamer acknowledges that "there lies behind this usage the notion of a reflection in a mirror."[52] By calling language speculative Gadamer does not mean that the structure of being is simply copied (*abgebildet*) in language. Rather "it is in the course (*Bahnen*) of language that the order and structure of our experience forms itself, at once originally and constantly changing."[53]

Let us consider again Gadamer's claim that language in a hermeneutical conversation with the text is the center that mediates the meaning of something open to question (*die Sache*) such that a meaning that is common emerges. By calling the center of language speculative, Gadamer is claiming that what is at issue (*die Sache*) and its meaning expressed in language belong together just as an object and its mirror image (*Spiegelbild*) belong together. Although the analogy is clearly limited to the extent that it need not be the case that an object be reflected in a mirror whereas it must be the case that the meaning of what is at issue be expressed and thus reflected in language, what Gadamer finds common is the specific mode of "belonging together," which he calls, after Hegel, a speculative unity.

To clarify this, he refers us back to his analysis of the mirror image (*Spiegelbild*) and its relation to the object that is reflected in the mirror in his earlier discussion of the ontological value of the picture (*Bild*). There he argues that the mirror image is an appearance and hence lacks being independently of the original object. As an appearance of the original object, the mirror image belongs together with the being of the original object. Although the mirror image and the original object seem to be two and distinct, they cannot in reality be distinguished: "It [the mirror image] is like a duplication that is still only one thing."[54] They belong together as a speculative unity. So also what is at issue (*die Sache*) and its meaning as expressed and reflected in language seem to be two and distinct. Nonetheless insofar as the meaning of what is at issue appears only as expressed and reflected in language, they belong together: "To be expressed in language does not mean that a second being is acquired. The way in which a thing presents itself is, rather, part of its own being. Thus everything that is language has a speculative unity: it contains a distinction, that between its being and the way that it presents itself, but this is a distinction that is not really a distinction at all."[55]

Let us look further at the relation between an object and its mirror image and consider what we shall call the double directionality present in a belonging together that is speculative. Gadamer has described earlier how the mirror image belongs together with the original object as a reflection of the original object in two senses. First of all, the mirror image is a reflection of the original object, where the "of" is to be taken as a subjective genitive. The object through its appearing *forth into* the mirror brings about the mirror image. Secondly, the mirror image is the reflection of the original object where the "of" is to be taken as an objective genitive. The reflection in the mirror, the mirror image, makes the object more, that is, it makes the object into the "original" rather than the "image." The object is more as a result of its being reflected *back from* the mirror image. In other words, as reflected *into* the mirror the object remains the same in its being as a result of its appearing. As reflected *back from* the mirror the object becomes other than it was. Now, as the original, it becomes more than its appearing, although it does so only in and through its appearing.[56]

Let us consider now what happens when the meaning of what is at issue (*die Sache*) is expressed and reflected in language in a hermeneutical conversation with the text. Given that the unity here is speculative, can we find evidence for a double directionality and increase in being similar to that made possible by the mirror image? Here Gadamer again turns to Hegel and through Hegel to Plato for evidence that the structure of language is speculative in this further sense. Gadamer is careful to qualify just how far he is in agreement with these thinkers. By working out what is speculative within Hegel and Plato, Gadamer does not mean to equate what is metaphysical within their dialectics with a hermeneutical conversation. Rather his intention is to recover the speculative structure of language by distinguishing it from what is metaphysical within their dialectics.

What Gadamer finds to be speculative within the metaphysical dialectics of Hegel and Plato is that in both cases the discursive articulation that constitutes the meaning of what is at issue is not "a movement performed by thought, but the movement of the object itself that thought experiences."[57] In this, the movement of the object itself that thought experiences is similar in its activity to the object's appearing forth into the mirror. Further, thought's experience, as something that it undergoes, is similar in its receptivity and passivity to the way the mirror receives its being reflecting, the image, from the object's appearing forth.

Gadamer focuses attention more precisely on the first directionality characteristic of the speculative in the following statement about Hegel: "In describing the true method, which is the activity of the thing itself, Hegel quotes Plato, who loved to show his Socrates in conversation with young men, because they were ready to follow Socrates' logical questions, without regard for current opinions. He [Hegel] illustrated his own method of dialectical development by these 'malleable youths', who avoided interfering with the path on which the things took them, and did not parade their own ideas."[58] What Hegel finds true about this way of conversing is not that the "malleable youths" follow Socrates. Rather what makes Socratic conversation a true method for Hegel is that the "malleable youths" are led by Socrates to follow the path "on which the thing itself took them." The thing itself, for example, justice or piety, is allowed to direct their thinking and to become present in thought for these youths. Their malleability enables them to be open for and mindful of the thing itself rather than mindful of themselves and their opinions. It is this being directed by the thing itself that is at issue (*die Sache*), which constitutes the first directionality of that which is speculative in the metaphysical dialectics of Plato and Hegel.

A hermeneutical conversation with the text is speculative in the same way in that the thing itself, the meaning of the text, directs the event of understanding. Comparable to being open to and mindful of the thing itself is the willingness to listen to what the text claims without insisting on the meaning one expects in accordance with one's own prejudices: "The unfolding of the totality of meaning towards which understanding is directed, forces us to make conjectures and to take them back again. The self-cancellation of the interpretation makes it possible for the thing itself—the meaning of the text—to assert itself."[59] Insofar as the meaning of the text asserts itself, it asserts its claim to truth. A hermeneutical conversation with the text bestows being to what is at issue (*die Sache*). What is open to question presents itself, that is, it finds its way into language.

Gadamer distinguishes two moments in the event of understanding: "[T]he dialectic of question and answer always preceeds the dialectic of interpretation."[60] The dialectic of question and answer ends with the question opened up by the text's claim to truth: "Only because between the text and its interpreter there is no automatic accord can a hermeneutical experience make us share in the text. Only because a text must be brought out of its alienness and become assimilated is there anything for the man who is seeking to understand to say. Only because the text calls for it does interpretation take place, and only in the way called for."[61]

The dialectic of interpretation begins with the response to the question that divides the interpreter from the text: "The apparently thetic beginning of interpretation is, in fact, a response and, like every response, the sense of an interpretation is determined by the question asked."[62] These two dialectics belong together as the double directionality of a speculative unity. We have seen that the dialectic of question and answer is speculative in the sense of first being directed by the meaning of the text that presents itself in its claim to truth. We have now to examine the dialectic of interpretation: "The paradox that is true of all transmitted material, namely of being one and the same and yet of being different."[63] This dialectic Gadamer also calls speculative, that is, speculative in the second sense of "having no tangible being of its own and yet throwing back the image that is presented to it."[64]

The dialectic of interpretation begins when the truth claimed by the text becomes an issue that must be worked out as an issue *for* the interpreter. It ends when the interpreter comes to terms with what the text calls into question, that is, reaches agreement about the matter at issue (*die Sache*) and its truth, which includes knowing where and why he disagrees with it. Here it is Hegel's "speculative proposition," which informs Gadamer's analysis of the speculative structure of the interpretative conversation with the text. Although Gadamer chooses Hegel to determine further the speculative structure of language, he argues first that it also can be found within Plato, who "took the first step" when he realized that "the word of language is both one and many,"[65] and second that it is to be found in Hölderlin, both in his poetry and in his theoretical fragment, "The Poetic Spirit's Mode of Proceeding."[66]

What makes Hegel's speculative proposition an appropriate model for the interpretative conversation with the text is not *that* it presents the truth as one and whole but rather *the way that* it presents the truth as one and whole. Gadamer reminds us here of Hegel's description of the speculative proposition in the preface to the *Phenomenology of Spirit*.[67] There Hegel distinguishes the speculative proposition from all judgments that predicate something of the subject. In the latter the subject-concept remains fixed while thought goes outside it to the predicate to relate something else back to it. In a speculative proposition, · however, the subject-concept disappears into the predicate, which becomes the truth of the subject. Thus a speculative proposition only appears to have the form of a judgment, that is, to relate a subject and a predicate. As soon as we attempt to determine the subject-concept of a speculative proposition further by taking something different and relating it back to the subject, we find that what appears to be different from the subject, namely, the predicate, instead already belongs to the nature of the subject.

Gadamer illustrates what he means by a speculative proposition in the following example: "'God is one' does not mean that it is a property of God's to be one, but that it is God's nature to be unity."[68] A speculative proposition is not simply analytic and an identity statement. "God is one" differs from "God is God" in that in the former *the setback* that thinking encounters when it fails to go beyond the subject-concept *makes present* what the subject-concept in truth is: "Starting from the subject, as if this remained the basis throughout, it [thinking] finds that, since the predicate is rather the substance, the subject has passed into the predicate and has thus been removed . . . The form of the proposition destroys itself since the speculative proposition does not state something of something, but presents the unity of the concept."[69] While for Hegel, the unity of the concept is ultimately metaphysical, that is, the unity that is God's nature, this unity needs to be *demonstrated* by explicitly presenting the setbacks that thought experiences that make present the unity of the concept. According to Gadamer, "This takes place in the account of the dialectical movement of the proposition. This is the *realization* of the speculative, and only its expression is speculative thinking."[70] For Gadamer, it is Hegel's concept of *demonstration* taken as the explicit presentation of both the setbacks that thought experiences and the self-destruction of the proposition that makes his speculative proposition a model appropriate for the interpretative conversation with the text.

In this conversation, what the interpreter understands about the issue in question differs from what the text claims to be true. The two claims are not the same in the way that the subject and the predicate in an identity statement are the same. Rather the two claims appear in their difference to be related externally to each other just as the predicate of a judgment is related externally to the subject of a judgment. The two claims remain externally related as long as the interpreter remains basically self-related and dissociated from the matter at issue. However once the interpreter experiences the matter at issue to be an issue *for him*, he experiences a setback to his own claim to the truth by the text's claim to the truth. In his interpretative conversation with the text, the interpreter expresses and presents the setbacks he experiences in coming to terms with what the text claims to be true. As in the speculative proposition, the experience of setbacks cancels the difference between the two claims to truth while making present the truth that is one and common. As a result of the interpretative conversation with the text, what is at issue (*die Sache*) has demonstrated itself, that is, it has emerged in its truth, a truth that is more than the truth originally claimed by the text and other than the truth originally claimed by the interpreter.

Language in the interpretative conversation with the text is speculative in three respects. It is speculative first of all because it presents the self-destruction of the difference between the two claims by explicitly presenting that truth which presents itself as one and common. It is speculative, secondly, because it makes present more truth than that claimed at first by the text: "Every assimilation of tradition is historically different."[71] That one and the same text can be different and mean more is because language in the interpretative conversation, like the mirror image, reflects back, that is, reflects back into the text and brings more of its meaning and truth into being. Finally, language in the interpretative conversation is speculative in that it appears only to disappear in the completion of the act of understanding the truth of what is at issue: "Paradoxically, an interpretation is right (*richtig*) when it is capable of disappearing in this way."[72] In this the language of the interpretative conversation most resembles the mirror image, which, having no real being on its own, appears only in reflecting back what is.

It is here where Gadamer seems so close to that transcendence of language that characterizes what is metaphysical in the dialectics of Plato and Hegel that he sets the limit to "*how far* the answer given there [in the tradition of Western metaphysics from Plato to Hegel] does justice to the problem"[73] he is concerned with. For both Plato and Hegel, the truth of what is stated in language is taken to be the identity of thought and being. The center of language disappears with the identity of thought and being in an intellect that is infinite. For Gadamer, however, being, which can be understood by an intellect that is finite and human, is and remains language. The language of the interpretative conversation with the text disappears therefore only when the language of the text comes to be understood to say more.

For Gadamer "all human speaking is finite in such a way that there is within it an infinity of meaning to be elaborated and interpreted."[74] While this means that there is in principle no absolute end to the interpretative conversation with the finite text and the written tradition, it does not mean that there is no possible completion to the event of understanding the text: "Certainly, there is here too for all understanding a criterion by which it is measured and a possible completion. It is the content of the tradition itself which expresses itself in language that is the sole criterion."[75] When Gadamer says that the content of the tradition, of the work to be interpreted, serves as a criterion for the completion of the event of understanding, he means that the work itself provides the measure of its truth insofar as it *continues to prove true*, that is, to present its truth for us. Thus an interpretative conversation with the text reaches its completion and ends not when the meaningful content of the text has been exhausted but rather when the meaningful content of the text matters and continues to matter more for us.

We have argued that Gadamer has turned to Hegel and through Hegel to Plato to recover from language conceived of metaphysically that structure of language which he calls speculative. Insofar as language is speculative, it bestows (*Stiften*) being in and through the word. In accordance with its double directionality, language lets what is at issue (*die Sache*) present itself as an issue first that matters and second that continues to matter more. The question we must return to now is that lifelong conversation between Gadamer and Heidegger about the speculative in Hegel,[76] and Gadamer's claim to be supplementing what Heidegger has disclosed about language.

Gadamer notes in his essay "Hegel and Heidegger" that the fact that Heidegger admits to the extraordinary contemporaneity of Hölderlin's thoughtful poetry for his own poetic thinking about language after *Being and Time* needs to be examined in light of the actual contemporaneity of Hölderlin and Hegel.[77] For Heidegger the need to overcome the language of metaphysics depends on the claim that philosophy as metaphysics is coming to an end: "The completion of metaphysics begins with Hegel's metaphysics of absolute knowledge as the Spirit of will."[78] It is important to note that for Heidegger metaphysics, strictly speaking, does not end but begins to come to completion with Hegel. It continues in Nietzsche and, beyond Nietzsche, as technology (*Technik*). In his lecture on Hölderlin's "Andeken" (1941–42), Heidegger contrasts Hölderlin with Nietzsche. Whereas Nietzsche remains rooted in modern metaphysics, Hölderlin *presages* the overcoming of *all* metaphysics.[79] In preparation for the new beginning at the end of philosophy taken as metaphysics, Heidegger turns away altogether from the language of metaphysics and to the language of Hölderlin's poetry.

The language of Hölderlin's poetry is not only what is to be thought insofar as it is thoughtful poetry but also is what is to guide our understanding of the language of thinking. When Gadamer asks later in the essay "Hegel and Heidegger" whether "in the end, is even the position which Heidegger tries to establish in opposition to Hegel trapped within the sphere of the inner infinity of reflection?"[80] He is questioning the language of Heidegger's "poetic" thinking, where "responding loses the character of questioning and becomes simple saying."[81] Gadamer is not suggesting that Heidegger's understanding of language after the *Kehre*, that language bestows (*Stiften*) being, has already been anticipated thematically by Hegel and is to be found within the scope of Hegel's reflection. The point of Gadamer's question is not to claim, as Derrida and his followers do, that Heidegger fails to overcome and falls back into the language of metaphysics. At issue in Gadamer's lifelong conversation with Heidegger is therefore not what Heidegger's thinking discloses about and on the way to language but rather Heidegger's particular *Sprachnot*,[82] that is, the extreme difficulty that we have in understanding the language of Heidegger's essays after the *Kehre*. It could be argued that Heidegger himself acknowledges this *Sprachnot* when he says, in the most poetic of his later essays, "The poetic character of thinking is still veiled over."[83]

For Gadamer, the impoverishment of Heidegger's language in his writings and lectures on language follows from his identification of philosophy with metaphysics and his attempt to overcome the language of philosophy through recourse to the language of poetry. Yet just as Heidegger's raising of the question of Being effects a new and renewed understanding of the tradition of philosophy, so also does his raising of the question of language effect a new and renewed understanding of the language of philosophy. Instead of the end of philosophy and the overcoming of the language of philosophy, Heidegger's "questioning" thinking opens up new possibilities for the hermeneutical conversation that we are: "an infinity of meaning to be elaborated and interpreted."[84] Thus when Gadamer asks whether Heidegger's poetic thinking about language remains "trapped within the sphere of the inner infinity of reflection," Gadamer is asking about the relation between the language of Heidegger's poetic thinking and the speculative language of Hegel. Here in this essay, and as we have seen in *Truth and Method*, Gadamer argues that when one follows Heidegger's turn to language, one returns to Hegel with the recognition that what Hegel calls the speculative, the inner infinity of reflection, is not bound to his metaphysics and to the end of the self-unfolding of the concept. Instead it is operative universally in and as the speculative structure of language.

In a recent essay, "Philosophie und Literatur" (1981), Gadamer sums up his understanding of the relation between philosphy and poetry and thus his response to Heidegger in the following way: "Perhaps the intrinsic proximity (*die innere Nachbarschaft*) of philosophy and poetry consists precisely in this: that they encounter one another in the most extreme countermovement: the language of philosophy constantly surpasses itself—the language of poetry (of every real poem) is unsurpassable and unique."[85] Although it was Heidegger who first raised the question of the proximity or neighborhood (*Nachbarschaft*) of the language of thinking and the language of poetry,[86] Heidegger, as we have said, turns to the poetry of Hölderlin, to his singing saying of the earth and sky, of the divinities and the mortals, to experience in thinking the center (*Mitte*) of language as the unity of the fourfold. Gadamer, in this essay and as we have shown in *Truth and Method*, does not follow Heidegger's turn to Hölderlin. Rather he returns to Hegel for his answer to Heidegger's question. That the language of philosophy and the language of poetry meet most closely where they most part, that they belong together intimately in the very extremity of their opposition indicates that the relation between the language of philosophy and the language of poetry is that relation which Hegel calls a speculative unity. Not only language in the hermeneutical conversation but language as such is speculative in its structure. As a center, language mediates the extremes represented by the language of philosophy and the language of poetry as well as all that falls between these extremes.

NOTES

1. M. Heidegger, *Frühe Schriften* (Frankfurt am Main: Vittorio Klostermann, 1972), p. 352f.
2. H.-G. Gadamer, *Hegel's Dialectic*, trans. P. Christopher Smith (New Haven: Yale University Press, 1971), p. 103.
3. *Truth and Method*, p. 237.
4. As M. Ermarth implies in "The Transformation of Hermeneutics: 19th Century Ancients and 20th Century Moderns," *Monist 64 (1981): 191.*
5. M. Heidegger, *Being and Time*, trans. J. Macquarrie and E. Robinson (New York: Harper and Row, Publishers, 1962), p. 209.
6. Ibid., p. 98ff.
7. F. de Saussure, *Course in General Linguistics*, ed. C. Bally and A. Sechehaye, trans. W. Baskin (New York: McGraw-Hill Book Company, 1959), p. 9ff.
8. J.R. Searle, *Speech Acts* (Cambridge: Cambridge University Press, 1980), p. 17: "It still might seem that my approach is simply, in Saussurian terms, a study of 'parole' rather than 'langue'. I am arguing, however, that an adequate story of speech acts is a study of *langue*." Further those who construe *parole* as *Rede* overlook the fact that it is not *Rede* but rather *Sprache, Wort*, and *Sage* that guide Heidegger's essays and lectures on language after *Being and Time*.
9. *Truth and Method*, p. 404.
10. F. Hölderlin, *Poems and Fragments*, trans. M. Hamburger (Cambridge: Cambridge University Press, 1966?, p. 439. Cf. also p. 429, "Conciliator, You That No Longer Believed In...."
11. *Truth and Method*, p. 321.
12. *Being and Time*, p. 159.
13. Ibid.

14. Ibid.
15. Ibid, p. 304ff.
16. See also M. Heidegger's lectures in "Hölderlins Hymnen 'Germanien' und Der Rhein" in *Gesamtausgabe* vol. 39 (Frankfurt am Main: Vittorio Klostermann, 1980), pp. 73 and 143, where Heidegger discusses being with another and others in terms of comradeship at the Front and *Volk*. Being with another so understood is later rejected by Heidegger.

17. *Truth and Method*, p. 321.
18. Ibid.
19. Ibid., p. 321f.
20. Ibid., p. 322.
21. Ibid.
22. Ibid.
23. Ibid., p. 323.
24. Ibid.
25. Ibid., p. 270.
26. Ibid., p. 323.

27. This is the meaning of effective-history (*Wirkungsgeschichte*).

28. *Hegel's Dialectic*, p. 58. The reference here is to G. W. F. Hegel, *Phänomenologie des Geistes* (Hamburg: Felix Meiner Verlag, 1952), p. 140. Emphasis added.

29. *Truth and Method*, p. 331.

30. Ibid. It is sometimes argued that Gadamer's understanding of a conversation with the text establishes the text as the authority and thus fails to realize the kind of reciprocity that is present in a living conversation. Here we should note that Gadamer assumes that we question the text. Reciprocity occurs when we let the text question us.

31. Ibid., p. 432, translation corrected.

32. M. Heidegger, "Hölderlin and the Essence of Poetry," trans. D. Scott, in *Existence and Being* (South Bend: Gateway Editions, Ltd., 1949), pp. 270ff.

33. Ibid., p. 277.

34. Ibid., p. 279.

35. Ibid., Cf. also "The Nature of Language," trans. P. Hertz in *On the Way to Language* (San Francisco: Harper and Row, Publishers, 1971), p. 78: "Those who have heard from one another—the ones and the others—are men and gods."

36. My translation; see also "Holderlin and the Essence of Poetry," p. 281: "Poetry is the establishing of being by means of the word."

37. *Truth* and Method, p. 427.

38. Ibid., p. 414, emphasis added.

39. Ibid.

40. Ibid., emphasis added.

41. Ibid., p. 418.

42. Ibid.

43. Ibid., p. 422.

44. Ibid., p. 239. Gadamer uses the same words to characterize Heidegger's preparation to the question of being in *Being and Time* and indicates thereby a practice common to both their hermeneutics.

45. Ibid., p. 415.

46. Ibid., p. 374.

47. Ibid.

48. Ibid.

49. Ibid., p. 373.

50. Ibid., p. 379.

51. Ibid., p. 377.

52. Ibid., p. 423.

53. *Truth and Method*, p. 415; translation corrected.

54. *Truth and Method*, p. 423. For his earlier discussion of the mirror image, see p. 123: "The mirror throws back an image (*Bild*) and not a copy (*Abbild*)." Throughout this and the later section, the translation is often misleading. *Darstellen* is not representing (*Vorstellen*); it is rather a presenting. Gadamer is aware that both Hegel and Heidegger are critical of representational thinking. That he chooses Hegel's alternative, the presenting (*Darstellen*) of inner reflec-

tion for his discussion of language, is part of the dialogue between Gadamer and Heidegger on the truth of Hegel.

55. Ibid., p. 432.

56. Ibid., p. 123. What is said here of the mirror image (*Spiegelbild*) is developed further by Gadamer for the picture of painting (*Bild*).

57. Ibid., p. 418. Using the language of Hegel, Gadamer also calls this "inner reflection."

58. Ibid., p. 421.

59. Ibid., p. 422.

60. Ibid., p. 429.

61. Ibid.

62. Ibid.

63. Ibid., p. 430.

64. Ibid., p. 431.

65. Ibid., p. 415.

66. F. Hölderlin, *Sämtliche Werke und Briefe*, vol. 1 (Munich: Carl Harser Verlag, 1978), pp. 864–69.

67. *Phänomenologie des Geistes*, pp. 48ff.

68. *Truth and Method*, pp. 423f.

69. Ibid., p. 424.

70. Ibid., p. 425, translation corrected.

71. Ibid., p. 430.

72. Ibid., p. 359.

73. Ibid., p. 414.

74. Ibid., p. 416.

75. Ibid., p. 430, translation corrected.

76. Cf. Gadamer's "Nachwort" and footnoes to *Das Erbe Hegel*. Cf. also R. Dottori, "Kristisches Nachwort zu '*Hegels Dialektik* von H.-G. Gadamer und zum Verhältnis Hegel—Heidegger—Gadamer," in *Bijdragen*, 38 (1977), pp. 176–92.

77. *Hegel's Dialectic*, p. 103.

78. M. Heidegger, "Overcoming Metaphysics," trans. J. Stambaugh in *The End of Philosophy* (New York: Harper and Row, Publishers, 1973), p. 89.

79. M. Heidegger, "Hölderlins Hymne 'Andenken'," in *Gesamtausgabe*, vol. 52 (Frankfurt am Main: Vittorio Klostermann, 1982), p. 143.

80. *Hegel's Dialectic*, p. 102.

81. "Science and Reflection," trans. W. Lovitt in *The Question Concerning Technology* (New York: Harper and Row, Publishers, 1977), p. 82.

82. "Philosophie und Literatur," in *Phänomenologische Forschung* 11 (1981): 43, for the *Sprachnot* that is inevitable in all philosophy in so far as ordinary language is "primarily determined for an orientation in the world" and not for questioning the given.

83. "The Thinker as Poet," trans. A. Hofstadter in *Poetry, Language, Thought* (New York: Harper and Row, Publishers, 1971), p. 12.

84. *Truth and Method*, p. 416.

85. "Philosophie und Literatur," p. 43. Author's translation. This essay

has recently appeared in English. See *Man and World* 18, (1985), pp. 241–159. (ed.).

86. Cp. M. Heidegger, "The Nature of Language," trans. P. D. Hertz in *On the Way to Language*, p. 90: "But we should become familiar with the suggestion that the neighborhood of poetry and thinking is concealed within this farthest divergence of their Saying. This divergence is their real face-to-face encounter."

MUST WE BE WHAT WE SAY? GADAMER ON TRUTH IN THE HUMAN SCIENCES

BRICE R. WACHTERHAUSER

We must be content then in speaking of such subjects and with such premises to indicate the truth roughly and in outline, and in speaking about things which are only for the most part true and with premises of the same kind to reach conclusions that are no better.

—Aristotle

It is extremely puzzling, to say the very least, that a work entitled *Truth and Method* should never discuss the question of truth in a direct and systematic manner. Gadamer's magnum opus says a great deal about the nature and conditions of understanding and interpretation in the human sciences (*Geisteswissenschaften*), but it does not explicitly address the problem of truth in these fields.

I find this lack all the more puzzling in light of Gadamer's claims that truth in the human sciences is somehow unique and different than truth in other disciplines, particularly the natural sciences. According to Gadamer, hermeneutics concerns itself "with modes of experience that lie outside of science: with the experience of philosophy, of art, and of history itself. These are all modes of experience in which a truth is communicated that cannot be verified by methodological means proper to science."[1] Gadamer promises "to develop . . . a concept of knowledge and of truth which corresponds to the whole of hermeneutic experience."[3]

One would hope that Gadamer would clarify exactly what these claims entail, but despite such claims he seems to fall short of fulfilling this hope. Throughout *Truth and Method* and in his other writings, Gadamer makes problematic references to such 'truths' as the truth of the art work,[3] the 'truth' of the literary work,[4] the 'truth' of practical reason,[5] and even the 'truth' of the philosophical tradition

219

in the West,[6] but whether there is one theory of truth behind such references remains unclear. However suggestive, I think these varied references to 'truth' remain intrinsically problematic because they are never systematically clarified in terms of a fully developed concept of truth. Consequently, such bold references to 'truth' threaten to obscure the issue of truth in the human sciences by raising an array of related but peripheral issues. To make matters even worse, when Gadamer does discuss various theories of truth he seems at times either to implicitly assume or explicitly affirm such conflicting accounts of truth as 'correspondence', 'coherence', and 'pragmatic' views of truth.

Given this state of affairs, one is tempted to agree with such critics as Rüdiger Bubner, Richard Rorty, Claus von Bormann, and Reiner Wiehl that there is no theory of truth in Gadamer's work.[7] One can revel in this fact and attempt to turn it into a provocative, if questionable, philosophical advantage, as does Rorty, or one can see Gadamer's deficiency as a philosophical weakness either awaiting theoretical redress of some kind (Bubner) or as intrinsically precluding such correction and clarification because of the inherent conceptual confusion in Gadamer's discussions of truth (Wiehl, von Bormann). At the very least, I think we must admit, whether or not we adopt the specific critical perspective on hermeneutics of any one of these philosophers, that Gadamer's own lack of clarity with regard to the notion of truth in the *Geisteswissenschaften* has been and is a legitimate object of criticism.

I think, however, that we must not dismiss the possibility that Gadamer has something of importance to say about truth in the human sciences. Although I agree with Gadamer's critics that one cannot argue that Gadamer offers us a clearly worked-out, fully developed theory of truth in the *Geisteswissenschaften*, I think the various things he says and suggests point to an interesting and important account of truth in this realm. I will argue, despite Gadamer's scattered remarks about different types of truth and the confusion about this issue which they suggest, that there is at least a consistent sketch of a significant theory of 'humanistic' truth running throughout his work. What follows is an interpretive hypothesis regarding that theory. It is my claim that if one reads Gadamer's varied references to truth in the human sciences in light of his most central and provocative claim, namely, that "Being that can be understood is language" (*Sein dass verstanden werden kann, ist Sprache*),[8] one will be able to see at least the outlines of a unique and significant theory of truth in the human sciences. Thus the primary purpose of this paper is interpretive rather than critical. Although hermeneutically speaking it is not legitimate to divorce interpretation from criticism (for in the hermeneutical circle they are distinct but inseparable activities), I wish to focus attention on one side of the hermeneutical task by attempting to make thematic what Gadamer only intimates and suggests.

In the first section of this paper I will sketch in the broadest and most general way possible what I take to be the most central tenets of a Gadamerian theory of truth in the human sciences. In the second section, I will attempt to deepen this broad sketch by a more detailed account of Gadamer's position on the nature of the self that the human sciences investigate and the type of truth it lends itself to. In the third section, I will discuss briefly some of the "guidelines" for pursuing truth in the *Geisteswissenschaften*, which seem suggested by Gadamer's account. The paper will end with a critical comment on what I take to be the most paradoxical and problematical consequences of Gadamer's theory of self-knowledge—the dispersal or possible dissolution of the self as a single, unified entity into the many ways of speaking about a self and its experience.

1

Gadamer's writings are replete with the claim that the *Geisteswissenschaften* offer us self-knowledge. Gadamer, in fact, never discusses the issue of truth in the human sciences apart from the issue of self-knowledge. In the human sciences, Gadamer claims, "what we know is, in the final analysis, ourselves. Knowledge in the human sciences always has something of self-knowledge about it."[9] As such, a Gadamerian theory of truth in the *Geisteswissenschaften* offers us both a perspective on the self as well as a perspective on what it means to speak of 'truth' about this self. This is no accident. Gadamer sees the nature of the self and the nature of truth about the self as inseparable issues. He insists that the type of reality that the self *is*, directly determines the type of truth that is possible about it.

Gadamer belongs to a tradition of ontological theories of truth that take their point of departure from the ontology of the subject matter. Aristotle, for example, argued that one cannot expect the same lawlike necessity that pertains to truths about the eternal order of the heavens to pertain to things human (*ta anthropina*).[10] Human affairs are largely if not wholly contingent and hence subject to radical change. Thus whatever truth is possible about us must not obscure this fundamental ontological truth but presuppose it and build upon it. Gadamer follows both the general methodological principle of all ontological theories of adjusting their theories of truth to 'fit' the reality[11] as well as Aristotle's caveat regarding the difference between human and 'cosmic' truths.[12] We can begin perhaps to see exactly how Gadamer's insight into the ontology of the self directs his theory of self-knowledge by looking briefly at his reasons for rejecting 'coherence' and 'correspondence' theories of truth in the human sciences.

Very briefly, Gadamer seems to reject a coherence theory of truth in the realm of self-knowledge because the historicity of the self precludes the possibility of 'coherence' functioning as an adequate criterion of truth. For example, Aristotle's account of the moral life may be internally coherent, but his notion of virtue is historically contingent, that is, it seems applicable only to a society such as Peraclean Athens. The fact that the self is subject to the contingencies of time make mere 'coherence' suspect as an adequate criterion of truth about ourselves.

More profoundly, Gadamer's position seems to entail a rejection of coherence theories of truth in the Geisteswissenschaften because he seems to hold the view that the self is not necessarily a 'system' or coherent whole. The self contains tensions and contradicitons in its very being, which, according to Gadamer, often make it impossible to describe in terms of one internally consistent account. Gadamer may have something in mind like Pascal's "The heart has its reasons, which reason knows not of" or the Kantian dichotomy between practical and theoretical reason or conflicting and irresolvable moral responsibilities that sometimes divide us, but whatever specific examples he may have in mind he does seem to reject the notion that the self must be described as a coherent whole. However, desirable consistency may be as a rational principle—Gadamer does not deny this—adequate phenomenological accounts of the self's experiences cannot always as a matter of principle be given in noncontradictory terms. In short, there are many linguistic accounts of the self no one of which can substantiate a claim to be the "one true account" or "the most fundamental account" of the self. Suffice it to say that Gadamer seems willing, at least in some cases, to defend a 'pluralistic' and 'antinomial' view of self-knowledge. In other words, on this view human beings do not possess a deep metaphysical or logical identity that guarantees our fundamental unity but, more often than not, we are 'many' striving to become 'one'. History itself, it seems, has left us with divided selves and conflicting accounts of our experience, which cannot easily, if ever, be unified. We will return to an argument about how this most disturbing aspect of Gadamer's position may be further explicated and defended up to a point, but before doing so let us look at Gadamer's reasons for rejecting a correspondence theory of truth in the human sciences.

The historicity of the self is also fundamental to understanding Gadamer's rejection of a correspondence theory of truth for the human sciences, although in a different way than mentioned above. The notion of truth as correspondence has certain presuppositions that make it unsuitable for understanding in what way there can be truth about ourselves. To begin with, the notion of truth as correspondence assumes that the truth about the object of inquiry is somehow given prior to and independently of some historically contingent linguistic account of ourselves, but awareness of some aspect of ourselves or of our experience seems inseparably tied up with some specific historically mediated way of speaking about it. In other words, there are no metalanguages of the self, that is, no language of the self that can be seen to be true in the same way at all times. This is so because the language of self-description is not 'ontologically neutral,' that is, the language of self-description does not leave the self substantially unaffected. This is so because every self is, in part, a social product. Who we are is inseparably tied up with the accounts about us which we inherit from our society. The great texts of *Geisteswissenschaften* are sometimes the direct source of these accounts but more often than not they are commentaries on them which extend and criticize them in various ways. Thus an account which offers us viable self-knowledge does not stand in relation to us as "a copy next to the real world, but it is the latter in the heightened truth of its being."[13] Instances of self-knowledge take us from our common social condition of being immersed in the deceptive half-light of everyday language and cultural biases and raise us to a heightened condition of self-awareness, which can be both a deepening of our involvement with these languages and a critical distancing of ourselves from them. For example, Gadamer points to the tragic drama in which the spectator may come to see her own situation in light of the disproportion between guilt and fate that marks the life of the tragic figure, but this seeing is not possible apart from a prior vocabulary about guilt and fate with which the spectator has already somehow identified and it does not entail an uncritical acceptance of such categories but may in fact expose their limitations. Gadamer describes this change as a 'deepening' of the spectator's 'continuity' with himself.[14] This deepening continuity that emerges from the tragedy makes it necessary to describe this truth as involving something more than 'correspondence.'

Gadamer's second reason for rejecting the correspondence theory has to do with his contention that the 'giveness' of the self is not, in principle, unchanging over time. According to Gadamer, we are so molded by our temporal circumstances that human beings can change substantially over time. Consider Gadamer's claim about the Western evolution of the self: "The history of our Western soul, which begins with the Socratic question, which deepens with Christian inwardness and which ends with the emphasis on freedom and personal right has shaped us irrevocably."[15] If this is so, there cannot be a metalanguage of the self, that is, an account of the self that is true in all its variations over time. So dependent is our being on the historical circumstances of our lives that Gadamer rejects, for example, existentialist accounts of our freedom as a spontaneous self-definition and insists instead that "the self we are does not possess itself; one could say that it happens."[16] As we have been saying, a principle way in which the self 'happens' in history is through the historically contingent languages of self-description that permeate our experience and thereby determine who we are. Language itself is the bearer of history or tradition and it is by participating in language that history often affects our self-identity.

One thing that remains obscure in this rejection of correspondence theories of truth in the realm of the human sciences is exactly how Gadamer's proposed alternative understanding of the relation between the self and the language of self-description can be spelled out in compelling detail. For example, it remains obscure how language hooks up with a human being in such an intimate way as to give rise to a sense of self. If language somehow determines the self, why is it the case that some language is obviously more adequate to the self? If language doesn't simply describe who we are but in some sense defines us, why can't any language about the self be adopted? An obvious response to this enigma would be to reject Gadamer's theory as absurd, on the grounds that some languages obviously do 'correspond' better to the self, hence their greater claim to truth. I think, however, such a response is premature. Gadamer suggests that although the self is linguistically structured in such a way that there is no metalanguage of the self, that is, no one account of the self true of all selves in all historical circumstances, it does not follow that we simply choose a language of self-description arbitrarily; a language of self-description is not chosen in a way analogous to the way some existentialists say we make a choice of a human project. On the contrary, the self is not chosen but always finds itself already somewhat determined by virtue of the fact that it exists, so to speak, *in medias lingua*, that is, in the midst of a native language, spoken in a certain cultural context with certain implicit understandings of the meaning of selfhood and its possibilities. This is not to say that we find ourselves fully determined and fully aware of who we are. Instead we find ourselves *in medias lingua*, that is, on the way to many different accounts of the self and its possibilities. This implies that the self as a linguisitically mediated reality is both determined and awaiting further determination and definition. In this sense Gadamer speaks of 'true' languages about the self as both describing us and defining us. I think this is what Gadamer means by the claim that certain languages are true of us by virtue of giving us a "deeper continuity with ourselves." This seems possible only if the self is neither an indeterminate 'nothing' nor a fully determinate 'essence'. Instead one may say that we find ourselves *in medias lingua* as *underdetermined*, that is, as a being with certain *finite* possibilities of self-understanding. Thus, according to Gadamer, language both limits who I am, by limiting how I can understand myself, and it opens up possibilities for who I might become by offering more than one possible 'true' linguistic amount of myself. This implies, on the one hand, that language always gives certain understandings of ourselves that are intractable and noncircumventable elements of our identity. On the other hand, these same inalienable linguistic inheritances can be mediated, that is, refined, criticized, and modified in such a way that they are transformed without ever being entirely left behind. Consider Gadamer's claim that "history does not belong to us, but we belong to it. Long before we understand ourselves through the process of self-examination, we understand ourselves in a self-evident way in the family, society and state in which we live."[17] If this is so, it suggests that there is something truly inalienable about the self-understanding inherent in everyday speech, which can be modified but never completely transcended. Thus there is a sense in which we are both given and awaiting further determination.

This is where Gadamer's understanding of the role of the human sciences in self-knowledge comes into clearer view. On the one hand, we are linguistic beings determined by the historically contingent possibilities for self-understanding inherent in our everyday speech. Everyday speech or ordinary language is, so to speak, the fount from which our self-understanding flows, but this source is in need of refinement, criticism, depth, etc. This original source of self-knowledge contains, in Hegel's words, "at once too much and too little,"[18] too many possible ways of understanding myself and too few sufficiently complex, consistent, and nuanced lines of self-understanding. In coming to terms with this situation of everyday speech, we cannot leave it behind, but we must find a way to mediate it, that is, to organize, sort out, deepen, and refine my initial sense of self. The great texts of the *Geisteswissenschaffen* offer us just the possibilities of self-understanding that everyday language lacks. Moreover by appropriating (or being appropriated by) some linguistic accounts of our experience, our sense of self evolves through history beyond its point of inception. The great texts of the *Geisteswissenschaften*—particularly philosophy and literature—contain the most refined, detailed, and multifaceted languages of the self that our culture has to offer. It is by appropriating these linguistic accounts (or aspects of them) that the self first gains a highly nuanced self-consciousness. When this happens the self begins to emerge in a richer intelligibility, one that, as it were, trades the breadth of ordinary language for the depth of some refined, nuanced, and critical language about ourselves. In this way, which I have described very roughly, the self gains a more highly mediated and historically limited sense of self, but one that is richer in specific detail and concrete sense of possibility. Through this process of 'linguistic mediation' the self begins a process of self-determination through language, which is potentially infinite or temporally open.[19]

Thus the human sciences have as their task not the discovery of some hidden but fully determinate human essence but the dialectical mediation of everyday speech about the self. In this way the human sciences attempt to "deepen our continuity with ourselves." The human sciences offer us more refined, more developed accounts of the possibilities of self-understanding inherent in ordinary language. In so doing, they do not cure us of the "bewitching" tendencies inherent in everyday speech, as Wittgenstein would define the task of philosophy. The therapeutic metaphor is misleading, for there is no way either to free ourselves from language or to so refine it as to escape its multifarious meanings. Thus the primary purpose of the human sciences is not purgative but involves a deepening of our involvement with language. Gadamer would describe this process as "speculative mediation," that is, the exploration, analysis, and further development of the meaing inherent in the different languages of self.

The human sciences, particularly philosophy and literature, are speculative in the original sense of a *speculum* or mirror, that is, their task is to show how language can be reflected back into itself in such a way that new meaning emerges.[20] Language is the mirror we hold up to language such that the play that results between different linguistic accounts generates new meaning.

Gadamer describes this process as both play (Spiel)[21] and dialogue (Gespräch)[22]. The human sciences are like a dialogue in that the participants must always presuppose some shared meaning and concern if they are to talk. Dialogue picks up on a topic always in the middle, that is, with a shared preunderstanding of the language and subject matter, and it is carried through successfully only when the participants give themselves to the possibilities of understanding or meaning that emerge between them. When participants give themselves to the meanings that emerge in the dialogue, it is like play in that the people involved become immersed in a self-sustaining dynamic that transcends the individual consciousness of each. In a manner analogous to the way in which the ball in various games dictates the movements of the players, so in a genuine dialogue the meanings that emerge in the dialogue propel each participant toward understandings that were not foreseen or intended. Thus the 'logic' of the dialogue often contains possibilities of meaning that emerge only in the dialogical context. In this sense, the self gains knowledge of itself by participating in language, that is, by allowing different aspects of our linguistic tradition to interface or dialectically mediate each other and thereby generate new insight and meaning. This interfacing can take place on many levels, but we are speaking of instances where it takes place primarily between 'everyday' accounts of the self's experience and the more highly complex accounts found in the texts of the human sciences.[23] When this happens the self participates in a movement of meaning in which it is articulated to itself on a variety of levels.

One can at least begin to get a sense of what this means if one reflects on how linguistic accounts affect and transform our relation to time. This same event of self-determination through language mediates historicity itself in such a way that the ephmerality and discrete, pointlike nature of the present movement is mitigated by language's capacity to open up a realm of ideal, intersubjective meaning. This enables the self to understand its being as persisting *through* time by reference to these linguistic accounts that structure the meaning of its experience *over* time. In other words, by allowing certain linguistic accounts to structure certain temporally discrete experiences analogously, I gain the possibility of a relatively stable, temporally unified sense of what these experiences mean. In short, I gain a sense of who I am (at least in these commonly structured experiences) through a linguistic account. Gadamer suggests that it is through a linguistically informed memory that I re-collect myself out of my fleeting experience and hence gain a sense of my continuity over time. Moreover it is by this linguistically informed memory that I imagine and anticipate the futrure. In this way all of my future-oriented actions are connected with a linguistically structured past. My whole life is held together by these linguistic accounts. As a result, the potential discreteness and uniqueness of every temporal moment is mitigated by transtemporal linguistic accounts that lift it not out of history but above a mode of temporality that is nothing but a series of unconnected, unintelligible, fleeting moments.

For example, by adopting a certain language of moral experience—Kant's for instance—my moral experience takes on a structure that classifies my motives in terms of 'heteronomous' and 'autonomous' motives and my acts in terms of their conformity (or lack therof) to the categorical imperative. Moreover, I gain the possibility of having a sense of moral self-development by learning to see my experiences in terms of the development of increasing 'autonomy' and 'good will.' In all of this I seem to gain a certain kind of linguistically mediated, intersubjective sense of self (as a member of the 'kingdom of ends') as well as a sense of a personal history that allows me to connect my discrete temporal experiences in terms of analogous structures of meaning and a particular *telos*.

2

This event of self-determination through language is, if my interpretation is valid, at the very center of Gadamer's understanding of the meaning and sources of self-knowledge. My rough description given above was not meant, however, to be a substitute for a more detailed analysis of Gadamer's view of the self and the arguments that can be given in its support. It is to this theory of the self that we now turn.

Two features are essential to Gadamer's ontology of the self: the nonsubstantial nature of the self and its thoroughgoing temporality. Let us begin with the former.

According to Gadamer, the self is nonsubstantial in that it is not a thing that somehow stands behind or under our changing experience. In this sense, the self is not identical with any natural type, like a member of the species homo sapiens, neither is it a soullike noumenal being that persists throughout time and perhaps beyond it. Gadamer is clear in his insistence that "there is neither 'I' nor 'thou' as isolated, substantial realities. I may say 'thou' or I may refer to myself over gainst a 'thou' but a *common understanding* precedes these situations."[24]

What this suggests but does not really make plain is that the self is inseparable from its self-understanding. The self is nonsubstantial because 'it' cannot be separated from its self-understanding. In this sense, when Gadamer speaks of 'self-consciousness' or coming to self-consciousness, he is not talking about the 'consciousness' of Husserl's phenomenology with its 'ego' or Sartre's pure 'spontaneity,' but he is talking about a sense or understanding of who I am as a being in a specific historical context who is engaged in certain linguistically mediated ways of life. Gadamer is not interested in the 'self' that is discussed and debated in the controversies between various forms of dualism and materialism. Rather than view the self as some mysterious substance either inhabiting a body or somehow 'produced' by and reducible to complex physical processes, Gadamer suggests we view ourselves more concretely as we really are in history, that is, as a specific 'nonsubstantial' way of existing that is informed, directed, and organized by a linguistically mediated awareness of what we are about.

This notion of self is highly reminiscent of Heidegger's claim that *Dasein* is that being which is its understanding. Gadamer owes a great deal to Heidegger's account of human being, as *Dasein*, that is, as a being that is what it is by taking up historically contingent possibilities of life and understanding and projecting them (and changing them in the process) toward an uncertain and open future. These possiblities are always understood in a historically specific way and projected in a historical situation that is not of our making. In committing ourselves consciously or unconsciously to some of the possibilities implicit in our linguistic and historical context, we gain simultaneously the beginnings of a self-understanding that will both guide us and change with us through time.[25]

Because all of us share in this prior, ineradicable relation to language Gadamer can argue that "the focus of subjectivity is a distorting mirror. The self-awareness of the individual is only a flickering in the closed circuit of historical life."[26] In other words, there is no 'pure' alinguistic intuition of the self but, according to Gadamer, all self-knowledge is linguistically mediated; there is no self-awareness as such but only various self-understandings that are inseparable from certain historically specific ways of speaking about the self.

Gadamer would argue that even the philosophical attempts to locate and describe the essential core of selfhood, the transcendental ego, failed to come up with an ahistorical metalanguage of the self. For example, Kant, Hegel, and Husserl all in some fashion speak of a transcendental 'I', but there is no body of univocal truths about this 'I' that can be distilled from their writings. In each case, the claim to have discovered a metalanguage of the self is dubious because the actual language of self-description that each thinker develops cannot be understood apart from the historical concerns of each philosopher.[27] In the case of Kant, the epistemological problems of Wolfe's scholastic rationalism, Hume's scepticism, Newtonian physics, and pietistic morality dominate his conception of the thinking self. In the case of Hegel, the overcoming of the tensions that existed between Enlightenment and romantic views of self and more fundamentally, the reconcillation of Greek and Christian cultures, undergird his concept of *Geist*. In the case of Husserl, the rise of 'psychologism', '*Lebensphilosophie*', 'existentialism', and the concommitant demise of 'European man' determine Husserl's concept of the transcendental ego. If this is so, the 'identity' that each of these thinkers investigated involved an inseparable element of historical contingency, that is, it can be shown that they did not understand the self apart from the historical circumstances in which they thought. The 'I' as such was never intuited directly, but every understanding of the 'I-think', whether it was the merely formal Kantian transcendental unity of apperception, Hegel's notion of *Geist*, or the Husserlian concept of a transcendental ego, presupposed a historically mediated 'we-speak' that, as it were, wove itself inseparably into the fabric of self-identity. Insofar as any understanding cannot be divorced from this 'we-speak', that is, the way in which the community of inquirers has come to speak about the self, self-understanding is inseparably tied to the historically contingent languages or linguistic accounts in terms of which we make ourselves intelligible to ourselves and others. More mundane examples may make the point plainer.

Many of us have appropriated (or been appropriated by) a language about who we are, which entails that we be 'productive' and 'self-sufficient'; that we 'pull our weight' and be a 'contributing member' of some social group. Many of us have in fact so 'identified' with this cliche-ridden language that it is impossible for us to think of the meaning and dignity of our lives without some such self-understanding and the practices it entails. This well-known 'work ethic' has become so fused into our identity that even though we may realize that this interpretive framework has historically contingent roots and that 'we' are logically distinct from this language, it may nevertheless be empirically impossible for us to 'locate' ourselves and others in terms completely devoid of our 'productive value'. In this sense, a very real aspect of who we *are* has been determined by the self-understanding or self-interpretation that we have in large part inherited from the historical circumstances into which we were born. Or consider as another example the fact that many of us have, in the course of our intellectual development and education, 'identified' with certain schools of thought to such an extent that although we can conceive of thinking otherwise, we nevertheless find ourselves coming back again and again to certain fundamental approaches to issues. This is not to say that intellectual change and development are impossible—such is obviously not the case—but once one has learned to think like a Kantian, Hegelian, Wittgensteinian, or Heideggarian, one often finds that despite one's intentions to be completely open-minded and objective that certain points of view and ways of approaching a problem suggest themselves almost as a matter of course. Whatever freedom one has in such matters is always limited and qualified in certain ways, because who we are is always a function of some linguistically mediated aspect of our historical situation.

One may respond that this argument concerning our failure to develop a metalanguage of the self is inconclusive because it rests on examples, which while not valid examples of a metalanguage of self, nevertheless logically do not preclude the development of such a metalanguage. This is a plausible response but one that Gadamer is prepared to meet. Gadamer can respond, quite plausibly, that all metalanguages, however formal or seemingly ahistorical, must be understood in historically specific, contingent contexts. It is from these changing contexts that the conditions necessary for translating any supposed metalanguage into concrete understanding derive. This is to say that the conditions of meaning of any language depend on the changing context into which it is spoken. If this is so, meaning will and must change with history, and hence there can never be a truly ahistorical metalanguage of the self.

This brings us to a consideration of the thoroughly temporal or historical nature of this nonsubstantial self. We can begin by pointing out that the self is historical in the sense that the possibilities it has for being-in-the-world are always inherited from the past, over which it has no control. Gadamer argues that this inheritance from the past implies that all human consciousness is always informed by 'prejudices' (*Vorurteile*).[28] The concept of 'prejudice' is intended by Gadamer to refer to the fact that "all self-knowledge proceeds from what is historically pregiven, what we call, with Hegel, 'substance', because it is the basis of all subjective meaning and attitude and hence both prescribes and limits every possibility of understanding."[29]

This implies that Gadamer understands 'prejudice' in the sense of an intersubjective prejudgment that informs our initial orientation toward things but not in terms of a one-sided, idiosyncratic, and necessarily irrational or false point of view. "Prejudices are not necessarily unjustified and erroneous, so that they inevitably distort the truth. In fact, the historicity of our existence entails that prejudices, in the literal sense of the word, constitute the initial directedness of our whole ability to experience. Prejudices are biases of our openness to the world."[30] Gadamer is not saying, however, that our prejudices cannot be altered or criticized from within language and history and not from some standpoint outside. In this way we can say that there is another sense in which our self-understanding is historical, namely, it is worked out *over* time. This is to say that the sense of ourselves that we initially inherit from the past is always powerfully present in our self-understanding, but in an evolving fashion. The influence of prejudice evolves and changes as our self-understanding changes. We work out our self-understanding in terms of the past, but the past is always understood and critically accessed in terms of the present with its (potentially) unique needs and genuinely new developments. Moreover I work out my self-understanding over time only as I project my evolving sense of self toward a contingent future, which may or may not allow my initial sense of self to continue to develop along lines that are unequivocally continuous with the past. Thus the past may always be with us in some sense, but we are not locked into a past understanding of ourselves that history, as it were, has condemned us to live out. History may limit our possibilities of self-understanding but it does not dictate them to us verbatim. We are historical in that we live out of a past and toward a future that is connected to it in essential ways, but neither as prisoners of time who are condemned to repeat an identical mirror image of the past nor as passive sufferers of a fate that we can in no way control. In a very rough way one might say that our intellectual freedom cannot be understood as either an ability to generate possibilities of understanding de nova or from some set of transcendental rules. Our intellectual freedom consists in the *limited* explanation, analysis, criticism, or development of possibilities of understanding that we have already inherited.[31] History imposes on our intellectual freedom a finitude in the sense that all understanding involves what Gadamer calls a "fusion of horizons" (*Horizontsver-schmelzung*)[32] between past, present, and future in which we are neither complete masters nor docile slaves but participants in a broader movement of meaning.

If the self *is* this historical way of being and not a substance with an inherent, unchanging, intelligible structure of its own, it is no wonder that it and the truth about it prove so elusive. The very number of possibilities I inherit and may realize, the variety of ways in which I may understand these possibilities, and the uncertainty of their eventual realization conspire to make my way of being in the world an elusive, tenuous, and possibly contradictory reality. Time itself keeps my way of being open to change. If this is so, any self-knowledge must be tentative and provisional. As Heidegger would say, there are no 'eternal truths' about Dasein. Moreover, history often leaves us with a way of being containing contradictions that may or may not be resolvable. In all cases, the self is guaranteed neither temporal closure nor logical unity. At best, history allows us to aspire to such goals but it does not necessarily foster their realization.

But if the self is so dependent on its linguistically mediated historical circumstances for its being, and these factors conspire to make its reality intrinsically tenuous, elusive, and possibly at odds with itself, one may wonder how the self can gain any valid understanding of itself at all. Given this state of affairs, there can be no doubt that we are in need of self-knowledge, but it is questionable whether we have the critical means to find our way in this linguistic-historical flux.

Gadamer is aware of this need and the problems that threaten its satisfaction. Although he never retracts his position on the dependency of the self on language and history, he suggests that we operate with a critical epistemic ideal that guides us in our search for self-knowlege. Gadamer calls this ideal the 'anticipation of completeness' (*Vorgriff der Vollkommenheit*).[33] This ideal suggests, I think, a set of practical guidelines that guide the pursuit of truth in the human sciences. The German '*Vollkommenheit*'[34] suggests minimally an ideal of 'comprehensiveness', that is, the ideal of approaching an exhaustive account of phenomenon in its present historical context; but I would suggest that the meaning of 'Vollkommenheit' extends beyond this ideal to include guidelines or "rules of thumb" such as depth, inclusivity, and architectonic structure or teleological order. It's important to point out, however, that these guidelines are *not* criteria or rules in the sense of either necessary or sufficient conditions. Gadamer does not think we can be this rigorous in the realm of self-knowledge. Instead these guidelines may be thought of as heuristic ideals that guide us in many situations of inquiry but do not bind us universally.

3

As we have already suggested , the first guideline may be called *comprehensiveness*. Very generally, this ideal insists that a true account of some aspect of experience address all *essential* aspects of phenomenon or realm of experience. This implies that a linguistic account that is truly able to effect truth in our lives must be comprehensive in the sense that it speaks to the essentials of my past experience in this realm as well as my present experience. In this sense, this guideline is not really formal, but historical; it bears on the *essentials* of some historically mediated experience. As such, it must not leave any essential aspect of this experience unaccounted for. Without this kind of comprehensiveness, any realm of experience will be one-sided, and as such its truth will be threatened by distortion.

But if *comprehensiveness* demands that a linguistic account address all the essentials of my past and present experience of some phenomenon, it also implies a certain ability to anticipate or deal with future experience. In this sense comprehensiveness implies a second "rule of thumb," namely, *semantic depth*. A true account of experience is not only comprehensive with regard to past and present experience, it also has depths or levels of meaning that either create new experience or that we are able to illuminate it as it arises from the fertile ground of history. A true account should be able to 'prove itself true' over time by extending the reader's present experience as it arises. Thus, for example, a text like Kant's *Critique of Practical Reason* has a kind of suggestive, near inexhaustible depth that makes it somehow able to enrich our moral experience over time as well as incorporate new experiences into the horizons of the account's intelligibility. If a linguistic account cannot do this, its truth is seen as limited and superficial. To the extent that a linguistic account fails to be deeply suggestive, its ability to cope with the new experience that may arise out of our historicity is greatly curtailed and its truth-value will be shortlived.

Semantic depth, however, also seems to include something like the inclusivity of an account. By *inclusivity* I understand the ability of a text to incorporate accounts of the same experience given by other texts into its accounts of the phenomenon. An account that is *inclusive* in this sense has a kind of comprehensiveness that demonstrates its superior truth over other texts in that it can give a more comprehensive interpretation of some phenomenon that is suggestive of both the strengths and weaknesses of other accounts. In this sense inclusivity is taken as a mark of truth because it has the potential to introduce an even greater consistency into experience insofar as it can incorporate the potentially conflicting accounts of other texts into one consistent, comprehensive, and suggestive account.

Lastly, a text that yields self-knowledge often functions *architectonically* or *teleologically* with respect to our experience. It functions architectonically in that it orders and structures our experience into an intelligible pattern. It does this, to speak very roughly, by ordering our experience in terms of primary, secondary, and tertiary aspects of experience or in terms of what is more important, less important, and least important for understanding some experience. It would seem that this kind of architectonic ordering can occur only vis-a-vis some *telos* by virtue of which different aspects of experience arrange themselves into an ordered whole. To appeal to Kant once again for an example, moral experience can organize itself in light of the development of 'good will'. The will that is concerned to do the right thing, simply because it is the right thing, is not concerned with the heteronomous motives of pleasure, pain, and personal profit. Such aspects of our moral experience are seen as secondary and not essential to the 'autonomous' grounds of duty.

4

There are many questions that should be asked at this point, if only space would allow it. Questions such as how does Gadamer propose we choose between conflicting accounts of some experience, all of which meet the conditions of *Vollkommenheit*? How do we choose, for example, between a Kant and a Nietzsche on the nature of the moral life or between a Hegel and a Wittgenstein on the proper goal of philosophical thought? Gadamer seems to admit that such choices exist, and the choice, he argues, is not made arbitrarily but pragmatically in terms of which account better meets the intellectual and/or practical needs of the historical moment. This is say that accounts that meet these conditions are taken as true and compelling only when an element of historical relevance is also present. This implies that 'truth' seems to come down to that which is 'binding' on inquiry, that which cannot be gainsaid or circumvented *in the present historical context*. In this sense, Gadadmer writes, "Experience teaches us to recognize reality. What is properly gained from all experience, then, is to know what is. But 'what is', here, is not this or that thing, but 'what cannot be done away with' (was nicht mehr umzustossen ist -Ranke)."[35]

Thus, it may be said that Gadamer gives a pragmatic twist to Hegel's dictum that "philosophy is its time grasped in thought."

Of course, this still leaves us with the possibility that more than one account will meet the standards of '*Vollkommenheit*', even when they are applied with an eye to historical context. This could leave us, in some cases, with a 'pluralistic' or maybe even an 'antinomian' truth. Suffice it to say that such a conclusion warrants further critical reflection, if for no other reason than that Gadamer's theory of self-knowledge threatens the dispersal and possible loss of the self through language.

It may be plausibly argued that Gadamer's rejection of the substantial ntature of the self in favor of a temporal account of the self as a linguistically mediated way of being-in-the-world seems helpful and plausible, particularly in light of how it is that the human sciences gives us self-knowledge. It does seem to be the case that we know ourselves only through certain linguisitc accounts of our experience, which not only structure that experience but contribute to its repeatability and development through time. But one can ask the question whether this account of the self doesn't implicitly divide the self against itself. I mean by this that insofar as there is no one language of experience, but only different languages about different realms of human experience, there seems to be no *one* self to which these various languages somehow refer. If the self is what it is in the linguistically mediated ways of being-in-the-world, and there are many ways of being-in-the-world (even for 'one' self), arent' we forced to conclude paradoxically that there are as many selves in each one of us as there are linguistically mediated ways of being? Isn't it possible—indeed, isn't it the case—that some people are, for example, Kantians in their account of knowledge and Nietzscheans in their account of the moral life? Or more mundanely, isn't it possible to have one kind of linguistically mediated understanding of one's self in one's career and another in one's family life and yet another in one's political or religious life? Gadamer's account of the self with its implication that we are as many selves as we are linguisitically mediated ways of being in the world may contain a truth—indeed it often seems that we are at odds with ourselves and we struggle constantly for a more unified sense of self—but it seems very paradoxical that an account of self-knowledge should come up with such a conclusion. Given this account can we talk of *a* self at all? The self as some kind of distinct unity seems to be lost in Gadamer's account. Ironically, perhaps our very linguistic habits about the self seem to presuppose a single self and not just many different ways of linguistically mediated being in the world. Hence our interminable discussions about personal identity. If Gadamer is right, such discussions can now be dismissed as discussions of a pseudoproblem. Nevertheless I doubt that the search for a unified self will die that easily. Gadamer's account of the self is not quite synonomous with Hume's theory of the self as a bundle of impressions, but the self according to Gadamer seems no more than a loose bundle of linguistically mediated, temporally extended experiences. This seems a marked improvement over Hume in that language in Gadamer's theory makes the self accessible but in Gadamer the self's knowability is very tenuous by virtue of the fact that the self remains scattered (*zerstreut*) through its various linguistic accounts. It seems the more we search for self-knowledge, that is, the more we allow the great linguistic accounts of the *Geisteswissenschaften* to mediate our experience, the further away we remain from our goal. The more we appropriate refined, nuanced, and varied accounts of our experience, the more our awareness of the nonunified nature of the self is brought home to us. Only a new "phenomenology of spirit" that would demonstrate the immanent and necessary telos of our ways of being would give a unified self but this kind of revival of Hegel Gadamer explicitly rejects.

Gadamer is fond of quoting Alcmaeon's words that "man perishes because he cannot join the beginning with the end." Perhaps this is a fitting way to summarize Gadamer's position. The idea of man as a unified being, even a potentially unified being, perishes if Gadamer is right, because there is no one language in which we can join our many ways of being into a comprehensive, comprehensible whole. In this sense, we may follow certain teleological lines of development without ever arriving at a *telos*;[36] we are, forever and always, "on the way."

NOTES

1. Hans-Georg Gadamer, *Truth and Method*, (New York: Seabury Press, 1975), pp. xii. Hereafter cited as *TM*. All quotes from this work are from this translation unless otherwise indicated.

2. *TM*, p. xiii.

3. See *TM*, pp. 73–152. An entire section of Gadamer's magnum opus is devoted to this issue.

4. Hans-Georg Gadamer, "Philosophy and Literature" *Man and World*, 18. See also TM, pp. 142ff.

5. Hans-Georg Gadamer, *Reason in the Age of Science*, trans. Frederick G. Lawrence, (Cambridge: MIT Press, 1982), pp. 69ff.

6. *TM*, p. xii.

7. Rüdiger Bubner, *Modern German Philosophy*, trans. Eric Mathews, (Cambridge: Cambridge University Press, 1981), p. 66. Richard Rorty, *Philosophy and the Mirror of Nature* (Princeton: Princeton University Press, 1979), pp. 357ff; Claus von Bormann, "Die Zweideutigkeit der Hermeneutische Erfahrung" in *Hermeneutik und Ideologiekritik* (Frankfurt: Suhrkamp Verlag, 1971), pp. 83–119; Reiner Wiehl, "Heidegger, Hermeneutics, and Ontology", pp. 460–484.

8. *TM*, p. 432.

9. Hans-Georg Gadamer, *Kleine Schriften*, vol. 1 (Tübingen: J. C. B. Mohr, 1967), p. 42. (Author's translation).

10. Aristotle, *Nichomachean Ethics*, 1094b, 15–20.

11. Gadamer's phenomenological background also inclines him in this ontological direction toward "the things themselves." This orientation may also be behind Gadamer's tendency to give priority to suggestive, concrete descriptions of instances of truth in the human sciences and thus to neglect some of the 'theoretical' implications of his insights.

12. Gadamer sees himself as reviving the Aristotelian notion of practical reason or 'phronesis' in order to broaden it into a model of human rationality as such. See *TM*, pp. 278ff; and Richard Bernstein, ''From Hermeneutics to Praxis,'' pp. 000–000.

13. *TM*, p. 117.

14. Ibid.

15. Hans-Georg Gadamer, ''Historical Transformation of Reason,'' in *Rationality Today* ed. by T.E. Geraets (Ottowa: University of Ottowa Press, 1979), p. 12.

16. Hans-Georg Gadamer, *Philosophical Hermeneutics*, ed. and trans. by David Linge (Berkeley: University of California Press, 1967), p. 55. Hereafter cited as *PH*.

17. *TM*, p. 245.

18. G.W.F. Hegel, *Phenomenology of Spirit*, trans. A. Miller (Oxford: Oxford University Press, 1977), p. 308–9. Gadamer's understanding of the role language plays in self-knowledge seems indebted to Hegel. Hegel certainly anticipated it. Consider Hegel's claim that language ''is the real existence of the pure self as self; in speech self-consciousness, qua independent, separate individuality comes into existence so that it exists for others; otherwise the 'I', this pure 'I' is non-existent, it is not there. Lanaguage, however, contains it, the real 'I' is . . . an objectivity which has in it the true nature of the 'I'. The 'I' as this particular 'I' but equally the universal 'I'.'' Ibid.

19. Gadamer describes himself as an advocate of the Hegelian ''bad infinite.'' See his *Reason in the Age of Science* (Cambridge: MIT Press, 1982), p. 40.

20. See *TM*, p. 425ff.

21. See Tm, pp. 41ff, 91ff, 114ff, and 446ff.

22. See TM, pp. 163, 165, 330ff, and 487ff.

23. Gadamer's insights into self-knowledge and language do not lead him to affirm a Derridean textualism—ontological appropriation makes reference to the self a possibility.

24.*PH*, p. 7. My emphasis.

25. Martin Heidegger, *Being and Time*, trans. John Macquarrie and Edward Robinson (New York: Harper & Row, 1962), pp. 150–53.

26. *TM*, p. 245.

27. See ibid. p. xxiv.

28. See *TM*, p. 238ff.

29. Ibid., p. 269.

30. *PH*, p. 9.

31. A possible example of how history both limits us and impels us toward new understanding can be found in the unique moral demands that living in a world with nuclear weapons places on all of us. Whatever 'solution' is possible to this dilemma will have to involve genuinely new perspectives on ourselves as well as perspectives that are somehow integrally related to past moral understandings.

32. *TM*, pp. 273ff, 337ff.

33. *TM*, p. 261. The ideal of '*Vollkommenheit*' seems reminiscent of the Kantian and Hegelian claim that reason is driven by the need for ever-greater comprehensiveness or exhaustiveness. So much so, in fact, that reason can be

content only with the 'infinite,' be that 'God' or the 'Absolute.' One may ask Gadamer, however, how he can speak of an ideal of 'Vollkommenheit' in light of his insistence on the intractable finitude of our condition?

34. 'Vollkommenheit' can be translated as 'perfection' or 'completeness.' 'Completeness' seems the more relevant translation, although context seems to allow for both.

35. TM, p. 320.

36. Gadamer seems to think of history as "teleological without a telos" in that certain events, developments, trends, etc., have an imminent telos without contributing in some way to an ultimate telos of history as such. This phrase, reminiscient of Kant's "purposiveness without purpose," is taken from Gadamer's critical discussion of Ranke. Despite the critical context, it seems to be applicable to Gadamer. See TM, p. 179.

Hermeneutics and Critical Theory

III

A Review of Gadamer's Truth and Method

Jürgen Habermas

Translated by Fred Dallmayr and Thomas McCarthy

1

General linguistics is not the only alternative to a historically oriented language analysis that immerses itself in the pluralism of language games without being able to justify the language of analysis itself. To break through the grammatical barriers of individual linguistic totalities we do not need to follow Chomsky in leaving the dimension of ordinary language. Not only the distance of a theoretical language from the primary languages secures the unity of analytical reason in the pluralism of language games. Apparently every ordinary language grammar itself furnishes the possibility to transcend the language it determines, that is, to translate from and into other languages. To be sure, the anguish of translation brings to consciousness in a particularly clear manner the objective connection of linguistic structure and world conception, the unity of word and thing. To procure a hearing for a text in a foreign language requires often enough a new text rather than a translation in the ordinary sense. Since Humboldt the sciences of language have been informed with the intention of demonstrating the close correlation of linguistic form and worldview. But even the demonstration of the individuality of linguistic structure, leading to resignation in the face of the ''un-translatability'' of traditional formulations, is based on the daily experience that we are never locked within a single grammar. Rather, the first grammar that we learn to master already puts us in a position to step out of it and to interpret what is foreign, to make comprehensible what initially is incomprehensible, to assimilate in our own words what at first escapes them. The relativism of linguistic worldviews and the monadology of language games are equally illusory. For we become aware of the boundaries drawn for us by the grammar of ordinary language by means of the same grammar—Hegel's dialectic of the limit formulates the experience of the translator. The concept of translation is itself dialectical; only where we lack transformation rules permitting the establishment of a deductive relation between languages through substitution and where an exact "translation" is excluded do we need that kind of interpretation that we commonly call translation. It expresses in one language a state of affairs that cannot be literally expressed in it but can nevertheless be rendered "in other words." H. G. Gadamer calls this experience, which is at best the basis of hermeneutics, the hermeneutic experience.

> Hermeneutic experience is the corrective through which thinking reason escapes the spell of language; and it is itself linguistically constituted. . . . To be sure, the multiplicity of languages with which linguistics is concerned also poses a question for us. But this is merely the single question: how is every language, in spite of its differences from other languages, supposed to be in a position to say everything it wants? Linguistics teaches us that every language does this in its own way. For our part, we pose the question: how does the same unity of thought and speech assert itself everywhere in the multiplicity of these ways of saying, in such a way that every written tradition can be understood?[1]

Hermeneutics defines its task as a countermove to the linguistic descriptions of different grammars. However, to preserve the unity of reason in the pluralism of languages, it does not rely on a metatheory of ordinary language grammars, as does the program of general linguistics. Hermeneutics mistrusts any mediatizing of ordinary languages and refuses to step out of their dimension; instead it makes use of the tendency to self-transcendence embedded in linguistic practice. Languages themselves possess the potential of a reason that, while expressing itself in the particularity of a specific grammar, simultaneously reflects on its limits and negates them as particular. Although always bound up in language, reason always transcends particular languages; it lives in language only by destroying the particularities of languages through which alone it is incarnated. Of course, it can cleanse itself of the dross of one particularity only in passing over into another. This intermittent generality is certified in the act of translation. It is reflected formally in a characteristic that is common to all traditional languages and guarantees their transcendental unity, namely, in the fact that they are in principle inter-translatable.

Wittgenstein, the logician, interpreted "translation" as a transformation according to general rules. Because the grammar of language games cannot be reconstructed according to general rules, he conceived linguistic understanding (*Sprachverstehen*) from the point of view of socialization, as training in a cultural form of life. It makes sense to conceive of the learning of "language in general" according to this model. But we can study the problem of linguistic understanding by focusing attention initially on the less fundamental process of learning a foreign language. To learn a language is not identical with learning to speak; it already presupposes the mastery of at least one language. With this primary language we have learned the rules that make it possible not only to achieve understanding within the framework of this one grammar but also to make foreign language understandable. In learning a specific language, we have at the same time learned how one learns languages in general. We assimilate foreign languages through translation. Of course, as soon as we have mastered them, we no longer need translation. Translations are necessary only when understanding is disturbed. On the other hand, difficulties in achieving understanding arise even in conversations within our own language. Communication takes place according to rules that are shared by the partners in discussion. But these rules not only make consensus possible; they also include the possibility of putting an end to situations of disturbed understanding. To converse means both to understand one another in principle and to be able to make oneself understood when necessary. The role of the discussion partner includes virtually the role of the interpreter, that is, of someone who can not only converse in one language, but can bring about an understanding between different languages. The role of the interpreter is not different in principle from that of the translator. Translation is only the extreme variant of an achievement upon which every normal conversation must depend.

> Thus the case of translation makes us conscious of linguisticality [*Sprachlichkeit*] as the medium in which understanding is achieved; for in translation understanding must first be artfully produced through an explicit contrivance. [It] is certainly not the the normal case of conversation. Translation is also not the normal case of our behavior toward a foreign language. . . . When

one really masters a language, there is no longer a need for translation; indeed translation seems impossible. To understand a language is thus not yet at all a real understanding and does not include any interpretative process; it is rather an accomplishment of life [Lebensvollzug]. For one understands a language in living in it—a proposition that holds true not only for living languages but, as is well known, for dead languages as well. The hermeneutic problem is thus not a problem of the correct mastery of language but one of correction coming to an understanding about what happens in the medium of language. . . . Only where it is possible to come to an understanding in language, through talking to one another, can understanding and coming to an understanding be at all a problem. Being dependent on the translation of an interpreter is an extreme case that doubles the hermeneutic process, the conversation: It involves a conversation of the interpreter with one's discussion partner and one's own conversation with the interpreter.[2]

The hermeneutic borderline case of translation, which at the same time provides the model for scientific interpretation, discloses a form of reflection that we implicitly carry out in every linguistic communication. It remains, to be sure, concealed in naive conversation, for understanding in reliably institutionalized language games rests on an unproblematic foundation of mutual understanding (Verständigtseins)—it is "not an interactive process, but an accomplishment of life."

Wittgenstein analyzed only the dimension of the language game as a form of life. For him understanding was limited to the virtual repetition of the training through which "native" speakers are socialized into their form of life. For Gadamer this understanding of language is not yet at all a "real understanding" (Verstehen) because the accompanying reflecton on the application of linguistic rules emerges only when a language game becomes problematic. Only when the intersubjectivity of the validity of linguistic rules is disturbed is an interpretative process set in motion that reestablishes consensus. Wittgenstein conflated this hermeneutic understanding with the primary process of learning to speak. Correspondingly, he was convinced that learning a foreign language has the same structure as growing up in one's mother tongue. This identification was necessary for him because he lacked a dialectical concept of translation. For translation is not a transformation that permits the reduction of statements in one language system to statements in another. Rather, the act of translation highlights a productive achievement to which language always empowers those who have mastered its grammatical rules: to assimilate what is foreign and thereby to further develop one's own linguistic system. This happens daily in situations in which discussion partners must first find a "common language." This language is the result of coming to an understanding (*Verständigung*), the structure of which is similar to translation.

> Coming to an understanding in conversation involves a readiness on the part of the participants and an attempt by them to make room for what is foreign and contrary. When this is mutually the case, and each partner weighs the counter-arguments while simultaneously holding fast to his own, then we can finally come to a common language and a common judgment in an imperceptible and spontaneous reciprocal transference of points of view. (We call this an exchange of opinions). In just the same way, the translator must hold fast to the rights of his mother tongue into which he translates and yet allows its own worth to what is foreign, even contrary, in the text and its mode of expression. But this description of the activity of the translator is perhaps already too abbreviated. Even in such extreme situations of translating from one language into another, the matter under discussion [*Sache*] can scarcely be separated from the language. Only that translator will translate in a truly genuine sense who gives voice to the subject matter disclosed in the text, but this means: who finds a language that is not his own but one adequate to the original.[3]

Gadamer sees in grammatical rules not only institutionalized forms of life but delimitations of horizons. Horizons are open, and they shift, we enter into them and they in turn move with us. This Husserlian concept presents itself as a way of accumulating the assimilative and generative power of language vis-a-vis its structural accomplishments. The life-worlds that determine the grammar of language games are not closed forms of life, as Wittgenstein's monadological conception suggests.

Wittgenstein showed how the rules of linguistic communication imply the conditions of possibility of their own application. They are at the same time rules for the instructional practice through which they can be internalized. But Wittgenstein failed to appreciate that the same rules also include the conditions of possibility of their interpretation. It is proper to the grammar of a language game not only that it defines a form of life but that it defines a form of life as one's own over against others that are foreign. Because every world that is articulated in a language is a totality, the horizon of a language also encompasses that which it is not—it discloses itself as particular among particulars. For this reason, the limits of the world that it defines are not irrevocable; the dialectical confrontations of what is one's own with what is foreign leads, for the most part imperceptibly, to revisions. Translation is the medium in which these revisions take place, and language is continuously developed further. The inflexible reproduction of language and form of life at the level of the immature is only a boundary case of the flexible renewal to which a transmitted language is continually exposed, in that those who have already mastered it bridge disturbances of communication, respond to new situations, assimilate what is foreign, and find a common language for divergent tongues.

Translation is necessary not only at the horizontal level, between competing linguistic communities, but between generations and epochs as well. Tradition (*Überlieferung*), as the medium in which languages propagate themselves, takes place as translation, namely, as the bridging of distances between generations.[4] The process of socialization, through which the individual grows into his language, is the smallest unity of the process of tradition. Against this background we can see the foreshortening of perspective to which Wittgenstein succumbed; the language games of the young do not simply reproduce the practice of the aged. With the first fundamental rules of language the child learns not only the conditions of possible consensus but at the same time the conditions of a possible interpretation of these rules, which permit him to overcome, *and thereby also to express*, distance. Linguistic understanding [*Sprachverstehen*] is based not only upon a primary mutual understanding [*Verständigtsein*] but also upon a hermeneutic understanding [*Verstehen*] that is articulated only when there are disturbances in communication.

Hermeneutic self-reflection goes beyond the sociolinguistic stage of language analysis marked by later Wittgenstein. When the transcendental construction of a pure language was shattered, language gained a new dimension through the pluralism of language games. The grammar of a language game no longer regulated only the connection of symbols but at the same time their institutionalized application in interaction. But Wittgenstein still conceived this dimension of application too narrowly. He saw only invariant linkages of symbols and activities and failed to appreciate that the application of rules includes their interpretation and further development. To be sure, Wittgenstein first made us aware—in opposition to the positivist bias—that the application of grammatical rules cannot in turn be defined at the symbolic level according to general rules; it can be inculcated only as a complex of language and practice and internalized as part of a form of life. But he remained enough of a positivist to conceive of this practice as the reproduction of fixed patterns—as if socialized individuals were subsumed under a total system composed of language and activities. In his hands the language game congeals to an opaque unity.

Actually, language spheres are not monadically sealed off but are inwardly as well as outwardly porous. The grammar of a language cannot contain a rigid design for its application. Whoever has learned to apply its rules has not only learned to express himself but also to interpret expressions in this language. Both translation (outwardly) and tradition (inwardly) must be possible in principle. Along with their possible application, grammatical rules simultaneously imply the necessity of interpretation. Wittgenstein failed to see this; as a consequence he conceived the practice of language games unhistorically. With Gadamer language gains a third dimension—grammar governs an application of rules, which, for its part, further develops the system of rules historically. The unity of language, submerged in the pluralism of language games, is reestablished dialectically in the context of tradition. Language exists only as transmitted (*tradierte*). For tradition mirrors on a large scale the lifelong socialization of individuals in their language.

Despite the abandonment of an ideal language, the concept of a language game remains bound to the unacknowledged model of formalized languages. Wittgenstein tied the intersubjectivity of ordinary language communication to the intersubjective validity of grammatical rules. To follow a rule means to apply it in the same way. The ambiguity of ordinary language and the imprecision of its rules are, for Wittgenstein, only apparent; every language games is completely ordered. The language analyst can rely on this order as a standard for his critique. Even though ordinary language cannot be reconstructed in formal language without being destroyed as such, its grammar is still no less precise and unequivocal than that of a calculus. This assumption is plausible only for someone who—contrary to Wittgenstein's own intention—has a prior commitment to the standard of formalized language. For one who ties linguistic analysis to the self-reflection of ordinary language the opposite is plainly the case. The unequivocal character of calculi is purchased with their monadological structure, that is, with a construction that excludes conversations. Strictly deductive systems permit implications, not communications. Dialogue is replaced, at best, with the transfer of information. Only dialogue-free languages have a complete order. Ordinary languages are incomplete and provide no guarantee for the absence of ambiguity. Consequently, the intersubjectivity of ordinary language communication is always "broken." It exists because consensus (*Einverständnis*) is in principle possible; and it does not exist because it is in principle necessary to achieve effective communicaton (*Verständigung*). Hermeneutic understanding (*Verstehen*) is applied to the point of rupture; it compensates for the brokenness of intersubjectivity.

Whoever starts from the normal case of conversation—and not from the model of a precision language—immediately grasps the open structure of ordinary language. An "unbroken" intersubjectivity of the grammar in force would certainly make possible identity of meaning, and thereby constant relations of understanding; but it would at the same time destroy the identity of the self in communication with others. Klaus Heinrich has examined ordinary language from this perspective of the dangers of a complete integration of individuals.[5] Languages that are no longer inwardly porous and have hardened into rigid systems remove the breaks in intersubjectivity and, simultaneously, the hermeneutic distance of individuals from one another. They no longer permit the vulnerable balance between separation and union in which the identity of every ego has to develop. The problem of an ego identity that can be established only through identifications—and this means through alienations (*Entäusserungen*) of identity—is at the same time the problem of a linguistic communication that permits the saving balance between speechless union and speechless alienations (*Entfremdung*), between the sacrifice of individuality and the isolation of the individualized. Experiences of imminent loss of identity refer to experiences of the reification of linguistic communication. In the sustained nonidentity of a successful communication the individual can develop a precarious ego identity and preserve it against the risks of reification or formlessness. Heinrich analyzes primarily one side: the conditions of protest against the self-destruction of a society sinking back into indifference, a society that obliterates through forced integration the distance of individuals from one another. This is the situation of dictated language regulation and unbroken intersubjectivity that cancels out the subjective range of application. Wittgenstein's conception of a language game would be realized in this way. For a strictly regulated language that inwardly closes all gaps must be monadically sealed off outwardly. The speech of protest is, thus, the other side of hermeneutic understanding, the latter bridges a sustained distance and prevents the breaking off of communication. The power of reconciliation is intrinsic to translation. It marshals the unifying power of language against its disintegration into a number of dispersed languages, which, as isolated systems, would exact the penalty of immediate unity.[6]

2

Gadamer uses the image of a horizon to capture the basic hermeneutic character of every concrete language—far from having a closed boundary, each concrete language can in principle incorporate what is linguistically foreign and at first incomprehensible. Each of the partners among whom communication must be brought about lives in a horizon. For this reason Gadamer represents effective hermeneutic communication (*Verständigung*) with the image of a fusion (*Verschmelzung*) of horizons. This holds true for the vertical plane in which we overcome historical distance through understanding as well as for the horizontal plane in which understanding mediates geographical or cultural linguistic distance. The appropriation (*Aneignung*) of a tradition through understanding follows the pattern of translation. The horizon of the present is not, so to speak, extinguished but fused with the horizon from which the tradition comes.

> To understand a tradition requires, to be sure, a historical horizon. But there can be no question of gaining this horizon by transposing oneself [*sich versetzen*] into a historical situation. It is, rather, necessary to have a horizon already if one is to be able to transpose oneself in this way. For what does it mean to "transpose oneself"? Certainly not simply to disregard oneself. Of course, this is necessary insofar as one must really keep the other situation before one's eyes. But one must bring *oneself* into this other situation. Only that consummates the meaning of "transposing oneself." Certainly not simply to disregard oneself. Of course, this is necessary insofar as one must really keep the other situation before one's eyes. But one must bring *oneself* into the other situation. Only that consummates the meaning of "transposing oneself." If one transposes oneself, for instance, into the situation of another, one will understand him, i.e., become conscious of the otherness, indeed the inextinguishable individuality of the others, precisely through transposing oneself into his situation. Such self-transposition is

neither the emphatic projection of one individuality into another nor the subjection of the other to one's own standards; it means, rather, rising to higher level of generality on which not only one's own particularity but that of the other is over-come. The concept of horizon presents itself here because it ex-presses the superior farsightedness that the one who is under-standing must possess. To acquire a horizon means that one learns to see beyond the near and the all-too-near not in order to overlook it but in order better to see it in a larger whole and with a more accurate sense of its proportions. Nietzsche's ac-count of the many changing horizons into which one needs to transpose oneself is not a correct description of historical con-sciousness. Whoever overlooks himself in this way has precise-ly no historical horizon. . . . To acquire a historical horizon cer-tainly demands effort on one's part. We are always preoc-cupied, hopefully and fearfully, with what is closest to us; and we always approach the testimony of the past within this bias. Thus we have continually to curb the precipitous assimilation of the past to our own expectations of meaning. Only then will one hear the tradition as it makes itself audible in its own, distinct meaning. . . . Actually, the horizon of the present is constantly being developed to the extent that we must con-tinually put our prejudices to the test. Not the least of these tests is the encounter with the past and the understanding of the tradition out of which we come. Thus the horizon of the present is not formed without the past. There is no more a separate horizon of the present than there are historical horizons that have to be acquired. Rather, understanding is always the process of fusing such supposedly self-sufficient horizons.[7]

This interlacing of horizons cannot be methodologically eliminated; it belongs to the very conditions of hermeneutic work. This becomes evident in the circular relation of prior understanding (*Vorverständnis*) to the explication of what is understood. We can decipher the parts of a text only if we anticipate an understanding—however diffuse—of the whole; and conversely, we can correct this anticipation (*Vorgriff*) only to the extent to which we explicate individual parts.

Thus the circle is not a formal circle. It is neither subjective nor objective but describes understanding as the interplay between the movement of tradition and that of the interpreter. The an-ticipation of meaning, that guides our understanding of a text is not an action of subjectivity; it is determined instead by the common bond that links us with the tradition. This common bond, however, is constantly being developed in our relation-ships to tradition.[8]

The interpreter is a moment of the same fabric of tradition as his object. He appropriates a tradition from a horizon of expectations that is already informed by this tradition. For this reason we have, in a certain way, already understood the tradition with which we are confronted. And only for this reason is the horizon opened up by the language of the interpreter not merely something subjective that distorts one interpretation. In opposition to the theoretically oriented language and analysis, hermeneutics insists that we learn to understand a language from the horizon of the language we already know. In a way, we repeat virtually those learning processes through which the native was socialized into his language. However, we are not drawn into these learning processes immediately (*unvermittelt*) but through the mediation of the rules that we internalized in our own socialization processes. Hermeneutics comprehends the mediation of what the interpreter brings with him, with what he appropriates, as a further development of the same tradition that the interpreter seeks to appropriate. Hermeneutics avoids the embarrassment of a language analysis that cannot justify its own language game, for it starts with the idea that learning language games can never succeed abstractly but only from the basis of the language games that the interpreter has already mastered. Hermeneutic understanding is the interpretation of texts in the knowledge of already understood texts. It leads to new learning processes (*Bildungsprozesse*) out of the horizon of already completed learning processes. It is a new step of socialization that takes previous socializations as its point of departure. In appropriating tradition, it continues tradition. Because hermeneutic understanding itself belongs to the objective context that is reflected in it, the overcoming of temporal distance cannot be interpreted as a construction of the knowing subject. The continuity of tradition already bridges the distance of the interpreter from his object.

From the perspective of hermeneutic self-reflection, the phenomenological and linguistic foundations of interpretive (*verstehenden*) sociology move to the side of historicism. Like the latter, they succumb to objectivism, because they claim for the phenomenological observer and the language analyst a purely theoretical attitude. But both are connected with their object domain through communication experience alone and cannot, therefore, lay claim to the role of uninvolved spectators. Impartiality is guaranteed only through reflected participation, that is, by monitoring the intitial situation (*Ausgangssituation*) of the interpreter—the sounding board from which hermeneutic understanding cannot be detached. At the level of communication, the possible objectivity of experience is endangered precisely to the degree that the interpreter is seduced by the illusion of objectivism into concealing from himself the methodologically indissoluble bond to the hermeneutic initial situation. Gadamer's first-rate critique of the objectivistic self-understanding of the cultural sciences (*Geisteswissenschaften*) hits not only historicism but also the false consciousness of the phenomenological and linguistic executors of its legacy. The pluralism of life worlds and language games is only a distant echo of the worldviews and cultures projected by Dilthey onto a fictive plane of simultaneity.

In the second part of his work, Gadamer discusses the romantic empathy theory of hermeneutics and its application to history (Scheiermacher and Droysen). Using Dilthey, he demonstrates the paradoxical consequences of a historical consciousness that—while transcending the psychological approach to understanding expressions in favor of an analysis of constellations of meaning—remains dependent on the deceptive capacity for an all-understanding reproduction of any objectivated meaning content whatever. Against Schleiermacher's and Dilthey's aestheticizing of history and against their aesthetizing of historical recollection, Gadamer brings to bear, subtly and relentlessly, Hegel's insight that the restitution of past life is possible only to the extent that it is a reconstruction of the present out of its past. In the place of an illusory reproduction of the past, we have its reflective mediation with present life.

> Subsequent understanding is in principle superior to the original production and can, therefore, be formulated as a "better understanding." This is not so much due to a subsequent bringing to consciousness that places us on a par with the author (as Schleiermacher thought). On the contrary, it describes the ineradicable difference between the author and the interpreter that is given with historical distance. Each time will have to understand a transmitted text in its own way; for the text belongs in the whole of the tradition that is of substantive interest to the age and in which it tries to understand itself. The actual meaning of a text, as it speaks to the interpreter, is not dependent on the occasion represented by the author and his original public. At least it is not exhausted by it; for the meaning is also determined by the historical situation of the interpreter and thus by the whole of the objective course of history. An author like Chladenius, who has not yet submerged understanding in past history, takes this naively and artlessly into account when he suggests that an author need not himself recognize the true meaning of his

text and, therefore, that the interpreter often can and must understand more more than he. But this is of fundamental significance. The meaning of a text goes beyond its author, not only occasionlly, but always. Understanding is therefore not merely reproductive but also productive.[9]

Objectivism conceals the complex of historical influences (*den wirkungsgeschichtlichen Zusammenhang*) in which historical consciousness itself is located. The principle of the historical influence (*Wirkungsgeschichte*) of a text becomes for Gadamer a basic methodological axiom for the interpretation of the text itself. This is not a question of an auxiliary discipline that supplies additional information but of research fundamental to the interpretation itself. For "historical influence" refers to the chain of past interpretations through which the prior understanding of the interpreter is objectively mediated with his object, even if behind his back. Transmitted (*überlieferte*) documents and historical events do not acquire their meaning—which hermeneutic understanding endeavors to grasp descriptively—independently of the events and interpretations that follow them. Meaning (*Sinn*) is an aggregate of sedimented significations (*Bedeutungen*) that continuously emerge from new retrospectives. Thus a transmitted meaning (*tradierter Sinn*) is in principle incomplete, that is, open for sedimentations from future perspectives. Historians and philologists who reflect on historical influences take into account the openness of the horizon of meaning. They anticipate that the progress of events will bring out new aspects of their object. This is the rational core of the philologist's experience that the content of transmitted texts is "inexhaustible."[10] Corresponding to this is the historian's experience that he cannot in principle give a conclusive description of any event. "Completely to describe an event is to locate it in all the right stories, and this we cannot do. We cannot because we are temporally provincial with regard to the future."[11]

A. C. Danto corroborates Gadamer's principle of historical influence through an analysis of the form of historical statements. Historical accounts make use of narrative statements. They are called narrative because they present events as elements of stories (*Geschichten*). Stories have a beginning and an end, they are held together by an action. Historical events are reconstructed wtihin the reference system of a story. They cannot be presented without relation to other, later events. Narrative statments are in general characterized by the fact that they refer to at least two events with different temporal indices, the earlier of these being the theme of the description. Narrative statements describe an event with the aid of categories under which it could not have been observed. The sentence "The Thirty Years War began in 1618" presupposes that at least those events have elapsed that are relevant for the history of the war up to the Peace of Westphalia, events that could not have been narrated by any observer at the outbreak of the war. According to the context, the expression "Thirty Years War" signifies not only a military happening that extended through three decades, but the political collapse of the German Empire, the postponement of capitalist development, the end of the Counter Reformation, and motif for a Wallenstein drama, etc., etc. The predicates with which an event is narratively presented require the appearance of later events in the light of which the event in question appears as a historical event. Consequently, the historical description of events becomes in the course of time richer than empirical observation at the moment of their happening.

In the reference system of theories of empirical science events are described only with categories that could be used to record an observation of these events. A scientifically predicted event can be identified only in an observation language that is neutral with respect to the time of its happening. A historical account of the same event—a solar eclipse, let us say—has to relate to the languages of interpretation of all those for whom it has acquired historical significance, that is, relevance in the framework of a story. If the historian wanted to proceed like the astronomer or physicist in describing an event and to use a temporally neutral observation language, he would have to assume the role of an ideal chronicler. Danto introduces this fiction; he places at the disposal of the historian a machine that records all events at each moment, stores them, and retrieves them. This ideal eyewitness notes down in an observation language everything that historically happens and how it happens. Notwithstanding, this fabulous machine would be almost worthless for our historian; for the perfect eyewitness reports would be meaningless if they were not constructions of at least one single living eyewitness who could make use of his narrative statements. The ideal chronicler is not in a position to describe intentional actions, for that would presuppose anticipating events beyond the time of observation. Such a machine is unable to establish causal relationships, for this would require that an event could be described retrospectively—the observation of a temporally later event is the necessary condition for identifying a previous event as its cause. The mechanical chronicler cannot tell a single story because relations between events with different temporal indices escape its observation; it cannot see the beginning, crisis, and end of an action complex because it lacks a point of view for possible interpretation.

Of course, the descriptions of the ideal eyewitness would also have to be interpretations. But a temporally neutral observation language excludes that mode of interpretation that alone makes it possible to comprehend an observed event as a historical event. Two successive historical events can be understood as the relation of a past-present to a past-future only by retrospectively applying the reference system of acting subjects who assess present conditions with a view to anticipated future conditions. When we speak of the outbreak of the Thirty Years War, we grasp the events of 1618 from the retrospective of a war ended thirty years later. For a contemporary of 1618 this expression could have had only a prospective significance. Thus we describe the event in categories that would have been relevant for a contemporary not as an observer but as an actor who could anticipate something of the future. To comprehend events historically, that is, to present them in the form of narrative statements, means that we comprehend them in the schema of possible action.

In doing this, the historian limits himself of course to the actual intentions of the actor. As someone who has been born later, he has already transcended the horizon of history as it presented itself to the actor. But even the unintended components and consequences of intentional complexes are grasped from the point of view of possible intentionality as soon as they enter the historical horizon of one who has come later. Gadamer demonstrates the transition from the psychological to the hermeneutic foundation of the cultural sciences with this point: "The problem of history is not how relationships are in general experienciable and knowable but how relationships that no one has experienced as such should be knowable."[12] Danto discusses this relation of subjectively intended meaning to objective meaning through the example of the romantic traits subsequently discovered in the works of classicism.

> It is a discovery for which we require the concept of romanticism and criteria for identifying the romantic. But a concept of romanticism would naturally not have been available in the heyday of classicism. . . . Whatever in classical writings turns out to fall under the concept of romanticism was doubtless put in those works intentionally. But they were not intentional under the description "putting in romantic elements," for the

authors lacked that concept. This is an important limitation on the use of *Verstehen*. It was not an intention of Aristarchus to anticipate Copernicus, nor of Petrarch to open the Renaissance. To give such descriptions requires concepts which were only available at a later time. From this it follows that even having access to the minds of the men whose action he describes will not enable the Ideal Chronicler to appreciate the significance of those actions.[13]

The historian does not observe from the perspective of the actor but describes events and actions out of the experiential horizon of a history that goes beyond the actor's horizons of expectations. But the meaning that retrospectively accrues to events in this way emerges only in the schema of possible action, that is, only if the events are viewed as if this meaning had—with the knowledge of those who were born later—been intended. Thus the language in which the historian presents events does not primarily express observations but the interrelations of a series of interpretations. The interpretation of contemporary observers is the last rung on a ladder of interpretations. Its first rung is the reference system of the historian, which, insofar as he is himself an acting subject, cannot be independent of his horizon of expectations. The ladder itself is the relationship of tradition that connects the historian with his object. It is constructed from the retrojections of those coming later who, knowing better, have reconstructed what happened in the schema of possible action. The historian is no chronicler restricted to observation; he is engaged in communicative experiences. Instead of the uninvolved recording of events, we have the task of hermeneutic understanding. At the level of historical presentation it proves to be meaningless to want to separate something like a pure description of the chronicler from interpretation. Danto criticizes such a conception

> that, in a way, accepts the ideal of imitation of the past but wants to insist that there is something beyond giving accounts, events, even perfect accounts, of the past or parts of the past, which is also the aim of history to do. For in addition to making true statements about the past, it is held, historians are interested in giving interpretations of the past. And even if we had a perfect account, the task of interpretation would remain to be done. The problem of just giving descriptions belongs to a humbler level of historical work, it is, indeed, the work of chroniclers. That is a distinction I am unable to accept. For I wish to maintain that history is all of a piece. It is all of a piece in the sense that there is nothing one might call a pure description in contrast with something else to be called an interpreta-

tion. Just to do history at all is to employ some overarching conception that goes beyond what is given. And to see that this is so is to see that history as an imitation or duplication of the past is an impossible ideal.[14]

A series of events acquires the unity of a story only from a point of view that cannot be taken from those events themselves. The actors are caught in their histories; even for them—if they tell their own stories—the point of view from which the events can take on the coherence of a story arises only subsequently. The story has a meaning, of course, only for someone who is in general capable of acting. As long as new points of view arise, the same events can enter into other stories and acquire new significations. We could give a definitive and complete description of a historical event only if we could be certain that new points of view would no longer appear, that is, that we could anticipate all the relevant points of view that would emerge in the future. In this sense, philosophy of history anticipates the point of view that could guide the last historian at the close of history as a whole. Because we are unable to anticipate the future course of events, we are also unable to anticipate, with good grounds, the point of view of the last historian. But without philosophy of history no historical event can be completely represented.

> Any account of the past is essentially incomplete. It is essentially incomplete, that is, if its completion would require the fulfillment of a condition that simply cannot be fulfilled. And my thesis will be that a complete account of the past would presuppose a complete account of the future so that one could not achieve a complete historical account without also achieving a philosophy of history. So that if there cannot be a legitimate philosophy of history, there cannot be a legitimate and complete historical account. Paraphrasing a famous result in logic, we cannot, in brief, consistently have a complete historical account. Our knowledge of the past, in other words, is limited by our knowledge (or ignorance) of the future, And this is the deeper connection between substantive philosophy of history and ordinary history.[15]

As long as the choice of descriptive expressions is determined by a theoretical system of reference, incompleteness of descriptions is no defect. Because, however, historians do not have at their disposal theories like those in the empirical sciences, their incomplete descriptions are in principle also arbitrary.

> Completely to describe an event is to locate it in all the right
> stores, and this we cannot do. We cannot because we are tem-
> porally provincial with regard to the future. We cannot for the
> same reasons that we cannot achieve a speculative philosophy
> of history. The complete description then presupposes a nar-
> rative organization, and narrative organization is something
> that we do. Not merely that, but the imposition of a narrative
> organization logically involves us with an inexpungeable sub-
> jective factor. There is an element of sheer arbitrariness in it.
> We organize events relative to some events which we find
> significant in a sense not touched upon here. It is a sense of
> significance common, however, to all narratives and is deter-
> mined by the topical interests of this human being or that.[16]

These implications are plausible, however, only if we accept the
ideal of complete description as a meaningful historiographical ideal.
Danto develops the *idea of all possible histories* through the hypothetical
role of the last historian. But for the last historian, as for every
historian before him, the series of past events can take the shape of a
story only from a point of view that he does not acquire from these
events themselves. Only if he himself acts in a horizon of expectations can he delineate the last of all possible reference systems for the
presentation of historical events. But as soon as the historian acts at
all, he produces new relationships that combine into a further story
from a new retrospective. The definitive and complete description
would thereby be subjected to a revision. Consequently, the historical
presentation of history as a whole would require a qualification that is
per se incompatible with the end of history. The ideal of complete
description cannot be consistently formulated, it ascribes to history a
claim to contemplation that it not only cannot redeem but that is illegitimate as a claim.

Every historian is in the role of the last historian. Hermeneutic
deliberations about the inexhaustibility of the horizon of meaning and
the new interpretations of future generations remain empty; they
have no consequences for what the historian has to do. For he does
not at all organize his knowledge according to standards of pure theory.
He cannot grasp anything that he can know historically independently of the framework of his own life practice (*Lebenspraxis*). In this context the future exists only as a horizon of expectations. And these expectations fuse hypothetically the fragments of previous traditions into an intuitively grasped totality of universal history, in the light of
which every relevant event can in principle be described as completely as is possible for the practically effective self-understanding of

a social life-world. Implicitly every historian proceeds in the way that Danto wishes to forbid to the philosopher of history. From the viewpoints of practice he anticipates end-states from which the multiplicity of events coalesces smoothly into action-orienting stories. Precisely the openness of history, that is, the situation of the actor, permits the hypothetical anticipation of history as a whole, without which the retrospective significance of the parts would not emerge. Dilthey already saw this.

> We grasp the significance of a moment of the past. It is significant insofar as a linkage to the future was achieved in it, through action or through an external event. . . . The individual moment [has] significance through its connections with the whole, through the relation of past and future, of individual being and mankind. But what constitutes the peculiar nature of this relation of part to whole within life? It is a relation that is never entirely completed. One would have to await the end of history to possess all the material needed for determining its significance. On the other hand, the whole is only there for us to the extent that it becomes comprehensible from the parts. Understanding moves constantly between these two modes of consideration. Our interpretation of the meaning of life changes constantly. Every plan of life is an expression of a comprehension of the significance of life. What we set as the goal of our future conditions the determination of the past's significance.[17]

Of course these goal settings, that is, the hermeneutic anticipations rooted in the interests of life practice, are not arbitrary. For they can hold good only to the degree that reality does not escape their grasp. Moreover, it is the peculiar achievement of hermeneutical understanding that—in relation to the successful appropriation of traditions —the prejudices that are attached to the initial situation of the interpreter are also rendered transparent in their emergence from tradition and thus absorbed into reflection.

3

Historical accounts that have the form of narrative statements can appear to be in principle incomplete and arbitrary only if they are measured against a mistaken ideal of description. The statements of empirical science do not themselves meet this standard of contemplative comprehension and corresponding representation. Their accuracy depends on criteria that determine the validity of technically utilizable knowledge. Correspondingly, if we examine the validity of hermeneutic statements in the framework proper to them, the framework of knowledge that has consequences for practice, then what Danto has to regard as a defect proves to be a transcendental condition of possible knowledge. Only because we project the provisional end-state of a system of reference out of the horizon of life-practice can the interpretation of events (which can be organized into a story from the point of view of the projected end) as well as the interpretation of parts (which can be described as fragments from the point of view of the anticipated totality) have any information content at all for that life practice. I find Gadamer's real achievement in the demonstration that hermeneutic understanding is linked with transcendental necessity to the articulation of an action orienting self understanding.

The immanent connection of understanding and application can be seen in the examples of theology and jurisprudence. Both the interpretation of the Bible in preaching and the interpretation of positive law in adjudication serve simultaneously as guideposts of how to apply the evidence in a given situation. The practical life relation to the self-understanding of the clients—the church congregation or the legal community—is not simply a subsequent corollary to the interpretation. Rather, the interpretation is realized in the application itself. Gadamer does not want to restrict the scope of this constitutive connection between understanding and practical transposition into life only to certain traditions that like the sacred texts of a canonical tradition or the valid norms of positive law are already insitutionally binding. Nor does he want to extend it merely to the interpretation of works of art on the explication of philosophical texts. He persuades us that the applicative understanding of distinguished traditions endowed with a claim to authority provides the model for hermeneutic understanding in general.

> The close relationship that originally linked philological hermeneutics with legal and theological hermeneutics was based on a recognition of application as an integrating moment of all understanding. Constitutive for both legal and theological hermeneutics is the tension between the fixed text—of the law or of revelation—on the one hand and, on the other hand, the meaning acquired through its application in the concrete instant of interpretation, whether in preaching or in the legal judgment. A law is not to be understood historically but is supposed to be concretized in its legal validity through interpretation. Similarly, a religious revelation is not to be interpreted

merely as a historical document but is supposed to be understood in such a way that it exercises its redemptive influence. In both cases, this involves that the text (the law or the message of salvation), if it is to be understood properly, i.e., corresponding to the claim that the text puts forward, must be understood anew and otherwise at each moment, i.e., in each concrete situation. Understanding is here always application. We took as our point of departure the knowledge that the understanding exercised in the cultural sciences is also essentially historical, that is, that there too a text is understood only if it is understood each time in another way. The task of a historical hermeneutics was characterized precisely by the fact that it reflects on the tension between the sameness of the shared reality [*Sache*] and the changing situation in which it is supposed to be understood.[18]

Gadamer explains the applicative knowledge engendered by hermeneutic understanding through the Aristotelian determinations of practical knowledge.[19] Hermeneutical knowledge has three features in common with the political-ethical knowledge that Aristotle distinguished from both science and technical knowledge.[20] *In the first place* practical knowledge has a *reflective* form; it is simultaneously "knowing oneself." For this reason we experience mistakes in the areas of practical knowledge in ourselves. False opinions have the habitual form of false consciousness. Deficient insight has the objective power of delusion. The *second* aspect is connected with this— practical knowledge is *internalized*. It has the power to fix drives and to shape passions. In contrast, technical knowledge remains external. We forget technical rules as soon as we fall out of practice. Practical rules, once mastered, become by constrast components of our personality structure. For this reason practical knowledge can also not be gained in the same presuppositionless way as theoretical knowledge; it must fasten on to a structure of prejudgments or prejudices (*Vorurteilsstruktur*). Only the hearer who has already acquired a foreknowledge (*Vorwissen*) on the basis of appropriated traditions and experienced situations can be enlightened by lectures in practical philosophy. Practical knowledge fastens on to a socialization process and develops it further. The *third* aspect becomes comprehensible at this point—practical knowledge is *global*. It refers not to particular aims that can be specified independently of the means for their realization. The action-orienting goals, as well as the ways in which they can be realized, are components of the same form of life (*bios*). This is always a social form of life that is developed through communicative action. Practical knowledge orients by way of rules of interaction. These transmitted (*tradierten*) rules are acquired by training; but the historically changing conditions of their use call for an application that, for its part, further develops the rules through interpretation.

If the hermeneutic sciences occupy the same position with respect to tradition as a practical philosophy that, enlightened by historical consciousness, has abandoned an ontologically grounded natural law, then the Aristotelian determinations can be claimed for hermeneutics as well:

> The interpreter who is occupied with a tradition seeks to apply the latter to himself. But here too this does not mean that the traditional text is for him given and understood in its general nature and only afterwards put to particular uses. Rather, the interpreter wants nothing other than to understand this general sense—the text, i.e., to understand what the tradition says, in what the meaning and significance of the text consist. In order to understand this, however, he cannot disregard himself and his concrete hermeneutic situation. He must relate the text to this situation if he wants to understand at all.[21]

Hermeneutic understanding is structurally oriented toward eliciting from tradition a possible action-orienting self-understanding of social groups. It makes possible a form of consensus on which communicative action depends. It eliminates the dangers of a communication breakdown in two directions: vertically, in one's own tradition, and horizontally, in the mediation between traditions of different cultures an groups. If these communication flows come to an end and the intersubjectivity of understanding either hardens or falls apart, an elementary condition of survival is disrupted—the possibility of agreement without constraint and recognition without force.

The dialectic of the general and the particular, which also obtains in the appropriation of traditions and the corresponding application of practical rules, shows once again the brokenness of intersubjectivity. That something like tradition exists at all involves an aspect of non-obligation—the tradition must also be revisable; otherwise what is nonidentical in the sustained group identity would be destroyed. Ego identities can be formed and maintained in linguistic communication only if the related group identity can constitute itself, vis-a-vis the collective other of its own past, as simultaneously identical with and different from it. For this reason the global generality of practical rules requires a concretizing interpretation through which, in the given situation, it is molded into a concrete generality that is intersubjectively valid.

A technical rule is abstractly general. It can be compared to a theoretical sentence whose conditions of application are formulated in general terms. Intersubjectivity is established at the theoretical level by a prior definition of fundamental predicates and at the operational level by invariant rules of application. The identification of states of affairs to which the sentence can be applied does not affect its semantic content. We can thus subsume cases under something abstractly general. It is otherwise with practical rules. We compare them with traditional meaning-contents, which are understood only when we have arrived at a consensus about their significance; only then do they have intersubjective validity in a social group. Understanding becomes a problem in this case because both the binding definition of fundamental predicates and the invariant rules of application are lacking. A prior understanding guides us in the search for states of affairs in which the meaning can be made precise; but this identification of the range of application qualifies in turn the semantic content. The global generality, which we must already have understood diffusely, determines the subsumed particular only to the degree to which it is itself first concretized by this particular. Only through this does it gain intersubjective recognition in a given situation; the recognition is tied to this situation. A new situation demands a renewal of intersubjectivity through repeated understanding. And intersubjectivity does not come to pass arbitrarily; it is, rather, the result of thoughtful mediation of the past with present life.

To be sure, Hegel could speak of thought in this connection with greater legitimacy than Gadamer. It is difficult to fix the moment of knowledge in hermeneutic understanding independently of the absolute movement of reflection. If the framework of tradition as a whole is no longer regarded as a production of reason apprehending itself, then the further development of tradition fostered by hermeneutic understanding cannot eo ipso count as rational. It would, however, be precipitous to take the logical dependence of interpretation on application and the interlacing of normative anticipation with cognitive experiences as sufficient cause for banishing hermeneutic understanding from the realm of substantial research and possible knowledge. At the level of hermeneutic understanding, the mobile relation that makes cognitive processes at all possible is not yet shut down—the relation between the formation of standards and description according to standards. The methodology of the empirical sciences pulls the two apart—theoretical constructions from the observations on which they can founder. But both aspects are previously coordinated in a transcendental framework. Protophysics makes an interpretation of reality binding, a reality that has been previously constituted under the conception of possible objects of technical control. With this constitution, the rules according to which theoretical sentences can be applied to facts are predecided, thus they are unproblematic within the sciences. Application is problematic and inseparable from interpretation wherever a transcendental framework that coordinates sentences and facts is not yet established once and for all but is undergoing transformation and must be determined ad hoc.[22]

The appropriation of traditional meaning-contents proceeds on a level at which schemata of possible world conceptions are decided. This decision is not made independently of whether such a schema proves itself in a given and preinterpreted situation. It is therefore senseless to assign hermeneutic understanding either to theory or to experience; it is both and neither. What we have called communicative experience will normally take place within a language whose grammar fixes a connection of such schemata. But the brokenness of intersubjectivity renders the continuous coordination of views in a common schema a permanent task. Only in extreme cases does this inconspicuously ever-present transformation and development of transcendental schemata of world interpretation become a problem that has to be explicitly mastered through hermeneutic understanding. Such cases appear when traditions are disrupted or foreign cultures are encountered—or when we analyze familiar traditions and cultures as if they were foreign. A controlled distanciation (*Verfremdung*) can raise understanding from a prescientific experience to the rank of a reflected procedure. In this way hermeneutic procedures enter into the social sciences. They are unavoidable as soon as data is gathered at the level of communicative experience. They are equally important for the selection of a categorical framework if we do not want to behave naively in the face of the unavoidably historical content of even the most general categories.

Gadamer unwittingly obliges the positivistic devaluation of hermeneutics. He joins his opponents in the view that hermeneutic experience "transcends the range of control of scientific method."[23] In the preface to the second edition of his work he sums up his investigations in the thesis "that the moment of historical influence is and remains effective in all understanding of tradition, even where the method of the modern historical sciences has gained ground and makes what has become historically into an "object" that has to be "ascertained" like an experimental finding—as if tradition were foreign and, humanly regarded, incomprehensible in the same sense as the object of physics."[24] This correct critique of a false objectivist self-understanding cannot, however, lead to a suspension of the methodological distanciation of the object, which distinguishes a self-reflective understanding from everyday communicative experience. The confrontation of "truth" and "method" should not have misled Gadamer to oppose hermeneutic experience abstractly to methodic knowledge as a whole. As it is, hermeneutic experience is the ground of the hermeneutic sciences. And even if it were feasible to remove the humanities entirely from the sphere of science, the sciences of action could not avoid linking empirical-analytic with hermeneutic procedures. The claim that hermeneutics legitimately makes good against the practically influential absolutism of a general methodology of the empirical sciences brings no dispensation from the business of methodology in general. This claim will, I fear, be effective *in* the sciences or not at all. The ontological—in Heidegger's sense—self-understanding of hermeneutics that Gadamer expresses in the preface mentioned above does not, it seems to me, suit his intentions.

> I did not want to develop a system of rules of skill that would be able to describe or even to guide the methodological procedure of the cultural sciences. It was also not my intention to investigate the theoretical foundations of work in the humanities in order to turn the knowledge gained to practical ends. If there is a practical implication of the investigations presented here, it is not an implication for unscientific "engagement" but for the "scientific" honesty to admit to oneself the engagement operative in every understanding. But my real claim was and is a philosophical one. Not what we are doing, not what we ought to be doing but what happens with us beyond our wanting and doing, is in question.[25]

This thesis is grounded with the statement: "Understanding itself should be thought of not so much as an action of subjectivity but as entering into the happening of tradition [*Überlieferungsgeschehen*] in which past and present are constantly mediated. It is this that must be acknowledged in hermeneutic theory, which is much too strongly dominated by the idea of a procedure, a method."[26] In Gadamer's view, ongoing tradition and hermeneutic inquiry merge to a single point. Opposed to this is the insight that the reflected appropriation of tradition breaks up the naturelike (*naturwüchsige*) substance of tradition and alters the position of the subject on it.[27] Gadamer knows that the hermeneutic sciences first developed in reaction to a decline in the binding character of traditions. When he emphasizes, nevertheless, that traditions are not rendered powerless by historical consciousness (p. xv), then he overlays the justified critique of the false self-understanding of historicism with the unjustified expectation that historicism is without consequences. Certainly, Scheler's grounding of the thesis that historical traditions lose their naturelike efficacy through scientific objectification is methodologically false. And compared with this, the hermeneutic insight is certainly correct, namely, the insight that understanding—no matter how controlled it may be—cannot simply leap over the interpreter's relationships to tradition. But from the fact that understanding is structurally a part of the traditions that it further develops through appropriation, it does not follow that the medium of tradition is not profoundly altered by scientific reflection. Even in traditions whose efficacy is unbroken, what is at work is not simply an authority detached from insight and blindly asserting itself. Every tradition must be woven with a sufficiently wide mesh to allow for application, that is, for prudent transposition with regard to changed situations. But the methodic cultivation of prudence in the hermeneutic sciences shifts the balance between authority and reason. Gadamer fails to appreciate the power of reflection that is developed in understanding. This type of reflection is no longer blinded by the illusion of an absolute, self-grounded autonomy and does not detach itself from the soil of contingency on which it finds itself. But in grasping the genesis of the tradition from which it proceeds and on which it turns back, reflection shakes the dogmatism of life-practices.

Gadamer turns the insight into the structure of prejudgments (*Vorurteilsstruktur*) involved in understanding into a rehabilitation of prejudice as such. But does it follow from the unavoidability of hermeneutic anticipation eo ipso that there are legitimate prejudices? Gadamer is motivated by the conservatism of that first generation, by the impulse of a Burke that has not yet been turned against the rationalism of the eighteenth century; he is convinced that true authority need not be authoritarian. It distinguishes itself from false authority through recognition (*Anerkennung*): "Indeed, authority has immediately nothing to do with obedience but with cognition [*Erkennt-nis*]."[28] This strikingly harsh statement expresses a basic philosophical conviction that is not covered by hermeneutics itself but at most by its absolutization.

Gadamer has in mind the type of educational process through which tradition is transferred into individual learning processes and appropriated as tradition. Here the person of the educator legitimates prejudices that are inculcated in the learner with authority—and this means, however we turn it around, under the potential threat of sanctions and with the prospect of gratifications. Identification with the model creates the authority that alone makes possible the internalization of norms, the sedimentation of prejudices. The prejudices are in turn the conditions of possible knowledge. This knowledge is raised to reflection when it makes the normative framework itself transparent while moving around in it. In this way hermeneutics also makes us conscious of that which is already historically prestructured by inculcated tradition in the very act of understanding. At one point Gadamer characterizes the task of hermeneutics as follows: it has to return along the path of Hegel's phenomenology of spirit in such a way that it demonstrates the substantiality that underlies and shapes all subjectivity.[29] However, the substantiality of what is historically pregiven does not remain unaffected when it is taken up in reflection. A structure of preunderstanding or prejudgment that has been rendered transparent can no longer function as a prejudice. But this is precisely what Gadamer seems to imply. That authority converges with knowledge means that the tradition that is effectively behind the educator legitimates the prejudices inculcated in the rising generation; they could then be confirmed only in this generation's reflection. In assuring himself of the structure of prejudgment, the mature individual would transfer the formerly unfree recognition of the personal authority of the guardian to the objective authority of a traditional framework. But then it would remain a matter of authority, for reflection could move only within the limits of the facticity of tradition. The act of recognition that is mediated through reflection would not at all have altered the fact that tradition as such remains the only ground of the validity of prejudices.

Gadamer's prejudice for the rights of prejudices certified by tradition denies the power of reflection. The latter proves itself, however, in being able to reject the claim of tradition. Reflection dissolves substantiality because it not only confirms but also breaks up dogmatic forces. Authority and knowledge do not converge. To be sure, knowledge is rooted in actual tradition; it remains bound to contingent conditions. But reflection does not wrestle with the facticity of transmitted norms without leaving a trace. It is condemned to be after the fact; but in glancing back it develops retroactive power. We can turn back upon internalized norms only after we have first learned, under externally imposed force, to follow them blindly. Reflection recalls that path of authority along which the grammars of language games were dogmatically inculcated as rules for interpreting the world and for action. In this process the element of authority that was simply domination can be stripped away and dissolved into the less coercive constraint of insight and rational decision.

This experience of reflection is the unforgettable legacy bequeathed to us by German Idealism from the spirit of the eighteenth century. One is tempted to lead Gadamer into battle against himself, to demonstrate to him hermeneutically that he ignores that legacy because he has taken over an undialectical concept of enlightenment from the limited perspective of the German nineteenth centry and that with it has had adopted an attitude that vindicated for us (Germans) a dangerous pretension to superiority separating us from Western tradition. But the matter is not this simple; Gadamer has a systematic argument at hand. The right of reflection demands that the hermeneutic approach restrict itself. It calls for a reference system that goes beyond the framework of tradition as such; only then can tradition also be criticized. But how could such a reference system be legitimized except, in turn, out of the appropriation of tradition?

4

Wittgenstein subjected linguistic analysis first to a transcendental and then to a sociolinguistic self-reflection. Gadamer's hermeneutics marks a third stage of reflection, the historical. At this stage the interpreter and his object are conceived as elements of the same complex. This objective complex presents itself as tradition or historical influence. Through it, as a medium of linguistic symbols, communications are historically propagated. We call this process "historical" because the continuity of tradition is preserved only through translation, through a large-scale philology proceeding in a naturelike manner. The intersubjectivity of ordinary language communication is broken and must be restored again and again. This productive achievement of hermeneutic understanding, whether implicitly or explicitly carried through, is for its part motivated by the tradition that it further develops in this way. Tradition is not a process that we learn to master but a transmitted language in which we live.

The mode of being of tradition is not, of course, one of sensuous immediacy. It is language; and the hearing that understands it in interpreting texts draws its truth into its own linguistic behavior-in-the-world [*Weltverhalten*]. Linguistic communication between the present and traditions is, as we have shown, the happening that extends its trajectory in all understanding. Hermeneutic experience must, as genuine experience, take on everything that is present to it. It does not have the freedom to select and disallow before the fact. But it also cannot claim an absolute freedom in that tolerant neutrality that appears to be specific to understanding. It cannot undo the happening that it is.[30]

The hermeneutic self-reflection of language analysis overcomes the transcendental conception that Wittgenstein clung to even in the face of the plurality of grammars of language games. As tradition, language encompasses all specific language games and promotes unity in the empirical multiplicity of transcendental rules. At the level of objective spirit, language becomes a contingent absolute. It can no longer comprehend itself as absolute spirit; it impresses itself on subjective spirit only as absolute power. This power becomes objective in the historical transformation of horizons of possible experience. Hegel's experience of reflection shrinks to the awareness of possible experience. Hegel's experience of reflection shrinks to the awareness that we are delivered up to a happening in which the conditions of rationality change irrationally according to time and place, epoch and culture. Hermeneutic self-reflection embroils itself in this irrationalism, however, only when it absolutizes hermeneutic experience and fails to recognize the transcending power of reflection that is also operative in it. Reflection can, to be sure, no longer reach beyond itself to an absolute consciousness, which it then pretends to be. The way to absolute idealism is barred to a transcendental consciousness that is hermeneutically broken and plunged back into the contingent complex of traditions. But must it for that reason remain stuck on the path of a relative idealism?

The objectivity of a "happening of tradition" that is made up of symbolic meaning is not objective enough. Hermeneutics comes up against the walls of the traditional framework from the inside, as it were. As soon as these boundaries have been experienced and recognized, cultural traditions can no longer be posed as absolute. It makes good sense to conceive of language as a kind of metainstitution on which all social institutions are dependent; for social action is constituted only in ordinary language communication.[31] But this metainstitution of language as tradition is evidently dependent in turn on social processes that are not reducible to normative relationships. Language is *also* a medium of domination and social power; it serves to legitimate relations of organized force. Insofar as the legitimations do not articulate the power relations whose institutionalization they make possible, insofar as these relations merely manifest themselves in the legitimations, language is *also* ideological. Here it is a question not of deceptions within a language but of deception with language as such. Hermeneutic experience that encounters this dependency of the symbolic framework on actual conditions changes into critique of ideology.

The nonnormative forces that infiltrate language as a metainstitution originate not only from systems of domination but also from social labor. In this instrumental sphere of action monitored by success, experiences are organized that evidently motivate linguistic interpretations and can change traditional interpretations through operational constraints. A change in the mode of production entails a restructuring of the linguistic worldview. This can be studied, for instance, in the expansion of the realm of the profane in primitive societies. Of course, revolutions in the reproductive conditions of material life are for their part linguistically mediated. But not only is a new practice set in motion by a new interpretation; old patterns of interpretation are also weakened and overturned "from below" by a new practice.[32] Today the institutionalized research practice of the empirical sciences secures a flow of information that was formerly accumulated prescientifically in systems of social labor. This information digests natural or contrived experiences that are constituted in the behavioral system of instrumental action. I suspect that the institutional changes brought about by scientific-technical progress indirectly exert an influence on the linguistic schemata of world-comprehension not unlike that formerly exerted by changes in the mode of production. For science has become first among the productive forces. The empirical sciences simply do not represent an arbitrary language game. Their language interprets reality from the anthropologically deep seated vantage point of technical mastery. Through them the factual constraints of the natural conditions of life impinge on society. To be sure, even the statements of the theories of empirical science refer in turn to ordinary language as final meta-language; but the system of activities that they make possible, the techniques of mastering nature, also react back on the institutional framework of society as a whole and alter the language.

An interpretive (*verstehende*) sociology that hypostasizes language to the subject of forms of life and of tradition ties itself to the idealist presupposition that linguistically articulated consciousness determines the material practice of life. But the objective framework of social action is not exhausted by the dimension of intersubjectively intended and symbolically transmitted meaning. The linguistic infrastructure of a society is part of a complex that, however symbolically mediated, is also constituted by the constraint of reality—by the constraint of outer nature that enters into procedures for technical mastery and by the constraint of inner nature reflected in the repressive character of social power relations. These two categories of constraint are not only the object of interpretations; behind the back of language, they also affect the very grammatical rules according to which we interpret the world. *Social actions can be comprehended only in an objective framework that is constituted conjointly by language, labor and domination.* The happening of tradition appears as an absolute power only to a self-sufficient hermeneutics; in fact it is relative to systems of labor and domination. Sociology cannot, therefore, be reduced to interpretive sociology. It requires a reference system that, on the one hand, does not suppress the symbolic mediation of social action in favor of a naturalistic view of behavior that is merely controlled by signals and excited by stimuli but that, on the other hand, also does not succumb to an idealism of linguisticality (*Sprachlichkeit*) and sublimate social processes entirely to cultural tradition. Such a reference system can no longer leave tradition undetermined as the all-encompassing; instead, it comprehends tradition as such and in its relation to other aspects of the complex of social life, thereby enabling us to designate the conditions outside of tradition under which transcendental rules of world comprehension and of action empirically change.

A descendent of Marburg neo-Kantianism, Gadamer is prevented by the residues of Kantianism still present in Heidegger's existential ontology from drawing the consequences that his own analyses suggest. He avoids the transition from the transcendental conditions of historicity to the universal history in which these conditions are constituted. He does not see that in the dimension of the "happening of tradition" he must always conceive as mediated what, according to the ontological difference, cannot be mediated—linguistic structures and the empirical conditions under which they change historically. Only on that account can Gadamer conceal from himself that the practical (lebenspraktische) connection of understanding with the hermeneutic vantage point of the interpreter makes necessary the hypothetical anticipation of a philosophy of history with a practical intent.[33]

NOTES

1. H. G. Gadamer, Wahrheit und Methode, 2nd ed. (Tübingen, 1965), p. 380.
2. Ibid., p. 362.
3. Ibid., p. 364.
4. (Editor's Note) Überlieferung is the nominal form of überliefern: deliver up, hand down, pass on, transmit. Because the German term retains the aspect of activity or process, of something that is done or happens, while the English "tradition" has largely lost the connotation of delivery or transmission present in its Latin roots, there are some difficulties in translation. In this sentence, for example, to speak of tradition as taking place or being carried out is odd; whereas a (literal) passing-on, handing-down or transmission might, perhaps, be spoken of in this way. When similar problems arise below, the German term will be noted in the text. As will become evident, Habermas uses Überlieferung and Tradition interchangeably.
5. K. Heinrich, Versuch über die Schwierigkeit nein zu sagen (Frankfurt, 1964).
6. Cf. my review of Heinrich reprinted in Zur Logik Sozialwissenschaften (Frankfurt, 1970), pp. 322ff. This examination shows that hermeneutic self reflection passes over freely into a dialectical theory of language. Bruno Liebrucks's planned six volume work, Sprache und Bewusstsein, promises to provide such a theory. To date there have appeared volume 1, Einleitung und Spannweite des Problems (Frankfurt, 1964), and volume 2, Sprache (Frankfurt, 1965). Liebrucks's critique of Gehlen's anthropology is important for the methodology of the sciences of action. Because Liebrucks accepts a restricted concept of practice—which he foreshortens to instrumental action—he ends up with an abstract opposition between language and action. The peculiar connection of language and practice, which Wittgenstein and Mead worked out in the symbolically mediated interaction of language games and of communicative action, has not yet been given its due in those volumes which have appeared.
7. Gadamer, Wahrheit und Methode, p. 288f. (Editor's Note) The German word translated here as "prejudices" is Vorurteile. This is somewhat misleading, since the English term now has an almost exclusively pejorative con-

notation, whereas Gadamer—while allowing for the similar connotation of the German term—attempts to elaborate a positive sense of the concept. A *Vor* + *urteil* is literally a prejudgment; as Gadamer uses the term, its meaning corresponds more closely to the etymological meaning of prejudice (Latin: *prae* + *judicium*) than to current usage. The accent here, as in the case of the other key hermeneutical concepts compounded from *vor*, is on this prefix (e.g., *Vorverständnis*—"prior understanding"; *Vorgriff*—"anticipation"; *Vorbegriffe*—"preconceptions"). This is meant to bring out the fact that the interpreter's own language, practice, form of life, etc., are preconditions for understanding. They belong to the initial situation (*Ausgangssituation*) from which interpretation proceeds. CF. *Wahrheit und Methode*, p. 255, for Gadamer's elucidation of the concept of a *Vorurteil*.

8. Gadamer, *Wahrheit und Methode*, p. 277.

9. Ibid., p. 280.

10. Cf. ibid., p. 355.

11. A. C. Danto, *Analytical Philosophy of History* (Cambridge, 1965), p. 142.

12. Gadamer, *Wahrheit und Methode*, p. 211.

13. Danto, *Analytical Philosophy of History*, p. 169.

14. Ibid., p. 115.

15. Ibid., p. 17 f.

16. Ibid., p. 112.

17. W. Dilthey, *Der Aufbau der geschichtlichen Welt in den Geisteswissenschaften*, in *Gesammelte Schriften*, vol. 3, p. 233.

18. Gadamer, *Wahrheit und Methode*, p. 292.

19. Cf. especially the *Nichomachean Ethics*, VI, 3–10.

20. The comparison *phronesis* and *techne* is particularly timely, since science —which was once reserved for contemplation—has become methodologically obligated to the attitude of the technician.

21. Gadamer, *Wahrheit und Methode*, p. 292.

22. (*Editor's Note*) Habermas's conception of the different "transcendental frameworks" guiding different types of inquiry is developed in his theory of cognitive interests. Cf. especially *Knowledge and Human Interests* (Boston, 1971). He argues there that "empirical analytic" inquiry is ultimately grounded in the structure of human labor whereas "historico-hermeneutic" inquiry is rooted in the structure of human interaction. Both "anthropologically deepseated structures of human action" give rise to "cognitive strategies" that determine the different logics of inquiry. In the one case there is an "orientation toward technical control," and in the other, an "orientation toward mutual understanding in the conduct of life."

23. Gadamer, *Wahrheit und Methode*, Introduction.

24. Ibid., p. xix.

25. Ibid., p. xiv.

26. Ibid., p. 274 f.

27. (*Editor's Note*) There is no precise English equivalent for the term *naturwüchsig*. The suffix -wüchsig (from *wachsen*: to grow) means literally "growing." The term is used by neo-Marxists to refer to processes that develop without reflection or plan. It is employed by way of contrast to consciously

directed processes or structures that are the result of human will and consciousness.

28. Gadamer, *Wahrheit und Methode,* p. 264.

29. Ibid., p. 286.

30. ibid., p. 439.

31. This is the point of view adopted by K. O. Apel in his critique of Gehlen's institutionalism. Cf. Apel "Arnold Gehlen's Philosophie der Institution," in *Philosophische Rundschau,* vol. 10 (1962), pp. 1ff.

32. Cf. J. O. Hertzler, *A Sociology of Language* (New York, 1965), especially chapter 7: "Sociocultural Change and Changing Language."

33. W. Pannenberg has seen this: "It is an odd spectacle to witness how a clearsighted and profound author has his hands full keeping his thoughts from taking the direction in which they themselves point. This spectacle is presented by Gadamer's book in its efforts to avoid Hegel's total mediation of present truth through history. These efforts are indeed grounded by the reference to the finitude of human experience, which can never be transcended in absolute knowledge. But strangely enough, the phenomena described by Gadamer push again and again in the direction of a universal conception of history which he—with Hegel's system before his eyes—would precisely like to avoid." (W. Pannenberg, "Hermeneutics and Universal History, pp. 111–146 above. In recent Protestant theology the reception of Ernst Bloch's work has, as far as I can see, given an impetus to overcoming the ontology of historicity (Bultmann, Heidegger) through a reflection on the dependence of the transcendental conditions of understanding on the objective complex of universal history. In addition to the works of Pannenberg, cf. also J. Moltmann, *Theologie der Hoffnung* (1964).

ON THE SCOPE AND FUNCTION OF HERMENEUTICAL REFLECTION

HANS-GEORG GADAMER

Translated by G. B. Hess and R. E. Palmer

INTRODUCTION

Philosophical hermeneutics takes as its task the opening up of the hermeneutical dimension in its full scope, showing its fundamental significance for our entire understanding of the world and thus for all the various forms in which this understanding manifests itself: from interhuman communication to manipulation of society; from personal experience by the individual in society to the way in which he encounters society; and from the tradition as it is built of religion and law, art and philosophy, to the revolutionary consciousness that unhinges the tradition through emancipatory reflection.

Despite this vast scope and significance, however, individual explorations necessarily start from the very limited experiences and fields of experience. My own effort, for instance, went back to Dilthey's philosophical development of the heritage of German romanticism, in that I too made the theory of the *Geisteswissenschaften* ("humanistic sciences and social sciences") my theme. But I hope to have placed it on a new and much broader footing linguistically, ontologically, and aesthetically; for the experience of art can answer the prevailing presumption of historical alienation in the humanistic disciplines, I believe, with its own overriding and victorious claim to contemporaneousness, a claim that lies in its very essence. It should be evident already from the essential linguisticality of all human experience of the world, which has as its own way of fulfillment a constantly self-renewing contemporaneousness. I maintain that precisely this contemporaneousness and this linguisticality point to a truth that goes questioningly behind all knowledge and anticipatingly before it.

And so it was unavoidable that in my analysis of the universal linguisticality of man's relation to the world, the limitations of the fields of experience from which the investigation took its start would unwittingly predetermine the result. Indeed, it paralleled what happened in the historical development of the hermeneutical problem. It came into being in encounter with the written tradition that demanded translation, for the tradition had become estranged from the present as a result of such factors as temporal distance, the fixity of writing, and the sheer inertia of permanence. Thus it was that the many-layered problem of translation became for me the model for the linguisticality of all human behavior in the world. From the structure of translation was indicated the general problem of making what is alien our own. Yet further reflection on the universality of hermeneneutics eventually made clear that the model of translation does not, as such, fully come to grips with the manifoldness of what language means in man's existence.[1] Certainly in translation one finds the tension and release that structure all understanding and understandability, but it ultimately derives from the universality of the hermeneutical problem. It is important to realize that this phenomenon is not secondary in human existence, and hermeneutics is not to be viewed as a mere subordinate discipline within the arena of the *Geisteswissenschaften*.

The universal phenomenon of human linguisticality also unfolds in other dimensions than those which would appear to be directly concerned with the hermeneutical problem, for hermeneutics reaches into all the contexts that determine and condition the linguisticality of the human experience of the world. Some of those have been touched upon in my *Truth and Method*; for instance, the *Wirkungsgeschichtliches Bewusstsein* ("consciousness of effective history," or the "consciousness in which history is ever at work") was presented in a conscious effort to shed light on the idea of language in some phases of its history. And of course linguisticality extends into many different dimensions not mentioned in *Truth and Method*.[2]

In rhetoric, linguisticality is attested to in a truly universal form, one that is essentially prior to the hermeneutical and almost represents something like the "positive" as over against the "negative" of linguistic interpretation. And in this connection the relationship between rhetoric and hermeneutics is a matter of great interest.[3] In the social sciences, one finds linguisticality deeply woven into the sociality of human existence, so that the theorists of the social sciences are now becoming interested in the hermeneutical approach.

Preeminently, Jurgen Habermas has recently established a relationship between philosophical hermeneutics and the logic of the social sciences in his significant contribution to the *Philosophische Rundschau*,[4] evaluating this relationship from within the epistemological interests of the social sciences. This relationship too raises important questions as to the proper interests and purposes of hermeneutical reflection as compared with those characteristics of the sciences and social sciences.

It seems advisable, then, if not imperative, to take up the question of the interdependence of rhetoric, hermeneutics, and sociology as regards the universalities that run through all three, and to try to shed some light on the various kinds of legitimacy possessed by these elements. This endeavor is the more important in view of the fact that the claim to being strictly a science is in all three cases rendered rather ambiguous because of an obvious relationship to praxis. Of course this relationship applies most openly and clearly to rhetoric and hermeneutics; but it also applies to sociology, as we shall see presently.

For it is clear that rhetoric is not mere thoery of forms of speech and persuasion; rather, it can develop out of a native talent for practical mastery, without any theoretical reflection about ways and means. Likewise, the art of understanding, whatever its ways and means may be, is not dependent on an explicit awareness of the rules that guide and govern it. It builds, as does rhetoric, on a natural power that everyone possesses to some degree. It is a skill in which one gifted person may surpass all others, and theory can at best only tell us why. In both rhetoric and hermeneutics, then, theory is subsequent to that out of which it is abstracted; that is, to praxis.

Historically it is worthy of note that while rhetoric belongs to the earliest Greek philosophy, hermeneutics came to flower in the romantic era as a consequence of the modern dissolution of firm bonds with tradition. Of course, hermeneutics occurs in earlier times and forms, but even in these it represents an effort to grasp something vanishing and hold it up in the light of consciousness. Therefore, it occurs only in later stages of cultural evolution, like later Jewish religion, Alexandrian philology, Christianity as inheriting the Jewish gospel, or Lutheran theology as refuting an old tradition of Christian dogmatics. The history-embracing and history-preserving element runs deep in hermeneutics, in sharp contrast to sociological interest in reflection as basically a means of emancipation from authority and tradition. Reflection in rhetoric, like that in hermeneutics, is a mediation about a praxis that is in itself already a natural and sophisticated one. I should like to recall something of the early history of both rhetoric and hermeneutics in order to characterize and compare the scope and functions of the two fields.

RHETORIC AND HERMENEUTICS

The first history of rhetoric was written by Aristotle, and we now possess only fragments of it. It is clear, however, that basically Aristotle's theory of rhetoric was developed to carry out a program originally projected by Plato. Plato, going back behind all the shallow claims put forward by the contemporary teachers of rhetoric, had discovered a genuine foundation for rhetoric that only the philosopher, the dialectician, could carry out: the task is to master the faculty of speaking in such an effectively persuasive way that the arguments brought forward are always appropriate to the specific receptivity of the souls to which they are directed. Certainly this statement of the task of rhetoric is theoretically enlightening, but implicit in it are two Platonic assumptions: first, that only he who has a grasp of the truth (that is, the ideas) can unerringly devise the probable *pseudos* of a rhetorical argument; second, that one must have a profound knowledge of the souls of those one wishes to persuade. Aristotelian rhetoric is preeminently an expansion of the latter theme. In it is fulfilled the theory of the mutual accommodation of speech and soul demanded by Plato in the *Phaedrus*, now in the form of an anthropological foundation for the art of speech.

Rhetorical theory was a long-prepared-for result of a controversy that represented the breaking into Greek culture of an intoxicating and frightening new art of speaking and a new idea of education itself: that of the Sophists. At that time an uncanny new skill in standing everything on its head, the Sicilian art of oratory, flowed in on the straitlaced but easily influenced youths of Athens. Now it became paramountly necessary to teach this new power (this great ruler, as Gorgias had called oratory) its proper limits—to discipline it. From Protagoras to Isocrates, the masters of rhetoric claimed not only to teach speaking, but also the formation of a civic consciousness that bore the promise of political success. But it was Plato who first created the foundations out of which a new and all-shattering art of speaking (Aristophanes has depicted it for us blatantly enough) could find its limits and legitimate place.

The history of understanding is no less ancient and venerable. If one acknowledges hermeneutics to exist wherever a genuine art of understanding manifests itself, one must begin if not with Nestor in the *Illiad*, then at least with Odysseus. One can point out that the new philosophical movement represented by the Sophists was concerned with the interpretation of sayings by famous poets and depicted them very artfully as pedagogical examples. Certainly this was a form of hermeneutics. Over against this, one can place the Socratic hermeneutics.[5] Still, it is far from a full-fledged theory of understanding. It seems, rather, to be generally characteristic of the emergence of the "hermeneutical" problem that something *distant* has to be brought close, a certain strangeness overcome, a bridge built between the once and the now. Thus hermeneutics, as a general attitude over against the world, came into its own in modern time, which had become aware of the temporal distance separating us from antiquity and of the relativity of the life-worlds of different cultural traditions. Something of this awareness was contained in the theological claim of Reformation biblical exegesis (in the principle of *sola scriptura*), but its true unfolding came about only when a "historical consciousness" arose in the Enlightenment (although it was influenced by the novel insights of Jesuit chronological information) and matured in the romantic period to establish a relationship (however broken) to our entire inheritance from the past.

Because of this historical development of hermeneutics hermeneutical theory oriented itself to the task of interpreting expressions of life that are fixed in writing, although Schleiermacher's theoretical working out of hermeneutics included understanding as it takes place in the oral exchange of conversation. Rhetoric, on the other hand, concerned itself with the impact of *speaking* in all its immediacy. It did of course also enter into the realm of effective *writing*, and thus it developed a body of teaching on style and styles. Nevertheless, it achieved its authentic realization not in the act of reading but in speaking. The phenomenon of the orally read speech occupies an in-between, a hybrid, position: already it displays a tendency to base the art of speaking on the techniques of expression inherent in the medium of writing, and thus it begins to abstract itself from the original situation of speaking. Thus begins the transformation into poetics, whose linguistic objects are so wholly and completely art that their transformation from the oral sphere into writing and back is accomplished without loss or damage.

Rhetoric as such, however, is tied to the immediacy of its effect. Now the arousing of emotions, which is clearly the essence of the orator's task,[6] is effectual to a vastly diminished degree in written expression, which is the traditional object of hermeneutical investigation. And this is precisely the difference that matters: the orator carries his listeners away with him; the convincing power of his arguments overwhelms the listener. While under the persuasive spell of speech, the listener for the moment cannot and ought not to indulge in critical examination. On the other hand, the reading and interpreting of what is written is so distanced and detached from its author—from his mood, intentions, and unexpressed tendencies—that the grasping of the meaning of the text takes on something of the character of an independent productive act, one that resembles more the art of the orator than the process of mere listening. Thus it is easy to understand why the theoretical tools of the art of interpretation (hermeneutics) have been to a large extent borrowed from rhetoric.[7]

Where, indeed, but to rhetoric, should the theoretical examination of interpretation turn? Rhetoric from oldest tradition has been the only advocate of a claim to truth that defends the probable, the *eikos* (verisimile), and that which is convincing to the ordinary reason, against the claim of science to accept as true only what can be demonstrated and tested! Convincing and persuading, without being able to prove—these are obviously as much the aim and measure of understanding and interpretation as they are the aim and measure of the art of oration and persuasion. And this whole wide realm of convincing "persuasions" and generally reigning views has not been gradually narrowed by the progress of science, however great it has been ; rather, this realm extends to take in every new product of scientific endeavor, claiming it for itself and bringing it within its scope.

The ubiquity of rhetoric, indeed, is unlimited. Only through it is science a sociological factor of life, for all the representations of science that are directed beyond the mere narrow circle of specialists (and, perhaps one should say, insofar as they are not limited in their impact to a very small circle of initiates) owe their effectiveness to the rhetorical element they contain. Even Descartes, that great and passionate advocate of method and certainty, is in all his writings an author who uses the means of rhetoric in a magnificent fashion.[8] There can be no doubt, then, about the fundamental function of rhetoric within social life. But one may go further, in view of the ubiquity of rhetoric, to defend the primordial claims of rhetoric over against modern science, remembering that all science that would wish to be of practical usefulness at all is dependent on it.

No less universal is the function of hermeneutics. The lack of immediate understandability of texts handed down to us historically or their proneness to be misunderstood is really only a special case of what is to be met in all human orientation to the world as the *atopon* (the strange), that which does not "fit" into the customary order of our expectations based on experience. Hermeneutics has only called our attention to this phenomenon. Just as when we progress in understanding the *mirabilia* lose their strangeness, so every successful appropriation of tradition is dissolved into a new and distinct familiarity in which it belongs to us and we to it. They both flow together into one owned and shared world that encompasses past and present and that receives its linguistic articulation in the speaking of man with man.

The phenomenon of understanding, then, shows the universality of human linguisticality as a limitless medium that carries *everything* within it—not only the "culture" that has been handed down to us through language, but absolutely everything—because (in the world and out of it) is included in the realm of "understandings" and understandability in which we move. Plato was right when he asserted that whoever regards things in the mirror of speech becomes aware of them in their full and undiminished truth. And he was profoundly correct when he taught that all cognition is only what it is as re-cognition, for a "first cognition" is as little possible as a first word. In fact, a cognition in the very recent past, one whose consequences appear as yet unforeseeable, becomes what it truly is for us only when it has unfolded into its consequences and into the medium of intersubjective understanding.

And so we see that the rhetorical and hermeneutical aspects of human linguisticality completely interpenetrate each other. There would be no speaker and no art of speaking if understanding and consent were not in question, were not underlying elements; there would be no hermeneutical task if there were no mutual understanding that has been disturbed and that those involved in a conversation must search for and find again together. It is a symptom of our failure to realize this and evidence of the increasing self-alienation of human life in our modern epoch when we think in terms of organizing a perfect and perfectly manipulated information—a turn modern rhetoric seems to have taken. In this case, the sense of mutual interpenetration of rhetoric and hermeneutics fades away and hermeneutics is on its own.

HERMENEUTICS AND THE SOCIAL SCIENCES

It is in keeping with the universality of the hermeneutical approach that hermeneutics must be taken into account with regard to the logic of the social sciences, and especially in relation to the intentional alienation and distancing present in sociological methodology. Jürgen Habermas in his article on the subject worked with my analysis of the *wirkungsgeschichtliches Bewusstsein* and the model of translation as both were given in *Truth and Method* with the hope that they could help to overcome the positivistic ossification of sociological logic and move sociological theory beyond its historical failure to reflect upon its linguistic foundations. Now Habermas's use of hermeneutics stands on the premise that it shall serve the methodology of the social sciences. But this premise is, in itself, a prior decision of greatest significance, for the purpose of sociological method as emancipating one from tradition places it at the outset very far from the traditional purpose and starting point of the hermeneutical problematic with all its bridge building and recovery of the best in the past.

Admittedly the methodological alienation that comprises the very essence of modern science is indeed to be found also in the *Geisteswissenschaften*, and the title of *Truth and Method* never intended that the antithesis it implies should be mutually exclusive.[9] But the *Geisteswissenschaften* were the starting point of my analysis in *Truth and Method* precisely because they related to experiences that have nothing to do with method and science but lie beyond science—like the experience of art and the experience of culture that bears the imprint of its historical tradition. The hermeneutical experience as it is operative in all these cases is not in itself the object of methodical alienation but is directed against alienation. The hermeneutical experience is prior to all methodical alienation because it is the matrix out of which arise the questions that it then directs to science. The modern social scientists, on the other hand, insofar as they recognize hermeneutical reflection as unavoidable, nevertheless advance the claim (as Habermas has formulated it) of raising understanding up out of a prescientific exercise to the rank of a self-reflecting activity by "controlled alienation"—that is, through "methodical development of intelligence."[10]

It has been the way of science from its earliest stages to achieve through teachable and controllable ways of proceeding what individual intelligence would also occasionally attain, but in unsure and uncheckable ways. But is this way to be absolutized and idolized? Is it right that social scientists should believe that through it they attain human personal judging and practice? What kind of understanding does one achieve through "controlled alienation"? Is it not likely to be an alienated understanding? Is it not the case that many social scientists are more interested in using the sedimented truisms inherent in linguisticality (so as to grasp "scientifically" the "real" structures, as they define them, of society) than in really understanding social life? Hermeneutical reflection will not, however, allow a restriction of itself to this function that is immanent in the sciences. And most especially it will not be deterred from applying hermeneutical reflection anew to the methodical alienation of understanding practiced by the social sciences, even though it exposes itself to positivistic detraction.

But let us examine first how the hermeneutical problematic applies within social scientific theory and how it would be seen from that vantage point. Habermas sees in its analysis of historicity one of the principal values of hermeneutics for social theory. So it is the claim of hermeneutics that the idea of *Wirkungsgeschichte* (effective history) furnishes a means of access to the realm of objects treated by sociology. The *wirkungsgeschichtliches Bewusstsein* ("consciousness of effective hiostry") seeks to be aware of its prejudgments and to control its own preunderstanding; and thus it does away with that naive objectivism that falsified not only the positive theory of science but also any project of laying either a phenomenological or language-analytical foundation for sociology.

Yet the question arises as to what hermeneutical reflection really does. Habermas answers this question in reference to universal history, a goal that unavoidably lifts itself out of the multiple goals and conceptions of goal in social actions. He asserts that if hermeneutical reflection were simply satisfied with general considerations, such as that nobody is able to reach beyond the limitedness of his own standpoint, then it would be ineffectual. The claim to a material philosophy of history may be contested by such a consideration, but historical consciousness nevertheless constantly will project an anticipated universal history. What is the good, after all, Habermas asks, of knowing merely that a projected futurity cannot be other than preliminary and essentially provisional? So, where it is effective and operational, what does hermeneutical reflection do? In what relationship to the tradition of which it becomes conscious does this "historically operative" reflection stand?

My thesis is—and I think it is the necessary consequence of recognizing the operativeness of history in our conditionedness and finitude—that the thing that hermeneutics teaches us is to see through the dogmatism of asserting an opposition and separation between the ongoing, natural "tradition" and the reflective appropriation of it. For behind this assertion stands a dogmatic objectivism that distorts the very concept of hermeneutical reflection itself. In this objectivism the understander is seen—even in the so-called sciences of understanding like history—not in relationship to the hermeneutical situation and the constant operativeness of history in his own consciousness, but in such a way as to imply that his own understanding does not enter into the event.

But this is simply not the case. Actually, the historian, even the one who treats history as a "critical science," is so little separated from the ongoing tradition (for example, those of his nation) that he is really *himself engaged in* contributing to the growth and development of the national state. He is one of the "nation's" historians; he belongs to the nation. And for the epoch of national states, one must say: the more he may have reflected on his hermeneutical conditionedness, the more national he knows himself to be. J. F. Droysen, for instance, who saw through the "eunuch-like objectivity" of the historian in all its methodololgical naivete, was himself tremendously influential for the national consciousness of bourgeoise nineteenth-century culture. He was, in any case, more effective than the epical consciousness of Ranke, which was inclined to foster the non-politicality appropriate to an authoritarian state. To understand, we may say, is itself a kind of happening. Only a naive and unreflective historicism in hermeneutics would see the historical-hermeneutical sciences as something absolutely new that would do away with the power of "tradition." On the contrary, I have tried to present in *Truth and Method*, through the aspect of linguisticality that operates in all understanding, an unambiguous demonstration of the continual process of mediation by which that which is societally transmitted (the tradition) lives on. For language is not only an object in our hands, it is the reservoir of tradition and the medium in and through which we exist and perceive our world.

To this formulation Habermas objects that the medium of science itself is changed through reflection, and that precisely this experience is the priceless heritage bequeathed us by German idealism out of the spirit of the eighteenth century. Habermas asserts that although the Hegelian procedure of reflection is not presented in my analysis as fulfilled in an absolute consciousness, nevertheless my "idealism of linguisticality" (as he calls it)[11] exhausts itself in mere hermeneutical appropriation, development, and "cultural transmission," and thus displays a sorry powerlessness in view of the concrete whole of societal relationships. This larger whole, says Habermas, is obviously animated not only by language but by work and action; therefore, hermeneutical reflection must pass into a criticism of ideology.

In taking such a position, Habermas is tying directly into the central motif in sociological interest in gaining knowledge. Rhetoric (theory) stepped forward against the bewitching of consciousness achieved through the power of speech, by differentiating between the truth and that which appears to be the truth (and which it teaches one to produce). Hermeneutics, being confronted with a disrupted inter-subjective understanding, seeks to place communication on a new basis and in particular to replace the false objectivism of alienated knowing with new hermeneutical foundations. Just as in rhetoric and hermeneutics so also in *sociological reflection* an emancipatory interest is at work that undertakes to free us of outer and inner social forces and compulsions simply by making us aware of them. Insofar as these forces and compulsions tend to legitimate themselves linguistically, Habermas sees the critique of ideology as the means of unmasking the "deceptions of language."[12] But this critique, of course, is in itself a linguistic act of reflection.

In the field of psychoanalytical therapy, too, says Habermas, we find the claims for the emancipatory power of reflection corroborated. For the repression that is seen through robs the false compulsions of their power. Just as in psychotherapy it is the goal to identify through a process of reflective development all our motives of action with the real meaning to which the patient is oriented (this goal is of course limited by the therapeutic task in the psychoanalytic situation, which therefore itself represents a limiting concept), so in social reality also (as Habermas would have it) hermeneutics would be at its best when such a fictitious goal situation is operative. For Habermas, and for psychoanalysis, the life of society and the life of the individual con-sists of the interaction of intelligible motives and concrete compul-sions, which social and psychological investigation in a progressive process of clarification appropriates in order to set man, the action and agent, free.

One cannot dispute the fact that this sociotheoretical conception has its logic. The question we must ask ourselves, however, is whether such a conception does justice to the actual reach of hermeneutical reflection: does hermeneutics really take its bearings from a limiting concept of perfect interaction between understood motives and consciously performed action (a concept that is itself, I believe, fictitious)? I maintain that the hermeneutical problem is universal and basic for all interhuman experience, both of history and of the present moment, precisely because meaning can be experienced even where it is not actually intended. The universality of the hermeneutical dimension is narrowed down, I think, when one area of understood meaning (for instance, the "cultural tradition") is held in separation from other recognizable determinants of social reality that are taken as the "real" factors. But is it not true that we can understand precisely *every* ideology as a form of false linguistic consciousness, one that may show itself not only to us as a conscious, manifest, and intelligible meaning but also may be understood in its "true" meaning? Take for example the interest in political or economic domination. In the individual life, the same thing applies to unconscious motives, which the psychoanalyst brings to conscious awareness.

Who says that these concrete, so-called real factors are outside the realm of hermeneutics? From the hermeneutical standpoint, rightly understood, it is absolutely absurd to regard the concrete factors of work and politics as outside the scope of hermeneutics. What about the vital issue of prejudices with which hermeneutical reflection deals? Where do they come from? Merely out of "cultural tradition"? Surely they do, in part, but what is tradition formed from? It would be true when Habermas asserts that "hermeneutics bangs helplessly, so to speak, from within against the walls of tradition,"[13] if we understand this "within" as opposite to an "outside" that *does not enter* our world—our to-be-understood, understandable, or nonunderstandable world—but remains the mere observation of external alterations (instead of human actions). Within this area of what lies outside the realm of human understanding and human understandings (our world) hermeneutics is not concerned. Certainly I affirm the hermeneutical fact that the world is the medium of human understanding or not understanding, but it does not lead to the conclusion that cultural tradition should be absolutized and fixed. To suppose that it does have this implication seems to me erroneous. The principle of hermeneutics simply means that we should try to understand everything that can be understood. This is what I means by the sentence: "Being that can be understood is language."[14]

This does not mean that there is a world of meanings that is narrowed down to the status of secondary objects of knowledge and mere supplements to the economic and political realities that fundamentally determine the life of society. Rather, it means that the mirror of language is reflecting everything that is. In language, and only in it, can we meet what we never "encounter" in the world, because we are ourselves it (and not merely what we mean or what we know of ourselves). But the metaphor of a mirror is not fully adequate to the phenomenon of language, for in the last analysis language is not simply a mirror. What we perceive in it is not merely a "reflection" of our own and all being: it is the living out of what it is with us—not only in the concrete interrelationships of work and politics but in all the other relationships and dependencies that our world comprises.

Language, then is not the finally found anonymous subject of all social-historical processes and action, which presents the whole of its activities as objectivations to our observing gaze; rather, it is by itself the game of interpretation that we all are engaged in every day. In this game nobody is above and before all the others; everybody is at at the center, is "it" in this game. Thus it is always his turn to be interpreting. This process of interpretation takes place whenever we "understand," especially when we see through prejudices or tear away the pretenses that hide reality. There, indeed, understanding comes into its own. This idea recalls what we said about the *atopon*, the strange, for in it we have "seen through" something that appeared odd and unintelligible: we have brought it into our linguistic world. To use the analogy of chess, everything is "solved," resembling a difficult chess problem where only the definitive solution makes understandable (and then right down to the last piece) the necessity of a previous absurd position.

But does this mean that we "understand" only when we see through pretexts or unmask false pretentions? Habermas's marist critique of ideology appears to presuppose this meaning. At least it seems that the true "power" of reflection is evident only when it has this effect, and its powerlessness when one would remain occupied with the supposed phantom of language and spin out its implication. The presupposition is that reflection, as employed in the hermeneutical sciences, should "shake the dogmatism of life-*praxis*."

Here indeed is operating a prejudice that we can see is pure dogmatism, for reflection is not always and unavoidably a step toward dissolving prior convictions. Authority is not *always* wrong. Yet Habermas regards it as an untenable assertion and treason to the heritage of the Enlightenment, that the act of rendering transparent the structure of prejudgments in understanding should possible lead to an acknowledgment of authority. Authority is by his definition a dogmatic power. I cannot accept the assertion that reason and authority are abstract antitheses, as the emancipatory Enlightenment did. Rather, I assert that they stand in a basically ambivalent relation, a relation I think should be explored rather than casually accepting the antithesis as a "fundamental conviction."[15]

For in my opinion this abstract antithesis embraced by the Enlightenment is a mistake fraught with ominous consequences. In it, reflection is granted a false power, and the true dependencies involved are misjudged on the basis of a fallacious idealism. Certainly I would grant that authority exercises an essential dogmatic power in innumerable forms of domination: from the ordering of education and the mandatory commands of the army and government all the way to the hierarchy of power created by political forces or fanatics. Now the mere outer appearance of obedience rendered to authority can never show why or whether the authority is legitimate, that is, whether the context is true order or the veiled disorder that is created by the arbitrary exercise of power. It seems evident to me that *acceptance* or *acknowledgment* is the decisive thing for relationships to authority. So the question is On what is this acknowledgment based? Certainly such acceptance can often express more a yielding of the powerless to the one holding power than true acceptance, but really it is not true obedience and it is not based on authority but on force. (And when anyone in an argument appeals to authority, he only pretends.) One need only study the processes of forfeiture and decline of authority (or its rise) to see what authority is and that out of which it lives and grows. It lives not from dogmatic power but from dogmatic acceptance. What is this dogmatic acceptance, however, if not that one concedes superiority in knowledge and insight to the authority, or for this reason one believes that authority is right? Only on this crucial concession, this belief, is acceptance founded. Authority can rule only because it is freely recognized and accepted. The obedience that belongs to true authority is neither blind nor slavish.

It is an inadmissable imputation to hold that I somehow meant there is no decline of authority or no emancipating criticism of authority. Of course, whether one can really say that decline of authority comes about *through* reflection's emancipatory criticism or that decline of authority is *expressed* in criticism and emancipation is a matter we shall leave aside (although we may say that it is perhaps a misstatement of the genuine alternatives). But what is really in dispute, I think, is simply whether reflection always dissolves substantial relationships or is capable of taking them up into consciousness.

In this regard, my presentation in *Truth and Method* of the teaching and learning process (referring principally to Aristotle's *Ethics*) is taken by Habermas in a peculiarly one-sided way. For the idea that tradition, as such, should be and should remain the only ground for acceptance of presuppositions (a view that Habermas ascribes to me) flies in the face of my basic thesis that authority is rooted in insight as a hermeneutical process. A person who comes of age need not—but he also from insight can—take possession of what he has obediently followed. Tradition is no proof and validation of something, in any case not where validation is demanded by reflection. But the point is this: Where does reflection demand it? Everywhere? I would object to such an answer on the grounds of the finitude of human existence and the essential particularity of reflection. The real question is whether one sees the function of reflection as bringing something to awareness in order to confront what is in fact accepted with other possibilities—so that one can either throw it out or reject the other possibilities and accept what the tradition de facto is presenting—or whether bringing something to awareness *always dissolves what one has previously accepted*.

The concept of reflection and bringing to awareness that Habermas employs (admittedly from his sociological interest) appears to me, then, to be itself encumbered with dogmatism, and indeed, to be a misinterpretation of reflection. For, from Husserl (in his doctrine of anonymous intentionalities) and from Heidegger (in demonstration of the ontological abridgement evident in the subject-object concept in idealism), we have learned to see through the false objectification inherent in the idealist conception of reflection. I would hold that there is most certainly an inner reversal of intentionality in reflection, which in no way raises the thing meant to be thematic object. Brentano, using Aristotelian insights, was aware of this fact. I would not know, otherwise, how the enigmatic form of the being of language could be grasped at all. Then one must distinguish "effective reflection" (*die "effektive" Reflexion*), which is that in which the unfolding of language takes place, from expressive and thematic reflection, which is the type out of which Occidental linguistic history has been formed.[15] Making everything an object and creating the conditions for science in the modern sense, this latter type of reflection establishes the grounds for the planetary civilization of tomorrow.

Habermas defends with extraordinary emotion the sciences of experience against the charge of being a random game of words. But who, from the vantage point of the technical power to place nature at our disposal, would dispute their necessity? The researcher may disclaim the technical motivation of his work and defend his relationship to pure theoretical interests—with full subjective justification. But nobody would deny that the practical application of modern science has fundamentally altered our world, and therewith also our language. But precisely so—"*also* our language." This by no means suggests, however, what Habermas inputes to me that the linguistically articulated consciousness claims to determine all the material being of life-practice. It only suggests that there is no societal reality, with all its concrete forces, that does not bring itself to representation in a consciousness that is linguistically articulated. Reality does not happen "behind the back" of language,[17] it happens rather behind the backs of those who live in the subjective opinion that they have understood "the world" (or can no longer understand it); that is, reality happens precisely *within* language.

Obviously this fact makes the concept of "natural situation" discussed by Habermas[18] highly questionable. Marx already persuasively held that this concept was the counteridea to the working world of modern class society, but Habermas willingly uses it not only in his reference to the "natural substance of tradition" but also to "the causality of natural patterns." I believe it is pure romanticism, and such romanticism creates an artificial abyss between tradition and the reflection that is grounded in historical consciousness. However, the "idealism of linguisticality" at least has the advantage that it does not fall into this sort of romanticism.

Habermas's critique culminates in questioning the immanentism of transcendental philosophy with respect to its historical conditions, conditions upon which he himself is dependent. Now this is indeed a central problem. Anyone who takes seriously the finitude of human existence and constructs no "consciousness as such" or "intellectus archetypus" or "transcendental ego," to which everything can be traced back, will not be able to escape the question of how his own thinking as transcendental is empirically possible. But within the hermeneutical dimension that I have developed I do not see this difficulty arising.

The well-known young theologian Wolfhart Pannenberg has presented a highly useful discussion of my book in his article "Hermeneutics and Universal HIstory,"[19] which relates to the question of immanentism but more particularly to the question of whether my philosophical hermeneutics necessarily but unconsciously rehabilitates the Hegelian concept of universal history (such as in the concept of fusion of horizons, where the ultimate horizon is, says Pannenberg, implied or presupposed in the direction of every individual event of fusion). In particular his discussion brought home to me the vast difference between Hegel's claim to demonstrate the presence of reason in history and the conceptions of world history, those constantly outstripped conceptions, in which one unconsciously always behaves like the latest historian.

Hegel's claim to a philosophy of world history can certainly be disputed. Hegel himself knew how finite it was and remarked that the feet of his pallbearers could already be heard outside the door,[20] and one finds that behind all the disavowals of world history the goal, the end-thought, of *freedom* possessed a compelling evidentness. One can as little get beyond this as one can get beyond consciousness itself.

But the claim that every historian must make and operate within, namely to tie the meaning of all events to today (and of course to the future of this today), is really a fundamentally more modest one than asserting a universal history or a philosophy of world history. Nobody can dispute that history presupposes futurity, and a universal-historical conception is unavoidably one of the dimensions of today's historical consciousness from a practical point of view, or for practical purposes (*"in praktischer Absicht"*). But does it do justice to Hegel to want to reduce him to the limitations implied by this pragmatic interpretive requirement that the present demands? "In praktischer Absicht"—nobody today goes beyond this claim, for consciousness has become aware of its finitude and mistrusts the dictatorship of ideas or concepts. Even so, who would be so foolish as to try to reduce Hegel to the level of practical purposes? I certainly would not, even while criticizing his claims to a philosophy of universal history. So on this point I think there is really no dispute between Pannenberg and myself, so far as I understand him. For Pannenberg does not propose to renew Hegel's claim either. There is only the difference that for the Christian theologican the "practical purpose" of all universal historical conceptions has its fixed point in the absolute historicity of the Incarnation.

All the same, the question [of universality] remains. If the hermeneutical problematic wishes to maintain itself in the face of the ubiquity and universality of rhetoric, as well as the obvious topicality and critiques of ideology, it must establish its own universality. And it must do so especially over against the claims of modern science to universality, and thus to its tendency to absorb hermeneutical reflection into itself and render it serviceable to science (as in the concept, for instance, of the "methodical development of intelligence" Habermas has in mind). Still, it will be able to do so only if it does not become imprisoned in the impregnable immanence of transcendental reflection but rather gives account of what its own kind of reflection achieves. And it must do it not only within the realm of modern science but also over against this realm, in order to show a universality that transcends that of modern science.

ON THE UNIVERSALITY OF HERMENEUTICAL REFLECTION

Hermeneutical reflection fulfills the function that is accomplished in all bringing of something to a conscious awareness. Because it does, it can and must manifest itself in all our modern fields of knowledge, and especially science. Let us reflect a bit on this hermeneutical reflection. Reflection on a given preunderstanding brings before me something that otherwise happens *behind my back*. Something—but not everything, for what I have called the *wirkungsgeschichtliches Bewusstsein* is inescapably more *being* than consciousness, and being is never fully manifest. Certainly I do not mean that such reflection could escape from ideological ossification if it does not engage in constant self-reflection and attempts at self-awareness. Thus only through hermeneutical reflection am I no longer unfree over against myself but rather can deem freely what in my preunderstanding may be justified and what unjustifiable.

And also only in this manner do I learn to gain a new understanding of what I have seen through eyes conditioned by prejudice. But this implies, too, that the prejudgments that led my preunderstanding are also constantly at stake, right up to the moment of their surrender—which surrender could also be called a transformation. It is the untiring power of *experience*, that in the process of being instructed, man is ceaselessly forming a new preunderstanding.

In the fields that were the starting points of my hermeneutical studies—the study of art and the philological-historical sciences—it is easy to demonstrate how hermeneutical reflection is at work. For instance, consider how the autonomy of viewing art from the vantage point of the history of style has been shaken up by hermeneutical reflection (1) on the concept of art itself, and (2) on concepts of individual styles and epochs. Consider how inconography has pressed from the periphery to the forefront, and how hermeneutical reflection on the concepts of experience and expression has had literary-critical consequences (even in cases where it becomes only a more conscious carrying forward of tendencies long favored in literary criticism). While it is of course evident how the shakeup of fixed presuppositions promises scientific progress by making new questions possible, it should be equally evident that this applies in the history of artistic and literary styles. And we constantly experience what historical research can accomplish through becoming conscious of the history of ideas. In *Truth and Method* I believe I have been able to show how historical alienation is mediated in the form of what I call the "fusion of horizons."

The overall significance of hermeneutical reflection, however, is not exhausted by what it means for and in the sciences themselves. For all the modern sciences possess a deeply rooted alienation that they impose on the natural consciousness and of which we need to be aware. This alienation has already reached reflective awareness in the very beginning stages of modern science in the concept of *method*. Hermeneutical reflection does not desire to change or eliminate this situation; it can, in fact, indirectly serve the methodological endeavor of science by making transparently clear the guiding preunderstandings in the sciences and thereby open new dimensions of questioning. But it must also bring to awareness, in this regard, the price that methods in science have paid for their own progress; the toning down and abstraction they demand, through which the natural consciousness still always must go along as the consumer of the inventions and information attained by science. One can with Wittgenstein express this insight as follows: The language games of science remain related to the metalanguage presented in the mother tongue. All the knowledge won by science enters the societal consciousness through school and education, using modern informational media, though maybe sometimes after a great—too great—delay. In any case, this is the way that new sociolinguistic realities are articulated.

For the *natural* sciences, of course, this gap and the methodical alienation of research are of less consequence than for social sciences. The true natural scientist does not have to be told how very particular is the realm of knowledge of his science in relation to the whole of reality. He does not share in the deification of his science that the public would press upon him. All the more, however, the public (and the researcher who must go before the public) needs hermeneutical reflection on the presuppositions and limits of science. The so-called humanities, on the other hand, are still easily mediated to the common consciousness, so that insofar as they are accepted at all, their objects belong immediately to the cultural heritage and the realm of traditional education. But the modern social sciences stand in a particularly strained relationship to their object, the social reality, and this relationship especially requires hermeneutical reflection. For the methodical alienation to which the social sciences owe their progress is related here to the human-societal world as a whole. These sciences increasingly see themselves as marked out for the purpose of scientific ordering and control of society. They have to do with "scientific" and "methodical" planning, direction, organization, development—in short, with an infinity of functions that, so to speak, determine from outside the whole of the life of each individual and each group. Yet this social engineer, this scientist who undertakes to look after the functioning of the machine of society, appears himself to be methodically alienated and split off from the society to which, at the same time, he belongs.

But is man as a political being the mere object of the techniques of making public opinion? I think not: he is a member of society, and only in playing his role with free judgment and politically real effectiveness can he conserve freedom. It is the function of hermeneutical reflection, in this connection, to preserve us from naive surrender to the experts of social technology.

Of course, a hermeneutically reflective sociologist like Habermas cannot conceive himself in these shallow terms of social engineering.

Habermas's lucid analysis of social-scientific logic has resolutely worked out the authentic epistemological interest, which distinguishes true sociologists from technicians of social structure. He calls it an *emancipating interest* (what a contrast to the interest of the social engineers!), which takes reflection alone as its objective. He points in this regard to the example of psychoanalysis. And it is in psychoanalysis, as a matter of fact, that hermeneutical reflection plays a fundamental role. This is because, as we have emphasized earlier, the unconscious motive does not represent a clear and fully articulable boundary for hermeneutical theory: it falls within the larger perimeter of hermeneutics. Psychotherapy could be described as the work of "completing an interrupted process of education into a full history (a story that can be articulated in language)", so in psychotherapy hermeneutics and the circle of language that is closed in dialogue are central. I think I have learned this fact, above all, from Jacques Lacan.[21]

All the same it is clear that even this is not the whole story, for the psychoanalytic approach turns out not to be universalizable even for the psychoanalyst himself. The framework of interpretation worked out by Freud claims to possess the character of genuine natural-scientific hypotheses, that is, to be a knowledge of acknowledged laws. This orientation inevitably shows up in the role that methodical alienation plays in his psychoanalysis. But although the successful analysis wins *its* authentication in its results, the claim to *knowledge* in psychoanalysis must not be reduced to mere pragmatic validation. And this means that psychoanalysis is exposed again to another act of hermeneutical reflection, in which one must ask How does the psychoanalyst's special knowledge relate to his own position within the societal reality (to which, after all, he does belong)?

The psychoanalyst leads the patient into the emancipatory reflection that goes behind the conscious superficial interpretations, breaks through the masked self-understanding, and sees through the repressive function of social taboos. This activity belongs to the emancipatory reflection to which he leads his patient. But what happens when he uses the same kind of reflection in a situation in which he is not the doctor but a partner in a game? Then he will fall out of his social role! A game partner who is always "seeing through" his game partner, who does not take seriously what they are standing for, is a spoilsport whom one shuns. The emancipatory power of reflection claimed by the psychoanalyst is a special rather than general function of reflection and must be given its boundaries through the societal context and consciousness, within which the analyst and also his patient are on even terms with everybody else. This is something that *hermeneutical reflection* teaches us: that social community, with all its tensions and disruptions, ever and ever again leads back to a common area of social understanding through which it exists.

Here, I think, the analogy Habermas suggests between psychoanalytical and, sociological theory breaks down, or at least raises severe problems. For where are the limits of this analogy? Where does the patient-relationship end and the social partnership in its unprofessional right begin? Most fundamentally: Over against what self-interpretation of the social consciousness (and all morality is such) is it in place to inquire *behind* that consciousness—and when is it not? Within the context of the purely practical, or of a universalized emancipatory reflection, these questions appear unanswerable. The unavoidable consequence to which all these observations lead is that the basically emancipatory consciousness must have in mind the dissolution of all authority, all obedience. This means that unconsciously the ultimate guiding image of emancipatory reflection in the social sciences must be an anarchistic utopia. Such an image, however, seems to me to reflect a hermeneutically false consciousness, the antidote for which can only be a more universal hermeneutical reflection.

NOTES

1. Thus what O. Marquard (Heidelberger Philosophiekongress, 1966) calls "das Sein zum Texte" does not at all exhaust the hermeneutical dimension—unless the word Texte is taken not in the narrow sense but as "the text that God has written with his own hand," i.e., the *liber naturae*, which consequently encompasses all knowledge from physics to sociology and anthropology. And even in this case the model of translation is implied, which is not fully adequate to the complexity of the hermeneutical dimension.

2. See Johannes Lohmann, *Philosophie und Sprachwissenschaft* and his review of my book in *Gnomon* 37 (1965): 709–18. Lohmann's treatment may be seen as a greatly expanded application of what I had briefly sketched as the imprint of the concept of *Sprache* (language in Occidental thought). He traces "the emergence of the concept (*Begriff*) as the intellectual vehicle by which given objects are momentarily subsumed under one cogitated form" (p. 74). He recognizes in the stem-inflecting verbs of Old Indo-Germanic the grammatical expression of this idea, especially in the copula. From this, he says, we can

deduce the possiblity of theory, which is a creation peculiar to the occident. The significance of this is more than historical; it also extends into the future. Not only does Lohmann take the transition from stem-inflecting to word-inflecting language types to interpret the history of thought in the occident by showing the development of language forms, he shows that this latter-day development to word-inflecting types makes possible science in the modern sense—science as the rendering disposable to us of our world.

3. I have considered some aspects of this in *Wahrheit und Methode* Tübingen: J. C. B. Mohr (Paul Siebeck), 1960, pp. 16ff (Hereafter cited as *WM*), but they can be greatly expanded see, for instance, the extensive supplements and corrections contributed by Klaus Dockhorn to the Göttingen "Gelehrten-Anzeiger" 208 Heft 314 (1966) 169–206.

4. *Philosophische Rundschau*, 14 Beiheft 5 (1967): pp. 149–180. Hereafter cited as *PhR*. See also his more recent book, *Knowledge and Human Interests*, (Boston: Beacon Press, 1972).

5. Hermann Gundert has done this in his contribution to *Hermeneia*, 1952, a Festschrift for Otto Regenbogen.

6. Klaus Dockhorn has shown, with profound scholarship, in "Gelehrten-Anzeigen," the extent to which the arousing of emotions has been considered the most important means of persuasion from Cicero and Quintilian to the political rhetoric of the eighteenth century in England.

7. I discussed this in my book, and Dockhorn, "Gelehrten-Anzeigen," has carried out the exploration on a much broader basis.

8. Henri Gouhier in particular has shown this in his *La Resistance au vrai*, ed. E. Castelli (Rome: 1955).

9. In this regard see the preface to the second edition (1965).

10. Cf. *Ph R*, 14:172–74.

11. Ibid., p. 179.

12. Ibid., p. 178.

13. Ibid., p. 177.

14. *WM*, p. 450.

15. *Ph R*, 14:172–74.

16. On this point I am agreeing with J. Lohmann in *Philosophie und Sprachwissenschaft*.

17. *PhR* 14:179.

18. Ibid., pp. 173–74.

19. Wolfhart Pannenberg, "Hermeneutik und Universalgeschichte," *Zeitschrift fur Theologie und Kirche* 60 (1963): 90–121. ET. Paul J. Achtemeier in *History and Hermeneutic*, ed. Robert W. Funk and Gerhard Ebeling (New York: Harper & Row, 1967), pp. 122–52.

20. Gadamer expresses this more picturesquely with a quote: "Die Füsse derer, die dich hinaustragen, sind schon vor der Türe" (translators).

21. See the collection of his writings now published as *Ecrits* (Paris: Editions du Seuil, 1966).

HERMENEUTICS AND THE
CRITIQUE OF IDEOLOGY

PAUL RICOEUR

The debate that is evoked by this title goes well beyond the limits of a discussion about the foundations of the social sciences. It raises the question of what I shall call the fundamental gesture of philosophy. Is this gesture an avowal of the historical conditions to which all human understanding is subsumed under the reign of finitude? Or rather is it, in the last analysis, an act of defiance, a critical gesture, relentlessly repeated and indefinitely turned against 'false consciousness', against the distortions of human communication that conceal the permanent exercise of domination and violence? Such is the philosophical stake of a debate that at first seems tied to the epistemological plane of the human sciences. What is at stake can be expressed in terms of an alternative: either a hermeneutical consciousness or a critical consciousness. But is it really so? Is it not the alternative itself that must be challenged? Is it possible to formulate a hermeneutics that would render justice to the critique of ideology, that would show the necessity of the latter at the very heart of its own concerns? Clearly the stake is considerable. We are not going to risk everything by beginning with terms that are too general and an attitude that is too ambitious. We shall, instead, focus attention on a contemporary discussion that presents the problem in the form of an alternative. Even if ultimately this alternative must be surpassed, we shall not be in ignorance of the difficulties to be overcome.

The principal protagonists in the debate are, on the side of hermeneutics, Hans-Georg Gadamer; and on the side of critique, Jürgen Habermas. The dossier of their polemic is now public, partially reproduced in the little volume entitled *Hermeneutik und Ideologiekritik*.[1] It is from this dossier that I shall extract the lines of force that characterize the conflict between hermeneutics and the critical theory of ideology. I shall take the assessment of *tradition* by each of these philosophies as the touchstone of the debate. In contrast to the positive assessment by hermeneutics, the theory of ideology adopts a suspicious approach, seeing tradition as merely the systematically distorted expression of communication under unacknowledged conditions of violence. The choice of this touchstone has the advantage of bringing to the fore a confrontation that bears upon the 'claim to universality' of hermeneutics. For the critique of ideology is of interest insofar as it is a nonhermeneutical discipline, situated outside the sphere of competence of a science or philosophy of interpretation and marking the fundamental limit of the latter.

In the first part of this essay, I shall restrict myself to presenting the contents of the dossier. I shall do so in terms of a simple alternative either hermeneutics or the critique of ideology. I shall reserve for the second part a more personal reflection, centered on the following two questions: (1) Can hermeneutic philosophy account for the legitimate demand of the critique of ideology, and if so at what price? Must it sacrifice its claim to universality and undertake a profound reformulation of its programme and its project? (2) On what condition is the critique of ideology possible? Can it, in the last analysis, be detached from hermeneutic presuppositions?

I hasten to say that no plan of annexation, no syncretism, will preside over this debate. I readily admit, along with Gadamer, that each of the two theories speaks from a different place; but I hope to show that each can recognize the other's claim to universality in a way that marks the place of one in the structure of the other.

THE ALTERNATIVE

Gadamer: The Hermeneutics of Tradition

We may go directly to the critical point—the *Brennpunkt*—that Habermas attacks in *Logik der Sozialwissenschaften*, namely the conception of historical consciousness and the provocative rehabilitation of the three connected concepts of prejudice, authority, and tradition. This text is by no means secondary or marginal. It goes directly to the central experience or, as I have just said, to the place from which this hermeneutics speaks and upon which it raises its claim to universality. This experience is the scandal constituted, on the level of modern consciousness, by the sort of *alienating distanciation—Verfremdung—*

that is not merely a feeling or a mood, but rather the ontological presupposition that sustains the objective conduct of the human sciences. The methodology of these sciences ineluctably implies an assumption of distance; and this, in turn, presupposes the destruction of the primordial relation of belonging—*Zügehorigkeit*—without which there would be no relation to the historical as such. The debate between alienating distanciation and the experience of belonging is pursued by Gadamer through the three spheres into which the hermeneutical experience is divided: the aesthetic sphere, the historical sphere and the sphere of language . . . So although we shall focus attention on the second part, it must be remembered that in a sense the debate is already played out in the aesthetic sphere, just as it only culminates in the lingual experience whereby aesthetic consciousness and historical consciousness are brought to discourse. The theory of historical consciousness is therefore an epitome of the work as a whole and microcosm of the great debate.

At the same time that hermeneutic philosophy declares the amplitude of its aim, so too it announces the locality of its point of departure. Gadamer speaks from a place that is determined by the history of attempts to resolve the problem of the foundation of the human sciences, attempts first undertaken in German romanticism, then in Dilthey's work, and finally in terms of Heidegger's ontology. This is readily acknowledged by Gadamer himself, even when he proclaims the universality of the hermeneutical dimension. For the universality is not abstract; it is, for each investigator, centered on a dominant problematic, a privileged experience. "My own attempt," he writes at the outset of "Rhetorik, Hermeneutik, und Ideologie-kritik," "is linked to the revival of the heritage of German Romanticism by Dilthey, insofar as he takes the theory of the human sciences as his theme, placing it on a new and broader foundation; the experience of art, together with the experience of contemporaneousness which is peculiar to it, provides the riposte to the historical distanciation of the human sciences."[2] Thus hermeneutics has an aim that precedes and surpasses any science, an aim testified to by "the universal linguality of behaviour relative to the world";[3] but the universality of the aim is the counterpart to the narrowness of the initial experience in which it is rooted. The fact that the localized nature of the initial experience is emphasized, as well as the claim to universality, is therefore not irrelevant to the debate with the proponents of the critique of ideology. It would have been equally possible to begin, not with historical consciousness as such, but rather with the interpretation of texts in the experiencing of reading, as the hermeneutics of Schleiermacher shows. In choosing this somewhat different point of departure, as I myself shall do in the second part of the essay, the problem of distanciation can be given a more positive significance than Gadamer suggests. Gadamer has specifically dismissed as less important a reflection on "being for the text" (*Sein zum Texte*), which he seems to reduce to a deliberation on the problem of translation, itself set up as a model of the linguality of human behavior toward the world. However, it is to this reflection that I shall return in the second part, in the hope of deriving therefrom an orientation of thought that is less subordinated to the problematic of tradition and more receptive to the critique of ideology.

By taking historical consciousness and the question of the conditions of possibility of the human sciences as the axis of reflection, Gadamer inevitably turned hermeneutic philosophy toward the rehabilitation of prejudice and the defense of tradition and authority, placing this philosophy in a conflictual relation to any critique of ideology. At the same time the conflict itself, in spite of the modern terminology, was returned to its original formulation, as expressed in the struggle between the spirit of romanticism and that of the *Aufklärung* ("Enlightenment"). The conflict had to take the form of a repetition of the same struggle along the course of an obligatory route, beginning with romanticism, passing through the epistemological stage of the human sciences with Dilthey, and undergoing the ontological transposition of Heidegger. In adopting the privileged experience of historical consciousness, Gadamer adopted also a certain philosophical route that, ineluctably, he had to reiterate.

The struggle between romanticism and the Enlightenment is the source of our own problem and the milieu in which the opposition between two fundamental philosophical attitudes took shape: on one side, the *Aufklärung* and its struggle against prejudices; on the other, romanticism and its nostalgia for the past. The problem is whether the modern conflict between the critique of ideology according to the Frankfurt School and the hermeneutics of Gadamer marks any progress in this debate.

So far as Gadamer is concerned, his declared intention is perfectly clear: the pitfalls of romanticism must be avoided. The second part of *Truth and Method*, which culminates in the famous theory of "consciousness exposed to the effects of history" (*wirkungsgeschichtliches Bewusstsein*), contains a sharp attack on romantic philosophy for having merely reversed the terms of the argument without displacing the problematic itself and without changing the terrain of the debate. For 'prejudice', in the double sense of precipitation (to judge too quickly) and predisposition (to follow custom or authority), is the category par excellence of the *Aufklärung*. Prejudice is what must be put aside in order to think, in order to dare to think—according to the famous adage *sapere aude*—so that one may reach the age of adulthood or *Mündigkeit*. To recover a less univocally negative sense of the word 'prejudice' (which has become virtually synonymous with unfounded or false judgment), and to restore the ambivalence that the Latin word *praejudicium* had in the juridical tradition prior to the Enlightenment, it would be necessary to question the presuppositions of a philosophy that opposes reason to prejudice. These are, in fact, the very presuppositions of a critical philosophy; it is for a philosophy of judgment —and a critical philosophy is a philosophy of judgment—that prejudice is a predominantly negative category. What must be questioned, therefore, is the primacy of judgment in man's behavior toward the world; and the only philosophy that sets up judgment as a tribunal is one that makes objectivity, as modeled on the sciences, the measure of knowledge. Judgment and prejudice are dominant categories only in the type of philosophy, stemming from Descartes, that makes methodical consciousness the key of our relation to being and to beings. Hence it is necessary to delve beneath the philosophy of judgment, beneath the problematic of subject and object, in order to effect a rehabilitation of prejudice that is not a simple negation of the spirit of the Englightenment.

It is here that romantic philosophy proves to be both a first foundation and a fundamental failure. A first foundation because it dares to challenge "the discrediting of prejudice by the *Aufklärung*,"[4] a fundamental failure, because it only inverts the answer without inverting the question. Romanticism wages its war on a terrain defined by the adversary, a terrain on which the role of tradition and authority in the process of interpretation are in dispute. It is on the same terrain, the same ground of inquiry, that the *mythos* is celebrated over the *logos*, that the old is defended against the new, historical Christendom against the modern state, the fraternal community against an administrative socialism, the productive unconscious against a sterile consciousness, the mythical past against a future of rational utopias, the poetic imagination against cold ratiocination. Romantic hermeneutics thus ties its destiny to everything that is associated with the Restoration.

Such is the pitfall that the hermeneutics of historical consciousness seeks to avoid. The question, once again, is whether Gadamer's hermeneutics has really surpassed the romantic point of departure of hermeneutics, and whether his affirmation that "the finitude of man's being consists in the fact that firstly he finds himself at the heart of tradition"[5] escapes from the play of inversions in which he sees philosophical romanticism, confronting the claims of critical philosophy, ensnared.

In Gadamer's view, it is only with the philosophy of Heidegger that the problematic of prejudice can be reconstituted as, precisely, a problematic. The Diltheyan stage of the problem is, in this respect, not at all decisive. On the contrary, we owe to Dilthey the illusion that the natural sciences and the human sciences are characterized by two scientificities, two methodologies, two epistemologies. Hence, in spite of his debt to Dilthey, Gadamer does not hesitate to write, "Dilthey was unable to free himself from the traditional theory of knowledge."[6] Dilthey still begins from self-consciousness; for him, subjectivity remains the ultimate point of reference. The reign of *Erlebnis* (lived experience) is the reign of a primordiality that I am. In this sense, the fundamental is the *Innesein*, the interior, the awareness of itself. It is thus against Dilthey, as well as the constantly resurging *Aufklärung*, that Gadamer proclaims: "the prejudices of the individual, far more than his judgements, constitute the historical reality of his being."[7] The rehabilitation of prejudice, authority, and tradition will thus be directed against the reign of subjectivity and interiority, that is, against the criteria of reflection. This antireflective polemic will help to give Gadamer's plea the appearance of a return to a precritical position. Yet however provoking—not to say provocative—this plea may be, it attests to the resurgence of the historical dimension over the moment of reflection. History precedes me and my reflection; I belong to history before I belong to myself. Dilthey could not understand that, because his revolution remained epistemological and his reflective criterion prevailed over his historical consciousness.

It may be asked nonetheless whether the sharpness of the remarks against Dilthey has the same significance as the attack on romanticism: Is not the fidelity to Dilthey more profound than the critique addressed to him? This would explain why the question of history and historicity, rather than that of the text and exegesis, continues to provide what I shall call, in a manner similar to Gadamer himself, the *primary* experience of hermeneutics. It is perhaps at this level that

Gadamer's hermeneutics must be interrogated, that is, at a level where his fidelity to Dilthey is more important than his critique. We shall reserve this question for the second part, restricting ourselves here to following the movement from the critique of romanticism and Dilthey's epistemology to the properly Heideggerian phase of the problem.

To restore the historical dimension of man requires much more than a simple methodological reform, much more than a mere epistemological legitimation of the idea of a 'human science' in face of demands from the sciences of nature. Only a fundamental upheaval that subordinates the theory of knowlege to ontology can bring out the real sense of the *Vorstruktur des Verstehens*—the forestructure (or structure of anticipation) of understanding—that is the condition for any rehabilitation of prejudice.

We are all familiar with the section of *Being and Time* on understanding (para 31),[8] where Heidegger, accumulating expressions that exhibit the prefix *vor (Vor-habe, Vor-sicht, Vor-griffe)*, proceeds to found the hermeneutical circle of the human sciences in a structure of anticipation that is part of the very position of our being within being. Gadamer expresses it well: "The point of Heidegger's hermeneutical thinking is not so much to prove that there is a circle as to show that this circle possesses an ontologically positive significance."[9] It is worth noting, however, that Gadamer refers not only to paragraph 31, which is still part of "the fundamental Analytic of *Dasein*" (the title of the first division), but also to paragraph 63, which clearly shifts the problematic of interpretation toward the question of temporality as such; it is no longer just a question of the *Da* [there] of *Dasein* [being-there], but of its 'potentiality-for-being-a-whole- (*Ganzseinskönnen*), which is manifested in the three temporal ecstases of care. Gadamer is right to "inquire into the consequences which follow for the hermeneutics of the human sciences from the fact the Heidegger derives the circular structure of understanding from the temporality of *Dasein*."[10] But Heidegger himself did not consider these questions, which would perhaps lead us back in an unexpected way to the critical theme that was allegedly expurgated along with purely epistemological or methodological concerns. If one follows the movement of radicalisation that leads, not only from Dilthey to Heidegger, but from paragraph 31 to paragraph 63 in the very interior of *Being and Time*, then it seems that the privileged experience (if one can still speak in this way) is no longer the history of the historians, but rather the history of the quest of the meaning of being in Western metaphysics. So it seems that the hermeneutical situation within which the interpretation unfolds is characterized by the fact that the structure of anticipation, in terms of which we interrogate being, is provided by the history of metaphysics; it is that which takes the place of prejudice. (Later we shall ask ourselves whether the critical relation that Heidegger establishes with respect to this tradition does not also involve a certain rehabilitation of the critique of prejudices). Heidegger thus effects a fundamental displacement of the problem of prejudice : Prejudice—*Vormeinung*—is part of the structure of anticipation.[11] Here the example of textual exegesis is more than a particular case; it is a development, in the photographic sense of the term. Heidegger may well call philological interpretation a "derivative mode", but it remains the touchstone. It is there that we can perceive the necessity of drawing back from the vicious circle in which philological interpretation turns, insofar as it understands itself in terms of a model of scientificity borrowed from the exact sciences, to the nonvicious circle formed by the anticipatory structure of the very being we are.

However, Heidegger is not interested in the movement of return from the structure of anticipation that constitutes us to the hermenutic circle in its properly methodological aspects. This is unfortunate, because it is on the return route that hermeneutics is likely to encounter critique, in particular the critique of ideology. Hence our own interrogation of Heidegger and Gadamer will begin from the difficulties raised by the movement of return, upon which the idea that philological interpretation is a "derivative mode of understanding" can alone be legitimated. Insofar as this derivation has not been attempted, it has still not been shown that the forestructure itself is fundamental. For nothing is fundamental, so long as something else has not been derived from it.

It is on this threefold basis—romantic, Diltheyan, Heideggerian—that *Gadamer's distinctive contribution to the problematic* must be placed. In this respect, Gadamer's text is like a palimpsest in which it is always possible to distinguish, as in the thickness of overlaid transparencies, a romantic layer, a Diltheyan layer, and a Heideggerian layer, and that may thus be read at each of these levels. Each level, in turn, is reflected on the views that Gadamer currently espouses as his own. As his adversaries have clearly seen, Gadadmer's distinctive contribution concerns, first, the link that he establishes, purely phenomenologically as it were, between prejudice, tradition, and authority; second, the ontological interpretation of this sequence in terms of the concept of *wirkungsgeschichtliches Bewusstein*, which I shall translate as "consciousness exposed to the effects of history" or "consciousness of historical efficacy"; and this, the epistemological or "metacritical" consequence, as Gadamer calls it in his *Kleine Schriften*, that an exhaustive critique of prejudice—and hence of ideology—is impossible, because there is no zero point from which it could proceed.

Let us consider each of these three points in turn: the phenomenology of prejudice, tradition, and authority; the ontology of consciousness exposed to the effects of history; and the critique of critique.

Gadamer's attempt to rehabilitate prejudice, tradition, and authority is not without a provocative aim. The analysis is 'phenomenological' in the sense that it seeks to extract from these three phenomena an essence that the *Aufklärung*, with its perjorative appraisal, has obscured. For Gadamer, prejudice is not the opposite pole of a reason without presupposition; it is a component of understanding, linked to the finite historical character of the human being. It is false to maintain that there are only unfounded prejudices, because there are, in the juridical sense, prejudgments that may or may not be subsequently grounded, and even 'legitimate prejudices'. So even if prejudices by precipitation are more difficult to rehabilitate, prejudices by predisposition have a profound significance that is missed by analyses conducted from a purely critical standpoint. Yet the prejudice against prejudice is rooted at a deeper level, namely, in a prejudice against authority, which is identified too quickly with domination and violence. The concept of authority brings us to the heart of the debate with the critique of ideology. Let us recall that this concept is also at the center of Max Weber's political sociology: the state is the institution par excellence that rests on a belief in the legitimacy of its authority and its right to use violence in the last instance. Now for Gadamer, the analysis of this concept has suffered, since the time of the *Aufklärung*, from a confusion between domination, authority, and violence. It is here that the analysis of essence is crucial. The *Aufklärung* posits a necessary connection between authority and blind obedience:

> But this is not the essence of authority. It is true that it is
> primarily persons that have authority; but the authority of per-
> sons is based ultimately, not on the subjection and abdication
> of reason, but on acceptance and recognition - rejection,

namely, that the other is superior to oneself in judgment and insight and that for this reason his judgment takes precedence, i.e., it has priority over one's own. This is connected with the fact that authority cannot actually be bestowed, but is acquired and must be acquired, if someone is to lay claim to it. It rests on consideration and hence on an act of reason itself which, aware of its own limitations, accepts that others have better understanding. Authority in this sense, properly understood, has nothing to do with blind obedience to a command. Indeed, authority has nothing to do with obedience; it rests on recognition.[13]

Thus the key concept is recognition (*Anerkennung*), which is substituted for the notion of obedience. We may note in passing that this concept implies a certain critical moment: "The recognition of authority," says Gadamer further on, "is always connected with the idea that what authority states is not irrational and arbitrary, but can be accepted in principle. This is the essence of the authority claimed by the teacher, the superior, the expert."[14] This critical moment offers the possibility of articulating the phenomenology of authority onto the critique of ideology.

However, this is not the aspect that Gadamer ultimately underlines. In spite of his earlier critique, it is to a theme of German romanticism that Gadamer returns, linking *authority* to *tradition*. That which has authority is tradition. When he comes to this equation, Gadamer speaks in romantic terms.

There is one form of authority that romanticism has defended with particular ardour: tradition. That which has been sanctioned by tradition and custom has an authority that is nameless, and our finite historical being is determined by the fact that always the authority of what has been transmitted—and not only what is clearly grounded—has power (*Gewalt*) over our attitudes and behaviour. All education depends on this [customs and traditions] are freely taken over, but by no means created by a free insight or justified by themselves. This is precisely what we call tradition: the ground of their validity. And in fact we owe to romanticism this correction of the enlightenment, that tradition has a justification that is outside the arguments of reason and in large measure determines our attitudes and behaviour. It is even a mark of the superiority of classical ethics over the moral philosophy of the modern period that is justifies the transition of ethics into 'politics', the art of right government, by the indispensability of tradition. In comparison with it, the modern enlightenment is abstract and revolutionary.[15]

(Notice how the word *Gewalt* ["power"] is slipped into the text behind *Autorität* ["authority"], as well as *Herrschaft* ["domination"] in the expression *Herschaft von Tradition*.[16]

Gadamer does not want, of course, to fall back into the rut of the irresolvable debate between romanticism and the Enlightenment. We must be grateful to him for attempting to reconcile, rather than oppose, authority and reason. The real meaning of authority stems from the contribution that it makes to the maturity of free judgement: "to accept authority" is thus also to pass through the screen of doubt and critique. More fundamentally still, authority is linked to reason insofar as "tradition is constantly an element of freedom and of history itself."[17] This point is missed if the 'preservation' (*Bewahrung*) of a cultural heritage is confused with the simple conservation of a natural reality. A tradition must be seized, taken up, and maintained; hence it demands an act of reason: "Preservation is as much a freely-chosen act as revolution and renewal."[18]

It may be noted, however, that Gadamer uses the word *Vernunft* ("reason") and not *Verstand* ("understanding"). A dialogue is possible on this basis with Habermas and Karl-Otto Apel, who are also concerned to defend a concept of reason distinct from the technocratic understanding that they see as subservient to a purely technological project. It may well be the case that the Frankfurt School's distinction between communicative action, the work of reason, and instrumental action, the work of technological understanding, can be sustained only by recourse to tradition—or at least to a living cultural tradition, as opposed to a tradition—is politicized and institutionalized. Eric Weil's distinction between the rationale of technology and the reasonableness of politics would be equally relevant here; for Eric Weil as well, what is reasonable emerges only in the course of a dialogue between the spirit of innovation and the spirit of tradition.

The properly 'ontological' interpretation of the sequence—prejudice, authority, tradition—is crystallized, as it were, in the category of *Wirkungsggeschichte* or *wirkungsgeschichtliches Bewusstsein*, which marks the summit of Gadamer's reflection on the foundations of the human sciences.

This category does not pertain to methodology, to historical *Forschung* (inquiry), but rather to the reflective consciousness of this methodology. It is a category of the awareness of history. Later we shall see that certain of Habermas's concepts, such as the regulative idea of unrestricted communication, are situated at the same level of the self-understanding of the social sciences. It is therefore important to analyze the category of the consciousness of historical efficacy with the greatest care. In general terms, it can be characterized as the con-sciousnes of being exposed to history and to its effects, in such a way that this action over us cannot be objectified, for the efficacy belongs to the very meaning of the action as a historical phenomenon. Thus in *Kleine Schriften* we read:

> By that I mean, first, that we cannot extricate ourselves from the historical process, so distance ourselves from it that the past becomes an object for us. . . . We are always situated in history. . . . I mean that our consciousness is determined by a real historical process, in such a way that we are not free to juxta-pose ourselves to the past. I mean moreover that we must always become conscious afresh of the action which is thereby exercised over us, in such a way that everything past which we come to ex-perience compels us to take hold of it completely, to assume in some way its truth.[19]

Let us analyze further the massive and global fact whereby con-sciousness, even before its awakening as such, belongs to and depends on that which affects it. This properly prevenient action, in-corporated into awareness, can be articulated at the level of philosophical thought in terms of four themes, which seem to me to converge in the category of the consciousness of historical efficacy.

To begin with, the concept must be placed together and in tension with the notion of *historical distance*. This notion, on which Gadamer elaborated in the paragraph preceding the one we quoted, is made in-to a methodological condition of *Forschung*. Distance is a fact; placing at a distance is a methodological attitude. The history of effects is precisely what occurs under the condition of historical distance. It is the nearness of the remote. Whence the illusion, against which Gadamer struggles, that 'distance' puts an end to our collusion with the past and creates a situation comparable to the objectivity of the natural sciences, on the grounds that a loss of familiarity is a break with the contingent. Against this illusion, it is important to restore the paradox of the 'otherness' of the past. Effective history is efficacy at a distance.

The second theme incorporated in the idea of historical efficacy is this: there is no *overview* that would enable us to grasp in a single glance the totality of effects. Between finitude and absolute knowledge, it is necessary to choose; the concept of effective history belongs to an ontology of finitude. It plays the same role as the 'thrown project' and the 'situation' play in Heidegger's ontology. Historical being is that which never passes into self-knowledge. If there is a corresponding Hegelian concept, it would not be *Wissen* ("knowledge"), but rather *Substanz*, which Hegel uses whenever it is necessary to speak of the unfathomable depths that come to discourse through the dialectic. To do justice to Hegel, one must retrace the course of *The Phenomenology of Mind*, rather than descend along the path toward absolute knowledge.

The third theme corrects somewhat the preceding point: if there is no overview, neither is there a situation that restricts us absolutely. Wherever there is a situation, there is a *horizon* that may contract or expand. As the visual circle of our existence attests, the landscape is organized into the near, the far, and the open. It is the same in historical understanding. At one time it was thought that the concept of horizon could be accounted for by assimilating it to the methodological rule of placing oneself in the other's point of view: the horizon is the horizon of the other. It was thus thought that history had been aligned with the objectivity of the sciences: to adopt the other's point of view while forgetting one's own, is that not objectivity? Yet nothing is more disastrous than this fallacious assimilation. For the text, thus treated as an absolute object, is divested of its claim to tell us something about something. This claim can be sustained only by the idea of a prior understanding concerning the thing itself. Nothing destroys more the very sense of the historical enterprise than this objective distancing, which suspends both the tension of points of view and the claim of tradition to transmit a true speech about what it is.

By restoring the dialectic of points of view and the tension between the other and the self, we arrive at the culminating concept of the *fusion of horizons*—our fourth theme. This is a dialectical concept that results from the rejection of two alternatives: objectivism, whereby the objectification of the other is premised on the forgetting of oneself; and absolute knowledge, according to which universal history can be articulated within a single horizon. We exist neither in closed horizons, nor within an horizon that is unique. No horizon is closed, because it is possible to place oneself in another point of view and in another culture. It would be reminiscent of Robinson Crusoe to claim that the other is inaccessible. But no horizon is unique, because the tension between the other and oneself is unsurpassable. Gadamer seems to accept, at one stage, the idea of a single horizon encompassing all points of view, as in the monadology of Leibniz.[20] This is, it seems, in order to combat Nietzsche's radical pluralism, which would lead to incommunicability and would shatter the idea, essential to the philosophy of *logos*, of a 'common understanding concerning the thing'. In this respect, Gadamer's account is similar to Hegel's, insofar as historical comprehension requires a 'common understanding concerning the thing' and hence a unique *logos* of communication; but Gadamer's position is only tangential to that of Hegel, because his Heideggerian ontology of finitude prevents him from transforming this unique horizon into a knowledge. The very word 'horizon' indicates an ultimate repudiation of the idea of a knowledge wherein the fusion of horizons would itself be grasped. The contrast in virtue of which one point of view stands out against the backcloth of others (*Abhebung*) marks the gulf between hermeneutics and any form of Hegelianism.

The unsurpassable concept of the fusion of horizons endows the the theory of prejudice with its most peculiar characteristic: prejudice is the horizon of the present, the finitude of what is near in its openness toward the remote. This relation between the self and the other gives the concept of prejudice its final dialectical touch: only insofar as I place myself in the other's point of view do I confront myself with my present horizon, with my prejudices. It is only in the tension between the other and the self, between the text of the past and the point of view of the reader, that prejudice becomes operative and constitutive of historicity.

The epistemological implications of the ontological concept of historical efficacy are easy to discern. They concern the very status of research in the social sciences: that is what Gadamer wanted to show. *Forschung*—inquiry—scientific research does not escape the historical consciousness of those who live and make history. Historical knowledge cannot free itself from the historical condition. It follows that the project of a science free from prejudices is impossible. History poses meaningful questions to the past, pursues meaningful research and attains meaningful results only by beginning from a tradition that interpellates it. The emphasis is on the word *Bedeutung* ("meaning") leaves no doubt: history as science receives its meaning, at the outset as well as the end of research, from the link that it preserves with a received and recognized tradition. The action of tradition and historical investigation are fused by a bond that no critical consciousness could dissolve without rendering the research itself nonsensical. The history of the historians (*Historie*) can only bring to a higher level of consciousness the very flow of life within history (*Geschichte*): "Modern historical research itself is not only research, but the transmisson of tradition."[21] Man's link to the past precedes and envelopes the purely objective treatment of historical facts. It remains to be seen whether the ideal of unlimited and unconstrained communication, which Habermas opposed to the concept of tradition, escapes from Gadamer's argument against the possiblity of a complete knowledge of history and, along with it, of history as an object in itself.

Whatever the outcome of this argument against the critique of ideology, hermeneutics ultimately claims to set itself up as a critique of critique, or metacritique.

Why metacritique? what is at stake in this term is what Gadamer calls, in the *Kleine Schriften*, "the universality of the hermeneutical problem." I see three ways of construing this notion of universality. It may be construed, first, as the claim that hermeneutics has the same scope as science. For universality is first of all a scientific demand, one that concerns our knowledge and our power. Hermeneutics claims to cover the same domain as scientific investigation, founding the latter in an experience of the world that precedes and envelopes the knowledge and the power of science. This claim to universality is thus raised on the same ground as the critique that addresses itself to the conditions of possibility of the knowledge of science and its power. So the first universality arises from the very task of hermeneutics: "to reconnect the objective world of technology, which the sciences place at our disposal and discretion, with those fundamental orders of our being that are neither arbitrary nor manipulable by us, but rather simply demand our respect."[22] To remove from our discretion what science places at our disposal: such is the first metacritical task.

It could be said, however, that this universality is still derived. In Gadamer's view, hermeneutics has a peculiar universality that can be attained, paradoxically, only by starting from certian privileged experiences of universal significance. For fear of becoming a *Methodik* ("methodology"), hermeneutics can raise its claim to universality only from very concrete domains, that is, from regional hermeneutics that must always be 'deregionalised'. In the process of deregionalisation, hermeneutics may encounter a resistance that stems from the very nature of the experiences with which it begins. For these are, par excellence, the experiences of *Verfremdung*—alienation—whether it be in the aesthetic, historical, or lingual consciousness. The struggle against methodological distanciation transforms hermeneutics into a critique of critique; it must always push the rock of Sisyphus up again, restore the ontological ground that methodology has eroded away. But at the same time, the critique of critique assumes a thesis that will appear very suspect to 'critical' eyes: namely that a *consensus* already exists, which founds the possibility of aesthetic, historical, and lingual relations. To Schleiermacher, who defined hermeneutics as the art of overcoming misunderstanding (*Missverständnis*), Gadamer riposts: "Is it not, in fact, the case that every misunderstanding presupposes a 'deep common accord'?"[23]

This idea of a *tragendes Einverständnis* is absolutely fundamental; the assertion that misunderstanding is supported by a prior understanding is the preeminent metacritical theme. It leads, moreover, to the third concept of universality that may be found in Gadamer's work. The universal element that permits the deregionalisation of hermeneutics is language itself. The accord that supports us is the understanding reached in dialogue—not so much the relaxed face-to-face situation, but the question-answer relation in its most radical form. Here we come across the primitive hermeneutical phenomenon: "No assertion is possible that cannot be understood as an answer to a question, and assertions can only be understood in this way."[24] Every hermeneutics thus culminates in the concept of *Sprachlichkeit* or the 'lingual dimension', although 'lanaguage' must be construed here, not as the system of language (*langues*), but as the collection of things said, the summary of the most significant messages, transmitted not only by ordinary language but by all of the eminent languages (*langages*), which have made us what we are.

We shall approach Habermas's critique by asking whether 'the dialogue which we are' is indeed the universal element that allows hermeneutics to be deregionalized, or if instead it constitutes a rather peculiar experience, enveloping both a blindness with respect to the real conditions of human communication, as well as a hope for a communication without restriction and constraint.

The Critique of Ideology: Habermas

I should like now to present the second protagonist of the debate, reduced for the sake of clarity to a simple duel. I shall discuss his *critique of ideology*, considered as an alternative to the *hermeneutics of tradition*, under four successive headings.

Whereas Gadamer borrows the concept of *prejudice* from philosophical romanticism, reinterpreting it by means of the Heideggerian notion of preunderstanding, Habermas develops a concept of *interest*, which stems from the tradition of Marxism as reinterpreted by Lukacs and the Frankfurt School (Horkheimer, Adorno, Marcuse, Apel, etc.).

Whereas Gadamer appeals to the human sciences, which are concerned with the contemporary reinterpretation of cultural tradition, Habermas makes recourse to the *critical social sciences*, directly aimed against institutional reifications.

Whereas Gadamer introduces *mis-understanding* as the inner obstacle to understanding, Habermas develops a theory of *ideology*, construed as the systematic distortion of communication by the hidden exercise of force.

Lastly, whereas Gadamer bases the hermeneutic task on an ontology of the 'dialogue which we are', Habermas invokes the *regulative ideal* of an unrestricted and unconstrained communication which does not precede us but guides us from a future point.

I present this very schematic outline of the alternative with the aim of clarification. The debate would be without interest if the two apparently antithetical positions did not share a zone of intersection that, in my view, ought to become the point of departure for a new phase of hermeneutics, a phase that I shall sketch in the second part. But first, let us take up each of the lines of disagreement.

1. The concept of interest invites us to say a few words about Habermas's relation to Marxism, which is roughly comparable with Gadamer's relation to philosophical romanticism. The Marxism of Habermas is of a quite specific sort, having little in common with Althusser's and leading to a very different theory of ideology. In *Knowledge and Human Interests*, published in 1968, Marxism is placed inside an archaeology of knowledge that, unlike Foucault's, does not aim to isolate discontinuous structures that could be neither constituted nor manipulated by any subject; on the contrary, it aims to retrace the continuous history of a single problematic, that of reflection, swamped by the rise of objectivism and positivism. The book seeks to reconstruct the 'prehistory of modern positivism', and thereby the history of the dissolution of the critical function, with a goal that could be called apologetic: namely, 'to recover the forgotten experience of reflection'.[25] Placed within the history of the achievements and the failures of reflection, Marxism can appear only as a very ambiguous phenomenon. On the one hand, it is part of the

history of critical reflection; it is at one extremity of a line that begins with Kant and passes through Fichte and Hegel. I do not have the time to describe how Habermas sees this series of radicalisations of the reflective task, across the successive stages of the Kantian subject, the Hegelian consciousness and the Fichtean ego, and culminating with the synthesis of man and nature in the activity of production. This way of formulating the filiation of Marxism from the question of critique is very revealing in itself. To conceive of Marxism as a novel solution to the problem of the conditions of possibility of objectivity and the object, to say that "in materialism labour has the function of synthesis," is to submit Marxism to a properly 'critical' reading, in the Kantian and post-Kantian sense of the word. Hence Habermas says that the critique of political economy has the same role in Marx's work as the logic has in idealism.

Thus placed within the history of critical reflection, Marxism cannot avoid appearing both as the most advanced position of the metacritique, insofar as man the producer takes the place of the transcendental subject and the Hegelian spirit, and as a stage in the history of the forgetting of reflection and the advance of positivism and objectivism. The defense of man the producer leads to the hypostatisation of one category of action at the expense of all others, namely instrumental action.

In order to understand this critique, which claims to be internal to Marxism, it is necessary to introduce the concept of interest. Here I shall follow the 1965 essay, included as an appendix to *Knowledge and Human Interests*, before returning to the latter work.

The concept of interest is opposed to all pretensions of the theoretical subject to situate itself outside the sphere of desire, pretensions that Habermas sees in the work of Plato, Kant, Hegel, and Husserl; the task of a critical philosophy is precisely to unmask the interests that underlie the enterprise of knowledge. It is evident that, however different the concept of interest may be from Gadamer's notions of prejudice and tradition, there is a certain family resemblance that will have to be clarified at a later stage. For the moment it will enable us to introduce the concept of ideology, understood as an allegedly disinterested knowledge that serves to conceal an interest under the guise of a rationalisation, in a sense similar to Freud's.

To appreciate Habermas's critique of Marx, it is important to realize that there are several interests, or more precisely *pluralism* of spheres of interest. Habermas distinguishes three basic interests, each of which governs a sphere of *Forschung*—of "inquiry"—and hence a group of sciences.

There is, first, the *technical* or *instrumental interest*, which governs the 'empirical-analytic sciences'. It governs these sciences in the sense that the signification of possible empirical statements consists in their technical exploitability: the relevant facts of the empirical sciences are constituted by an *a priori* organization of our experience within the behavioral system of instrumental action. This thesis, close to the pragmatism of Dewey and Peirce, will be decisive for understanding the functions of what Habermas, following Marcuse, regards as the modern ideology, namely science and technology themselves. The imminent possiblity of ideology arises from this correlation between empirical knowledge and the technical interest, which Habermas defines more exactly "the cognitive interest in technical control over objectified processes."[26]

There is, however, a second sphere of interest, which is no longer technical but *practical*, in the Kantian sense of the word. In other writings, Habermas opposes communicative action to instrumental action; it is the same distinction; the practical sphere is the sphere of subjective communication. He correlates this sphere with the domain of the "historical-hermeneutic sciences." The signification of propositions produced in this domain does not proceed from possible prediction and technical exploitability, but from understanding meaning. This understanding is accomplished through the interpretation of messages exchanged in ordinary language, by means of the interpretation of texts transmitted by tradition, and in virtue of the internalization of norms that institutionalize social roles. It is evident that here we are closer to Gadamer than to Marx. Closer to Gadamer, for, at the level of communicative action, understanding is subsumed by the interpreter to the conditions of preunderstanding, which in turn is constituted on the basis of the traditional meanings incorporated into the seizure of any new phenomenon. Even the practical emphasis that Habermas gives to the hermeneutical sciences is not fundamentally foreign to Gadamer, insofar as the latter linked the interpretation of what is distant and past to the 'application' (*Anwendung*) here and now. Closer to Gadamer, we are also further from Marx. For the distinction between the two levels of interest, technical interest and practical interest, between the two levels of action, instrumental action and communicative action, between the two levels of science, empirical-analytic science and historical-hermeneutic science, provides the starting point for the internal critique of Marxism (here I return to the main text of *Knowledge and Human Interests*). The critique claims to be internal in the sense that Habermas discerns in the work of Marx himself the outlines of his own distinction between the two types of interest, action and science. He sees this is in the famous distinction between 'forces of production' and 'relations of production', the latter designating the institutional forms in which productive activity is carried out. Marxism in fact rests on the disjunction between force and form. The activity of production should engender one unique self-productive humanity, one unique 'generic essence' of man; but the relations of production split the producing subject into antagonistic classes. Therein Habermas sees the beginnings of his own distinction, in the sense that the phenomena of domination and violence, as well as the ideological dissimulation of these phenomena and the political enterprise of liberation, take place in the sphere of the *relations* of production and not that of the *forces* of production. An awareness of the distinction between instrumental and communicative action is therefore necessary in order to account for the very phenomena that Marx analyzed: antagonism, domination, dissimulation, liberation. But such an awareness is precisely what Marxism, in the understanding that it has of its own thought, lacks. In subsuming forces and relations to the same concept of *production*, it precludes the real separation of interests, and hence also that of levels of action and spheres of science. In that respect, Marxism belongs explicitly to the history of positivism, to the history of the forgetting of reflection, even though implicitly it is part of the history of the awareness of reifications which affect communication.

2. We have still not spoken of the third type of interest, which Habermas calls the *interest in emancipation*. He connects this interest with a third type of science, the *critical social sciences*.

Here we touch upon the most important source of disagreement with Gadamer; whereas the latter takes the 'human sciences' as an initial point of reference, Habermas invokes the 'critical social sciences'. This initial choice is heavy with consequences. For the 'human sciences' are close to what Gadamer calls *humaniora*, ''the humanities''; they are essentially sciences of culture, concerned with the renewal of cultural heritage in the historical present. They are thus by nature sciences of tradition—of tradition reinterpreted and reinvented in terms of its implications here and now, but of continuous tradition nonetheless. From the outset, the destiny of

Gadamer's hermeneutics is tied to these sciences. They can incorporate a critical moment, but they are inclined by nature to struggle against the alienating distanciation of the aesthetic, historical, and lingual consciousness. Consequently, they forbid the elevation of the critical instance above the recognition of authority and above the very tradition reinterpreted. The critical instance can be developed only as a moment subordinated to the consciousness of finitude and of dependence upon the figures of preunderstanding that always precede and envelop it.

The situation is quite different in the critical social sciences. They are critical by constitution; it is this which distinguishes them from the empirical-analytic sciences of the social order, as well as from the historical-hermeneutic sciences described above. The task of the critical social sciences is to discern, beneath the regularities observed by the empiriacl social sciences, those 'ideologically frozen' relations of dependence that can be transformed only through critique. Thus the critical approach is governed by the interest in emancipation, which Habermas also calls *self-reflection*. This interest provides the frame of reference for critical propositions: self-reflection, he says in the sketch of 1965, frees the subject from dependence on hypostatised powers. It can be seen that this is the very interest that animated the philosophies of the past; it is common to philosophy and the critical social sciences. It is the interest in *Selbstständigkeit*, in autonomy, in independence. But ontology concealed this interest, buried it in the ready-made reality of a being which supports us. The interest is active only in the critical instance that unmasks the interests at work in the activities of knowledge, which shows the dependence of the theoretical subject on empirical conditions stemming from institutional constraints and orients the recognition of these forms of constraint toward emancipation.

The critical instance is thus placed above the hermeneutical consciousness, for it is presented as the enterprise of 'dissolving' the constraints arising not from nature, but from institutions. A gulf therefore divides the hermeneutical project, which puts assumed tradition above judgment, and the critical project, which puts reflection above institutionalized constraint.

3. We are thus led, step by step, toward the third point of disagreement, which is the focus of our debate. I shall state the point as follows: the concept of ideology plays the same role in a critical social science as the concept of misunderstanding plays in a hermeneutics of tradition. It was Schleiermacher who, before Gadamer, tied

hermeneutics to the concept of misunderstanding. There is hermeneutics where there is misunderstanding. But there is hermeneutics because there is the conviction and the confidence that the understanding that precedes and envelops misunderstanding has the means to reintegrate misunderstanding into understanding by the very movement of question and answer on the dialogical model. Misunderstanding is, if I may say so, homogenous with understanding and of the same genre; hence understanding does not appeal to explanatory procedures, which are relegated to the excessive claims of 'methodologism'.

It is otherwise with the concept of ideology. What makes the difference? Here Habermas constantly resorts to the parallel between psychoanalysis and the theory of ideology. The parallel rests on the following criteria.

First trait: in the Frankfurt School and in a tradition that could still be called Marxist in a very general sense, distortion is always related to the repressive action of an authority and therefore to violence. The key concept here is 'censorship', an originally political concept that has returned to the critical social sciences after passing through psychoanalysis. The link between ideology and violence is crucial, for it introduces into the field of reflection dimensions that, without being absent from hermeneutics, are not accentuated by it, namely the dimensions of labor and power. We may say, in a broad Marxist sense, that the phenomena of class domination appear with the emergence of human labor, and that ideology expresses these phenomena in a way that will be explained shortly. In Habermas's terms, the phenomenon of domination takes place in the sphere of communicative action; it is there that language is distorted as regards its conditions of application at the level of communicative competence. Hence a hermeneutics that adheres to the ideality of *Sprachlichkeit* finds its limit in a phenomenon that affects language as such only because the relation between the three dimensions—labor, power, and language—is altered.

Second trait: because the distortions of language do not come from the usage of language as such but from its relation to labor and power, these distortions are unrecognizable by the members of the community. This misrecognition is peculiar to the phenomenon of ideology. It can be analyzed phenomenologically only by appealing to concepts of a psychoanalytic type: to *illusion* as distinct from error, to *projection* as the constitution of a false transcendence, to *rationalisation* as the subsequent rearrangement of motivations according to the appearance of a rational justification. To say the same thing in the sphere of critical social science, Habermas speaks of "pseudocommunication" of "systematically distorted communication," as opposed to mere misunderstanding.

Third trait: if misrecognition is insurmountable by the directly dialogical route, then the dissolution of ideologies must pass through the detour of procedures concerned with explaining and not simply, with understanding. These procedures invoke a theoretical apparatus that cannot be derived from any hermeneutics that remains on the level of the spontaneous interpretation of everyday speech. Here again psychoanalysis provides a good model: it is developed at length in the third part of *Knowledge and Human Interests* and in the article entitled "Der Universalitätsanspruch der Hermeneutik."[27]

Habermas adopts Alfred Lorenzer's interpretation of psychoanalysis as *Sprachanalyse*, according to which the 'understanding' of meaning is accomplished by the 'reconstruction of a 'primitive scene', placed in relation with two other 'scenes': the 'symptomatic scene' and the 'artificial scene of transference'. Certainly, psychoanalysis remains in the sphere of understanding, and of an understanding that culminates in the awareness of the subject; hence Habermas calls it a *Tiefenhermeneutik*, a 'depth hermeneutics'. But the understanding of meaning requires the detour of a 'reconstruction' of the processes of 'desymbolisation', which psychoanalysis retraces in the inverse direction along the routes of 'resymbolization'. So psychoanalysis is not completely external to hermeneutics, because it can still be expressed in terms of desymbolization and resymbolization; rather it constitutes a *limit-experience*, in virtue of the explanatory force linked to the 'reconstruction' of the 'primitive scene'. In other words, to 'understand' the *what* of the symptom, it is necessary to 'explain' its *why*. This explanatory phase invokes a theoretical apparatus, which establishes the conditions of possibility of explanation and reconstruction: topographical concepts (the three agencies and the three roles), economic concepts (the defence mechanism, primary and secondary repression, splitting-off), genetic concepts (the famous stages and the successive phases of symbol organization). As regards the three agencies (*ego, id, superego*) in particular, Habermas says that they are connected to the sphere of communication by the dialogical process of analysis, through which the patient is led to reflect upon himself. The metapsychology, concludes Habermas, "can be founded only as meta-hermeneutics."[28]

Unfortunately, Habermas tells us nothing about the way in which the explanatory and metahermeneutical scheme of psychoanalysis could be transposed onto the plane of ideology. It would have to be said, I think, that the distortions of communication that are linked to the social phenomena of domination and violence also constitute phenomena of desymbolization. Habermas sometimes speaks, very appropriately, of "excommunication," recalling the Wittgensteinian distinction between public and private language. It would also have to be shown in what sense the understanding of these phenomena requires a reconstruction that would recover certain features of 'scenic' understanding, or indeed of the three 'scenes' as such. In any case, it would be necessary to show that understanding requires an explanatory stage, such that the sense is understood only if the origin of the non-sense is explained. Finally, it would have to be shown how this explanation invokes a theoretical apparatus comparable to the Freudian topography or economics, and that the central concepts of this apparatus could be derived neither from the dialogical experience within the framework of ordinary language, nor from a textual exegesis grafted onto the direct understanding of discourse.

Such are the major characteristics of the concept of ideology: the impact of violence in discourse, a dissimulation whose key eludes consciousness, and the necessity of a detour through the explanation of causes. These three characteristics constitute the ideological phenomenon as a *limit-experience* for hermeneutics. Since hermeneutics can only develop a natural competence, we need a meta-hermeneutics to formulate the theory of the deformations of communicative competence. Critique is this theory of communicative competence, which comprises the art of understanding, the techniques for overcoming misunderstanding, the techniques for overcoming misunderstanding and the explanatory science of distortions.

4. I do not want to end this very schematic presentation of Habermas's thought without saying something about what is perhaps the most profound divergence that separates him from Gadamer.

For Habermas, the principal flaw of Gadamer's account is to have *ontologised* hermeneutics; by that he means its insistence on understanding or accord, as if the *consensus* which precedes us were something constitutive, something given in being. Doesn't Gadamer say that understanding is *Sein* [being] rather than *Bewusstsein* [consciousness]? Does he not speak, with the poet, of the 'dialogue which we are' (*das Gespräch, das wir sind*)? Doesn't he regard *Sprachlichkeit* as an ontological constitution, as a milieu within which we move? More fundamentally still, does he not anchor the hermeneutics of understanding in an ontology of finitude? Habermas can have nothing but mistrust for what seems to him to be the ontological hypostatisation of a rare experience, namely the experience of being preceded in our most felicitous dialogues by an understnading which supports them. This experience cannot be canonised and made into the paradigm of communicative action. What prevents us from doing so is precisely the ideological phenomenon. If ideology were only an internal obstacle to understanding, a mere misunderstanding which the exercise of question and answer could resolve, then it could be said that 'where there is misunderstanding, there is a prior understanding'.

A critique of ideology must think in terms of anticipation where the hermeneutics of tradition thinks in terms of assumed tradition. In other words, the critique of ideology must posit as a regulative idea, in front of us, what the hermeneutics of tradition conceives as existing at the origin of understanding. It is at this point that the third interest which guides knowledge, the interest in emancipation, comes into play. This interest, as we have seen, animates the critical social sciences, providing a frame of reference for all the meanings constituted in psychoanalysis and the critique of ideology. Self-reflection is the correlative concept of the interest in emancipation. Hence self-reflection cannot be founded on a prior *consensus*, for what is prior is precisely a broken communication. One cannot speak with Gadamer of the common accord which carries understanding without assuming a convergence of traditions that does not exist, without hypostatising a past which is also the place of false consciousness, without ontologising a language which has always only been a distorted 'communicative competence'.

The critique of ideology must be placed, therefore, under the sign of a regulative idea, that of unlimited and unconstrained communication. The Kantian emphasis is evident here; the regulative idea is more what ought to be than what is, more anticipation than recollection. It is this idea which gives meaning to every psychoanalytic or sociological critique. For there is desymbolisation only within the project of resymbolisation, and there is such a project only within the revolutionary perspective of the end of violence. Where the hermeneutics of tradition sought to extract the essence of authority and to connect it to the recognition of superiority, the interest in emancipation leads back towards the eleventh of the *Theses on Feuer-*

bach: 'the philosophers have only interpreted the world; the point, however, is to change it'. An eschatology of non-violence thus forms the ultimate philosophical horizon of a critique of ideology. This eschatology, close to that of Ernst Bloch, takes the place of the ontology of lingual understanding in a hermeneutics of tradition.

TOWARDS A CRITICAL HERMENEUTICS

Critical Reflection on Hermeneutics

I should like now to offer my own reflections on the presuppositions of each position and tackle the problems posed in the introduction. These problems, we said, concern the significance of the most fundamental gesture of philosophy. The gesture of hermeneutics is a humble one of acknowledging the historical conditions to which all human understanding is subsumed in the reign of finitude; that of the critique of ideology is a proud gesture of defiance directed against the distortions of human communication. By the first, I place myself in the historical process to which I know that I belong; by the second, I oppose the present state of falsified human communication with the idea of an essentially political freedom of speech, guided by the limiting idea of unrestricted and unconstrained communication.

My aim is not to fuse the hermeneutics of tradition and the critique of ideology in a supersystem that would encompass both. As I said at the outset, each speaks from a different place. Nonetheless, each may be asked to recognize the other, not as a position that is foreign and purely hostile, but as one that raises in its own way a legitimate claim.

It is in this spirit that I return to the two questions posed in the introduction: (1) Can hermeneutic philosophy account for the demands of a critique of ideology? And if so, at what price? (2) On what condition is the critique of ideology possible? Can it, in the last analysis, be detached from hermeneutical presuppositions?

The first question challenges the capacity of hermeneutics to account for a critical instance in general. How can there be critique within hermeneutics?

I shall note to begin with that the recognition of a critical instance is a vague desire constantly reiterated but constantly aborted, within hermeneutics. From Heidegger onward, hermeneutics is wholly engaged in *going back to the foundations*, a movement that leads from the epistemological question concerning the conditions of possibility of the human sciences to the ontological structure of understanding.

It may be asked, however, whether the return route from ontology to epistemology is possible. For it is only along this route that one could confirm the assertion that questions of exegetico-historical critique are 'derivative', and that the hermeneutical circle, in the sense of the exegetes, is 'founded' on the fundamental anticipatory structure of understanding.

Ontological hermeneutics seems incapable, for structural reasons, of unfolding this problematic of return. In the work of Heidegger himself, the question is abandoned as soon as it is asked. Thus in *Being and Time* we read this:

> In the circle of understanding . . . is hidden a positive possibility of the most primordial kind of knowing. We genuinely take hold of this possibility only when, in our explication (*Auslegung*), we have understood that our first, last, and constant task is never to allow our fore-having, fore-sight, and fore-conception to be presented to us by fancies (*Einfälle*) and popular conceptions (*Volksbegriffe*), but rather to make the scientific theme secure by working out these anticipations in terms of the things themselves.[29]

Here we find, posed in principle, the distinction between an anticipation according to the things themselves and an anticipation springing from fancies (*Einfälle*) and popular conceptions (*Volksbegriffe*); these two terms have a visible link with prejudices by 'precipitation' and by 'predisposition'. But how can this distinction be pursued when one declares, immediately afterwards, that "the ontological presuppositions of historiological knowledge transcend in principle the idea of rigour held in the most exact sciences,"[30] and thereby eludes the question of the rigor proper to the historical sciences themselves? The concern to anchor the circle more deeply than any epistemology prevents the epistemological question from being raised on ontological ground.

Is that to say that there is not, in the work of Heidegger himself, any development that corresponds to the critical moment of epistemology? Indeed there is, but the development is applied elsewhere. In passing from the Analytic of *Dasein*, which still includes the theory of understanding and interpretation, to the theory of temporality and totality, which includes the second meditation on understanding (par. 63), it seems that all critical effort is spent in the work of *deconstructing metaphysics*. The reason is clear: because hermeneutics has become the hermeneutics of being—of the meaning of being—the anticipatory structure appropriate to the question of the meaning of being is given by the history of metaphysics, which thus takes the place of prejudice. Henceforth, the hermeneutics of being deploys all its critical resources in the debate with classical and medieval substance, with the Cartesian and Kantian *cogito*. The confrontation with the metaphysical tradition of the West takes the place of a critique of prejudices. In other words, from a Heideggerian perspective, the only internal critique that can be conceived as an integral part of the enterprise of disclosure is the deconstruction of metaphysics; and a properly epistemological critique can be resumed only indirectly, insofar as metaphysical residues can be found at work in the sciences that claim to be empirical. But this critique of prejudices that originates in metaphysics cannot take the place of a real confrontation with the human sciences, with their methodology, and with their epistemological presuppositions. The obsessive concern with radicality thus blocks the return route from general hermeneutics toward regional hermeneutics: toward philology, history, depth-psychology, etc.

As regards Gadamer, there is no doubt that he has perfectly grasped the urgency of this 'descending dialectic' from the fundamental toward the derived. Thus he proposes, as we noted above, to "inquire into the consequences which follow for the hermeneutics of the human sciences from the fact that Heidegger derives (*Ableitung*) the circular structure of understanding from the temporality of *Dasein*."[31] It is precisely these 'consequences' that interest us. For it is in the movement of derivation that the link between preunderstanding and prejudice becomes problematic and the question of critique is raised afresh, in the very heart of understanding. Thus Gadamer, speaking of the texts of our culture, repeatedly insists that these texts signify by themselves, that there is a 'matter of the text' that addresses us. But how can the 'matter of the text' be left to speak without confronting the critical question of the way in which preunderstanding and prejudice are mixed?

It seems to me that Gadamer's hermeneutics is prevented from embarking upon this route, not simply because, as with Heidegger, all effort of thought is invested in the radicalization of the problem of foundation, but because the hermeneutical experience itself discourages the recognition of any critical instance.

The *primary* experience of this hermeneutics, determining the very place from which it raises its claim to universality, involves the refutation of the 'alienating distanciation'—*Verfremdung*—which commands the objectifying attitude of the human sciences. Henceforth the entire work assumes a dichotomous character that is indicated even in the title, *Truth and Method*, wherein the disjunction overrides the conjunction. It is this initial dichotomous situation that, it seems to me, prevents Gadamer from really recognizing the critical instance and hence rendering justice to the critique of ideology, which is the modern post-Marxist expression of the critical instance.

My own interrogation proceeds from this observation. Would it not be appropriate to shift the initial locus of the hermeneutical question, to reformulate the question in such a way that a certain dialectic between the experience of belonging and alienating distanciation becomes the mainspring, the key to the inner life, of hermeneutics?

The idea of such a shift in the initial locus of the hermeneutical question is suggested by the history of hermeneutics itself. Throughout this history, the emphasis has always come back to exegesis or philology, that is, to the sort of relation with tradition that is based on the *mediation* of texts, or documents and monuments that have a status comparable to texts. Schleiermacher was exegete of the New Testament and translator of Plato. Dilthey located the specificity of interpretation (*Auslegung*), as contrasted with the direct understanding of the other (*Verstehen*), in the phenomenon of fixation by writing and, more generally, of inscription.

In thus reverting to the problematic of the text, to exegesis and philology, we appear at first sight to restrict the aim and the scope of hermeneutics. However, because any claim to universality is raised from somewhere, we may expect that the restoration of the link between hermeneutics and exegesis will reveal its own universal features that, without really contradicting Gadamer's hermeneutics, will rectify it in a manner decisive for the debate with the critique of ideology.

I should like to sketch four themes that constitute a sort of critical supplementation to the hermeneutics of tradition.

The distanciation in which this hermeneutics tends to see a sort of ontological fall from grace appears as a positive component of being for the text; it characteristically belongs to interpretation, not as its contrary but as its condition. The moment of distanciation is implied by fixation in writing and by all comparable phenomena in the sphere of the transmission of discourse. Writing is not simply a matter of the material fixation of discourse; for fixation is the condition of a much more fundamental phenomenon, that of the autonomy of the text. A threefold autonomy: with respect to the intention of the author; with respect to the cultural situation and all the sociological conditions of the production of the text; and finally, with respect to the original addressee. What the text signifies no longer coincides with what the author meant; verbal meaning and mental meaning have different destinies. This first form of autonomy already implies the possibility that the 'matter of the text' may escape from the author's restricted intentional horizon, and that the world of the text may explode the world of its author. What is true of psychological conditions is also true of sociological conditions, even though he who is prepared to liquidate the author is less prepared to perform the same operation in the sociological sphere. The peculiarity of the literary work, and indeed of the work as such, is nevertheless to transcend its own psychosociological conditions of production and thereby to open itself to an unlimited series of readings, themselves situated in sociocultural contexts that are always different. In short, the work *decontextualizes* itself, from the sociological as well as the psychological point of view, and is able to *recontextualize* itself differently in the act of reading. It follows that the mediation of the text cannot be treated as an extension of the dialogical situation. For in dialogue, the vis-a-vis of discourse is given in advance by the setting itself; with writing, the original addressee is transcended. The work itself creates an audience, which potentially includes anyone who can read.

The emancipation of the text constitutes the most fundamental condition for the recognition of a critical instance at the heart of interpretation; for distanciation now belongs to the mediation itself.

In a sense, these remarks only extend what Gadamer himself says, on the one hand, about 'temporal distance' that, as we have seen above, is one aspect of 'consciousness exposed to the efficacy of history'; and on the other hand, about *Schriftlichkeit*, which, according to Gadamer himself, adds new features to *Sprachlichkeit*. But at the same time as this analysis extends Gadamer's, it shifts the emphasis somewhat. For the distanciation revealed by writing is already present in discourse itself, which contains the seeds of the distanciation of the *said* from the *saying*, to follow Hegel's famous analysis at the beginning of *The Phenomenology of Mind*: the *saying* vanishes, but the *said* persists. In this respect, writing does not represent a radical revolution in the constitution of discourse but only accomplishes the latter's profoundest aim.

2. If hermeneutics is to account for a critical instance in terms of its own premises, then it must satisfy a second condition: it must over-

come the ruinous dichotomy, inherited from Dilthey, between 'explanation' and 'understanding'. As is well known, this dichotomy arises from the conviction that any explanatory attitude is borrowed from the methodology of the *natural sciences* and illegitimately extended to the *human sciences*. However, the appearance of semiological models in the field of the text convinces us that all explanation is not naturalistic or causal. The semiological models, applied in particular to the theory of the narrative, are borrowed from the domain of language itself, by extension from units smaller than the sentence to units larger than the sentence (poems, narratives, etc.) Here discourse must be placed under the category, no longer of writing but rather of the work, that is, under a category that pertains to praxis, to labor. Discourse is characterized by the fact that it can be produced as a work displaying structure and form. Even more than writing, the production of discourse as a work involves an objectification that enables it to be read in existential conditions that are always new. But in contrast to the simple discourse of conversation, which enters into the spontaneous movement of question and answer, discourse as a work 'takes hold' in structures calling for a description and an explanation that mediate 'understanding'. We are here in a situation similar to that described by Habermas: *reconstruction* is the path of understanding. However, this situation is not peculiar to psychoanalysis and to all that Habermas designates by the term 'depth hermeneutics'; it is the condition of the work in general. So if there is a hermeneutics—and here I oppose those forms of structuralism that would remain at the explanatory level—it must be constituted across the mediation rather than against the current of structural explanation. For it is the task of understanding to bring to discourse what is initially given as structure. It is necessary to have gone as far as possible along the route of objectification, to the point where structural analysis discloses the *depth semantics* of a text, before one can claim to 'understand' the text in terms of the 'matter' that speaks therefrom. The *matter* of the text is not what a naive reading of the text reveals, but what the formal arrangement of the text mediates. If that is so, then truth and method do not constitute a disjunction but rather a dialectical process.

3. The hermeneutics of texts turns toward the critique of ideology in a third way. It seems to me that the properly hermeneutical moment arises when the interrogation, transgressing the closure of the text, is carried toward what Gadamer himself calls "the matter of the text," namely the sort of *world* opened up by it. This can be called the

referential moment, in allusion to the Fregean distinction between sense and reference. The sense of the work is its internal organization, whereas the reference is the mode of being unfolded in front of the text.

It may be noted in passing that the most decisive break with romantic hermeneutics is here; what is sought is no longer an intention hidden behind the text, but a world unfolded in front of it. The power of the text to open a dimension of reality implies in principle a recourse against any given reality and thereby the possibility of a critique of the real. It is in poetic discourse that this subversive power is most alive. The strategy of this discourse involves holding two moments in equilibrium: suspending the reference of ordinary language and releasing a second-order reference, which is another name for what we have designated above as the world opened up by the work. In the case of poetry, fiction is the path of redescription; or to speak as Aristotle does in the *Poetics*, the creation of a *mythos*, of a 'fable', is the path of *mimesis*, of creative imitation.

Here again we are developing a theme sketched by Gadamer himself, particularly in his magnificent pages on *play*. But in pressing to the end this meditation on the relation between *fiction* and *redescription*, we introduce a critical theme that the hermeneutics of tradition tends to cast beyond its frontiers. The cirtical theme was nevertheless present in the Heideggerian analysis of understanding. Recall how Heidegger conjoins understanding to the notion of 'the projection of my ownmost possibilities'; this signifies that the mode of being of the world opened up by the text is the mode of the possible, or better of the power-to-be: therein resides the subversive force of the imaginary. The paradox of poetic reference consists precisely in the fact that reality is redescribed only insofar as discourse is raised to fiction.

A hermeneutics of the power-to-be thus turns itself toward a critique of ideology, of which it constitutes the most fundamental possibility. Distanciation, at the same time, emerges at the heart of reference: poetic discourse distances itself from everyday reality, aiming towards being as power-to-be.

4. In a final way, the hermeneutics of texts indicates the place for a critique of ideology. This final point pertains to the status of subjectivity in interpretation. For if the primary concern of hermeneutics is not to discover an intention hidden behind the text but to unfold a world in front of it, then authentic self-understanding is something that, as Heidegger and Gadamer wish to say, can be instructed by the 'matter of the text.' The relation to the world of the text takes the

place of the relation to the subjectivity of the author, and at the same time the problem of the subjectivity of the reader is displaced. To understand is not to project oneself into the text but to expose oneself to it; it is to receive a self enlarged by the appropriation of the proposed worlds that interpretation unfolds. In sum, it is the matter of the text that gives the reader his dimension of subjectivity; understanding is thus no longer a constitution of which the subject possesses the key. Pressing this suggestion to the end, we must say that the subjectivity of the reader is no less held in suspense, no less potentialized, than the very world that the text unfolds. In other words, if fiction is a fundamental dimension of the reference of the text, it is equally a fundamental dimension of the subjectivity of the reader: in reading, I 'unrealize myself'. Reading introduces me to imaginative variations of the *ego*. The metamorphosis of the world in play is also the playful metamorphosis of the *ego*.

In the idea of the 'imaginative variation of the *ego*', I see the most fundamental possibility for a critique of the illusions of the subject. This link could remain hidden or undeveloped in a hermeneutics of tradition that introduced prematurely a concept of appropriation (*Aneignung*) directed against alienating distanciation. However, if distanciation from oneself is not a fault to be combated, but rather the condition of possibility of understanding oneself in front of the text, then appropriation is the dialectical counterpart of distanciation. Thus the critique of ideology can be assumed by a concept of self-understanding which organically implies a critique of the illusions of the subject. Distanciation from oneself demands that the appropriation of the proposed worlds offered by the text passes through the disappropriation of the self. The critique of *false consciousness* can thus become an integral part of hermeneutics, conferring upon the critique of ideology that metahermeneutical dimension that Habermas assigns to it.

Hermeneutical Reflection on Critique

I should like now to offer a similar reflection on the critique of ideology, with the aim of assessing the latter's claim to universality. I do not expect this reflection to return the critique of ideology to the fold of hermeneutics but rather to confirm Gadamer's view that the two 'universalities', that of hermeneutics and that of the critique of ideology, are interpenetrating. The question could also be presented in Habermas's terms: On what conditions can critique be formulated as metahermeneutics? I propose to follow the order of the theses in terms of which I sketched Habermas's thought.

1. I shall begin with the theory of interests that underlies the critique of the ideologies of transcendental phenomenology and positivism. It may be asked what authorizes the following theses: that all *Forschung* is governed by an interest that establishes a prejudicial frame of reference for its field of meaning; that there are three such interests (and not one or two or four): namely, the technical interest, the practical interest, and the interest in emancipation; that these interests are anchored in the natural history of the human species, but that they mark the emergence of man out of nature, taking form in the spheres of labor, power, and language; that in self-reflection, knowledge and interest are one; that the unity of knowledge and interest is attested to in a dialectic that discerns the historical traces of the repression of dialogue and that reconstructs what has been suppressed.

Are these 'theses' empirically justifiable? No, for then they would fall under the yoke of the empirical-analytic sciences that pertain to *one* interest, the technical interest. Are these theses a 'theory', in the sense given to this word by psychoanalysis for example, that is, in the sense of a network of explanatory hypotheses permitting the reconstruction of a primitive scene? No, for then they would become regional theses as in any theory and would again be justified by *one* interest, the interest in emancipation perhaps; and the justification would become circular.

Is it not necessary to recognize henceforth that the disclosure of interests at the roots of knowledge, the hierarchical ordering of interests and their connection to the trilogy of labor-power-language, are dependent upon a philosophical anthropology similar to Heidegger's Analytic of *Dasein*, and more particularly to his hermeneutics of 'care'? If that is so, then these interests are neither observables, nor theoretical entities like the *ego*, the *super-ego* and the *id* in Freud's work, but rather 'existentiales'. Their analysis depends upon hermeneutics, insofar as they are at once 'the closest' and 'the most concealed', so that they must be disclosed in order to be recognized.

The analysis of interests could be called 'metahermeneutical', if it is supposed that hermeneutics is primarily a hermeneutics of discourse, indeed an idealism of lingual life. But we have seen that it has nothing to do with this, that the hermeneutics of preunderstanding is fundamentally a hermeneutics of finitude. Hence I am quite willing to say that the critique of ideology raises its claim from a different place than hermeneutics, namely from the place where labor, power, and, language are intertwined. But the two claims cross on a common ground: the hermeneutics of finitude, which secures a priori the correlation between the concept of prejudice and that of ideology.

2. I should like now to consider afresh the pact that Habermas establishes between critical social science and the interest in emancipation. We have sharply contrasted the positions of the critical social sciences and the historical-hermeneutic sciences, the latter inclining toward recognition of the authority of traditions rather than toward revolutionary action against oppression.

Here the question that hermeneutics addresses to the critique of ideology is this: Can you assign the interest in emancipation a status as distinct as you suppose with respect to the interest that animates the historical-hermeneutic sciences? The distinction is asserted so dogmatically that it seems to create a gulf between the interest in emancipation and the ethical interest. But the concrete analyses of Habermas himself belie this dogmatic aim. It is striking that the distortions that psychoanalysis describes and explains are interpreted, at the metahermeneutical level where Habermas places them, as distortions of communicative competence. Everything suggests that the distortions relevant to the critique of ideology also operate at this level. Recall how Habermas reinterprets Marxism on the basis of a dialectic between instrumental and communicative action. It is at the heart of communicative action that the institutionalization of human relations undergoes the reification that renders it unrecognizable to the participants of communication. It follows that all distortions, those which psychoanalysis discovers as well as those which the critique of ideology denounces, are distortions of the communicative capacity of men.

So can the interest in emancipation be treated as a distinct interest? It seems not, especially if one considers that taken positively as a proper motif and no longer negatively in terms of the reifications that it combats, this interest has no other content than the ideal of unrestricted and unconstrained communication. The interest in emancipation would be quite empty and abstract if it were not situated on the same plane as the historical-hermeneutic sciences, that is, on the plane of communicative action. But if that is so, can a critique of distortions be separated from the communicative experience itself, from the place where it begins, where it is real and where it is exemplary? The task of the hermeneutics of tradition is to remind the critique of ideology that man can project his emancipation and anticipate an unlimited and unconstrained communication only on the basis of the creative reinterpretation of cultural heritage. If we had no experience of communication, however restricted and mutilated it was, how could we wish it to prevail for all men and at all institutional levels of the social nexus? It seems to me that critique can be neither the first instance nor the last. Distortions can be criticized only in the name of a *consensus* that we cannot anticipate merely emptily, in the manner of a regulative idea, unless that idea is exemplified; and one of the very places of exemplification of the ideal of communication is precisely our capacity to overcome cultural distance in the interpretation of works received from the past. He who is unable to reinterpret his past may also be incapable of projecting concretely his interest in emancipation.

3. I arrive at the third point of disagreement between the hermeneutics of tradition and the critique of ideology. It concerns the abyss that seems to separate simple misunderstanding from pathological or ideological distortion. I shall not reconsider the arguments, already mentioned above, that tend to attenuate the difference between misunderstanding and distortion; a depth-hermeneutics is still a hermeneutics, even if it is called metahermeneutical. I should like instead to emphasize an aspect of the theory of ideology that owes nothing to the parallel with psychoanalysis. A large part of Habermas's work is addressed not to the theory of ideology taken abstractly, but to contemporary ideologies. Now when the theory of ideology is thus developed concretely in terms of a critique of the present, it reveals aspects that call for a concrete—and not simply a theoretical—*rapprochement* between the interest in emancipation and the interest in communication.

For what is, according to Habermas, the dominant ideology of the present day? His answer is close to that of Herbert Marcuse and Jacques Ellul: it is the ideology of science and technology. Here I shall not discuss Habermas's interpretation of advanced capitalism and of developed industrial societies; I shall go straight to the principal characteristic that, in my view, imperiously returns the theory of ideology of science and technology. The modern state is a state dedicated no longer to representing the interests of an oppressing class,) once used for the justification of power have been replaced by an ideology of science and technology. The modern state is a state dedictaed no longer to representing the interests of an oppressing class, but rather to eliminating the dysfunctions of the industrial system. To justify surplus-value by concealing its mechanism is thus no longer the primary legitimating function of ideology, as it was in the epoch of liberal capitalism described by Marx, quite simply because surplus-value is no longer the principal source of productivity and its appropriation the dominant feature of the system. The dominant feature of the system is the productivity of rationality itself, incorporated into self-regulating systems; what is to be legitimated, therefore, is the maintenance and growth of the system itself. It is precisely for this purpose that the scientific-technological apparatus has become an ideology, that is, a legitimation of the relations of domination and inequality that are necessary for the functioning of the industrial system, but that are concealed beneath all sorts of gratifications provided by the system. The modern ideology thus differs appreciably from that described by Marx, which prevailed only during the short period of liberal capitalism and possessed no universality in time. Nothing now remains of prebourgeois ideology, and bourgeois ideology was expressly linked to the camouflaging of domination in the legal institution of the free labor contract.

Granted this description of the modern ideology, what does it signify in terms of interest? It signifies that the subsystem of instrumental action has ceased to be a subsystem, and that its categories have overrun the sphere of communicative action. Therein consists the famous 'rationalization' of which Max Weber spoke: not only does rationality conquer new domains of instrumental action, but it subjugates the domain of communicative action. Max Weber described this phenomenon in terms of 'disenchantment' and 'secularization'; Habermas describes it as the obliteration of the difference between the plane of instrumental action, which is also that of labor, and the plane of communicative action, which is also that of agreed norms, symbolic exchanges, personality structures, and rational decision-making procedures. In the modern capitalist system, which here seems identical with the industrial system as such, the ancient Greek question of the 'good life' is abolished in favour of the functioning of a manipulated system. The problems of praxis linked to communication—in particular the desire to submit important political questions to public discussion and democratic decision—have not disappeared; they persist, but in a repressed form. Precisely because their elimination is not automatic and the need for legitimation remains unfulfilled, there is still the need for an ideology to legitimate the authority that secures the functioning of the system; science and technology today assume this ideological role.

But the question that hermeneutics then addresses to the critique of contemporary ideology is this: granted that ideology today consists in disguising the difference between the normative order of communicative action and bureaucratic conditioning, hence in dissolving the sphere of interaction mediated by language into the structures of instrumental action, how can the interest in emancipation remain anything other than a pious vow, save by embodying it in the reawakening of communicative action itself? And upon what will you concretely support the reawakening of communicative action, if not upon the creative renewal of cultural heritage?

4. The ineluctable link between the reawakening of political responsibility and the reanimation of traditional sources of communicative action leads me to say a few words, in conclusion, about what appeared to be the most formidable difference between the hermeneutical consciousness and the critical consciousness. The first, we said, is turned toward a *consensus* that precedes us and, in this sense, that exists; the second anticipates a future freedom in the form of a regulative idea that is not a reality but an ideal, the ideal of unrestricted and unconstrained communication.

With this apparent antithesis, we reach the liveliest but perhaps the most futile point in the debate. For in the end, hermeneutics will say From where do you speak when you appeal to *Selbstreflexion*, if it is not from the place that you yourself have denounced as a non-place, the non-place of the transcendental subject? It is indeed from the basis of a tradition that you speak. This tradition is not perhaps the same as Gadamer's; it is perhaps that of the *Aufklärung*, whereas Gadamer's would be romanticism. But it is a tradition nonetheless, the tradition of emancipation rather than that of recollection. Critique is also a tradition. I would even say that it plunges into the most impressive tradition, that of liberating acts, of the Exodus and the Resurrection. Perhaps there would be no more interest in emancipation, no more anticipation of freedom, if the Exodus and the Resurrection were effaced from the memory of mankind . . .

If that is so, then nothing is more deceptive than the alleged antinomy between an ontology of prior understanding and an eschatology of freedom. We have encountered these false antinomies elsewhere: as if it were necessary to choose between reminiscence and hope! In theological terms, eschatology is nothing without the recitation of acts of deliverance from the past.

In sketching this dialectic of the recollection of tradition and the anticipation of freedom, I do not want in any way to abolish the difference between hermeneutics and the critique of ideology. Each has a privileged place and, if I may say so, different regional preferences: on the one hand, an attention to cultural heritages, focused most decidedly perhaps on the theory of the text; on the other hand, a theory of institutions and of phenomena of domination, focused on the analysis of reifications and alienations. Insofar as each must always be regionalized in order to endow their claims to universality with a concrete character, their differences must be preserved against any conflationist tendency. But it is the task of philosophical reflection to eliminate deceptive antinomies that would oppose the interest in the reinterpretation of cultural heritages received from the past and the interest in the futuristic projections of a liberated humanity.

The moment these two interests become radically separate, then hermeneutics and critique will themselves be no more than . . . ideologies!

NOTES

1. Here roughly is the history of the debate. In 1965 the second edition of Hans-Georg Gadamer's *Wahrheit und Methode* (Tübingen: J.C.B. Mohr; hereafter cited in the text as *WM*) appeared, published for the first time in 1960. [English translation: *Truth and Method* (London: Sheed and Ward, 1975; hereafter cited in the text as *TM*).] This edition contains a preface which replies to a first group of critics. Habermas launched an initial attack in 1967 in *Zur Logik der Sozialwissenschaften* (Frankfurt: Suhrkamp), an attack directed against the section of *Wahrheit und Methode* on which we shall concentrate, namely the rehabilitation of prejudice, authority and tradition, and the famous theory of the 'historical-effective consciousness'. The same year Gadamer published, in *Kleine Schriften* I (Tübingen: J.C.B. Mohr), a lecture from 1965 entitled 'Der Universalität des hermeneutischen Problems' [English translation: 'The universality of the hermeneutical problem', translated by David E. Linge, in *Philosophical Hermeneutics* (Berkeley: University of California Press, 1976)] as well as another essay, 'Rhetorik, Hermeneutik und Ideologiekritik'. Habermas replied in a long essay, 'Der Universalitäts-anspruch der Hermeneutik', published in the *Festschrift* in honour of Gadamer entitled *Hermeneutik und Dialektik* I (Tübingen: J.C.B. Mohr, 1970). (The latter two essays are reprinted in a collection edited by Habermas and others entitled *Hermeneutik und Ideologiekritik* (Frankfurt: Suhrkamp, 1971).) But the principal work of Habermas which we shall consider is called *Erkenn-*

tnis und Interesse (Frankfurt: Suhrkamp, 1968) [English translation: *Knowledge and Human Interests*, translated by Jeremy J. Shapiro (London: Heinemann, 1972)]; it contains in the appendix an important exposition of principles and methods published in 1965 as 'A general perspective'. His conception of the contemporary form of ideology is found in 'Technik und Wissenschaft als "Ideologie"', offered to Herbert Marcuse on his seventieth birthday in 1968 [English translation: 'Technology and science as "ideology"', translated by Jeremy J. Shapiro, in *Toward a Rational Society* (London: Heinemann, 1971)].

2. Hans-Georg Gadamer, *Hermeneutik und Ideologiekritik*, p. 57. Hereafter cited as *HI*.

3. Ibid.

4. The title of pp. 241–5 in *Truth and Method*.

5. *WM*, p. 260; *TM*, p. 245.

6. *WM*, p. 261; *TM*, p. 245.

7. *WM*, p. 261; *TM*, p. 245.

8. Martin Heidegger, *Sein und Zeit* (Tübingen: Max Niemeyer, 1927; hereafter cited in the text as SZ) [English translation: *Being and Time*, trans. John Macquarrie and Edward Robinson (New York: Harper & Row, 1962; hereafter cited in the text as *BT*)].

9. *WM*, p. 251; *TM*, p. 236.

10. *WM*, p. 251; *TM*, p. 235.

11. See *SZ*, p. 150; *BT*, p. 190.

12. *SZ*, p. 152; *BT*, p. 194.

13. *WM*, p. 264; *TM*, p. 248.

14. *WM*, p. 264; *TM*, p. 249.

15. *WM*, p. 265; *TM*, p. 249.

16. *WM*, p. 265; *TM*, p. 250.

17. Ibid.

18. *WM*, p. 266; *TM*, p. 250.

19. Hans-Georg Gadamer, *Kleine Schriften* I, p. 158. Hereafter cited as *KS-I*.

20. *WM*, p. 288; *TM*, p. 271.

21. *WM*, p. 268; *TM*, p. 253.

22. *KS-I*, p. 101.

23. Ibid, p. 104.

24. Ibid, p. 107.

25. Jurgen Habermas, *Knowledge and Human Interests*, p. 9.

26. Ibid, p. 309.

27. *HI*, p. 120ff.

28. Ibid, p. 149.

29. *SZ*, p. 153; *BT*, p. 195.

30. *SZ*, p. 153; *BT*, p. 195.

31. *WM*, p. 251; *TM*, p. 235.

Hermeneutics and 'Post-Modernism'

IV

WHAT IS THE DIFFERENCE THAT MAKES A DIFFERENCE? GADAMER, HABERMAS, AND RORTY

RICHARD J. BERNSTEIN

If we take the whole history of philosophy, the systems reduce themselves at a few main types which under all the technical verbiage in which the ingenious intellect of man envelopes them, are just so many visions, modes of feeling the whole push, and seeing the whole drift of life, forced on one by one's total character and experience, and on the whole preferred—*there is no other truthful word*—*as one's best working attitude.*

William James

There are many ways to characterize what we are talking about when we speak of modernity and post-modernity. But one description—as it pertains to philosophy—might go something like this. The "core problem" for philosophy in the modern world has been to resolve what Michael Dummett has called the "scandal" of philosophy— "the scandal caused by philosophy's lack of a systematic methodology." Characterizing this scandal, Dummett tells us:

> It has been a constant preoccupation of philosophers to remedy that lack, and a repeated illusion that they had succeeded in doing so. Husserl believed passionately that he had at last held the key which would unlock every philosophical door, the disciples of Kant ascribed to him the achievement of devising a correct philosophical methodology: Spinoza believed that he was doing for philosophy what Euclid had done for geometry; and before him, Descartes supposed that he had uncovered the one and only proper philosophical method. I have mentioned only a few of the many examples of this illusion; for any outsider to philosophy far the safest bet would be that I am suffering from a similar illusion by making the same claim for Frege.

343

To this I can offer only the banal reply which any prophet has
to make to any skeptic: time will tell.[1]

Dummett expresses a primary concern of modern philosophy that
has persisted from Descartes until the present: to turn philosophy
into a "rigorous science," to discover its real foundations, its proper
object, its systematic methodology; to overcome the situation where
philosophy appears to be the endless battleground among competing opinions (doxoi) and finally becomes a legitimate form of
knowledge (episteme). This search to discover some basic constraints
is not only characteristic of philosophy but it pervades the entire
range of the cultural disciplines. Hovering in the background of this
pursuit is what may be called "the Cartesian anxiety"—the fear or apprehension that if there are no such basic constraints, no foundations,
no determinate "rules of the game," then we are confronted with intellectual and moral chaos where anything goes. But recently there
has been another analysis of the "scandal" of philosophy—that the
real scandal is that we are still taken in and mesmerized by the very
conception of philosophy that Dummett embraces: where we presuppose that there is a "proper object" of philosophy; that there are
philosophic problems that are to be solved once and for all; and that
there is a "systematic methodology" for doing this. If we really want
to overcome the scandal of philosophy, then what is needed is a form
of philosophical therapy that will rid us of the illusion and the self-
deception that philosophy is or can be such a foundational discipline.
What characterizes so much of what is sometimes called postmodernity is a new playful spirit of negativity, deconstruction, suspicion,
unmasking. Satire, ridicule, jokes, and punning become the
rhetorical devices for undermining "puritanical seriousness." This
esprit pervades the writings of Rorty, Feyerabend, and Derrida.
Where an earlier generation of philosophers like Sartre were telling
us that the human predicament is one of unhappy consciousness
with no possibility of overcoming it, it almost seems as if we are now
being told that our condition is one of "absolute dialectical unrest,"
which Hegel took to be the essence of skeptical self-consciousness.

Using an older positivist and emotivist terminology, we may say
that those who take a "pro-attitude" (one that bears a strong affinity
with a domesticated Nietzsche) toward this new phenomenon think
of it as a liberating spirit that releases us from the tyranny of western
metaphysics—what Heidegger called "the onto-theo-logical constitution of metaphysics." And those who have an "anti-attitude" toward

this destruction and deconstruction think of it as opening the floodgates to nihilism, irrationalism, subjectivism, and rampant relativism.

Frequently the opposing poles that I am sketching have been characterized by traditional binary oppositions: rationalism/irrationalism; objectivism/subjectivism; absolutism/relativism. But we are increasingly coming to realize that these traditional dichotomies obscure more than they illuminate, and that they gain their power from an entire mode of thinking, acting, and feeling that is itself being called into question. There is an almost desperate attempt to break out of and move beyond the dichotomies that have characterized modern thought together with an enormous amount of confusion and uncertainty about what this even means.

It is against this background that I want to take a close look at *some* of the characteristic themes and emphases in the work of Rorty, Gadamer, and Habermas. What initially strikes us are the crucial and consequential differences among them—the hard and fast barriers that seem to separate them. At one extreme there is Habermas, who some may think of as the "last" great rationalist. Habermas has attempted to resolve the scandal of philosophy by showing us that the legacy of the philosophic tradition is redeemed in a new reconstructive science—a comprehensive theory of rationality that focuses attention on the centrality of communicative action and discourse, and that can serve as a ground for a critical theory of society. At the other extreme is Rorty, who mocks the very idea of such a "theory" and thinks that it is just another misguided variation of the discredited foundational project of modern philosophy.

Although Rorty appropriates the term "hermeneutics," he tells us "it is not the name for a discipline, nor for a method of achieving the sorts of results which epistemology failed to achieve, nor for a program of research. On the contrary, hermeneutics is an expression of the hope that the cultural space left by the demise of epistemology will not be filled—that our culture should become one in which the demand for constraint and confrontation is no longer felt."[2] From Gadamer's perspective this is a very strange sort of hermeneutics. For what Gadamer takes to be basic for philosophical hermeneutics is that it points the way to an "entirely different notion of knowledge and truth"[3] that is revealed and realized through *understanding*. So from Gadamer's perspective, Rorty's hermeneutics is mutilated or castrated, for it is a hermeneutics without the claim to knowledge and truth.

The thesis that I want to play out is that when we take a closer look at what is going on here, what at first appear to be dramatic and consequential differences begin to look more like differences of emphasis. I am not saying that the three of them are really saying the same thing, or that the differences that divide them are unimportant, but I will try to show how different these differences look once we start probing. I want to show this by concentrating on the themes of praxis, practice, practical truth, and discourse as they appear in their thinking. Let met begin with Gadamer and then move on the Habermas and Rorty in order to show the play—the *spiel*,—that takes place here.

1

The most intriguing and most central theme in Gadamer's understanding of philosophical hermeneutics in his fusion of hermeneutics and praxis. In the context of *Wahrheit und Methode* this becomes evident when Gadamer takes up the issue of "application" and argues for the relevance of Aristotle's *Ethics* in order to clarify "the rediscovery of the fundamental hermeneutic problem." Against an older tradition of hermeneutics that sought to divide it into three distinct subdisciplines: *subtilitas intelligendi* ("understanding"), *subtilitas explicandi* ("interpretation") and *subtilitas applicandi* ("application") Gadamer argues that these are three moments of the *single* process of understanding.[4] They are internally related so that all genuine understanding involves not only interpretation but also application. What Gadamer means is revealed through his own interpretation and appropriation of *phronesis*, which is to be carefully distinguished from theoretical knowledge or *episteme* on the one hand, and technical skill or *techne*, on the other hand. *Phronesis* is a form of reasoning and practical knowledge in which there is a distinctive type of mediation between the universal and the particular where *both* are codetermined. It is not the application of *Method* or the subsumption of particulars under fixed determinate rules or universals. Furthermore, what is distinctive about such practical knowledge is that it involves "the peculiar interlacing of being and knowledge, determination through one's own becoming, *Hexis*, recognition of the situational Good, and *Logos*."[5]

Gadamer claims that Aristotle's analysis of *phronesis* and the ethical phenomenon is a "kind of model of the problems of hermeneutics." For as he tells us:

We, too, determined that application is neither subsequent nor a merely occasional part of the phenomenon of understanding, but codetermines it as a whole from the beginning. Here too application was not the relating of some pre-given universal to the particular situation. The interpreter dealing with a traditional text seeks to apply it to himself. But this does not mean that the text is given to him as something universal, that he understands it as such and only afterwards uses it for particular applications. Rather, the interpreter seeks no more than to understand this universal thing, the text, i.e. to understand what this piece of tradition says, what constitutes the meaning and importance of the text. In order to understand that, he must not seek to disregard himself and his particular hermeneutical situation. He must relate the text to his situation, if he wants to understand at all.[6]

Most of the fundamental themes in philosophical hermeneutics are implicit in this passage or can be related to it. Gadamer's major critique of nineteenth-century hermeneutics is that it neglected the *positive* role that forestructures, prejudgments, and prejudices play in *all* understanding. He claims that it was only with Heidegger that the positive enabling role of forestructures was fully appreciated, and this ontological insight requires a new understanding of the famous hermeneutical circle. This is the basis of Gadamer's *apologia* for prejudice against the "Enlightenment's prejudice against prejudices." Prejudices that are constitutive of our being and our historicity are not only unfounded, negative, and blind; they can also be "justified" and enabling; they open us to experience (*Erfahrung*).[7] We are always being shaped by effective history (*Wirkungsgeschichte*); consequently to understand is always to understand *differently*. Because all understanding involves a dialogical encounter between the text or the tradition that we seek to understand and our hermeneutical situation, we will always understand the "same thing" differently. We always understand from our situation and horizon, but what we seek to accomplish is to enlarge our horizon, to achieve a fusion of horizons (*Horizontverschmelzung*). Gadamer stresses that horizons—whose medium is language—are not self-enclosed; they are essentially open, porous, and fluid. Against subjectivist, relativist, and historicist misinterpretations of our hermeneutical situation, Gadamer stresses the need to situate our horizon within a larger horizon; to open ourselves to the claim to truth that works of art, texts, and tradition make upon us; to allow them to "speak to us."[8] All of this can be taken as a commentary on the meaning of our finitude and historicity.

For there is no Archimedean point, no transcendental position, no theoretical perspective that lies outside of our historicity. Consequently there can never be absolute knowledge, finality in understanding, or complete self-transparency of the knower. We always find ourselves in an open dialogical or conversational situation with the very tradition and history that is effectively shaping us.

If we closely examine Gadamer's writings since the publication of *Wahrheit und Methode,* we can discern a subtle but important shift that has taken place—a change of emphasis that marks a return to concerns of his earliest writings. For in *Wahrheit und Methode* Gadamer introduces *phronesis* and praxis in order to elucidate the character of philosophical hermeneutics. Ethics and politics are not thematic in the book. The interpretation of works of art, texts, and history is thematic. But since the publication of *Wahrheit und Methode* Gadamer has been increasingly concerned with moving in the other direction, with exploring the consequences of hermeneutics for praxis. He claims that "hermeneutic philosophy is the heir to the older tradition of practical philosphy," that "practical and political reason can only be transmitted dialogically," that the "chief task of philosophy is to justify this way of reason and to defend practical and political reason against the domination of technology based on science. That is the point of philosophical hermeneutic. It corrects the peculiar falsehood of modern consciousness; the idolatry of scientific method and the anonymous authority of the sciences and it vindicates again the noblest task of the citizen—decision-making according to one's own responsiblity—instead of conceding that task to the expert."[9]

Gadamer, in the spirit of dialogical encounter that is so central to his thinking, has sought to learn from and appropriate the "truth" from his critics and dialogical partners. Indeed, in his writings during the past twenty years, Gadamer begins to sound more and more like Habermas. Fundamental to both of them has been the categorical distinction between the technical and the practical (Habermas even acknowledges that in part it was Gadamer's work that made him sensitive to the importance and centrality of this distinction). Gadamer like Habermas has been critical of the deformation of praxis where praxis is taken to be the application of science to technical tasks. Gadamer too tells us that "in modern technological society public opinion itself has in a new and really decisive way become the object of very complicated techniques—and this, I think, is the main problem facing our civilization."[10] The theme that is so central from

Habermas—that there is a categorical distinction between purposive-rational action and communicative action, and that there are different types of rationalization processes corresponding to the different levels of action and rationality—is echoed in Gadamer. There is in fact a latent radical strain—a supplement—in Gadamer's thinking that at times he fails to realize. This becomes evident when he tells us that "genuine" solidarity, authentic community, should be realized,"[11] or when in answering the question What is Practice? he declares, "Practice is conducting oneself and acting in solidarity. Solidarity, however, is the decisive condition and basis of all social reason."[12] There are even passages in Gadamer that sound like the echoes of the older Frankfurt School. For exmaple, he describes Hegel's legacy as follows:

> The principle of freedom is unimpugnable and irrevocable. It is no longer possible for anyone still to affirm the unfreedom of humanity. The principle that all are free never again can be shaken. But does this mean that on account of this, history has come to an end? Are all human beings actually free? Has not history since then been a matter of just this, that the historical conduct of a man has to translate the principle of freedom into reality? Obviously this points to the unending march of world history into the openness of its future tasks and gives no becalming assurance that everything is already in order.[13]

I am fully aware of the nuances that separate Gadamer and Habermas even when they use the same expressions—"dialogue," "solidarity," and "freedom." But that is just the point that I want to make—that what at first appears to be so extreme and confrontational begins to look like differences of emphasis. The fundamental thesis that I want to advance is that despite Gadamer's manifest (and real) conservative strain, his fear of the "dogmatism" and potential "terror" of what he calls "planning reason," there is a powerful latent radical strain in his thinking that is constantly pulling us in a different direction. Gadamer's entire project philosophical hermeneutics can be read as an attempt to recover what he takes to be the deepest and most pervasive theme in Western philosophy and culture—that the quintessence of our being is to *be dialogical*. This is not just the "mode of being" of the "few," but is a real potential of every person—a potential that *ought* to be actualized. It is this dialogical character of what we truly are that is deformed and threatened by modern technological society. A cardinal principle of Gadamer's hermeneutics is that when we seek to understand a text the vital question is what the text *says*, its meaning and its truth—this meaning is not to be confused or identified with the psychological intentions of the author. If we apply this principle to Gadamer's own texts, then we detect a tension or conflict between what the texts "say" and what he has "meant." This tension is even exhibited in Gadamer's self-conscious integration of Aristotelian, Platonic, and Hegelian motifs. The appeal to *phronesis* as a model of practical wisdom has traditionally had elitist connotations from the time of Aristotle through Burke right up to the contemporary vogue of neo-Aristotelianism. Aristotle himself never thought of *phronesis* as an "intellectual virtue" that could be ascribed to *all* human beings, but only to a few, only to those rare and gifted individuals who had been properly educated. Gadamer softens this elitist aura of *phronesis* by blending it with his understanding of dialogue and conversation that he appropriates from Plato. When this is integrated with the Hegelian "truth"—"the principle that *all* are free never again can be shaken"— then the implicit "radicalization" of *phronesis* becomes evident. It is Gadamer who tells us that "the point of philosophical hermeneutics is to vindicate the noblest task of the citizen—decision-making according to one's own responsibility."

There is an implicit *telos* here, not in the sense of what *will* work itself out in the course of history, but rather in the sense of what *ought* to be realized. So if we take the theme of application or appropriation to *our* historical situation concretely, then this sets a task for us that can guide our practical lives, that is, to attempt to realize that type of society in which the *idea* of open authentic dialogue and conversation becomes a concrete reality in which *all* have the *real* opportunity to participate. Considering the fragility and the conditions required for such dialogue, it would be a gross perversion of Gadamer's phenomenological insight to think that such an idea can serve as an *organizational* principle of society. Nevertheless, the very idea of such a dialogical rationality is a regulative ideal that can and ought to orient our praxis.

This is why I think that if we want to get at the important differences that still separate Gadamer and Habermas, it is more perspicuous to focus our attention on the meaning and role of *truth* and *criticism* for each of them rather than on the slogan Hermeneutics versus Critique of Ideology. But even here the differences turn out to be different from what at first seems so apparent. Consider the concept of truth, which is not only the most central theme in Gadamer's work but also the most elusive. At first it looks as if what Gadamer means by "truth" is a blending of motifs that he has appropriated from Hegel and Heidegger. Like them, Gadamer rejects and criticizes the dominant conception of truth as *adequatio intellectus et rei*—at least when it comes to understanding the type of truth that pertains to hermeneutical understanding. But Gadamer also carefully distances himself from both Hegel and Heidegger. He categorically rejects what Hegel took to be the ground of his own understanding of truth, that the "true is the whole," which is realized in *Wissenschaft*.[14] It is also evident that Gadamer draws back Heidegger's "radical" thinking about the meaning of *alethia*.[15] But what is even more important and revealing is that when Gadamer appeals to the concept of truth to justify what he has to say about the relevance of Aristotle, *phronesis*, and the tradition of practical philosophy to our hermeneutical situation, he is implicitly appealing to a concept of truth that (pragmatically speaking) comes down to what can be *argumentively validated by a community of interpreters*.[16]

If we focus our attention on the meaning of "criticism" for Gadamer, he tells us "it is a grave misunderstanding to assume that the emphasis on tradition which enters all understanding implies an uncritical acceptance of tradition and sociopolitical conservatism. . . . In truth the confrontation of our historic tradition is always a critical challenge to this tradition. . . . Every experience is such a confrontation."[17] But however sympathetic one may be with Gadamer's critique of objectivism, foundationalism, and the search for an Archimedian point that lies outside of our historicity, there is a question that he never adequately answers for us. All criticism presupposes some principles, standards, or criteria of criticism, no matter how open, tentative, and historical these may be. Tradition itself is not a seamless whole, and what is most characteristic of *our* hermeneutical situation is that there are *conflicting* traditions making conflicting claims upon us. We need to gain some clarity about what are and what ought to be the standards for "a critical challenge" to tradition. It may be true, but it certainly isn't sufficient to tell us that there are no fixed rules or determinate universals that can serve as standards for criticism. If reason is "social reason"—or is genuinely intersubjective—then we need to elucidate the intersubjective principles that can guide our individual criticisms and decisions. Furthermore, to insist, as Gadamer himself does, that the principles, laws, *nomoi* are themselves "handed down" to us from the tradition and demand concrete application does not help us to resolve questions concerning the *conflict* of these *nomoi*, or questions that arise when traditional *nomoi* no longer seem to "bind" us.

The perspective that I think is most illuminating for understanding the differences that make a difference between Gadamer and Habermas is one that emphasizes how much they share in common in the "application" theme. Already, in Habermas's initial review of *Wahrheit und Methode*, he declared, "I find Gadamer's real achievement in the demonstration that hermeneutic understanding is linked with transcendental necessity to the articulation of an action-orienting self-understanding."[18] It is instructive to see how this is worked out and transformed in Habermas's own attempt to develop a comprehensive theory of communicative action and rationality. For Habermas, no less than Gadamer, we cannot escape from our own horizon in seeking to understand what appears to be alien to us. This has crucial significance for the entire theory of rationality, for Habermas too argues that it is an illusion to think that we can assume the position of disinterested observers and theoreticians when it comes to understanding other forms of life and what purport to be other standards of rationality. One never escapes the situation of taking an *evaluative* stance toward the validity claims made by others. If we want to "describe" other forms of life, or ealier stages of our social development, then one can do this only by adopting a "performative" attitude of one who *participates* in a process of mutual understanding.[19] In this respect, the theme of our historicity in which we are always applying or appropriating what we seek to understand to our historical situation is no less fundamental for Habermas than it is for Gadamer. But for Habermas, unlike Gadamer, the primary problem becomes how can we reconcile this performative participation with the type of intersubjective understanding that makes the claim to objectivity. When Habermas seeks to develop a comprehensive theory of communicative action, a universal pragmatics, he is *not* claiming that we do this *sub species aternitatus*, or that we assume the position of an "infinite intellect." Rather he is claiming that from within the horizon of our hermeneutical situation we can seek to elucidate the "unavoidable" conditions and principles of communicative action, discourse, and rationality. We aspire to universality recognizing that any such claim is eminently fallible. If one were to translate Habermas's project into Gadamerian terms, it might be put like this: Gadamer, you yourself have argued that all understanding involves application, and furthermore that our hermeneutical horizon is not closed and limited. Indeed you emphasize the very openness of language that is the condition for all understanding. So the question becomes What is it about the linguistic medium within which we participate that allows for such appropriation and understanding? How are we to account for the fact that we can in principle always understand that which strikes us as alien and strange? What is it about the very character of language and rationality that enables us to grasp the possibility of the type of dialogue, conversation, and questioning that you yourself have so penetratingly elucidated?

Now it may seem as if what I am trying to show is that if we press Gadamer's claims and insights we are led to the very concerns that are central for Habermas. I do think this is true, but it needs to be carefully qualified because it can suggest a misleading asymmetry whereby an "immanent critique" of Gadamer inevitably leads to Habermas's project. But I also think that such a critique can be *reversed*, that we can use Gadamer to highlight some of the latent tensions in Habermas's project. But before turning to what I take to be internal conflicts within Habermas, let me try to pin down the way in which the differences between Habermas and Gadamer now appear. Habermas can be interpreted as highlighting difficulties and lacunae in what Gadamer has accomplished—difficulties concerning the question of truth, especially as it pertains to practical discourse; and difficulties concerning the practice of criticism, whether it be the criticism of the traditions that have formed us or the criticism of present society. Furthermore, Habermas can be used to highlight some of the difficulties in the very appeal to *phronesis*. For Gadamer himself has stressed that *phronesis* involves a mediation and codetermination of the universal and the particular. In the context of ethical and political action, by the "universal" Gadamer means those principles, norms, and laws that are funded in the life of a community and orient our particular decisions and actions. Gadamer stresses how all such principles and laws require judgment and *phronesis* for their concrete application. This makes good sense when there are shared *nomoi* that inform the life of a community. But what happens when there is a breakdown of such principles, when they no longer seem to have any normative power, when there are deep and apparently irreconcilable conflicts about such principles, or when questions are raised about the very norms and principles that ought to guide our praxis? What type of discourse is appropriate when we question the "universal" element—the *nomoi*—that is essential for the practice of *phronesis*? These are the issues that Habermas pursues, and they are not just Habermas's questions but ones that Gadamer raises for us.

2

But now let me turn directly to Habermas and explore how a hermeneutical perspective can sharpen our perception of the tensions that lie at the heart of his thinking. In this context I want to discuss the very *idea* of a theory of communicative action. What kind of theory or intellectual endeavor is it, and how is it to be justified or warranted? Habermas speaks with "two voices," which might be called the "pragmatic" and the "transcendental." Alternatively, I can clarify what I mean by employing a distinction that Charles Taylor makes between "strict dialectics" and "interpretative dialectics" in his book on Hegel. Taylor distinguishes two ways in which a dialectical argument can command our assent. "There are strict dialectics, whose starting point is or can reasonably claim to be undeniable. And then there are interpretative or hermeneutical dialectics, which convince us by the overall plausiblity of the interpretation they give."[20] This is a most unHegelian type of distinction because Hegel's *claim* to truth, system, and *Wissenschaft* depends ultimately on the validity of "strict dialectics." Yet I agree with Taylor that Hegel's most valuable and enduring contribution is what he revealed through interpretative or hermeneutical dialectics. Precisely how is this distinction relevant to Habermas?

At times, especially during the period when Habermas was writing *Erkenntnis und Interesse*, he slips into the language of "strict dialectics" or "strict transcendental argument." This is apparent in the original discrimination of the three "quasitranscendental" cognitive interests and is also evident in his earlier attempts to argue that there are four types of validity claims implicit in communicative action. Habermas's constant use of "necessity," what "must be presupposed," what is "unavoidable" easily leads one to think that he is advancing a transcendental argument in the tradition of Kant, even when he stresses his differences with Kant. But in the years since the publication of *Erkenntnis und Interresse*, Habermas has qualified his project to disassociate himself from this *strong* transcendental strain—and with good reason. Not only have there been powerful objections pressed against the possibility of transcendental arguments or strict dialectics, Habermas has seen more clearly that a theory of communicative action is not intended to be a transcendental a priori theory. In stating his reasons for abandoning the expression "transcendental," Habermas tells us that "adopting the expression *transcendental* could conceal the break with the apriorism that has been made in the meantime. Kant had to separate empirical from transcendental analysis sharply."[21] It is just this dichotomy that a reconstructive theory of communicative action is intended to *overcome*. This is why Habermas now prefers to speak about the logic of reconstruction or reconstructive analysis, and to argue that *within* the domain of scientific theories we must distinguish between empirical-analytic theories and reconstructive theories—the latter types illustrated by the work of Chomsky, Piaget, and Kohlberg. A theory of communicative action is intended to be a *scientific* reconstructive theory of this type. There is still a crucial ambiguity here that needs to be resolved. Even if we accept this distinction between empirical-analytic and reconstructive analyses, how are we to understand this distinction? Habermas emphasizes—and this is vital for his entire project—that the distinction is one of alternative research strategies within the domain of scientific knowledge. Questions concerning empirical evidence, confirmation, and falsification (when properly formulated) are just as central for validating reconstructive hypotheses and theories as they are for empirical-analytic disciplines. If we turn to the critical literature concerning those reconstructive disciplines that Habermas takes to be paradigmatic, we find extensive discussion of whether the empirical and experimental evidence does or does not support the hypotheses advanced by Chomsky, Piaget, and Kohlberg. From a methodological perspective it is still an open issue whether in the long run reconstructive strategies or empirical-analytic strategies will prove scientifically more fruitful. I agree with Habermas that there are no a priori or conceptual reasons that are sufficient to rule out the viability of scientific reconstructive analyses. But there are also no a priori reasons for ruling out the possibility that such analyses may be replaced or displaced by new sophisticated empirical-analytic approaches. The important point here is that insofar as we are concerned with advancing scientific knowledge, it is methodologically prudent to be open to different types of research strategy. Habermas can draw support from the postempiricist philosophy of science—that it is important to keep ourselves open to alternative research programs or traditions, especially in the early stages of the development of a new research program. I am stressing what Habermas himself emphasizes when he defends the claim that a theory of communicative action or a universal pragmatics is a *scientific* theory, one in which "the distinction drawing on a priori knowledge and a posteriori knowledge becomes blurred."[22] But when we turn our attention to the details of the theory of communicative action, and in particular to some of the strong claims that Habermas makes, the scientific status of such a theory becomes dubious and questionable. Consider some of the key claims that Habermas makes about practical truth and normative validity. The idea of practical truth is intended to be the analogue to the idea of theoretical truth; and both sorts of truth can be redeemed and warranted through appropriate forms of substantive argumenation.[23] When questions concerning the appropriateness and legitimacy of claims to universal normative validity are raised, no matter how these questions and potential conflicts are resolved, the participants are unavoidably committed to the idea that such claims can be resolved by argumentative discourse. However sympathetic one may be to this as a regulative ideal that ought to be approximated, it isn't clear in what sense this is an "unavoidable" or "necessary" presupposition that is somehow grounded in the very nature of intersubjectivity. Certainly someone who denies it is not involved in a logical contradiction, nor is it clear in what sense, if any, there is an "existential" or "pragmatic" contradition.

Sometimes it seems as if what Habermas is doing is surreptiously defining "practical discourse" in such a manner that although one can always opt out of such discourse, once he commits himself to it then he is already committed to the discursive redemption of normative validity claims. But Habermas has not established that such a commitment is "built into" the very nature of practical discourse. It is not helpful to say, that however counterfactual the ideal speech situation may be, it is *anticipated* and *presupposed* in every appropriate speech act. There is, of course, nothing objectionable about the appeal to counterfactuals in scientific theories; establishing them is just as central to empirical-analytic sciences as they are to reconstructive sciences. But there is something very peculiar about Habermas's counterfactual claims; for it isn't at all clear what type of scientific evidence is relevant for supporting or refuting such claims. In this context the Popperian demand for refutability or falsifiability is perfectly appropriate. If we are dealing with a scientific theory, one wants to know what could possibly count as a falsification or a refutation of the theory. What evidence would be relevant to refute the counterfactual claims that despite all signs to the contrary, every speaker who engages in communicative action is committed to the presupposition of the discursive redemption of normative validity claims?

One can also criticize Habermas from the opposite point of view. If a universal pragmatics is intended to be a genuine scientific theory that is hypothetical, fallible, and refutable, then what would be the consequences—especially concerning the redemption of universal claims of normative validity, practical truth, and practical discourse—if it turned out to be the case that such a theory is refuted or falsified? Does this mean that the issue of the type of communicative ethics that Habermas advocates and the decisionism that he opposes is a *scientific* issue to be decided by the success of rival research programs? Habermas gets himself into these and related apori as the more he insists on the scientific status of a theory of communicative action.[24] From Rorty's perspective it looks as if Habermas is guilty of succumbing to the temptation that Rorty so brilliantly exposes in another context—to come up with a "successor discipline" to traditional epistemology that claims to do better what epistemology has failed to accomplish.[25]

I have suggested that there is an alternative reading of Habermas when I referred to his pragmatic voice and to interpretative dialectics (which are to be contrasted with his transcendental voice and to strict dialectics). What is fascinating and confusing about Habermas are the ways in which these two voices are superimposed on each other. To explain what I mean about this other voice in Habermas—this other way of reading him—let me cite a passage from Thomas McCarthy's judicious study of Habermas. He opens his study by telling us:

> His contributions to philosophy and psychology, political science and sociology, the history of ideas and social theory are distinguished not only by their scope but by the unity of perspective that informs them. This unity derives from a vision of mankind, our history and our prospects, that is rooted in the tradition of German thought from Kant to Marx, a vision that draws its power as much from the moral-political intention that animates it as from the systematic form in which it is articulated.[26]

When McCarthy speaks of a vision that draws its power from "the moral-political intention that animates it," he comes very close to what William James means by vision in the passage that I cited at the beginning of this essay. The reading of Habermas that I am suggesting is one that emphasizes this aspect of his thinking, that sees his work *not* as another (failed) attempt at strict dialectics, transcendental argument, or even as proposing a rival scientific theory and research program. Rather, it is a perspective that emphasizes that what he is really doing is interpretative dialectics that seeks to command our assent "by the overall plausibility of the interpretation that they give."

Whether we focus our view on Habermas's early reflections on the relation of theory and praxis, his delineation of the three primary cognitive interests, his probing of the question of legitimacy, or his most recent attempts to elaborate a reconstruction of historical materialism and a theory of communicative action, these analyses can be viewed as stages in the systematic articulation and defense of "a vision of mankind, our history and our prospects." For the interpretations that Habermas develops in each of these different but interrelated problematics is animated by the same "moral-political intention"—to show us that there is a *telos* immanent in the forms of life that have shaped us and the forms of communication in which we participate. This is not to be understood as a *telos* that represents the march of world history, one that must and will be realized, but rather as a "gentle but obstinate, a never silent although seldom redeemed claim to reason, a claim that must be recognized de facto whenever and wherever there is to be consensual action."[27]

To argue, as I have been doing, for a reading of Habermas that stresses his pragmatic voice and his practice of interpretative dialectics is not *yet* to make a judgment about how *plausible* his interpretations and narratives really are. I do not think there is any wholesale way of doing this. For this requires that we actually work through the several interrelated problematics and *show* precisely what are the strengths and weaknessses of his interpretations. Here too there is an important lesson to be learned from Gadamer. It is all too frequently assumed that if we can not come up with universal fixed criteria to measure the plausibility of competing interpretations, then this means that we have no *rational* basis for distinguishing better and worse, more plausible or less plausible interpretations, whether these be interpretations of texts, actions, or historical epochs. One does not have to neglect the tangled problems that arise when confronted with evaluating conflicting or competing interpretations to appreciate that in concrete cases we can and do make comparative judgments and seek to support them with *arguments* and the appeal to *good reasons*. [28]

The reading of Habermas that I am advocating can be stated in a slightly different manner. Returning to Gadamer, we can see how he is always pulling us back and reminding us of the inescapability of understanding and interpretation from our historical and hermeneutical horizon. We know, of course, that there are always dangers in doing this; we can be guilty of ethnocentrism, of subtly rewriting history from a Whiggish perspective, of being insufficiently self-critical and reflective about "our standards of rationality." But as Hegel reminds us, sometimes we need to be mistrustful of the very fear of falling into error for a typical reaction to this fear of falling into error because we are always understanding from the perspective of our hermeneutical horizon is to imagine that we can assume the position of an "infinite intellect"[29] or the type of disinterested transcendental point of view that deceives itself into thinking that it is "outside" of history. Alternatively we can flirt with that form of relativism that thinks that we can bracket all prejudgments and our own performative attitude in seeking to understand alien forms of life or earlier stages of our own history. Both Gadamer and Habermas see through the speciousness of these flights from our historical situation. Both, although in different ways, have argued that we can take our historical situation and the practices that are constitutive of it seriously, and at the same time we can develop a critical perspective on it that is at once informed by an undertanding of our history and is oriented to an open projective future. Both reject the thesis that Popper calls "The Myth of the Framework"—that we are prisoners caught in the framework of "our theories; our expectations; our past experiences; our language" where there is *no* possibility of overcoming these limitations.[30] But this commonness between Gadamer and Habermas points to a double irony. For I am claiming that we can employ Gadamer's analysis of what constitutes hermeneutical understanding, which includes the moments of interpretation and application, to get a clearer grasp of what Habermas is actually *doing* (as distinguished from what he sometimes says he is doing); and I am also suggesting—although I cannot adequately substantiate it here—the Habermas elaborates a more comprehensive, plausible, and powerful interpretation of *our* historical hermeneutical situation than does Gadamer. There is even a further twist here. For in the interpretation of Gadamer that I have proposed, we see that there is a latent radical thrust or *telos* in his thinking that points to the demand for the type of society in which every citizen has the opportunity to engage in the open dialogue, conversation, and questioning that he takes to be constitutive of what we are. Gadamer's own analysis and interpretation of modern society, and the main problems confronting it, can be used to *support* the vision of a society in which there is a practical attempt to overcome the forms of systematically distorted communication that block authentic dialogue. Shortly I will try to show how we can also use Rorty to clarify and support the readings of Habermas and Gadamer that I have been adumbrating.

But once again what *initially* strikes us are the sharp differences between Rorty, on the one hand, and Habermas and Gadamer, on the other.

3

Rorty has dropped enough hints in his published writings for us to know how he would "go after" both Habermas and Gadamer. There is a dazzling brilliance in Rorty's deconstructions of what he takes to be the misguided pretensions of philosophical discourse. He is certainly sympathetic with Habermas's plea for undistorted communication but scornful of what happens when "Habermas goes transcendental and offers principles."[31] By constantly leading us to think what we really need is some sort of *theory* in order to *ground* communication and conversation, Habermas is making the same sorts of mistakes that philosophers have always made in their desperate (and failed) attempts to *discover* real constraints and foundations. Habermas is a victim of the illusion that has haunted modern thinkers—that they must dignify the contingent social practices that have been hammered out in the course of history with something that pretends to be more solid and substantial. I suspect that he may even accuse Habermas of being guilty of the "mistake" that Habermas ascribes to so many other thinkers—of being caught in a "scientific misunderstanding" of what he is doing. Underlying Habermas's "technical verbiage" of a new scientific theory of communicative action is nothing more and nothing less than a "moral-political vision." What is perhaps even more misguided from Rorty's perspective is that the constant emphasis in Habermas on consensus and the expectation of the redemption of validity claims through argumentation is really retrogressive. When this is unmasked, it turns out to be only another version of what has been the primary bias of modern epistemology, that is, the assumption that "all contributions to a given discourse are commensurable." "Hermeneutics" as Rorty uses this polemical expression, is "largely a struggle against this assumption."[32] If Rorty is right about what characterizes the conversation of the West, then we should not fool ourselves into thinking that there are any a priori limitations or any hidden constraints on the invention of new vocabularies and new forms of abnormal discourse. It is the very appeal to something like the idea of a rational consensus that has always been used to block, stifle, or rule out "revolutionary" turns in the conversation. To speak of the argumentative redemption of validity claims through the appropriate level of discourse is either potentially stifling or sheer bluff. It *either* becomes a glorification and reification of what are our *existing* contingent social practices and forms of life *or* a pious and vacuous generality. We don't have the slightest idea—before the fact—of what "rules" of argumentation (if any) will be applicable to new abnormal modes of discourse. Habermas fails to realize that he is just giving expression to the old positivist hope that we can come up with determinate rules that will once and for all tell us (in princple) what will count as legitimate and illegitimate (or meaningless) discourse.

Rorty's major complaint against Habermas can be put in still another way, which becomes prominent in Rorty's *apologia* for a neopragmatism (shaped more by his reading of James and Dewey than Peirce and Mead). The heart of this neopragmatism is a "defense" of the Socratic virtues—"willingness to talk, to listen to the people, to weigh the consequences of our actions upon other people."[33] The point for Rorty is that these "are *simply* moral virtues," and there is no metaphysical or epistemological guarantee of success. "*We do not even know what 'success' would mean except simply continuance*" of the conversation that is "merely *our* project, the European intellectual's form of life."[34] What Nietzsche has helped us to see is that there is no "metaphysical comfort" to be found that *grounds* or secures these moral virtues—and we must resist the temptation to find such comfort. The antipragmatist (and in this respect Habermas would be seen as an antipragmatist) thinks that "the question of whether loyalty to our fellow human beings presupposes that there is something permanent and unhistorical which explains *why* we should continue to converse in the manner of Socrates, something which guarantees convergence to agreement."[35] As Rorty tells us, "For the traditional, Platonic or Kantian, philosopher [and he would include Habermas in this tradition] the possibility of *grounding* the European form of life—of showing it to be more than European, more than a contingent human project—seems to be the central task of philosophy [or a new reconstructive science of communicative action].[36] And while Rorty concedes that he has not presented an "argument" for pragmatism or answered the deep criticism that "the Socratic virtues cannot as a practical matter, be defended save by Platonic means, that without some sort of metaphysical comfort nobody will be able *not* to sin against Socrates,"[37] he leaves little doubt that no one from Plato on has even come close to "succeeding" in *grounding* these virtues. So what has been Habermas's main preoccupation ever since the publication of *Erkenntnis und Interesse* (and seems to be his project from his earliest writings), to show that we can "ground" critical theory, is only another version of the old Platonic urge to "escape from conversation to something atemporal which lies in the background of all possible conversations."[38]

Rorty is no less devastating in his critique of Gadamer. He would find all the talk of "an entirely different notion of truth and knowledge," which is revealed by hermeneutic understanding, a form of mystification. Despite Gadamer's own incisive critiques of epistemology and the Cartesian legacy that he claims has infected and distorted even nineteenth-century hermeneutics, Gadamer himself is unwittingly a victim of the Cartesian persuasion that he is reacting against. For Gadamer is constantly playing on the idea that it is *really* philosophical hermeneutics and not epistemology, Method, or science that can achieve what philosophy has always promised us—some profound access to "truth" that is not available to us by the limited and normal methods of science. Gadamer fits right into the tradition of metaphysical idealism, whose principal legacy is "the ability of literary culture to stand apart from science, to assert its spiritual superiority to science, to claim to embody what is most important for human beings."[39] The trouble with Gadamer is that he is only a "half-hearted pragmatist"—what Rorty calls a "weak textualist." "The weak textualist—the decoder—is just one more victim of realism, of the 'metaphysics of presence.' He thinks that is he stays within the boundaries of a text, takes it apart, and shows how it works, then we will have 'escaped the sovereignty of the signifier,' broken with the myth of language as a mirror of reality, and so on. But in fact he is just doing his best to imitate science—he wants a *method* of criticism, and he wants everybody to agree he has cracked the code."[40] Despite Gadamer's claim that the essential problem of philosophical hermeneutics is not a problem of method at all, and despite Gadamer's claim that to understand and to interpret is always to understand and interpret *differently*, he too wants the "comforts of consensus"—even if it is only the comforts of the consensus of the community of interpreters within the same historical horizon who have the proper *Bildung*.

Rorty, too, would "go after" the central and all-important distinction in Gadamer between Method and Truth. For again, despite Gadamer's claims that he never intended to play Method off *against* Truth, and that he wants to acknowledge the legitimacy of science when it is limited to its proper domain, nevertheless the very dichotomy of Method and Truth is suspect. For Rorty would claim that when we take a close look at what goes on in science and what goes on in hermeneutic understanding, we discover that the distinction here in only a pragmatic distinction of differences of degree (or a difference in what is contingently taken to be normal and abnormal discourse). Science itself is more like hermeneutical understanding than Gadamer realizes, and disputes about rival hermeneutical interpretations are more like "Method" than Gadamer acknowledges.

I have sought to portray Rorty's critique of Gadamer and Habermas in the strongest and most vivid manner because here we really *seem* to have some differences that really make a difference. Rorty's "strong" criticisms would no doubt be matched by an equally "strong" rebuttal. Both Gadamer and Habermas would see Rorty as expressing a new, sophisticated version of a very old form of relativism—the type of relativism that *each* has sought to expose and defeat. And if they wanted to get really nasty, they may accuse Rorty of failing to realize the unintended consequences of what he is saying. They may draw on their own respective appropriations of Hegel to accuse Rorty of failing to see how easily a playful relativism that seems so innocent in "civilized" discourse turns into its opposite in the practical realm— how the restless esprit of unrestrained dialectical negativity becomes a potent force for unrestrained destruction. Rorty's "techniques" of deconstruction can be turned against himself. For when decoded, his celebration of relativism is perhaps more honestly revealed by Feyerabend when he tells us:

> Reason is no longer an agency that directs other traditions, it is a tradition in its own right with as much (or as little) claim to the center of the stage as any other tradition. Being a tradition it is neither good nor bad, it simply is. The same applies, to all traditions—they are neither good nor bad, they simply are. They become good or bad (rational/irrational; pious/impious; advanced/primitive; humanitarian/vicious; etc.) only when looked at from the point of view of some other tradition. 'Objectively' there is not much to choose between anti-semitism and humanitarianism. But racism will appear vicious to a humanitarian while humanitarianism will appear vapid to a racist. *Relativism* (in the old simple sense of Protagoras) gives an adequate account of the situation which thus emerges.[41]

I have raised the specter of relativism not because I want to explore it here, but because I want to get rid of it. I agree with a recent statement of Albrecht Wellmer that "relativism" is a confused response to a whole set of issues that need to be disentangled and carefully discriminated. One of the troubling aspects of recent discourse is the ease with which this appellation gets tossed around without much conceptual clarification about what it really means. Rorty himself attempts to deflate the issue when he says:

> Relativism is the view that every belief on a certain topic or perhaps about *any* topic, is as good as every other. No one holds this view. Except for the occasional cooperative freshman, one cannot find anybody who says that two incompatible opinions on an important topic are equally good. The philosophers who get *called* relativists are those who say that the ground for choosing between opinions is less algorithmic than had been thought. . . . So the real issue is not between people who think one view is as good as another and people who do not. It is between those who think our culture, or purposes, or intuitions, cannot be supported except conversationally, and people who still hope for other sorts of support.[42]

In the conflict between Rorty on the one hand, and Gadamer and Habermas on the other, we really seem to have differences that make a difference. There appears to be no way of reducing the gap between what Rorty is telling us and what Gadamer and Habermas are saying. If Rorty is right, then Gadamer and Habermas must both be wrong. One may even be inclined to say that both Gadamer and Habermas are representatives of modernity—at least insofar as they believe that philosophy (when properly reconstructed) still holds out the promise of *knowledge* and *truth*, even when all necessary concessions are made to the realization of human finitude, fallibility, openness, and historicity; while Rorty is a postmodern thinker who seeks to root out the last buried vestiges of the "metaphysics of presence." Or using Rorty's terminology, we may say that both Habermas and Gadamer are "weak textualists," while Rorty sides with the "strong textualists" who try to live without "metaphysical comfort." The strong textualist "recognizes what Nietzsche and James recognied, that the idea of *method* presupposes that a *privileged vocabulary*, the vocabulary which gets to the essence of the object, the one which expresses the properties which it has in itself opposed to those which are read into it. Nietzsche and James said that the notion of such a vocabulary was myth—that even in science, not to mention philosophy, we simply cast around for a vocabulary which lets us get what we want."[43] But is this yet the "last word"? Are we simply faced with an irreconcilable and incommensurable opposition? I think not, and I now will show that when we probe what Rorty is saying, we will see once again how different the differences begin to look.

In order to decode what Rorty is saying, let me introduce a rough but important distincton between Rorty's metacritique of therapeutic analysis of philosophy and his rhetorical apologia for pragmatism. Thus far I have been stressing Rorty's metacritique of the projects of both Gadamer and Habermas. This type of metacritique has become something of an obsession in Rorty. But there is also a subtext, something of what Derrida calls a "supplement" in his work. Rorty has attempted to block any suggestion that he is laying the foundations for a new type of philosophy, a new constructive program. His deliberate use of such vague distinctions as the normal and abnormal, the familiar and unfamiliar, or even systematic and edifying philosophy are rhetorical devices employed to cure us of the expectation or belief that philosophy must be "constructive." Still one keeps asking Where does Rorty really stand? What is the basis for his metacritique? Is he an "epistemological behaviorist"? a "holist"? a "pragmatist"? Are not these really substantive philosophic positions that need to be defended? Rorty is acutely aware that these are the types of questions that will be raised about his project. Every time we think we can really pin him down, he nimbly dances to another place.

"Epistemological behaviorism" and "holism" are not to be taken as names of new philosophic "positions," but rather as expressions that are intended to call epistemology and the project of modern philosophy into question.[44] He even tells us that "pragmatism is, to speak, oxymoronically post-philosophical philosophy."[45] One of the deepest aspirations of thinkers since Hegel—including Kierkegaard, Nietzsche, Marx, Freud, Heidegger, Wittgenstein, Foucault, and Derrida has been to "end" philosophy (and the meaning of the end of the philosophy has been played out in all its variations). Rorty places himself in this tradition with a further ironical twist about the meaning of the "end of philosophy."[46] This also helps to make sense of what can be called his cryptopositivism, which he ironically employs for rhetorical shock value. This becomes manifest when Rorty, for example, tells us "physicalism is probably right in saying that we shall someday be able, 'in principle,' to predict every movement of a person's body (including those of his larynx and his writing hand) by reference to microstructures within his body,"[47] or when he says about Hegel that "under cover of Kant's invention, a new super-science called 'philosophy,' Hegel invented a literary genre which lacked any trace of argumentation."[48] After all these are just the claims that positivists have always made. I do not want to suggest that Rorty doesn't mean what he is saying. He means *precisely* what he is saying, but the irony becomes clear when we realize that whereas the positivists made these sorts of claims against a background where the "tough-minded" natural scientist is taken to be the cultural hero of our time, Rorty is sympathetic with those strong textualists who, without denigrating science, seek to replace the scientist with the poet and the literary critic as the new cultural heros. In short, Rorty wants to show us how little is said when, to use the positivist turn of phrase, we extract the "cognitive content" of what the positivist is saying. Science is nothing more nor less than a very effective vocabulary for coping, one that is likely to win out over philosophy or any other cultural discipline when it comes to matters of *prediction* or following relatively clear patterns of argumentation. The point is not to get trapped into thinking that it is the *only* vocabularly available to us, or getting seduced into thinking that somehow philosophy or any other cultural discipline ought to be able to beat science at its own "game."

But let me turn directly to what I have called Rorty's subtext, his rhetorical apologia for pragmatism. I speak of it as a *rhetorical apologia* because Rorty does not want to claim that one can argue for it, if we *mean* by argument what goes on in science or what the positivists sought to reify as the standards for all "genuine" argumentation. The content of this pragmatism can be characterized as a defense of the Socratic virtues, "the willingness to talk, to listen to other people, to weigh the consequences of our actions upon other people." It means taking conversation seriously (and playfully) without thinking that the only type of conversation that is important is the type that aspires to put an end to conversation by reaching some sort of "rational consensus," or that all "genuine" conversations are really inquiries about "truth." It means not being fooled into thinking or feeling that there is or must be something more fundamental than the contingent social practices that have been hammered out in the course of history. It means resisting tthe "urge to substitute theoria for *phronesis*" and appreciating that there are no constraints on inquiry save conversational ones and that even these conversational constraints "cannot be anticipated." One of the possible consequences of this type of pragmatism would be a "renewed sense of community."[49] "Our identification with our community—our society, our political tradition, our intellectual heritage—is heighened when we see this community as *ours* rather than nature's, *shaped* rather than *found*, one among many that men have made. In the end, the pragmatists tell us, what matters is our loyality to other human beings clinging together against the dark, not our hope of getting things right."[50] It would be a mistake and a slander to think that such a meditation on human finitude entails or leads to an acceptance of the status quo. The critical impulse in Rorty is no less strong than it is in Habermas or even Gadamer. Rorty is constantly criticizing what he takes to be the specter of prevailing illusions and self-deceptions, and he provides "a hint of how our lives might be changed."[51] There *is* a profound moral-political vision that informs his work and suggests what our society and culture may *yet* become. Rorty's deepest sympathies, as well as his tentativenes, are expressed when he draws a distinction between two types of "strong textualists."

> Pragmatism appears in James and Bloom as an identification with the struggles of finite men. In Foucault and Nietzsche it appears as contempt for one's own finitude, as a search for some mighty inhuman force to which one can yield up one's identity. . . . I have no wish to defend Foucault's inhumanism, and every wish to praise Bloom's sense of our common human lot. But I do not know how to back up this preference with argument, or even with a precise account of the relevant differences. To do so, I think, would involve a full-scale discussion of the possibility of combining private fulfillment, self-realization, with public morality, a concern for justice.[52]

Now if one brackets Rorty's metacritique and pays close attention to his own" preface" and "vision," there is something very remarkable about it when we compare what he is saying with Gadamer and Habermas. For there is a significant overlap or family resemblance in these respective visions. This, of course, does not diminish the significance of the differences between Rorty, on the one hand, and Gadamer and Habemas, on the other. But once again, these differences now begin to look very different.

We can even find suitable translations for Rorty's key points in Gadamerian and Habermasian terms. For we can say that as Rorty interprets the "application" theme to our hermeneutical situation, this means that we accept the radical contingency of the social practices that define what we are. To say that they are radically contingent does not mean that they are *arbitrary*, if by this we mean that we can somehow leap out of our historical situation and blithely accept some other set of social practices. Rorty is calling for an honest recognition of what constitutes our finitude and historicity and giving up the false "metaphysical comfort" that these practices are grounded in something more fundamental. We can appreciate the extent to which *our* sense of community is threatened and distorted not only by the "material conditions" that characterize our lives, but by the faulty epistemological doctrines that fill our heads. The *moral* task of the philosopher or the cultural critic is to defend the openness of human conversation against all those temptations and real threats that seek closure—to keep open the "cultural space left by the demise of epistemology." Even Rorty's neopragmatism has undergone a subtle shift in the course of his intellectual development. Rorty's first published article was a defense of Peirce and an attempt to show the family resemblances between Peirce and the postpositivist musings of the later Wittgenstein.[53] In *Philosophy and the Mirror of Nature*, it is Dewey as the critic of foundationalism who replaces Peirce as the hero of pragmatism. And in some of Rorty's most recent writings, it is James's humanistic pragmatism that he emphasizes. The line of development here is one in which there is "breaking with the Kantian epistemological tradition."[54] There is a certain strain or tension in Rorty's appropriation of the views of the pragmatists. For Peirce, Dewey, and even James, it was still the scientist who was the cultural hero. They sought to imbue philosophy with what they took to be the quintessence of the scientific experimental spirit. But unlike theirs, Rorty's deepest affinities are with what he calls "literary culture." The narrative that he unfolds is one where representatives of literary culture such as Bloom, Foucault, and Derrida replace professional philosophers as the dominant voice in the present conversation of mankind. Dewey is one of Rorty's heros, but Rorty does not follow Dewey in his sociopolitical critiques of the "problems of men." But although Rorty himself has not practiced the type of sociopolitical critique that became so central for Dewey, he expresses deep sympathy with it. Rorty too is an apologist for those very democratic virtues that were so central for Dewey and that he sought to make concrete. There is an important difference of emphasis here between Rorty and Habermas—one that also reveals the common ground that they share. For Rorty's descriptions of what characterizes the social-political practices of our time are rather "thin" when compared with the "thick" descriptions of Habermas (or even with the highly illuminating analyses of micropractices by Foucault). If, as Rorty tells us, the legacy of the pragmatists is to call for a change of orientation on how we can best cope with the world, how to live our lives so that we can "combine private fulfillment, self-realization, with public morality, a concern with justice," then this demands a critical analysis of the *conflicts* of the social and cultural practices that shape our lives.[55] Further, this change of orientation requires confronting the practical tasks for achieving what Dewey once delineated as the primary task of democracy—"the creation of a freer and more humane experience in which all share and to which all contribute."[56] I suggested earlier that we can use Rorty to get a clearer "fix" on what Habermas is really doing. In Rorty's terms, Habermas's importance is to be found in his "vision of mankind, our history and its prospects." Habermas is a "cultural critic" who has helped to clarify what is *our* human project and who has developed a "moral-political vision" that highlights the demand for the concrete achievement of the very Socratic virtues that Rorty himself defends.

4

It may be legitimately asked where does this *Spiel* of Gadamer, Habermas, and Rorty leave us. Let me first emphasize what I take to be the wrong conclusions to draw. It would be wrong to say that I am suggesting that all three are basically saying the same thing: they are not. It would be a mistake to think that there are no differences among them that make a difference. And it would be just as faulty and misleading to think that their respective voices can be *aufgehoben* into a grand synthesis. Drawing on the central notion of a conversation that is so vital for all three of them, we can say that we must do as much justice to their differing emphases as to what they share in common. The appeal to the "model" of a conversation can be illuminating. For in any living vital conversation (which is not just the babble of incommensurable opinions), there will always be important differences among the participants; it behooves us to listen carefully to what each is saying to catch the nuances of their inflections. What I have tried to show is how different these differences appear once we start probing and listen carefully. But the other side of differences is the common ground that *emerges*. In this final section, it is this common ground that I want to highlight. For I think it tells us something important about our hermeneutical situation and the *agon* between modernity and postmodernity.

Labels in philosophy and cultural discourse have the character that Derrida ascribes to Plato's *pharmakon*:[57] they can poison and kill, and they can remedy and cure. We *need* them to help identify a style, a temperament, a set of common concerns and emphases, or a vision that has a determinate shape. But we must also be wary of the ways in which they can blind us or can reify what is fluid and changing. The label that I would use to *name* the common project of Rorty, Habermas, and Gadamer is "nonfoundational pragmatic humanism," and I want to comment on each of the expressions in this label. I do not think that much needs to be said about the expression "nonfoundational." For here we find a convergence in the major traditions of contemporary philosophy. One line can be drawn that runs from Peirce, James, Dewey, Mead, Wittgenstein, Quine, Sellars, and Rorty. "Nonfoundational" is perhaps too weak a term to characterize this movement of thought because it is essentially "*anti*foundational." Already in his famous papers of 1868, Peirce laid down the main lines of the contemporary attack on the Cartesian legacy. He had the perspicacity to see that carrying out this project would lead us to a revolutionary understanding of human inquiry, signification, and the human condition. This attack on the Cartesian legacy and persuasion is echoed and perhaps deepened in sustained critique of this tradition of "modern subjectivism" in the *thinking* of Heidegger and Gadamer. Of course, Rorty so presses this antifoundationalist motif that Habermas (and even Peirce) begin to look like foundationalists from his perspective. But I think that a fairer and more generous interpretation of Habermas would emphasize that he too has been motivated to root out this tendency in the Hegelian-Marxist tradition with which he identifies. Although there are still some rearguard skirmishes, I think we can say, using James's phrase, that the "choice" between foundationalism and nonfoundationalism is no longer a "living option"; it is a "dead option."

Both Rorty and Habermas would feel comfortable with the appellation, "pragmatic," although I suspect Gadamer would not. It is to Habermas's credit that he has been one of the few German philosophers who (along with Apel) has been able to break out of those blinding prejudices that have been a barrier for continental philosophers to appreciate the vitality, *esprit*, and relevance of what is best in the American pragmatic tradition. It is not just that Habermas has creatively drawn on the work of Peirce and Mead in developing his own understanding of communicative action, discourse, and rationality, but the American pragmatist with whom Habermas shares the deepest affinity is John Dewey; indeed I think that Habermas is closer in spirit to Dewey than Rorty is. Habermas pursues what Dewey took to be the aim of the reconstruction of philosophy, which enables us to cope with the concrete "problems of men" in their sociopolitical context.

For all Gadamer's erudition, there is no evidence that he has ever grappled with the American pragmatic tradition. He seems to share Heidegger's prejudice about this tradition.[58] But this "blindness" need not get in the way of seeing the affinity between the best of Gadamer and the best of American pragmatism. Of course, the pragmatists have always been more sympathetic with the promise of science in helping us to cope with human problems. But one can find in pragmatism a similar highlighting of what Gadamer calls *phronesis* —practical knowledge and wisdom. Furthermore, there are structural parallels between Gadamer's attack on the Cartesian legacy and that of the pragmatists. But the affinity is more profound than the attack on a common enemy. For just as Gadamer seeks to overcome the misleading epistemological associations of the subject-object distinction that pervades modern thought, this is also true of the pragmatists. Gadamer's suggestion that the "mode of being" of play provides a more penetrating understanding of the way we are in the world corresponds to Dewey's analysis of the dynamic to-and-fro transactional character of "situations." And what Gadamer tells us about the meaning of human finitude, the fallibility of all understanding, and the essential openness of experience to future experience are themes that are just as central to the pragmatic tradition.

"Humanism," the third term in the label I am proposing, has become something of a dirty word in recent times. It has been used by its critics to identify everything that they think is wrong in the modern world. The *locus classicus* for the contemporary critique of humanism is Heidegger's infamous "Letter on Humanism," but the attack on humanism has been helped along by the way in which "humanism" has become a whipping boy for Althusser and Foucault. From Foucault's perspective, "humamism," which the modern world takes to be its greatest contribution to culture, turns out to be the *pharmakon* that kills—it names everything that is wrong, stolid, self-deceptive, and bleak in the modern world. When unmasked it seems to be the ideology of the new regime of power/knowledge—the ideology of the "disciplinary society," "the age of bio-power," the "caceral archipelago." In the new postmodern, poststructuralist Manichean theology, "humanism" seems to function as the name for the Kingdom of Darkness. Given the bad press that humanism has received recently from such diverse sources, it may seem best to drop this signifier altogether in favor of something that doesn't evoke such strong emotive reactions. But it is more than a matter of perversity to hold on to this notion and *not* to abandon it in the face of such varied criticisms. One doesn't have to believe in the deification of man (or woman) to be a humanist, or to be guilty of the hubris that neglects the limitations of human finitude, or to be an apologist for the "caceral archipelago" to be a humanist. This is not the place for a scholarly disquisition on the history and vicissitudes of the meaning of "humanism." But one can recognize with Rorty that it is a fitting expression for the "Socratic virtues," or with Gadamer that it signifies the essential dialogical, conversational, questioning character of what we are. One can agree with Habermas that it is a "fiction to believe that Socratic dialogue is possible everywhere and at any time" and be alert to the material conditions that distort and deform such dialogue and prevent its actualization in society. Such a humanism points to the urgency of the practical tasks that confront us in trying to make the world a bit more humane, where our social practices actually become practices where we can engage in rational persuasion and *phronesis*, rather than manipulation and strategic maneuvering; where we seek to root out all hidden forms of domination. It directs us to what Rorty calls a "renewed sense of community" and to working toward a society in which the type of dialogue and *phronesis* that Gadamer celebrates are not mere abstractions. It provides no blueprints for how to accomplish this (for there are none), and it eschews all forms of false "metaphysical comfort." It means seeking to eliminate the real obstacles that stand in the way of distorted communications—whether these come from the secret police or more subtle and frequently more effective forms of power/knowledge. The common ground that emerges in the play of Rorty, Gadamer, and Habermas—their nonfoundational pragmatic humanism—may yet serve as a vision that can move us, "a mode of feeling the whole push, and seeing the whole drift of life" that can enable us to cope with the darkness of our times and orient our praxis.

NOTES

1. Michael Dummett, "Can Analytical Philosophy Be Systematic, and Ought It to Be?" in *Truth and Other Enigmas* (London: Duckworth, 1978), p. 458.

2. Richard Rorty, *Philosophy and the Mirror of Nature* (Princeton: Princeton University Press, 1979), p. 315.

3. Hans-Georg Gadamer, "The Problem of Historical Consciousness," *Interpretative Social Science: A Reader*, eds. P. Rabinow and W. Sullivan (Berkeley: University of California Press, 1979), p. 113.

4. See *Truth and Method* (New York: Seabury Press, 1975), pp. 274ff. See also Gadamer's discussion of The Hermeneutical Problem and Aristotle's Ethics, in "The Problem of Historical Consciousness," pp.135ff.

5. "The Problem of Historical Consciousness," p. 107.

6. *Truth and Method*, p. 289.

7. See the discussion of the positive role of prejudices (*Vorurteile*) in *Truth and Method*, pp. 235ff.

8. Gadamer writes, "The best definition for hermeneutics is: to let what is alienated by the character of the written word or by the character of being distantiated by cultural or historical distances speak again," in "Practical Philosophy as a Model of the Human Sciences," *Research in Phenomenology* 9: p. 83.

9. "Hermeneutics and Social Science," *Cultural Hermeneutics* 2 (1975): 316.

10. Ibid., pp. 313-14.

11. "What is Practice?," *Reason in the Age of Science* (Cambridge: MIT Press, 1982), p. 80.

12. Ibid., p. 87.

13. "Hegel's Philosophy and its Aftereffects," *Reason in the Age of Science*, p. 37.

14. See, for example, the following passage, which is typical of Gadamer's distancing himself from Hegel.

> For Hegel it is necessary, of course, that the movement of consciousness, experience should lead to a self-knowledge that no longer has anything different or alien to itself. For him the perfection of experience is 'science,' the certainty of itself in knowledge. Hence his criterion of experience is that of self-knowledge. That is why the dialectic of experience must end with the overcoming of all experience, i.e., in the complete identity of consciousness and object. We can not understand why Hegel's application to history, insofar as he saw it as part of the absolute self-consciousness of philosophy, does not do justice to the hermeneutical consciousness. The nature of experience is conceived in terms of that which goes beyond it; for experience itself can never be science. It is in absolute antithesis to knowledge and to that kind of instruction that follows from general theoretical or technical knowledge. The truth of experience always contains an orientation towards new experience. . . . The dialectic of experience has its own fulfillment not in definitive knowledge, but in that openness to experience that is encouraged by experience itself. *Truth and Method*, p. 319

15. In his published work, Gadamer is usually respectful and cautious in his comments on Heidegger. But occasionally he indicates his strong disagreements with Heidegger. See the foreward to the second edition of *Truth and Method*, xxv. See also his correspondence with Leo Strauss (which was not intended for publication), *Independent Journal for Philosophy*, 2 (1978), pp. 5–12.

16. See my discussion of this in "From Hermeneutics to Praxis," *The Review*

of Metaphysics 35 (June 1982). This article presents a fuller critical discussion of Gadamer's philosophical hermeneutics. Also in this volume, pp. 87–110.

17. "The Problem of Historical Consciousnes," p. 108.

18. "A Review of Gadamer's *Truth and Method,*" *Understanding and Social Inquiry,* eds. Fred R. Dallmayr and Thomas McCarthy (Notre Dame: University of Notre Dame Press, 1977?, p. 351 (and p. 262 above).

19. It is important to distinguish different roles or types of evaluation in this context. Habermas's main point is that "classifying" or "describing" speech acts (whether such speech acts are made in our own or an alien language) *presupposes* that we understand the types of validity claim that they make. An interpreter must have the ability to make clear to himself or herself the implicit reasons that move participants to take the positions that they do take. In order to *understand* an expression, the interpreter must bring to mind the reasons with which the actor would under suitable circumstances defend its validity. Consequently the interpreter is drawn into the process of *assessing* validity *claims.* But this process of determining that a validity claim has been made and assessing it is not *yet* to make an evaluative judgment about the soundness of the validity claim. Habermas's point can be illustrated by appealing to the now famous example of Zande witchcraft. We could not even begin to understand Zande witchcraft unless we had the ability to discriminate what the Azande consider to be reasons for acting in one way or another. To do this requires a *preunderstanding* on our part of what it means to make a validity claim. This is the sense in which describing or understanding the *meaning* of what the Azande are doing requires *assessing* validity claims. But it is a different (although related question) to evaluate whether the reasons given by the Azande are good or bad reasons, and even here we need to make an important distinction. For understanding of the practice of Zande witchcraft requires that we can discriminate what the Azande *themselves* consider good or bad reasons for acting. (Presumably the Azande themselves can make *mistakes.*) This judgment can also be distinguished from a judgment whether (and in what sense) the *types* of reasons that the Azande give are adequate. Habermas is, of course, aware of the ever-present danger of ethnocentrism, of unreflectively imposing alien standards of judgment and thereby missing the *point* or *meaning* of a practice. But it is an illusion to think that we can escape from ethnocentrism by thinking that we can *describe* alien liinguistic practices without assessing the validity claims that are implicitly made in speech acts. For one of the clearest statements of this point about the internal relation between understanding *meaning* and *assessing* validity claims and its significance for a theory of rationality, see Jürgen Habermas, *Theorie des Kommunikativen Handelns,* vol. 1 (Frankfurt: Suhrkamp Verlag, 1981), pp. 152ff.

Although there are important points of disagreement, Habermas can draw support for this thesis about what is required for describing and understanding the meaning of "alien" languages from Donald Davidson's argument in "On the Very Idea of a Conceptual Scheme," *Proceedings of the American Philosophical Association,* 1974.

20. Charles Taylor, *Hegel* (Cambridge: Cambridge University Press, 1975), p. 218.

21. "What is Universal Pragmatics?" *Communication and the Evolution of Society* (Boston: Beacon Press, 1979), p. 24.

22. Ibid., p. 24.

23. For a perceptive analysis of Habermas's theory of argumentation and its relation to a theory of truth, see Gunnar Skirbekk, "Pragmatism in Apel and Habermas," *Chronicle for Institut Unternational de Philosophie (forthcoming).*

24. Habermas betrays an insight that was central to his earlier work when he argued that critique is not to be assimilated to either *science* or *philosophy.*

25. See Rorty's critical discussion of such successor theories in *Philosophy and the Mirror of Nature,* chaps. 5 and 6.

26. Thomas McCarthy, *The Critical Theory of Jürgen Habermas* (Cambridge, Mass.: MIT Pres, 1978), p. ix.

27. "Historical Materialism and the Development of Normative Structures," *Communication and the Evolution of Society,* p. 97.

28. For a discussion of the complexities involved in evaluating conflicting and competing interpretations, see Charles Taylor, "Interpretation and the Sciences of Man"; and Paul Ricouer, "The Model of the Text: Meaningful Action Considered as a Text." Both essays are reprinted in *Interpretative Social Science,* eds. Paul Rabinow and William M. Sullivan (Berkeley: University of California Press, 1979.)

One of the primary reasons why critics of hermeneutics have been suspicious of its claim to "cognitive legitimacy" is that the decision or choice among competing interpretations has been contrasted with science where there are presumably clear determinate rules or criteria for choosing among rival theories or paradigms. But despite internal disputes among postempiricist philosophers and historians of science, there has been a growing rational consensus that this is a *myth.* Kuhn, Lakatos, Feyerabend, Toulmin (and many others) have emphasized the essential openness or indeterminacy of the criteria in choosing among rival theories, paradigms, or research programs. All of the above would agree with Kuhn's famous claim that "there is no neutral algorithm for theory-choice, no systematic decision procedure that, properly applied, must lead each individual in the group to the same decision." Thoms Kuhn, *The Structure of Scientific Revolutions* (Chicago: University of Chicago Press, 1970), p. 200. Kuhn himself realizes how many claims that he has been making bear a close affinity with those which have been central to contemporary hermeneutics. See his preface to *The Essential Tension* (Chicago: University of Chicago Press, 1977), and his essay, "Objectivity, Value Judgment and Theory Choice."

29. "Gadamer-Strauss Correspondence," *Independent Journal for Philosophy.*

30. Karl Popper, "Normal Science and Its Dangers," *Criticism and the Growth of Knowledge,* ed. Imre Lakatos and Alan Musgrave (Cambridge: Cambridge University Press, 1970), p. 56.

31. Richard Rorty, "Pragmatism, Relativism, and Irrationalism," *Proceedings and Addresses of the American Philosophical Association,* (1980), p. 736.

32. *Philosophy and the Mirror of Nature,* p. 316.

33. "Pragmatism, Relativism, and Irrationalism," p. 734.

34. Ibid., p. 734.

35. Ibid., p. 733.

36. Ibid., pp. 734–35.

37. Ibid., p. 737.

38. Ibid., p. 737.

39. Richard Rorty, "Nineteenth-Century Idealism and Twentieth-Century Textualism," *The Monist* 64, no. 2 (April 1981): 165.

40. Ibid., p. 167.

41. Paul Feyerabend, *Science in a Free Society* (London; NLB, 1978), pp. 8–9.

42. "Pragmatism, Relativism, and Irrationalism," pp. 727–28.

43. "Nineteenth-Century Idealism and Twentieth-Century Textualism," pp. 167–68.

44. See the discussion of "epistemological behaviorism" and "holism" in my paper "Philosophy in the Conversation of Mankind," *The Review of Metaphysics* 33, no. 4 (June 1980).

45. "Nineteenth-Century Idealism and Twentieth-Century Textualism," p. 159.

46. See Rorty's discussion of the "end of philosophy in the final chapter of *Philosophy and the Mirror of Nature*.

47. *Philosophy and the Mirror of Nature*, p. 354.

48. "Nineteenth-Century Idealism and Twentieth-Century Textualism," p. 162.

49. "Pragmatism, Relativism, and Irrationalism," pp. 724ff.

50. Ibid., p. 727.

51. Ibid., p. 738.

52. "Nineteenth-Century Idealism and Twentieth-Century Textualism," p. 51.

53. "Pragmatism, Categories, and Language," *The Philosophical Review* 70 (April 1961).

54. "Pragmatism, Relativism, and Irrationalism," p. 719. See the opening section of this address for Rorty's understanding of pragmatism.

55. I have developed this critique of Rorty in "Philosophy in the Conversation of Mankind."

56. John Dewey, "Creative Democracy—The Task Before Us," in *Classic American Philosophers*, ed. Max Fisch (New York, 1951), p. 394.

57. "Plato's Pharmacy," *Dissemination* (Chicago: University of Chicago Press, 1981).

58. For a discussion of the similarities and differences between Heidegger and the pragmatists, see Richard Rorty, "Overcoming the Tradition: Heidegger and Dewey," *The Review of Metaphysics* 30 (1976); and "Heidegger Against the Pragmatists" (unpublished ms.).

TEXT AND INTERPRETATION [a.]

HANS-GEORG GADAMER

Translated by Dennis J. Schmidt

The problems of hermeneutics were initially developed from the point of departure of the special sciences, from theology and jurisprudence in particular, and in the end even from the historical sciences. Yet, already in German romanticism we find the profound insight that Dilthey formulated in remarking that understanding and interpretation not only come into play in expressions of life that are fixed in writing, but rather concern the general relation of people to one another and to the world. In German this has even left an imprint upon words that are derived from the word for 'understanding' [*Verstehen*], such as the word for 'communication' [*Verständnis*].[b.] Thus, 'Verstehen' also means 'für etwas Verständnis haben'. The

---

a. *Translator's note:* An earlier version of this paper was delivered on November 20, 1982 as part of the "Perspectives of Interpretation" series in the conferences on the philosophy of the human sciences at Temple University. A subsequent, and greatly expanded, development of this paper and its themes was delivered in Paris a year later. That paper, along with a commentary by Derrida and Gadamer's reply to Derrida has been published in Philippe Forget, ed. *Text und Interpretat* (München: Fink Verlag, 1984), pp. 25-55. This version is printed with permission from the author.

---

b. *Translator's note:* There is no equivalent in English for the linguistic example given here. *Verständnis* can mean 'understanding', 'comprehension', 'communication', 'intelligence', 'sympathy'; *Verstehen* is the nominative form of the verb 'to understand'; *für etwas Verständnis haben* means 'to have an appreciation for something.'

ability to understand is a fundamental endowment of man, one that sustains his communal life with others and, above all, one that takes place by way of language and the partnership of conversation. In this respect, the universal claim of hermeneutics is beyond all doubt. On the other hand, however, the linguisticality of the communicative event [*Verständigungsgeschehen*], which is in play between people, signifies nothing less than an insurmountable barrier, the metaphysical significance of which was also evaluated positively for the first time by German romanticism. It is formulated in the sentence: *Individuum est ineffabile*. This sentence points to a limit of ancient ontology (at any rate, it cannot be documented in the medieval period). However, for the romantic consciousness it meant that language never touches upon the last, insurmountable secret of the individual person. This expresses the feeling for life that characterized the romantic age in a particularly telling manner, and it points to an inherent law of linguistic expression, which not only sets the limits of linguistic expression but also determines its significance for the formation of the common sense that unites people.

I believe that it is helpful to recall these historical antecedents of our present formulation of the question. The consciousness of method found in the historical sciences, which flourished as a result of romanticism, and the influence exerted by the successful model of the natural sciences led philosophical reflection to restrict the universality of the hermeneutical experience to its scientific form. The full extent of the fundamental hermeneutical experience is to be found neither in Wilhelm Dilthey, who attempted to ground the social sciences in their historicality by way of the conscious continuation of the ideas of Friedrich Schleiermacher and his romantic compatriots, nor in the neo-Kantians, who worked toward an epistemological justification of the human studies within the framework of a transcendental critique of culture and values. This lack of any view encompassing the full extent of hermeneutic experience might even have been more pronounced in the homeland of Kant and transcendental idealism than in countries where 'les Lettres' played a meaningful role in public life. In the end, however, philosophical reflection everywhere went in a similar direction.

Thus I took as my own point of departure the critique of the idealism and methodologism of the epistemological era. Heidegger's extention of the concept of understanding to an existential, that is to a fundamental categorical determination of human existence, was of particular importance for me. That was the impetus that motivated me to critically go beyond the discussion of method and to expand the formulation of the hermeneutic question so that it not only took science into account, but the experience of art and of history as well. With a critical and polemical intent in his analysis of understanding, Heidegger followed the example of former discussions of the hermeneutic circle, maintaining it in its positivity and conceptualizing it in his analysis of *Dasein*. However, one should not forget that what is at stake in this issue is not a matter of circularity as a metaphysical metaphor, but rather the structure of a logical concept that finds its real place in the theory of scientific proof as the doctrine of *circulus vitiosus*. The hermeneutic circle says that in the domain of understanding there can be absolutely no derivation of one from the other, so that here the logical fallacy of circularity does not represent a mistake in procedure, but rather the most appropriate description of the structure of understanding. Thus, Dilthey introduced the discussion of the hermeneutical circle as a means of separating himself from the post-Schleiermachian scientific epoch. If, along with this, one bears in mind the true extend that everyday speech accords to the concept of understanding, then one sees that the discussion of the hermeneutic circle is in fact directed toward the structure of Being-in-the-world itself, that is toward the overcoming of the subject-object bifurcation that was the primary thrust of Heidegger's transcendental analysis of Dasein. Just as one who uses a tool does not treat that tool as an object, but works with it, so too the understanding in which Dasein understands itself in its Being and in its world is not a way of comporting itself toward definite objects of knowledge, but is rather the carrying out of Being-in-the-world itself. With this the hermeneutical doctrine of method, which bore the imprint of Dilthey, transformed itself into a hermeneutics of facticity, which was guided by Heidegger's inquiry into Being and which included the retrospective questioning of historicism and of Dilthey.

As is well known, the later Heidegger completely discarded the concept of hermeneutics because he realized that he would never be able to break through the sphere of transcendental reflection in this manner. His philosophizing, which in the 'Kehre' attempted to complete this withdrawal from the concept of the transcendental, increasingly encountered such difficultires with language that many readers of Heidegger came to believe that there was more poetry than philosophical thought to be found in his work. I believe of course that this view is a mistake, and so one of my own motives was to look for ways in which Heidegger's discussion of Being, which is not the Being of beings, can be legitimated. That effort led me once again to intense work on the history of classical hermeneutics, and it compelled me to emphasize what new insights were brought to light by the critique of this history. It seems to me that my own contribution to these insights is the discovery that no conceptual language, not even what Heidegger called the 'language of metaphysics', represents an unbreakable constraint upon thought if the thinker only allows himself to trust language; that is, if he engages in dialogue with other thinkers and other ways of thinking. Thus, in full accord with Heidegger's critique of the concept of subject, whose hidden ground he revealed as substance, I tried to conceive the original phenomenon of language in dialogue. This effort entailed a hermeneutical reorientation of dialectic, which had been developed by German Idealism as the speculative method, with respect to the art of the living dialogue in which the Socratic-Platonic movement of thought took place. This reorientation of dialectic was not intended to lead to a merely negative dialectic even though it was always conscious of the fundamental incompletability of the Greek dialectic. Rather, it represented a correction of the ideal of method that characterized modern dialectic as fulfilling itself in the idealism of the Absolute. This same interest led me to search for the hermeneutical structure in the experience of art and of history itself, which the so-called social sciences have as their 'objects', rather than initially in the experience that is treated by science. No matter how much the work of art may appear to be an historical given, and thus a possible object of scientific research, it is always the case that it says something to us, and it does so in such a way that its statement can never finally be exhausted in a concept. Likewise, in the experience of history we find that the ideal of the objectivity of historical research is only one side of the issue, in fact a secondary side, because the special feature of historical experience is that we stand in the midst of an event without knowing what is happening to us before we grasp what has happened in looking backwards. Accordingly, history must be written anew by every new present.

Ultimately, the same basic experience holds true for philosophy and its history. Plato, who wrote only dialogues and never dogmatic texts, is not alone in teaching us this lesson. For, in what Hegel calls the speculative element in philosophy (which was at the basis of his own observations of the history of philosophy), we are constantly confronted with a challenge to bring into view this same element in the dialectical method. Thus I tried to hold fast to the inexhaustibility of the experience of meaning by developing the implications for hermeneutics of the Heideggerian insight into the central significance of finitude.

In this context, the encounter with the French philosophical scene represents a genuine challenge for me. In particular, Derrida has argued against the later Heidegger that Heidegger himself has not really broken through the Logo-centrism of metaphysics. Derrida's contention is that insofar as Heidegger asks about the essence of truth or the meaning of Being, he still speaks the language of metaphysics which looks upon meaning as something preexisting that is to be discovered [*vorhandenen und aufzufindenen*]. This being so, Nietzsche is said to be more radical. His concept of interpretation does not entail the discovery of a preexisting meaning, but the positing of meaning in the service of the 'Will to Power'. Only then is the Logo-centrism of metaphysics really broken. In order to be consistent this development and continuation of Heidegger's insight, which Derrida views as its radicalization, must discard Heidegger's own presentation and critique of Nietzsche. In this view Nietzsche is not regarded as the extreme case of the forgetfulness of Being that culminates in the concepts of value and will, but as representing the true overcoming of metaphysics, the very metaphysics within with Heidegger remains trapped when he asks about Being, or the meaning of Being, as if it were a Logos to be discovered. Thus it was not enough that the later Heidegger developed his special quasipoetical language in order to escape the language of metaphysics; a language that with each new essay by Heidegger seemed to be a new language and was always one that required that each reader be constantly engaged as one's own translator of this language. To be sure, the extent to which one can succeed in finding the language that fulfills this task is problematic; however, the task is set, it is the task of 'understanding'. Since my confrontation with the French continuation of Heideggerian thought, I have become aware that my own efforts to 'translate' Heidegger testify to my own limits and especially indicate how deeply rooted I am in the romantic tradition of the humanities and its humanistic heritage. But it is precisely this very tradition of 'historicism' that supports me, against which I have tried to take a critical stand. In a letter that has since been published, Leo Strauss got to the heart of the matter in saying that for Heidegger it is Nietzsche, while for me it is Dilthey, who forms the focal point of critique. It could be said that the distinctive feature of Heidegger's radicality is that his own critique of the Husserlian brand of neo-Kantianism put him in the position of recognizing in Nietzsche the extreme culmination of that which he called the history of the forgetfulness of Being. But this critical observation is immanent and is one that rather than being inferior to Nietzsche's thought goes beyond him. I find that the French followers of Nietzsche have not grasped the significance of the seductive and tempting challenge of Nietzsche's thought. It seems to me that only in this way could they come to believe that the experience of Being that Heidegger tried to uncover behind metaphysics is exceeded in radicality by Nietzsche's extremism. In truth, however, there is a deep ambiguity that characterizes Heidegger's image of Nietzsche in that he follows Nietzsche into the most extreme positions and precisely at that point he finds the excesses [Un-wesen] of metaphysics at work insofar as in the valuing and revaluing of all values Being itself becomes a value-concept in the service of the 'Will to Power'. Heidegger's attempt to think Being goes far beyond such disintegration of metaphysics in the thinking of values, or better yet, he goes back behind metaphysics itself without finding the satisfaction that Nietzsche found in the extreme of its self-disintegration. Such retrospective questioning does not do away with the concept of Logos and its metaphysical implications, rather it recognizes its one-sidedness and concedes its superficiality. In this regard it is of decisive importance that 'Being' does not unfold totally in its self-manifestation, but rather withholds itself and withdraws with the same originality with which it manifests itself. This is the deep insight that was first maintained by Schelling in opposition to Hegel's logical idealism. Heidegger takes up this question once again while applying to it the conceptual powers that Schelling lacked.

Thus my own efforts were directed toward not forgetting the limit that is implied in every hermeneutical experience of meaning. When I wrote the sentence "Being which can be understood is language," it was implied thereby that that which is can never be completely understood. This is implied insofar as everything that goes under the name of language always refers beyond that which achieves the status of a proposition. That which is to be understood is that which comes into language, but of course it is always that which is taken as something, taken as true [wahr-genommen]. This is the hermeneutical dimension in which Being 'manifests itself'. In this sense I retained the expression the "hermeneutics of facticity," and expression that signifies a transformation of the meaning of hermeneutics. Of course, in my attempt to describe the problems I followed the lead of the experience of meaning that occurs in language in order to point to the limits that are posited for it. The Being-toward-the text from which I took my orientation is certainly no match for the radicality of the limit experience found in Being-toward-death, and just as little does the incompletable question of the meaning of art or the meaning of history as that which happens to us signify a phenomenon that is as original as the question put to human *Dasein* of its own finitude. I can, therefore, understand why the later Heidegger (and Derrida would presumably agree with him on this point) was of the opinion that I never really abandoned the sphere of phenomenological immanence to which Husserl consistently held fast and which formed the basis of my early training in neo-Kantianism. I can also understand why one could believe that it is possible to recognize methodological 'immanence' in the holding fast to the hermeneutical circle; in fact, it seems to me that the desire to break out of the circle cannot be fulfilled, indeed such a demand is truly absurd. For this immanence is after all nothing other than what it was for Schleiermacher and his successor Dilthey, that is, a description of what understanding is. In view of the scope of understanding, the circularity that moves between the one who understands and that which he understands can lay claim to genuine universality, and it is precisely on this point that I believe that I have followed Heidegger's critique of the phenomenological concept of immanence, a critique that is addressed against Husserl's notion of an ultimate transcendental justification. The dialogical character of language, which I tried to work out, leaves behind the starting point in the subjectivity of the subject, even that of the meaning-directed intentions of the speaker. What we find happening in speaking is not a mere reification of intended meaning, but an endeavor that continually modifies itself, or better: a continually recurring temptation to engage oneself in something or to become involved with someone. But that means to expose oneself and to risk oneself. Genuinely speaking one's mind has little to do with a mere explication and assertion of our prejudices; rather, it risks our prejudices—it exposes oneself to one's own doubt as well as to the rejoinder of the other. Who has not had the experience—especially before the other whom we want to persuade—of how the reasons that one had for one's own view, and even the reasons that speak against one's own view rush into words. The mere presence of the other before whom we stand helps us to break up our own bias and narrowness even before he opens his mouth to make a reply. What becomes a dialogical experience for us here is not restricted to the sphere of arguments and counterarguments the exchange and unification of which may be the end meaning of every confrontation. Rather, as the experiences that have been described indicate, there is something else in this experience, namely, a potentiality of otherness [*Andersseins*] that lies beyond every coming to agreement about what is common. This is the limit that Hegel did not exceed. To be sure, he did recognize the speculative principle that holds sway in 'Logos', and he even introduced proofs of the identity of this principle in dramatically concrete ways: he unfolded the structure of self-consciousness and of 'self-knowledge in the Being of the other' as the dialectic of recognition and brought this to the point of the struggle of life and death. In a similar fashion, Nietzsche's penetrating psychological insights brought into view the 'Will to Power' as the substrate even in all devotion and self-sacrifice: "There is the will to power even in the slave." However, for me, Heidegger remains definitive when he finds the Logo-centricism of Greek ontology in the self-centeredness of this tension between self-abandonment and self-insistence to be continued in the sphere of arguments and counter-arguments, and in the factual confrontation wherein it is embedded.

A limit of the Greek modes can be detected here, one that was critically advanced by the Old Testament, Saint Paul, Luther, and their modern reinterpreters. In the discovery of the celebrated Socratic dialogue as the basic form of thought this dimension of dialogue still does not come into conceptual consciousness. This fits in quite well with the fact that a writer with the poetic imagination and linguistic powers of Plato knew to portray the charismatic figure of a Socrates so that the erotic tension that vibrates about the person is really brought into view. But because Plato's presentation of Socrates shows that when leading the conversation Socrates always insisted upon demanding an account from the other and upon leading others back to themselves by convicting them of their pretended wisdom, it is presupposed that the Logos is common to all and does not belong to Socrates' alone. Yet, as we already indicated, the true depth of the dialogical principle first enters philosophical consciousness in the twilight of metaphysics, in the epoch of German romanticism, and then is rehabilitated in our century in opposition to the subjective bias that characterized idealism. This is the point from which I proceeded in asking two further questions. First, How do the communality of meaning [*Gemeinsamkeit des Sinnes*], which is built up in conversation, and the impenetrability of the otherness of the other mediate each other? Second, What, in the final analysis, is linguisticality? Is it a bridge or a barrier? Is it a bridge over which one communicates with the other and builds sameness over the flowing stream of otherness? Or is it a barrier that limits our self-abandonment and that cuts us off from the possiblity of ever completely expressing ourselves and communicating with others?

In the framework of this general formulation of the question, the concept of the text presents a special sort of challenge. That is something that unites and perhaps even divides us from our French colleagues. However that may be, this was my motivation in confronting the theme "Text and Interpretation" once again. How does the text stand in relation to language? What is communication [*Verständigung*] between speakers? And why is it that something like texts can be given to us in common? What does it mean that in this process of communication with one another something emerges that, like texts, is one and the same thing for us? How has the concept of the text been able to undergo such a universal extension? It is obvious to anyone who watches the philosophical tendencies of our century that more is at stake in this theme than reflections upon the methodology of the philological sciences. Text is more than a title for the subject matter of literary research. Interpretation is more than the technique of scientifically interpreting texts. In the twentieth century, both of these concepts have acquired a new importance in the role that they play in our view of knowledge and the world.

Of course, this shift is connected with the role that the phenomenon of language has come to occupy in our thought. But such a statement is tautological. That language has acquired a central position in philosophical thought is, on its part, related to the turn that philosophy took in the course of the last decades. That the ideal of scientific knowledge, which modern science follows, came out of the model of nature as mathematically ordered (a model that was first developed by Galileo in his mechanics) meant that the linguistic interpretation of the world, that is, the experience of the world that is linguistically sedimented in the lived-world, no longer formed the point of departure and the point of reference for the formulation of questions or the desire for knowledge; rather, it meant that the essence of science was constituted by that which could be accounted for, or analyzed by, rational laws. In this way natural language lost its unquestioned primacy, even if it did retain its own manner of seeing and speaking. A logical consequence of the implications of this modern mathematized natural science was that in modern logic and the theory of science the ideal of language was replaced by the ideal of unequivocal notation. Thus, it is due to the nexus of limit experiences, which restrict the claim to universality of the scientific access to the world, that meanwhile natural language as a universal has recaptured the center of philosophy.

Of course, this does not signify a mere return to the experiences of the lived world and their linguistic sedimentation, which we know as the dominant theme of Greek metaphysics, the logical analysis of which led to Aristotlean logic and to *grammatica speculativa*. Rather, it is no longer the logical achievement of language that is being considered, but language as language and as the schematization of our access to the world. In this way, the original perspectives displace one another. Within the German tradition, this led to a resumption of romantic ideas—of Schlegel, Humboldt, and others. Neither in the neo-Kantians nor in the first phenomenologists do we find the problem of language considered at all. Only in a second generation did the midworld [*Zwischenwelt*] of language become a theme, thus we find it in Ernst Cassirer and especially in Martin Heidegger, and in the interesting contributions of Hans Lipps. In the British tradition something similar is to be found in the developments that Wittgenstein made from his starting point in Russell. To be sure, the issue here is not really one of a philosophy of language that is constructed upon the basis of comparative linguistics, or of the ideal of constructing a language that takes its place in a universal theory of signs; rather, the issue is at the enigmatic connection between thinking and speaking.

Thus, on the one hand, we have the theory of signs and linguistics, which have led to new knowledge about the way in which linguistic systems function and are constructed; and, on the other hand, we have the theory of knowledge, which realized that it is language that mediates any access to the world. Both theories cooperate in reinforcing the point of departure of a philosophical justification of the scientific access to the world. The assumption in this point of departure is that the subject takes hold of empirical reality with methodological self-certainty by means of its rational mathematical construction, and that it then expresses this reality in propositional statements. In this way the subject fulfills its true epistemological task, and this fulfillment climaxes in the mathematical language with which natural science defines itself as universally valid. The midworld [*Zwischenwelt*] of language is left out of consideration here in principle. Insofar as it is once again coming into view as such, it demonstrates against mathematical language the primary mediatedness of all access to the world, and more than this, it demonstrates the inviolability of the linguistic schema of the world. The almost mythical status of self-consciousness, which was adopted in its apodictic self-certainty as the origin and justification of all validity, and the ideal of a final justification [*Letztbegrundung*] in general, over which a priorism and empiricism fight, loses its credibility in the face of the priority of the domain of language that we cannot undermine and in which all consciousness and all knowledge articulates itself. From Nietzsche we learned to doubt the grounding of truth in the self-certainty of self-consciousness. Through Freud we became acquainted with the astonishing scientific discoveries that resulted from taking these doubts seriously. And in Heidegger's fundamental critique of the concept of consciousness we have seen the conceptual prejudice that stems from Greek Logos-philosophy and that, in the modern turn, put the concept of the subject in the center. All of this contributed to the rediscovery of the priority of the 'linguisticality' of our experience of the world. Over against the illusion of self-consciousness as well as the naivity of a positive concept of facts, the midworld of language has proven itself to be the true dimension of that which is given.

From this one can understand the rise of the concept of interpretation. It is a word that originally arose out of the mediating relation, the function of the intermediary between speakers of different languages; that is, it originally concerned the translator and was then transferred to the deciphering of texts that are difficult to understand. In that moment when the midworld of language presented itself to philosophical consciousness in its predetermined meaning, it had to take a sort of pivotal position in philosophic interpretation. The career of the word began with Nietzsche and become something of a challenge to all positivism. Does this given exist from whose certain point of departure knowledge can search for the universal, the law, the rule, and so find its fulfillment? Is the given not in fact the result of an interpretation? It is interpretation that performs the never fully complete mediation between man and world, and to this extent the sole actual immediacy and givenness is that we understand something as something. The faith in *Protokollsätze* as the fundament of all knowledge did not last long even in the Vienna Circle. Even in the domain of the natural sciences the hermeneutical consequences of grounding of knowledge cannot be evaded, that is, that the so-called given is not separable from interpretation.

Only in the light of interpretation does something become a fact, and an observation show itself to be expressible. Heidegger's critique of the phenomenological concept of consciousness and—similarly in Scheler—of the concept of pure perception as dogmatic revealed itself to be even more radical. Thus the hermeneutical understanding-of-something-as-something was discovered even in the so-called perception itself. In the final analysis, however, this means that interpretation is not an additional or appended procedure of knowing but constitutes the original structure of 'Being-in-the-world'.

But does this mean that interpretation is an insertion [*Einlegen*] of meaning and not a discovery [*Finden*] of meaning? This is obviously the question, posed by Nietzsche, that decides the rank and extent of hermeneutics as well as the objections of its opponents. In any case, one need admit that the concept of text first comes to constitute a central concept in the structure of linguisticality from out of the concept of interpretation; indeed, the special mark of the concept of the text is that it shows itself only in connection with interpretation and, from the point of view of interpretation, as the authentic given that is to be understood. This is true even in the dialogical process of coming to an understanding insofar as one lets the disputed statements be repeated and thereby pursues the intention to a binding formulation, an event that culminates in reification of communication by way of a transcript. In a similar manner the interpreter of a text asks what is really in the text. This too can lead to a biased and prejudicial response to the extent that everyone who asks a question tries to find a direct confirmation of his own assumptions in the answer. But, in such an appeal to that which is in the text, the text itself still remains the first point of relation over and against the questionality, arbitrariness, or at least multiplicity of the possibilities of interpretation that are directed towards the text.

This is confirmed by the history of the word. The concept of 'text' has entered into modern speech from essentially two fields. On the one hand, as the text of a written work whose interpretation was carried out in sermons and church doctrine so that the text represents the basis of all exegesis, which in turn presupposes the truths of faith. The other natural use of the word 'text' we find in connection with music. Here it is the text for song, for the musical interpretation of words, and here too such a text is not so much a pregiven as it is a residue of the performance of the song. Both of these natural ways of using the word 'text' point back to the linguistic usage of the Roman jurists of late antiquity who, by the codification of the laws, tried to overcome the disputability of its interpretation and application. From here the word found a wider extention so that it covered all that which resists integration in experience and represents the return to the supposed given that would then provide a better orientation for understanding.

The metaphorical talk of the book of nature rests upon the same foundations. It is that book the text of which was written by the hand of God and that the researcher is called upon to decipher, namely to render readabale and comprehensible by way of his interpretation. Thus, we find the hermeneutical return to the text at work whenever we encounter resistance to our primordial assumption of the meaningfulness of the given. The intimacy with which text and interpretation are entangled is thoroughly apparent insofar as even the tradition of a text is not always reliable as a basis for an interpretation. Indeed, it is often interpretation that first leads to the critical restoration of the texts. There is therefore a methodological advantage to be gained in making this inner relation of interpretation and text clear. The methodological advantage, which results from this observation made about language, is that here 'text' must be understood as a hermeneutical concept. This implies that the text is not regarded from the perspective of grammar and linguistics, and as divorced from any content that it might have; that is, that it is not to be viewed as an end product the production of which is the object of an analysis whose intent is to explain the mechanism that allows language as such to function at all. From the hermeneutical standpoint—which is the standpoint of every reader—the text is a mere intermediate product [*Zwischenprodukt*], a phase in the event of understanding that, as such, certainly includes a definite abstraction, namely the isolation and reification of this very phase. But this abstraction moves in precisely the reverse direction from the one upon which linguists rely. The linguist does not want to enter into the discussion of the topic which is spoken of in the text; rather, he wants to shed light upon the functioning of language as such, whatever the text may say. He does not make that which is communicated in the text his theme, but instead asks how it is possible to communicate anything at all by whatever means of punctuation and symbolization that occur.

For the hermeneutical approach, on the other hand, comprehending what is said is the sole concern. For this, the functioning of language is mere precondition. Thus, a first precondition is that an expression be acoustically intelligible, or that a printed text be decipherable, so that the comprehension of what is spoken, or written, is at least possible. The text must be readable.

Once again the use of words offers us an important clue. In a rather pretentious sense, we speak of the readability of a text when we want to express a minimum qualification for the estimation of a text or in the judgment of a translation. Naturally, this is a figurative way of speaking. But, as is often the case with such speech, it makes things thoroughly clear: the negative correspondence here is unreadability, and that always means that as a written expression the text did not fulfill its task of being understood without any difficulties. We find further confirmation here that we always already look ahead to an understanding of that which is said in the text. It is only from this point that we grant and qualify a text as readable.

From philological work this is well known as the task of restoring a readable text. However, it is clear that this task always only appears in such a way that a point of departure is made from some sort of understanding of the text. Only where the text is already deciphered, and the deciphered does not allow itself to be unhesitatingly transformed into understandability, are questions raised about what is really in the text and whether or not the traditional reading, that is, the commonly accepted reading, was correct. The treatment of the text by the philologist who produces a readable text corresponds completely to that which happens in direct, yet not only acoustical, auditory transmission. We say therefore that one has heard when one can understand. The uncertainty in the acoustical transmission of an oral message corresponds to the uncertainty of a reading [Lesart]. In both cases a feedback [Rückkoppelung] comes into play. Preunderstanding, anticipation of meaning, and thereby a great many circumstances that do not appear in the text as such, play their role in reading of the text [Auffassung des Textes]. This becomes completely clear when it is a matter of translation from foreign languages. Here the mastery of foreign language is a mere precondition. If the 'text' can be spoken of at all in such cases, then it is because it not only has to be understood but also to be conveyed into another language. In this manner it becomes a 'text', for that which is said is not simply understood, rather it becomes an object—the point is to reproduce that which was intended against the multiplicity of possible intentions. There is still another indirect hermeneutical relation here: every translation, even the so-called literal reproduction, is a sort of interpretation.

In sum, that which the linguist makes his theme in refraining from trying to understand the content of the text represents a mere limit case for understanding itself. In opposition to this view of the linguist, that which makes understanding possible is precisely the forgetfulness of language as that in which the discourse or the text is formally encased. Only where the language is disrupted, that is, where understanding will not succeed, are questions asked about the wording of the text, and only then can the reconstruction of the text become a task. In everyday speech we differentiate between the wording of the text and the text itself, but it is not accidental that both of these designations can also always act as a substitute for the other. In Greek, too, language and writing go together in the conept of *"grammatike"*. Indeed the extension of the concept of the text is hermeneutically well grounded. In every case, whether spoken or written, the understanding of the text remains dependent upon communicative conditions that, as such, reach beyond the reified meaning content of what is said. One can almost say that if one needs to reach back to the wording of the text, that is, to the text as such, then this must always be motivated by the peculiarity of the situation of understanding. This can be seen in the current use of the word 'text' just as clearly as it can be demonstrated in the history of the word 'text'. Doubtless, there is a sort of vanishing point [*Schwundstufe*] of the text that we could hardly ever call a text, such as one's own notes that provided a support for one's recollections. Here the question of the text is posed only when memory fails and the notes appear alien and incomprehensible, and it is necessary to refer back to the signs and writing; that is, it is necessry to refer back to the notes as text. Generally, however, notes are not a text because they appear as the mere trace of memory, the return of which was intended by the entry.

But there is another extreme case of understanding that, in general, does not provoke a discussion of the text. Here I am referring to something like scientific communication, which presupposes definite conditions of understanding from the outset. The reason for this is to be found on the manner of its address. It is directed toward the specialist. As was true in the case of notes, which are only for myself, so too is scientific communication, even when it is published, not for everyone. It only tries to be understandable for one who is well acquainted with the level and language of research. When this condition is fulfilled, the partner will not generally return to the text qua text. He does that only when the information expressed seems to be implausible and he must ask whether or not there is a misinterpretation somewhere. The situation is, of course, different from the historian of science for whom the same scientific documents really are texts precisely because they require interpretation to the extent that the interpreter is not the intended reader, so that the distance that exists between him and the original reader must be bridged. For the same reasons one generally does not speak of the text of a letter when one is its recipient. Then one enters smoothly into the written situation of conversation as it were, so long as no special disruption of understanding makes it necessary to refer back to the exact text. Thus, a written conversation demands basically the same fundamental condition that holds true for an oral exchange. Both partners must have the good will to try to understand one another. Thus, the question becomes How far is this situation and its implications given if no particular addressee or group is intended, but rather a nameless reader—or perhaps an outsider—wants to understand a text? The writing of a letter is another form of attempting a conversation and, as in the case of immediate linguistic contact or in all smoothly functioning exchanges, only a disruption in communication provides a motive for reaching back to the text as the 'given'. In any event, like one who is in a conversation, the writer tries to impart what he means, and that includes the pre-view of the other with whom he shares presuppositions and upon whose understanding he relies. The other takes that what is said as it is intended, that is, he understands because he fills out and concretizes what is said and because he does not take what is said in its abstract literal meaning. That is also the reason why one cannot say certain things in letters as one can in the immediacy of conversation, even when one sends them to a partner with whom one is very close. There is too much that is omitted in a letter that, in the immediacy of conversation, carries the proper understanding; and furthermore, in conversation one always has the opportunity to clarify or defend what was meant on the basis of some response. That is recognized especially in Socratic dialogue and the Platonic critique of writing. *Logoi*, which present themselves absolved from the situation of communication [*Verständigungssituation*] (and this is collectively true of written words), risks misuse and misunderstanding because they dispense with the obvious corrections of living conversation.

Here we find a consequence suggested that is essential to hermeneutical theory. If every printed text is cut off from the communicative situation, then this implies something for the intention of writing itself. Because as a writer one knows all of the problems of putting words in print, one is always steered by the pre-view of the recipient with whom one wants to reach an equivalent understanding. While in living conversation one tries to reach understanding through the give-and-take of discussion, which means that one searches for those words (and accompanies them with intonation and gesture) that one expects will get through to the other, in writing the openness that is implied in seeking the words cannot be communicated because it is printed. Therefore a virtual horizon of interpretation and understanding must be opened in writing the text itself, one that the reader must fill out. Writing is more than a repetition of the spoken in print. To be sure, everything that is fixed in writing refers back to what was originally said, but it must equally look forward, for all that is said is always already directed toward understanding and includes the other in itself.

Thus we speak of the text of a transcript, because, from the start, it is intended as a document, and that means that what is fixed in it is to be referred to. Precisely for this reason, a transcript requires the special mark and signature of the partner. The same is true of the closing of contracts in business and politics.

With this we come to a comprehensive concept that lies at the basis of all constitution of texts and simultaneously makes clear the embeddedness of the text in the hermeneutical context: every return to the text (whether it concerns a printed text or merely the repetition of what is expressed in conversation) refers to that which was originally announced or pronounced and that should be maintained to be a meaningful identity. What prescribes to all reifications in writing their task is precisely that this 'information' should be understood. The printed text should fix the original information [*Kundgabe*] in such a way that its sense is unequivocally understandable. Here the task of the writer corresponds to that of the reader, addressee, interpreter, that is, to achieve such an understanding and to let the printed text speak once again. To this extent, reading and understanding mean that the information is led back to its original authenticity. The task of interpretation always poses itself when the meaning content of the printed work is disputable and it is a matter of attaining the correct understanding of the 'information.' However, this 'information' is not what the speaker or writer originally said, but what he wanted to say indeed even more: what he would have wanted to say to me if I had been his original interlocutor. It is something of a command for interpretation that the text must be followed 'according to its meaningful sense' [Sinnsgemäss] (and not literally). Accordingly we must say that a text is not a given object, but a phase in the execution of the communicative event.

This general state of affairs is particularly well illustrated by judicial codification and correspondingly in judicial hermeneutics. Judicial hermeneutics functions as a sort of model with good reason: here the transference into written form and the continual reference to the text are in special proximity. From the outset that which is established as law serves to settle or avoid disputes. To this extent, the parties of the dispute who seek justice, as well as the findings of justice, the court, are always motivated to return to the text. The formulation of laws, of legal contracts or legal decisions, is thus especially exacting, and the fact that it is put into print makes it all the more so. Here a verdict or an agreement is to be formulated so that its judicial sense emerges from the text univocally and so that misuse or distortion is avoided. 'Documentation' demands that an authentic interpretation must succeed, even if the authors themselves, the legislator or a party to the contract, are not available. This implies that from the outset the written formulation must take into account the interpretive free space that arises for the 'reader' of the text who has to employ this space. Here—whether by proclamation or codification—it is always a question of avoiding strife, excluding misunderstandings and misuse, and making univocal understanding possible. In opposition to the mere proclamation of law or the actual closing of a contract, putting the law or contract into print is only an effort to secure an additional guarantee. This implies, however, that here too there remains a free space of meaningful concretization, a concretization that has to carry out the interpretation for the purpose of practical application. That it is like a text, whether it is codified or not, rests in the claim to validity of the legal statute. Therefore, law, like the statute, constantly requires interpretation for practical application, and conversely this means that interpretation has already entered into every practical application. There is, therefore, a creative legal function that is always accorded to legal decisions, to precedents, or to the prevailing administration of the law. To this extent, the judicial example shows with exemplary clarity just how much every preparation of a text is already related to interpretation, that is, to its correct, analogous application. It should be remembered that the hermeneutical problem between oral and written discourses is basically the same. One may think of the example of taking testimony from witnesses. In order to guarantee their neutrality witnesses are not supposed to be initiated into the larger context of the investigation and the rigors of the process of making a judgment. So they encounter the question put to them with the abstractness of the 'text', and the answer that they have to give is equally abstract. This means that it is like a written utterance. This comes out in the discontentedness with which a witness admits to the written transcript of his testimony. He certainly cannot dispute his language, but he does not want to let it stand in such isolation and would prefer to interpret it right away himself. To the witness the duty of the court stenographer in making the transcript is to render an account so that when the transcript is read back every possible justice is done to the intended meaning of the speaker. Conversely, this example of the testimony of a witness shows how written proceedings (namely the written component in proceedings) feed back into the way in which the conversation is handled. The witness, who is isolated as a result of his testimony, is, so to speak, already isolated as a consequence of the results of the investigation being put into print. A similar state of affairs obviously holds true in such cases where one has given a promise, an order, or a question in writing: this situation also contains an isolation of the original communicative situation and must express the original living sense in the style of something reified in writing. The reflexive relation to the original situation of communication remains apparent in all of these instances.

This can also be done by way of additional punctuation, which facilitates the proper understanding that was found meanwhile in the record. Thus, the question mark, for example, is such an indication of how the recorded sentence really must be articulated. The very appropriate Spanish custom of putting a question between two question marks makes this basic intent clear in a persuasive manner: one already knows at the beginning of the sentence how one has to articulate the relevant phrases. On the other hand, the dispensibility of such punctuation aids, which were not to be found at all in many ancient cultures, confirms how understanding is, nevertheless, possible solely through the printed text. The mere sequence of written symbols without punctuation represents communicative abstraction in the extreme.

Doubtless, there are many forms of communicative linguistic comportment that can not be subjugated to this finality; for instance, texts (inasmuch as they can obviously be regarded as such) that have been divorced from their addressee—in order to be examined as a literary presentation—but that in the communicative event itself resist being put into a text. Instances of such discourse are jokes, or the empty redundance of the speaker, or the camouflaging of unconscious tendencies that takes place in the effort to recount a dream, or communication that is distorted ideologically. In these cases the interpreter has no original hermeneutic function whatsoever toward the text: he transforms the utterance into an 'object' that it does not want to be. This results in the celebrated 'hermeneutics of suspicion'.

On the other hand, the interpreter who tries to follow the 'intentionality' of the discourse has a function that incorporates his mediating discourse [Zwischenrede] in the communicative event. His assistance in the process of understanding does not restrict itself to the purely linguistic level but goes beyond this to a mediation of content that attempts to balance the rights and limits of the parties with one another. The 'intervening speaker' becomes the 'mediator'. It seems to me that an analogous relation exists between the text and the reader. When the interpreter overcomes the foreign element in a text his own withdrawal does not imply a disappearance in a negative sense, but rather his entry into communication in such a way that the tension between the horizons of the text and the reader is dissolved. This is what I have called the fusion of horizons. Like the different standpoints, the separate horizons enter into one another. Therefore, the understanding of a text tends to interest the reader in what the text says, which is precisely the point at which the reader vanishes. The sense in which the literary text does not vanish, the sense in which its comprehension is a communicative event, and the role that falls to the interpreter in this case poses a new theme: the theme of the 'eminent text'. I have already made some contributions on this issue in English.

MUST WE SAY WHAT WE MEAN?
THE GRAMMATOLOGICAL
CRITIQUE OF HERMENEUTICS

DAVID COUZENS HOY

Are there texts that it is impossible to understand and interpret? Is there a minimal set of conditions that must be satisfied before an interpreter can claim to have understood a text? Those familiar with the problems of interpreting the writings of antiquity will know that these are old questions, perhaps as old as the writing themselves. The Anaximander fragment, for instance, is a notorious example of the difficulties of interpretation, and it has had widely variant readings, such as Nietzsche's, or Heidegger's (who generated his reading by criticizing Nietzsche's blindness to the proximity of Nietzsche's own metaphysics to Anaximander's). The Anaximander fragment is thus now part of an intricate web of readings, or of what has recently been called intertextuality. Presumably we are so enmeshed in this web that is impossible to read the text independently of its intertextual toils. Our entrapment in this famous hermeneutic circle is so complete that we should perhaps not even desire to escape.

Recently, however, the question of the limits of interpretation has been raised in a provocative way by the French poststructuralist Jacques Derrida. Both *Of Grammatology* (Baltimore, 1976) and *Spurs: Nietzsche's Styles* (Venice, 1976) represent a thoroughgoing challenge to hermeneutical philosophy. In *Spurs* Derrida makes his point with a curious example—one that is closely related to Heidegger's reinterpretation of both Anaximander and Nietzsche through a rereading of the Anaximander passage. Derrida's example is a piece of scrap paper from Nietzsche's *Nachlass* on which is written, in quotation marks, "I have forgotten my umbrella." Derrida suggests, probably correctly, that no amount of traditional philological interpretation will enable us to decide the meaning of this "text." It thereby becomes for him a paradigm case, one that can be elaborated infinitely through his own method of deconstruction even though the text itself is beyond the limits of "interpretation," traditionally understood. This particular text is a paradigm precisely because it has, in Derrida's words, "no decidable meaning."

This undecidability is both the bane of hermeneutical philosophy and the hallmark of grammatological philosophy. Grammatology is thus conceived as the antidote to the traditional metaphysical assumptions about the nature of language, meaning, and truth. These assumptions are not simply matters about which only philosophers should worry because they bias the practical procedures of all the interpretive disciplines.

Whether the grammatological attack on hermeneutics really has such a sweeping critical scope as Derrida implies must, however, be questioned. Hermeneutical philosophy itself has a history, and criticism of older versions do not necessarily apply to newer ones. To avoid misunderstanding, then, a brief explanation of "hermeneutics" as it is currently conceived is in order.

HERMENEUTICS AND GRAMMATOLOGY

Hermeneutics is essentially the philosophical concern with the theory of understanding and interpretation. For philosophers the primary interest in hermeneutics depends on whether it can generate a successful critique of traditional epistemology. Since Kant epistemology has been conceived as a foundationalist enterprise— one that attempts to separate knowledge from other forms of belief, with the intention of ascertaining what is objectively certain. Hermeneutics, in contrast, rejects the idea that the primary task of philosophy is to supply foundations and guarantee certainty. It sees knowledge as pragmatically relative to contexts of understanding. The paradigm of the phenomenon of understanding is the interpretation of texts, and hermeneutical theory maintains that although there is no physicalistic "fact of the matter" to be properly or improperly *represented* by interpretations, nevertheless, there *are* determinate constraints on what gets taken as proper or improper interpretation.

Perhaps only because the theory of knowledge (epistemology) and the theory of understanding (hermeneutics) have traditionally been preoccupied with different paradigms, they have evolved into competing views about what philosophical theories must do. An extremely condensed account of the contrast between them can be given by characterizing them in terms of four presuppositions on which they differ. The traditional notion of knowledge presupposes (1) a privileged standpoint as the guarantee of certainty; (2) perception as the paradigm case; (3) the atemporal truth of instances of knowledge claims; and (4) the impotence of reflection to disrupt self-evident tenets. In contrast, hermeneutics maintains that understanding is always interpretive, and thus, (1) that there is no uniquely privileged standpoint for understanding; (2) that reading rather than seeing is the paradigm case for the phenomenon of understanding; (3) that understanding changes, and thus interpretations require continual reexamination; and (4) that any interpretive understanding is laden with self-understanding, however implicit, so that changes in the latter eventuate in changes in the former.

To the confirmed epistemologist hermeneutical philosophy will sound like yet another version of relativism or idealism. To this the hermeneutical theorist should reply not by defending relativism against objectivism, intertextuality against historical realism, coherence against correspondence, but rather by pointing out that even seeing these as the only *philosophical* alternatives involves a peculiarly Kantian or epistemological "theory of theories"—one that unwarrantedly believes that various fields of inquiry are in a state of crisis if *philosophy* has not proved that mind can mirror nature, or that the reader can be sure of capturing a particular poem and not some other poem in the one right interpretation. In fact, "realism" and "nominalism" are more relevant to a debate *within* hermeneutics than they are as philosophical labels to be attached to either hermeneutics or epistemology when these are viewed from *outside* each other. A heavy infusion of Peirce into recent hermeneutical literature seems to have reintroduced that traditional philosophical quandary into debates about the propriety of interpretations and the limits on readings. Derrida's apparent nominalism can be viewed as as attempt to take post-Heideggerian philosophy in a different direction from that taken by hermeneutic philosophers like Hans-Georg Gadamer. Both camps are allied in their opposition to traditional epistemology, but more interesting are their radical internal differences.

Both grammatology and hermeneutics are theories of understanding as reading, and they emphasize reception and intertextuality (not psychological response). The semiotic notion of intertextuality involves, however, a different theory of language from that found in Gadamer's notion of linguisticality. Whereas Gadamer thinks of texts as being engaged in dialogues with one another—thus relying on the Platonic notion of dialogue as a concern with the truth of the matter—the poststructuralists' notion of discourse prescinds from terms like "meaning," "reference," "significance," and "intention." The semiotic notions of text and intertext represent a fundamental challenge to the traditional aesthetic conceptions of the nature of the work of art, conceptions that the semioticians think are still retained by contemporary hermeneutic theorists who follow Heidegger. Hermeneutics, like Heidegger, is accused of presupposing, contrary to its intentions, a philosophy of presence, that is, an implicit ontological (or "onto-theo-logical") commitment of the sort that Heidegger wanted to overcome. This commitment manifests itself in the fact that when hermeneutics insists that the tradition (*Wirkungsgeschichte*) inevitably influences the understanding and interpretation of artworks, it does not question sufficiently the traditional metaphysical assumptions built into the very concepts of artwork and tradition.

The grammatologist replaces the notion of the *work* of art, "l'oeuvre," or "the book," with the more neutral notion of the *text*, and it substitutes the concept of intertextuality for that of tradition. "Text" and "intertext" are thus technical terms in the vocabulary of the poststructuralist research program, and their usefulness can be appreciated, it would seem, only after giving up the traditional metaphysical vocabularly still retained by hermeneutics.

According to the grammatological critique of hermeneutics, the concept of the *work* of art entails that any written work that is properly literary must be characterized by five features: (1) unity, (2) autonomy, (3) intentionality, (4) self-referentiality, and (5) a self-conscious literariness. This last feature summarizes the previous four in that it depends on a sharp distinction between the literary and the literal, between artistic and ordinary language. This distinction is itself possible only if the interpretation of a work can show it to have an internal unity and an autonomous uniqueness. This conception of the artwork gives interpretation its task of investigating both the intrinsic structure of the work and the extrinsic sources and setting of the work's production. Precisely because what is under investigation is a work, and a work is assumed to be a production by somebody, the intentionality that pervades the work can be a guide to the interpretation. But because the work is a work of *art*, the interpretation need not be limited by the reference of the work to the world in which it is produced if the work itself can be said to produce its own world.

Given these features, the grammatologist's technical term "text" does not simply substitute for the hermeneutical term "work" because the grammatologist's or semiotician's research program is not committed to these traditional assumptions. Instead of "interpretation" the grammatologist's investigation is characterized as "deconstruction" or "dissemination." It does not search for the hidden intentional unity of the text, but it decodes the lack of such unity by searching out the tensions, oppositions, and even the incoherence that propagates further writing. Literary language is no longer privileged over ordinary language because both are characterized by the same possibilities. Thus, self-referentiality is not a special feature of literary language alone, and there is also nothing like a "hidden meaning" that the hermeneutic interpretation must uncover. The text is not autonomous but is the interplay of an infinity of other texts.

For the grammatologist, who starts from the linguistic, Saussurean notion of the "arbitrariness of the sign," the text is only a chain or a fabric of signs. Derrida's "fabric of signs" metaphor works like the more familiar "web of beliefs" metaphor in that there is no independent access to the fact of the matter, to the thing represented, to the transcendental signified, to Being, or to whatever other transcendental ineffable one wants to substitute. Signs refer only to other signs, and Derrida thus cites Peirce's claim that "we think only in signs." This arbitrariness of the sign leads both Saussure and Derrida to stress what Derrida calls the "immotivation and discontinuity" of the structure of the sign.[1] These features are carried over into the conception of the text, which is not a "work"—that is, a unity generated by a producer's intention. The text, like all language, is discontinuous within itself. It is itself enmeshed in a fabric of texts, in a system of systems, which is now called intertextuality.

Working in a research program in which tradition is a central concept requires the interpreter to be aware of the influences on the genesis of the work, and perhaps of the work's own influence on other works (that is, the history of its reception). Understanding a work can thus be helped by understanding both its sources and its own importance as a source. In the alternative research program "intertextuality" replaces such traditional "source study," although it is not to be taken as being identical in practice to source study and is not merely a more fashionable way of describing the tradition. For the grammatologist "tradition" is linked conceptually with a theory of history and historical development containing vestiges of teleological, holistic metaphysics.

As the totality of works, tradition presupposes the notions of (1) continuity, (2) commensurability, (3) charity, (4) commonality, and (5) progress (toward consensus). That none of these associations accompany the concept of intertextuality can be seen by taking each feature in turn.

Continuity

Although historians and philologists recognize historical changes resulting in differences over time, they ordinarily assume that history is continuous. "Tradition" may not be as sweeping a term as "history" because history includes many traditions, but it is nevertheless true that tradition is of a piece. Recently, however, historians have become more skeptical of such holistic assumptions, and many have come to suspect that the unity linking historical events into a causal chain is really more a function of the historian's narrative than of the observable, empirical events. This skepticism is not new, of course, since it goes back to the historian David Hume, but poststructuralist theorists like Michel Foucault have added new rhetorical twists. Against the usual assumption by historians of ideas that history is continuous, Foucault spells out in *The Archaeology of Knowledge* (New York, 1976) a methodology suggesting the thesis that history is discontinuous.

Hermeneutic theorists like Gadamer argue that the interpreter's own tradition necessarily conditions his or her understanding of the past. The hermeneutic theorist could not insist on the inevitability of such conditioning, and of the hermeneutic circle, unless the process leading from past to present were continuous. Because the poststructuralist methods of historiography are designed to avoid the very idea of continuous development, there would appear to be a basic disagreement between hermeneutics and poststructuralism.

Although there may in fact be differences between those who use the methods of the annalists and those who do not, these differences do not in fact result from a real philosophical issue of the sort Foucault raises. His point is best taken as saying that "continuity" and "discontinuity" are not features of the empirical events but rather as regulative ideas for the historiographical writing itself. Some historians will think, of course, that if another historian such as Foucault identifies a discontinuity, a break or rupture, in the historical process being described, then the research has not been completed. Rather, the research has just begun, according to the historian of continuity, because now one must explain that discontinuity, showing how it came about and how it could have been produced out of what preceded it.

This is, however, only a practical question and not a theoretical one. There is always more to be explained, and all historians must limit the scope of their accounts (whether temporally in terms of dates or methodologically in terms of what is to be described). Foucault overstates his case against the traditional historian by implying that the claims that history is continuous and that it is not continuous are contradictories. Presumably no one could say that history as a whole (or even a subdivision of history, like *the* history of thought) is continuous, and this observation should make it clear that the predicates "is continuous" and "is discontinuous" apply not so much to the events themselves as to the historian's "story." Because there is no standpoint from which these predicates could be applied to all of history, they should be taken as reflections on the success or the limits of particular narratives. "Some histories are continuous" and "some histories are discontinuous" would then not be misunderstood as logical contradictories. They are at best logical subcontraries, which means that although both cannot be false, *both* may very well be true.[2]

Commensurability

This long discussion of the notion of continuous development should help to deflate some of the rhetoric involved in worries about terms like "discontinuity," "rupture," or "paradigm shift," and to elucidate the other components of the traditional notion of tradition. Tied to the assumption that a tradition is essentially continuous is the belief that it consists of entities that can be circumscribed in a commensurate discourse, no matter how diverse these entitites are from one another. One may think, for instance, that the very idea of a history of art or of literature is paradoxical because a work of art or literature is supposed to be a unique, autonomous whole and therefore to have no internal links with preceding or subsequent works or with external reality.[3] Individual works, or perhaps individual groupings of works (whether by author or by period), are thus incommensurate with one another.

Such hermeneutical incommensurability would indeed seem to make adequate understanding an impossible ideal. As a further consequence, would interpretation also become "undecidable"? To make this grammatological inference would be to conflate "adequate understanding" with "assimilation." The hermeneutic theorist can block this move by insisting that we can understand another culture or cultural artifact adequately even if we do not share that culture's beliefs. Much the same point has been made about understanding primitive societies or other religions. Similarly, we can understand and be moved by literary work against the background of our understanding of other ones that may be temporally and generically quite different. Although the strategies for construing a history of literature or of art may be complex and debatable, the discontinuity of history and the concomitant incommensurabilty of various discourses do not constitute a *practical* obstacle to our understanding of other times and discourses.

Charity

Derrida's and Foucault's arguments sometimes indicate, however, a way in which the incommensurability of discourses may constitute a *theoretical* obstacle for the hermeneutical theory of understanding. Their position is often expressed in terms of a theory of language that has as a consequence the rejection of what philosophers call the principle of charity. This principle is a constraint on translation such that if a purported translation did not preserve the maximal number of truths, or the least number of falsehoods, in English (that is, as determined from *our* point of view), then it would not be a proper translation. It would have to be discounted a priori as an implausible attempt that simply failed to understand the other language.

However essential this principle may be as a constraint on translation, it would not be a desirable regulative principle in a theory of understanding and interpretation. As such, charity would be like the old hermeneutical view that we could not be said to have understood a work of the past (the Bible, for example) until we have interpreted everything that seemed strange about it into familiar terms. Derrida often criticizes hermeneutics in general for wanting to make the strange familiar, and his program of deconstruction is designed, it would seem, to preserve the strangeness of the text and even to make familiar texts become strange. Yet a modern hermeneutics could readily accept this method of reading as a strategy that is useful in preventing us from reading our own expectations into everything. This strategy would make us more aware of our expectations so that we do not become overly enclosed in the circle of our own subjective understanding. Deconstruction may thus be a necessary moment of the hermeneutic circle, which is a ceaseless, open-ended activity. The deconstructive movement away from what is familiar should not, however, obscure the equally necessary movement back toward a hermeneutic self-recognition in the text. There must be *some* shared belief if there is to be any understanding at all. The hermeneutic theorist can say this and still balk at accepting the principle of charity as a necessary condition of understanding. Because charity is the assumption that *most* of the beliefs must be shared. It is a much stronger claim than is required by a plausible theory of understanding.[4]

Commonality

When charity is taken as a psychological rather than a semantic principle, it raises a difficulty that is familiar from the history of hermeneutics. Charity presupposes the essential commonality between the author and the reader such that whether the hermeneutical theory emphasizes genesis or response, it is describing psychological processes in individual minds. Although the hermeneutic philosophies of Schleiermacher and Dilthey go beyond the Enlightenment assumption that people are everywhere and always the same, their theories rely on notions like empathy to bridge the hermeneutical gap between the author and the interpreter.

This psychologism is attacked by critics of hermeneutics like Derrida and Foucault, who prefer to think of the object of their investigations as "discourses" and "texts" rather than "minds." This is not, however, a fundamental criticism of hermeneutic theory as such, but only of an outdated version of it. In varying degrees, contemporary theorists like Gadamer and Habermas have taken philosophical criticisms of psychologism into account and formulated their hermeneutical theories in such a way that there is no real conflict with the poststructuralists' linguistic methods.

Progress and Consensus

More to the point than the charge of psychologism is the criticism of hermeneutics for being encumbered with the vestiges of an undesirable teleology. Thinking of history as a developmental process in which all epochs are linked by common characteristics in such a way that improvement is possible leads naturally to a belief in progress. This notion of progress can be a weak one, as in Habermas's Peircean theory of the ideal speech situation. The original intuitions of hermeneutics were indeed that if everybody were able to think and discuss an issue in an unconstrained way, such discussion would inevitably result in agreement and thus in convergence on the truth, the *consensus omnium*, the universally commensurating discourse about all possible discourses.

This view of Habermas's, however, has been contested by other hermeneutic theorists, including Gadamer, who posits instead an indefinitely open-ended development. Progress thereby becomes a more spectific notion. Whether progress has been made could not be decided in global terms, but only in regard to specific social institutions, whose existence in and of themselves is not a priori necessary. Because there would be no transhistorical standpoint from which history or civilization could be said to have progressed, this piecemeal but plausible outlook would not be guilty of presupposing an implicitly teleological metaphysics like that found in most developmental theories of history.[5]

INTERTEXTUALITY AND INTENTIONALITY

Whether there is a real opposition between hermeneutics and grammatology, and whether the standard conceptions of the literary work and the literary tradition are indeed undermined by the interpretive undecidability implied by the concepts of text and intertextuality has not been sufficiently argued by the poststructuralists. Much depends on how such notions as intertextuality are taken. Is there, for instance, a real theoretical and practical difference between a methodology relying on the notion of intentionality and one relying on intertextuality? If there is, then the grammatological critique of hermeneutics may entail a genuine alternative. If there is not, then whether particular grammatological criticisms of traditional ways of doing research in the humanities are valid is still an important matter, but one that is better decided in terms of particular disciplines and interpretations.

Focusing attention specifically on the field of literary criticism, then, it should be emphasized that unlike the term "undecidability," which is part of Derrida's metaphilosophical polemics, the term "intertextuality" names a specific concept in a research program of practical criticism. It is used particularly by semiotic theorists like Julia Kristeva, Roland Barthes, and Michael Riffaterre. Kristeva defines the concept succinctly in *Semiotike*: "Le texte poétique est produit dans le mouvement complexe d'une affirmation et d'une négation simultanées d'un autre texte."[6] She also claims that it is a "fundamental law" that "les textes poétiques de la modernité . . . se font en absorbant et en détruisant en même temps les autres texts de l'espace intertextuel." [7] Her view is thus comparable to Harold Bloom's theory of poetic influence as a patricidal series of misreadings. Kristeva's and Bloom's approaches are of a different order in practice, however, and Jonathan Culler has argued convincingly that Bloom's conception of intertextuality is too general and "Romantic," lacking the practical specificity of the semiotic notion.[8] Intertextuality has even been applied outside of literature, and the historians Hayden White and Michel Foucault clearly rely on related strategies.

Derrida's relation to these practical pursuits is rather complex. As a historian of philosophy he could be said to be putting the notion of intertextuality to use in that specific area. As a philosopher in his own right he is mapping out the grammatological theory without which the notion of intertextuality would lose its force. In fact, there is a disturbing tendency for both literary critics and historians to say that since *philosophy* has now *proved* that nothing exists but texts, or that we think only in signs, or that "die Sprache spricht," this now makes the methodology of intertextuality applicable to all scientific inquiry, and even perhaps all there is to any science.

This reasoning would indeed be guilty of hasty ontologizing, and it would lead too quickly toward an unabashed nominalism. It goes against the grain of Derrida's own metaphilosophical view that philosophy cannot "prove" anything and certainly not anything ontological. There are thus two ways to take the philosophical import of the notion of intertextuality. The wrong way is to think Derrida's famous claim that "il n'y a pas de hors-texte"[9] is a new version of idealism (perhaps in the vein of Cassirer's or Whorf's *Sprachidealismus*). Grammatology would then be an ontological overdramatization of what literary critics call formalism. A better way to take intertextuality is as the basic concept of a research program that is only exercising an option to choose its vocabulary and to restrict itself to specific kinds of analysis. This program thus abandons any ontological claims because it is rather an attempt to deontologize its object of study by avoiding laden terms like "intention," "author," "meaning," "meaningfulness," "value," and "reality" as well as the distinction between metaphorical and literal, or serious and nonserious discourse.

A research program is certainly entitled to select its own vocabularly, but the next question is whether it will have practical results that are not parasitic on the alternative vocabulary. Citing Bakhtine, Kristeve in *Semiotike* notes that the importance of intertextuality is that it replaces intersubjectivity.[10] Because intertextual criticism does not want itself confused with traditional source study, it will go to any lengths to avoid the concept of intention. It even makes the poet's knowledge of other texts irrelevant. Harold Bloom goes so far as to say that the ephebe need not have read the precursor poem that his own poem "misreads."[11] Presumably Bloom is saying more than he really means, however, for he is probably imagining that the ephebe knows some of the precursor's poetry but may not happen to know a specific "central" poem—central to both the precursor and the ephebe precisely because its centrality may be perceivable only after the ephebe's own poems have caused a swerve in the history of poetry. The poem, although not known, could plausibly be said to have been inferable, and Bloom's claim is not as paradoxical as it sounds.

The irrelevance of what the poet knew or intended is also apparent among the French critics. Like Kristeva, Roland Barthes also dissolves the concept of subjectivity into that of the text: "Je n'est pas un sujet innocent, antérieur au texte. . . . Ce "moi" qui s'approche du texte est déjà lui-même une pluralité d'autres textes, de codes infinis, ou plus exactement: perdus (dont l'origine se perd)."[12] Barthes's claim makes clear that the intertext implied within a text need not be another literary text (contrary to Bloom). That it often is, however, is seen by Barthes himself in *The Pleasure of the Text*:

> I recognize that Proust's work, for myself at least, is *the* reference work, the general *mathesis*, the *mandala* of the entire literary cosmogony—as Mme de Sévigné's letters were for the narrator's grandmother, tales of chivalry for Don Quixote, etc; this does not mean that I am in any way a Proust "specialist": Proust is what comes to me, not what I summon up; not an "authority," simply a *circular memory*. Which is what the intertext is: the impossibility of living outside the infinite text— whether this text be Proust or the daily newspaper or the television screen: the book creates the meaning, the meaning creates life.[13]

These two passages from Barthes reveal how difficult it is to break completely with the concept of subjectivity. Whereas the first passage says the "I" is not anterior to the text but is already a plurality of other texts, this does not seem to be *all* that is true about the "I" in the second passage. Although it is impossible to live outside the infinite text, can the "I" be just the infinite text? If the "I" is an infinity of texts, then it lacks the identity necessary to being an "I." If the identity is provided by a primary intertext, as Proust's is for Barthes, then who or what does the reading, the expanding of the text's infinite relations?

The semiotic notion of the text as an infinity of connections with other texts, as a universe that is both microcosm and macrocosm, is troubling. Kristeva also says that "tout texte est d'emblée sous la juridiction des autres discours qui lui imposent un univers."[14] This metaphorical insistence on the network of texts as an infinite universe is obviously more theoretical than practical. It follows from Saussure's thesis of the arbitrariness of the sign, but it is applied rather differently at the level of practical criticism. As Culler aptly points out, "It is difficult to make the universe as such the object of attention."[15] He notices that Kristeva herself pays attention to which editions an author could have known when that would make an interpretive difference. The intertextual domain thus in practice becomes narrowed down to specific texts, and perhaps even to one text.

Exactly what principle governs this narrower selection of the relevant intertext is not clear from the theory itself. The advantage of the alternative research program making use of intention is that it can state precisely what its principle of selection is and how it will handle hard cases. For instance, in one of the better formulations of intentionalist interpretation, namely, Stanley Cavell's *Must We Mean What We Say?* the critic can decide when he or she is properly attributing an implied reference in the text (or film) and when that allusion is merely being read into the text arbitrarily. "It makes sense," Cavell argues, "to say Fellini intended (that is to say, Fellini can have intended) the reference to Philomel if he knew the story and now sees its relevance to his own, whether or not the story and its relevance occurred to him at the time."[16] Cavell thus maintains that although there can be inadvertent intentions such as this case illustrates, knowing is still a necessary (but not a sufficient) condition for intending.

Some principle such as this would also be required by the intertextual critics when they move from the infinite universe of intertextual reference down to the selection of specific texts and codes. If their choice of interpretant is not just arbitrary, there must be constraints on it. Without a specific principle stated in a nonintentionalist vocabulary the intertextual research program risks being in practice merely parasitic on the traditional philological program.

Whether one should want to be entirely free from criticism based on the vocabulary of intersubjectivity depends upon how restrictive that vocabulary actually is. Derrida himself has been interpreted as denying the role of intention altogether, but in fact his view about intention is more subtle, as is evident in his exchange with the American philosopher of language, John Searle.[17] In the course of criticizing both hermeneutics and speech act theory, which make comparable mistakes, Derrida says he does not wish to get rid of the concept of intention but only to give it a different place, a less privileged one.[18] Intention will no longer be constitutive of the meaning of the work. The lack of any sufficient condition for the reading of a written text will allow Derrida to replace "interpretation" with "deconstruction" or "dissemination," an infinite play of possibilities built into the play of the text. "Play" is itself a technical term for the absence of a transcendental signified—the goal of traditional interpretive searches for "the meaning" of the work.

To condense the debate between Searle and Derrida one can invert Cavell's titular question and ask: Must we say what we mean? On Searle's theory it turns out that in a certain sense we *must* say what we mean, because what a sentence says is a function of the speaker's or the author's intentions. For Searle sentences just are "fungible intentions," and "to the extent that the author says what he means the text is the expression of his intentions."[19] In contrast, Derrida's view seems to be that we *cannot* say what we mean, and often he purposefully does not say what he means or does so only ironically. He rejects the idea that the intention necessarily determines the meaning of the text on the grounds that the intention is in fact more problematically disjointed or divided within itself than intentionalist theorists realize. Derrida maintains that intention is never fully present to itself and is not transparent, even to the intender. The nonserious, the *oratio obliqua*, will thus never be excluded from even the most ordinary language, contrary to what Austin and Searle seem to think.

More interesting than the differences between Searle and Derrida are the differences between Derrida and Cavell. Whereas Searle and Derrida have nonequivalent concepts of intention, Derrida and Cavell appear to agree, especially since Cavell can allow for inadvertent intentions. Yet although Cavell emphasizes the importance of the appeal to intention, Derrida diminishes it. To understand why this is so, one must first understand that there is considerable agreement between Derrida and Cavell about the nature of philosophical theories. This agreement may also explain the obvious metaphilosophical disagreement between Derrida and Searle.

Cavell's question is: Must we mean what we say? His answer is: it depends. In the essay "A Matter of Meaning It," he says, contra Beardsley, that the appeal to the intention of an utterance is sometimes inappropriate as an explanation. The appeal to the intention is for Cavell much like the attempt to explain any remark or action in order to determine reponsibility. Intention is useful in figuring out "the point of the work," or "why it is as it is." But Cavell also thinks the attempt to explain the work by determining its intention forces one further *into* the work. So there is a significant difference between his intentionalism and the view Beardsley is attacking. To avoid confusion Cavell should perhaps have been willing to speak of the text's rather than the author's intentions. That he did not do so is explained by the fact that this view is not a different theory of intention so much as a different view of philosophy from Beardsley's. Seeing the critic making implicit or explicit intentional claims when faced with the question "Why this?" Cavell thinks the philosopher has two choices: either to repudiate this description of the activity of criticism "on the ground that they [the intentional claims] *cannot* be true (because of his philosophical theory—in this case of what poems are and what intentions are and what criticism is)," or to "accept them as data for his philosophical investigation, learning from them what it is his philosophizing must account for."[20] On the one hand, then, philosophers like Beardsely and Searle who think of philosophy as a prescriptive, foundationalist enterprise reject certain descriptions of literary criticism because their theories tell them that things cannot be that way. On the other hand, philosophers like Cavell and Derrida who think of philosophy as nonprescriptive, antifoundationalist writing look at what is being done, note how philosophy makes false problems out of its own ruminations, and develop their own view more as a critical undercutting of the philosophical theory that does not question itself than as an ideal guide for the practical discipline in question. In the latter theory intention is not a constitutive entity but a procedural strategy of reading. As such it can be emphasized or ignored to the extent that the reading requires.

Of course, Cavell and Derrida do have their differences, but probably only because the critics Derrida is reading now are quite different from those Cavell was reading in 1957 or even in 1965 (the dates of the two essays by Cavell under discussion). Derrida is not faced with critics who worry about the question "Why this?" whereas "Why?" is the paradigm question for the philosophical literature on the theory of action (such as Anscombe's 1957 work, *Intention*). To Cavell's claim that we need to appeal to intention to explain the *point* of the work, Derrida could replay his theme that there is no way the critic can "faire le point" ("mark the point," or better, "take bearings") because there is no punctual position, no unilinear text signed by a "single" (singly intentioned, or "single-minded") author. Even Cavell's procedural notion of intention as that which forces the reader to go further into the text may be met with skepticism. Go further into the text, says Geoffrey Harmann in his *Georgia Review* essay on Derrida's *Glas*, and you only encounter the essential unintelligibility of the literary work.[21] The metaphysics of presence is insidious, Derrida could say, and still contaminates Cavell's thought insofar as he believes intention to be equivalent to what the poem means and appeals to it as the basis for explaining the "unity of the work" and "trust in someone as an artist."[22]

Derrida's distrust of these traditional aesthetic categories leads him to make his own claims sound more controversial than they probably are. Something like *Sprachidealismus* may seem to be implied by such statements as "there is nothing outside of the text" and "the thing itself a sign." "Reality" itself becomes merely a textual entity, a construct in the text of philosophy, because there is no "natural attachment" to a real referent, no "flesh and bone" referents even for proper names. These claims are to be true not only of literary writing, as we would normally assume, but of all kinds of writing, not just the doubling commentary of the literary interpreter, but also the writing of "the philosopher, the chronicler, the theoretician in general, and at the limit everyone writing."[23]

Of course, nobody really thinks he or she is merely a fictional entity, so Derrida's point must be overstated. His claim that there is no signified outside the text, no real referents, is a rather dramatic way of saying there is no such thing as *the* signified, no transcendental signified entirely independent of the signifier-signified relation. Take Derrida's own suggested cases, the historian and the philosopher. Unlike the novelist they both seem to write with a commitment to the actual existence of real events or definite truths. They write so that their signifiers *will* disappear into the signified. In conversation one historian tried to defend the idea of intertextuality by denying that there were real events in the past. The fall of the Bastille and the shooting of John Kennedy were for him to be *only* textual constructs. When asked contentiously whether being shot himself would be only a textual event, the historian's amusing reply was to insist that the "event" could be said to have occurred only when people started talking about it. What, however, would the first person who said anything be talking about? And what would the wounded man himself have experienced?

Clearly the more adequate response is not to deny that there are real events but to insist that any event is only ever captured in a description, that is, in a context that is itself not an event but a discursive variable. Derrida himself in his reply to Searle insists that he does not deny the necessity of having some context or other, but only the idea that any given context is more necessary or privileged than any other. Derrida's point thus appears to be the quite plausible one that all we have access to in interpreting texts is the system of inferences formulatable from the text and others, or at least from other textlike constructs such as Barthes's television screen. The assertion that there are real events is trivial and uninformative if it is also true that events are only ever comprehended under a description. Derrida need not deny that there are real events, or that there is a "flesh and bone" genesis of the text, and indeed he does not.[24] When he says, for instance, that "what opens meaning and language is writing as the disappearance of natural presence"[25], he is not asserting the nonexistence of natural presence.[25] He is implying only that anything said after that is not a matter of fact but of interpretation. In the history of philosophy we are used to the idea of natural presence disappearing right at the beginning—as it does, for instance, with sense-certainty in Hegel's *Phenomenology of Spirit*.

Derrida's theory of reading is thus not so radical that it rejects the classical exigencies of traditional criticism. These still do obtain, and reading, "must be intrinsic and remain within the text." Given this admission, however, it is then quite legitimate for Derrida to insist that reading not restrict itself to repeating or doubling "the conscious, voluntary, intentional relationship that the writer institutes in his exchanges with the history to which he belongs."[26] Reading must open the text by supplementing it. This supplement is not a capricious addition by the reader, though, for it must already be contained in the text, which is never fully present to itself, even from the beginning.

Derrida's philosophy is not as complete a break with the history of philosophy as many would like to believe. On the contrary, he is best understood as the latest development of a tradition going back to Kant and Hegel, a tradition that includes contemporary hermeneutics as well. Of course, to see Derrida as part of a tradition is itself a hermeneutical move—one that may manifest a desire to control his texts by making what is strange in them appear quite familiar. To conclude this would be to underestimate the complexity of the hermeneutic process, however, because the act of finding a tradition for his work—or alternatively expressed, finding the particular intertextural matrix in which his texts are determinate intersections—is only the start of the uncertain task of interpreting them. This difficulty is compounded by a writer who does not wish "to say what he means" and does not think that "saying what one means" is even desirable as a regulative ideal. Such compounding, however, does not make interpretation impossible. There may well be texts impossible to interpret in practice, but there is no reason to think that anything readily identifiable as a text is uninterpretable in principle.

NOTES

1. Jacques Derrida, *Of Grammatology* (Baltimore, 1976), p. 326.

2. See Hans Michael Baumgartner, *Kontinuität und Geschichte: Zur Kritik und Metakritik der historischen Vernunft* (Frankfurt, 1972), pp. 301–12.

3. For further discussion of the paradox of literary history, see chap. 5 of the author's *The Critical Circle: Literature, History, and Philosophical Hermeneutics* (Berkeley, Los Angeles, and London, 1978).

4. The principle of charity could also be accused of repeating a concealed ideology, namely, that implicit in the idea of the social melting pot, where it is assumed, of course, that "they" will become like "us" rather than "we" like "them." Ian Hacking makes a similar point in *Why Does Language Matter to Philosophy?* (Cambridge, 1975), p. 149. For further discussion see D. C. Hoy, "Forgetting the Text: Derrida's Critique of Heidegger," *Boundary* 2 (Fall 1979); and "Hermeneutic Circularity, Indeterminacy, and Incommensurability," *New Literary History* No. 1 (Autumn 1978): 161–73.

5. For further discussion see D. C. Hoy, "Taking History Seriously: Foucault, Gadamer, Habermas," *Union Seminary Quarterly Review* 34, no. 2 (Winter 1979): 85–95.

6. Julia Kristeva, *Semiotiké* (Paris, 1969), p. 257.

7. Ibid.

8. Jonathan Culler. "Presupposition and Intertextuality," *MLN* 91 (1976): 1380–96. Hereafter cited as Culler, "PI". My thanks to both Jonathan Culler and Cynthia Chase for a helpful discussion of this paper.

9. Derrida, *Grammatology*, p. 158.

10. Kristeva, *Semiotiké*, p. 146.

11. Harold Bloom, *The Anxiety of Influence* (New York, 1973), p. 70.

12. Roland Barthes, *S/Z* (Paris, 1970), p. 16; cited by Culler, "Presupposition and Intertextuality," p. 1382.

13. Roland Barthes, *The Pleasure of the Text* (New York, 1975), p. 36.

14. Cited by Culler, "PI", p. 1384.

15. Ibid.

16. Stanley Cavell, *Must We Mean What We Say?* (New York, 1969), p. 233. Hereafter cited as Cavell.

17. For the Searle-Derrida exchange see J. Derrida, "Signature Evenement Contexte," in *Marges de la philosophie* (Paris, 1972): English translation in *Glyph* 1 (Baltimore, 1977). pp. 172–97, which is then followed by J. Searle, "Reiterating the Differences: A Reply to to Derrida" (pp. 198–208). Hereafter cited as "Reiterating..." Derrida's rejoinder. "Limited Inc: a b c..." appears in *Glyph* vol. 2 (Baltimore, 1977), pp. 162–254.

18. Derrida, "Signature Event Context," p. 192. One must keep in mind that in French the verb for "to mean" is *vouloir-dire*.

19. J. Searle, "Reiterating...," p. 202.

20. Cavell, p. 227.

21. Geoffrey Hartman, "Monsieur Texte II: Epiphony in Echoland," *The Georgia Review* 30, no. 1 (Spring 1976): 182.

22. Cavell, p. 237.

23. Derrida, *Grammatology*, pp. 49, 46, 159, and 160.

24. Derrida's position is in spirit not that remote from Nelson Goodman's nominalism. In like manner one could say that in *Ways of Worldmaking* Goodman goes too far when he speaks of there being not one but many worlds. It would seem perfectly adequate to speak of a plurality of world-versions. His point, though, is that if there is no other access to a world than through a particular version, the term "the world" has no use except one internal to a version.

25. Derrida, *Grammatology*, p. 159.

26. Ibid., pp. 159, and 158.

HERMENEUTICS AS THE RECOVERY OF MAN

JOHN D. CAPUTO

When Constantine Constantius—the Kierkegaardian pseudonym—undertook a return trip to Berlin, he made an experiment in "repetition" that was, I want to argue, of some consequence for hermeneutics. I believe that what we nowadays call "hermeneutics"—Heideggerian and post-Heideggerian hermeneutics—defends the view that repetition is possible and indeed that everything in hermeneutics turns on its possibility. On this account, hermeneutics is always a work of retrieval (*Wiederholung*) a laying out (*auslegen*) that fetches back (*wiederholen*), an explicating that retrieves what is latent and puts it into words for the first time, as Heidegger says.[1] Hermeneutics is set on restoring something that has remained withdrawn, on bringing out into the open something that has been closed off. And that is what I mean by speaking of hermeneutics as a philosophy of "recovery," from the Latin *recuperare*, which means to recoup, to retrieve or restore, and also to recuperate. It means at once to get back something lost or latent, and also to get "better," to get over an illness (in our case, of the spirit).[2]

Now I will devote my time in the present essay—which is part of a larger project—to the word "recovery," although I appreciate the fact that the word "man" in my title is not uncontroversial, especially today when we not only want to overcome humanism but even to be pitiless about the death of man. I will say here only this much about the word "man" in my title. I stand with Heidegger's *Letter on Humanism*, and I believe that Derrida is right to say that Heidegger's treatise remains in a sense still a species of humanism, albeit of a higher sort. Derrida is right, I think, but I do not take that to be a

416

criticism of Heidegger. I am worried more by the "end of man" than by remaining within a humanism of a higher sort.[3]

The point of the present essay then will be to thematize the project of recovery, to probe and unfold it, and to defend its role in an adequately conceived hermeneutics. I will argue as follows. There are two philosophies of recovery or retrieval that feed into the hermeneutic strategy of *Being and Time*—the Kierkegaardian notion of exitential "repetition" and the phenomenological return to beginnings in Husserl. In *Being and Time*, Heidegger demonstrates that these two versions of retrieval are of a piece, that they represent as it were twin circles. I will show that the one circle—existential repetition—belongs to what Kierkegaard calls the "founding of metaphysics," while Husserlian phenomenology, as Derrida shows so well, remains under the spell of the metaphysics of presence. I will argue that Kierkegaardian repetition controls and decisively modifies the phenomenological element in *Being and Time*,[4] and hence that the hermeneutics that is at work in this book has broken with metaphysics. After Heidegger, hermeneutics means a recovery of origins, a return to the more primordial, which has nothing to do with the "nostalgia for presence" but on the contrary everything to do with what Kierkegaard calls the "courage" for repetition. Finally, without pretending to know what Derrida in the long run wants to say, and fully cognizant that I may be deconstructed on the spot, I want to conclude that Derrida's critique of Heideggerian hermeneutics is misled by the Husserlian element in *Being and Time*. It is a mistake, I will contend, to make the critique of presence into a critique of the whole project of retrieval, and hence a mistake to think that hermeneutics is a matter of the free play of signs—even as it is a mistake for Rorty to think that hermeneutics has to do merely with keeping the lines of communication open between the diverse "language games."[5]

KIERKEGAARD'S EXISTENTIAL REPETITION

The hermeneutic circle is the oldest official—if the office of philosophy was instituted with the Platonic Socrates—philosophical theory about man and knowledge. The Being of the soul is to return whence it came, to recover its origins in the sphere of primordial Being, to recover its lost home in the sphere of pure presence. The Being of the soul is circular, belonging primordially to the supersensible world, falling into the sensible things, and destined for return.[6] And if the Being of the soul is circular, then knowledge too has a circular structure; knowledge is recollection, the reactivation of a former cognition that has somehow lost its life. Philosophy opened its doors with the doctrine of the circle.

But in Platonism the circle is through and through metaphysical; indeed Platonism inaugurated metaphysics and it is more or less what metaphysics has meant for over two thousand years. Aristotle made his reputation, in part, by showing what had gone wrong with the Platonic undertaking, but the price of the Aristotelian critique is high—the replacement of the circle with the hypothesis of the tabula rasa. What was needed was a thinker with Aristotelian instincts who understood the dynamics of the circle. That, I contend, is what we find in Kierkegaard, and if it is true that it is found in Heidegger, as I think it is, that is in no small measure due to Kierkegaard.[7]

Kierkegaard made a penetrating critique of the metaphysical version of the circle—"recollection"—and opposed it to the authentically Christian version, which was for him the opposite of metaphysics, and this he called "repetition." In the book that bears that title, Constantine Constantius writes:

> . . .repetition is a decisive expression for what "recollection" was for the Greeks. Just as they taught that all knowledge is a recollection, so will modern philosophy teach that the whole of life is a repetition. . . . Repetition and recollection are the same movement, only in opposite directions; for what is recollected has been, is repeated backwards, whereas repetition properly so called is recollected forwards. Therefore repetition, if it is possible, makes a man happy, whereas recollection makes him unhappy.[8]

The common problem to which both recollection and repetition are addressed is the transition from time to eternity, and that is why Constantine says that they are the same movement. How does the existing, temporal individual make his way from time to eternity? The Greek solution, Constantine says, is to move *backward*, from time to an eternal preexistence. Now there are two things to be emphasized about this characterization. In the first place, it holds that eternity is, or has been already, present and that its presence has been lost. Eternity is in the past; it is a lost actuality. Secondly, the backward movement signifies for Constantine the attempt to extricate oneself from time, to back oneself *out* of it. That is why in the *Postscript* Johannes Climacus says that Platonic recollection is the "temptation" to recollect oneself out of existence, and that it belongs to the greatness of (the historical) Socrates to have resisted this temptation.[9] Recollection then is a nostalgia for a lost eternity that sees the temporal as copy, imperfection, transiency, and it wants to extricate itself from time by means of speculative thought. Recollection is metaphysics, and metaphysics wants to be disengaged speculation.

Repetition, on the other hand, is the way from time to eternity that is taken by existence itself. Eternity in this sense is not a metaphysical object but a religious goal, the whole point of Christian life. Now for the existing individual eternity is the *vita ventura*, the life that is to come—in this *ventura* we already hear Heidegger's *Zukommen*—the life that is promised to those who fight the good fight, who set their hands to the plow without looking back. That is why Constantine calls repetition a movement forward, not backward. For it does not have to do with a past actuality, with a presence lost, but with a presence that is yet to be realized, with the *possible*. It is not a matter of reawakening a recollection of a previous existence, but of bringing about a new life. In repetition what is to be repeated has not previously existed, has never enjoyed a prior presence, but remains something to be brought about. Whence if the backward movement of recollection signifies evasion, escape, disinterest, retreat; then repetition moves forward, presses forth, engages the battle, pushes ahead, resolves upon the one thing necessary and clings to that resolve even unto death. In the Christian conception, time (temporality) is a trial and test that sorts out the wheat from the chaff. If metaphysics wants to think its way out of time, Christian life in time is a test in which every moment is urgent, every moment an occasion for a decisive action, for a decision upon which everything—that is to say, all eternity—hangs in the balance. Whence the Christian sees time in terms of futurity and decisiveness. Christian time is futural; the Christian labors each day for the *vita ventura*, the life that is to come. But in metaphysics time is an imperfection, an imitation, not something to be worked through; it lacks urgency, decisiveness. Nothing is decided in time; the point is rather to transcend time for the sake of eternity, to put it out of action.

Platonic recollection therefore belongs to—indeed inaugurates—the metaphysics of presence. Platonism remains for Kierkegaard under the spell of the Eleatics, whereas Kierkegaard bids us to think in terms of *kinesis*, movement.[10] In an astonishing commentary on Aristotelian *kinesis*, Kierkegaard writes in his private papers, "When even Aristotle said that the transition from possibility to actuality is *kinesis* he was not talking about logical possibility and actuality but about the possibility and actuality of freedom, and therefore he quite rightly posits motion."[11] Kierkegaard wants us to think not in terms of permanent presence but in terms of movement where movement means principally existence and freedom.

That is why Kierkegaard sees no essential difference between Platonic and Hegelian recollection, even though Hegel wants to think Being in terms of time and motion. The doctrine of *Aufhebung* does not constitute an essential improvement over *anamnesis*. For Hegelian time is not authentic, radical, Christian temporality, in which everything hinges on the moment, the decision; it is not a time in which we are exposed to the flux and contingency. Hegel's is a time made safe by eternity, underwritten by reason, regulated by necessity. It lacks what is uniquely proper to time: contingency, freedom, exposure to the future. It makes only a show of embracing *kinesis* while in fact subordinating it to a rational teleology of history. Hegel's time is a time reworked by metaphysics, made over into its image and likeness, and in which the groundlessness of radical freedom is covered up.[12]

The proper element of repetition is time. Repetition moves through time, grapples with it, exposes itself to the flux. But if it cannot, like recollection, simply negate time and nullify the flux, neither can repetition merely submit to time and turn itself over to the flux. Its unique task is to persevere in time and to maintain its constancy, identity, and continuity. What was a theoretical question for Hume and Kant concerning the "identity" of the epistemological subject became for Kierkegaard the concrete problem of how the existing individual achieves identity as an ethicoreligious agent. Hence if Kierkegaard wanted a philosophy of *kinesis* and not pure presence, this was to be a *kinesis* with constancy, with identity, with "repetition."[13] The lack of repetition for Kierkegaard means momentariness, opportunism, the inconstancy that busies itself from moment to moment. Just as in Nietzsche's conception of eternal return, in repetition we fuse Being and becoming, not in the fraudulent manner of the Hegelian *Aufhebung*, but existentially, by maintaining constancy within the flux of time.[14]

That also is why the love of repetition is happy, for it presses forward robustly to victory; the happiness of repetition is the exhilaration that comes of an earnest struggle. But the love of recollection is unhappy, for it is a melancholy longing for a lost paradise, dreamy will-lessness. The unhappiness of recollection lies in its nostalgia for a presence lost. Recollection is flaccid and voluptuous, while repetition is courage, reality, the seriousness of life.[15]

Repetition, we said, has the courage to impose constancy on the flux, the constancy of the circle in which in the midst of change, we return to the same. It fuses Being and becoming, constancy and novelty. But what precisely is the constancy of the circle of repetition? Does it mean the return of the same, repetition in the *literal* sense? Not at all, for literal repetition remains within the metaphysics of presence; literal repetition is re-presentation, making present again a presence lost. Indeed, the point of Constantine's treatise is to show that the attempt to repeat the same, to reenact a moment that is over, is doomed to failure. That is why repetition is impossible on the aesthetic level. One can never repeat a pleasure that has flown by: there are too many contingencies, too many fortuitous contributions for us to be able to bring them all together again; whereas aesthetics must practice the rotation method, and it dreads repetition.[16] Constantine Constantius's return visit to Berlin ends in failure; this whole whimsical tale, Kierkegaard writes, is a parody of true repetition.[17]

Kierkegaard wants to show that true repetition is possible only in the religious sphere, in the sphere of the inner man, and that means that it belongs to the category of existence and freedom. It has an existential sense, and it has nothing to do with the recurrence of something present (*vorhanden*). The circle of repetition therefore is the circle in which freedom works itself out. It is the process by which freedom becomes what it already is, by which it becomes itself. Repetition does not mean that we get something external (*vorhanden*) back—that we are able to make present again a presence flown—but that "consciousness (is) raised to the second power." It does not signify the repossession of lost goods or even, as Kierkegaard learned to his regret, that one gets one's fiancee back, but rather that one gets one's freedom back.[19] But not precisely "back," for repetition does not move backward; rather one acquires freedom for the first time. But then what is repeated? An innermost potentiality, the latent possibilty to be or become oneself, which we have neglected, overlooked, "forgotten." In repetition the existing individual learns that to regain his soul he must suffer the loss of the whole world. Repetition is a growth in freedom, a shattering of worldly ambitions and selfish goals in order to be brought back to the one thing necessary, to one's innermost and utmost potentiality.

This is made clear in the young man's use of the story of Job in the second part of the book. Kierkegaard thinks that Job and Abraham— he uses Abraham of course in *Fear and Trembling*—as great as they are, are only fighting out border skirmishes on the outskirts of faith, and are not full-fledged "heroes" of faith.[20] Their sufferings are only a temporary "trial," and hence a merely probationary period after which their goods will be restored, made present again. Abraham and Job recuperate their losses—Abraham gets Isaac back, and Job's goods and reputation are also restored. But the condition of true repetition is the permanent loss of presence. Freedom must suffer shipwreck; it must undergo the agony of absence. The genuinely religious individual must be prepared to lose all. In this way he will learn that God, Who is the true teacher of repetition, is leading him back to himself, wondrously directing him on a wholly unsuspected course by means of which he discovers what he did not realize he even sought—himself. He seeks the world but in losing it, finds himself; he seeks to restore something external and in the process recovers his own inner freedom. In Kierkegaardian repetition there is neither a prior presence nor literal recurrence, but rather the emergence of the new from the possible. Repetition is not the re-presentation of a presence lost, as in Platonic *anamnesis*, nor the making explicit of what was necessarily and logically implicit, as in Hegelian *Aufhebung*. It is rather freedom's discovery of itself, a self that was latent, unknown, although it was known all along to God, Who has mysteriously led us back to ourselves. We should neither have known it by ourselves, nor found it by ourselves. But it "is" there—where "is" does not mean "present"—all along, calling us, beckoning to us. God alone elicits it from us, prompts us, moves us, casting us down only to lift us up anew, reborn, remade in the new man who has all along stirred within us. Repetition is the self's recovery of itself.

It is clear then, and let us conclude our sketch of Kierkegaard on this point, that the movement of repetition eludes the metaphysics of presence, that it is an overcoming of metaphysics. This is pointed out by Constantine Constantius himself. He writes, "Repetition is the *interest* of metaphysics"—that is, that point in modern thought at which metaphysics realizes that it can no longer remain disinterested speculation—"and at the same time the interest upon which metaphysics founders"—that is, the point at which metaphysics, which is necessarily speculative and necessarily a philosophy of presence, breaks down and gives way to the philosophy of concrete existence.[21] Metaphysics looks on, with the detachment of the disinterested spectator, at the spactacle of presence. But repetition is not a speculative problem, and it cannot be resolved by speculative means. It does not have to do with restoring the fullness of presence but with the abyss of freedom. It has nothing to with Greek ousiology but with saving oneself only by first losing oneself.[22]

When *Repetition* was translated into German in 1909 in the Diedrichs edition, the Danish title *Gentagelse* was rendered *Wiederholung*, and it was that early German edition, which Heidegger knew, that stands in a decisive way behind the hermeneutic phenemonology of *Being and Time*.[23] Now one cannot proceed directly from Kierkegaard to Heidegger without first passing through Husserl, to whom we turn now. But I have offered this reading of this Kierkegaardian text in order to underline something essential about Heidegger's hermeneutic strategy in *Being and Time*, something that is threatened today by those who, like Rorty and Derrida, often speak as though they were continuing what Heidegger has set in motion.

HUSSERL'S RETURN TO BEGINNINGS

The work of retrieval in *Being and Time* is multilayered. It has to do not only with existential retrieval—it is not only an existential hermeneutic—but also with phenomenological retrieval: it is also a hermeneutic phenomenology. As an existential hermeneutic it wants to recall us to ourselves, to restore our authentic selfhood and being-with others (*Selbstsein, Mit-sein*). As a hermeneutic phenomenology it invokes a new methodological consciousness that says that to philosophize is to recover an understanding in which we already stand. Now if the inspiration of Heidegger's existential hermeneutic is Kierkegaard's notion of repetition, the inspiration of his hermeneutic phenomenology is Husserl's phenomenology, on which account it is proper to regard Husserl's work as a proto-hermeneutics. We have said that the genius of *Being and Time* was to find a way of bringing these two levels of retrieval together and to make of them a single garment. For of themselves they are at odds with one another on the issue of the "metaphysics of presence." Hence we want to see not only how

Heidegger draws upon Husserlian phenomenology in constituting his new hermeneutics, but how the Husserlian element is controlled by the "foundering" or destruction of metaphysics.

Husserl had given an account of perceptual consciousness that maintained that everything in perception turns on the decisive role played by the "horizon" or field to which the perceptual object belongs. We are conscious of the orchestra playing, not of the silence in the rest of the hall; of the film we are viewing, not of the darkness in the theater. The phone ringing in the stillness of the night is alarming even though it is commonplace for the same phone, with the same decibel level, to ring in the middle of a busy day. A word or a sentence taken out of context takes on a wholly new sense. A severed human hand is ghastly, even though it is well preserved and "looks no different" than a living member of a whole body. The facade of a building that is being leveled is no longer the same but stands as a mute testimony to the ravages of urban progress. We pay explicit attention to the object that appears within the bounds of the horizon while the horizon itself remains implicit, playing a decisive but mute role. "The focal is girt about with a "zone" of the marginal; *the stream of experience can never consist wholly of focal actualities.*"[24] The stream of experience is thus a complex of actualities (focal, thematic), and an inactual, nonthematic halo that surrounds and decisively affects the structure of the thematic object.

Now it is always possible to shift the arrow of intentional attention away from the focal to the nonfocal and to make the inactual actual. That is the task of reflection. Rays of attention, Husserl says, can be sent by the ego to penetrate the "dimly apprehended depth or fringe of indeterminate reality," piercing its vagueness and "fetching out" from it the hitherto inactual.[25] And here, in this fetching out (*herausholen*) carried out by transcendental reflection, Heidegger encountered another form of that fetching back (*wiederholen*) that makes the implicit explicit, that turns the phenomenological look from the thematic entity to its implicit horizon. Here, in this Husserlian distinction between actual object and inactual horizon,[26] Heidegger found the housing for the ontological distinction between the entity and its Being, which he had learned from his years of study of scholasticism and Aristotle.

Now it is clear that transcendental horizonal consciousness moves in a circle. It is only in virtue of the prethematic and implicitly grasped horizon that it is possible to grasp an object; yet it is only by scrutinizing our consciousness of the object that we find it in the lines that reach out to the horizon. The work of phenomenology is carried out by moving back and forth between horizon and object, between thematic and prethematic. Nor is there anything vicious in this circle, for the implicit horizon is the *causa essendi* of the thematic object, while our consciousness of the object is the *causa cognoscendi* of our discovery of the horizon. The viciousness of the circle is removed as soon as one takes into account the distinction between implicit and explicit.

Husserl himself considered the work of fetching objects back off the horizon as an infinite task, an idea in the Kantian sense. It is in principle possible, even if it not so factually, to make the absent horizon present. Whence if the experienced object is a complex of actuality and inactuality, presence and absence, this is not to be conceived in opposition to the principle of all principles, the principle of self-givingness, but as a task imposed upon reflection to bring every component in our experience to explicit consciousness. Derrida would insist, and rightly in our opinion, that Husserl's argument actually worked against his own purposes, and that he had in fact established the opposite: that there is no pure presence, no purely self-giving object, and that presence is only possible on the horizon of absence.[27] It is precisely the absence of the horizon, its implicit, prethematic status, that makes the presence of the object possible. What if, Heidegger would ask, our capacity for reflection, our capacity to convert absence into presence, is finite? What if the infinite task is not merely a dream but a misunderstanding of the facticity of Dasein?[28]

Somewhere shortly after 1920, Husserl began to pay more attention to the "world" as the horizon of horizons and at the same time to consider the genetic and historical dimensions of his theory of intentionality. This joint emphasis on world and history gave rise to the famous *Lebenswelt* phenomenology that has so decisively influenced continental philosophies of this century. I want here to pull but one thread in the rich texture of Husserl's later philosophy that is of special importance to the story we are presently telling and that seems to have decisively affected Heidegger's hermeneutics of retrieval, and that is Husserl's theory of predication.

Husserl had always held to the perceptual base of all knowledge and defended a stratified theory in which objects of a higher order are founded (*fundiert*) upon the lower order, and ultimately perceptual objects. In *Formal and Transcendental Logic*, and especially in *Experience and Judgment*, Husserl traced with meticulous care the lineage of judgments of higher order in perceptual experience. Perhaps because of a renewed appreciation for Dilthey, Husserl came to realize that this perceptual base, after it is a perception of material objects, is also a cultural-perceptual world and hence is historically qualified; the perceptual ground upon which judgments of higher order are founded has a historical coefficient. Whence not only are the higher order predications of mathematical physics founded on perception—that had always been his position—but furthermore science has a history and the world of reduction cannot be separated from the history of the formation of scientific judgments. And so when he argued in *Krisis* that the Galilean science had simply taken over naively and without transcendental reflection mathematical cognitions of a higher order, this constituted a failure in historical retrieval. What is missing in modern physicalist objectivism is a capacity to fetch back the historico-epistemic (a new alliance!) beginnings of its own cognitions. The failure to carry out the reduction now means a failure in historical sense, an incapacity for the historical reduction—which means retrieval, repetition, or, as Husserl puts it, reactivation. Reactivation is Husserlian repetition. Our incapacity for this reduction allows the abstract constructions of modern physics to lead a life of its own, to acquire an autonomous voice, and to speak imperiously to modern man. We have forgotten their origins, forgotten to repeat to their beginnings, and that failure in repetition has precipitated the contemporary crisis.

And so everything in phenomenology turns on retrieval. From the very start, phenomenology meant for Husserl a search for beginnings, for forgotten origins; and the method it used, reduction, *reducere*, meant a leading back to beginnings. Reduction, reactivation—these are the Husserlian versions of recovery and repetition. What is reduction if not retrieval? And what is the naiveté of the natural attitude if not forgetfulness? The transcendental ego leads an anonymous life, forgotten in the midst of our preoccupation with the natural life that it makes possible. We live out our intentional life, inhabit our intentional acts, without heeding the transcendental activity that gives shape to our world. And transcendental phenomenology recalls us out of this oblivion, back to the hidden and forgotten origins of our world. If transcendental phemenology always had a genetic sense, it was inevitable that it would finally take a historical turn; hence there could have been no more consistent outcome to Husserl's development.[29] Transcendental reduction was all along destined to become historical retrieval.

But what is the charcter of this retrieval? Does it amount to a making-present-again, a literal representation, or it is a repetition that endures the loss of presence? I think it is to Derrida's credit to have shown that this phemenology remains a captive of the metaphysics of presence. We have already seen how this was the case with the phenomenology of horizons; and it is also the case with the task of historical retrieval. This I take to have been ably demonstrated in Derrida's commentary "The Origin of Geometry."[30] In the historical reduction, everything turns on leading the structures of higher order back to their foundations in the living present, in the primordial perceptual experiences of the first geometers who initially gave sense to our inherited mathematical idealizations. At the beginning of our scientific tradition there lie rich and pregnant experiences that have nourished the whole subsequent history. It is all a matter of returning to this limpid moment—one that we can determine a priori without recourse to factual information; this is the way it "must have been"— in which a light dawned upon the first geometer and he was motivated to pass from a practical concern to an idealized reconstruction of it. Here was a moment of transcendental truth, now long forgotten and buried over by a history of neglect and naiveté. The transcendental—historical reduction breaks the spell of this naiveté and we reenter the region of pristine light.

The reduction turns out to be recollection in the Kierkegaardian sense, recaapturing a lost world, moving backward to a former presence, reinstating a past actuality. The circle moves from presence to absence, and from absence to presence restored. The work of phenomenology is to make present again what has lost its presence. Now on this point—which goes to the heart of the thesis of this paper —we must say that Kierkegaard was the more radical thinker who understood that repetition in the literal sense is impossible. One cannot restore a presence lost. That is the illusion of metaphysics. Kierkegaard understood the foundering of metaphysics; his "thunderstorm" had taught him the limitations of repetition. Constantine Constantius had undertaken repetition—if we may paraphrase Merleau-Ponty's famous remark about the reduction—precisely in order to discover the impossibility of carrying it out literally. He learned that repetition must become a more oblique recovery, one that instead of retrieving pure presence learns to endure the harshest absence.

HEIDEGGER'S HERMENEUTICS OF RETRIEVAL

What Heidegger saw in *Being and Time* was that the two philosophies of retrieval by which he had been affected so deeply—Kierkegaard's philosophy of repetition and Husserl's return to beginnings—belonged together. He saw that the circle of repetition, the self's recovery of itself, belonged together with the circle of understanding, the phenomenological recovery of the implicit and prethematic. He saw that the existential-ontological recovery, by which Dasein hands itself back to itself futurally, is of a piece with the hermeneutic-phenomenological recovery. The philosophy of retrieval provides a determination not only of the Being of man but also of the method of investigation,[31] whence there are always two tiers of retrieval at work in the existential analytic, two distinguishable but related circles—the one ontological, the other methodological; the one existential and the other hermeneutic. And each mirrors the other. The ontological circle grounds the hermeneutic; and the hermeneutic circle befits a being with the Being of Dasein.

We have seen, however, that in their original and native settings—in Kierkegaard and in Husserl—these philosophies of retrieval are not of a kind. For the one, Kierkegaard's, has made a breach with the metaphysics of presence, and the other, Husserl's, wanted to make present again the anonymous ego, the sedimented sense, the implicit horizon, to bring everything into the clarity of a philosophy of intuition and self-givenness. And so we want to interrogate *Being and Time* as to the sense of the retrieval that is at work there, as to the character of the hermeneutics that it practices and its relationship to metaphysics. Is this a retrieval in the traditional metaphysical sense that wants to reinstate a lost presence and bring it into the light of the day—as the word "phenomenology" indicates—or has it made its break with metaphysics so that it understands the loss of presence?

Now it has been our contention all along that the relationship of Heidegger to Kierkegaard is much more intimate than either Heidegger himself or his commentators have been prepared to admit. In our view, the genius of Kierkegaard, the academic renegade and tormented "exception," is amplified by the genius of Heidegger, the German professor, a species about whom Kierkegaard had not a few things to say. We want to show that Heidegger's proximity to Kierkegaard is the controlling element on this question of retrieval and that his hermeneutics is not a philosophy of presence. In *Being and Time* there is, of course, no question of making one's way from time to eternity, but rather from fallenness and inauthentic time to authentic being-a-self. The *vita ventura* becomes authentic futurity. But structurally the positions are the same: the call of conscience is a call back to our thrown Being-in-the-world. The caller of the call of conscience is Dasein itself (in its authentic Being), and that which is called is also Dasein itself (in its inauthenticity), and what is said to Dasein in the call is to become itself, to be the being that it already is, to take up its authentic potentiality for Being. Here there is an existential circle: Dasein calls itself to become itself. Just as in Kierkegaard, Dasein is not Being but *kinesis*, and the structure of the movement is circular: from Dasein to Dasein; to become the being that we already are, to be (*wesen*, taken verbally) that which we have been all along (*gewesen*).

It is in virtue of this existential circularity of Dasein's Being that Heidegger can claim both that authenticity is a modification of inauthenticity, and also that inauthenticity is a modification of authenticity. Ontologically, in the order of Being, inauthenticity is a falling out of, and hence derivative from, authenticity: in its average day-to-day-ness, Dasein fails to be true to its ontological makeup and falls in among things. But on the other hand, ontically and factually, authenticity is a modification of inauthenticity: finding itself factually dispersed among things, the transition to authenticity is a movement back to existential-ontological Being, a retrieval of its thrown-projection into the world.

Now the essential point here, for our purposes, is that this recovery is not to be construed as making-present-again of a lost presence; it is not the restoration of a past actuality. On the contrary, it does not recover presence but absence; it recovers Dasein's own absence from which it has all along been in flight.[33] The call says "nothing," precisely so: no-thing. It recalls Dasein to the brute contingency of its Being, the thrownness about the origin of which Dasein has nothing to say. It recalls Dasein to the nothingness of its potentiality for Being: Dasein is all along a null project, a project into death, running forth (*vorlaufen*) into the end. This is a recovery that Dasein would just as soon forgo. This is no return ticket for a trip to Berlin but an invitation to take up the anxiety of Abraham and Job. It is more like the *memento mori* of Christianity, enjoining us to recall our finitude and death. This is a retrieval of absence, of the abyss. Inauthenticity on the other hand clings to the present, the actual, and it moves like the aesthete in volume 1 of *Either/Or* from one actuality to the next, practicing the rotation method, avoiding true repetition in favor of the curiosity of the ever-new. But authentic Dasein, which has the courage for anxiety, the courage of repetition, recovers the absence that underlies this presence; it breaks the grip of the actual upon its Being and in so doing recovers its freedom. The freedom of Dasein is that it is no longer held fast by the actual; it is a transcendence beyond things that stretches out into the Nothing.[34]

This is not to say that Dasein's freedom is an impotent, brooding over finitude, that it is nihilism or Stoic freedom. On the contrary, freedom is a taking action which liberates the possible.[35] Hence, in the breach with everyday Dasein's preoccupation with the actual (presence), in order to confront its own nothingness (absence), Dasein uncovers the true Being of the possible. The Being of Dasein is neither presence (*Vorhandensein*) nor absence, but possibility (*Seinkönnen*). Dasein projects itself into a potentiality for Being, not a free-floating and wholly untrammeled possibility, but a possibility into which it has been thrown. Dasein's recovery of itself, its self-retrieval (*Wiederholung*), is then not a recollection of a previous state as in Platonism, nor a reactivation in Husserl's sense, which makes actual again. It is on the contrary the initiation of something new, a retrieval in which Dasein discovers (uncovers, recovers) what it is capable of , what it has all along been "sent" to do. We must hear the *schicken* in Heidegger's use of the words *Schicksal* and *Geschick* in *Being and Time*. These words have nothing to do with fate and determinism, but with sending, *mittere*, mission. The authenticity of Dasein lies in retrieving what is has been sent or commissioned to do in this historical situation, in taking up that for which it has all along been sent. Recovery is the repetition of the possible.[36]

Just as in Kierkegaard, repetition does not consist in restoring a lost possession—it does not mean we get the girl back. Rather, we are led by it into a new sphere, one that is unexpected, unforeseen, previously unknown, but yet somehow always mysteriously familiar, obliquely and darkly preunderstood. And we are brought into this sphere not solely by our own resources. For, as in Kierkegaard, Dasein requires a teacher of repetition. If in Kierkegaard this teacher is God, in Heidegger it is the historical situation itself, the movement of history in which and by which we see the traces and hear the echoes of a forgotten possibility, a possibility that can indeed be felt only by those who have the eyes to see and the ears to hear, that is, by resolute Dasein bent on recovering itself.[37]

We are now in a position to situate Heidegger's hermeneutic method in *Being and Time*. I want now to show that Heidegger's hermeneutics is through and through a philosophy of retrieval, and hence that the methodology of *Being and Time* is a mirror image of its ontology. And I then want to argue that this means that the Kierke-gaardian moment controls the Husserlian, that the ontology of finitude modifies the phenomenology of presence, reshapes it and gives it a new sense, which nowadays goes under the name of "hermeneutic phenomenology."

Ontologically, the call of conscience is a call *back* from inauthenticity and fallenness in order to make its way *back* to Dasein's authentic con-stitution. Dasein's Being is characterized by a certain drift or tend-ency to fall in among things, to de-generate in the literal sense of becoming more and more removed from its origins.[38] We tend to drift further and further from ourselves, ontologically, even though on-tically we are this very being. But if fallenness is a certain *Zug*—drift, pull, tendency—then hermeneutics must be the *Gegen-zug*, the counterpull, the countertendency; any adequate interpretation of Da-sein can come about only by countering this tendency, reversing this drift, wrenching Dasein in the opposite direction. That means that in-terpretation, *Aus-legung*, is a forceful setting free (*Freilegung*) of Da-sein that checks its tendency to fall and makes its way back to its primordial or originary (*ursprünglich*) makeup: "The setting free of Dasein's primordial Being (*ursprünglichen Seins*) must rather be *wrested* from Dasein by following the *counter-tendency (im Gegen-zug)* from that taken by the falling ontico-ontological tendency of interpre-tations."[39] On the existential level, authentically being oneself (*eigentliches Selbstsein*) is the countertendency to inauthentically being like everyone else (*das 'Man'*). On the hermeneutic level—that is, on the level of a thematic interpretation such as is undertaken by the author of *Being and Time*—an authentic interpretation of Dasein in terms of existence and temporality is the countertendency to a falling interpretation of Dasein in terms of presence. Our prethematic fallen-ness (as existing begins) is mirrored in a fallen ontology. If on the prethematic level fallen Dasein takes refuge in the *actual*, then on the level of an explicit hermeneutic thematization this results in a meta-physics of presence. Hence we need an interpretative moment that corresponds on the hermeneutic level to existential resoluteness, which cuts through the ontology of presence even as resoluteness breaks the grip of the actual. That is what Heidegger means by hermeneutics, and that is why hermeneutics is this countertendency (*Gegenzug*).

This mirroring of anticipatory resoluteness in hermeneutics also explains why hermeneutics proceeds by way of forestructures.[40] The methodological forestructure, the preunderstanding, reflects the existential-ontological being-ahead-of-itself; *Vorstruktur* reflects *Vorwegsein*. Hermeneutic forestructures cut through the disguises of fallness and make their way back to Dasein's originary structure, even as resoluteness returns Dasein to itself. They are a movement *back* to Dasein's structure precisely because they are a projective movement *forward*. Inasmuch as they projectively sketch ahead the horizon within which Dasein (or whatever being is under interpretation) can appear, they are at the same time a movement back to Dasein's concealed Being. The forestructures carry out the regress. To mimic the later Heidegger: *Vorstruktur und Rückgang: dasselbe.* Here then is the dynamics of the circle: the fall into the dominant ontology of presence is a falling out, an *exitus*, an ontological de-generation, while the hermeneutic projection is a *reditus*, return, retrieval. Hermeneutics is the thematic recovery of Dasein, even as resoluteness is its prethematic recovery.[41] Hermeneutics is methodological repetition, even as resoluteness is existential repetition.[42]

But what guarantee is there that the projective forestructures effect the *reditus*, that they manage to recapture the being in its primordial Being, that they are drawn from the things themselves and are not arbitrary fancies? As Heidegger puts it: "But is not anything of this sort *guided* and *regulated* in a way of its own? Where are ontological projects to get the evidence that their 'findings' are phenomenally appropriate? Ontological interpretation projects the entity presented to it upon the Being which is that entity's own, so as to conceptualize it with regard to its structure. Where are the sign-posts to direct the projection, so that Being will be reached at all?"[43] The only positive response to this question is to be found in Heidegger's notion of the preunderstanding,[44] and it is here that Heidegger's Husserlian strategy comes into play. The legitimacy of the forestructures is secured only if the forestructures, which are to be structures that reach forth beyond the being to its Being, also reach *back* and *link up* without preunderstanding. *This linking up is the only possible control in hermeneutic phenomenology.* We can ensure that the forestructural violence will be a wresting loose, a setting free, and not simly sheer caprice, only by insisting that such forestructures effect a movement of return to or retrieval of a prior understanding, a preunderstanding that Heidegger simply takes to be constitutive of Dasein. That is what Dasein *is*: a being that always and already is possessed of an understanding of Being—and hence of its own Being, of the Being of others, and the Being of things. If this preunderstanding is denied or undermined, the whole edifice of hermeneutic phenomenology collapses. This is not to say that this preunderstanding is not at times badly defaced or distorted, but even then it remains at work in everything that Dasein does: "No matter how far removed from an ontological concept the distinction between existence and reality may be, no matter even if Dasein proximally understands existence as reality, Dasein is not just present-at-hand but has already understood itself, however mythical or magical the interpretation which it gives may be."[45] Here Heidegger invokes the dynamics of Husserl's phenomenology of horizons and the distinction between the inplicit, prethematic horizon and the explicitly thematic object. We live and move about within a certain horizonal understanding, and these "forgotten" horizons make our explicit awareness possible. Heidegger takes over this Husserlian structure and gives it a more properly ontological cast. The horizon within which Dasein moves about is its understanding of its own Being (and of Being in general), an understanding (*Verstehen*) that does not get to be a concept (*Begriff*), which remains anonymous, even though its effects are felt in every corner of our experience. The hermeneutic forestructures then are "guided and regulated" by this preunderstanding. Their role is to explicate it, to bring it out into the open, to give it explicit, thematic shape where previously it remained anonymous and prethematic. The work of hermeneutics is *aus-legen, ex-ponere*, to lay out in the sense of drawing out into the open, to make exlicit what we all already implicitly understand.

Notice then how Heidegger has redefined the traditional hermeneutic circle along Husserlian lines (and at the same time drawn Husserl into the hermeneutic circle). He has transformed the old circle of the whole and the parts into a phenomenological circle of implicit and explicit, of prethematic and thematic, of anonymous horizon and explicitly named object. And he saw that these phenomenological dynamics obey the laws of repetition and retrieval. That is why there is nothing vicious in hermeneutic circularity: it conforms to classical phenomenological science, and Derrida is certainly right to say that the hermeneutic circle in *Being and Time* is controlled by the logic of implicit and explicit.[46] Phenomenology is already a protohermeneutics, for its work of fetching out (*herausholen*) what is only horizonally given, or pregiven, is a work of laying-out (*auslegen*) an understanding in which we already stand.

A primordial interpretation, Heidegger says, "will let that which is to be interpreted *put itself into words for the very first* time."[47] Where understanding previously remained vague and inarticulate, in interpretation it becomes articulated and explicit. But that means that in hermeneutics everything comes down to recognition—*recognitio, Wiedererkennung, Anerkennung*—knowing which comes back to what we already know. A knowing again, renewing our primordial acquaintance with ourselves. Everything comes down to our capacity for retrieval and repetition; there is no proving and disproving in hermeneutics, but only a self-examination, a self-discovery, in which we find ourselves in the account or fail to do so. Hermeneutics provides this prior understanding with the words with which to come into language. In so doing, it brings us to stand in the place that we already occupy. It returns us to ourselves, brings us home. It is appropriation and homecoming: coming into our own again.

But we have said that the hermeneutic phenomenology is the mirror image of the existential ontology,[48] and hence that this Husserlian moment is controlled by the Kierkegaardian. Hence we must not make the mistake of thinking that in this hermeneutics we want to make everything present and explicit, to restore presence everywhere. For the ontology of existence culminates in resoluteness that is a readiness for anxiety, openness to the absence. And so that too is mirrored in the hermeneutics.

To see how this is so, we must follow up the clue that is provided us by the ontology of existence. When resolute Dasein returns to itself from fallenness, it does not seize again a lost presence, nor recapture a pure but hitherto concealed Being. On the contrary, it returns to the nothingness of its Being and faces up to that from which it has all along been in flight, its own nullity (*Nichtigkeit*). By the same token, if hermeneutic phenomenology projects the Being of this being in terms of existence and temporality and claims thereby that it has drawn this projection from primordial sources, that it has thereby entered the circle "wholly and primordially" (*ganz und ursprünglich*[49]) it has not claimed to have made Dasein's being *transparent*. It does not claim to have restored a lost presence and brought it out into the light but rather to have restored the mystery, the absence, the "lethic" element in Dasein. Hence the effect of this hermeneutic retrieval is to have recovered our "openness for the mystery" (*Offenheit zum Geheimnis*)[50] of existence. Retrieval for Heidegger does not mean the retrieval of presence, the recovery of a lost actuality, but precisely the opposite. For his grievance with metaphysics has all along been that it turns Being into presence. It treats Dasein as a fully definable thing, a circumscribable presence, which, however much we qualify it with uplifting predicates (person, spirit, etc.), remains something present. But the Being of Dasein is finitude, contingency, nothingness, lacking a secure grasp of its whence and its whither, thrown and mortal. Whence what is brought to words for the first time in this projection of Dasein is a self-understanding of ourselves as mortals. Heidegger wants to recover the mystery of mortality; the retrieval is a *memento mori*, the recovery of the abyss. The *terminus ad quem* of this retrieval of this phenomenological *Rückgang*, is no transcendental ego, no res cogitans or absolute spirit, but the being whose Being is a nullity. Heidegger's hermeneutic is bent on restoring our finitude, mortality, and humanity—if *homo* means *humus*.

In Husserl the recovery of origins is intended as a transcendental movement, as a movement of pure freedom, in which the ego disengages itself from its situatedness within the horizon of the world. The movement from thematic to prethematic is made possible because of the ability of the reflecting ego (*das reflectierende ich*) to loosen the grip of any worldly horizon and thereby to secure for the ego reflective clarity. But in Heidegger there can be no question of loosening ourselves *from* our horizonal situatedness but rather of awakening ourselves *to* our situatedness, awakening our sense of *being* situated. In *What is Metaphysics?* he argues that we cannot thematize the world as such and as a whole by some pure effort of thought—for that would result in an unphenomenological and vacuous construction—but we can, through anxiety, become profoundly attuned to our situatedness *within* an encompassing (and hence nonbracketable) totality.[51] Husserl's phenomenology of horizons is meant to be part of a presuppositionless science that would reduce every prethematic horizon (in princple, if not in fact) to thematic awareness. But Heidegger means instead to unfold and penetrate our horizons, not to entertain the illusion that we can disengage them. The task is not to deny our presuppositions, he said, but to penetrate them more deeply.[52]

Heidegger stands with Kierkegaard on this point, not Husserl. And his critique of Husserl is an echo of Kierkegaard's critique of Plato, Platonic recollection, Hegelian remembering (*Erinnerung*) of the forms through which the spirit has passed, Husserlian *epoche*—all of these are so many versions of what Kierkegaard called "distinterest," which he regarded as a fantastic creation. The project of repetition and of retrieval is radically interested, and the metaphysics of presence founders on this interest: "Repetition is the *interest* of metaphysics and at the same time the interest upon which metaphysics founders."[53] As long as one remains on the level of interest—*inter-esse*, being betwixt and between, being caught up in the world, Being-in-the-world, existence—there can be no illusion of transparency. Transparency and pure presence are illusions of distance, illusions induced by the impossible attempt to shut down the workings of existence, to disengage the existing self, to forget that one exists, as Johannes Climacus put it. And it is to this forgetting that retrieval and recovery are opposed, so that when one recalls existence, one has dismissed the illusion of presence and thereby restored the mystery of existence.

That is also why, I should add here, concrete and practicing hermeneutics—the hermeneutics of texts in the usual sense, as opposed to the exclusively ontological hermeneutics we have pursued here—must guard against the same illusion of objective presence. We have seen that existential retrieval means that Dasein recovers not a lost actuality but a possibility, and that hermeneutic retrieval recovers not a transparent presence but the enigma of a thrown project. But that implies that concrete, working hermeneutics must aim its interpretations, not principally at restoring lost monuments and documents, but at what is possible in a text. Its goal cannot be to reconstruct a past actuality, to restore it to its original condition, but, as Gadamer argues, to find out its possible sense for us today, to find out what it says to us, here and now.[54] We shall do this in any case, as Gadamer argues—or else interpretations would not have a history. As Nietzsche says in *The Advantage and Disadvantage of History for Life*, the strong one knows how to assimilate the past and to bring it into the service of the present and future, and he does so at the expense of pure objectivity.[55] Indeed pure objectivity, were it ever possible—and not instead an ontological folly that flies in the face of the facticity of Dasein—would be of no use at all. We would then have to learn how to wean ourselves away from such things as from a form of escapism. The perfect reconstruction of past actuality would leave us speechless and must, insofar as we are existing beings, and would be of no use to life, as Nietzsche would say. This is not to say that the reading of a text is a capricious affair in which any reading is allowed. That is precisely what Heidegger rules out when he criticizes the notion of a free-floating construction.[56] We have seen that the one decisive hermeneutic control is what we called the *linking* up of a projection with the preunderstanding. Unless the being in terms of which a being is projected reaches back and articulates a preunderstanding, then it is groundless and uprooted. And that means that the labors of a concrete, working hermeneutics must be enlisted in the service of articulating our self-understanding. The interpretation of a past historical epoch, of a work of art, or of a scriptural text, must be governed by their ability to tell us who we are, to say something to use here and now about the beings that we ourselves are or, better, must become. All hermeneutics, on whatever level, is the recovery of man and is governed by the existential imperative to become oneself.

DERRIDA'S CRITIQUE OF RETRIEVAL

We have made everything in the hermeneutic strategy initiated by *Being and Time* turn on the dynamics of retrieval. We have followed the complex interweaving of two levels of retrieval, the one existential the other phenomenological. And we have said that everything depends upon our ability to make the transition from fallenness—whether into the naivete of the natural attitude or the tranquility of everydayness—to Dasein's primordial Being. But Derrida wants to deconstruct this very distinction between the primordial and the fallen on the grounds that it too belongs to the metaphysics of presence:

> Yet is not the contrast between primordial and derivative properly metaphysical? Is not a demand for an *arche* in general—whatever precautions are taken with the concept—the essential operation of metaphysics? Is there not at least some Platonism in the notion of *Verfallen*?[57]

On Derrida's view, Heidegger's notions of authenticity and primordiality remain under the spell of the metaphysics of presence:

> The primordial and the authentic are determined as the proper (*eigentlich*)—i.e., as the *near* (*prope, proprius*), the present in the proximity of presence to self. It could be shown how this value of proximity and presence to self enters, at the beginning of *Being and Time* and elsewhere, into the decision to pose the question of the meaning of Being starting from the existential analytic of Dasein. The force of metaphysics in such a decision and in the credit accorded here to the value of presence to self could also be demonstrated.[58]

For Derrida the very structure of retrieval is metaphysical, for it implies a movement from a temporary absence to a permanent presence. Dasein is at first dissipated and dispersed among things, estranged from itself, then it returns to itself, *gathers* itself up into a unity and self-identity, a unity that is of course at the expense of difference, of differance.

That is what leads Derrida, at the conclusion of "The Ends of Man," to distinguish two different sorts of deconstruction. The first, Heidegger's, attempts deconstruction "without changing ground, by repeating what is implicit in the founding concepts and original problematics, by using against the edifice the instruments or the stones available in the house." The second, Derrida's extension (and deconstruction) of Heidegger, goes further: "To decide to change ground, in a discontinuous and eruptive manner, by stepping abruptly outside and by affirming absolute rupture and difference."[59] Heidegerrian deconstruction is at fault precisely because it is an attempt at retrieval, at repeating the primordial beginnings, because it wants to go back and find what is primordial. Derrida's undertaking is however a more pitiless breaking with every possible form of metaphysics and humanism and stands altogether outside it. There is no question of repeating or retrieving its innermost sense, but of breaking with the very illusion of an innermost sense. Heidegger's overcoming befits the higher man, but not the Übermensch himself: it is not pitiless enough.[60]

I should like to respond to this criticsm by taking my point of departure from a text from *Vom Wesen des Grundes*, which, in conjunction with the argument we have developed in this paper, throws Derrida's reading of Heidegger into doubt. Here Heidegger says that insofar as Dasein is characterized by "existence," "transcendence," and "possibility"—words drawn from metaphysics but that acquire a new and unmetaphysical sense in Heidegger—then, far from being a being of nearness, as Derrida would have it, Dasein is precisely a being of distance (*ein Wesen der Ferne*):

> And so man, as an existing transcendence which bounds forth towards possibilities, is a *being of distance*. Only through the primordial distances he establishes in his transcendence towards all beings does true nearness to things arise in him. And only being able to hear into the distance, effects in Dasein as a self an awakening to the answer of Dasein-with, in being-with which Dasein can surrender its egoism (*Ichheit*) in order to win itself as an authentic self.[61]

This text flatly contradicts the attempt to define authentic Dasein in terms of self-presence, self-nearness, self-identity. For authentic Dasein is characterized by transcendence: it is stretched out beyond itself— beyond its factual presence or present factuality—into the possible, into its uttermost potentiality for Being. And it is precisely this self-absence, its being held out into Nothingness (*Gehaltensein in das Nichts*),[62] from which inauthentic Dasein is in flight. Inauthenticity is the flight from absence to presence. Inauthenticity is a refusal of transcendence, of that stretching forth into the possible that constitutes its genuine Being; it is a flight into the actual. Authentic Dasein, on the other hand, has the courage for absence, for the uncanny; it is ready for anxiety, for the nullity of its ground and of its projects, for the possibility of its own nullity, which it cultivates precisely as a possibility. In the langauge of metaphysics this ec-statis stretching out of Dasein's Being is called transcendence, and that means, Heidegger says here in a language beyond metaphysics, self-distancing. Dasein is what it is only by staying open to the distance that constitutes its very Being. To be a self is to have the courage for self-distancing, to keep the wound of finitude open— whereas inauthenticity collapses upon itself, collapsing into the present and the actual. The controlling metaphor in all of Heidegger's diverse accounts of Dasein over the years is not nearness but openness, disclosedness, and that always means keeping itself open or stretched out into the distance.[63] Authenticity is a matter of distance, not of nearness. (And it is this same distance—*ec-statis.Ausstehen*—that constitutes the projectedness of Dasein upon which all Heideggerian hermeneutics turns.)

In my view, Derrida has been misled by his critique of Husserl. He rightly—quite brilliantly, I think—saw in Husserl's phenomenology a metaphysics of presence, and he showed in his "Introduction" to *The Origin of Geometry* that Husserl wanted a metaphysical making-present-again, that he wanted to reactivate a lost meaning, to repeat it literally. Whence he says in the essay on Descartes and Foucault; "The attempt to write the history of the decision, division, difference runs the risk of construing the division as an event or a structure subsequent to the unity of an original presence, thereby confirming metaphysics in its fundamental operation."[64] But if this movement from presence to absence, and then from absence to presence restored, holds true of Husserl's teleology of reason, it cannot be said either of the retrieval of authenticity in *Being and Time* or of the step back into the origin of metaphysics in the later writings. For the recovery of the primal and primordial of which Heidegger speaks— whether in his early writings or late—is never the recovery of a primal presence. It is the recovery of a primordial *experience (Erfahrung)*, but this is always an experience of finitude and absence. In other words, and here one can put our counterpoint to Derrida succinctly, *in Derrida the critique of presence tends to pass over surreptitiously into a critique of retrieval itself*. And that is what I deny. For the one is not the other. Retrieval can indeed take the metaphysical form of a retrieval of presence—that is what Platonic recollection, Hegelian *Erinnerung*, and Husserlian *Reaktivierung* surely are. But a more radical doctrine of retrieval, such as we find in Heidegger, has given up this nostalgia for presence and has become instead a readiness for anxiety; and openness; a self-exposure to finitude, limit, and negativity. It wants precisely to return us to the finitude from which we have all along been in flight and for which metaphysics is constantly seeking the cure. In Heidegger the movement of *return* means having the courage to face up to the nothingness that inhabits Being and the thought of Being. It is not nostalgia but courage for the hard and inhospitable. It is the acknowledgment of our finitude, fallibility, and mortality. It is a recovery of man; for man, *homo*, means *humus*. This recovery is the call to remember, man, what you are: *memento homo, cineris est et in cinerem reverteris*. It is the recovery of the *memento mori*. And that is a recovery that we would soon enough do without. If it is nostalgia, it is a pathological nostalgia.

Whence the critique of presence cannot be passed off as a critique of all return and all retrieval, not if retrieval, instead of meaning the restoration of presence, means the restoration of the mystery, of the wholly other, of the nameless. Derrida thinks that repetition means you get the girl back.[65] But he has not taken adequately into account the Kierkegaardian element in repetition. He gets no further in the understanding of repetition than Constantine Constantius, who has an aesthetic theory, and not as far as the anxiety of Job and Abraham. Indeed, even Job and Abraham remain only on the outskirts of true repetition: for their deferral and difference were only temporary; they got their goods back. Genuinely religious, genuinely nonmetaphysical repetition means the agony of real and permanent loss, means that the recovery of the self is carried out only in the agony of absence.

If retrieval means the recovery of the abyss, of the mystery, of the absence that inhabits human experience, that is also what I take hermeneutics to be. Hermeneutics thinks—contrary to Derrida (and Rorty)—that there is something deeper to be sought, something more primal. Hermeneutics turns on this commitment to the primordial. The movement of its circle is always circling back on something more essential. Hermeneutic violence is always practiced in the service of retrieval. If recovery is the life of hermeneutics, then deconstruction is but a moment through which it passes. And that is why I reject the disjunction that Derrida proposes:

> There are thus two interpretations of interpretation, of structure, of sign, of play. The one seeks to decipher, dreams of deciphering a truth or an origin which escapes play and the order of the sign, and which lives the necessity of interpretation as an exile. The other, which is no longer turned towards the origin, affirms play and tries to pass beyond man and humanism, the name of man being the name of that being who, throughout the history of metaphysics or of ontotheology —in other words throughout his entire history—has dreamed of full presence, the reassuring foundation, the origin and end of play.[66]

For in this dichotomy Derrida has fused the search for the originary with the nostalgia for presence, and that is precisely what I deny. We have seen in Heidegger the search for something originary that is not the fullness of presence but that has the courage for the abyss. In Heidegger, both early and late, the return to the primordial has nothing to do with escaping from the play in which Dasein (or Being) is caught up. On the contrary, it is entering into that play and taking one's stand within it. As a readiness for anxiety, it is precisely the acknowledgment that Dasein is the being whose Being is at stake, whose Being is not secured by an *essentia* or *natura*, not underwritten by *eidos* or ousia, but is precisely an issue for Dasein.

And who can deny that this very confrontation with the abyss of Dasein is a return to origins, a recovery of that more primordial Being from which everyday Dasein is in flight, which is at the same time a denial of presence, a readiness for the void.

And so everything comes down to the question with which we began, about whether repetition is possible. Hermeneutics has all along maintained that it is, and the point of hermeneutic violence has always been to wrest loose what tends of itself to remain concealed. Deconstruction belongs in the service of retrieval; active forgetting— as Nietzsche himself says[67]—belongs together with recalling. Whether it is taken on the ontological level, which we have pursued here, or on the concrete level of an interpretation of texts, hermeneutics always means that there is a deeper sense, a latent understanding, that needs to be brought to words. That means, for example, that the interpretation of a classical text, or of a work of art, of a moment in human history, is never finished, never exhausted. There is always a new and primordial way for these things to speak to us. And in each case they speak to us about ourselves; they tell us who we are and recall us to our finitude. The texts of the great metaphysicans always address the question of our finitude, whether to embrace it or to find a way around it. The works of the great artists sing the song of our incarnation and mortality. The sacred texts recall us to our dependence upon an encompassing power. It is the task of hermeneutics, as I see it, to give words to this self-understanding, to bring it into language, and that means into appearance. These are words that we would sooner leave unsaid in favor of the public interpretation of our lives. Such words are neither a mere play of signs nor a monument to ageless presence and pure Being; they are words that hermeneutics enlists in the service of the *Sache selbst*, words of elemental power, words that have put themselves at the disposal of a primordial *hermeneuein*.

NOTES

1. *SZ*, sect. 63, 314–15/362. SZ = Martin Heidegger, *Sein und Zeit*, 10. Aufl. (Tübingen: Niemeyer, 1963); the pagination after the slash refers to the English translation, *Being and Time*, trans. J. Macquarrie and E. Robinson (New York: Harper and Row, 1962).

2. Hence one can connect this sense of *recuperare* with the Husserlian "crisis," which is an illness of the spirit.

3. Jacques Derrida, "The Ends of Man," *Philosophy and Phenomenological Research* 30 (1969):31–57.

4. With the notable exception of Calvin Schrag, Heidegger commentators tend to keep a safe distance from acknowledging the Kierkegaardian element in Heidegger's work, for fear, no doubt, of being declared "ontic." That is a serious mistake, not because Heidegger's work is indeed ontic, but because a good deal of Heidegger's "ontological" revolution is prepared for by Kierkegaard. I might also recommend in this connection William Spanos, "Heidegger, Kierkegaard and the Hermeneutic Circle: Towards a Postmodern Theory of Interpretation as Disclosure," *Boundary 2* 4 (Winter 1976):455–88, which is one of the few essays I know which has seen the connection between Kierkegaardian repetition and Heideggerian hermeneutics. The point of this essay, which is obscured by the highly opaque style in which it is written, is that "existential" hermeneutics means self-appropriation, a point we heartily endorse although it is not the point of the present essay.

5. See my "The Thought of Being and the Conversation of Mankind; the Case of Heidegger and Rorty," forthcoming in *The Review of Metaphysics*.

6. In the Middle Ages this became the basis of a mystical circle of *exitus* and *reditus* — e.g. in Meister Eckhart. See my "Fundamental Themes in Meister Eckhart's Mysticism." *The Thomist* 42 (1978):197–225.

7. This point has been pursued in a penetrating way in various essays by Thomas Sheehan; see his "Heidegger's Topic: Excess, Access, Recess," *Tijdschrift voor Philosophie* 41, no. 4 (December 1979):615–35.

8. Rep., p. 33. *Rep.* = Soren Kierkegaard, *Repetition: an Essay in Experimental Psychology*, trans. with introduction and notes by Walter Lowrie (New York: Harper and Row, The Cloister Library, 1964).

9. Soren Kierkegaard, *Concluding Unscientific Postscript*, trans. Walter Lowrie and David Swenson (Princeton: University Press, 1941), 184–85, including the "note."

10. See note 7, supra.

11. Rep., 21.

12. Rep., 20 and 52.

13. It is precisely this problematic which occupies Heidegger in SZ, § 64.

14. There is an important doctrine of repetition in Nietzsche, which goes under the name of eternal recurrence.

15. Rep., 33–35.

16. Ibid., 23.

17. Ibid., 14.

18. Ibid., 135.

19. It is painfully obvious that Kierkegaard has in mind here his own loss of Regine. When he wrote *Repetition*, he still entertained the hope that he would be reunited with her, only to find, shortly after he had completed the book, that she had married Schlegel. Whence Kierkegaards' unpleasant introduction to the shortcomings of the philosophy of presence. But here it seems to me is a classical case of having to kill the author and to forget Kierkegaard himself.

20. Rep., 115.

21. Rep., 52. Interest for Kierkegaard means *inter-esse*, being in the midst of, and clearly anticipates Heidegger's *in-der-Welt-sein*. See Kierkegaard, *Johannes Climacus or De omnibus dubitandum est* and *A Sermon*, trans. T.H. Croxall (Stanford: University Press, 1958), pp. 151–52.

22. For more on Kierkegaard's notion of repetition, see the bibliography under the entry "Repetition," in *Soren Kierkegaard's Journals and Papers*, 5 vols., vol. 3, ed. and trans. Howard and Edna Hong (Bloomington: Indiana University Press, 1975), pp. 20–22.

23. See *Soren Kierkegaard: International Bibliografi*, ed. Jens Himmelstrup (Copenhagen: Nyt Nordisk Forlag—Arnold Busck, 1961), no. 808, p. 26; and Hans-Georg Gadamer, *Philosophical Hermeneutics*, trans. David Linge (Berkeley: Univ. of California Press ,1976), p. 214.

24. Edmund Husserl, *Ideas: General Introduction to Pure Phenomenology*, trans. W. Boyce Gibson (New York: Collier Books, 1962), p. 107.

25. Ibid., p. 92.

26. For more on Husserl's discussion of horizon, see ibid., §§ 27–28, 44, 47, 63, 69 and 83; see also the distinction between attentional actuality and the wakeful ego, on the one hand, and implicit, nonattention, potential consciousness of the horizon in §§ 35 and 37.

27. This kind of argument runs throughout Derrida's Husserl interpretations; but see, e.g., Derrida, *Speech and Phenomena*, trans. David Allison (Evanston: Northwestern University Press, 1973), pp. 81–83.

28. See Heidegger's letter to Husserl of 22 October 1927, in Edmund Husserl, *Phänomenologische Psychologie*, Husserliana IX (The Hague: Martinus Nijhoff, 1962), pp. 600–3. One should beware of overstating the opposition between Husserl and Heidegger, which is in part the point of the present discussion.

29. Derrida makes this point in "'Genesis and Structure' and Phenomenology," in *Writing and Difference*, trans, with an introduction by Alan Bass (Chicago: University Press, 1978), pp. 154–68.

30. Jacques Derrida, *Edmund Husserl's "Origin of Geometry:" An Introduction*, trans. John Leavey, ed. David Allison (Stony Brook: Nicholas Hays, 1978).

31. Heidegger does not censor the word "method," as Gadamer does. See *Der Satz vom Grund* (Pfüllingen: Neske, 1957), p. 111.

32. Cf. *SZ*, sect. 27, 130/168; and sect. 64, 317/365.

33. Thomas Sheehan, "On Movement and the Destruction of Ontology," *The Monist* 64 (OCtober 1985):539–40.

34. See *What is Metaphysics?* in *Martin Heidegger: Basic Writings*, ed. David Krell (New York: Harper and Row, 1977), p. 101.

35. *SZ*, sect. 59, 294/340–41.

36. *SZ*, sect. 74.

37. Heidegger writes: "The resoluteness which comes back to itself and hands itself down, then becomes the *repetition* of a possibility of existence that has come down to us. *Repeating is handing down explicitly* — that is to say, going back into the possibilities of the Dasein that has-been-there" (*SZ*, § 74, 385/437).

38. "… in the field of ontology, any 'springing-from' (*ent-springen*) is degeneration" (*SZ*, par. 67, 334/383).

39. *SZ*, § 63, 311/359.

40. That of course is why Gadamer claims that in *Being and Time* hermeneutics is given ontological foundation.

41. Actually, interpretation (*Auslegung*) may be either thematic or prethematic, but the work of the author of *Being and Time* is clearly meant to be a thematization.

42. That is why the word "*Wiederholung*" can be used to apply either to Dasein's own existential self-actualization (par. 74) or to the reading of the history of ontology — in *Kant and the Problem of Metaphysics*, trans. James Churchill (Bloomington: Indiana University Press, 1962), pp. 211–12.

43. *SZ*, § 63, 312/359.

44. Part of the answer to this question is negative: if a conception has become popular, common (*volkisch*, SZ, § 32, 153/195), then we may be sure that it is de-generate, diluted, commonplace, fallen out of its elemental

power. But such a negative criterion will ensure only that our forestructures will be exotic, not necessarily recuperative, restorative of the things themselves. It is a necessary but not a sufficient condition.

45. SZ, § 63, 313/361.

46. Derrida, "Ends of Man," pp. 47–48.

47. SZ, § 63, 314–15/362.

48. Whence either the ontology or the methodology may be called hermeneutic.

49. SZ, § 63, 315/363.

50. Martin Heidegger, *Discourse on Thinking* (New York: Harper and Row, 1966), p. 55.

51. *What is Metaphysics?* p. 101.

52. SZ, § 62, 310/358.

53. Rep., 53.

54. Whence Gadamer's critique of historical objectivism is in the essential spirit of *Being and Time*.

55. See Friedrich Nietzsche, *The Advantage and Disadvantage of History for Life*, trans. Peter Preuss (Indianapolis: Hackett Publishing Co., 1980), pars. 2 and 6.

56. SZ, § 7, 28/50.

57. Jacques Derrida, "*Ousia* and *gramme*: a note to a Footnote in *Being and Time*," trans. Edward Casey, in *Phenomenology in Perspective*, ed. Joseph Smith (The Hague: Martinus Nijhoff, 1970), p. 89.

58. Derrida, "Ousia," p. 90, n. 36.

59. Derrida, "Ends," p. 56.

60. In the same spirit, Rorty speaks of Heidegger's "fatal attachment to the tradition," a "pathetic notion." See his "Overcoming the Tradition: Heidegger and Dewey," in *Heidegger and Modern Philosophy*, ed. Michael Murray (New Haven: Yale University Press, 1978), p. 256.

61. Martin Heidegger, *The Essence of Reasons*, A Bilingual Edition, incorporating the German text of *Vom Wesen des Grundes*, trans. T. Malick (Evanston: Northwestern University Press, 1969), pp. 130–31.

62. *What is Metaphysics?* p. 105.

63. There is a threefold distancing at work here: (1) Dasein stretches out toward its own potentiality for Being, which makes its *Selbstsein* possible; (2) toward the Being of others, which makes its *Mit-sein* possible, and (3) toward *Vorhandensein* and *Zuhandensein*, which makes its every day *in-sein* possible. All three of these ecstases are made possible by its primordial projection of Being itself.

64. *Writing and Difference*, p. 40.

65. There is to be sure a thematic of "repetition" in Derrida, but it is always in the sense of the supplement, trace or vestige, but not in the genuine sense of Kierkegaard and Heidegger. See the concluding pages of *Of Grammatology*, trans. G.C. Spivak (Baltimore: Johns Hopkins University Press, 1974), esp. p. 312.

66. Derrida, "Structure, Sign and Play in the Disclosure of the Human Sciences," in *Writing and Difference*, p. 292.

67. Nietzsche, "Advantage and Disadvantage," par. 1, p. 10.

HERMENEUTICS AND NIHILISM: AN APOLOGY FOR AESTHETIC CONSCIOUSNESS

GIANNI VATTIMO

The work that ushered into contemporary thought what has come to be called ontological hermeneutics is H.-G. Gadamer's *Truth and Method*. It begins with a long first section dedicated to "the clarification of the truth of artistic experience," a problem that finds its theoretical nucleus in a chapter devoted to "the recovery of the problem of the truth in art" and to the critique of the abstract nature of aesthetic consciousness. With this critique of aesthetic consciousness, Gadamer develops in a very original manner the results of Heidegger's meditation on art, which sees the work of art as "the truth of Being setting itself to work."[1] Gadamer's critique aims to show the historical character of aesthetic experience; he sees aesthetic experience as a type of historical experience.

The twenty years that have gone by since the publication of Gadamer's book have seen important developments in ontological hermeneutics. In Germany some of these developments—and I am thinking specifically of the work of K. O. Apel—have emphasized the nature of hermeneutics as a sort of "philosophy of social communication." It is, in fact, well known that Apel has attempted to realize a synthesis between the philosophy of language, of empiricist and pragmatic origin and the philosophy of existence, of Heideggerian inception, precisely by holding out firmly for the a priori of generalized communication. Other more recent elaborations of hermeneutics such as, for example, H. R. Jauss's literary hermeneutics, seem to be oriented in a direction that emphasizes the historically constructive character of the philosophy of interpretation. Whereas for Apel the ideal of *Verstehen* that guides hermeneutics becomes the model to attain a society freed from the opacity of neurosis, inequality, and want, for Jauss a more pervasive hermeneutic awareness is desired in order to establish a more comprehensive literary and artistic criticism, especially from the point of view of placing the work of art in a historical context, be it that which witnessed the coming into being of the work or that into which the work carries over and in which it still continues to act. Jauss does, in fact, speak of an aesthetics of artistic reception.

Jauss and Apel (and we might add Ricoeur) seem to be noteworthy examples of a ''constructive interpretation'' of hermeneutics. They develop and carry out in a coherent manner premises already contained in Gadamer's work. In these constructive developments, however, hermeneutics seems ever so distant from its Heideggerian origins. We can see an example of this in Apel himself. Apel rethinks the hermeneutic problem in neo-Kantian terminology and from a neo-Kantian perspective. He speaks, in fact, of an a priori of limitless communication, whereas it is precisely neo-Kantianism that constitutes Heidegger's constant negative and polemical point of reference. Although Gadamer would not identify himself with these neo-Kantian developments, the premises for their possibility are already contained in *Truth and Method*. The book opens with a ''critique of aesthetic consciousness,'' which displaces all the nihilistic implications of Heidegger's ontology and by doing so opens up the possibility of hermeneutics becoming a philosophy of history, a philosophy that is fundamentally humanistic, that is, ultimately, neo-Kantian.

We can, however, leave aside for the moment these general observations, which should lead to a critical revision of many of the results obtained by modern hermeneutics. The specific topics of this paper are the following: (1) to bring out what appear to be the nihilistic aspects of Heidegger's hermeneutics or hermeneutic ontology: (2) to show by the nihilistic components of this hermeneutics that the ''aesthetic consciousness,'' so harshly criticized by Gadamer for its links with nineteenth- and twentieth-century subjectivistic philosophy, must be rescued from this critique and reevaluated (reinstated?) as an experience of truth precisely insofar as this experience is essentially nihilistic.

2

One generally assumes that Heidegger provides the basis for hermeneutic ontology insofar as he affirms the connection—to some almost an identification—of Being and language. But beyond this connection—in itself rather ambiguous and difficult to formulate as a thesis—there are other aspects of Heidegger's philosophy that have a fundamental importance for hermeneutics and that can be summarized as follows: (1) the analysis of *Dasein* ("Being-there") in *Sein und Zeit*, as a hermeneutic totality; (2) in the later works, the effort of defining the extrametaphysical way of thinking in terms of *Andenken*, "re-collection" ("keeping in mind"), and more specifically, in terms of the relationship to tradition (*Über-lieferung*).

It is precisely these two elements that impart content to the general connection between *Sein* and *Sprache*, giving it what I perceive to be a nihilistic meaning.

2.1.

The first nihilistic element in Heidegger's hermeneutic theory can be found in his analysis of Dasein as a hermeneutic totality. Dasein fundamentally means *Being-in-the-world*; but this, in turn, can be understood only as the threefold existential structure of state of mind (*Befindlichkeit*), Understanding-Interpreting, (*Verstehen-Auslegung*) and *Discourse* (*Rede*).

The circle of understanding and interpretation is the very center of Dasein's being-in-the-world. Being-in-the-world, in fact, doesn't mean being in actual contact with all the different things that constitute the world, but rather being always already (*immer schon*) familiar with a totality of meanings, that is, with a context of references. In Heidegger's analysis of the world-character of the world, things give themselves to Dasein only as a moment of a project, or, as Heidegger says, as instruments, tools. *Being-there* exists in the form of a project in which things are insofar as they belong to this project, insofar as they have meaning in this context. This preliminary familiarity, identical with the very existence of Dasein, is what Heidegger calls understanding or preunderstanding (*Vorverstehen*). Every act or manifestation of knowledge is nothing but an articulation or interpretation of this preliminary familiarity with the world. Nevertheless this formulation of the hermeneutic structure of existence is not complete.

The second section of the part of *Sein und Zeit* takes up this problem once again and treats it in a way that eliminates any possibility of reading *Sein und Zeit* from a neo-Kantian perspective. The hermeneutic totality that Dasein is (or exists) does not identify itself with some a priori Kantian structure. The world with which Dasein is always familiar is not a transcendental screen or a categoric scheme; it is always already given to Dasein in a historic-cultural *Geworfenheit* ("throwness") profoundly tied to its mortality. Heidegger finally manages to demonstrate the connection between the project of *Being-there* and *Being-toward-death* at the beginning of the second section of *Sein and Zeit*, where he posits the problem of the totality of the structures of Dasein. Dasein can be a totality only by anticipating and preparing itself for its own death. Among all possibilities that make up Dasein's project, that is its *being-in-the-world*, dying is the only possibility that Dasein cannot evade. Moreover, as long as Dasein is, death is also that possibility which remains *pure* possibility. But it is precisely because of its remaining a permanent possibility, which, by realizing itself, would render impossible all other concrete possibilities this side of death which man lives de facto, that death acts as the factor that allows all other possibilities to manifest themselves as possibilities. And it is death, therefore, that confers to existence the mobile rhythm of a *dis-cursus*, of a context whose sense constitutes itself as a musical whole, always in movement without ever stopping on a single note.

Thus, Dasein founds itself as a hermeneutic totality only insofar as it lives continually in the possibility of not being there. We can describe this condition by saying that the foundation of Dasein coincides with its *breaking-through* or its groundlessness; the hermeneutic totality of *Being-there* exists solely in virtue of its constitutive possibility of not being there anymore.

2.2

This relationship between founding and breaking-through, introduced in *Sein und Zeit* in the analysis of being-toward-death, is a constant in all of Heidegger's successive developments, though the problematic of death seems almost to disappear in his later writings. Founding and breaking-through are the basis for the notion of *Ereignis*, the event of being, a term upon which, in the later Heidegger, most of the problems related to the notion of *Eigentlichkeit*, or authenticity, are transferred. In *Vorträge und Aufsätze*, for instance, *Ereignis* is the *disclosure of appropriation*, the event within which the thing is given *als etwas*, as something. But the thing can let itself be taken or *made one's own* (zueignen) only insofar as it is caught in "the mirror-play of the world," in a "round dance" (*Reigen*) where, while it appropriates itself, it is also ex-propriated (ent-eignet), so that the appropriation is always, in the end a *Über-eignen*, a trans-propriating. This conception of the event as *ereignen*, which ultimately is a *übereignen*—and this for the same reasons expounded in *Sein und Zeit*—where the thing comes to being only as an aspect of a total project, which, as it allows it to appear, consumes and dissolves it in a network of references. This concept of *übereignen* corresponds, in the work of the later Heidegger, to what was the nexus between founding and breaking-through in *Sein und Zeit*. As we saw, in *Sein und Zeit* the hermeneutic totality was founded only in relation to the possibility of its not being there anymore; here, each thing appears as such, as what is, only insofar as it dissolves into a circular reference to all other things, which does not have the nature of a dialectic insertion within a founding totality but has the character of violence or whirl that has the character of a "round dance" as the essay "The Thing," included in *Vorträge and Aufsätze*, explicitly says.

2.3.

In what sense can this vision of the hermeneutic constitution of Dasein be called nihilistic? First of all, in one of the meanings attributed to the term by Nietzsche, in a note placed by the editors at the beginning of the 1906 edition of *Der Willie Zur Macht*, nihilism is that situation in which, as in the Copernican revolution, "man rolls aways from the center toward X." For Nietzsche, this means that nihilism is the situation whereby man is explicitly aware of the absence of a foundation as constitutive of his condition (what in other terms Nietzsche calls the death of God). Now, the nonidentification of Being and foundation (*Grund*) is one of the most obvious points in all of Heidegger's ontology: Being is not the foundation, for each foundational relationship is always already given within the particular epochs of Being and the epochs as such are opened, not founded, by Being. Moreover elsewhere in *Sein und Zeit* Heidegger speaks explicitly of the necessity to "leave Being conceived in terms of foundation alone" if we wish to draw near a thinking that is no longer metaphysically or objectively oriented.

It seems, at any rate, that Heidegger's thinking manifests itself as the opposite of nihilism, at least in that sense of nihilism as the process that not only eliminates Being as foundation but that forgets Being *tout court*. Nihilism, according to a page in Heidegger's *Nietzsche*, is that process in which "in the end there is nothing left of Being as such." In this latter sense, is it legitimate to go against Heidegger's own text and call Heideggarian hermeneutics nihilistic? In order for use to see how even this second meaning of the concept of nihilism can be applied to Heidegger's thought, we must go on to the second of the two "nihilistic tracts" I have indicated as fundamental in Heidegger and his hermeneutics, that is, his conception of thinking as *An-denken*.

2.4.

As we noted above, *An-denken* is the form of thought that Heidegger opposes to metaphysical thought, dominated by the forgetfulness of Being. *An-denken* is also what he himself has attempted to do in the works after *Sein und Zeit*, in which he no longer pieces together any systematic discourse, but limits himself to retracing the great moments of the history of metaphysics as expressed in the sentences of poets and thinkers. It is a great error to consider this going over the history of metaphysics as a simple preparatory exercise toward the construction of some subsequent positive ontology. Re-memoration or recalling to mind as a going over again of the decisive moments of the history of metaphysics is the definitive form of the thinking of Being bestowed on us as a gift and the highest form possible for us to realize. *An-denken* corresponds to what in *Sein und Zeit* was described as the anticipating resoluteness that accepts one's death and that was meant to be at the base of authentic existence. In *Sein und Zeit* this decision was indicated only as a possibility and actually remained very vaguely defined. The fact of mortality, which founds the hermeneutic totality of existence, is developed and rendered clear in the later Heidegger as *An-denken*, which in English we can render as recollective thinking. It is by going over again the history of metaphysics as the forgetfulness of Being that Dasein decides for its own death and as such founds itself as a hermeneutic totality, the foundation of which consists of the absence of a foundation.

One of the few places where Heidegger in his later works speaks of death and of mortality is a page from *Satz vom Grund*. Here the appeal of the principle of sufficient reason to indicate a cause for every phenomenon, and thus give a rational ordering of the world, is reversed, and Heidegger treats it as an appeal to leap into the *Abgrund*, into the abyss in which, as mortals, we already find ourselves. This leaping is nothing more than *An-denken*; it means thinking from the point of view of the *Geschick*, i.e., from the task-destiny-gift of being, and that implies an entrusting oneself to the liberating link that places us within the tradition of thinking. Even though Heidegger himself does not make the connection clear, it is fair to assume that what was the anticipating decision toward death in *Sein und Zeit* has become in the later works thinking as re-memoration (or recollection), which realizes itself insofar as Dasein entrusts itself to the liberating link that places it in the *Über-lieferung* ("tradition"). *An-denken*, or the recollection that is counterpoised to the forgetting of Being, is thus defined as a leap into the abyss of mortality, or, what amounts to the same think, as an entrusting oneself to the liberating link of tradition. Thinking that eludes metaphysical forgetting is not, then, a thinking that has access directly to Being, re-presenting it, making and re-making it present. This is, if anything, exactly what constitutes the metaphysical thinking of objectivity; Being is never quite thought of as presence. The thinking that doesn't forget Being is the thinking that *recalls* Being, that is to say, thinks it as always-already gone, disappeared, absent.

In a sense, then, what Heidegger says about nihilism is true also of thinking as re-collecting, for in such thinking "there is nothing left of Being as such." Hence the importance of tradition. Tra-dition (Über-lieferung), the handing down of linguistic messages that constitute the horizon within which Dasein is thrown as a historically deter-mined project, attains preeminence because Being as an opening horizon where things appear can unfold only as the trace of words that have been spoken, and trans-mitted (and we can see how the literal resonances of the term *Geschick* (mittance) are at work here, for *Geschick* stands for both destiny and sending). Such handing down is strictly connected with the morality of Dasein: only because genera-tions follow one another in the natural rhythm of birth and death, is Being the *fore*-telling that is handed down, that is trans-mitted.

2.5.

The task accomplished by hermeneutics with respect to tradition is never a making-present, in any sense of the term. Above all, it doesn't have the historicist sense of reconstructing the origin of a cer-tain state of affairs or things in order to allow us a more suitable ap-propriation of the past, which would be the traditional notion of knowing as knowledge of causes and principles. What "sets free" or liberates in this entrusting to tradition is not the cogent evidence of principles, of *Gründe*, having established which we could finally clearly explain to ourselves what is happening; what "sets free" is in-stead the leap into the abyss of mortality. This takes place in Heideg-ger's etymological reconstructions of the great words of tradition;

the relationship with tradition does not offer a steady support but rather forces us into a retracing *in infinitum*, where the imposing cogency of the historical horizons that we inhabit is made fluid, and the present order of beings—which in the objectifying thinking of metaphysics pretended to be identified with Being—is unveiled as a *particular* historical horizon. But this is not a purely relativistic dimension: what Heidegger has in mind is always the meaning of Being and not the irreducible relativism of the epochs. Through this retracing *in infinitum* and the making fluid of historical horizons, it is the meaning of being that is re-collected. This meaning that is given us only insofar as it is bound to mortality, to the handing down of linguistic messages from generation to generation, is the opposite of the metaphysical conception of Being as stability, force, *energeia*. This meaning is that of a *weak*, declining Being that unfolds in the concealing, that *Gering*, unpretentious, not sought after, spoken of in the discussion of "The Thing" in *Vorträge and Aufsätze*.

If this is so, the hermeneutic constitution of *being-there* is nihilistic, not only because man is founded by rolling away from the center toward the X, but also because the meaning of Being that man attempts to re-collect tends to identify itself with nothingness, with the fleeting traits of an existence enclosed by the boundaries of birth and death.

2.6.

In contrast, hermeneutic experience as defined in Gadamer's work can hardly be considered as a leap into the *Abgrund* of mortality, at least in the sense of the Heidegger of *Satz Vom Grund*. This ought to be obvious if we recall the critique of aesthetic consciousness carried out by Gadamer in the first section of *Wahrheit und Methode*. Aesthetic consciousness, *aesthetische Bewusstsein*, is the term that sums up the conceptions of aesthetic experience worked out by the neo-Kantian philosophies of the early part of the twentieth-century. The aesthetic quality of a natural object or of a human artifact is the correlate of a deliberate attitude, taken by consciousness, which is purely contemplative and does not assume, with respect to the object, a theoretical or practical position. Now whereas in Kant, where the conception originates, disinterested contemplation was focused on objects conceived and created as works of genius, that is, as realizaitons of a creative force imbedded in nature iself, twentieth-century neo-Kantism has done away with the theory of genius. Aesthetic quality is no longer ontologically rooted and remains defined only negatively, as lacking any practical or cognitive points of reference, and is intrinsically tied to a precise position assumed by the observer. Gadamer at this point recalls Valery's "hermeneutic nihilism": "mes vers ont le sens qu'on leur prête." We can also bring to mind certain aspects of Croce's aesthetics, with its characterization of pure intuition as distinct from any type of cognitive, ethical, or political values. The domination of art is thus constituted as a dimension of "aesthetic experience" abstractly considered, whose sense is nothing more than the concretization of a given social taste (gout), and which, moreover, appreciates beauty as a sort of fetish, unrelated to any effective historical and existential consideration. The museum as a public institution corresponds to this notion of aesthetic consciousness and it is no mere chance that this phenomenon developed in recent centuries, parallel to the genesis of aesthetic subjectivism. The museum, where works of art of the most diverse styles and schools are gathered, is the place where this abstract and historically uprooted notion of aesthetic quality is most evident; whereas the personal private collection of the princes or the courts used to represent a certain taste and qualified preferences, the museum went on to accumulate everything that is "aesthetically valid," and for the very reason that the objects were endowed with "contemplability," totally severed from historical experience.

Aesthetic quality thus abstractly defined is given to the individual in a perspective that has the nature of the *Erlebnis*, of a precise, momentary, and ultimately epiphantic event. Gadamer quotes a relevant passage from Dilthey's *Leben Schleiermachers*, where we read: "Each one of the *Erlebnisse* is complete in itself, it is a particular image of the universe which eludes any explicative connection."[2] But this meaning of the romantic *Erlebnis* is still linked to a pantheistic vision of the universe. The *Erlebnis* of twentieth-century culture, and of Dilthey himself, becomes an experience whose meaning it totally subjective, devoid of any ontological justification: whether in a verse, in a landscape, or in a musical score, the sovereign subject distills the totality of meaning in an entirely arbitrary and casual way, leaving it devoid of any organic connection with its existential and historical situation or with the "reality" within which it lives.

Says Gadamer: "Basing aesthetics on the concept of *Erlebnis* leads to an absolute series of points that suppresses the unity of the work, the identity of the artist with himself, and the identity of the interpreter or spectator."[3] Thus understood, aesthetic consciousness subsumes those negative traits that Plato had already pointed out when he distrusted tragic actors who can feign any type of sentiment, losing somehow their own identity. And it also comprises the nihilistic and self-destructive traits that Kierkegaard described as belonging to the aesthetic phase of existence. To the aesthetic consciousness understood as pointlike temporariness and ephemeral experience, as in Kierkegaard's *Don Juan*, Gadamer wants to substitute an experience of art characterized by the historical continuity and constructivity that Kierkegaard had located in the ethical choice of marriage. Gadamer's aim is to *retrieve* art as an experience of truth. In this, he is going against the scientistic current of contemporary thinking that has limited truth to the field of the mathematical sciences of nature, relegating all other experiences more or less explicitly to the domains of poetry, aesthetic momentaeity, and the *Erlebnis*. In order to free art from this predicament, it is necessary to replace the notion of truth as conformity of proposition to a thing, with a more comprehensive notion founded on the concept of *Erfahrung*, that is, on experience as a modification that the subject undergoes when he encounters something that has real relevance for him. We can then say that art is experience of truth if it is 'true' or authentic experience, if the encounter modifies the observer.

This notion of experience is quite obviously of Hegelian origin. Its model is the itinerary of the *Phenomenology of Spirit*. And the Hegelian influence can be deeply felt insofar as in order to be lived as an experience of truth, the encounter with the work of art must be couched in the dialectical continuity of the subject with himself and with his own history. The work does not speak to us in the pointlike, instaneous abstraction of the *Erlebnis*: the work is a historical event, and our encounter with it is historical in that we are *other* when we leave the work, just as the new interpretation of the work makes it other and has a bearing upon its being, which extends it in the act of interpretation. In fact, all this characterizes the aesthetic experience *as* an authentic historical experience and, furthermore, in ultimately identifying art experience with historical experience the specificity of the work can no longer be perceived. There is, after all, a reason why one of the central concepts of Gadamer's hermeneutics is that of the ''classic.'' The classic work of art is one whose aesthetic quality is recognized as *founding* and which is therefore the exact opposite of any pointlike *Erlebnis*. Aesthetic quality is the power of historical founding, the capacity to exercise a *Wirkung* that shapes not only taste, but also language, and therefore the realms of existence of future generations.

2.7.

A distich by Hölderlin, ever present to Heidegger, says "Voll Verdienst, doch dichterisch/wohnet der Mensch auf dieser Erde." Full of merit, yet poetically, does Man dwell upon this earth. But why "doch?" (yet)? From Gadamer's standpoint, in which the work of art and the encounter with it are fully couched in the continuity of effects, that is, of the *Wirkungen* that make up the texture of history, we cannot see why there should be an opposition between the merit—that is, work and the production of historical effects—and the poetic quality of man's dwelling upon the earth. Yet Heidegger insists on this opposition continually. In fact, in his hermeneutics and in the aesthetics that it supports, there is a conception of the truth of art that does not allow itself to be reduced to the historical constructive terms defined by Gadamer. As a result of this, it calls as well for a revision of the critique of aesthetic consciousness.

We could assert, anticipating the conclusion, that the instantaneousness and ephemeral quality of aesthetic consciousness, so studiously criticized by Gadamer, express precisely the sense of Hölderlin's *doch*: what takes place in the work of art is a particular instance of "breaking-through" historicity, which announces itself along with the suspension of the hermeneutic continuity of the subject with himself and with history. The pointlike nature of aesthetic consciousness is the mode by which the subject lives the leap into the *Ab-grund* of his own mortality.

2.8.

When Heidegger speaks of the work of art as "the setting of truth to work," he explains that it is such insofar "as it sets up (*stellt auf*) a world," and "it sets forth (*her-stellt*) the earth." The setting up of a world is that historical disclosure that the work has. We can read this disclosing function of the work both in the utopian sense that would bring this aspect of Heidegger's aesthetics close to that of Bloch or Adorno, or in a more transcendental sense, as the capacity of the work to project alternative possibilities of existence as pure possibility, as for instance it was worked out by Ricoeur.

The setting up of a world is (also) the truth of art as Gadamer sees it in *Truth and Method*. But what is the setting forth of the earth? In Heidegger's language, it is the fact of "bringing it into the open as the self-secluding . . . as that which is by nature undisclosable, that which shrinks from every disclosure and instantly keeps itself closed up."[4] If we look elsewhere in Heidegger's works for some indication to better understand what meaning ought to be attributed to the earthy nature of the work of art, we find the use of the term *Erde* in the doctrine of the *Geviert*, of the "four-fold" of the world, the unveiling of sky and earth, of mortals and divinities. Although the *Geviert* is one of the most difficult points of the conceptual terminology Heidegger uses, the texts are clear at least concerning the following: that the earth is inhabited by mortals insofar as they are mortals. From the earth we are therefore sent back to mortality. And mortality constitutes, as we saw, the basic nihilistic trait of Dasein as a hermeneutic totality.

We shall then say that the work of art is the truth of Being setting itself to work because it sets up historical worlds; it announces or foretells, as an original linguistic event, the possibility of historical existence *but showing this always with a reference to mortality*. The union of founding and breaking-through that runs through all of Heidegger's ontology is realized in the work of art, in the nexus it constitutes between earth and world. The Greek temple of which the essay "Origin of the Work of Art" speaks exhibits all its own proper historical meanings solely on the basis of a staying physically within nature, registering on its own stony body the changes of the weather, that is, the passing of the seasons, and with it the passing of historical time. So it is, in the same essay, with the peasant's shoes in Van Gogh's painting, which Heidegger takes as an example in his discussion on the concept of thing: they show some cracks that are not seen, according to Heidegger, as realistic representations of life in the fields, but rather as the presence of the earth as lived temporarily, being born, getting old, and dying.

Already in *Holzwege*, therefore, the earthly element shows itself to be the most radically natural aspect of the work of art; it has to do with its being matter, but matter in which there lives the *physis*, which is always conceived of as ripening, *Zeitigung*, the growth of an organism that is born and is destined to die. Unlike practical products the work of art shows forth its earthiness, its mortality, its being subject to the action of time—for instance, the film that accumulates on paintings, or the growing corpus of interpretations or the vicissitudes of the appearing and disappearing of some works according to the vicissitudes of taste—not as a limit, but as a positively constitutive aspect of its meaning.

2.9.

This presence of mortality cannot, at any rate, be articulated in the interpretations of the work of art unless it bcomes a limiting term. We can seek help at this point in Adorno's use (in his aesthetic theory) of the term "expression." For Adorno, the term serves to point out the fact that in the work there exists, beyond its structure, techniques and even dissonances, a "something more" that is its expressivity. Now, insofar as this "something more" does not become discourse—that is, it doesn't allow itself to be caught in the network of conceptual mediation—it may just correspond or may be the precise correlative of the aesthetic *Erlebnis*. That sense in which the work of art is always also a "symbol" of the experience of birth and death is something that interpretation and critical discourse cannot articulate, except at the risk of tautology, unutterability, stammerings.

And yet our aesthetic experience bears witness to the fact that all the discursive toil of interpretation and criticism would be vain if it did not lead to that "final" moment, which is perhaps what was meant, in Aristotle's *Poetics*, with the notion of *catharsis*. In each work of art there is an earthy element that does not become world, doesn't turn into discourse or meaning unveiled in discourse: this element alludes to mortality, often at the level of the contents of the work (for instance, in the archetypes one can isolate), other times at the level of its material nature (the film or patina of time, the fortunes a work goes through, the corruption of its substance). This earthy (or *terrestrial*) element, insofar as it cannot be the object of any possible "dis-cursus," is given to pointed experience describably only as *Erlebnis*.

But it isn't true, however, that once the *Erlebnis* is freed from the romantic metaphysics of genius and its ontological foundation in nature, it must perforce fall back into the horizon of subjectivism. It is precisely the analysis of *being-there* (Dasein) that Heidegger carried out in *Sein und Zeit* that allows us to see the constitutive structure of existence independently of the subjectivity/objectivity opposition. In the experience of the constitution of Dasein as a hermeneutic totality, in the experience of recollective thinking, and in the encounter with the work of art as the truth of Being setting itself to work there is an element of "breaking-through" inseparable from the founding of a world. Art is in fact defined as the truth of Being setting itself to work precisely because it keeps the conflict between earth and world alive, that is to say, because it founds the world while showing at the same time its foundationlessness.

In order to describe, on a subjective level, this experience of the "breaking-through", or of the leap into the *Ab-grund* of mortality in which we already and always are, the only model we have at our disposal is precisely that of *Erlebnis*, of aesthetic consciousness in its pointed ahistoricity and discontinuity; in other words, in the characteristics it manifests as an experience of mortality.

Even if in this momentary experience Dasein does not encounter the ontological transcendence present in the work of genius, as the romantics believed, it doesn't follow that Dasein encounters only itself as subject: it encounters itself instead as existing, as mortal, as something that in its capacity of dying, experiences Being in a radically different manner than that which is familiar to the metaphysical tradition.

NOTES

1. cf. Martin Heidegger, *Poetry, Language, Thought*. Trans. A. Hofstadter New York: Harper and Row (1971), p. 81. Hereafter cited as *Poetry*.
2. Hans-Georg Gadamer, *Truth and Method*. New York: Seabury Press (1975), p. 58.
3. Ibid., p. 85.
4. *Poetry*., p. 97.

HEIDEGGER, HERMENEUTICS, AND ONTOLOGY

Translated by Brice R. Wachterhauser

Heidegger's thinking concerns itself with the fundamental question of European metaphysics. What is strange and unusual about this thinking is above all its contention that European metaphysics has not yet 'authentically' asked in any way its own most fundamental and defining question. Insofar as it has not yet even expressly entertained it, Heidegger claims that European metaphysical thought has been without a conception of its own essence and remains without a conception of itself. The question, which until now has not been authentically thought, is the question concerning the Being of beings, the question of the meaning of Being posed in terms of the ontological difference between Being and beings. This provocative thesis is formulated by Heidegger in ever new approaches and variations and is constantly repeated. Through willful interpretations of the classic components of European metaphysics he attempts to confirm it. Accordingly, all the classical thinkers of European metaphysics, whether Plato or Descartes, Leibniz or Kant, Hegel or Husserl, failed to consider that basic question 'authentically'; they failed to think it fundamentally. Their obvious 'forgetfulness of Being' led them to philosophical answers that failed to address the authentic and original question of metaphysics. Moreover, within the limits of metaphysical thought this failure remained, with a certain inevitability, unintelligible.

Heidegger's interpretations of metaphysics, which have not become classic, do not intend simply to undergird his contention concerning the hidden and unthought essence of this metaphysics. Heidegger intended above all that these interpretations open up new ways of thinking Being that, while allowing this unthought to be thought, simultaneously allow it to be preserved in its status as "that which cannot be thought before" (*Unvordenklichkeit*). This demand to bring the unthought, as opposed to the thought, into the circle of the thinkable, the evident paradox of making this unthought into the thinkable and that which is thought and doing it in such a way that it simultaneously retains its not being thought (*Ungedachtsein*) is a strong challenge to philosophical thinking. One can say that this challenge directly or indirectly finds its present-day response in a highly stimulating hermeneutical activity directed at the classical texts of traditional metaphysics. But this answer to the provocation of Heidegger's thinking must remain inadequate as long as the individual interpretations, however intelligent and subtle, do not say where they stand with respect to the alleged unthought of previous metaphysics.

Heidegger himself clearly saw the dangers and the risk of failure in his own thinking of Being. It was not just modesty and discretion regarding method when he described this thinking as being-on-the-way and thereby set it in sharp opposition to a thinking that develops from an absolute starting point to a definitive goal. And it was not simply a renunciation of audacity or pure prudence when he spoke of a "step back" when he could have spoken of a "step forward." It could very well be—he ponders the possibility in his philosophical discussion with Hegel—that this 'step back' may fail given the frantic development of modern technology, the heir of the old metaphysics. And still another danger could bring the new thinking of Being to naught, namely the danger that lies hidden in our facility to mistake the thinking of Being for the traditional contents of metaphysics so that "everything that gives itself along the way of this 'step back' will only be used and processed as a result of representational thinking." In either case, he feared that the 'step back' will have possibly been in vain.

But is this testimony to the dangers of failure that threaten the new thinking of Being perhaps only the expression of an extreme and unredeemable demand made upon thought? Did Heidegger himself perhaps sense that such a thinking, which wants to think the unthought as such, that which is forgotten in the entire tradition of metaphysics, may easily get lost in the limitless realm of that which is not binding (*das Unverbindliche*)? Is the marked refusal of every possible mediation (*Vermittlung*) between the thought and the unthought, the renunciation of the production of a conceptual relation between the one and the other, a sign of disdain for that hermeneutical enterprise in which the interpretation is more important than an authentic understanding of the subject matter (*Sache*)? Or does the preservation of the irreducible difference between thought and the unthought, between the manifest and the hidden, concern something else? What is at issue—a philosophical truth or, ultimately, a philosophical error?

Heidegger's testimony to the dangers that threaten the new thinking of Being refers to an aporia basic to this thinking. On the one hand, like every thinking that aims at insight into some questionable issue (*Sache*), this thinking must try to gain an appropriate distance from this issue so that it can show itself in its proper light. Hence it is justly demanded of this new thinking of Being that a distance, appropriate to the sought-after essence of metaphysics, be gained as a condition of the possibility of being able to think this essence. The 'step back' must meet this condition by gaining the proper distance, which involves a step away from and possibly beyond metaphysics. But where does this step lead? Which way out does such a thinking intend to take? For on the other hand such a thinking of Being comes from the metaphysical tradition and it is, thanks to this origin, a metaphysical thinking that is grounded in the essence of metaphysics and it is to this essence that his thinking must correspond. Must not such a thinking lose the ground under its feet when it attempts to distance itself from its own essence for the sake of a supposedly 'objective' distance? Can the thinking of Being as a metaphysical thinking take the required step back at all if it is true metaphysical being is the final and most primordial Being? Does this not demonstrate that Heidegger's attempt to think the unthought of traditional metaphysics is, even before the possiblity of failure, from the very outset meaningless, even absurd?

Now it is no exaggeration to say that no one saw this aporia so clearly or brought it so unmistakably to general awareness than Heidegger himself. He interpreted this aporia as the fate of metaphysics in our time. The most characteristic traits of his new thinking of Being are connected directly with this interpretation. Hence his refusal to characterize his own thinking as a metaphysical thinking; hence, also, his peculiar formulation of coming to grips with (*Verwindung*) metaphysics, which mitigates (*ablösen*) the talk of 'overcoming' (*Überwindung*) and 'destruction' (*Destruktion*). In particular the 'hermeneutical ambiguity' that attaches to all of his interpretations of traditional meltaphysics corresponds to this aporia and its interpretation of the history of Being. All of these interpretations say basically one and the same thing: that in all that metaphysics has hitherto thought there is an unthought that is not to be mistaken for the thought and that does not allow dialectical mediation. Thus, this contradiction between the thought and unthought, the manifest and the hidden, shows up in all forms of traditional metaphysics. Hermeneutical ambiguity defines the human way of relating in terms of a relation to Being and the world. But this ambiguity just as much defines the relation of thinking to metaphysics. Heidegger sees an essential belonging-together between both ambiguities, for the essence (*Wesen*) of man and the essence of thinking Being belong together for him. Both ambiguities are sedimented in human language, for language expresses itself both in our relation to Being and world and in thinking the Being of beings. Heidegger attempted in the language of his thinking to correspond to both these hermeneutical ambiguities and to the aporia described and its own interpretation of the history of Being. Hence his language of thinking seems to vacillate between a literal faithfulness to the language of metaphysics and another unfamiliar (*unvertraute*) language of the new thinking of Being. These languages, however, are inseparable. They are only apparently different languages. Both intend the same: they intend to intimate something in their very hiding of something. They intend to leave something unexpressed in their refering to it. In short, they intend to correspond to the essence of truth.

What these two inseparable ways of speaking intend simultaneously to intimate and hide is not ultimately the feared-for loss of meaning of the traditional language of metaphysics and the hoped-for gain in meaning from the language of this new thinking of Being. Both expressions of thinking intend much more to preserve the essence of human thought and thereby to make further thinking possible. The question concerning the possible success or failure of Heidegger's thinking of Being is accordingly inseparable from the other question: Are the characteristically winding and strange paths of this new thinking attempts to overcome the aporia of metaphysical thinking and thereby to arrive on the other side of metaphysics on the firm ground of an unquestionable valid knowledge? Or is this thinking with its constant being-on-the-way and its concomitant unending attempts at new approaches satisfied if it illuminates this aporia, addressed simply as the fate of metaphysics in our present age, without any demand to resolve this aporia, but, instead, rejecting every attempt to explicitly develop the conditions of its possible transcendence (*Aufhebung*)? Is Heidegger's apparently extremely demanding thinking in the final analysis in a specific sense undemanding? Heidegger makes it intentionally difficult for his readers to decide one way or another. He plays with both possibilities of either making or renouncing this demand, perhaps for the sake of the authentic hermeneutical ambiguity, which must leave undecided whether the thinking of Being today has stepped out of the ambit of traditional metaphysics, or whether it even can.

And yet even with the value that this intentionally ambiguous thinking and speaking places upon consistency, one question cannot be dismissed out of hand: Hasn't Heidegger taken too seriously this aporia of metaphysical thinking that we have described? Hasn't he blocked off without reason all paths to its resolution through his arbitrary interpretation of the history of Being? What really compels us to comprehend this aporia as the inescapable fate of metaphysics in our day? Why not see it instead as a possible occasion and contingent point of departure for metaphysical knowledge in our age?

It is not by accident that this aporia reminds us of the old argument of indolent reason, according to which learning is absurd because without a presupposed knowledge it is impossible but with such knowledge it is superfluous. There appears to be a real kinship between this and the old sophistic game of unmediated opposites. For while we have, in the case of these sophistries the unmediated opposites of being and nothing being played upon in order to produce the appearance of the impossibility of becoming and movement, we have in the case of Heidegger a conceptual game concerned with the absolute difference between essence and ground (*Grund*), a difference that threatens concept and knowledge with absence of sufficient reason (*Grundlosigkeit*) and unfathomableness (*Abgründigkeit*). Must one not ask in the face of this kinship and in light of the lack of mediations (*Vermittlungen*) whether Heidegger hasn't simply revived the ancient sophisms and lent them a profundity through his admittedly epochal interpretation of the history of Being that, for all that, is not beyond question? Or is this kinship and proximity something superficial, only a deceptive illusion that obscures the real meaning of Heidegger's thinking of Being?

Already ancient philosophy, particularly Plato's, noticed this strange proximity between the then modern sophistry and the ancestral speculative mythology, and it saw in this neighborly mingling a danger to well-grounded knowledge and clear human insight. Against this danger Plato developed the idea of a philosophical knowledge and the concept of a clear, well-grounded knowledge. He grounded this idea on both experience and thought and linked up this concept of cognition with the modes of thought, that is, the thought of experience and the thought of beings. And finally he elaborated this mode of thought into the first attempt at a philosophical, fundamental science, the science of dialectic. The thinking of experience, the recollecting of the perceived and the supposedly known, created, when methodically pursued, a counterweight against the nonbinding and seductive thought games played with sophistical and mythologizing paradoxes. Moreover, the thought of beings as beings served not only as an instrument to disentangle the confused and to illuminate the dark and obscure, but it made it possible to lay foundations of a philosophical science concerned with first principles and causes. Ever since Plato's initial founding of a philosophical science of first principles, all metaphysics has been based on these two fundamental supports; on experience and on thought. These two, however, are bound together by common principles.

2

Heidegger's new thinking of Being, however, has contrasted these two fundamental instances of secured and well-grounded knowledge to his own; the thought of experience with the experience of thought and the thought of beings with the remembrance of Being. But what does such a contrast mean? What insight can thereby be gained? Do these constrasts point to the possibility of a new speculative mythology, in the manner of pre-Socratic thought, through which the tradition of metaphysics as a science of first principles will be overcome? Or is this characterization of the new thinking of Being as speculative mythology one-sidedly influenced through the critical perspective of Plato? Is this opposition and contrast in any way sufficiently determined to answer questions of this sort?

One is tempted to see in the philosophical hermeneutics founded by H.-G. Gadamer a counterproposal to the Heideggarian thinking of Being, and in his relationship to the latter to see something like a repetition of the old philosophical history of the Platonic critique of speculative mythology and its sophistic application. But the history of philosophy knows pure repetition, in the strict sense of the word, just as little as actual history does. Instead we find both stronger and weaker analogies in the basic traits of different histories, as well as progression and even regression in problems and their solutions. In fact, Gadadmer's hermeneutics is far removed from a renewal of traditional metaphysics and from a revival of its idea of a philosophical science of first principles. To be sure, this hermeneutics has contributed to the defusing and neutralization of the ontohistorical aporia of Heidegger's thinking. Gadamer himself wants to see in his historical hermeneutics no unbridgable opposition to Heidegger's thinking of Being. Rather, he sees the essential difference to be in the posing of questions and problems. But this difference points unintentionally in the direction of an opposing position.

A sign of this can be seen in the loss of significance that the fundamental aporia of the metaphysical thought of Being suffers in historical hermeneutics. For a loss of significance always inevitably occurs when a single and absolute essence (*Wesen*) splinters into a multiplicity, thereby losing the original unity of its essence. Gadamer's hermeneutics has, in fact, replaced the one and single history of the thinking of Being with a multiplicity of histories of interpretations and so has apparently relativized the meaning of the one absolute history of Being. For the manifold histories of understanding Being and self-understanding do not initially present a unity subsisting in and for itself. Rather in each of these different, individual histories a distinct historical context of effects (*Wirkungszusammenhang*) constitutes itself from one or more other histories. In such a context of effects, the different histories that belong to it form a historical relation of ideal simultaneity, regardless of their lack of real simultaneity. A definite, particular history, regardless of what kind, allows its determinate character as such to be known in the mirror of other histories that project a spectrum of this character. A history that allows the character of another history to be known acts as its "effective-history" (*Wirkungsgeschichte*). The temporal relation of an "effective-history" is a dual relation involving being past (*Nachzeitigkeit*) and being simultaneous (*Gleichzeitigkeit*) with respect to all histories over against which it functions as an effective-history. Accordingly, there belongs an effective historical reflection to each history, with respect to the determination of its character. Hence the character of a history can present itelf with many shadings in accordance with the number of effective-histories that belong to the history in question.

The absolute ontological history of thinking (*Seinsgeschichte des Denkens*) is, from the standpoint of historical hermentutics, only a particular history, even if a meaningful history. Thus what is binding in principle for each history binds it as well. The possibility of knowing its character is dependent on effective-historical reflection. This character can display itself in innumerable shadings in one of many other histories. Given this in-principle infinite multiplication of the one absolute ontological history of thinking, (*Seinsgeschichte des Denkens*) the absolute and irreducible difference between the determination of essence and the ground of essence loses that eminent significance which that history possessed as its constitutive aporia. In the splintering and multiplication of the one absolute history of Being, that one major aporia splinters and multiplies itself into innumerable lesser aporias. These in no way lose their meaning only because of their indeterminate number. Their relation to *understanding* differentiates itself from the relation of that fundamental aporia to *thinking*. This thinking intends to preserve the absolute difference between essence and ground for its own sake and for the sake of Being. It leaves this difference, and with it the aporia, as it is, and it always only gives it new expression.

In contrast, understanding looks always for agreement in communication. In the attempt to come to an understanding, historical hermeneutics asks a question for which an answer is sought. Such an approach implies that an answer can be found even if it is not completely convincing, even if it leaves behind something not understood or even, perhaps, if something not understood is engendered. The relation between a history and its effective-history presents itself in respect to this immanent aporia as a relation of question and answer. In its context of effects with other histories effective-history forms a structural whole of question and answer. The difference between Gadamer's historical hermeneutics and Heidegger's thinking of the history of Being is not just a difference in the estimation of the history of Being in comparison to other histories, nor is it simply a difference in the weight given to the two fundamental concepts of understanding and thinking within the whole structure of the human comportment toward Being. These differences in estimation refer rather to specific differences in the determination of basic, historical relations of the relation between absolute and relative Being, between the unity and multiplicity of beings, and further, between question and answer, Being and self, and between truth and mediation.

Initially, specific differences of this kind find an unified expression in a different position with regard to the problem of ontology. Gadamer consciously gives his hermeneutical philosophy an ontological foundation in order to mark itself off from a methodological hermeneutics, that is, from a technique or method. In contrast, the idea of an ontological grounding of Heidegger's thinking of Being runs counter to the meaning of this thinking, to its self-characterization as being-on-the-way, as well as in the consistency with which it maintains its irresolvable hermeneutical ambiguity. For this ambiguity claims that in this epochal thinking of Being it cannot be definitely decided whether thinking still moves within the essential realm of traditional European metaphysics or whether it has already reached the ground of this essence and thereby has pushed beyond the sphere of its validity and influence. And it cannot be definitely decided whether that which has been thought in the metaphysical tradition is being thought about further in another form and way of speaking or whether Heidegger is not already in the realm of the unthought when he attempts to think in these new forms of experession and ways of speech. In the face of such an indecisiveness and undecidability, the talk of a new ontology as opposed to the old is, at least provisionally, meaningless.

In contrast to this, what is the meaning of the ontological self-grounding of hermeneutics? What we find first of all, instead of hermeneutical ambiguity (*Zweideutigkeit*) in relation to the thinking of Being in traditional metaphysics is a certain manifold of ambiguities (*Vieldeutigkeit*)* which determines Gadamer's relation to traditional metaphysics and distinguishes it from Heidegger's ambiguity, even when this 'many-sided' ambiguity is often superimposed on Heidegger's ambiguity. This many-sided ambiguity marks certain strengths and weaknesses of ontological hermeneutics, particularly in comparison to the strengths and weaknesses of Heidegger's thinking of Being. Hermeneutical ontology defines itself as a universal ontology of experience and language. With this self-grounding hermeneutics certainly neither intends a new ontology in the place of the traditional one, nor does it intend simply to take over traditional ontology just as it is and to undergird itself with this foundation. Gadamer's herme-

---

*Wiehl is obviously playing here on the difference between *zwei* (two) and *viel* (many). Both *Zweideutigkeit* and *Vieldeutigkeit* can be translated as "ambiguity." The latter, however, suggests in this context a more complex, many-sided ambiguity.—Trans.

neutical ontology of experience and language cannot be forced into a dichotomous framework that separates old and new. In this 'neither-nor' it is analogous to the hermeneutical ambiguity of Heidegger's thinking of Being.

But the many ambiguous ways it relates to traditional ontology and metaphysics points in yet another direction. It remains undetermined whether the ontological region of experience and language is primary to the region of traditional ontology only according to time or also according to Being and knowledge. In its ontological foundations philosophical hermeneutics leaves a question unanswered that presented a key problem for traditional metaphysics to which it sought an answer in the form of a methodologically basic principle, namely, the principle of the difference between that which is 'for us' and that which is 'in and for itself' the first and most original principle. The old metaphysics was well aware that a region of Being preceded it, a sphere of experience, of everyday language and pragmatic behavior from which it took its own point of departure. But is recognized the priority of this region only in a limited sense, namely in the sense of a certain temporal priority. While in its own sphere—the sphere of true and authentic knowledge of first principles—it claimed absolute priority. This absolute priority is a priority in a three-fold sense, namely a priority in respect to *Being* and to *time* as well as to *knowledge*. Now certainly the historical hermeneutics of our day is in no way a stranger to the classical principle of methodological mediation, of the systematic ordering of beings according to basic priorities. On the contrary, this hermeneutics makes a specific hermeneutical use of this principle in its effective-historical ontology and its logic of question and answer. In this respect, a given effective-history consequently has, in a certain sense, priority for us vis-a-vis its preceding history and in another sense it does not. Similarly, with regard to the relation of question and answer, there are priorities in more than one sense and in more than one respect. In this sense it follows that a given effective-history is prior to its prehistory (*Vorgeschichte*) with respect to *knowledge*, but not in a temporal sense. And it is this priority of a knowledge 'for us', considered as effective-historical, that allows us to see the point of departure of a question in this effective-history, which seeks its answer in the historical context in which it has its ontological and logical locus. At the same time, it appears that the hermeneutical use of this classical principle of mediation is not limited to its application in the sphere of effective-historical ontology and the logic of question and answer. On the contrary, it seems that this principle is being applied beyond these realms to the relation of hermeneutics as a whole to traditional metaphysics. For the hermeneutical ontology of experience and language advances the claim to be both more original and more comprehensive than traditional metaphysics. It claims absolute priority over traditional metaphysics.

From the standpoint of such absolute priority, traditional metaphysics necessarily appears as derivative and secondary. Paradoxically, it takes on the appearance of a particular ontology insofar as hermeneutics presents itself as a general, that is, universal, ontology. The strength of Gadamer's hermeneutical philosophy over against Heidegger's thinking of Being lies in this definition of its own fundamental relationship to traditional metaphysics. While Heidegger's thinking of Being takes a path that remains continually on-the-way to and beyond the ground of thinking, hermeneutical philosophy gives itself from the start such a primordial and comprehensive foundation that it must appear meaningless to want to think beyond it toward something still more primordial. It is this apparently absolute primordiality and breadth that lends hermeneutics its specific distance from metaphysics and thereby makes possible the conditions of a possible critique of metaphysical thought. In this manner, hermeneutics places itself within the traditional ambit of contemporary philosophical critiques of metaphysics.

Moreover, the breadth of its foundation also opens up worlds of experience and linguistic expression that demand a new right and significance of their own over the predominance of metaphysical thinking. These are worlds of nonmetaphysical experience and language within a general culture shared with metaphysics, as well as the nonmetaphysical worlds of experience and language of other cultures. In this respect, Gadamer's hermeneutics is related to Cassirer's *Philosophy of Symbolic Forms*. In a similar fashion, hermeneutics seeks insight in to the comprehensive foundations of cross-cultural research; in a similar fashion, hermeneutics is a philosophy of culture and a general cultural anthropology. On the other hand, hermeneutics shares with Heidegger's thinking of Being the attempt to come to grips (*verwinden*) with metaphysics. In this, hermeneutics shows itself to be, in a certain respect, more successful in gaining a theoretical distance to metaphysics than Heidegger's unfathomable (*abgründigen*) thinking of Being.

But how are we to interpret the intellectual proximity of hermeneutical philosophy to such opposing positions as those of Cassirer and

Heidegger? Does the former succeed in bridging these extremes? Is hermeneutical philosophy in any way suited to such a task? What differentiates how hermeneutics comes to grips with metaphysics from a transcendental-philosophical critique of metaphysics in the style of late Neo-Kantianism? The strength of philosophical hermeneutics is, as it is with any philosophical theory, simultaneously somehow its weakness. Thus the laying of the philosophical foundation of a hermeneutical praxis in a universal ontology of experience and language certainly could not be thought out more comprehensively. At any event, it has extended and enriched the region of prelinguistic worlds of expression through presenting it as a special kind of language world.

But this extraordinary *breadth* of the hermeneutical grounding has been paid for with a loss of *depth*. At least this picture forces itself upon us when one compares this self-grounding with the unfathomableness (*Abgründigkeit*) of Heidegger's thinking of Being, which places the whole essence of a ground (*Grund*) in question. If Heidegger wins depth at the cost of breadth, Gadadmer reverses this relationship. And in both cases signs of the trivial begin to show themselves, as it always does where philosophical thought can do one only at the cost of the other. Thus even hermeneutics has its characteristic triviality which lies precisely in its ontological self-grounding. Its actual weakness, however, lies in its failure to clearly distinguish between philosophical theory and a theoretical principle, between ontology and an ontological principle. An ontological principle no more makes an ontology than a logical principle makes a logic. This pertains to both the ontological principle of effective-history and to the logical principle of the correspondence of question and answer. Both principles are not by themselves sufficient to 'ground' an ontology and an ontological logic.

3.

An ontology is an interrelated whole, a system of ontological principles formulated with respect to definite manifold of beings, which is, in turn, determined by these principles. This interrelation demands a manifold of logical principles for its systematic presentation. This systematic unity of these principles belongs to that ontology and they present us with a constitutive logic for the same. An ontological logic belongs to every ontology that makes up the form of its presentation that is intrinsic to it as its inner form. An ontology is universal with respect to the universality of its principles and with respect to the universality of the manifold of beings for which the same principles are valid as universal principles. Hermeneutical philosophy's neglect of the difference between an ontology and an ontological principle makes its ontological foundation ambiguous in many ways (*Vieldeutigkeit*). The hermeneutical ontology of experience and language is ambiguous both in terms of its concept and in terms of its function. This ambiguity allows a series of different interpretations. According to one such interpretation, hermeneutical philosophy is not an ontology at all in the strict and proper sense of the word. Rather, it specifies several general conditions that form the outer limits for a possible universal ontology that, before all else, requires future elaboration in conjunction with the development of a hermeneutical, ontological logic. Accordingly, both the principle of effective-history would have to be developed into a universal ontology of histories and historical relations, and the logical principle of question and answer would have to be elaborated as an universal theory of forms and structures. In this way, the universal ontology of histories and the logic of forms and structures would form an interconnected theoretical whole. Then the infinite multiplicity of human experiences and linguistic forms of expression would allow themselves to be thought as embedded in determinate historical relations and as formed and structured in respect to determinate structural relations.

A second possible way of interpreting a hermeneutical ontology is based on the supposition that certainly in theory one must differentiate between an ontology and one or more ontological principles or, more exactly, between an ontology and an indeterminate multiplicity of ontological principles, but that in each concrete case no such difference can be made without qualification and with sufficient clarity. On this supposition rests the distinction between 'strong' and 'weak' ontologies. An ontology is strong inasmuch as it can make this difference clearly visible and it is all the more strong the better it succeeds in doing so. Thus we can take as a model of such a strong ontology those which satisfy the following conditions: an undetermined multiplicity of principles is developed into an unified ontological framework within which each individual principle, as an ontological principle, is, with respect to every other principle, univocally determined according to its concept, position, and function. At the same time, this ontological framework makes it possible to recognize the completeness of all the principles, as well as their general and special validity for a certain region of being. And finally, it holds for this model of a 'strong' ontology, that it can bring any other principle that has no well-defined logical place within it into a well-defined logical relation with those principles that belong to it, be it into a relation of a specific compatibility or of specific incompatibility.

In contrast, 'weak' ontologies are those that do not satisfy the general conditions of a strong ontology. And they are all the weaker the further they remain from the model of a strong ontology, and the less they are in a position to develop an indeterminate manifold beyond a mere "rhapsody" of general principles into a well-defined ontological framework. Even if the difference between a strong and a weak ontology has been sketched only provisionally and, in reality, remains a relative difference, still this definition suffices to enable us to characterize hermeneutical philosophy with regard to its self-grounding as a very weak ontology.

This characterization holds by no means only in comparison to the paradigmatic strong ontologies of traditional metaphysics, such as, for example, Hegel's ontology, which has always been recognized, even by Heidegger and Gadamer, as a paradigm of a very strong ontology. Hermeneutics is also a weak ontology compared to itself insofar as it is considered not only as an actual ontology but also a possible ontology for which it provides a general context of meaning. Both these ontological interpretations of hemeneutical philosophy have primarily a theoretical character. According to each, the infinitely many-sided, in each case concrete hermeneutical practice of communication and interpretation retains a theoretical basis, be it in the form of the conditions of a possible strong ontology, be it in the form of an actual, even if weak ontological foundation. Here the individual ontological principles function as theoretical elements whose validity extends to the infinite multiplicity of the possibility of human experience and expression as the matter and content of hermeneutical practice.

Besides such a primarily theoretical interpretation of the foundations of hermeneutical philosophy a pragmatic-ontological interpretation is also possible. In this case the ontological principles do not function as theoretical building blocks of a possible or actual ontological foundation but as pragmatically valid principles of an ontological interpretation. A pragmatically valid principle, such as effective-history, is not to be confused with a methodical rule of procedure for understanding or interpretation. Rather, it presents, so to speak, a metahermeneutical principle, which is in one way or another applicable to interpretative contexts, which are more or less regulated in various ways. Despite their differences, all three ontological interpretations of hermeneutical philosophy agree in their claim that the presupposed ontological principles are valid for the comprehensive contents of human experience and expression and that they function for these contents as formal principles of the most general sort.

From such an ontological interpretation of the self-grounding of hermeneutics, we may now distinguish an interpretation that which, from the point of view of its actual content, may be called the ontological self-interpretation of hermeneutics. Here we must seek the universal ontological foundation of concrete hermeneutical practice in the complete range of the possibilities of experience and expression. And correspondingly we find here that within this given complete framework the individual experiential and expressive elements function as ontological principles in regard to the comprehensive multiplicity of possible interpretative contexts.

Analogous to the three formal-ontological interpretations of hermeneutical philosophy presented above we can think of three interpretations that are content-oriented. The first provides only the general boundaries for the conditions of a possible ontology of experience which is to be formulated with respect to the multiplicity of experiential and expressive possibilities. The second implies what can be called a 'weak' ontology of experience. This weakness can be defined analogously to the aforementioned weakness, namely as inadequately differentiating between the context of the experience and an individual experience. In the third, we have finally the pragmatic-ontological interpretation according to which the individual principles of experience function as principles of a pragmatic-ontological interpretation of all possible contexts of interpretation.

By means of this fundamental difference between form and content within the ontological self-interpretation of hermeneutical philosophy, we can discern a further fundamental ambiguity. It remains an open issue whether the hermeneutical-ontological principles have the character of general thoughts and basic concepts or whether they pertain to general experiences and modes of expression or whether we have to do with mixtures of one with the other. Accordingly, hermeneutical philosophy leaves the fundamental ontological relation between thinking and experience undetermined. Thereby possibilities of distinguishing between the thinking of experience and the experience of thinking are left open. As we have already said, an ontological logic belongs implicitly or explicitly to a philosophical ontology, and its principles serve the systematic development of ontological principles in their mutual conceptual and functional determination. In this, we must take into account throughout that the principles of this logic may be distinguished from the corresponding ontological principles only in regard to their function, not, however, in regard to their conceptual determination and logical space. To this extent, the difference between an ontology and an ontological logic has a purely functional character. But however one distinguishes between an ontology and its ontological logic, the ambiguity of one brings in its wake a corresponding ambiguity in the other. Thus analogous to the three, or, as the case may be, six ontological interpretations of hermeneutics, we can think of a corresponding plurality of interpretations of that hermeneutical-ontological logic that belong to hermeneutics. According to the first, such a logic serves only to provide the general framework of the conditions for a possible ontological logic; according to the second, we have to do with a weak logic, the weaknesses of which corresponds to that of the ontology to which it belongs; according to the third, we deal finally with a pragmatic-hermeneutical logic. Over against the pure theoretical differences between thoughts and experiences, between conceptual and linguistic realities, the logical principles of hermeneutics behave like the ontological principles, ambivalently.

This is not the least of reasons why the relation between ontology and ontological logic remains open and relatively inexact in hermeneutical philosophy. The hermeneutical ambiguity of the principles affects especially the ontological and logical function of essences, justifications, and definitions. Contemporary hermeneutics gives at least the appearance of assigning absolute priority to understanding and interpretation over thought and knowledge. Such a move has conditionally disabled the essentially different priorities of traditional metaphysics and its epistemology; perhaps even turned them upside down into their opposites. Along with this change of epistemological priorities, a change in attitude took place simultaneously with regard to the traditional validity claims of the principles of 'essence', 'justification', and 'definition'. Thought, for traditional metaphysics, was directed toward the determinate goal of knowledge of essences, of adequate justification and conclusive definitions. In contrast, understanding and interpretation cannot be said without qualification to be built on a universally binding and definitive ideal of knowledge. Of course, every attempt at understanding and communication has its provisional, immanent goal that regulates it in this instance. And such an attempt must satisfy certain criteria and conditions if it is finally to be recognized as a successful, as a sufficient, and an an ultimately true understanding. Nevertheless in such a process of understanding it always remains at first an open issue to what extent these criteria and conditions are valid only in this and not other process, and to what extent they can claim beyond this a general or even an absolutely general binding validity. In any case, these criteria and conditions do not without qualification simply correspond to those of an essential, basic, and definitive knowledge of truth. Rather, it appears that much understanding can reach its goal even without any insight into essence or without adequate self-justification. But this does not mean that the principles of true knowledge can be fundamentally divorced from the processes of understanding and interpretation.

If philosophical hermeneutics grants an absolute priority to understanding and interpretation over thinking and knowledge, then it seems that it is in a position to claim that an unmistakable freedom has accrued to the first-mentioned epistemological procedures in their relation to the principles of thinking and knowledge, that is, to essences, justifications, and definitions. Thus it can be that these principles never come directly into view in the attempt to understand. But it can also be the case that this attempt to understand directs itself specifically and consciously toward a pre-given essence, toward a given justification or definition, as its determinate object and content. On the other hand, a specific understanding can present itself in the form of an essential insight, a specific justification or definition. And neither can we rule out the possibility that understanding, regardless of the difference between form and content, will orient itself at least indirectly by those principles, at least unconsciously and in a unfathomable (*abgründige*) manner.

But is understanding's relative independence of the principles of thought and knowledge sufficient to justify the priority of understanding over thought and knowledge? Have we thereby found sufficient means to differentiate one of these epistemological attitudes (*Verhalten*) from the other? The position of hermeneutical philosophy with respect to the principles of 'essence', 'justification', and 'definition' is, as it is with respect to any principles, frought with a many-sided ambiguity. Thus it remains entirely open whether or not and to what extent these principles play a specific role in the event of understanding and interpretation. Moreover, this ambiguity, which in general characterizes the hermeneutical use of principles, does not disappear even if we presuppose that philosophical hermeneutics allows these principles at least a certain limited meaning in the processes of understanding. Also in the case of the principles of 'essence', 'justification', and 'definition', one can clearly distinguish conceptually what neither hermeneutical praxis nor its ontological self-justification sufficiently distinguishes, namely the general conditions of the possible validity of principles, so-called weak principles, and the pragmatic use of principles.

What is 'weak' in such principles is not to be confused with the mere insufficiency of their conceptual and functional determination. 'Weak' also implies even here a particular form of indeterminacy and ignorance. We must differentiate a weak essence from a definition of an essence that is obviously insufficient, just as we must distinguish a weak reason from an insufficient justification, and a weak definition from an inadequate definition. A weak essence is, furthermore, not to be confused with a concept of essence, such as we find in nominalism, where essence is seen as a subjective-linguistic posit (*Setzung*) without objectively real content. Rather in this context we take a weak essence to be an essential unity of coherent phenomena and essential determinations of a subject matter (*Sache*), which, despite the obvious unity of this evidence, does not allow itself to be known on this basis, whether because, as an essential unity of this questionable subject matter, it does not have sufficient state of stable determination (*hinreichenden Bestand*) or whether because it points beyond its unity to a primordial unity of determinations, even if this turns out to be a hidden essential ground of the matter at issue. Analogous determinations of weakness, as opposed to mere inadequacy, obtain for justification and definitions.

Weak principles, as we have denoted them here, can also be characterized as aporetic principles. This aporetic character determines the indeterminate and unknowable nature of weak principles. Inasmuch as the hermeneutical use of these principles leaves open to what extent they do or do not fulfill their function, it also leaves undecided the direction in which thinking led by these principles takes understanding. We cannot decide whether it is in a direction of growing insight into essence or in increasing distance from such; whether it is in the direction of an always adequate justification or in the opposite direction; whether it is in the direction of a conclusive definition or back to a conceptual tentativeness.

4

This presentation of the many-sided ontological-logical ambiguity of hermeneutical philosophy in its use of principles is not an end in itself. More than anything else it should help us gain a critical perspective on the problems of Heidegger's thinking of Being, his intentional obscurities, and his hermeneutical ambiguities. Before all else, the consideration of the hermeneutical ambiguity (*Zweideutigkeit*) of this thinking of Being, mirrored in the manifold of ontological ambiguities (*Vieldeutigkeit*) of Gadamerian hermeneutics, should make clear how the strenuous attempt of that thinking to think the unthought in traditional metaphysics unavoidably calls forth of itself its own thought. As we have said, Heidegger's hermeneutical ambiguity has its own strengths and weaknesses as does Gadamer's manifold of ontological ambiguities. A comparison of both promotes, at first, that which is common or at least the appearance of a fundamental commonality. This is the thought of the absolute priority of Being, of Being over thinking and knowledge, over consciousness and human existence. In light of this absolute priority of Being one is tempted to speak of the highest ontological principle of hermeneutics and the thinking of Being under which all other ontological and logical principles, from whatever source, are subsumed. This highest ontological principle presents itself under many names and in many forms, sometimes under its own name, sometimes as the principle of finitude and limitation, sometimes as the principle of substantiality and existence. However these principles are related to the highest principle, however they represent it, in any case certain priorities are posited through time. Priority is given to finitude over infinitude, to the conditioned over the absolute, to thing-like substantiality over self-conscious subjectivity, to the concrete, individual existence over the abstract and general essence.

It was not without reason that Gadamer stressed the internal consistency and unity of this thought with the much discussed 'Kehre' in Heidegger's thinking of Being, which occurred after *Sein und Zeit*. He maintained that it was not first after the 'Kehre' but already in his magnum opus that Heidegger placed the absolute priority on the question of Being before all other questions of metaphysical thought. In this interpretation, Gadamer shows where despite the difference in their questions, he sees the essential common element of his hermeneutical thought with Heidegger's thinking of Being, that is, in the recogntion of the absolute priority of Being as the highest ontological principle. From such a vantage point the *'Kehre'* seems to be the essential common concern of their thought. The *'Kehre'* is first of all and primarily a turn in opposition to that turn of thought that Kant termed 'Copernican' and took as a general characteristic of his newly founded critical transcendental philosophy. Kant's 'revolution' was also in a certain sense a turn, namely a reversal of the traditional priority of Being over knowledge in favor of the opposite absolute priority of thought, of the knowledge of objects, of the conscious knowing subject over Being. In light of Kant's Copernican revolution, the turn of both hermeneutical thinking and the thinking of Being appears as a 'return' to the original thought of Being before that turn, as a 'step back'.

But doesn't this commonality of a turn (*Kehre*) of thinking, of a step back in hermeneutical thinking and in thinking of Being, hide an essential difference? What is to say that this step back takes a different direction in each case; in one case back to the dialectical ontology of Plato and in the other case still farther back to the beginnings of Greek ontological thought in the Presocratics? Isn't this different direction of the 'step back', that is, the different region that is reached by each 'step back', an indication perhaps of the significance of the difference between the many-sided ontological ambiguity of hermeneutics and the hermeneutical ambiguity of the thinking of Being?

This question is directly related to another: Have we adequately understood the meaning of this 'turn' (*Kehre*) of thought, of this 'step back' in general? Is not the interpretation addressed above at the very least misleading? Is not the observed proximity addressed above at the very least misleading? Is not the observed proximity of Gadamer's hermeneutics to the philosophy and anthropology of culture of late neo-Kentianism not the only thing that speaks against this interpretation? Does not Heidegger's high regard for Kant's thesis that 'being is not a predicate', a thesis that he brought into express proximity to his own thought, just as much argue against this interpretation? In fact, both Heidegger and Gadamer have essentially promoted this misleading interpretation. And it is just this interpretation that has produced the no less misleading impression of a kinship with other very influential tendencies of thought in our time. Hence, in Marxism, economic 'Being' is given priority over the political and cultural 'Being' of human beings. Thereby an absolute priority of Being over thought, of objectivity over subjectivity is claimed. In a similar manner, psychoanalysis—as metapsychology and therepeutic practice—makes use of this absolute principle of Being in that conscious knowledge gives place to the conditioned priority of the unconscious being of the modern psyche. Existentialism and structuralism also belong among those theories that give precedence to Being absolutely and to absolute Being over knowledge: the first in the form of the priority of concrete existence over abstract essence; the second in the form of the priority of structural over subjective Being. It is this elementary use of the absolute foundational principle of Being that gives the appearance of a real commonality between these highly divergent and different theoretical frames and thus has enabled their incidental syntheses. But is the use of this fundamental ontological principle in such an elementary way really meaningful? Is the use of this principle in any way sufficiently defined in order to speak of a theoretical foundation thanks to its employment? It seems that the employment of such a principle draws its alleged meaning from the completely meaningful task of correcting the widespread self-overvaluation of human consciousness and thereby of counteracting the genesis of a false consciousness of the theoretical and practical capabilities of human beings. But is this fundamental principle useful at all for such a task? Are not maxims of reason much more effective in promoting theoretical and practical insight in the life practices of human beings than an abstract conceptual formula? In fact, this absolute principle of Being finds its application as a critical court of appeal over philosophical theories that overestimate human consciousness, which appear to aid and abet the human spirit, such as, in particular, the philosophical theories of transcendental and speculative idealism. But is this critical use against traditional theories any better justified? Is it anymore effective in its critical intent? Is it true at all that philosophical idealism necessarily fosters the overestimation of the human spirit against the power of nature? Or does this interpretation hold only for a certain reductive reading of idealism? Does not idealism after all make something clear to humans other than their own essential determination?

This positing of a highest and absolute foundational principle is in no way sufficient to render powerless an ontology as whole and this even to a lesser extent if, as in the case of idealism, this principle is integrated into its opposed position in a determinate way. For in this idealism, the priority of Being over thought is not a meaningless idea. Rather, it is conceived in connection with the opposed priority and this in a carefully differentiated and methodically harmonized manner. The theoretical foundational relation of nature and spirit rests here on a general ontological foundation whose individual ontological priorities are ordered according to the priorites of Being, of time, and of knowledge—for us and in and for themselves.

There are many deficiencies observable in the use of this ontological foundational principle in the postidealistic and antiidealistic movements of the recent and most recent past. Such a deficiency lies already in the isolating and absolutizing of a single foundational principle. For the positing of the absolute priority of Being yields in general no ontological principle, but instead only a quite general concept of such a principle, without any content and without any guidance in how to obtain such a content. Instead, the unmethodical use of this absolute principle of Being fosters the resuscitation of those old metaphysical errors that Kant set out to definitively defeat in his critique of reason and its 'Copernican revolution'. These are the old metaphysical errors of confusing principles and categories that now present themselves again in different forms and contents. Such confusions are, as always, the confusion between form and content, of possibility and actuality, and ultimately all the confusions that are possible between the abstract and the concrete.

A further deficiency in the use of this absolute foundational principle arises from the consistency of its isolation. In its absolute autonomy, in its isolated use without those complementary principles, which give this use a determinate meaning in the first place, we see the general loss of the validity of this principle that we have denoted as the principle of mediation, that is, the systematic ordering of beings according to well-ordered priorities. In place of the methodically interconnected context of things, worked out according to well-differentiated priorities of Being, time, and knowledge—priorities on the one hand for us and on the other hand in and for themselves—we find, henceforth, individual contingent positings of this or that absolute priority. And this methodical foundational principle of traditional ontology appears only in a reduced form, be it as the difference between the priorities time and knowledge *or* of Being and time. The widespread and widely recognized talk of the decline of the great systems of modern philosophy in the course of the nineteenth century signifies by no means only that the universal ontological foundation dissolves and that its corresponding conceptual vocabulary loses its general binding force, but it also signifies that philosophy suffers the loss of a universally recognized method. In place of this loss we find isolated and occasional use of this or that principle and as a consequence of these uses, ambiguities, and confusions about principles.

Heidegger's thinking of Being and Gadamer's philosophical hermeneutics have, more or less, consciously placed themselves squarely within this effective context of this recent and most recent history of metaphysics. To this extent, the hermeneutical ambiguity of Heidegger and the ontological ambiguities of Gadamer are reflections of this effective context. *Being and Time* is not only the title of Heidegger's magnum opus, it is also a key for understanding this effective context that emphasizes the loss of validity of that methodical foundational principle of traditional ontology: 'Being and Time' and *not* 'Being and time and knowledge in relation to us and in and for itself.'

The hermeneutical ambiguity of Heidegger's thinking of Being corresponds to the paradoxical situation in which an ontological principle as a foundational principle is opposed to a degenerate (*verfallenden*) ontology. It is paradoxical because such degeneration requires no counterforce and because that which is valid cannot be disarmed through an isolated and contingent principle. But the many-sided ontological ambiguity of hermeneutics also corresponds in its own way to the effective-historical context in which it stands. It is not difficult to recognize in the manifold of ambiguities of the ontological self-grounding of this thought, the ambiguity of its use of ontological and logical principles in the above-named movements of the past and present century, which, like hermeneutics, rest on the foundational principles of Being.

But have we adequately understood Heidegger's hermeneutical ambiguity and Gadamer's ontological ambiguity in taking them as reflections of an effective history? What is the specific difference between these reflections?

Heidegger has attempted to think the hermeneutical ambiguity that he discovered as the destiny of metaphysics; not simply its most recent destiny, but rather its ancient destiny implicit from its inception. Yet hasn't he simply repeated in another form Nietzsche's thought that the destiny of European metaphysics, and with it the destiny of European culture, it nihilism? Is the hermeneutical ambiguity in the end only another expression for the completely primordial skepticism, for an unfathomable (*abgründig*) nihilism? Without a doubt, Heidegger had other intentions. It was not by chance that he characterized Nietzsche as the last metaphysician. He did so to avoid having to characterize himself as the last. His thinking of Being aims

to go beyond nihilism in that he conceives this to be the most conclusive form of metaphysics; namely, as the ultimate consequence of
the attempt of thought to gain a sufficient ground. For this reason his
thinking of Being seeks no sufficient grounding. Rather, it intends to
think the essence of a sufficient ground in order to think beyond this
essence. But does this thinking succeed in getting beyond the thinking of this unfathomable nothing (*abgründigen Nichts*)? Can it think
beyond nihilism? Does it enable us to think our way around nihilism?
Didn't Nietzsche himself run aground precisely on this problem?
Hermeneutical ambiguity corresponds to fundamental, ontological,
hermeneutical truth. This is more primordial than the truth of metaphysics, which in the end turns out to be only the result of a successful thought process, a successful act of knowing that brings to light
nihilism. This hidden and late-emerging nihilism in the truth of metaphysics is not, however, the unthought-of metaphysics. Were it so, it
could not appear as the ultimate consequence of metaphysics. Hermeneutical truth intends to open a place for the secret, for the unthought, for the ineffable on the other side of the effable nothing of
nihilism. But is the unthought really thought in this thinking of truth,
in the thoughtful preservation of its countertrait of "disclosedness"?

Gadamer's historical hermeneutics has integrated this fundamental
ontological and hermeneutical concept of truth into his own hermeneutical thought and displacaed it into its own conceptual space of
ontological and logical ambiguities. Truth, in Gadamer's hermeneutical philosophy, is as ambiguous as the ontology and the hermeneutical use of ontological and logical principles. Hermeneutical
truth contains something of that idea of a critique that limits human
knowledge to that which is humanly possible. But, on the other
hand, we can not fail to overhear an emphatic augmentation of our
experience found in the completed fullness of inexhaustible being,
which is experienced in the essence of the work of art. Lastly, we
should not fail to recognize a sobering significance of a truth that appears in connection with the many ambiguities, in that it exhorts us to
the idea of univocal and complete determination. All these
descendents of the hermeneutical concept of truth have a great deal
in common with the concept of truth in traditional metaphysics.

In comparison to all these many ambiguities, the strength of
Heidegger's thinking of Being lies in "the univocity of hermeneutical
ambiguity". But is this ambiguity really so 'univocal' as it appears? In
fact, it only superfically conceals all those ontological ambiguities

previously developed. Every one of their possible meanings can be considered in light of hermeneutical truth. A particular affinity appears to exist between 'weak' ontologies and weak principles on the one hand and hermeneutical truth on the other. But in order to think the unthought-of metaphysics, Heidegger's thinking of Being attempts to avoid ontological thinking. He attempts to avoid the use of ontological and logical principles by thinking these principles in light of hermeneutical truth, that is, in terms of their own hermeneutical ambiguity. In this respect, thinking of Being is fundamentally different from hermeneutics, which, with all of its many-sided ambiguities, remains within the ontological, logical realm of principles and possible justification. In contrast, Heidegger attempts to avoid the many ontological and logical ambiguities of traditional metaphysics and its effective history in order to be able to think the unthought. In this manner he shows, whether intentionally or unintentionally, not the unthought of metaphysics but rather the unthought of his own thinking of Being.

Notes on the Contributors

Richard J. Bernstein is T. Wistar Brown Professor of Philosophy at Haverford College. His many publications in prominent journals have dealt with American pragmatism, Hegel, Social and Political Theory, and Hermeneutics. He has served as editor of the *Review of Metaphysics* and *Praxis International*. He is the author of seven books and monographs, among which is *Beyond Objectivism and Relativism: Science, Hermeneutics, and Praxis*.

John D. Caputo is Professor of Philosophy at Villanova University. In addition to many articles on Heidegger, Mysticism, and Phenomenology, he is the author of two books entitled *The Mystical Element in Heidegger's Thought* and *Heidegger and Aquinas: An Essay on Overcoming Metaphysics*.

Hans-Georg Gadamer is Professor of Philosophy Emeritus at Ruprecht-Karls-Universität, Heidelberg. Besides *Truth and Method*, which can be called the seminal work of philosophical hermeneutics, he is the author of many works on Plato, Hegel, and the German philosophical tradition.

Marjorie Grene is Professor of Philosophy Emeritus at the University of Caifornia at Davis. Her many books and articles on the history of philosophy and on contemporary philosophy have earned her an international reputation.

Jürgen Habermas is Professor of Philosophy at the University of Frankfurt and Director of the Max Planck Institut fur Sozialwissenschaften in Munich. His many books and articles have appeared in many languages and are currently at the center of worldwide debate.

David Couzens Hoy is Professor of Philosophy at the University of California at Santa Cruz. In addition to articles on Heidegger, hermeneutics, and deconstruction, he is the author of a book on hermeneutics and literary criticism entitled *The Critical Circle*.

485

Charles Larmore is Assistant Professor of Philosophy at Columbia University. His publications have been in the area of the history of modern philosophy, ethics, and epistemology.

Wolfhart Pannenberg is Professor of Theology at the University of Munich. His many books and articles have made important contributions to theology and philosophy.

Paul Ricoeur has an international reputation for work done in philosophy, theology and literature. His many works include *Interpretation Theory: Discourse and the Surplus of Meaning* and *Freud and Philosophy: An Essay on Interpretation*. He holds appointments at both the Université de Paris and the University of Chicago.

Gianni Vattimo is Professor of Philosophy, University of Turin, Italy. His many articles on Nietzsche, deconstruction, Heidegger, and hermeneutics have gained him an international audience. He is currently working on a book about hermeneutics and nihilism.

Brice R. Wachterhauser is Assistant Professor of Philosophy at Saint Joseph's University, Philadelphia, Pennsylvania. He has published articles on Husserl, the problem of evil, and the hermeneutics of textual interpretation.

Merold Westphal is Professor of Philosophy at Hope College. In addition to his many publications in the areas of Hegel and 19th and 20th European philosophy, he is the author of two books, *History and Truth in Hegel's Phenomenology* and *God, Guilt, and Death*.

Reiner Wiehl is Professor of Philosophy at the Ruprecht-Karls-Universitat, Heidelberg. His many publications have been primarily in the areas of German Idealism and Contemporary German philosophy.

Kathleen R. Wright is Associate Professor of Philosophy at Haverford College. Her publications have been primarily on Hegel. She is currently working on a manuscript on the problem of language in Heidegger and Gadamer.

Bibliography

Abel, Theodore. "The Operation Called *Verstehen.*" *American Journal of Sociology* 54 (1948): 211–18.

———. "Verstehen I and Verstehen II." *Theory and Decision*, vol. 6.

Albert, Hans. "Verstehen und Geschichte." *Zeitschrift für Allgemeine Wissenschaftstheorie*, vol. 1.

———. *Pladoyer für Kritischen Rationalismus.* Munich: Piper, 1971.

Albrecht, Erhard. *Beiträge zur Erkenntnistheorie und das Verhältnis von Sprache und Denken.* Halle: Neimeyer, 1959.

Apel, Karl-Otto. "Das Verstehen." *Archiv für Begriffsgeschichte* 1 (1955): 142–99.

———. "Szientifik, Hermeneutik, Ideologie-Kritik: Entwurf einer Wissenschaftslehre in erkenntnisanthropologischer Sicht." *Man and World* I (1968): 36–63.

———. "Communication and the Foundation of the Humanities." *Acta Sociologica.* Vol. 15.

———. *Transformation der Philosophie.* 2 vols. Frankfurt: Suhrkamp, 1973.

———. "Types of Social Science in the Light of Human Interests of Knowledge." *Social Research* 44, no. 3: 425–70.

———. "The Common Presuppositions of Hermeneutics and Ethics," *Research and Phenomenololgy* 9 (1979): 35–53.

———. *Towards a Transformation of Philosophy.* Translated by Glyn Adey and David Frisby. London: Routledge & Kegan Paul, 1980.

———. *Understanding and Explanation: A Transcendental Pragmatic Perspective.* Translated by Georgia Warnke. Cambridge: MIT Press, 1985.

Arthur, Christopher E. "Gadamer and Hirsch: The Canonical Work and the Interpreter's Intention", *Cultural Hermeneutics* 4 (1977): 183–97.

Ast, Friedrich. *Grundriss der Philologie.* Landshut: Krull, 1808.

Ball, Terrence, ed. *Political Theory and Praxis: New Perspectives.* Minneapolis: University of Minnesota Press, 1977.

Bar-Hillel, Y. "Critique of Habermas' Hermeneutic Philosophy of Language," *Iyyon* (1973): 276–88.

Bauman, Zygmut. *Hermeneutics and Social Science.* New York: Columbia University Press, 1978.

Bernstein, Richard J. *Beyond Objectivism and Relativism: Science, Hermeneutics, and Praxis.* Philadelphia: University of Pennsylvania Press, 1983.

———. "Hannah Arendt: The Ambiguities of Theory and Practice." In Ball, *Political Theory and Praxis.*

———. *Praxis and Action.* Philadelphia: University of Pennsylvania Press, 1971.

———. *The Restructuring of Social and Political Theory.* New York: Harcourt Brace Jovanovich, 1976.

———. "Why Hegel Now? *Review of Metaphysics* 31 (1977): 29–60.

———. "Philosophy in the Conversation of Mankind." *Review of Metaphysics* 33 (1980): 745–76.

———. "From Hermeneutics to Praxis." *Review of Metaphysics* 35 (1982): 823–45.

———. "What is the Difference That Makes a Difference? Gadamer, Habermas, and Rorty." In *PSA 1982.* Vol. 2. Proceedings of the 1982 Biennial Meeting of the Philosophy of Science Association. Edited by P. D. Asquith and T. Nickles. East Lansing, Mich.: Philosophy of Science Association, 1983.

Betti, Emilio. *Zur Grundlegung einer allgemeinen Auslegungslehre* Reprinted from *Festschrift für Ernst Rabel.* Tübingen: 2 J.C.B. Mohr, 1954; 79–168.

———. *Die Hermeneutik als allgemeine Methodik der Geisteswissenschaften.* Tübingen: J.C.B. Mohr, 1962.

———. *Teoria general della interpretazione.* 2 vols. Milan: Giuffre, 1965. Translated into German by Betti as *Allegemeine Auslegungslehre als Methodik der Geisteswissenschaften.* Tubingen: J.C.B. Morh, 1967.

Blanchette, Oliva. "Language, the Primordial Labor of History: A Critique of Critical Social Theory in Habermas." *Cultural Hermeneutics* 1 (February 1974): 325–82.

Bleicher, Josef. *Contemporary Hermeneutics: Hermeneutics as Method, Philosophy and Critique.* London: Routledge & Kegan Paul, 1980.

———. *The Hermeneutic Imagination: Outline of a Positive Critique of Scientism and Sociology.* Boston: Routledge & Kegan Paul, 1982.

Boeckh, A. *Enzyklopadie und Methodenlehre der philologischen Wissenschaften.* (Edited by Bratuscheck, 1877). Darmstadt: Wissenschaftliche Verlagsanstalt, 1966.

Boehler, Dietrich. "Zum Problem des 'Emancipatorischen Interesses' und seiner gesellschaftlichen Wahrnemung." *Man and World* 3 (May 197): 26–53.

———. "Das Dialogische Prizip Als Hermeneutische Maxime." In *Man and World* 11 (1978): 131–64.

Bollnow, Otto Friedrich. "Über das Kritische Verstehen" *Deutsche Vierteljahresschrift für Literaturwissenschaft.* Vol. 22, pp. 1–29.

———. *Das Verstehen: Drei Aufsätze zur Theorie der Geisteswissinschaften.* Mainz: Kirchheim, 1949.

———. *Die Methode der Geisteswissenschaften.* Mainz: Gutenberg, 1950.

———. *Die Lebensphilosophie.* Berlin: Springer, 1958.

———. *Dilthey: Eine Einführung in seine Philosophie.* 3d rev. ed. Stuttgart: Kohlhammer, 1968.

———. "What Does it Mean to Unverstand a Writer Better than He Understood Himself?" *Philosophy Today* 23 (1979): 16–28.

Bourgeois, Patrick. "Paul Ricoeur's Hermeneutical Phenomenology." *Philosophy Today* 16 (1972): 20–27.

Bubner, Rüdiger. "On Hegel's Significance for the Social Sciences." *Boston Studies in the Philosophy of Science* Ed. by Marx Wartofsky.

———. "Was ist Kritische Theorie?." *Philosophische Rundschau,* (December, 1969) pp. 213–248.

———. *Theorie und Praxis, eine nachhegelsche Abstraktion.* Frankfurt am Main: V. Klostermann, 1971.

———. "Action and Reason." *Ethics,* 83, (1973), pp. 224–236.

———. "Theory and Practice in the Light of the Hermeneutic-Criticism Controversy." *Cultural Hermeneutics.* Vol. 5. 2, 4.

———. *Modern German Philosophy* translated by Eric Mathews. Cambridge: Cambridge University Press, 1981.

———. Cramer, K.; Wiehl, R.; eds. *Hermeneutik und Dialektik.* Vols. 1 and 2. Tübingen: J.C.B. Mohr, 1970.

Burian, Richard M. "More than a Marriage of Convenience: On the Inextricability of History and Philosophy of Science." *Philosophy of Science* 44 (1977): 1–42.

Byrum, Charles Stephen. "Philosophy as Play." *Man and World* 8 (1975): 315–26.

Caputo, John D. "Hermeneutics as the Recovery of Man." *Man and World* 15 (1982): 343–67.

———. "Husserl, Heidegger, and the Question of a 'Hermeneutic' Phenomenology." *Husserl Studies* 1 (1984): 157–78.

Carr, David. *Phenomenology and the Problem of History.* Evanston: Northwestern University Press, 1974.

———. "Interpretation and Self-Evidence." *Analecta Husserliana* 11 (1980): 133–48.

Carrington, Robert S. "A Comparison of Royce's Key Notion of the Community of Interpretation with the Hermeneutics of Gadamer and Heidegger." *Transactions of the Charles S. Peirce Society* 20 (1984): 279–302.

Coreth, Emrich. *Grundfragen der Hermeneutik.* Freiburg: Herder, 1969.

Crowther, Paul. "Experience of Art: Some Problems and Possibilities of Hermeneutical Analysis." *Philosophy and Phenomenological Research* 43 (1983): 347–62.

Dallmayr, Fred R. "Reason and Emancipation: Notes on Habermas." *Man and World* (Fall 2972): 79–109.

———. *Polis and Praxis: Exercises in Contemporary Political Theory.* Cambridge: MIT Press, 1985.

———, ed. *Materialien zu Habermas'* Erkenntnis und Interesse. Frankfurt: Suhrkamp, 1974.

———, and McCarthy, Thomas A., eds. *Understanding and Social Inquiry*. Notre Dame, Ind.: University of Notre Dame Press, 1977.

Davidson, Donald. "On the Very Idea of a Conceptual Scheme." *Proceedings and Addresses of the American Philosophical Association* 47 (1973–74): 5–20.

Davidson, Donald. *Inquiries into Truth and Interpretation*. Oxford: 1984.

Derrida, Jacques. *Of Grammatology*. Translated Gayatri Chakravorty Spivak. Baltimore: The Johns Hopkins University Press, 1974.

———. "Structure, Sign, and Play in the Discourse of the Human Sciences." *The Structuralist Controversy*. Baltimore: The Johns Hopkins University Press, 1968.

———. *Speech and Phenomena*. Translated by David B. Allison. Evanston, Ill.: Northwestern University Press, 1973.

———. *Writing and Difference*. Translated by Alan Bass. Chicago: University of Chicago Press, 1978.

Dilthey, Wilhelm, *Gesammelte Schriften*. 18 vols. Stuttgart: B.G. Teubener; Göttingen Vandenhoeck & Ruprecht, 1914–77.

———. "The Rise of Hermeneutics." Translated by Fredric Jameson. *New Literary History* 3 (1972): 229–44.

———. *Selected Writings*. Translated and edited by H.P. Rickman. Cambridge University Press, 1976.

Dockhorn, Klaus. "Hans-Georg Gadamer's *Truth and Method*." *Philosophy and Rhetoric* 13 (1980): 160–80.

Doppelt, Gerald. "Kuhn's Epistemological Relativism: An Interpretation and Defense." *Inquiry* 21 (1978): 33–86.

Droysen, Johann Gustav. *Outline of the Principles of History* E. Benjamin Andrews, Translator. Boston: Ginn & Co., 1893.

———. *Historik: Vorlesungen über Enzyklopedie und Methodologie der Geschichte* edited by Rudolph Hubner. 3d ed. Darmstadt: Wissenschaftliche Buchgellschaft, 1958.

Edie, James . *Speaking and Meaning: The Phenomenology of Language*. Bloomington, Indiana: Indidana University Press, 1976.

Ermarth, Michael. "The Transformation of Hermeneutics." *Monist* 64 (1981): 175–94.

———. *Wilhelm Dilthey: The Critique of Historical Reason*. Chicago: University of Chicago Press, 1982.

Ernesti, Johann August. *Institutio interpretis Novi Testamenti* 4th edition with observations by Christopher Fr. Ammon. Leipzig: Weidmann, 1792. English translation by Moses Stuart, *Elements of Interpretation* 3d ed.; Andover: M. Newman, 1827. 4th ed. Another English translation by Charles H. Terrot, *Principles of Biblical Interpretation*. 2 vols.; Edinburgh: T. Clark, 1832–33.

Farrar, Fredric W. *History of Interpretation*. Grand Rapids, Mich.: Baker Book House, 1961,

Feyerabend, Paul. *Against Method: Outline of an Anarchistic Theory of Knowledge*. London: NLB, 1975.

Fish, Stanley. *Is There A Text In This Class?* Cambridge: 1980.

Flanagan, Kieran. "Hermeneutics: A Sociology of Misunderstanding," *Philosophical Studies* (Ireland) 30 (1984): 270–81.

Floistad, Guttorm. "Social Concepts of Action: Notes on Habermas's Proposal for a Social Theory of Knowledge." *Inquiry* 13 (1970): 175–98.

Follesdal, Dagfinn. "Experience and Meaning." In *Mind and Language*. Edited by Samuel Guttenpan. Oxford: Clarendon Press, 1975.

―――. "The Status of Rationality Assumptions in Interpretation and in the Explanation of Explanation." *Dialectica* 36 (1982): 302–16.

―――. "Hermeneutics and the Hypothetico-Deductive Method." *Dialectica* 33 (1979): 39–336.

Forget, Phillipe, ed. *Text und Interpretation* München: Fink Verlag, 1948.

Franklin, James. "Natural Sciences of Textual Interpretation: The Hermeneutics of the Natural Sign." *Philosophy and Phenomenological Research* 44 (1984): 509–20.

Frei, Hans W. *The Eclipse of Biblical Narrative: A Study of Eighteenth and Nineteenth Century Hermeneutics*. New Haven: Yale University Press, 1974.

Fruchon, Pierre. *Hermeneutique, Language Et Ontologie: Un Disiernment Du Platonisme Chez H.-G. Gadamer*. Paris: 1975.

Funke, Gerhard. "Problem und Theorie der Hermeneutik." *Zeitschrift fur Philosophische Forschung*. Vol 14: 2.

Gadamer, Hans-Georg. "Jusqu'a quel point la preforme-t-elle la pensee?" in *Demitizzazio-ne e Ideologia*.

―――. "The Problem of Historical Consciousness." In Rainbow and Sullivan, *Interpretive Social Science: A Reader*. Berkeley: University of California Press.

―――. *Platos dialektische Ethik: Phänomenologische Interpretationen zur* "*Philebos.*" Habilitation Lectures. Leipzig: Meiner, 1931.

―――. *Plato und die Dichter*. Frankfurt: Klostermann, 1934.

―――. *Volk und Geschichte im Denken Herders* Lecture given in Paris on May 29, 1941. Frankfurt: Klostermann, 1942.

―――. *Wahrheit und Methode*. Tübingen: J.C.B. Mohr, 1960. "Hermeneutik und Historismus," *Philosophische Rundschau* 9 (1962): 241–76. Republished as an appendix to the 2d ed. of *WM*.

―――. *Le Probleme de la conscience historique*. Lectures presented in Louvain, 1959. Louvain: Publications universitaires de Louvain, 1963.

―――. *Kleine Schriften I and II*. Tübingen, 1967.

―――. "La Philosophie dans la Societe Modern." *Archives de Philosophie* 31 (January-March 1968): 5–16.

―――. "Hermeneutik," in Kilbansky, 1969.

―――. "The Power of Reason." *Man and World* 3 (February 1970): 5–15.

―――. "Replik," in Apel et al., 1971, pp. 283–317.

―――. "The Continuity of History and the Existential Moment." *Philosophy Today* 16 (Fall 1971): 230–40.

―――. *Kleine Schriften III*. Tübingen, 1972.

―――. "La Morte come Problema." *Giornale Critico della Filosoffia Italiana* 52 (April-June 1973): 221–32.

————. "Summation." *Cultural Hermeneutics* 2 (1975): 329–30.

————. *Truth and Method.* New York: Seabury, 1975.

————. *Philosophical Hermeneutics.* Edited and translated by David E. Linge. Berkeley: University of California Press, 1976.

————. *Hegel's Dialectic.* Translated by P. Christopher Smith, New Haven: Yale Univerisity Press, 1976.

————. *Kleine Schriften IV.* Tübingen, 1977.

————. *Philosophische Lehrjahre.* Frankfurt am Main: Vittorio Klosterman, 1977.

————. *Poetica.* Frankford, 1977.

————. *Die Aktualitat des Schönen*, Stuttgart, 1977.

————. *Die Idee des Guten zwischen Platon und Aristoteles.* Heidelberg: C. Winter Universitätsverlag, 1978.

————. "Historical Transformations of Reason." In *Rationality Today*, edited by Theodore F. Geraets. Ottawa: University of Ottawa Press, 1979.

————. *Plato. Texte zur Ideenlenre*, Frankfurt, 1978.

————. "Signification De la 'Logique' De Hegel." *Archives de Philosophie.* 1970.

————. "Heidegger's Paths." *Philosophie Exchange* 2 (1979): 80–91.

————. "Religious and Poetical Speaking." In Olson, A., ed. *Myth, Symbol and Reality*, Notre Dame, 1980.

————. *Dialogue and Dialectic.* P. Christopher Smith. New Haven: Yale University Press, 1980.

————. *Reason in the Age of Science.* Translated by Fredrick G. Lawrence. Cambridge, Mass.: MIT Press, 1981.

————. "On the Problematic Character of Aesthetic Consciousness." *Graduate Faculty Philosophy Journal* 9 (1982): 31–40.

————. "The Hermeneutics of Suspicion." *Man and World* 17 (1984): 313–24.

————. *Philosophical Apprenticeships.* Translated by Robert R. Sullivan. Cambridge: MIT Press, 1985.

————, ed. *Das Problem der Sprache.* Muenchen: Wilhelm Fink Verlag, 1967.

————, and H. Kuhn, eds. *Philosophische Rundschau: Eine vierteljahresschrift fur philosophische Kritik.*

Gall, Robert S. "Between Tradition and Critique," *Auslegung* 8 (1981): 5–18.

Garrett, Jan Edward. "Hans-Georg Gadamer On 'Fusion of Horizons'." *Man and World* 19 (1978): 392–400.

Geertz, Clifford. "From the Native's Point of View: On the Nature of Anthropological Understanding." In Rabinow and Sullivan, *Interpretive Social Science: A Reader.* Berkeley: University of California Press, 1979.

————. *The Interpretation of Culture.* New York: Basic Books, 1973.

Giddens, Anthony. *New Rules of Sociological Method.* London: Hutchinson, 1976.

————. *Profiles and Critiques in Social Theory.* Berkeley: Univerisity of California Press, 1982.

Gram, Moltke S. "Gadamer on Hegel's Dialectic: A Review Article." *Thomist* 43 (1979): 332–30.

Griswald, Charles. "Gadamer and the Interpretation of Plato," *Ancient Philosophy* 2 (1981): 121-28.

Grondin, Jean. "La Conscience Du Travail De L'histoire Et Le Problem La Verite En Hermeneutique." *Archives de Philosophie* 44 (1981): 435-54.

———. *Hermeneutische Wahrheit?* Königstein: Athenäum, 1982. Bern: Francke, 1947.

Grunbaum, Adolf. *The Foundations of Psychoanalysis.* Berkeley: 1984.

Grunder, K.R. "Hermeneutik und Wissenschaftstheorie." *Philosophisches Jahrbuch der Gorres-Gesellschaft.* 75: 152-65.

Gutting, Gary. "Paradigms and Hermeneutics: A Dialogue on Kuhn, Rorty and the Social Sciences." *American Philosophical Quarterly* 21 (1984): 1-16.

Habermas, Jürgen. "A Review of Gadamer's *Truth and Method.*" In Dallmayr and McCarthy, *Understanding and Social Inquiry,* pp. 335-63.

———. *Theorie und Praxis,* 4th rev. ed., 1971). Framkfurt: Suhrkamp, 1967.

———. *Erkenntnis und Interesse.* Frankfurt: Suhrkamp, 1968.

———. *Technik und Wissenschaft als 'Ideologie'.* Frankfurt: Suhrkamp, 1969.

———. *Protestbewegung und Hochschurlreform.* Frankfurt: Suhrkamp, 1969.

———. *Zur Logik der Sozialwissenschaften.* Frankfurt: Suhrkamp, 1970.

———. *Knowledge and Human Interests.* Translated by Jeremy J. Shapiro, Boston: Beacon Press, 1971.

———. *Theory and Practice.* Boston: Beacon Press, 1973.

———. *Legitimation Crisis.* Translated by Thomas McCarthy. Boston: Beacon Press, 1975.

———. "Hannah Arendt's Communications Concept of Power." *Social Research* 44 (1977): 3-24.

———. *Communicaton and the Evolution of Society.* Translated by Thomas McCarthy. Boston: Beacon Press, 1979.

———. *Theorie des Kommunikativen Handelns* 2 vols. Frankfurt: Suhrkamp, 1981.

———. *Philosophical-Political Profiles.* Cambridge: MIT Press, 1981.

———, Henrich, Luhman, Hrsgb. *Hermeneutik und Ideologiekritik.* Mit Beitragen von Karl- Otto Apel, Calus v. Bormann, Rudiger Bubner, Hans-Georg Gadamer, Hans Joachim Giegel, Jurgen Habermas. Framkfurt am Main: Suhrkamp Verlag, 1971.

Hans, James S. "Hans-Georg Gadamer and Hermeneutic Phenomenology." *Philosophy Today* 22 (1978): 3-19.

———. "Hermeneutics, Play, Deconstruction." *Philosophy Today* 24 (1980): 299-317.

Harney, Maurita. "Psychoanalysis and Hermeneutics." *Journal of the British Society of Phenomenology* 9 (1978): 71-81.

Haw, Alan R. "Dialogue as Productive Limitation in Social Theory: The Habermas—Gadamer Debate" *Journal of the British Society of Phenomenology* 11 (1980): 131-43.

Heelan, Patrick A. "Horizon, Objectivity and Reality in the Physical Sciences." *International Philosophical Quarterly* 7 (Summer 1967): 375-412.

——. "The Logic of Framework Transpositions." *International Philosophical Quarterly* 11 (Summer 1971): 314–34.

——. "Towards a Hermeneutics of Science." *Main Currents,* 28 (January-February 1971): 85–93.

——. "Continental Philosophy and Philosophy of Science" in Asquith, P.ed., *Current Research in Philosophy of Science,* Ann Arbor: Edwards, 1979.

——. "Perception as a Hermeneutical Art." *Reivew of Metaphysics* 37 (1983): 61–76.

Heidegger, Martin. *Sein und Zeit.* Tübingen Niemeyer, 1977.

——. *Platons Lehre von der Wahrheit: Mit einem Brief über den "Humanismus."* Bern: Francke,

——. "Hegels Begriff der Erfahrung," in *Holzwege.* Frankfurt: Klostermann, 1950.

——. *Erläuterungen zu Hölderlins Dichtung* 2d ed. Frankfurt: Klostermann, 1951.

——. *Vorträge und Aufsätze.* Pfüllingen: Neske, 1954.

——. *Identität und Differenz.* Pfüllingen: Neske, 1957.

——. *Unterwegs zur Sprache.* Pfüllingen: Neske, 1959.

——. *Existence and Being.* Chicago: Regnery, 1949; paperback, 1961.

——. *Being and Time.* New York: Harper & Row, 1962.

——. *Holzwege,* 4th ed. Frankfurt: Klostermann, 1963.

——. *Vom Wesen des Grundes* 5th ed. Translated by T. Malick. Frankfurt: Klostermann, 1965.

——. *Discourse on Thinking.* New York: Harper & Row, 1966.

——. *Vom Wesen der Wahrheit,* 5th ed. Frankfurt: Klostermann, 1967.

——. *What is Called Thinking.* Translated by J. Glenn Gray. New York: Harper and Row, 1968.

——. "The Age of the World View." *Boundary II* 4, no. 2 (Winter, 1976).

——. *Basic Writings.* Edited by David Farrell Krell. New York: Harper & Row, 1977.

Hekman, Susan. "Action as a List: Gadamer's Hermeneutics and the Social Scientific Analyses of Action." *Journal for the Theory of Social Behavior* 14 (1984): 333–54.

Held, David. *Introduction to Critical Theory.* Berkeley: 1980.

Heinrich, D., Schultz, W., Volkmann-Schluck, K-H., Hrsgb. *Die Gegenwart der Griechen im neueren Denken: Festschrift für Hans-Georg Gadamer zum 60, Geburtstag.* Tübingen: J.C.B. Mohr, 1960.

Henrichs, Norbert. *Bibliographie der Hermeneutik und ihrer Anwendungsbereiche zeit Schleiermacher. Kleine Bibliographien aus dem Philosophischen Institut der Universität Dusseldorf.* Dusseldorf: Philosophia-Verlag, 1968.

Hinman, Lawrence M. "Gadamer's Understanding of Hermeneutics." *Philosophy and Phenomenological Research* 40 (1980): 512–35.

Hirsch, E. D., Jr. "Truth and Method in Interpretation." *Review of Metaphysics,* March, 1965. 489–507.

Hirsch, E. D., Jr. *Validity in Interpretation.* New Haven: Yale University Press, 1967.

——. *The Aims of Interpretation.* Chicago: University of Chicago Press, 1976.

Hogan, John. "Gadamer and the Hermeneutical Experience." *Philosophy Today* 20 (1976): 3–12.

Holborn, Hajo. "Wilhelm Dilthey and the Critique of Historical Reason." *Journal of the History of Ideas*, vol. 2.

Howard, Ray T. *Three Faces of Hermeneutics: An Introduction to Current Theories of Understanding.* Berkeley: University of California Press, 1982.

Hoy, David Couzens. *The Critical Circle: Literature and History in Contemporary Hermeneutics.* Berkeley: University of California Press, 1978.

———. "Hermeneutic Circularity, Indeterminacy and Incommensurability." In *New Literary History*, 1978.

———. "Must We Say What We Mean?" *Review of the University of Ottowa* 50 (1980): 411–26.

Hyde, Michael J. "Philosophical Hermeneutics and the Communicative Experience," *Man and World* 13 (1980): 81–98.

Ihde, Don. *Hermeneutic Phenomenology.* Evanston: Northwestern University Press, 1971.

———. "Interpreting Hermeneutics." *Man and World* 13 (1980): 325–44.

Ijsseling, Samuel. "Hermeneutics and Textuality." *Research in Phenonenolgy* 9 (1979): 1–16.

Ineichen, Hans. *Erkenntnistheorie und geschichtlichgesselschaftliche Welt: Diltheys Logik der Geisteswissenschaften.* Frankfurt a.M: Klostermann, 1975.

Ingram, David. "The Historical Genesis of the Gadamer-Habermas Controversy." *Auslegung* 10 (1983): 86–151.

———. "Hermeneutics and Truth." *Journal of the British Society for Phenomenology* 15 (1984): 62–76.

Jalbert, John E. "Hermeneutics or Phenomenology: Reflections on Husserl's Historical Mediations as a 'Way' into Transcendental Phenomenology." *Graduate Faculty Philosophy Journal* 8 (1982): 98–132.

Jameson, Fredric. "The Rise of Hermeneutics," *New Literary History*: 3, 2.

Jauss, Hans Robert. "The Limits and Tasks of Literary Hermeneutics." *Diogenes* 17 (1980): 92–119.

Jauss, Hans Robert, and Godzich, Wlad. *Aesthetic Experience and Literary Hermeneutics.* Minneapolis: University of Minnesota Press, 1982.

Jay, Martin. "Should Intellectual History Take a Linguistic Turn? Reflections on the Habermas-Gadamer Debate." In *Modern European Intellectual History.* Edited by Dominick LaCapra and Stephen L. Kaplan. Ithaca: Cornell University Press, 1982.

Jenner, Donald. "Hermeneutic Philosophy: History as the Singular Ground of Thought." *Cogito* 1 (1983): 88–108.

Johnson, Patricia. "The Task of the Philosopher: Kierkegaard/Heidegger/Gadamer." *Philosophy Today* 28 (1984): 3–19.

Juhl, P. D. *Interpretation: An Essay in Literary Criticism.* Princeton: 1980.

Kamper, Dietmar. "Hermeneutik—Theorie einer Praxis?" *Zeitschrift fur Allegmeine Wissenschaft* 5 (1974): 39–53.

Kemp, Peter. "Phänomenologie und Hermeneutik in der Philosophie Paul Ricoeurs." *Zeitschrift für Theologie und Kirche* vol 67: 335–47.

Kermode, Frank. *The Genesis of Secrecy: On the Interpretation of Narrative.* Cambridge, Mass.: Harvard University Press, 1979.

Kiblansky, Raymond. *Contemporary Philosophy. A Survey*, vol. 3. Florence: La Nuova Italia Editrice, 1969.

Kimmerle, Heinz. "Hermeneutische Theorie oder ontologische Hermeneutik." *Zeitschrift für Theologie und Kirche* LXI (1962): 114–30.

———. "Metahermeneutik, Application, hermeneutische Sprachbildung." *Zeitschrift für Theologie und Kirche*. 61 (1964): 221–35.

———. "Die Funktion der Hermeneutik." *Zeitschrift fur Wissenschaftstheorie*, vol. 5.

Kisiel, Theodore. "The Happening of Tradition: The Hermeneutics of Gadamer and Heidegger." *Man and World*, vol. 2, 1969, pp. 358–85.

———. "Hegel and Hermeneutics." In *Beyond Epistemology*. Edited by F. G. Weiss. The Hague: Martinus Nijhoff, 1974.

Knapke, Margaret Lee. "The Hermeneutical Focus of Heidegger and Gadamer: The Nullity of Understanding." *Kinesis* 12 (1981): 3–18.

Kockelmans, Joseph J. *Martin Heidegger: A First Introduction to His Philosophy*. Pittsburg: Duquesne University Press, 1965.

———. *On Heidegger and Language*. Evanston: Northwestern University Press, 1972.

———. "On Myth and Its Relationship to Hermeneutics." *Cultural Hermeneutics* 1 (April 1973): pp. 47–86.

———. "Toward an Interpretive or Hermeneutic Social Science." *Graduate Faculty Philosophy Journal* 5 (1975): 73–96.

———. "Destructive Retrieve and Hermeneutic Phenomenology in *Being and Time*." *Research in Phenomenology* 7 (1977): 106–37.

Kolakowski, Leszek. *Husserl and the Search for Certitude*. New Haven: Yale University Press, 1975.

Krausser, Peter. "Dilthey's Revolution in the Theory of the Structure of Scientific Inquiry and Rational Behavior." *Review of Metaphysics* 22 (1968): 262–80.

Krüger, Gerhard. *Grundfragen der Philosophie. Geschichte, Wahrheit, Wissenschaft*. Frankfurt: Klostermann, 1965.

Kuhn, Thomas S. *The Structure of Scientific Revolutions* 2d ed. enl. Chicago: University of Chicago Press, 1970.

———. *The Essential Tension: Selected Studies in Scientific Tradition and Change*. Chicago: University of Chicago Press, 1977.

———. "Reflections on My Critics." In Lakatos and Musgrave, *Criticism and the growth of Knowledge*.

Kuypers, K. "Hermeneutik und die Interpretation Der Logos-Idee." *Revue Internationale de Philosophie* 29 (1970): 52–77.

Ladgrebe, Ludwig. "Wilhelm Diltheys Theorie der Geistwissenschaften: Analyse ihrer Grundbegriffe." *Jahrbuch für Philosophie und phänomenologische Forschung* 6 (1928): 238–366.

———. "Vom geisteswissenschaftlichen Verstehen." *Zeitschrift für Philosophie der Gegenwart*. Frankfurt a.M.: Ullstein Verlag, 1958.

Lawrence, Fred. "Self-Knowledge in History in Gadamer and Lonergan." In *Language, Truth, and Meaning*. Edited by Philip McShane. Notre Dame: University of Notre Dame Press, 1972.

————. "Dialectic and Hermeneutic: Foundational Perspectives on the Relationship between Human Studies and the Project of Human Self-Constitution." In "Philosophy and Social Theory, A Symposium." *Stony Brook Studies in Philosophy,* I (1974) pp. 37–59.

————. "Gadamer and Lonergan: A Dialectical Comparison," *International Philosophical Quarterly* 20 (1980): 25–47.

Linge, David E. "Dilthey and Gadamer. Two Theories of Historical Understanding." *Journal of the American Academy of Religion.* 41: 536–53.

Lipps, Hans. *Untersuchungen zu einer hermeneutischen Logik.* Frankfurt: Klostermann, 1959. 144 pp.

Löwith, Karl. *Meaning in History: The Theological Implications of the Philosophy of History.* Chicago: University of Chicago Press, 1949.

————. *Gessammelte Abhandlungen: Zur Kritik der geschichtlichen Existenz.* Stuttgart: Kohlhammer, 1960.

————. *From Hegel to Nietzsche: The Revolution in Nineteenth-Century Thought.* New York: Holt, Rinehart and Winston, 1964.

Lohmann, Johannes. "Gadamer's *Wahreit und Methode,*" *Gnomon* 38 (1965): 709–18.

————. *Philosophie und Sprachwissenschaft.* Berlin: Duncker and Humblot, 1965.

Lyotard, Jean-Francois. *The Postmodern Condition: A Report on Knowledge.* Translated by Geoff Bennington and Brian Mussumi, Minneapolis, 1984.

MacIntyre, Alasdair. "Contexts of Interpretation." *Boston University Journal* 24, no. 1 (1976): 431–46.

MacIntyre, Alasdair. "Epistemologigal Crises, Dramatic Narrative and the Philosophy of Science." *Monist* 60 (1977): 453–72.

Macomber, W. B. *Anatomy of Disillusion.* Evanston: Northwestern University Press, 1967.

Maddox, Randy L. "Hermeneutic Circle-Viscious or Victorious?" *Philosophy Today* 27 (1983).

Makkreel, Rudolph A. *Dilthey: Philosopher of the Human Studies.* Princeton, Princeton University Press, 1975.

Mandelbaum, Maurice. *The Problem of Historical Knowledge: An Answer to Relativism.* New York: Harper & Row, 1967.

————. *History, Man and Reason: A Study in Nineteenth-Century Thought.* Baltimore: Johns Hopkins University Press, 1971.

Maraldo, John C. *Der Hermeneutische Zirkel: Untersuchungen zu Schleiermacher, Dilthey and Heidegger.* Freiburg und Muenchen: Verlag Karl Alber, 1974.

Marx, Werner. *Heidegger and the Tradition.* Evanston: Northwestern University Press, 1971.

Mazzeo, John Anthony. *Varieties of Interpretation.* Notre Dame: University of Notre Dame Press, 1978.

McCarthy, Thomas. 'On Misunderstanding "Understanding."' *Theory and Decision* 3 (June 1973): 351–69.

————. "The Operation Called *Verstehen*: Towards a Redefinition of the Problem." In *PSA 1972*.

————. *The Critical Theory of Jürgen Habermas*. Cambridge, Mass: MIT Press, 1978.

Meier, Georg Freidrich, *Versuch einer allgemeinen Auslegungskunst*. Dusseldorf: Stern-Verlag, 1965. 136 pp.

Meinecke, Freidrich. *Historism: The Rise of a New Historical Outlook*. Translated by J.E. Anderson. London: Routledge & Kegan Paul, 1972.

Mendelson, Jack. "The Habermas-Gadamer Debate." *New German Critique* 18 (1979): 44–73.

Misgeld, Dieter. "Critical Theory and Hermeneutics: The Debate between Habermas and Gadamer." In *On Critical Theory*. Edited by John O'Neill. New York: Seabury Press, 1976.

————. "Discourse and Conversation: The Theory of Communicative Competence and Hermeneutics in Light of the Debate between Habermas and Gadamer." *Cultural Hermeneutics* (1977): 321–44.

————. "On Gadamer's Hermeneutics." *Philosophy of the Social Sciences* 9 (1979): 221–39.

Murray, Michael. "The New Hermeneutic and the Interpretation of Poetry." *Review of the University of Ottawa* 50 (1980): 374–94.

Nicholson, Graeme. "The Role of Interpretation in Phenomenological Reflection." *Research in Phenomenology* 14 (1984).

Nielson, Kai. "Probing Critical Theory." *International Studies in Philosophy* 13 (1981): 81–92.

Okrent, Mark. "Hermeneutics, Transcendental Philosophy and Social Science", *Inquiry* 27 (1984).

Orth, Ernest Wolfgang. "Historical and Systematic Remarks on the Relation between Description and Hermeneutics in Phenomenology: A Critique of the Enlarged Use of Hermeneutics." *Research in Phenomenology* 14 (1984).

Palmer, Richard. *Hermeneutics: Interpretation Theory in Schleiermacher, Dilthey, Heidegger, and Gadamer*. Evanston, Ill.: Northwestern University Press, 1969.

————. "Phenomenology as Foundaiton for a Post-Modern Philosophy of Literary Interpretation." *Cultural Hermeneutics* 1 (July 1973): 207–22.

————. "Allegorical, Philological and Philosophical Hermeneutics." *Review of the University of Ottawa* 50 (1980): 338–60.

Pannenberg, Wolfhart. "Hermeneutic and Universal History." In *Basic Questions in Theology*, vol. 1. Translated by George H. Kehm. Philadelphia: Fortress Press, 1970.

————. *Theology and the Philosophy of Science*. Translated by Francis McDonagh. Philadelphia: Westminster Press, 1976.

Pavlovic, K.R. "Science and Autonomy: The Prospects for Hermeneutic Science." *Man and World* 14 (1981): 127–40.

Pöggeler, Otto. "Hermeneutiche Philosophie und Theologie." *Man and World* 7 (1974): 158–176.

Rabinow, Paul, and Sullivan, William M., eds. *Interpretive Social Sciences: A Reader*. Berkeley: University of California Press, 1979.

Radnitzky, Gereard. *Contemporary Schools of Metascience*. Lund, Sweden: Berlingska Boktryckeriet, 1970.

Rasmussen, David M. *Mythic-Symbolic Language and Philosohpical Anthropology: A Constructive Interpretation of the Thought of Paul Ricoeur*. The Hague: Martinus Nijhoff, 1971.

———. "Between Autonomy and Sociality." *Cultural Hermeneutics* 1 (April 1973): 3–45.

Reagan, Charles E. *Studies in the Philosophy of Paul Ricoeur*. Athens: Ohio University Press, 1979.

Renthe-Fink, Leonhard. "Geschichtlichkeit." *Abhandlungen der Akademie der Wissenschaften in Göttingen*. Kl. 59 (1964).

Ricoeur, Paul. "Existence et Hermeneutique." In *Festschrift für Romano Guardini*. Würzburg: Echtor Verlag.

———. "Philosophie et Langage", in Kilbansky, 1969, pp. 272–95.

———. *Freud and Philosophy: An Essay on Interpretation*. Translated by Denis Savage. New Haven: Yale University Press, 1970.

———. "The Model of the Text: Meaningful Action Considered as a Text." *Social Research* 38, no. 3, (1971).

———. "Hermeneutique et des Critique des ideologies." In Castelli, 1973.

———. *The Conflict of Interpretations: Essays in Hermeneutics*. Evanston: Northwestern University Press, 1974.

———. "Le Metaphore Vivre. L'ordre philosophiique". Paris: Editions du Seuil, 1975.

———. *Interpretation Theory: Discourse and the Surplus of Meaning*. Fort Worth, Texas: Texas Christian University Press, 1976.

———. *Paul Ricoeur: Hermeneutics and the Social Sciences*. Edited and translated by John B. Thompson. Cambridge, England: Cambridge Uniaversity Press, 1981.

———. "Narrative and Hermeneutics." In Fischer, John, ed., *Essays on Aesthetics: Perspectives on the work of Monroe Beardsley*. Philadelphia: Temple University Press, 1983.

———, and Gadamer, Hans-Georg. "The Conflict of Interpretations," in Bruzina, R., ed., *Phenomenology Dialogues & Bridges*. Albany: SUNY Press, 1982.

Rockmore, Tom. "Ideality, Hermeneutics and the Hermeneutics of Idealism." *Idealistic Studies* 12 (1982): 92–102.

Rodi, Frithjof. "Diesseits der Progmatik: Gedanken zu Einer Funktioinsbestimmung der Hermeneutischen Wissenschaften," *Zeitschrift für Allgemeine Wissenschaft* 10 (1979): 288–315.

———. "Dilthey, Gadamer and 'Traditional' Hermeneutics," *Reports on Philosophy* 7 (1983): pp. 3–12.

Rorty, Richard. "The World Well Lost." *Journal of Philosophy* 69 (1972): 649–65.

———. *Philosophy and the Mirror of Nature*. Princeton: Princeton University Press, 1979.

———. "Nineteenth Century Idealism and Twentieth Century Textualism." *Monist* 64 (1981): 155–74.

———. *Consequences of Pragmatism*. Minneapolis: University of Minnesota Press, 1982.

Russen, Jorn. "Wahrheit und Methode in der Geschichtswissenschaft-philosophische Probleme der Historik." *Philosophische Rundschau* 18 (1972): 267–89.

Sandkühler, Hans Jorg. *Praxis und Geschichtsbewusstsein, Fragen einer dialektischen und historisch-materialistischen Hermeneutik.* Frankfurt: Suhrkamp, 1973.

Schleiermacher, F. D. E. *Hermeneutik und Kritik: mit besonderer Beziehung auf das Neue Testament.* Edited by F. Luecke. in Sämmtliche Werke. vol. VII. Beling: Reimen, 1838.

———. *Hermeneutik.* Edited and with an introduction by Heinz Kimmerle. Heidelberg: Carl Winter, Universitätsverlag, 1959.

———. *Hermeneutics: The Handwritten Manuscripts.* Edited by Heinz Kimmerle. Translated by James Duke and Jack Forstman. Missoula, Montana: Scholars Press, 1977.

Schrag, Calvin O. *Radical Reflection and the Origin of the Human Sciences.* West Lafayette: Purdue University Press, 1980.

Schreiter, Jorg. "Die Hermeutik als Bestandteil der Gegenwärtigen Burgerlichen Philosophie." *Deutsche Zeitschrift für Philosophie* 32 (1984): 237–45.

Schrift, Alan. "Nietzsche's Hermeneutic Significance." *Auslegung* 10 (1983): 39–47.

Schucman, Paul. "Aristotle's Phronesis and Gadamer's Hermeneutics." *Philosophy Today* 23 (1979): 41–50.

Schultz, Walter. "Anmerkungen zur Hermeneutik Gadamers." In Bubner et al., *Hermeneutik und Dialektik*, 1970.

Seebohm, Thomas M. *Zur Kritik der hermeneutischen Vernunft.* Bonn: Bouvier, 1972.

———. "The Problem of Hermeneutics in Recent Anglo-American Literature: Part I." *Philosophy and Rhetoric* 10 (1977): 180–98.

Seigfried, Hans. "Phenomenology, Hermeneutics and Poetry." *Journal of the British Society for Phenomenology* 10 (1979): 94–100.

Seung, T. K. *Semiotics and Thematics in Hermeneutics.* New York: Columbia University Press, 1982.

Siemek, Marek. "Marxism and the Hermeneutic Tradition." *Dialectics and Humanism* (1975), pp. 87–103.

Silverman, Hugh J. "For a Hermeneutic Semiology of the Self." *Philosophy Today* 23 (1979): 199–204.

———. "Phenomenology: From Hermeneutics to Deconstruction." *Research in Phenomenology* 14 (1984).

Skinner, Quentin. "Meaning and Understanding in the History of Ideas." *History and Theory* 8 (1969): 1–53.

———. "Motives, Intentions and the Interpretation of Texts." *New Literary History* 3 (1972): 393–408.

Skjervheim, Hans. "Objectivism and the Study of Man," *Inquiry*, vol. 17; pp 213–239; and vol. 18, pp 265–302.

Smith, P. Christopher. *Hermeneutics as a Theory of Human Finitude: Studies on H.G. Gadamer.* Forthcoming.

———. "Gadamer on Language and Method in Hegel's Dialectic." *Graduate Faculty Philosophy Journal* 5 (1975): 53–72.

———. "H.-G. Gadamer's Heideggarian Interpretation of Plato." *Journal of the British Society of Phenomenology* 12 (1981): 211–30.

Taylor, Charles. "Interpretation and the Sciences of Man." In *Review of Metaphysics* 25 (1971): pp. 3–51.

Thompson, John B. *Critical Hermeneutics.* Cambridge, England: Cambridge University Press, 1981.

———, and Held, David, eds. *Habermas: Critical Debates.* Cambridge, Mass.: MIT Press, 1982.

Tugendhat, Ernst. *Traditional and Analytic Philosophy: Lectures on the Philosophy of Language.* Translated by P. Gortner. Cambridge University Press, 1982.

———. "The Fusion of Horisons." *Times Literary Supplement* 19 (May 1978).

Velkley, Richard. "Gadamer and Kant: The Critique of Modern Aesthetic Consciousness," *Interpretation* 9 (1981):353–64.

Wach, Joachim. *Das Verstehen.* 3 vols. Tübingen: J.C.B. Mohr, 1926–33.

Wachterhauser, Brice. "Interpreting Texts: Objectivity or Participation?" *Man and World*, forthcoming.

———. "Must We Be What We Say? Gadamer on Truth in the Human Sciences" in Brice Wachterhauser, ed. *Hermeneutics and Modern Philosophy.* Albany: SUNY Press, 1986.

Wallulis, Jerald. "Philosophical Hermeneutics and the Conflict of Ontologies." *International Philosophical Quarterly* 24 (1984): 283–302.

Warnach, Viktor, ed. *Hermeneutik als Weg heutiger Wissenschaft.* Salzburg, Austria: Anton Pustet, 1972.

Weinsheimer, Joel C. *Gadamer's Hermeneutics*, New Haven: Yale University Press, 1985.

Wellmer, Albrecht. *Critical Theory of Society* Translated by John Cumming. New York: Herder & Herder, 1971.

Wolf, Friedrich August. *Vorlesung uber die Enzklopadie der Altertumwissenschaft.* Leipzig: Lehnhold, 1831.

Wolff, Janet. *Hermeneutic Philosophy and the Sociology of Art.* London: Routledge & Kegan Paul, 1975.

Wolff, Kurt. "Surrender and the Body." *Cultural Hermeneutics* (1974): pp. 19–60.

———. "Surrender-And-Catch and Hermeneutics." *Philosophy and Social Criticism* 10 (1984): 10–16.

Wright, Georg von. *Explanation and Understanding.* Ithaca: Cornell University Press, 1971.

Wright, Kathleen. "Gadamer on the Speculative Structure of Language." In *Hermeneutics and Modern Philosophy*, Brice Wachterhauser, ed. New York: State University of New York Press, 1986.

Zaner, Richard M. *The Context of Self*. Athens: Ohio University Press, 1981.

Zockler, Christofer. *Dilthey und die Hermeneutik*. Stuttgart: Metzler Verlag, 1975.

Index